Aviation
Authority

LAS SECTION

LICENSING, ADMINISTRATION and STANDARDISATION

ORS SECTION

OPERATING REQUIREMENTS and SAFETY

Safety Regulation Group
CAA Personnel Licensing Department

Civil Aviation Authority

LASORS 2007

Published by TSO (The Stationery Office) on behalf of the UK Civil Aviation Authority.

Printed copy available from:

TSO, PO Box 29, Norwich NR3 1GN

www.tsoshop.co.uk
Telephone orders/General enquiries: 0870 600 5522
E-mail: customer.services@tso.co.uk
Fax orders: 0870 600 5533
Textphone: 0870 240 3701

TSO Shops:

123 Kingsway, London, WC2B 6PQ
Tel: 020 7242 6393
Fax: 020 7242 6394

16 Arthur Street, Belfast BT1 4GD
Tel: 028 9023 8451
Fax: 028 9023 5401

71 Lothian Road, Edinburgh EH3 9AZ
Tel: 0870 606 5566
Fax: 0870 606 5588

TSO@Blackwell and other Accredited Agents

Enquiries regarding the content of this publication should be addressed to:-

Civil Aviation Authority
Personnel Licensing Department
Aviation House
Gatwick Airport South
West Sussex RH6 0YR

ISBN-10 0 11 790697 2

ISBN-13 978 0 11 790697 6

This year's cover features additional photography from Brian Barr, Iain Davies and Mike Page.
Pictures are reproduced with kind permission of Pilot Magazine www.pilotweb.co.uk

WELCOME TO LASORS

From a list of very wise old sayings there is one that every pilot must learn:

'Don't assume - check!'

And that is where LASORS scores over every other publication for the GA pilot. It has brought together the most readable, educational and up to date safety and licensing information around. If you need further inspiration to read on, then consider that guidance to avoid just about every one of the UK's annual toll of aviation accidents is contained in LASORS Safety Sense Leaflets. Each of these is the latest version, amended to capture the lessons of history:

'Those who choose to ignore the lessons of history are destined to re-live them'

The LAS section brings together in one easily understandable book all the flight crew licensing information otherwise found in JAR-FCL, the UK ANO, AICs and the old CAPs 53/54. Regulations and procedures do change between the annual publishing of LASORS and these updates are notified by AICs and published on our web site www.caa.co.uk/srg/licensing. The ORS section is also by no means in its definitive format. If it can be enhanced to make the whole book more valuable to the pilot it will be. The aim is to give pilots a one-stop reference for all aspects of safe aeroplane operation. Consider these two sayings:

'No matter how many hours you have in your log book, or your position in the hierarchy of life, you are only as good as your performance on your last flight'

and

'The superior pilot is the one using his superior knowledge and his superior judgement to avoid those situations that otherwise would require him to display his superior skill'

So read on, LASORS really does have a lot to offer, apply the knowledge and prepare to enjoy the benefits of being a better pilot than those who just assume they know.

IMPORTANT NOTE: CURRENT STATUS OF JAR-FCL

JAR-FCL 1 (Aeroplane) **Amendment 6** and JAR-FCL 2 (Helicopters) **Amendment 4** were published on 1 August 2006 and are now available on the Joint Aviation Authorities web site at www.jaa.nl. Both these documents contain changes introduced as a result of the NPA process, and in particular NPA 25, which includes a major change to the structure of helicopter licensing and theoretical knowledge syllabi and examinations for both aeroplane and helicopter licence applicants.

Because these changes will have a possible legal and financial effect on UK licence holders and applicants for a licence, it will be necessary to consult with aviation industry before these measures can be implemented. Consequently, and for the immediate future, the UK will continue to use previous issues of JAR-FCL 1 and 2 as the basis for licensing requirements and guidance within this document.

For aeroplanes, JAR-FCL 1 **Amendment 5** and for helicopters JAR-FCL 2 **Amendment 3** will remain the effective versions used by the Authority. Article 155 of the Air Navigation Order (2005) will, from December 2006, refer to these documents.

We will advise when industry consultation is completed whether the measure introduced by NPA FCL-25 and subsequent NPAs are to be introduced in the UK and the timescale for doing so by Aeronautical Information Circular.

LIST OF CHANGES FROM LASORS 2006

This section identifies any notable amendments made to the previous edition following changes in policy, or adoption of Notice of Proposed Amendments (NPA) or adoption of new amendments to JAR-FCL, and gives a precis of the change. Minor amendments relating to clarification of text have also been made but are not listed below.

Section	Title	Revision
Section A2	JAR-FCL Concept and Mutual Recognition	New paragraph added regarding the current status of JAR-FCL and the version that the CAA is using. Also information regarding NPA25
Section A2	JAR-FCL Concept and Mutual Recognition	Austria now approved for JAR-FCL 1 & 3 Croatia now approved for JAR-FCL 1, 2 & 3 Estonia now approved for JAR-FCL 1, 2 & 3 France now approved for JAR-FCL 2 Latvia now approved for JAR-FCL 1, 2 & 3 Lithuania now approved for JAR-FCL 1, 2 & 3 Poland now approved for JAR-FCL 1, 2 & 3
Section A8	State of Licence Issue	Policy regarding training and testing in other JAA Member States added
Section A10	Minimum Requirements for the Issue of a JAR-FCL Licence on the basis of a National Licence	Change in policy regarding the Skill Test requirements for UK CPL(A)/IR holders upgrading to a JAR-FCL ATPL(A)
Section A10	Minimum Requirements for the Issue of a JAR-FCL Licence on the basis of a National Licence	Change in policy regarding the Skill Test requirements for UK CPL(H)/IR holders upgrading to a JAR-FCL ATPL(H)
Section A17	Administration Procedures (Personnel Licensing)	Further amendments made
Section A20	ICAO Language Proficiency	Information regarding the language proficiency requirement ICAO are introducing with effect from 5th March 2008
Section A Appendix A	Definitions and Abbreviations	Further additions and amendments made
Section A Appendix C	Forms List	Further additions made
Section A Appendix D	List of Publications which applicants for flight training and pilot licence examinations may find helpful	Further Publications added

Section A Appendix E	Useful Addresses	Further amendments made
Section A Appendix G	Flight Instruction & Skill Testing in Aeroplanes/ Helicopters - Limitations for Holders of Class 1 Medical Certificate with Operational Multi-Crew Limitation (OML)	Amendments to table made
Section B	Flight Radio Telephony Operator's Licence	Various amendments made including further clarification on Non-UK FRTOL conversions
Section C1	JAR-FCL PPL (Aeroplane)	Further clarification of partial PPL(A) training completed in another JAA Member State
Section C1	JAR-FCL PPL (Aeroplane)	Policy regarding holding an appropriate medical certificate at the time of Skill Test
Section C1	JAR-FCL PPL (Aeroplane)	Change of Policy relating to the definition of a Service Pilot for the purposes of gaining a PPL(A) only
Section C2	JAR-FCL PPL (Helicopter)	Further clarification of partial PPL(H) training completed in another JAA Member State
Section C2	JAR-FCL PPL (Helicopter)	Policy regarding holding an appropriate medical certificate at the time of Skill Test
Section C3	UK PPL (Gyroplane)	Clarification of 4 hours differences training and wheel balancing exercises
Section D1	JAR-FCL CPL(Aeroplane)	Further clarification on training in another JAA Member State
Section D1	JAR-FCL CPL(Aeroplane)	Further clarification of policy regarding ICAO CPL(A)/ATPL(A) conversion to a JAR-CPL(A)
Section D1	JAR-FCL CPL(Aeroplane)	Change in policy regarding credits towards the CPL(A) modular course for holders of a valid Instrument Rating
Section D1	JAR-FCL CPL(Aeroplane)	Further clarification of JAR-FCL Theoretical Knowledge Acceptance period
Section D1	JAR-FCL(Aeroplane)	Amendments made relating to requirements for CPL(A) and IR(A) Skill Tests
Section D2	JAR-FCL CPL(A) Restricted to UK Registered Aircraft	Policy change added regarding acceptance of former UK BCPL(A) theory exams for JAR-FCL CPL(A)(R)
Section D4	JAR-FCL CPL(Helicopter)	Further clarification of policy regarding ICAO CPL(H)/ATPL(H) conversion to a JAR-CPL(H).
Section D4	JAR-FCL CPL(Helicopter)	Further clarification on training in another JAA Member State.

Section D8	UK CPL (Airships)	Amendment made to night flying requirements
Section D9	Licence Re-issue	Clarification of medical requirements for licence re-issue
Section E1	Instrument Rating (Aeroplane)	Further clarification of policy regarding ICAO IR conversions to JAR-FCL IR
Section E1	Instrument Rating (Aeroplane)	Policy added regarding IR(A) training conducted in other JAA Member States
Section E1	Instrument Rating (Aeroplane)	Further clarification of JAR-FCL Theoretical Knowledge acceptance period
Section E2	Instrument Rating (Helicopter)	Clarification of policy regarding ICAO IR conversions to JAR-FCL IR
Section E2	Instrument Rating (Helicopter)	Policy added regarding IR(H) training conducted in other JAA Member States
Section E2	Instrument Rating (Helicopter)	Further clarification of JAR-FCL Theoretical Knowledge acceptance period
Section E Appendix A	UK IMC Rating - Ground Examination Syllabus	Minor amendments made
Section F	Type and Class Ratings (Aeroplanes and Helicopters)	Details of the piloting of Ex Military (Aeroplanes and Helicopters) added
Section F	Type and Class Ratings (Aeroplanes and Helicopters)	Details of differences training for aeroplanes fitted with Single Power Lever Controls added
Section F	Type and Class Ratings (Aeroplanes and Helicopters)	Details of differences training for aircraft fitted with Electronic ('Glass') Instruments added
Section F3	Multi-Engine Piston (Land) Class Rating (Single-pilot) and Multi-Engine Centre-Line Thrust Privileges	Clarification of requirements to add Multi-Engine Centre-Line Thrust Privileges
Section F4	Multi-Pilot Aeroplane Type Rating	Further clarification relating to the required take-offs and landings and a reduction based on experience on similar types
Section F4	Multi-Pilot Aeroplane Type Rating	Further clarification for revalidation and renewal of type ratings for Qualified Service Pilots
Section F4	Multi-Pilot Aeroplane Type Rating	New Policy added regarding pre-requisite conditions for training for QSP(A)'s with a Green Instrument Rating
Section F7	Seaplane Rating	Further clarification of Seaplane Skill Test
Section F8	Helicopter Type Ratings (Single and Multi-Pilot)	Further clarification for revalidation and renewal of type ratings for Qualified Service Pilots

Section F9	Transfer of Type/Class Ratings	Further clarification on Transfer of Military Type Ratings and subsequent revalidations/ renewals.
Section F Appendix A	Guide to studying for the Seamanship Examination	Change to pass mark for Seamanship Examination
Section F Appendix G	SEP(SEA) Class Rating Skill Test Schedule	New Appendix added
Section G1	JAR-FCL ATPL(Aeroplane)	Further clarification of policy regarding ICAO ATPL(A) conversion to a JAR-FCL ATPL(A)
Section G3	JAR-FCL ATPL (Helicopter)	Further clarification of policy regarding ICAO ATPL(H) conversion to a JAR-FCL ATPL(H)
Section G5	Licence Re-issue	Clarification of medical requirements for licence re-issue
Section H1	JAR-FCL FI(A) & FI(H) Ratings	Further clarification regarding FI(A)/(H) Privileges and Requirements
Section H1	JAR-FCL FI(A) & FI(H) Ratings	Policy added regarding proficiency check required for first revalidation after initial issue
Section H1	JAR-FCL FI(A) & FI(H) Ratings	Policy changes regarding military concessions for the issue of a FI(A)/(H) rating
Section J	JAR-FCL Theoretical Knowledge Examination Requirements	Amendments to whole section relating to exam attendance, exam bookings, regulations and examination results
Section J Appendix A	Examination Timetable for 2007	New Timetable for 2007 added
Section J Appendix B	Examination Briefing	Amendments made to the Examination Briefing
Section K	Flight Engineer Licence	Clarification of theoretical knowledge acceptance period for RAF Air Engineers
Section 2 - ORS	AICs Pink and Yellow	AICs updated
Section 2 - ORS	Safety Sense	Amendments and updates made to Safety Sense Leaflets
Section 2 - ORS	Safety Sense	New leaflet added entitled Flight in Controlled Airspace
Section 2 - ORS	Practical Guidance	Amendments made

INDEX TO LASORS

LASORS will comprise of 2 sections:

Section 1, Licensing Administration and Standardisation (LAS), will encompass the licensing and standardisation procedures employed by Safety Regulation Group in their role of regulating these. It will give guidance on how licences and ratings are obtained, revalidated or renewed. The use of subparts is purposely intended to allow the reader to link the information to its location within JAR-FCL documentation.

SECTION 1 - LAS

Section 2, Operating Requirements and Standards (ORS) will be developed as an aviators personal data source for those best practices and standard procedures in the preparation for flight. Its material will be sourced form well known products such as AICs (Pink), Safety Sense leaflets, etc.

Subject headings are grouped around phases of preparation, flight and other information

SECTION 2 - ORS

INDEX BY SECTION

WELCOME TO LASORS

SECTION 1 – LAS

SECTION 2 – ORS

ORS AIC's Pink and Yellow

SAFETY SENSE - GENERAL AVIATION

HANDLING SENSE LEAFLETS

SECTION A

GENERAL INFORMATION

A1 INTRODUCTION

The Civil Aviation Authority (CAA) is empowered by the Air Navigation Order (ANO) to grant Joint Aviation Authority (JAA) and United Kingdom (UK) flight crew licences and associated ratings, where it is satisfied that the applicant is a fit person to hold the licence or rating concerned and is appropriately qualified to act in the capacity to which it relates. A holder of a JAR-FCL Licence is entitled to act as a member of flight crew in an aircraft registered in JAA member states within the privileges of the licence or rating. A holder of a United Kingdom national licence is entitled to act as a member of flight crew in aircraft registered in the UK within the privileges of the licence or rating concerned. Where no JAA licence or ratings exist the CAA may grant UK National licences with privileges restricted to UK registered aircraft, and in some cases, UK airspace.

This publication explains the privileges of JAA and UK National licences and associated ratings, sets out the requirements which have to be met for their grant and describes the administrative procedures for their issue, revalidation and renewal. It also explains the credits, which may be given towards certain requirements to persons with previous flying experience. Where exemption of the holder of a non-UK licence or rating is mentioned, such exemption is only available where the licence or rating was issued by a Contracting State whose own qualifying requirements meet the published minimum requirements of the International Civil Aviation Organisation (ICAO).

Extensive use of abbreviations is made to make this document more readable and to avoid repetition where this can be accomplished without causing confusion. A list of abbreviations used is at Section A, Appendix A.

Nothing in this publication is meant to conflict with aviation legislation. Where there is any doubt the legislation must be regarded as definitive. The precise privileges of licences and ratings are set out in Schedule 8 of the Air Navigation Order (please refer to Section A, Appendix F).

A2 JAR-FCL CONCEPT AND MUTUAL RECOGNITION

Background to JAR-FCL

European aviation systems had developed in the past with great variations in structures and details. Therefore, it has been necessary to write harmonised requirements.

The Civil Aviation Authorities of certain European States have agreed common comprehensive and detailed aviation requirements, referred to as the Joint Aviation Requirements (JAR). The aim is to minimise type certification problems on joint ventures, to facilitate the export and import of aviation products, to make it easier for maintenance carried out in one European State to be accepted by the Civil Aviation Authority in another European State and to regulate commercial air transport operations, and for the issuance and maintenance of pilot and flight engineer licences.

JAR–FCL is the code developed for all categories of pilot and flight engineer licences so as to permit use of licences and ratings without further formality in any participating States.

JAR-FCL 1	applies to aeroplane licences
JAR-FCL 2	applies to helicopter licences
JAR-FCL 3	applies to medical Requirements
JAR-FCL 4	will apply to Flight Engineers
JAR-FCL 5	will apply to balloon and Glider licences

ICAO Annex 1 has been selected to provide the basic structure of JAR–FCL, the JAR for licensing, but with additional sub-division where considered appropriate. The content of Annex 1 has been used and added to where necessary by making use of existing European regulations.

JAR–FCL has been issued with no national variants. It has been accepted that JAR–FCL should be applied in practice and the lessons learned embodied in future amendments. The Civil Aviation Authorities of the JAA are therefore committed to early amendment in the light of experience.

Future development of the requirements of JAR–FCL will be in accordance with the JAA's Notice of Proposed Amendment (NPA) procedures. These procedures allow for the amendment of JAR–FCL to be proposed by the Civil Aviation Authority of any of the participating countries and by any organisation represented on the Joint Steering Assembly.

The Civil Aviation Authorities have agreed they should not unilaterally initiate amendment of their national codes without having made a proposal for amendment of JAR–FCL in accordance with the agreed procedure.

Amendments to the text in JAR–FCL are usually issued initially as 'Orange Paper' amendments. Orange Paper amendments are pages containing revised paragraphs, following NPA adoption. The issue of such pages avoids the need to re-paginate whole Subparts and are a clear method of identifying new texts.

Twenty-nine states from within the European Union (EU), European Free Trade Association (EFTA) and Eurocontrol blocks set out to pursue JAA membership. At the end of October 2006 the following nations had passed the Licensing Inspection to become fully approved JAA Member states:

Austria	- JAR-FCL 1 & 3
Belgium	- JAR-FCL 1, 2 & 3
Croatia	- JAR-FCL 1, 2 & 3
Czech Republic	- JAR-FCL 1, 2 & 3
Denmark	- JAR-FCL 1,2, 3 & 4
Estonia	- JAR-FCL 1, 2 & 3
Finland	- JAR-FCL 1,2 & 3
France	- JAR-FCL 1,2, 3 & 4
Germany	- JAR-FCL 1, 2, 3 & 4
Greece	- JAR-FCL 1 & 3
Iceland	- JAR-FCL 1,2 &3
Ireland	- JAR-FCL 1, 2, 3 & 4
Italy	- JAR-FCL 1, 2 & 3
Latvia	- JAR-FCL1, 2 & 3
Lithuania	- JAR-FCL 1, 2 & 3
Malta	- JAR-FCL 1 & 3
Netherlands	- JAR-FCL 1, 2, 3 & 4
Norway	- JAR-FCL 1,2 & 3
Poland	- JAR-FCL 1, 2 & 3
Portugal	- JAR-FCL 1, 2 & 3
Romania	- JAR-FCL 1, 2 & 3
Slovenia	- JAR-FCL 1 & 3
Spain	- JAR-FCL 1, 2 & 3
Sweden	- JAR-FCL 1, 2 & 3
Switzerland	- JAR-FCL 1 & 3
Turkey	- JAR-FCL 1 & 3
United Kingdom	- JAR-FCL 1,2 & 3

A definitive list of Full Member States currently recommended for mutual recognition is available on the JAA web site www.jaa.nl. Please refer to the web site for any updates made since publication.

Current Status of JAR-FCL

JAR-FCL 1 (Aeroplane) Amendment 6 and JAR-FCL 2 (Helicopter) Amendment 4 were published on 1 August 2006 and are now available on the Joint Aviation Authorities web site at www.jaa.nl. Both these documents contain changes introduced as a result of the NPA process, and in particular NPA 25, which includes a major change to the structure of helicopter licensing and theoretical knowledge syllabi and examinations for both aeroplane and helicopter licence applicants.

Because these changes will have a possible legal and financial effect on UK licence holders and applicants for a licence, it will be necessary to consult with aviation industry before these measures can be implemented. Consequently, and for the immediate future, the UK will continue to use previous issues of JAR-FCL 1 and 2 as the basis for licensing requirements and guidance. For aeroplanes, JAR-FCL 1 **Amendment 5** and for helicopters JAR-FCL 2 **Amendment 3** will remain the effective versions used by the Authority. Article 155 of the Air Navigation Order (2005) will, from December 2006, refer to these documents.

We will advise when industry consultation is completed whether the measure introduced by NPA FCL-25 and subsequent NPAs are to be introduced in the UK and the timescale for doing so by Aeronautical Information Circular.

Mutual Recognition

JAR-FCL 1.015/2.015 states 'Where a person, an organisation or a service has been licensed, issued with a rating, authorisation, approval or certificate by the Authority of a JAA Member State in accordance with the requirements of JAR-FCL and associated procedures, such licences, ratings, approvals or certificates shall be accepted without formality by other JAA Member States'.

Whenever a reference is made to a JAA Member State for the purpose of mutual recognition of licences, ratings, authorisations, approvals or certificates, this means a JAA Full Member State.

Validity of Licences and ratings

A licence holder shall not exercise the privileges granted by any licence or rating issued by a JAA Member State unless the holder maintains competency by meeting the relevant requirements of JAR-FCL.

The validity of the licence is determined by the validity of the ratings contained therein and the medical certificate. The licence will be issued for a maximum period of 5 years.

Applicability

Whenever licences, ratings, authorisations, approvals or certificates are mentioned in JAR-FCL, these are meant to be licences, ratings, authorisations, approvals or certificates issued in accordance with JAR-FCL. In all other cases these documents are specified as e.g. ICAO or national licences.

Whenever a reference is made to aeroplanes this does not include microlights as defined nationally, unless otherwise stated.

A3 BASIC AUTHORITY TO ACT AS A FLIGHT CREW MEMBER

A person shall not act as a flight crew member of a civil aeroplane/helicopter registered in a JAA Member State unless that person holds a valid licence and rating complying with the requirements of JAR–FCL and appropriate to the duties being performed, or an authorisation as set out in JAR–FCL 1.085/2.085 and/or 1.230/2.230. The licence shall have been issued by:

- A JAA Member State; or
- Another ICAO Contracting State and rendered valid in accordance with JAR–FCL 1.015/2.015(b) or (c).

Pilots holding national motor gliders licences/ratings/ authorisations are also permitted to operate touring motor gliders under national regulations.

Pilots holding a restricted national private pilot's licence are permitted under national regulations to operate aeroplanes registered in the State of licence issue within that State's airspace.

Exercise of privileges

The holder of a licence or rating shall not exercise privileges other than those granted by that licence, rating or authorisation.

A4 HOW TO BE A PILOT UNDER JAR- FCL

To earn your living as a pilot you will need to hold a Professional Pilot Licence. The way in which a Professional Pilot Licence is obtained has significantly changed due to the harmonisation of European licensing requirements.

The CAA is a member of the JAA. One of the main aims of the JAA is to achieve a common standard of flight crew licensing amongst the JAA member states and facilitate the mobility of flight crew between the states.

There are three types of licence, the Private Pilot Licence, the Commercial Pilot Licence and the Airline Transport Pilot Licence.

The Commercial Pilot Licence can be obtained via two routes:-

- the integrated course route
- the modular route

Starting a Course

Before embarking on a course of training it is important to ensure that you are medically fit for the licence being sought. The Flying Training Organisation (FTO) is tasked with ensuring that you have sufficient knowledge of mathematics, physics and the English language to facilitate an understanding of the instruction given on the course.

The educational standard assumed for the full time Commercial Pilot Licence Integrated course is at least 5 GCE 'O' Level or 5 GCSE 'C' Level passes, including English Language, Mathematics and a Science subject. However, the minimum educational requirements are actually left to the discretion of the FTO concerned. You will probably find that for sponsorship, an airline will require at least 2 GCE 'A' Level or 2 GCSE 'H' Level passes.

Important Note: **If you intend to train for a licence in another JAA Member State, you should refer to our policy as detailed in Section A8 State of Licence Issue.**

The Private Pilot Licence (Aeroplane and Helicopter)

The Private Pilots Licence (PPL) is a recreational licence and can be achieved by completing a course of a minimum of 45 hours flying training. The privileges of this licence allow you to fly, but not for remuneration, as pilot-in-command or co-pilot of any aircraft, for which an appropriate rating is held, engaged in non-revenue flights. A PPL is obtained through a training organisation registered with the Authority. Adding further ratings to the licence may extend the privileges. (Please refer to Section C1 and C2 for further details).

Integrated Courses (Aeroplane and Helicopter)

The Integrated Course is a full time course of ground and flying training run by a FTO approved to conduct such courses. These fully residential courses offer the quickest means of qualifying for a Professional Pilot's Licence, but they are expensive. You should contact the approved FTO's for details of their current charges. Because of the high cost of integrated courses, sponsorship by an airline is the only way for most young people to achieve their ambition by this route. Details of sponsorship schemes available can be obtained from individual airlines and are also sometimes advertised in the aviation press.

The Integrated Courses available are:-

AEROPLANE

Commercial Pilot Licence (Aeroplane) Integrated Course

The aim of this course is to train pilots to the level of proficiency necessary for the issue of a CPL(A), excluding flight instructor training and instrument rating instruction. This course consists of a minimum of 150 hours of flying training and 300 hours (reduced to 200 hours for PPL holders) of theoretical knowledge instruction. (Please refer to Section D1.2A for further details).

Commercial Pilot Licence (Aeroplane) with Instrument Rating Integrated Course

The aim of this course is to train pilots to the level of proficiency necessary to operate single pilot, single-engine or multi-engine aeroplanes in commercial air transportation and to obtain the CPL(A)/ IR.

This course consists of a minimum of 180 hours of flying training and 500 hours of theoretical knowledge instruction. (Please refer to Section D1.2B for further details).

Airline Transport Pilot Licence (Aeroplane) Integrated Course

The aim of this course is to train pilots to the level of proficiency necessary to enable them to operate as Co-Pilot on multi-pilot, multi-engine aeroplanes in commercial air transportation and to obtain the CPL(A)/ IR with ATPL theoretical knowledge and Multi-Crew Co-operation credit.

The course consists of a minimum of 195 hours of flying training and 750 hours of theoretical knowledge instruction. The course also includes training in multi-crew co-operation for the operation of multi-pilot aeroplanes. (Please refer to Section D1.2C for further details).

HELICOPTER

Commercial Pilot Licence (Helicopter) Integrated Course

The aim of this course is to train pilots to the level of proficiency necessary for the issue of a CPL(H) but not the Instrument rating or any further specialisation.

The course consists of a minimum of 135 hours of flying training and 550 hours (reduced to 500 hours for PPL holders) of theoretical knowledge instruction. (Please refer to Section D4.2A for further details).

Airline Transport Pilot Licence (Helicopter) Integrated Course

The aim of this course is to train pilots to the level of proficiency necessary to enable them to operate as Co-pilot on multi-pilot, multi-engine helicopters in commercial air transportation and to obtain the CPL(H)/ IR but not any further specialisation.

The course consists of a minimum of 195 hours of flying training and 750 hours of theoretical knowledge instruction. The course also includes training in multi-crew co-operation for the operation of multi-pilot helicopters. (Please refer to Section D4.2B for further details).

MODULAR COURSES

The modular courses are designed for individuals who do not wish to undertake a full time course of integrated training or who wish to stagger their training by completing 'modules' of approved training over a period of time, having already gained their Private Pilot Licence. The Modular Courses available are:-

Commercial Pilot Licence (Aeroplane) Modular Course

The aim of this course is to train PPL(A) holders to the level of proficiency necessary for the issue of a CPL(A).

Before commencing a JAR-FCL CPL(A) approved modular course an applicant shall be the holder of a PPL(A) issued in accordance with ICAO Annex 1. Prior to commencing the flight training an applicant shall have completed 150 hours of flight time as a pilot and have complied with JAR-FCL 1.225 and 1.240 if a multi-engine aeroplane is to be used on the skill test. The course consists of a minimum of 25 hours of flying training (30 hours for applicants without a night flying qualification (aeroplane)) and 200 hours of theoretical knowledge instruction. The flying training may be reduced by 10 hours for holders of valid Instrument Rating.

Before taking the CPL(A) Skill Test at the end of the course applicants will be required to provide evidence of having completed an appropriate level of theoretical knowledge examinations. An approved course of training for the examinations must have been undertaken prior to attempting them. (Please refer to Section D1.2D for further details).

Commercial Pilot Licence (Helicopter) Modular Course

The aim of this course is to train PPL(H) holders to the level of proficiency necessary for the issue of a CPL(H) but not the instrument rating or any further specialisation.

Before commencing a JAR-FCL CPL(H) approved modular course an applicant shall be the holder of a PPL(H) issued in accordance with ICAO Annex 1. Prior to commencing the flight training an applicant shall have completed:

- 155 hours flight time as pilot of helicopters, including 50 hours as PIC of helicopters of which 10 hours shall be cross-country; or
- 135 hours as pilot of helicopters if holder of a PPL(A); or
- 105 hours as pilot of helicopters if holder of a CPL(A).

The course consists of a minimum of 30 hours of flying training (35 hours for applicants without a night flying qualification (helicopter)) and 500 hours of theoretical knowledge instruction.

Before taking the CPL(H) Skill Test at the end of the course applicants will be required to provide evidence of having completed an appropriate level of theoretical knowledge examinations. (Please refer to Section D4.2C for further details).

Instrument Rating (Aeroplane and Helicopter) Modular Course

The aim of the IR modular flying training course is to train pilots to the level of proficiency necessary to operate aeroplanes or helicopters as appropriate under IFR and in IMC.

Holders of a PPL(A)/(H) or CPL(A)/(H) as appropriate, either licence(s) to include the privileges to fly by night, issued in accordance with ICAO Annex 1 may commence the flight training on, an approved JAR-FCL IR modular course.

The course shall comprise of 50 hours instrument flying for Single-Engine IR(A)/IR(H) or 55 hours instrument flying for Multi-Engine IR(A)/IR(H).

Prior to the IR Skill Test a candidate will be required to produce evidence of having passed the appropriate level of theoretical knowledge examinations required for an Instrument Rating. (Please refer to Sections E1 and E2 for further details).

ATPL Theoretical Knowledge Modular Course

The aim of this course is to train pilots who have not received the theoretical knowledge instruction during an integrated course, to the level of theoretical knowledge required for the ATPL(A)/(H). An applicant wishing to undertake an ATPL modular course shall be the holder of a PPL(A)/(H) issued in accordance with ICAO Annex 1 as appropriate and complete 650 hours of instruction in ATPL theory at an approved FTO. (Please refer to Section D for further details).

Holders of a CPL(A)/IR may have the ATPL(A) theoretical instruction reduced by 350 hours.

Holders of a CPL(A) may have the ATPL(A) theoretical instruction reduced by 200 hours.

Holders of an Instrument Rating (Helicopters) may have the ATPL(H) theoretical instruction reduced by 200 hours.

Theoretical Knowledge Examination Bookings

All applications for a booking for any ATPL, CPL or IR examination (including re-sits) must be recommended and countersigned by the Chief Ground Instructor (or authorised signatory) of an approved training provider. A candidate who qualifies for exemption from approved theoretical knowledge training (i.e. some non-JAA ATPL conversions) will not be subject to this requirement. (Please refer to Section J for further details).

Multi-Crew Co-operation

The aim of this course is to train pilots in the functioning of the flight crew as a team of co-operating members led by the pilot-in-command on multi-pilot aircraft, and its completion is required to endorse an initial multi-pilot aircraft type on to a licence. This course may be completed as part of the approved ATPL integrated course, as a stand-alone course or as part of the initial multi-pilot type rating training course. The MCC course shall comprise of at least 25 hours of theoretical knowledge instruction and exercises and 20 hours of MCC training. Students attending an ATPL integrated course may have the practical training reduced by 5 hours. Wherever possible, the MCC training should be combined with the initial type rating course on multi-pilot aircraft. For further details on the MCC course or claiming an MCC course credit, please refer to Section F10.

A5 MEDICAL

Medical fitness

In order to apply for, or to exercise the privileges of a licence which is accepted without formality by other mutually recognised JAA Member States, the applicant or licence holder shall hold a medical certificate issued in accordance with the provisions of JAR–FCL 3 (Medical), appropriate to the privileges of the licence and shall be mentally and physically fit to exercise safely the privileges of the applicable licence.

Note: Applicants for a licence are strongly advised to ensure they meet the medical requirements for that licence before committing themselves to any substantial expense in satisfying other licensing requirements.

A student pilot must hold a valid Medical Certificate or Medical Declaration (as appropriate to licence sought) before he will be permitted to fly solo.

Medication

Pilots taking medication on a regular or occasional basis should check with their AMEs to see whether the medication or the condition for which it is being taken for, are acceptable for aviating duties. This includes non-prescription medication (also known as "Over the Counter" medication.

JAR-FCL Medical Certificates

There are two standards of JAR medical certificate: JAR Class 1 for a professional flying licence; JAR Class 2 for a private flying licence.

The initial JAR-FCL Class 1 medical examination is conducted at the UK CAA Aeromedical Centre at Gatwick. Holders of a JAR-FCL Class 1 medical certificate issued by another mutually recognised JAA Member State should either contact the CAA Aeromedical Centre at Gatwick or refer to the CAA-SRG web site for details on acceptability and mutual recognition.

The initial JAR-FCL Class 2 medical examination can be obtained from by any UK CAA Authorised medical Examiner (AME), or by an AME in a mutually recognised JAA Member State.

For further details on medical examinations and medical examiners and for JAA Member States which have been 'mutually recognised' please refer to the CAA-SRG web site www.caa.co.uk.

UK (National) Medical Requirements

The UK has special arrangements for pilots flying balloons, airships, microlights, gyroplanes, and single-engine piston under 2000kg. For up to date information please refer to the CAA SRG web site: www.caa.co.uk

Decrease in medical fitness

GENERAL

Every holder of a medical certificate issued in accordance with JAR–FCL 3 (Medical) who is aware of:

- any significant personal injury involving incapacity to function as a member of a flight crew; or
- any illness involving incapacity to function as a member of a flight crew throughout a period of 21 days or more; or
- being pregnant,

shall inform the CAA in writing of such injury or pregnancy, and as soon as the period of 21days has elapsed in the case of illness. The medical certificate shall be deemed to be suspended upon the occurrence of such injury or the elapse of such period of illness or the confirmation of the pregnancy, and:

in the case of injury or illness the suspension shall be lifted upon the holder being medically examined under arrangements made by the CAA and being pronounced fit to function as a member of the flight crew, or upon the CAA exempting, subject to such conditions as it thinks fit, the holder from the requirement of a medical examination; and;

in the case of pregnancy, the suspension may be lifted by the CAA for such period and subject to such conditions as it thinks fit and shall cease upon the holder being medically examined under arrangements made by the CAA after the pregnancy has ended and being pronounced fit to resume her functions as a member of the flight crew.

Instructors/Examiners (Aeroplanes and Helicopters)

With certain exceptions, instructors and examiners are required to hold a professional pilot's licence, including a Class 1 medical certificate, in order to receive remuneration for their services. In some cases, a minor or temporary decrease in medical fitness will require the Class 1 medical certificate to be restricted by an Operational Multi-crew Limitation (OML). This restricts the holder to flying solely in a multi-crew environment where the other pilot is qualified to act as pilot-in-command or co-pilot on that flight. Flight instruction and skill tests for the initial grant of a licence or rating are undertaken in a multi-crew environment, even when conducted on a single-pilot aircraft, but the pilot under instruction or test is not qualified to act as pilot-in-command or co-pilot other than in the capacity of a student pilot.

Note: The conditions detailed in this document apply only to flights in aircraft, NOT to training or skill tests conducted in synthetic training devices.

In all cases, the instructor or examiner who is subject to an OML must brief the student on the procedure to be followed in the event of incapacitation. For further details please refer to Section A Appendix G.

A6 FLIGHT CREW LICENCES (JAR AND UK NATIONAL)

Flight crew licences issued in accordance with JAR–FCL will conform to JAR-FCL specifications and may only be replaced with a JAR-FCL licence. Licences issued in accordance with UK National arrangements will, where applicable, remain valid until their date of expiry and may be renewed after this date. The UK National Licence will continue to be available to those who have previously held the licence. There is no necessity for UK national licence holders to convert to a JAR-FCL equivalent licence unless they wish to do so. The only circumstance in which all holders of a UK national licence would need to obtain a JAR-FCL licence would be if the EU mandated such a move. Until such time as EC Directive 91/670/EEC is withdrawn, a UK National licence can still be validated in other EU States.

Holders of UK national licences do not need to surrender their licence upon issuance of a JAR-FCL equivalent.

A7 NON-JAA LICENCE HOLDERS

Validation of Licences issued by Non-JAA States

A licence issued by a non-JAA State may be rendered valid at the discretion of the Authority of a JAA Member State for use on aircraft registered in that JAA Member State in accordance with Appendix 1 to JAR-FCL 1.015/2.015.

Validation of a professional pilot's licence shall not exceed one year from the date of validation, provided that the basic licence remains valid. Any further validation for use on aircraft registered in any JAA Member State is subject to agreement by the JAA Member States and to any conditions seen fit within the JAA. The user of a licence validated by a JAA Member State shall comply with the requirements stated in JAR–FCL.

For further information regarding validations, please contact PLD for advice.

The requirements stated in the above shall not apply where aircraft registered in a JAA Member State are leased to an operator in a non-JAA State, provided that the State of the operator has accepted for the period of lease the responsibility for the technical and/or operational supervision in accordance with JAR–OPS 1.165. The licences of the flight crews of the non-JAA State operator may be validated at the discretion of the Authority of the JAA Member State concerned, provided that the privileges of the flight crew licence validation are restricted for use during the lease period only on nominated aircraft in specified operations not involving a JAA operator, directly or indirectly, through a wet lease or other commercial arrangement.

Exercising the privileges of a Non-UK Licence in UK registered aircraft

Article 26, of the ANO 2005, states that a pilot must hold an appropriate licence granted either by the CAA or by a foreign authority and rendered valid under the ANO to fly a UK registered aircraft.

A JAA licence is deemed to be a licence rendered valid under the ANO unless the CAA in the particular case gives direction to the contrary. A JAA licence is a licence issued in accordance with licensing and medical requirements of JAR-FCL by a full JAA Member State that has been recommended for mutual recognition by Central JAA (JAA Headquarters).

A licence issued by any other ICAO Contracting State (including a JAA State that has not yet been recommended for mutual recognition) is also deemed to be valid under the ANO for the purposes of flying a UK registered aircraft, providing that the licence and medical are valid in accordance with the rules/laws of the issuing State, and the CAA does not in the particular case give direction to the contrary. However, the ANO 2005 Article 26 (4) (a) states that the holder of such a licence **cannot**:

1. act as a member of the flight crew of any aircraft flying for the purpose of public transport or aerial work or on any flight in respect of which he receives remuneration for his services as a member of the flight crew; or

2. in the case of a pilot's licence, to act as a pilot of any aircraft flying in controlled airspace in circumstances requiring compliance with the Instrument Flight Rules or to give any instruction in flying.

Conversion of a licence issued by a non-JAA State

A licence issued by a non-JAA State may be converted to a JAR–FCL licence provided that an arrangement exists between the JAA and the non-JAA State. This arrangement shall be established on the basis of reciprocity of licence acceptance and shall ensure that an equivalent level of safety exists between the training and testing requirements of the JAA and the non-JAA State. Any arrangement entered into will be reviewed periodically, as agreed by the non-JAA State and the JAA. A licence converted according to such an arrangement shall have an entry indicating the non-JAA State upon which the conversion is based. Other Member States shall not be obliged to accept any such licence.

Details on licence conversion terms can be found in the relevant section pertaining to the licence being sought.

Credit given to a holder of a licence issued by a non-JAA State

An applicant for a JAR-FCL licence and IR, if applicable, already holding at least an equivalent licence issued in accordance with ICAO Annex 1 by a non-JAA State shall meet all the requirements of JAR-FCL, except that the requirements of course duration, number of lessons and specific training hours may be reduced. The CAA may be guided as to the credits to be granted on the basis of a recommendation from an appropriate training organisation.

A8 STATE OF LICENCE ISSUE

JAR-FCL 1.065/2.065 states that an applicant shall demonstrate the satisfactory completion of all requirements for licence issue to the Authority of the 'State of Licence Issue'.

Training/Testing in other JAA Member States

In circumstances agreed by both Authorities, an applicant who has commenced training under the responsibility of one Authority may be permitted to complete the requirements under the responsibility of the other Authority.

The agreement shall allow for:

1. theoretical knowledge training and examinations*;
2. medical examination and assessment;
3. flight training and testing.

The Authorities shall agree the 'State of Licence Issue'.

*The UK CAA does not recognise JAR-FCL PPL(A)/ (H) examinations completed in another JAA Member State for the purpose of issuance of a UK JAR-FCL PPL(A)/ (H) as these examinations are produced "nationally" and are not compiled using the JAA Central Question Bank.

Note: Applicants should be aware that whilst there is provision in JAR-FCL to allow training/testing to be carried out between JAA Member States, each State may have their own policy regarding the acceptance of training/testing completed in another State. Therefore, prior to commencement of training, applicants are advised to contact the intended 'State of Licence Issue' to confirm their policy on this matter (for UK Policy see below).

Further ratings (e.g. type/class/instrument/instructor) may be obtained under JAR-FCL requirements in any JAA Member State and will be entered into the licence by the 'State of Licence Issue'. For endorsement of the rating onto a UK issued licence, this is on the proviso that a full course of training and testing is completed at a JAA Approved Training provider. Applicants who qualify for the reduced Instrument Rating conversion requirements as detailed in Section E1.2/E2.2 may conduct the specified course of training in another JAA Member State.

UK Policy

JAR-FCL Theoretical Knowledge Exams completed in another JAA Member State (other than the UK)

The UK CAA will recognise a valid pass in JAR-FCL Theoretical Knowledge Examinations (except PPL as mentioned above) completed in another JAA Member State towards the issue of a UK JAR-FCL Licence. This is subject to the applicant completing a course of flying training and testing at a UK approved Flying Training Organisation. In addition, the applicant will require written confirmation from the Authority of the other JAA State confirming that the examinations taken were in accordance with JAR-FCL, and that they have no objection with the UK being the State of Licence Issue. This confirmation shall be submitted to the UK CAA at the time of licence issue together with copies of the appropriate JAR-FCL Theoretical Knowledge Examinations. Applicants will also be required to obtain a UK issued JAR-FCL Medical Certificate.

Previous JAR-PPL Training completed in another JAA Member State (other than the UK)

An applicant who has commenced training for a JAR-FCL PPL(A)/(H), who intends to continue with their training with a UK Registered Facility of Flying Training Organisation, must in the first instance contact the Authority of the Member State in which training was commenced. The applicant should confirm with that other State that they will allow them to continue their training with a UK training provider, and agree that the UK will be the 'State of Licence Issue'. If the other State agrees then the applicant will be required to obtain written confirmation to this effect in order for all previous PPL training to be recognised by the UK CAA. The applicant should also arrange with the other JAA State for any PPL training records to be forwarded onto the new Registered Facility or FTO. If the other State does not give agreement then the UK CAA will only recognise up to a maximum of 10 hours of the previous training towards the overall 45 hour requirement for licence issue. The applicant will in this case be required to complete the further 35 hours as specified in Section C1.2/C2.2 - Flying Training Requirements. It should also be noted that the UK CAA does not recognise JAR-PPL examinations completed in another JAA Member State (see above), and the applicant will be required to retake and pass all of these examinations.

JAR-FCL CPL Modular Course of Flying Training completed in another JAA Member State (other than the UK)

An applicant who has a valid pass in JAR-FCL Theoretical Knowledge Examinations completed through a UK Approved Training provider, wishing to complete a CPL modular course of flying training in another JAA Member State should in the first instance contact the Authority of that Member State. The applicant should confirm with that other State that they are willing to recognise their JAR-FCL Theoretical Knowledge Examinations and that they will be the 'State of Licence Issue'.

Transfer State of Licence Issue

For administrative convenience (e.g. revalidation), the licence holder may subsequently transfer a licence issued by the 'State of Licence Issue' to another JAA Member State, provided that employment or normal residency is established in that State. That State would thereafter become the 'State of Licence Issue' and would assume the responsibility for licence issue referred to above. An applicant shall hold only one JAR-FCL aeroplane or JAR-FCL helicopter licence and one medical certificate at any time.

An applicant may only apply to change the state of licence issue of a JAR-FCL licence provided that employment or normal residency is established in that state. **Normal residency** means the place where a person usually lives for at least 185 days in each calendar year because of personal and occupational ties or, in the case of a person with no occupational ties, because of personal ties which can show close links between that person and the place where she or he is living.(JAR-FCL 1.070/2.070 refers).

Procedures for holders of JAR-FCL pilot's licences to transfer state of licence issue to the United Kingdom

To begin the process to transfer the state of licence issue you are required to fill in form SRG\1136 'Application to Change State of Issue of a JAR-FCL Licence to the United Kingdom' and send it to the CAA at the address on the form, along with copies of your JAR-FCL licence(s), JAR-FCL medical certificate, any JAR-FCL examination passes (if completed) and the required fee. To conform with the "Normal Residency" requirement mentioned above details of employment with a UK Operator or residency in the UK will also be required to be submitted. Information concerning the transfer of your medical details is available on the SRG web site at www.caa.co.uk. Your application will be acknowledged.

The CAA will then approach the existing state of licence issue, for information, to effect the change. A certified copy of your form SRG\1136 will accompany the application to the JAA member state.

Upon return of the documentation from the original state of licence issue to the CAA, a decision will be made to accept or reject the request that the CAA become the state of issue or your JAR-FCL licence(s). You will be notified in writing of the decision.

If your application is accepted you will be requested to submit your original JAR-FCL licence(s) and medical certificate. Only upon receipt of the original licence(s) will the UK issue new licences.

Your original JAR-FCL licence(s) can be submitted to the CAA Personnel Licensing Department (PLD) by post or handed in at our public counter.

Finally, your original JAR-FCL licence(s) will be returned to the original State of licence issue for destruction along with confirmation that the CAA has issued the new licence(s).

In the event the request is rejected, the original state of issue will be advised of this and your fee will be refunded.

By making an application to change the state of licence issue to the UK, you consent to the CAA contacting the original state of licence issue as outlined in the procedure detailed in earlier. You will be required to pay an issue fee for each JAR-FCL licence issued by the CAA. A licence will be issued for a period of five years. At the end of the five years a fee for revalidation/ renewal will be charged.

Procedures for holders of UK JAR-FCL pilot's licences to transfer state of licence issue to another JAA member state.

The licence holder shall apply directly to the new State of licence issue and provide details and documentation as required by that State. When notified by the new State of licence issue, a standard form of information (Standard Document No.155) will be supplied by the CAA to verify relevant details of the licence holder.

The applicant will initially provide sight of the existing licence (or photocopy) and provide logbook(s) or photocopies of relevant period as required by the new State of licence issue. The new State of licence issue will provide an application form that will include a declaration of accuracy and a cautionary warning regarding a false representation. The declaration may be accepted in lieu of logbook evidence of flying experience, at the discretion of the intended State of licence issue. The application form will specify any further information required by the new State of licence issue (e.g. proof of [employment or residency] in accordance with JAR-FCL 1.070 and 2.070.In addition to that included in the standard JAR-FCL transfer form (Document No.155).

In order to comply with laws concerning privacy, confidentiality and data protection, licence holders shall agree on the application form to the transfer of all required licensing information to the new State of licence issue. The original or a certified copy of the application form shall be sent to the CAA when requesting the standard transfer of information (Document No.155).

The CAA will, as requested by the new State of licence issue, transfer all relevant licensing information relating to all pilot licences currently held by an individual, and shall indicate if the licence holder is the subject of past or pending licence enforcement action. New States of licence issue may refuse to issue a licence on the grounds of information presented by the CAA on the applicant. If your application is accepted then the new licence will only be used on surrender of the existing licence, which shall be returned to the CAA for destruction.

A9 CURTAILMENT OF PRIVILEGES OF LICENCE HOLDERS AGED 60 YEARS OR MORE

Age 60–64. The holder of a pilot licence who has attained the age of 60 years shall not act as a pilot of an aeroplane engaged in commercial air transport operations except:

- as a member of a multi-pilot crew and provided that,
- such holder is the only pilot in the flight crew who has attained age 60.

Age 65. The holder of a pilot licence who has attained the age of 65 years shall not act as a pilot of an aeroplane engaged in commercial air transport operations.

It should be noted that in some other JAA Member States privileges of licence holders aged 60 years or more may differ.

A10 MINIMUM REQUIREMENTS FOR THE ISSUE OF A JAR-FCL LICENCE ON THE BASIS OF A NATIONAL LICENCE

Licences and ratings, authorisations, approvals or medical certificates issued in accordance with the national regulations of JAA Member States before 1 July 1999 shall continue to be valid with the same privileges, ratings and limitations, if any. After 1 January 2000 all requirements for revalidation or renewal of such licences or ratings, authorisations, approvals or medical certificates are in accordance with the requirements of JAR–FCL, except as specified for the medical restriction below.

Holders of a licence issued in accordance with the national regulations of a JAA Member State who do not fully meet the [Section 1 requirements of JAR-FCL 3] (Medical) shall be permitted to continue to exercise the privileges of the national licence held.

There is no necessity for holders of a UK national pilot licence to convert to a JAR-FCL equivalent licence unless they wish to do so. Details for the issue of a JAR-FCL Pilot Licence on the basis of an existing National (UK) Pilot Licence are detailed as follows.

A10.1 Minimum Requirements for the issue of a JAR-FCL pilot licence (aeroplane) on the basis of a national (UK) pilot's licence (aeroplanes)

A Pilot licence issued by the CAA in accordance with national requirements may be replaced by a JAR-FCL licence subject, where applicable, to conditions. For the replacement of such licences the holder shall:

1. Complete as a proficiency check, the type/class and instrument rating (IR if applicable) revalidation requirements of JAR-FCL 1.245 **(**(b)(1), 1.245(c)(1)(i) or 1.245(c)(2)**)** relevant to the privileges of the licence held;
   - Only a <u>valid</u> Licensing Proficiency Check (LPC) or Licensing Skill Test (LST) is acceptable.
   - An Operator Proficiency Check (OPC) as required by JAR-OPS is <u>not</u> acceptable.
   - **This requirement does not apply for the issue of a JAR-FCL PPL(A)**
2. **For CPL(A) and ATPL(A) only**
   Demonstrate to the satisfaction of the CAA that a knowledge of the relevant parts of JAR-OPS 1 and JAR-FCL (see AMC FCL 1.005 and 1.015) has been acquired;
   - Applicants will satisfy this requirement by signing a declaration contained in the application form for the licence.

   For PPL(A) only
   Demonstrate to the satisfaction of the CAA that a knowledge of the relevant parts of JAA Requirements (see AMC FCL 1.125) has been acquired:
   - Applicants will satisfy this requirement by signing a declaration contained in the application form for the licence.
3. Demonstrate a knowledge of English in accordance with JAR-FCL 1.200 if Instrument Rating (IR) privileges are held;
   - This shall be demonstrated by having graduated from an IR course given in English.
4. Hold a valid JAR-FCL Medical Certificate;
   - Class 1 for CPL(A) or ATPL(A)
   - Class 1 or 2 for PPL(A).
5. Comply with the experience requirements and any further requirements as set out in the table overleaf.

Whenever a reference is made to aeroplanes this does not include microlights as defined nationally unless otherwise specified.

National licence held (1)	Total flying experience (hours) (see note 1) (2)	Any further JAA requirements (3)	Replacement JAR-FCL licence and conditions (where applicable) (4)	Removal of conditions (5)	
ATPL (A)	>1500 as PIC on multi-pilot aeroplanes	None	ATPL(A)	Not applicable	a
ATPL (A)	>1500 on multi-pilot aeroplanes	None	as in (c)(4)	as in (c)(5)	b
ATPL (A)	>500 on multi-pilot aeroplanes	(i) demonstrate to the Authority a knowledge of flight planning and performance as required by Appendix 1 to JAR- FCL 1.470 **(see note 2)**	ATPL(A), with type rating restricted to co-pilot. **(see note 3)**	demonstrate ability to act as PIC as required by JAR-FCL Appendix 2 to JAR-FCL 1.240	c
CPL(A)/ IR & passed ICAO ATPL theory test in JAA Member State of licence issue	>500 on multi-pilot aeroplanes or in multi-pilot operations on single-pilot aeroplanes JAR-FAR 23 commuter category in accordance with JAR-OPS 1 or equivalent national operational requirements **(see Note 4)**	(i) demonstrate to the Authority a knowledge of flight planning and performance as required by Appendix 1 to JAR- FCL 1.470 **(see note 2)** (ii) have at least 100 hours as PIC of aeroplanes. (iii) have a valid multi-engine IR.	CPL(A)/IR with JAR-FCL ATPL theory credit	Not applicable	d
CPL(A)/ IR	>500 on multi-pilot aeroplanes or in multi-pilot operations on single-pilot aeroplanes JAR-FAR 23 commuter category in accordance with JAR-OPS 1 or equivalent national operational requirements	(i) pass an examination for JAR-FCL ATPL knowledge in the JAA Member State of licence issue. * **(see text below table)** (ii) have at least 100 hours as PIC of aeroplanes. (iii) have a valid multi-engine IR.	CPL(A)/IR with JAR-FCL ATPL theory credit	Not applicable	e
CPL(A)/ IR	>500 as PIC on single pilot aeroplanes	None	CPL(A)/IR with type/class ratings restricted to single pilot aeroplanes	Obtain a multi-pilot type rating as required by JAR-FCL 1.240	f
CPL(A)/ IR	<500 as PIC on single pilot aeroplanes	(i) demonstrate to the Authority a knowledge of flight planning and flight performance as required by Appendix 1 to JAR- FCL 1.470 **(see note 6)**	as (4)(f)	Obtain a multi-pilot type rating as required by JAR-FCL 1.240	g
CPL(A)	>500 as PIC on single pilot aeroplanes	(i) Night qualification, if applicable	CPL(A), with type/class ratings restricted to single-pilot aeroplanes	Obtain a multi-pilot type rating as required by JAR-FCL 1.240	h
CPL(A)	<500 as PIC on single pilot aeroplanes	(i) Night qualification, if applicable (ii) as (3)(g)	as (4)(h)	Obtain a multi-pilot type rating as required by JAR-FCL 1.240	i
PPL(A)/ IR	≥75 hrs. in accordance with IFR	(i) Night qualification	PPL(A)/IR (the IR restricted to PPL)	(i) demonstrate to the Authority a knowledge of flight performance & planning as required by AMC FCL 1.470(c)	j
PPL(A)	≥70 hrs. on aeroplanes	(i) demonstrate the use of radio navigation aids. **(see note 7)**	PPL(A)	Not applicable	k

Notes:

1. Multi Pilot and Single Pilot Aeroplanes are defined in Section A, Appendix A.

2. UK CPL (A) or ATPL (A) holders who have passed, or were credited, the UK Flight Planning examination at ATPL level and Performance A will be deemed to have satisfied this requirement.

3. All aircraft ratings included in a UK ATPL (A) will be transferred to the JAR-FCL as Pilot-in-Command (PIC) ratings (unless specifically restricted to 'Co-pilot only' in the UK licence), as applicants will have already demonstrated the ability to act as PIC on each type/class. In this case, the JAR-FCL ATPL (A) will not be issued with type/class ratings restricted to co-pilot.

4a. UK CPL (A)/IR holders who have passed UK ATPL (A) theory examinations, and have 500 hours flying experience in multi-pilot operations will be credited the JAR-FCL ATPL(A) theoretical knowledge examinations for the purpose of JAR-FCL ATPL(A) licence issue. This credit will remain valid for a period of 7 years from the most recent validity date of the IR (A). To upgrade to a JAR-FCL ATPL (A), applicants must either:

   i. Obtain a multi-pilot type rating (if not already held) in accordance with JAR-FCL 1.240, meet the experience requirements of JAR-FCL 1.280 and pass the ATPL (A) Skill Test on a multi-pilot type with an authorised Examiner. The ATPL(A) Skill Test may serve at the same time as a skill test for the issue of the licence and a proficiency check for the revalidation of the type rating for the aeroplane used in the test and may be combined with the skill test for the issue of a multi-pilot type rating; or

   ii. Obtain a multi-pilot type rating (if not already held) in accordance with JAR-FCL 1.240, meet the experience requirements of a UK ATPL (A) as detailed below (even though such a licence can no longer be issued) **AND** meet the requirements for conversion of a UK ATPL (A) to JAR-FCL ATPL (A) in accordance with Appendix 1 to JAR-FCL 1.005 (see previous table).

   1500 hours as pilot of flying machines which must include the following requirements:

   - 250 hours PIC of aeroplanes of which up to a maximum of 150 hours may be as Co-pilot acting as PIC U/S of aeroplanes;
   - 50 hours cross-country as PIC or PIC U/S of aeroplanes or helicopters of which not less than 35 hours must be as PIC of aeroplanes including a 300nm flight with landings at not less than 2 intermediate and different aerodromes;
   - Further 150 hours cross-country as PIC, PIC U/S or Co-pilot in aeroplanes or helicopters, of which not less than 65 hours must be in aeroplanes;
   - 100 hours night flying as PIC, PIC U/S or Co-pilot in aeroplanes (up to 50 hours may be flown in helicopter), of which not less than 25 hours must be cross-country as PIC or PIC U/S, including 2 flights as PIC terminating at an aerodrome not less than 65nm from point of departure. The night flying must include 5 hours and 10 take-offs and landings as PIC.
   - 75 hours flying as pilot by sole reference to instruments, (50 hours must be in aeroplanes, the remainder may be in helicopters or approved simulator.

4b. UK CPL (A)/IR holders who have passed UK ATPL(A) theory examinations, and have less than 500 hours flying experience in multi-pilot operations do not qualify for the JAR-FCL ATPL(A) theory credit. However, UK ATPL (A) theory will be accepted (i) to endorse the first multi-pilot type rating onto the JAR-FCL CPL (A) licence, and (ii) for the subsequent issue of a JAR-FCL ATPL (A) **provided** applicants meet the experience requirements of a UK ATPL (A) (even though such a licence can no longer be issued) **and** meet the requirements for conversion of a UK ATPL (A) to JAR-FCL ATPL (A) in accordance with Appendix 1 to JAR-FCL 1.005 (see previous table). The UK ATPL (A) theory will remain valid for a period of 7 years from the most recent validity date of the IR (A) for the issue of a JAR-FCL ATPL (A).

5. UK CPL (A) holders already holding a type rating for a multi-pilot aeroplane are not required to have passed the ATPL theoretical knowledge examinations whilst they continue to operate that same aeroplane type, but will **not** be given ATPL theory credit for a JAR-FCL licence. If a type rating for a different multi-pilot aeroplane is required, applicants must pass the JAR-FCL ATPL theoretical knowledge examinations.

6. UK CPL (A) holders who have passed, or were credited the UK Flight Planning examination at CPL level and have passed Performance C, D, E

or U will be deemed to have satisfied this requirement.

7. Demonstration of the use of radio navigation aids should be to the satisfaction of a Chief Flying Instructor. Successful demonstration should be certified by the CFI in the applicant's personal flying logbook

A10.2 Minimum requirements for the issue of a JAR-FCL pilot licence (helicopter) on the basis of a national (UK) pilot's licence (helicopters)

A pilot licence issued by the CAA in accordance with national requirements may be replaced by a JAR-FCL licence, subject to conditions. For the replacement of such licences the holder shall:

1. Complete, as a proficiency check, the type (and instrument rating (IR) if applicable) revalidation requirements of JAR-FCL 2.245 (b) relevant to the privileges of the licence held;
    - Only a valid Licensing Proficiency Check (LPC) or Licensing Skill Test (LST) is acceptable.
    - An Operator Proficiency Check (OPC) as required by JAR-OPS is not acceptable.
2. **For CPL (H) and ATPL (H) only**
Demonstrate to the satisfaction of the CAA that a knowledge of the relevant parts of JAR-OPS 3 and JAR-FCL (see AMC FCL 2.005 and 2.015), has been acquired; applicants will satisfy this requirement by signing a declaration contained in the application form for the licence.
3. **For PPL (H) only**
Demonstrate to the satisfaction of the CAA that knowledge of the relevant parts of JAA Requirements (see AMC FCL 2.125) has been acquired; applicants will satisfy this requirement by signing a declaration in the application form for the licence.
4. Demonstrate acknowledge of English in accordance with JAR-FCL 2.200 if Instrument Rating (IR) privileges are held;
    - This shall be demonstrated by having graduated from an IR course given in English.
5. Hold a valid JAR-FCL Medical Certificate.
    - Class 1 for CPL (H) or ATPL (H)
    - Class 1 or 2 for PPL (H)
6. Comply with the experience requirements and any further requirements as set out in the table:

1 of 2

National licence held (1)	Total flying hours experience (2)	Any further JAA requirements (3)	Replacement JAR-FCL licence and conditions (where applicable) (4)	Removal of conditions (5)	
ATPL (H) (valid IR(H))	>1000 as PIC on multi-pilot helicopters	none	ATPL (H)	Not applicable	a
ATPL (H) (no IR(H) privileges)	>1000 as PIC on multi-pilot helicopters	none	ATPL (H) restricted to VFR privileges	Obtain an IR (H) in accordance with JAR-FCL 2 Subpart E	b
ATPL (H) (valid IR (H))	>1000 on multi-pilot helicopters	none	ATPL (H) with type rating restricted to co-pilot (**see Note 2**)	demonstrate ability to act as PIC as required by JAR-FCL Appendix 1 to JAR-FCL 2.240 and 2.295 paras 9 to 15	c
ATPL (H) (no IR (H) privileges)	>1000 on multi-pilot helicopters	none	ATPL (H) restricted to VFR privileges and type rating restricted to co-pilot (**see Note 2**)	(i) Obtain an IR (H) in accordance with JAR-FCL 2 Subpart E (ii) demonstrate ability to act as PIC as required by Appendix 1 to JAR-FCL 2.240 and 2.295 paras 9 to 15	d
ATPL (H) (valid IR (H))	>500 on multi-pilot helicopters	demonstrate to the Authority a knowledge of flight planning and flight performance as required by Appendix 1 to JAR- FCL 2.470	ATPL (H) with type rating restricted to co-pilot (**see Note 2**)	demonstrate ability to act as PIC as required by JAR-FCL Appendix 1 to JAR-FCL 2.240 and 2.295 paras 9 to 15	e
ATPL (H) (no IR (H) privileges)	>500 on multi-pilot helicopters	demonstrate to the Authority a knowledge of flight planning and flight performance as required by Appendix 1 to FCL 2.470	ATPL (H) restricted to VFR privileges and type rating restricted to co-pilot (**see Note 2**)	(i) Obtain an IR (H) in accordance with JAR-FCL 2 Subpart E (ii) demonstrate ability to act as PIC as required by Appendix 1 to JAR-FCL 2.240 and 2.295 paras 9 to 15	f
CPL/IR (H) and passed an ICAO ATPL (H) theory test in the JAA Member State of licence issue	>500 multi-pilot helicopters	(i) demonstrate to the Authority a knowledge of flight planning and flight performance as required by Appendix 1 to JAR- FCL 2.470 (ii) meet remaining requirements of JAR-FCL 2.250(a)	CPL/IR(H) with JAR-FCL ATPL(H) theory credit	Not applicable	g

2 of 2 *(cont'd from previous page)*

National licence held (1)	Total flying hours experience (2)	Any further JAA requirements (3)	Replacement JAR-FCL licence and conditions (where applicable) (4)	Removal of conditions (5)	
CPL/IR (H)	>500 as PIC on multi pilot helicopters	(i) to pass an examination for JAR-FCL ATPL(H) theoretical knowledge in the JAA Member State of licence issue *(see text below table) (ii) meet remaining requirements of JAR-FCL 2.250(a)	CPL/IR (H) with JAR-FCL ATPL(H) theory credit	not applicable	h
CPL/IR (H)	>500 as PIC on single pilot helicopters	none	CPL/IR (H) with type ratings restricted to single-pilot helicopters	obtain multi-pilot type rating as required by JAR-FCL 2.240	i
CPL (H)	<500 as PIC on single pilot helicopters	demonstrate to the Authority a knowledge of flight planning and flight performance as required by Appendix 1 to JAR-FCL 2.470	as (4)(h)		j
CPL (H)	>500 as PIC on single pilot helicopters	night qualification, if applicable	CPL(H) with type ratings restricted to single pilot helicopters		k
CPL(H)	<500 as PIC on single pilot helicopters	night qualification, if applicable, demonstrate to the Authority a knowledge of flight performance and planning as required by Appendix 1 to JAR-FCL 2.470	as (4) (j)		l
PPL/IR (H)	≥75 hrs. in accordance with IFR	night qualification; if night flying privileges are not included in the instrument rating	PPL/IR (H) (the IR restricted to PPL)	demonstrate to the Authority a knowledge of flight performance and planning as required by Appendix 1 to JAR-FCL 2.470	*m*
PPL (H)	≥75 hrs. on helicopters	demonstrate the use of radio navigation aids	PPL (H)		n

Notes:

1. Multi Pilot Helicopters are defined as helicopters certificated for operation with a minimum crew of at least two pilots **or** required to be operated by a crew of at least two pilots in accordance with JAR-OPS.

   Single-Pilot Helicopters are defined as helicopters certificated for operation by one pilot.

2. All Aircraft Ratings included in a UK ATPL (H) will be transferred as a Pilot-in-Command (PIC) ratings to the JAR-FCL licence (unless specifically restricted to 'Co- pilot only' in the UK licence) as applicants will have already demonstrated the ability to act as PIC on each helicopter type. In this case, the JAR-FCL ATPL (H) will not be issued with type ratings restricted to co-pilot.

3a. UK CPL(H)/IR holders who have passed UK CPL(H) theory examinations, <u>and</u> have 500 hours flying experience in multi-pilot operations will be credited the JAR-FCL ATPL(H) theoretical knowledge examinations for the purpose of JAR-FCL ATPL(H) licence issue. This credit will remain valid for a period of 7 years from the most recent validity date of the IR (H). To upgrade to a JAR-FCL ATPL (H), applicants must either:

   i. Obtain a multi-pilot type rating (if not already held) in accordance with JAR-FCL 2.240 (**see Note 1**), meet the experience requirements of JAR-FCL 2.280 and pass the ATPL (H) Skill Test on a multi-pilot type with an authorised Examiner. The ATPL (H) Skill Test may serve at the same time as a skill test for the issue of the licence and a proficiency check for the revalidation of the type rating for the helicopter used in the test and may be combined with the skill test for the issue of a multi-pilot type rating; or

   ii. Obtain a multi-pilot type rating (if not already held) in accordance with JAR-FCL 2.240 (see Note 1), meet the experience requirements of a UK ATPL (H) (even though such a licence can no longer be issued) **AND** meet the requirements for conversion of a UK ATPL (H) to JAR-FCL ATPL (H) in accordance with Appendix 1 to JAR-FCL 2.005.

3b. UK CPL (H)/IR holders who have passed UK CPL(H) theory examinations, and have <u>less than</u> 500 hours flying experience in multi-pilot operations do not qualify for the JAR-FCL ATPL(H) theory credit. However, the UK CPL (H) theory will be accepted for the issue of a JAR-FCL ATPL (H) **provided** applicants meet the experience requirements of a UK ATPL (H) as detailed below (even though such a licence can no longer be issued) **and** meet the requirements for conversion of a UK ATPL (H) to JAR-FCL ATPL (H) in accordance with Appendix 1 to JAR-FCL 2.005. The UK CPL (H) theory will remain valid for a period of 7 years from the most recent validity date of the IR(H) for the issue of a JAR-FCL ATPL(H).

   *CPL holders already holding a type rating for a multi-pilot helicopter are not required to have passed an examination for ATPL theoretical knowledge whilst they continue to operate that same helicopter type, but will not be given ATPL theory credit for a JAR-FCL licence. If they require another type rating for a different multi-pilot helicopter, they must pass an examination in JAR-FCL ATPL(H) knowledge in the JAA Member State of licence issue.

FLYING EXPERIENCE REQUIREMENTS FOR UK ATPL(H)

1200 hours as pilot of flying machines which must include the following requirements:

400 hours PIC of Helicopters, **or alternatively;**

- 50 hours PIC of Flying Machines, which must include 35 hours PIC of Helicopters, plus 165 hours PIC or Co-Pilot acting as PIC U/S of Helicopters; plus 200 hours PIC or Co-pilot) of Helicopters.
- 50 hours Cross-country flying, must include 10 hours Pilot-in-Command of Helicopters, must include One flight by day of at least 50 nm and One flight by night of at least 50 nm.
- 40 hours PIC or PIC U/S of Aeroplanes or Helicopters, must include 15 hours PIC or PIC U/S of Helicopters.
- 20 hours Night flying as PIC, PIC U/S or P/UT of Helicopters, must include 3 hours Dual instruction, must include 1 hour Cross-country flying, 10 hours PIC or PIC U/S, must include 5 hours PIC, must include 5 take-offs, circuits and landings without assistance.
- 10 hours instruction in Instrument flying in Helicopters.

4. UK CPL (H) holders already holding a type rating for a multi-pilot helicopter are not required to have passed the ATPL theoretical knowledge examinations whilst they continue to operate that same helicopter type, but will **not** be given ATPL theory credit for a JAR-FCL licence. If a type rating for a different multi-pilot helicopter is required, applicants must pass the JAR-FCL ATPL theoretical knowledge examination.

5. Demonstration of the use of radio navigation aids should be to the satisfaction of a Chief Flying Instructor. Successful demonstration should be certified by the CFI in the applicant's personal flying logbook.

6. A Night Qualification in accordance with Appendix 4 to JAR-FCL 2.125.

A11 SPECIAL CIRCUMSTANCES (EXEMPTIONS TO JAR-FCL)

It is recognised that the provisions of all parts of JAR-FCL will not cover every possible situation. Where the application of JAR–FCL would have anomalous consequences, or where the development of new training or testing concepts would not comply with the requirements, an applicant may ask the Authority concerned for an exemption. An exemption may be granted only if it can be shown that the exemption will ensure or lead to at least an equivalent level of safety.

Exemptions are divided into short term exemptions and long term exemptions (more than 6 months). The granting of a long term exemption may only be undertaken in agreement with the JAA FCL Committee/ LST. Where applicable, text has been changed within this document to incorporate the change within the exemption. A full list of exemptions to JAR-FCL can be found on the JAA web site at www.jaa.nl.

A12 CREDIT FOR MILITARY SERVICE

UK Military flight crew members applying for licences and ratings specified in JAR–FCL shall apply to the CAA. The knowledge, experience and skill gained in military service will be credited towards the relevant requirements of JAR–FCL licences and ratings at the discretion of the CAA. The privileges of such licences shall be restricted to aircraft registered in the State of licence issue until the requirements set out in the Appendix 1 to JAR–FCL 1.005/2.005 are met.

Further details can be found in the relevant section appropriate to the licence or rating being sought.

NOTE: Your medical certificate and certificate of test pages should be transferred to this licence

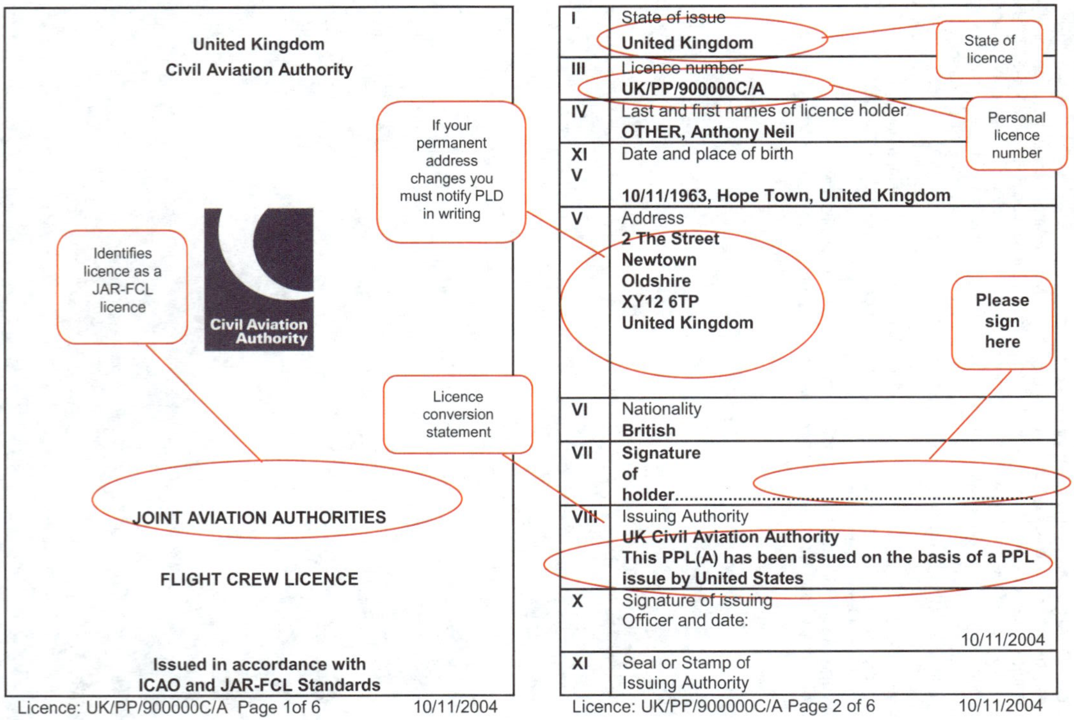

II	Title of licence, date of initial issue and country code **PPL(A)** **10/11/2004** **UK**
IX	Validity. This licence is to be re-issued not later than **09/11/2009.** The privileges of the licence shall be exercised only if the holder has a valid medical certificate for the required privilege. By the application of JAR- FCL 1.015(a)(1), the licence holder is entitled to exercise licence privileges on aircraft registered in any Member State of the Joint Aviation Authorities. A document containing a photo shall be carried for the purposes of identification of the licence holder. The privileges of this licence may be exercised at night.
XII	**Radiotelephony privileges:** Flight Radiotelephony Operator's Licence held. See Flight Radiotelephony Operator's Licence for details.
XIII	**Remarks:** OSL - Valid only with Safety Pilot and in aircraft with dual controls.

Licence: UK/PP/900000C/A Page 3 of 6 10/11/2004

This licence is valid until this date

Type of licence

PPL & BCPL
A night qualification will appear here if held.

CPL & ATPL
Night privileges are an integral part of these licences and this entry does not appear

Any relevant licence remarks/ restrictions

XII	Ratings to be revalidated
Class/Type/IR	**Remarks/Restrictions**
SEP (Land)	**Nil**
B737 300-900	**Nil**
MEP (Land)	**Nil**
EMB 110	**Nil**
Instrument	**Nil**
No further entries	**No further entries**

Nil indicates that there are no restrictions within the privileges of the rating, i.e. Co-pilot only

Ratings included in this licence, all as listed in App 1 to JAR FCL 1.215/1.220

Instructor	**Remarks/Restrictions**
FI(A)	**SP SE and ME only in accordance with JAR-FCL 1.330.**
No further entries	**No further entries**

Licence: UK/PP/900000C/APage 4 of 6 10/11/2004

3 of 4

Attachment indicating UK National ratings included in licence

	Attachment to licence number
	UK/PP/900000C/A
IV	**Last and first names of licence holder** **OTHER, Anthony Neil**
XII	**National ratings to be revalidated**

Rating	**Remarks/Restrictions**
IMC	**Nil**
No further entries	**No further entries**

Licence: UK/PP/900000C/A Page 5 of 6 10/11/2004

NOTE

On licences that have no national ratings, Page 5 will appear blank with the text

INTENTIONALLY BLANK

This does not mean the page is missing

Abbreviations used in licences	
ATPL	Airline Transport Pilot Licence
CPL	Commercial Pilot Licence
PPL	Private Pilot Licence
IR	Instrument Rating
(A)	Aeroplane
(H)	Helicopter
SE	Single - engine
ME	Multi - engine
MPA	Multi - pilot aeroplane
SPA	Single - pilot aeroplane
R/T	Radio Telephony
MEP	Multi - engine piston aeroplanes
SEP	Single - engine piston aeroplanes
FI	Flight Instructor
CRI	Class Rating Instructor
TRI	Type Rating Instructor
IMC	Instrument Meteorological Conditions
IRI	Instrument Rating Instructor

Licence: UK/PP/900000C/A Page 6 of 6 10/11/2004

CERTIFICATE OF REVALIDATION PAGE

Any certificate of test/experience/revalidation with current entries should be retained. It is advised that all certificate pages with entries are retained for possible future reference.

Last and first names: OTHER, Anthony Neil
RATING - CERTIFICATE OF REVALIDATION **Licence No. UK/PP/900000C/A**

Rating	Date of test/ check (if applicable)	Valid until	Examiner Authorisation no.	Examiners Signature
SEP (Land)	N/A	09/05/2008	UK/CRE/862619B	C Watts
B737-300/IR	23/05/2006	22/05/2007	UK/CRE/862619B	C Watts
EMB 110/IR/MPA	15/06/2006	14/06/2007	UK/CRE/871445B	A Simple
MEP (Land)	14/07/2006	13/07/2007	UK/CRE/790480L	B Little
IR-SPA-SE	14/07/2006	13/07/2007	UK/CRE/961953D	B George
FI(A)	01/07/2006	04/04/2009	UK/FIE/862619B	C Watts

Types/classes as listed on JAR-FCL 1. Entries as per guidance to Examiners.

Check conducted in revalidation period.

Correct Examiner authorisation stated

All entries to be made in ink

Licence: UK/PP/900000C/A Rating validity page 10/11/2004

Last and first names: OTHER, Anthony Neil
NATIONAL RATING - CERTIFICATE OF REVALIDATION Licence No. UK/PP/900000C/A

Rating	Date of test/ check (if applicable)	Valid until	Examiner Authorisation no.	Examiners Signature
IMC	04/10/2006	03/11/2008	UK/CRE/862619B	C Watts

Specific revalidationpage for National ratings only.

All entries to be made in ink

Licence:UK/PP/900000C/A National Rating validity page 10/11/2004

A14 TRAINING ORGANISATIONS

Training organisations and registered facilities

Requirements for the establishment, manning and approval of all training organisations can be found in Standards Documents.

Flying training organisations (FTO's) offer training for professional licences and associated ratings.

Type Rating Training Organisations (TRTO's) offer training for type ratings only for licence holders.

Facilities offer training for PPL only shall register for that purpose with the CAA FTO's may also conduct training for the PPL; TRTO's may also conduct training for PPL holders seeking a type rating.

Organisations specialising in theoretical knowledge instruction will be approved by the CAA relevant to the specialised knowledge instruction they are providing.

For details of approved organisations, PPL Registered Facilities and Standards Documents, please refer to CAA-SRG web site www.caa.co.uk.

Finance

It should be noted that the UK CAA is not empowered to verify the financial viability of a registered facility. Registration does not imply any financial protection or guarantee that a registered facility's finances are adequate. A training organisation seeking approval (FTO or TRTO as detailed above) is required by the JAA to satisfy to the UK CAA that sufficient funding is available to conduct courses of flying or ground training to the approved standards but prospective trainees should be aware that this does not imply any protection of fees paid to training organisations.

Methods of paying for courses of training can vary. For example, some organisations may require a lump sum payment in advance some may offer a discount for payment in advance, others may accept staged payments. Whatever method is used, prospective trainees are strongly advised to give careful consideration to their financial commitment before entering in an agreement.

A15 APPEALS AND ENFORCEMENT

A JAA Member State may at any time, in accordance with its national procedures, act on appeals, limit privileges, or suspend or revoke any licence, rating, authorisation, approval or certificate it has issued in accordance with the requirements of JAR–FCL if it is established that an applicant or a licence holder has not met, or no longer meets, the requirements of JAR–FCL or relevant national law of the State of licence issue.

If a JAA Member State establishes that an applicant or licence holder of a JAR–FCL licence issued by another JAA Member State has not met, or no longer meets, the requirements of JAR–FCL or relevant national law of the State in which an aircraft is being flown, the JAA Member State shall inform the State of licence issue and the Licensing Division of the JAA Headquarters. In accordance with its national law, a JAA Member State may direct that in the interest of safety an applicant or licence holder it has duly reported to the State of licence issue and the JAA for the above reason may not pilot aircraft registered in that State or pilot any aircraft in that State's airspace.

Review of licensing decisions by the CAA

Where an application for a licence or a rating is refused, or is granted in terms other than those requested, the applicant may, under the provisions of the Civil Aviation Authority Regulations 1991, request that the case be reviewed by the CAA, that is by one or more members of the CAA, who are appointed by the Secretary of State, as opposed to officials acting on its behalf.

Similarly, an applicant who has failed a test or examination which he is required to pass before he is granted or may exercise the privileges of a licence or rating, may request that the CAA determine whether the test or examination was properly conducted.

Any request under these provisions should be made to the CAA, Head of Personnel Licensing Department (PLD), at the address given in Appendix A, within 14 days of receipt by the applicant of the notice of refusal to grant a licence or rating, or notice to grant it in terms other than those requested, or receipt of notice of failure of an examination or test.

Reference should be made to the Civil Aviation Authority Regulations, 1991, for further information.

A16 RECORD OF TRAINING

Any Registered Facility or FTO should keep the records of flying and ground training involved in a student's training. Irrespective of how many Registered Facilities have been involved in a PPL applicant's training, the person signing the certificate of training on the application form is normally responsible for verifying that all the required training has been satisfactorily completed.

The CAA may require to inspect a student's training records before issuing a licence or rating. All records thus required will be returned. Records are to be kept for at least five years following completion of training. A student is required to maintain an accurate record in his personal flying log book of any training undertaken. Exercises should be annotated and the time spent should be recorded in the 'Remarks' column whenever the exercise forms only a part of a particular sortie.

On completion of any course of training, the Chief Flying Instructor (CFI) (or his representative) should certify the student's logbook as a true record of the training completed.

An FTO shall maintain and retain records for a period of at least 5 years and a Registered Facility shall retain the records for a period of 3 years.

Recognised Syllabus

All required training for the issue of a JAR-FCL licence or associated ratings must be conducted in accordance with the syllabus published in JAR-FCL 1 or 2. For a National licence or rating, training must be conducted to a syllabus recognised by the CAA. Once a syllabus is recognised any proposed modification to it must be submitted to the CAA for approval. Training for a JAR-FCL PPL and associated ratings must be conducted at a Registered Facility (RF) and training for a Professional Pilot Licence must be conducted at an organisation authorised to conduct CAA and JAR-FCL approved courses of flight and ground training.

A17 ADMINISTRATION PROCEDURES (PERSONNEL LICENSING)

This section details the administration procedures when applying to the CAA, for a particular service. Applications should be sent to the CAA, PLD. (Full address in Section A, Appendix E). All of our application forms can be downloaded from the SRG web site at www.caa.co.uk. For a full list of application forms please refer to Section A, Appendix C.

Applying for a service

When an application form is submitted to PLD, the Licensing Operations Team will check your application on receipt to ensure that all requirements have been met. You will then be advised the day after assessment whether the application has been accepted or rejected.

When an application is accepted this will mean that we have fully assessed all relevant requirements including flying experience, written examinations, flight tests and that all administrative requirements have been met. To avoid delay customers should follow carefully our **'Application Checklists',** which are on our application forms, which details the documentation to be submitted with the application.

To indicate how long we are currently taking to process applications, details of turnround times are available on our web site and are updated weekly. We are aware how important it is for customers to know how long their applications may take but, while we always plan to issue the licence within our published CAA Code of Practice timescale, there may be variations in actual delivery times. We also regret that we are unable to expedite individual applications as all applications are dealt with in date order of receipt.

When an applicant has failed to meet a licensing requirement the application will be rejected and a letter detailing why will be sent by return. Once the applicant has met all requirements the item will be processed in **date order from the initial application.**

Computerised Logbooks

Computerised Logbooks are acceptable, provided that they are submitted in hard copy paper format and contain the relevant information (as specified in ANO, currently in force, Article 35) with each page certified as true and signed by the applicant.

Evidence of Identity and Nationality

Applicants applying for the issue of a UK National licence are required to provide evidence of nationality and the date/place of birth and are required to submit their original birth certificate or actual passport with their application for licence issue. Photocopies are not acceptable.

Applicants applying for the issue of a JAR-FCL licence are required to provide evidence of identity and are required to submit their passport or birth certificate. Photocopies are acceptable provided the relevant information is clearly presented and certified by the Head of Training (or authorised signatory) of the approved training provider. In instances where approved training (i.e. National to JAR PPL Conversions/ECAC) has not been completed then the applicant will be required to submit their original documents for us to verify their identity. QSP's may submit photocopies certified by the OC Flying/ Squadron Commander. Existing holders of UK professional flight crew licence or holders of another JAR-FCL pilot's licence can ignore this requirement.

Scheme of Charges

Details of our scheme of charges can be found on the CAA-SRG web site at www.caa.co.uk.

Public Counter Service

PLD provides a counter service at Aviation House, dealing with customer enquiries. The counter opening times are 09:00 am to 16:00 pm.

The Department provides the following 'while you wait' services:-

- Addition of a Type or Class Rating to a Licence;

- Renewal of a Licence;
- UK National to JAR-FCL Licence Conversions;
- Inclusion of the Flight Instructor Rating*;
- Removal of restrictions from the Flight Instructor Rating.

* FI Ratings accompanied by a letter from the employer will be considered for same day issue.

Providing that individuals present themselves with the relevant documentation before midday, we are normally able to provide a 'same day' service, on a 'first come first served basis'. The length of time that an individual will have to wait is dependant on the number of ratings received prior to their arrival at the counter. We have allocated a finite amount of manpower to provide this same day service and therefore, we may not be able to accommodate all requests. We apologise for any inconvenience that this may cause.

On occasions, we have had pilots from major airlines arriving after midday expecting their rating to be endorsed the same day, as they are requested to fly on line the following day. We are aware of crew rostering and flight operational constraints and we try to accommodate these requests, however it may not always be possible to process same day items received after midday.

Therefore, all pilots who are currently undertaking aircraft type training and require their type rating endorsements urgently, should present themselves at our counter before midday. Failure to do so will result in a delay in the processing of the rating. Alternatively, the rating can be treated as a postal application and returned within 10 working days.

In addition, any multiple rating applications (four or more) made by one person/company should be agreed beforehand with the Customer Service Team Manager. Requests should be made in writing or by fax on 01293 573996. Please note, in order to maintain the service we provide we are not able to pre-book slots therefore multiple ratings will be processed for the end of the working day.

We are unable to provide a 'same day' service for applications for licence issue.

All other applications for services may be handed in at the counter but cannot be issued the same day.

Change of Address

Changes of address should be made in writing by letter, fax or by change of address notification (available on the SRG web site at www.caa.co.uk). You should quote your CAA reference number together with details of your new permanent address. There is no need for you to submit your licence, so you may continue to fly whilst the address change is being processed. Once we have actioned the change, we will despatch new licence pages for you to sign and insert into your licence. There is no fee for this service.

Change of Name

Individuals who have changed their name are required to notify the CAA in writing of the change. If the change of name is through marriage then you are also required to submit the original marriage certificate. There will be no charge for this service.

If the change of name is other than by marriage then you are required to submit either an original passport, original change of name deed, Statutory Declaration or original decree absolute. There will be a charge for changing personal particulars (other than by marriage); please refer to the current Scheme of Charges.

Lost Flight Crew Licence

Individuals who have lost their pilot licence are required to submit an application form SRG\1117 for a duplicate licence, together with the appropriate fee (as per current Scheme of Charges).

Where a pilot is required to operate an aircraft and has lost their licence or does not have the licence with them, the operating company should make a request in writing for an exemption to be issued, together with the appropriate fee (as per the Scheme of Charges) to allow the pilot to operate without their licence being carried on the aircraft.

The request from the operating company may be made by fax to 01293 573996, and should include the following information:-

- Name and Licence Number of the pilot.
- Name of the operating company.
- Type and series of aircraft to be operated without the licence in hand.
- Nature of Operation.
- Length of time exemption is required.

(please note that exemptions are issued for a short period until such time as the pilot is able to locate his/her licence or a duplicate licence has been issued, in the case of a lost licence).

An exemption to fly will **not** be issued to a pilot who does not hold the appropriate licence or rating.

Lost Flying Logbook

Individuals who have lost their logbook(s) and are intending to obtain further licences/ratings will be required to obtain a Sworn Affidavit, completed through a solicitor or Commissioner of Oaths, detailing their flying hours to the best of their knowledge. The flying hours should be detailed into categories in conjunction with the applicable licence requirements. This is required in order for us to be able to confirm flying experience when a further licence is applied for.

Individuals who do not intend to obtain any further licence (i.e. ATPL holders) are not required to obtain a Sworn Affidavit, but may wish to start a new logbook.

A18 INTENDING TO FLY OVERSEAS

As a result of recent events, increased global security measures have been adopted by an increased number of National Aviation Authorities.

In the past, production of a valid ICAO pilot licence and current medical certificate to any ICAO Authority would usually result in an immediate authorisation enabling the pilot to exercise the privileges of a PPL in that country. This practice has mostly ceased. Some National Authorities are requesting that holders of ICAO licences not issued by that Authority have their licences and medical certificates verified by the issuing authority; prior to the pilot exercising the privileges of his/her licence in the specific National Authorities airspace/aircraft.

As such the UK CAA have implemented a standard licence verification process for all UK licence holders who require a verification to fly/train in another country where the ICAO Authority of that country requires it.

The UK CAA is working closely with other National Authorities and together have agreed a relatively simple verification procedure. The CAA form SRG\1160 must be completed by each individual and sent direct to the UK CAA. Upon receipt of both the SRG\1160 and the official request from the overseas National Authority a verification will be issued directly to that Authority. This is normally sent by e-mail or fax to keep delays to a minimum. While appearing a simple procedure, for the UK it produces significant problems because of data protection and disclosure of information legislation. Please refer to the Scheme of Charges for the current fee for this service on the SRG web site at www.caa.co.uk.

It is still the case that non-UK ICAO licence holders may exercise the privileges of their licence in UK registered aircraft, albeit subject to restrictions, without the need for any verification. Details of the restrictions imposed on non-UK licence holders can be found in Section A7.

Holders of a UK issued JAR-FCL licence intending to fly in a different JAA Member State do not need to have their licences verified. Full details of the licence verification process can be found on the SRG web site at www.caa.co.uk.

A19 TRAINING AND TESTING ON FOREIGN REGISTERED AIRCRAFT

Flight tests and training in foreign registered aircraft in the UK are subject to both airworthiness and licensing restrictions. If 'valuable consideration' is to be given to the examiner or instructor then the aircraft is being used for aerial work and the flight is subject to ANO Article 140. Prior to undertaking such a flight, the operator of the foreign registered aircraft must obtain an Operating Permit from the Department for Transport (contact 020 7944 5806/5847). The Department for Transport will only consider granting these Operating Permits under certain limited circumstances. This requirement applies equally to JAA member state registered aircraft as to any other state registrations.

In addition, before acting as pilot-in-command of a foreign registered aircraft, the licensing requirements of the state of registration must be met in accordance with ANO Article 26(3). For 'N' registered aircraft, U.S. Federal Air Regulations (FARs) 61.3(a)(1) states that 'when the aircraft is operated within a foreign country a current pilot licence issued by that country in which the aircraft is operated may be used'. In the case of 'Mutually Recognised' JAA member state aircraft, a valid JAA licence should be sufficient; however, the holders of JAA licences and UK National licences must still meet the requirements of ANO Article 26(3) and ensure that their licences 'rendered valid' by the foreign licensing authority. In all cases the requirements of Article 36 must also be met with regard to the entitlement to give instruction and to examine in such aircraft.

Also to comply with JAR-FCL 1 and 2, approval has to be sought from the Approvals Section of Personnel Licensing Department or Flight Operations Department, as appropriate, who may require an inspection of the aircraft and its documentation to ensure it is fit for the purpose. An application for a licence or rating should be accompanied with copies of all supporting paperwork.

A20 ICAO LANGUAGE PROFICIENCY

A new ICAO Annex 1 requirement has been introduced regarding Language Proficiency. As of 5 March 2008, applicants for a licence and licence holders who are required to use the radio telephone will be required to demonstrate the ability to speak and understand the language used for radiotelephony communications. The language proficiency required must be at least Operational Level (level 4).

These new requirements will be introduced in NPA FCL-26 but at this time the full details regarding the implementation of these requirements by the UK are being formulated. We will advise industry in due course by Aeronautical Information Circular.

APPENDICES TO SECTION A

APPENDIX A DEFINITIONS AND ABBREVIATIONS

1 of 8

Abbreviations	Definitions
A	Aeroplane
A/C	Aircraft
ADF	Automatic Direction Finding
AFI	Assistant Flying Instructor
AIC	Aeronautical Information Circular
AIP	Aeronautical Information Publication
AIS	Aeronautical Information Services
AMC	Aeromedical Centre
AMC	Acceptable Means of Compliance
AME	Authorised Medical Examiner
AMS	Aeromedical Section
ANO	Air Navigation Order
AOC	Air Operator's Certificate
AOPA	Aircraft Owners and Pilots Association
ATC	Air Traffic Control
ATC	Air Training Corps
ATP	Airline Transport Pilot
ATPL	Airline Transport Pilot Licence
ATSU	Air Traffic Service Units
BBAC	British Balloon and Airship Club
BCPL(A)	Basic Commercial Pilot's Licence (Aeroplanes)
BGA	British Gliding Association
BHGA	British Hang Gliding Association
BINA	British Isles and North Atlantic
BITD	Basic Instrument Training Device
BMAA	British Microlight Aircraft Association
CAA	Civil Aviation Authority (United Kingdom)
CAP	Civil Aviation Publication
Category (of aircraft)	Categorisation of aircraft according to specified basic characteristics, e.g. aeroplane, helicopter, glider, free balloon
CCQ	Cross Crew Qualification

2 of 8 *(cont'd from previous page)*

Abbreviations	Definitions
CFI	Chief Flying Instructor
CFS	Central Flying School (of the Royal Air Force)
CG	Centre of Gravity
CGI	Chief Ground Instructor
C of A	Certificate of Airworthiness
C of E	Certificate of Experience
C of R	Certificate of Revalidation
C of T	Certificate of Test
Complex type	An aeroplane certificated for the carriage of at least four persons, have a variable pitch propeller and retractable landing gear
Conversion (of a licence)	The issue of a licence on the basis of a licence issued by a non-JAA State
Co-pilot	A pilot operating other than as pilot-in-command, an aircraft for which more than one pilot is required under the list of types of aeroplanes as listed in Appendix 1 to JAR-FCL 1.220) or the type certification of the aircraft, or the operational regulations under which the flight is conducted, but excluding a pilot who is on board the aircraft for the sole purpose of receiving flight instruction for a licence or rating
CP	Co-pilot
CPL	Commercial Pilot Licence
CQB	Central Question Bank
CR	Class Rating
CRE	Class Rating Examiner authorised to conduct Skill Tests, Proficiency Checks for aircraft and instrument ratings on Single-Pilot Aeroplanes (SPA)
CRI	Class Rating Instructor
CRM	Crew Resource Management
DAAIS	Danger Area Activity Information Service
DACS	Danger Area Crossing Service
DEFTS	Defence Elementary Flying Training School
DHFS	Defence Helicopter Flying School
DME	Distance Measuring Equipment
Dual instruction time	Flight time or instrument ground time during which a person is receiving flight instruction from a properly authorised instructor
ECAC	European Civil Aviation Conference
ECG	Electrocardiograph
EFIS	Electronic Flight Instrument System
EFT	Elementary Flying Training
EFTA	European Free Trade Association

3 of 8 *(cont'd from previous page)*

Abbreviations	Definitions
EU	European Union
FADEC	Full Authority Digital Engine Control
FCL	Flight Crew Licensing
FE	Flight Examiner authorised to conduct tests and examinations and sign Certificates of Test and Revalidation in accordance with the privileges stated on the individual authorisation.
F/E	Flight Engineer
F/EL	Flight Engineer Licence
FI	Flight Instructor
FI(R)	Flight Instructor (Restricted)
FIC	Flight Instructor Course
FIE	Flight Instructor Examiner
FIH	Flight Information Handbook
FIS	Flight Information Service
Flight and Navigation Procedures Trainer - Type I (FNPT I)	A ground based training device which represents the flight deck environment of a class of aeroplanes.
Flight and Navigation Procedures Trainer - Type II (FNPT II)	A ground based training device which represents the flight deck environment of a multi-engine aeroplane type or class to the extent that the systems appear to function as in an aeroplane. It incorporates a visual system providing an out of the flight deck view.
Flight Simulator (FS)	A full size replica of a specific type or make, model and series aeroplane flight deck, including the assemblage of all equipment and computer programmes necessary to represent the aeroplane in ground and flight operations, a visual system providing an out of the flight deck view, and a force cueing motion system. It is in compliance with the minimum standards for Flight Simulator Qualification.
Flight time (aeroplane)	The total time from the moment that an aeroplane first moves for the purpose of taking off until the moment it finally comes to rest at the end of the flight.
Flight time (helicopter)	The total time from the moment a helicopters rotor blades start turning until the moment the helicopter finally comes to rest at the end of the flight and the rotor blades are stopped
Flight Training Device (FTD)	A full size replica of an aeroplane's instruments, equipment, panels and controls in an open flight deck area or an enclosed aeroplane flight deck, including the assemblage of equipment and computer software programmes necessary to represent the aeroplane in ground and flight conditions to the extent of the systems installed in the device. It does not require a force cueing motion or visual system. It is in compliance with the minimum standards for a specific FTD Level of Qualification.
FN	Flight Navigator
FNPT	Flight and Navigation Procedures Trainer
FRTOL	Flight Radio Telephony Operator's Licence

4 of 8 *(cont'd from previous page)*

Abbreviations	Definitions
FTO	Flying Training Organisation (Approved to conducted JAA Courses)
GST	General Skill Test (National Private Pilot's Licences)
GPS	Global Positioning System
H	Helicopter
HPA	High Performance Aeroplane
HT	Head of Training
ICAO	International Civil Aviation Organisation
IEM	Interpretative and Explanatory Material
IFR	Instrument Flight Rules
ILS	Instrument Landing System
IMC	Instrument Meteorological Conditions
Instrument time	Instrument flight time or instrument ground time
Instrument flight time	Time during which a pilot is controlling an aircraft in flight solely by reference to instruments
Instrument ground time	Time during which a pilot is receiving instruction in simulated instrument flight in synthetic training devices (STDs)
IR(A)	Instrument Rating (Aeroplane)
IR(H)	Instrument Rating (Helicopter)
IRE	Instrument Rating Examiner
IRI	Instrument Rating Instructor
IRT(A)	Instrument Rating Test (Aeroplanes)
IRT(H)	Instrument Rating Test (Helicopters)
IRVR	Instrumented Runway Visual Range
JAA	Joint Aviation Authorities
JAR	Joint Aviation Requirements
JAR-FCL	Joint Aviation Requirements – Flight Crew Licensing
JOC	Jet Orientation Course
LARS	Lower Airspace Radar Service
LPC	Licensing Proficiency Check
LOFT	Line Orientated Flight Training
LST	Licensing Skill Test
MATZ	Military Aerodrome Traffic Zone
MCC	Multi Crew Co-operation - the functioning of the flight crew as a team of co-operating members led by the pilot-in-command

5 of 8 *(cont'd from previous page)*

Abbreviations	Definitions
MCCI	Multi Crew Co-operation Instructor
MCQ	Multiple Choice Questions
ME	Multi-engine
MEP	Multi-engine Piston
MET	Multi-engine turbo-prop
MGIR	Motor Glider Instructor Rating
MPA	Multi-pilot aeroplanes – aeroplanes certificated for operation with a minimum crew of at least two pilots
MPH	Multi-pilot Helicopter – helicopters certificated for operation with a minimum crew of two pilots
MTWA	Maximum Total Weight Authorised
NAA	National Aviation Authority
NDB	Non-Directional Beacon
NFT	Navigation Flight Test (UK National Licences)
NFU	National Farmers Union
Night	The period between the end of evening civil twilight and the beginning of morning civil twilight, or such other period between sunset and sunrise as may be prescribed by the appropriate Authority.
nm	Nautical Miles
NOTAM	Notice to Airmen
NPLG	National Pilot Licensing Group (NPLG) Ltd.
NPPL	National Private Pilot's Licence
NSUs	Nominated Service Units
OCM	Organisational Control Manual
OML	Operational Multicrew Limitation
OPC	Operator Proficiency Check
OSL	Operational Safety Pilot Limitation
Other training devices (OTD)	Training aids other than flight simulators, flight training devices or flight and navigation procedures trainers which provide means for training where a complete flight deck environment is not necessary.
P2	Co-pilot
PF	Pilot Flying
PIC	Pilot-in-command
PIC U/S	Pilot-in-command, under supervision
PLD	Personnel Licensing Department
PNF	Pilot not flying

Abbreviations	Definitions
PPL	Private Pilot Licence
PPL(BAL)	A PPL Examiner authorised to conduct Flight Tests and ground examinations for Balloons
PPL(GR)	A PPL Examiner authorised to conduct ground examinations and sign Cs of E for aeroplanes
PPL(GRH)	A PPL Examiner authorised to conduct ground examinations and sign Cs of E for helicopters
PPL(GRM)	A PPL Examiner authorised to conduct ground examinations and sign Cs of E for microlights
PPL(R)	A PPL Examiner authorised to sign Cs of E
PPL(X GYRO)	A PPL Examiner authorised to conduct Flight Tests, ground examinations and sign Cs of T for Gyroplanes and also sign Cs of E
PPL(XMG)	A PPL Examiner authorised to conduct Flight Tests and ground examinations and sign Cs of T for SLMGs and sign Cs of E
PPL(XPP)	A PPL Examiner authorised to conduct Flight Tests and ground examinations and sign Cs of T for Powered Parachutes and also sign Cs of E
Private pilot	A pilot who holds a licence which prohibits the piloting of aircraft in operations for which remuneration is given
Professional pilot	A pilot who holds a licence which permits the piloting of aircraft in operations for which remuneration is given
Proficiency checks	Demonstrations of skill to revalidate or renew ratings, and including such oral examination as the examiner may require
P U/T	Pilot Under Training
QFI	Qualified Flying Instructor (Military)
QSP(A)	Qualified Service Pilot (Aeroplanes)
QSP(H)	Qualified Service Pilot (Helicopters)
RAS	Radar Advisory Service
RASA	Radar Advisory Service Area
Rating	An entry in a licence stating special conditions, privileges or limitations pertaining to that licence
RBI	Relative Bearing Indicator
Renewal (of e.g. a rating or approval):	The administrative action taken after a rating or approval has lapsed that renews the privileges of the rating or approval for a further specified period consequent upon the fulfilment of specified requirements
Revalidation (of e.g. a rating or approval):	The administrative action taken within the period of validity of a rating or approval that allows the holder to continue to exercise the privileges of a rating or approval for a further specified period consequent upon the fulfilment of specified requirements
RF	Registered Facility
RMI	Radio Magnetic Indicator

Abbreviations	Definitions
Route Sector	A flight comprising take-off, departure, cruise of not less than 15 minutes, arrival, approach and landing phases
R/T	Radiotelephony
RTF	Radiotelephony
RVR	Runway Visual Range
SAR	Search and Rescue
SE	Single-engine
SEP	Single-Engine Piston
Simple SEP	For the purposes of the National Private Pilot's Licence a single engine piston aeroplane with a maximum take-off weight authorised not exceeding 2000kgs and which is not a microlight aeroplane or a self-launching motor glider.
SET	Single-engine turbo-prop
SFE	Synthetic Flight Examiner
SFI	Synthetic Flight Instructor
Skill tests	Skill tests are demonstrations of skill for licence or rating issue, including such oral examination as the examiner may require
SLMG	Self Launching Motor Glider
Solo flight time	Flight time during which a pilot is the sole occupant of an aircraft
SPA	Single Pilot Aeroplane – an aeroplane certificated for operation by one pilot
SPH	Single-pilot helicopters – a helicopter certificated for operation by one pilot
SPLC	Single Power Lever Control
SSEA	Simple Single Engine Aeroplane
STD	Synthetic Training Device - a training device that is either a Flight Simulator (FS), a Flight Training Device (FTD), a Flight & Navigation Procedures Trainer (FNPT), or an Other Training Device (OTD)
STI	Synthetic Training Instructor
Student pilot-in-command (SPIC)	Flight time during which the flight instructor will only observe the student acting as pilot-in-command and shall not influence or control the flight of the aircraft. SPIC hours can only be accredited for graduates of Integrated Courses for ATPL (A)/(H) and CPL(A)/IR
TGL	Temporary Guidance Leaflet
TMG	Touring Motor Glider - A motor glider having a certificate of airworthiness issued or accepted by any JAA Member State having an integrally mounted, non-retractable engine and a non-retractable propeller It shall be capable of taking off and climbing under its own power according to its flight manual.
TR	Type Rating
TRE	Type Rating Examiner
TRE (A)	Type Rating Examiner (Aeroplane)

Abbreviations	Definitions
TRE (E)	Type Rating Examiner (Flight Engineer)
TRE (H)	Type rating Examiner (Helicopter)
TRI	Type Rating Instructor
TRI (A)	Type Rating Instructor (Aeroplane)
TRI (E)	Type Rating Instructor (Flight Engineer)
TRI (H)	Type Rating Instructor (Helicopter)
TRTO	Type Rating Training Organisation
Type (of aircraft)	All aircraft of the same basic design, including all modifications except those modifications that result in a change of handling, flight characteristics or flight crew complement.
UAS	University Air Squadron
UIR	Upper Information Region
UKAIP	United Kingdom Aeronautical Information Publication
VDF	VHF Direction Finding
VFR	Visual Flight Rules
VHF	Very High Frequency
VMC	Visual Meteorological Conditions
VOR	VHF Omni Range
ZFT	Zero Flight Time
ZFTT	Zero Flight Time Training

APPENDIX B

RECORDING OF FLIGHT TIME

General information

Pilot logbooks must be kept in accordance with the provisions of the UK ANO currently in force and should also conform to JAR-FCL (IEM FCL 1.080/2.080 refers).

Details of flights flown under JAR-OPS 1, may be recorded in an acceptable computerised format maintained by the operator. In this case an operator shall make the records of all flights operated by the pilot, including differences and familiarisation training, available on request to the flight crew member concerned.

Recommended information

The record shall contain the following information:

1. Personal details:

   a. Name and address of the holder;

   b. Particulars of each flight during which the holder of the logbook acted as either a member of the flight crew of an aircraft or for the purpose of qualifying for the grant or renewal of a licence under the Air Navigation Order.

2. For each flight:

   a. Name of Pilot-in-command.

   b. Date (day, month, year) of flight.

   c. Place and time of departure and arrival (times (UTC) to be block time).

   d. Type (aeroplane make, model and variant) and registration of aeroplane.

   e. SE, ME.

   f. Total time of flight.

   g. Accumulated total time of flight.

3. Operational conditions:

   a. Night

   b. IFR

4. Particulars of any test or examination undertaken whilst in flight.

Recording of pilot function

1. Pilot-in-command flight time:

   a. The holder of a licence may log as pilot-in-command time all of the flight time during which he is the pilot-in-command.

   b. The applicant for or the holder of a pilot licence may log as pilot-in-command time all solo flight time and flight time as student pilot-in-command provided that such SPIC time is countersigned by the instructor and is part of an approved syllabus of training.

   c. The holder of an instructor rating may log as pilot-in-command all flight time during which he acts as an instructor in an aeroplane or supervises SPIC flying. (For further details please refer to **Student Pilot-in-Command** paragraph at the end of this Appendix).

   d. The holder of an examiner's authorisation may log as pilot-in-command all flight time during which he occupies a pilot's seat and acts as an examiner in an aeroplane;

   e. A co-pilot acting as pilot-in-command under the supervision of the pilot-in-command on an aeroplane on which more than one pilot is required under the type certification of the aeroplane or as required by JAR-OPS provided such pilot-in-command time under supervision (see '5' below) is countersigned by the pilot-in-command. (For further details please refer to **Co-pilot** paragraph at the end of this Appendix).

   f. If the holder of a licence carries out a number of flights upon the same day returning on each occasion to the same place of departure and the interval between successive flights does not exceed thirty minutes, such series of flights may recorded as a single entry.

2. Co-pilot flight time: The holder of a pilot licence occupying a pilot seat as co-pilot may log all flight time as co-pilot flight time on an aeroplane on which more than one pilot is required under

the type certification of the aeroplane, or the regulations under which the flight is conducted. (For further details please refer to **Co-pilot** paragraph at the end of this Appendix).

3. Cruise relief co-pilot flight time: A cruise relief co-pilot pilot may log all flight time as co-pilot when occupying a pilot's seat. (For further details please refer to **Cruise Relief Pilot** paragraph at the end of this Appendix).

4. Instruction time: A summary of all time logged by an applicant for a licence or rating as flight instruction, instrument flight instruction, instrument ground time, etc. shall be certified by the appropriately rated and/or authorised instructor from whom it was received.

5. PICUS (Pilot-in-command under supervision): Provided that the method of supervision is acceptable to the Authority, a Co-pilot may log as PIC flight time flown as PICUS, when all of the duties and functions of PIC on that flight were carried out, such that the intervention of the PIC in the interest of safety was not required. (For further details please refer to **Co-Pilot** paragraph at the end of this Appendix).

6. A remarks column will be provided to give details of specific functions e.g. SPIC, PICUS, instrument flight time* etc.

   *A pilot may log as instrument flight time only that time during which he operates the aircraft solely by reference to instruments, under actual or simulated instrument flight conditions.

Presentation of flight time record

The holder of a licence or a student pilot shall without undue delay present his flight time record for inspection upon request by an authorised representative of the Authority.

A student pilot shall carry his flight time record logbook with him on all solo cross-country flights as evidence of the required instructor authorisations.

Aeroplane flight time

An aeroplane shall be deemed to be in flight from the moment the aircraft moves under its own or external power for the purpose of taking off until the moment it comes to rest at the end of the flight.

Helicopter flight time

The total time from the moment a helicopters rotor blades start turning until the moment the helicopter finally comes to rest at the end of the flight and the rotor blades are stopped.

Flight simulator time

Particulars of any training session, test or examination undertaken whilst in a flight simulator shall be recorded in the logbook, including, for each flight simulator or FNPT session:

a. the date of the session, test or examination (d/m/y);

b. type and qualification number of training device;

c. synthetic training device instruction;

d. the capacity in which the holder acted;

e. the nature of the session, test or examination;

f. total time of session;

g. accumulated total time.

STD time is creditable towards courses and licence issue but is not flight time and must not be recorded as such. STD time must be logged separately from flight time recorded in the logbook.

Military flight time

The civil aviation interpretation of a Pilot-in-Command is defined in the Air Navigation Order as a person who, for the time being, is in charge of the piloting of the aircraft without being under the direction of any other pilot in the aircraft. For civil licensing purposes, this is regarded as being the person named as pilot-in-command on the CA 48 (the ATS flight plan) or where flying hours are logged as 'Captain' of the aircraft by a Qualified Service Pilot (QSP) in military aircraft.

When a QSP is Captain of the aircraft, the flying hours logged in military terminology as 'First Pilot' equates to the civil definition of pilot-in-command. (Note: in civil terminology PIC and P1 are the same). If the captain of a military aircraft is not a QSP, then the flying hours logged as first pilot may be claimed as PIC towards licence experience requirements.

In summary:

Civil Aviation Operating Capacity	Military Equivalent
Pilot-in-Command (PIC)	P1(Captain)/1st Pilot (Nimrod) P1
PIC under Supervision (PIC U/S)	P1 (Non-Captain)/ Co-pilot P1/2nd Pilot P1 (Nimrod)
Co-pilot (P2)	Co-pilot/2nd Pilot (Nimrod)

Recording of Military Flying Times – Taxi-time allowances

It is normal practice for pilots in civil aviation to record their flying hours on a "chock-to-chock" basis. However, UK military flight crew are required only to record "airborne" time – this practice being linked to Service engineering procedures and is unlikely to change.

The CAA has always been aware of this discrepancy, and of the fact that it led to Service pilots being slightly disadvantaged compared to their civilian colleagues when they left the Services.

In recognition of this, the CAA worked with the MOD (Training Policy Unit) to devise a system that would give some credit for military taxi times.

The system that was decided upon was the taxi-assessment system. The Service pilot adds a taxi-time allowance (see table 1 below) to each sector flown as entered in his Service logbook - the taxi-time allowance being dependant on the type of sortie flown by the pilot. The taxi-time allowances built up throughout a career are then entered into a table (see table 2 below) to arrive at a total for their career. Prior to leaving the Services this table should be placed in the pilot's logbook and signed by his last Squadron Commander. **Please note that this arrangement cannot be used for CAA licence issue purposes.**

It should be emphasised that when canvassed, most UK airlines said they were aware of the discrepancy between the Service and CAA method of recording flying hours, and took this into account in the recruitment process. Where this is the case, any hours calculated by the individual Service pilot in excess of 75 hours should be taken into account by the individual airline.

The taxi-time allowance that the CAA is prepared to recognise for licence issue purposes is 5% of the total military "airborne" hours up to a maximum credit of 75 hours for ATPL(A) issue and 10 hours for CPL(A) issue. This corresponds to the average amount of taxi hours credited for civil pilots under the "chock to chock" system. When the Service pilot submits his application for licence issue, this taxi-time allowance (where required to meet minimum experience requirements) may be added to the recorded military airborne hours and the new total declared on the application form. Effectively it will mean that a military pilot will be required, inter alia, to acquire 1425 hours of military "airborne" flight time for ATPL(A) issue and 190.5 hours for CPL(A) issue. **Note:** this allowance <u>cannot</u> be used to satisfy the eligibility requirements for any of the QSP licence accreditation schemes detailed elsewhere in this publication.

Table 1

Taxi Allowance Times	
Fixed-Wing Training Aircraft	10 mins
Fast Jets	10 mins
Multi-engine Transport Aircraft	15 mins
Display Flying	5 mins
Wheeled Helicopter – Airfield Operations	5 mins
- Field Operations	Nil
Skidded Helicopters	Nil
Aircraft Carrier Operations	Nil

Table 2

Table 2

Example of "taxi-assessment" to be included in a Service pilot's logbook at the end of his career.

Summary for (…….Name…….)   (…….Date…….) to (……Date……)

Date:………………………………………………………

Signature:…………………………………………………

Appointment:………………………………………………

Aircraft Type	Sorties Flown	Taxi Allowance	Total
Grand Total			

Guide to logbook annotation

1 of 2

Case 1	Operating Capacity 2	Non-pilot licence requirements 3	Designation in logbook under 'Holder's Operating Capacity' 4	Recording of item in logbook 5
A	Pilot-in-Command	N/A	PIC or P1	Enter time in 'P1' column.
B	Co-pilot performing the duties of PIC under supervision of pilot-in-command (see Notes)	N/A	PIC U/S or P1 U/S	Enter time in 'P1' column. Counted in full toward licence experience requirements subject to certification by the pilot-in-command.
C	Co-pilot (see Notes)	N/A	P2	Enter time in 'Second pilot' or in 'Co-pilot (P2)' column.
D	Co-pilot whilst holding PPL	N/A	P2	As for 'C'.
E	Pilot acting as: (i) Systems Panel Operator (SPO) in aircraft certificated for optional operation by three pilot crew; (ii) Flight Engineer in aircraft certificated for optional or mandatory operation by two pilots + FE crew.	N/A FE licence with rating	SPO E1	Enter time in the 'F Eng', 'Any other flying' or spare column and annotate 'SPO' or 'F Eng' as appropriate.
F	Pilot on flight deck but not as P1, P2, SPO or FE: (i) Acting as 'required' Flight Navigator (under the Air Navigation Order); (ii) Pilot supervising Co-pilot activities; (iii) No duties assigned (Supernumerary);	F/N licence N/A N/A	N1 P2 SNY	Enter time in the 'F/Nav', 'Any other flying' or spare column and annotate 'N1'. Enter as for case C. Enter time in 'Any other flying' or spare column and annotate 'SNY'.
G	Pilot under instruction for the purpose of gaining a licence or rating, or for conversion to an aircraft type within an aircraft rating group or class.	N/A	P/UT	Enter time in 'Dual' column.
H	Student Pilot-in-Command. (Pilot acting as pilot-in-command during a approved integrated course of training, under the supervision of a flight instructor. The flight instructor shall only observe the student acting as pilot-in-command and shall not control the flight of the aircraft). (see Notes)	N/A	SPIC	Enter time in 'P1' column.

2 of 2 *(cont'd from previous page)*

Case 1	Operating Capacity 2	Non-pilot licence requirements 3	Designation in logbook under 'Holder's Operating Capacity' 4	Recording of item in logbook 5
J	Pilot undergoing any form of flight test with a JAA or CAA Authorised Examiner (other than case K).	N/A	PIC U/S for successful test P/UT for unsuccessful test	Enter time in 'P1' column and have it certified by aircraft commander. Enter time in 'Dual' column.
K	Pilot undergoing a flight test in the capacity of co-pilot.	N/A	P2	As for case C.
L	Student pilot flying as the sole occupant of an aircraft during training for the grant of a PPL or CPL.	N/A	PIC or P1	Enter time in 'P1' column.
M	Student pilot flying as pilot-in-command during training for a CPL accompanied by a Safety Pilot.	N/A	PIC or P1	As for case L.
N	Pilot acting as Safety Pilot	N/A	SNY	As for case F(iii).
P	Pilot undergoing Flight Instructor Course training as pilot-in-command accompanied by: Pilot acting as 'student' for instructional purposes.	N/A N/A	PIC or P1 SNY	Roles in column 2 are interchangeable between pilots. Time spent as 'P1' to be entered as case L. Time spent as 'student' to be entered and count as case F(iii).
R	Pilot acting as 'Cruise Pilot' only (see Notes)	N/A	See Notes on 'heavy' crew below	See Notes on 'heavy' crew below

Notes: The terms Pilot-in-Command, Co-pilot, Flight Crew and Crew shall have the interpretation given them by Article 129 (1) of the Air Navigation Order 2005.

1. Whenever two members of flight crew acting in the same capacity share a particular operating duty, each performing such duty for particular periods only and neither acting under the supervision of the other, only the time during which the duty was performed is to be recorded in the appropriate column of the personal flying log book.

2. A pilot claiming time spent as co-pilot performing the duties and functions of pilot-in-command, under the supervision of the pilot-in-command, toward meeting the licence requirements as given in Case B, will be credited with that flight time only if:

   a. the flight was conducted in an aircraft having a Certificate of Airworthiness that requires its flight crews to include not less than two pilots;

   b. he was responsible for checking the accuracy of the flight plan, load sheet and fuel calculations for the flight;

   c. he ensured that all crew checks were carried out in accordance with the laid down operation procedures;

   d. throughout the flight he carried out all the duties and functions of pilot-in-command and conducted the take-off and the landing;

   e. he resolved all meteorological, communication and air traffic control problems;

   f. the pilot-in-command did not have to overrule any course of action proposed or taken by the co-pilot;

   g. the pilot-in-command certifies in the co-pilot's flying log book against the entry for that flight that it was carried out by the co-pilot acting as pilot-in-command under supervision. Such certification will be taken as confirming that all the foregoing conditions were met.

3. A pilot claiming flying hours as co-pilot towards meeting the overall flying experience requirements for a licence, as provided for in cases C,D, F(ii)or K, will only be credited with that flight time if holding an appropriate licence to perform co-pilot duties, and if:

   a. the flight was conducted in an aircraft required by its Certificate of Airworthiness, or by Article 25(3) of the Air Navigation Order, to carry a crew of not less than two pilots; or

   b. the flight was conducted by an AOC holder choosing to operate a particular aircraft as a two pilot operation and provided that the specific duties that the second pilot was required to perform on all flights in respect of the operation of the aircraft were contained in the Operations Manual relating to the aircraft; or

   c. it was conducted in a military aircraft normally flown bý more than one pilot; or

   d. exceptionally in Cases C and D, and subject to prior agreement with the CAA, it was conducted in an aircraft not required to carry two pilots but which was fitted with full dual controls for that flight, and the pilot-in-command certifies in the co-pilot's log book that the flight was conducted as a genuine two pilot operation.

   Flight time as PIC US, apart from as specifically provided for under Case J above, will only be allowable for the holder of a PPL subject to the terms of a prior agreement with the CAA.

'Heavy' Crew

When an aircraft crew consists of more than the required number of pilots i.e. a 'heavy' crew the rules for logging of flight time are as per JAR-FCL 1.080, but for clarification the following should apply.

Pilot in Command

The designated commander of the aeroplane may log as pilot in command all the flight time. This includes rest taken on board.

Co-Pilot

- The designated co-pilot of the aeroplane may log as co-pilot all the time he acts as co-pilot whilst sitting in a pilot's seat.
- He may log as PIC U/S all the time he occupies a pilot's seat and acts as pilot-in-command under the supervision of the pilot in command or a cruise relief pilot substituting for the pilot in command.
- He may also log as pilot in command all the time he is acting as pilot in command and substituting for the designated commander of the aircraft when he is taking rest.
- He may not log as flight time any periods during which he does not occupy a pilot's seat.

Cruise Relief Pilot

- A cruise relief pilot may log as pilot in command all the time he occupies a pilot's seat as relief for the designated commander.
- He may log as co-pilot all the time he occupies a pilot's seat as relief for the co-pilot.
- He may log as PIC U/S all the time he occupies a pilot's seat and acts as pilot in command under the supervision of the designated commander or his relief.

Student Pilot-in-Command

A student on a CPL(A)/IR, CPL(H) or ATPL(A)/(H) Integrated Course of flying training may log flight time as SPIC when they are receiving instrument flight instruction from an appropriately qualified instructor. The instructor must be the holder of a valid professional licence, instructor rating, instrument rating and IRI privileges. SPIC time shall be credited as pilot-in-command time, unless the flight instructor had reason to control any part of the flight. A ground de-briefing by the flight instructor does not affect the crediting as pilot-in-command.

APPENDIX C FORMS LIST

When applying to the CAA for a service, you are required to complete the appropriate application. Details of the forms currently in use are detailed below. Check lists of other documentation to be submitted are also included in most application forms and applicants are strongly advised to follow these to avoid delay in processing. The most up-to-date list of forms are available on the SRG web site at www.caa.co.uk or may be requested by E-mail: fclweb@srg.caa.co.uk.

1 of 3

Form Number	Description
SRG1101	Professional UK National Flight Crew Licence
SRG1102	Private/Professional Flight Crew Licence Renewal - Application
SRG1103	Request for a Statement of Requirements for a UK FE/JAR ATPL(A) (restricted to UK aircraft only)
SRG1104	JAR-FCL Pilot Licence Application on Conversion of an existing National (UK) Licence
SRG1105	JAR-FCL Private Pilot Licence (Aeroplane) – Application
SRG1106	Flight Radio Telephony Operator's Licence Grant or Renewal – Application
SRG1108	JAR-FCL ATPL (Aeroplanes) Theoretical Knowledge Examination - Application
SRG1109	Type Rating Training Programme – Approval or Revalidation Application (TRTOP)
SRG1110	Type Rating Training Organisation – Approval or Revalidation Application
SRG1111	Registration to Conduct Training for a Private Pilot licence in Accordance with JAR-FCL 1 (Aeroplane) and JAR-FCL 2 (Helicopter)
SRG1114	Approval and Re-Approval of a Flying or Ground Training Organisation Offering Courses or Training for a Professional Pilot's Licence, Single Pilot Multi-Engine Piston Class Rating, Instrument Rating or Flight Instructor (Restricted) rating – Application
SRG1115	Balloons and Airships – Application for Private Pilot Licence
SRG1117	Duplicate Flight Crew Licence – Application
SRG1118	Validation of Flight Crew Licences Issued By ICAO Contracting States Issue and Renewal
SRG1119	Additional Aeroplane Type/Class Rating- Single/Multi Pilot and Revalidation/Renewal of UK/JAA Type/Class and or Instrument Rating (Aeroplane) - Application
SRG1120	JAR-FCL ATPL (Helicopters) Theoretical Knowledge Examination - Application
SRG1121	JAR-FCL CPL (Aeroplane) Theoretical Knowledge Examination – Application.
SRG1122	Air Law Validation Examination - Application
SRG1123	JAR-FCL Commercial Pilot's Licence – Application
SRG1125	Private Pilot Licence (Aeroplanes) Instrument Meteorological Conditions Rating – Application

2 of 3 *(cont'd from previous page)*

Form Number	Description
SRG1126	Night Qualification (Aeroplane or Helicopter) Application
SRG1127	JAR-FCL Private Pilot's Licence (Helicopter) – Application
SRG1128	Examiner Authorisation Issue/reissue/Variation Application.
SRG1130	JAR-FCL Professional Pilot Licence (Aeroplane) Application (For use only by UK Qualified Service Pilots qualifying under CAA/MOD accreditation arrangements)
SRG1131	Instructor Form 1: JAR-FCL 1 (Aeroplane) and JAR-FCL 2 (Helicopter) – Application
SRG1132	Instructor Form 1: National Fixed Wing Application
SRG1133	Instructor Form 2: JAR-FCL 1 (Aeroplanes), JAR-FCL 2 (Helicopter) – Application
SRG1134	Flight Instructor Rating: Request for Statement of Requirements
SRG1135	Instructor Form 3: Instructor Rating Revalidation/Renewal
SRG1136	JAR-FCL Licence – Application to change the State of Issue to United Kingdom
SRG1137	JAR-FCL Airline Transport Pilot Licence – Application
SRG1138	JAR-FCL Commercial Pilot Licence (Aeroplane) Restricted – Application
SRG1139	JAR-FCL Commercial Pilot Licence (Helicopter) Restricted – Application
SRG1140	Instructor Approval – Application
SRG1142	Commercial Pilot's Licence (Balloons) Examinations Application
SRG1143	Approval to conduct Assistant Flying Instructor Rating Course (Microlight) Renewal of Course Approval(s) - Application
SRG1144	JAR-FCL ATPL (Aeroplanes/Helicopters) Theoretical Knowledge Examination Application (UK Qualified Service Pilots Qualifying Under CAA/MOD Accreditation Arrangements)
SRG1147	JAR-FCL CPL (Helicopters) Theoretical Knowledge Examination – Application
SRG1149	JAR-FCL ATPL (Aeroplanes) Additional Performance Examination – Application
SRG1151	Theoretical Knowledge Examination for the Grant of an Instrument Rating (Aeroplanes) and (Helicopters) – Application
SRG1152	Seamanship Examination - Application
SRG1153	JAR-FCL and JAR-OPS – Demonstration of Knowledge Requirements
SRG1155	Radiotelephony Flight Examiners Authorisation/Reauthorisation - Application
SRG1156	JAR-FCL Professional Pilot Licence (Helicopter) Application (For use only by UK Qualified Service Pilots qualifying under CAA/MOD accreditation arrangements)
SRG1157	SPA Skill Test and Proficiency Check Schedule – Examiner's Record
SRG 1158	MPA Type Rating, Skill Test and Proficiency Check Schedule – Examiner's Record

3 of 3 *(cont'd from previous page)*

Form Number	Description
SRG1160	UK Licence Verification Authorisation for Licence Validation
SRG1161	Inclusion of an Instrument Rating Aeroplane/Helicopter in a UK/JAR-FCL Pilot Licence - Application
SRG1162	Flight Radiotelephony Operator's Licence - ATC Licence Holders - Exemption Certificate
SRG1163	Removal of the restriction from a JAR-FCL Commercial Pilot Licence (Restricted) - Application
SRG1164	Multi-Crew Co-operation Course Training Credit - Application
SRG1165	JAR-FCL Private Pilot's Licence Aeroplanes/Helicopters Theoretical Knowledge Examination - Application
SRG1167	Form 170A Signatory Authorisation Helicopter - Application
SRG1168	Certificate of Training and Competence for the Professional Pilot Licence and/or Instrument Rating - Form 170A
SRG1169	Flight Instructor Test/Check Schedules - Examiner's Record
SRG1171	Flight Radiotelephony (Communications) Training Syllabus - Training Record
SRG1173	Type/Instrument Rating Skill Test for Single and Multi Pilot Helicopter JAR-FCL and UK Licences Initial Issue - Application
SRG1174	Type/Instrument Rating Proficiency Check for Single and Multi Pilot Helicopter JAR-FCL and UK Licences Revalidation/Renewal - Application
SRG1176	UK IMC Rating Skill Test - Examiner's Record
SRG1177	Helicopter Instructor Test/Check Schedules - Examiner's Record
SRG1180	FTO/TRTO Personnel Form
SRG1181	JAR-FCL Airline Transport Pilot's Licence (Aeroplanes) Theoretical Knowledge Bridging Examination - Application
SRG1182	Balloon/Airship Examiner Authorisation Issue/Reissue/Variation - Application
SRG1187	PLD Payment Method Form

APPENDIX D LIST OF PUBLICATIONS WHICH APPLICANTS FOR FLIGHT TRAINING AND PILOT LICENCE EXAMINATIONS MAY FIND HELPFUL

This appendix contains a list of publications that users may find helpful in preparing themselves for flight training and pilot licence ground examinations. The following list does not claim to be comprehensive, or necessarily to give the best treatment of particular subjects, but has been drawn from commercial sources as reference material. It should be noted that the Authority exercises no editorial control over their content or accuracy and all examination applicants are recommended to take advice from an approved FTO.

The following series of books include material for more than one subject although no individual series necessarily includes material for all subjects.

In addition, users can also obtain information from the following web sites:-

- UK Aeronautical Information Circulars - www.ais.org.uk
- UK CAPs - www.caa.co.uk
- JAA Documents - www.jaa.nl
- EASA Documents - www.easa.eu.int
- ICAO Documents - www.icao.int

General

Aeronautical Information Circulars

The Air Pilot's Manual Vol. 1–7
T Thom

The Private Pilot's Licence Course Vol. 1–3
AFE

JAR Professional pilot studies (CPL) - Phil Croucher

Ground Studies for Pilots - Series of 5 books
Blackwell Science

AP 3456 Vol. 1-9
Ministry of Defence

The Commercial Pilot's Study Manual Series Vol. 1-4
M Burton

Instructional Techniques for the Flight Instructor
John Halstead and Alan Newton

Pilots Weather
Editor Brian Cosgrove, Airlife Publishing Ltd.

Radio Aids Navigation Tutor (RANT) - Instrument Navigation computer program
(Oddsoft: www.oddsoft.co.uk

e-mail: info@oddsoft.co.uk

Private Pilots Guides JAR PPL (5 volumes)
Pooleys

Pre-flight briefing
Pooleys

010 – Aviation Law and ATC Procedures

Aviation Law for Pilots (10th edition)
R B Underdown and Tony Palmer

ICAO Documents and annexes as listed in the appropriate syllabus and learning objectives (LOs)

JAR-FCL 1, 2 & 3

ANO in plain English
Phil Croucher

JAR-OPS in plain English
Phil Croucher

JAR PPL Aviation Law & Operational Procedures
Pooleys

021 – Airframe and Systems

Aircraft Basic Science
Bent and McKinley

Aircraft Instruments
E H J Pallett

Aviation Fuel Properties
Coordinating Research Council Inc

Aircraft Systems
Moir and A Seabridge

Aircraft Systems for Pilots
D D Remer

Aircraft Electrical Systems (3rd edition)
E H J Pallett

Aircraft Electricity and Electronics (4th edition) Eismen/Bent/McKinley

Aircraft Instruments and Integrated Systems
E H J Pallett

Aircraft Hydraulic Systems (3rd edition)
William A Neese

Aircraft Hydraulic Systems EA-AH-1
Aviation Technician Training

Aircraft Powerplants
Bent/McKinley

Aircraft Landing Gear Systems
JA Tanner

Aircraft Oxygen Systems EA-AOS
Scheppler/Crane (A/T Trg Co.)

Aircraft wheels, Brakes and Anti-skid systems EA
AWB Aviation

Airframe and Powerplant Mechanics General Handbook AC65-9A
US Dept. of Transport/FAA

Airframe and Powerplant Mechanics Powerplant Handbook AC65-12A
US Dept. of Transport/FAA

From Logic to Computers
P J Thewlis and B N T Foxon

General Aviation Safety Information Leaflet

Handling the Big Jets
D P Davies

Hydraulics (Vol. 1)
H G Conway (published by The Royal Aeronautical Society)

Airframe and Powerplant Mechanics
Airframe Handbook AC65-15A
US Dept. of Transport/FAA

Aircraft Maintenance and Repair
Kroes/Watkins/Delp

Hydraulics/Undercarriages (Vol. 2)
HG Conway (Published by The Royal Aeronautical Society)

Into Thin Air
EW Still (published by Normalair-Garrett Ltd., Yeovil)

Performance Requirements Manual
R V Davies

The Jet Engine
Rolls Royce

Transport Category Aircraft Systems
Thornas W Wild

CAA Fire Safety at Work Leaflet

EASA CS-25 (Large Aeroplanes)

CAP 434 Aviation Fuel at Aerodromes

CAP 74 Aircraft Fuelling

CAP 562 (CAAIP) - 5 - 7 Tyres: 5 - 8 Wheels and Brakes: 6 - 3 Structures

EASA CS-29 (Large Helicopters)

AP 3456 Vol. 9
Executive Editor AP3456

AP 3456 Vol. 2
Executive Editor AP3456

Gas Turbine Engine
Pratt and Whitney

JAR PPL Aircraft General and Principles of Flight
Pooleys

022 – Instruments

Aircraft Instruments and Integrated Systems
E H J Pallet

Aircraft Instruments
E H J Pallett

Aircraft Electricity and Electronic (4th edition)
Eisman/Bent/McKinley

Automatic Flight Control
E H J Pallett

A&P Airframe Handbook AC 65-15A
US Dept. of Transport/FAA

CAP 359 (UK Operating Requirements for all weather operations)

Manual of Avionics: Introduction to the Electronics of Civil Aviation
B Kendall. (Granada)

031 – Mass and Balance

JAR-OPS 1/3

Airframe Systems for Pilots
DD Remer

Airframe and Powerplant Mechanics Handbook AC65-15A
US Dept. of Transport/FAA

Aircraft Basic Science
Bent and McKinley

CAP 696 – Mass and Balance Manual (Specimen charts)

BCAR Section A CAP 553

Weight and Balance of Aircraft CAAIP Leaflet 1-4

Helicopter Manual (specimen charts) to be issued

032 – Performance

Handling the Big Jets
D P Davies

CAP 698 Performance Manual (Specimen Charts)

The Aircraft Performance Requirements Manual
R V Davies

Aircraft Performance Theory
PJ Swatton (Blackwell Scientific)

JAR- OPS 1/3 - JAA

EASA CS-23 (normal, utility, aerobatic & Commuter aeroplanes)

EASA CS-25 (Large Aeroplanes)

Helicopter Manual (specimen charts) to be issued

JAR PPL Flight Planning & Performance
Pooleys

033 – Flight Planning

CAP 697 Flight Planning Manual
(Specimen charts)

JAR Ops 1/3 -JAA

Helicopter Manual (specimen charts) to be issued

034 – Performance (Helicopters)

Specimen Performance Charts (to be issued)

040 – Human Performance and Limitations

Aeromedicine for Aviators
K E E Reed (Pitman)

Aviation Medicine Manual CAP 567 (CAA)

Single Pilot CRM
Phil Croucher

Ernsting's Aviation Medicine
David J Rainford and David P Gradwell

Aviation Medicine
J Ernsting and P King (Butterworths)

Aviation Psychology
RS Jensen (Gower Techinical)

Fit to Fly
BALPA Medical Study Group
(Granada Publishing)

Human Factors in Flight
F H Hawkins (Gower Technical Press)

Human Factors for General Aviation
S R Trollip and R S Jensen (Jepperson Sanderson)

Human Factors for Pilots
Roger G Green (Ashgate Publishing)

Human Performance and Limitations in Aviation
R D Campbell and M Bagshaw (BSP Professional Books)

Handbook of Human Factors
Gavriel Salvendy (John Wiley and Sons)

Human Factors in Air Transportation
McFarland (McGraw-Hill Book Co)

Human Factors in Aviation
EL Wiener and DC Nagel (Academic Press)

Tasks, Errors and Mental Models Goodstein, Anderson and Olsen (Taylor and Francis)

"Briefings" A Human Factors course for Pilots - Rene Amalberti

Basic Flight Physiology
Richard O Reinhart (McGraw-Hill)

Human Factors in Multi-Crew Flight Operations Harry W Orlady and Linda M Orlady (Ashgate)

Aerospace Medicine
Roy L De Host (Lippincott Williams & Wilkins)

050 – Meteorology

Atmosphere, Weather and Climate
RG Barry and R J Chorley (Methuen)

Ground Training for the Private Pilot: Air Navigation and Aviation Meteorology.
R D Campbell. (Granada)

Handbook of Aviation Meteorology (HMSO) Third Ed 1994
(TSO Tel. 0870 600 5522)

ICAO Doc 8400 Codes (including the Q code)

Meteorology for Pilots
M Wickson (Airlife)

The Meteorological Glossary (Met 0 842/AP 897) (TSO Tel. 0870 600 5522)

Climatology for Airline Pilots

HR Quantick (Blackwell Science)

Meteorology and Flight
Tom Bradbury (A & C Black)

ICAO Annexe 3

JAR PPL Meteorology
Pooleys

The following web site may also be of use:
www.booty.demon.co.uk

061 – General Navigation

Aircraft Electricity and Electronics (4th edition)
Eisman/Bent/McKinley

Aircraft Instruments and Integrated Systems
E H J Pallett

Ground Studies for Pilots – Navigation

R B Underdown and Tony Palmer (Blackwell Science)

AP 3456 Vol. 7

JAR PPL Navigation
Pooleys

062 – Radio Navigation

Manual of Avionics: Introduction to the Electronics of Civil Aviation
B Kendall. (Granada)

The VOR and ADF including DME
M Cass (Airlife)

Ground Studies for Pilot's Radio Aids
R B Underdown and David Cockburn (Blackwell Science)

The following web sites may also be of use:
GPS: www.igeb.gov/sps-2001-final.pdf
RNav: www.ecacnav.com

071 – Operational Procedures

Aircraft Systems
Imoir and A Seabridge

Aircraft Oxygen Systems EA-AOS
Scheppler/Crane (A/T Trg Co.)

Aircraft Powerplants
Bent/McKinley

Airframe and Powerplant Mechanics Handbook AC 65-15A

Operational Flying - Phil Croucher

Transport Category Aircraft Systems
Thornas W Wild

The Jet Engine
Rolls Royce

JAR-OPS 1 (A) or 3 (H) - JAA

EASA CS-25 - (Large Aeroplanes)

AP 3456 Vol. 2
Executive Editor AP3456 See above

CAP 562 (CAAIP part 5)

The Helicopter Pilot's Handbook
Phil Croucher

081 – Principle of Flight (Aeroplanes and Helicopters)

Aerodynamics for Naval Aviators
H H Hurt Jr, US Navy

Aircraft Flight
R H Barnard and D R Philpott

CAP 467

Flight Theory and Aerodynamics
C E Dole

Flight Theory for Pilots
C E Dole

Handling the Big Jets
D P Davies

EASA CS-25 (Large Aeroplanes)

Mechanics of Flight 10th edition
AC Kermode

The Illustrated Guide to Aerodynamics
HC "Skip" Smith

Flightwise – Principles of Aircraft Flight
Chris Carpenter

Section B Section C Section D Section E Section F Section G Section H Section I Section J Section K Index

Fundamentals of Flight
Richard S Shevell

Introduction to Flight
John D Anderson Jr

JAR PPL Aircraft General & Principles of Flight
Pooleys

082 – Principles of Flight (Helicopters)

Basic Helicopter Aerodynamics
J Seddon

Basic Helicopter Handbook AC 61-13B
US Dept. of Transport/FAA

The Helicopter and How it Flies
J Fay

Helicopter Aerodynamics
R W Prowty

Principles of Helicopter Flight
W J Wagtendonk

091/092 – Communications (VFR & IFR)

ICAO Documents and Annexes as listed in the syllabus and learning objectives

CAP 413

APPENDIX E

USEFUL ADDRESSES

All enquiries concerning licensing requirements, charges, Instructor Ratings and Examiner Authorities (with the exception of the NPPL):

Personnel Licensing Department (PLD)
Civil Aviation Authority
Safety Regulation Group
Aviation House (GE)
Gatwick Airport South
West Sussex
RH6 OYR

Tel: 01293 573700
Fax: 01293 573996
e-mail: fclweb@srg.caa.co.uk
web: www.caa.co.uk

CAA Publications may be viewed at:
www.caa.co.uk/publications

JAA documents may be obtained from:

RAPIDOC (and Technical Indexes Ltd)
Willoughby Road
Bracknell
Berkshire
RG12 8DW

Tel: 01344 426 311
Fax: 01344 71440
e-mail: rapidoc@techindex.co.uk
web: www.techindex.co.uk/rapidoc

AICs, UKAIPs, NOTAMs, etc. may be obtained from:

Aeronautical Information Service
National Air Traffic Services Ltd.
Control Tower Building
London Heathrow Airport
Hounslow
Middlesex
TW6 1JJ

Tel: :UK AIP section: 020 8745 3456
NOTAM & PIB info: 020 8745 3450/3451
General enquiries: 020 8745 3464
e-mail: ais.supervisor@nats.co.uk
web: www.ais.org.uk

Medical enquiries, booking medical examinations:

Medical Department
Civil Aviation Authority
Safety Regulation Group
Aviation House (GW)
Gatwick Airport South
West Sussex
RH6 0YR

Tel: 01293 573700
Fax: 01293 573995
e-mail: medicalweb@srg.caa.co.uk
web: www.caa.co.uk

The ANO may be viewed at:
www.hmso.gov.uk (SI 2005 No. 1970)

The ANO, with associated legislation, is also available in loose-leaf form as CAP 393 from:

The Stationery Office
PO Box 29
St. Crispins House
Duke Street
Norwich
NR3 1GN

Tel: 0870 600 5522
Fax: 0870 600 5533
web: www.clicktso.com
e-mail: customer.services@tso.co.uk

Representative Bodies:

Aircraft Owners and Pilots Association (AOPA)
50A Cambridge Street
London
SW1V 4QQ

Tel: 020 7834 5631
Fax: 020 7834 2623
e-mail: info@aopa.co.uk
web: www.aopa.co.uk

British Balloon and Airship Club General enquiries:

The British Balloon and Airship Club
c/o P.R.O Hannah Cameron
St. John Street
Bedminster
Bristol
BS3 4NH

Tel: 0117 9531 231
e-mail: information@bbac.org
web: www.bbac.org

Technical enquiries:

The British Balloon and Airship Club
c/o Vice Chairman Mr Wyn Morgan
14 Swansea Road
Penllergaer
Swansea
SA4 1AQ

Tel: 01792 899 333
Fax: 01792 899 444
web: www.technical@bbac.org

British Gliding Association (BGA)
Kimberley House
Vaughan Way
Leicester
LE1 4SE

Tel: 0116 253 1051
Fax: 0116 251 5939
e-mail: bga@gliding.co.uk
web: www.gliding.co.uk

For technical enquiries only relating to NPPL SLMG - Mr Pete Stratten

British Microlight Aircraft Association (BMAA)
Deddington
Banbury
Oxfordshire OX15 OTT

Tel: 01869 338 888
Fax: 01869 338116
e-mail: general@bmaa.org
web: www.bmaa.org

Popular Flying Association (PFA) Ltd
Turweston Aerodrome
Nr Brackley
Northamptonshire
NN13 5YD

Tel: 01280 846786
Fax: 01280 846780
e-mail: office@pfa.org.uk
web: www.pfa.org.uk

British Helicopter Advisory Board
Graham Suite
Fairoaks Airport
Surrey
GU24 8HX

Tel: 01276 856 100
Fax: 01276 856 126
e-mail: info@bhab.org
web: www.bhab.flyer.co.uk

British Hang Gliding and Paragliding Association (BHPA) Ltd
Old School Room
Loughborough Road
Leicester
LE4 5PJ

Tel: 0870 873 6490
Fax: 0870 873 0850
e-mail: office@bhpa.co.uk
web: www.bhpa.co.uk

British Business & General Aviation Association (BBGA)
19 Church Street
Brill
Aylesbury
HP18 9RT

Tel: 01844 238 020
Fax: 01844 238 087
e-mail: ga@gamta.org
web: www.gamta.org

Guild of Air Pilots and Air Navigators (GAPAN)
9 Warwick Court
Grays Inn
London
WC1R 5DJ

Tel: 020 7404 4032
Fax: 020 7404 403
e-mail: gapan@gapan.org
web: www.gapan.org

National Pilot's Licensing Group Ltd (NPLG)
Turweston Aerodrome
Nr Brackley
Northants
NN13 5YD

Tel: 01280 846786

NPPL telephone enquiries should be directed to:

- For administration matters relating to NPPL SSEA and SLMG - contact NPLG
- For technical enquiries only relating to NPPL SSEA - contact AOPA
- For technical enquiries only relating to NPPL SLMG - contact Mr Pete Stratten at BGA
- For administration and technical matters relating to NPPL Microlight - contact BMAA

PPL/IR Europe
Le Clos au Comte Catel
Guernsey
Channel Islands
GY5 7QG

Tel: 01481 252565
e-mail: memsec@pplir.org
web: www.pplir.org

APPENDIX F **SCHEDULE 8 OF AIR NAVIGATION ORDER 2005**

SCHEDULE 8

Articles 27, 28, 29, 30 and 31

Flight crew of aircraft - Licences, Ratings, Qualifications and Maintenance of Licence Privileges

PART A - FLIGHT CREW LICENCES

Section 1
United Kingdom Licences

Sub-section 1 - Aeroplane Pilots

Private Pilot's Licence (Aeroplanes)

Minimum age - 17 years

No maximum period of validity

Privileges:

1. Subject to paragraph (2), the holder of a Private Pilot's Licence (Aeroplanes) shall be entitled to fly as pilot in command or co-pilot of an aeroplane of any of the types or classes specified or otherwise falling within an aircraft rating included in the licence.

2. He shall not -

   a. fly such an aeroplane for the purpose of public transport or aerial work save as hereinafter provided:

      i. he may fly such an aeroplane for the purpose of aerial work that consists of:

         aa. the giving of instruction in flying, if his licence includes a flying instructor's rating, class rating instructor rating, flight instructor rating or an assistant flying instructor's rating; or

         bb. the conducting of flying tests for the purposes of this Order;

      in either case in an aeroplane owned, or operated under arrangements entered into, by a flying club of which the person giving the instruction or conducting the test and the person receiving the instruction or undergoing the test are both members;

      ii. he may fly such an aeroplane for the purpose of aerial work that consists of -

         aa. towing a glider in flight; or

         bb. flight for the purpose of dropping of persons by parachute;

      in either case in an aeroplane owned, or operated under arrangements entered into, by a club of which the holder of the licence and any person carried in the aircraft or in any glider towed by the aircraft are members;

   b. receive any remuneration for his services as a pilot on a flight save that if his licence includes a flying instructor's rating, a flight instructor rating or an assistant flying instructor's rating by virtue of which he is entitled to give instruction in flying microlight aircraft or self-launching motor gliders he may receive remuneration for the giving of such instruction or the conducting of such flying tests as are specified in sub-paragraph ((a) (i)) in a microlight aircraft or a self-launching motor glider.

   c. unless his licence includes an instrument rating (aeroplane) or an instrument meteorological conditions rating (aeroplanes), fly as pilot in command of such an aeroplane:

      i. on a flight outside controlled airspace when the flight visibility is less than 3km;

      ii. on a special VFR flight in a control zone in a flight visibility of less than 10km except on a route or in an aerodrome traffic zone notified for the purpose of this sub-paragraph; or

      iii. out of sight of the surface;

   d. as pilot in command of such an aeroplane at night unless his licence includes a night rating (aeroplanes) or a night qualification (aeroplanes);

   e. unless his licence includes an instrument rating (aeroplane), fly as pilot in command or co-pilot of such an aeroplane flying in Class A, B or C airspace in circumstances that require compliance with the Instrument Flight Rules;

   f. unless his licence includes an instrument rating (aeroplane) or an instrument meteorological conditions rating (aeroplanes), fly as pilot in command or co-pilot of such an aeroplane flying in Class D or E airspace in circumstances that require compliance with the Instrument Flight Rules; or

g. fly as pilot in command of such an aeroplane carrying passengers unless within the preceding 90 days he has made three take-offs and three landings as the sole manipulator of the controls of an aeroplane of the same type or class and if such a flight is to be carried out at night and his licence does not include an instrument rating (aeroplane) at least one of those take offs and landings shall have been at night.

Basic Commercial Pilot's Licence (Aeroplanes)

Minimum age - 18 years

Maximum period of validity - 10 years

Privileges:

1. The holder of a Basic Commercial Pilot's Licence (Aeroplanes) shall be entitled to exercise the privileges of a United Kingdom Private Pilot's Licence (Aeroplanes).

2. Subject to paragraphs (3) and (7), he shall be entitled to fly as pilot in command of an aeroplane of a type or class on which he is so qualified and which is specified in an aircraft rating included in the licence when the aeroplane is engaged on a flight for any purpose whatsoever.

3. He shall not -

a. fly such an aeroplane on a flight for the purpose of public transport if he has less than 400 hours of flying experience as pilot in command of aeroplanes other than self-launching motor gliders or microlight aeroplanes;

b. fly such an aeroplane on a flight for the purpose of public transport if its maximum total weight authorised exceeds 2300 kg;

c. fly such an aeroplane on any scheduled journey;

d. fly such an aeroplane on a flight for the purpose of public transport except a flight beginning and ending at the same aerodrome and not extending beyond 25 nautical miles from that aerodrome;

e. fly such an aeroplane on a flight for the purpose of public transport after he attains the age of 60 years unless the aeroplane is fitted with dual controls and carries a second pilot who has not attained the age of 60 years and who holds an appropriate licence under this Order entitling him to act as pilot in command or co-pilot of that aeroplane;

f. fly such an aeroplane at night, unless his licence includes a night rating (aeroplanes) or a night qualification (aeroplane);

g. unless his licence includes an instrument rating (aeroplane) or an instrument meteorological conditions rating (aeroplanes), fly as pilot in command of such an aeroplane -

i. on a flight outside controlled airspace when the flight visibility is less than 3km;

ii. on a special VFR flight in a control zone in a flight visibility of less than 10 km except on a route or in an aerodrome traffic zone notified for the purposes of this sub-paragraph; or

iii. out of sight of the surface.

h. unless his licence includes an instrument rating (aeroplane), fly as pilot in command or co-pilot of such an aeroplane flying in Class A, B or C airspace in circumstances that require compliance with the Instrument Flight Rules;

i. unless his licence includes an instrument rating (aeroplane) or an instrument meteorological conditions rating (aeroplanes), fly as pilot in command or co-pilot of such an aeroplane flying in Class D or E airspace in circumstances that require compliance with the Instrument Flight Rules; or

j. fly as pilot in command of such an aeroplane carrying passengers unless within the preceding 90 days he has made three take-offs and three landings as the sole manipulator of the controls of an aeroplane of the same type or class and if the flight is to be undertaken at night and his licence does not include an instrument rating (aeroplane) at least one of those take offs and landings shall have been at night.

4. Subject to sub-paragraph (5), he shall be entitled to fly as pilot in command of an aeroplane of a type or class specified in an instructor's rating included in the licence on a flight for the purpose of aerial work which consists of -

a. the giving of instruction in flying; or

b. the conducting of flying tests for the purposes of this Order;

in either case in an aeroplane owned, or operated under arrangements entered into, by a flying club of which the person giving the instruction or conducting the test and the person receiving the instruction or undergoing the test are both members.

5. He shall not be entitled to exercise the privileges contained in paragraph (4) other than in an aeroplane that he is entitled to fly as pilot in command on a private flight, an aerial work flight or a public transport flight pursuant to the privileges set out in paragraph (1) or (2) of these privileges.

6. Subject to paragraph (7) he shall be entitled to fly as co-pilot of any aeroplane of a type specified in an aircraft rating included in the licence when the aeroplane is engaged on a flight for any purpose whatsoever provided that he shall not be entitled to fly as co-pilot of an aeroplane which is engaged on a flight for the purpose of public transport unless he has more than 400 hours of flying experience as pilot in command of aeroplanes other than self-launching motor gliders and microlight aeroplanes and the aeroplane is certificated for single pilot operation.

7. He shall not at any time after he attains the age of 65 years act as pilot in command or co-pilot of any aeroplane on a flight for the purpose of public transport.

Commercial Pilot's Licence (Aeroplanes)

Minimum age - 18 years

Maximum period of validity - 10 years

Privileges:

1. The holder of a Commercial Pilot's Licence (Aeroplanes) shall be entitled to exercise the privileges of a United Kingdom Private Pilot's Licence (Aeroplanes) which includes an instrument meteorological conditions rating (aeroplanes) and a night rating (aeroplanes) or night qualification (aeroplane), and shall be entitled to fly as pilot in command of an aeroplane -

   a. on a special VFR flight notwithstanding that the flight visibility is less than 3km;

   b. when the aeroplane is taking off or landing at any place notwithstanding that the flight visibility below cloud is less than 1800 metres.

2. Subject to paragraphs (3) and (7), he shall be entitled to fly as pilot in command of an aeroplane of a type or class on which he is so qualified and which is specified in an aircraft rating included in the licence when the aeroplane is engaged on a flight for any purpose whatsoever.

3. He shall not -

   a. unless his licence includes an instrument rating (aeroplane), fly such an aeroplane on any scheduled journey;

   b. fly as pilot in command of an aeroplane carrying passengers unless he has carried out at least three take-offs and three landings as pilot flying in an aeroplane of the same type or class or in a flight simulator, approved for the purpose, of the aeroplane type or class to be used, in the preceding 90 days;

   c. as co-pilot serve at the flying controls in an aeroplane carrying passengers during take-off and landing unless he has served as a pilot at the controls during take-off and landing in an aeroplane of the same type or in a flight simulator, approved for the purpose, of the aeroplane type to be used, in the preceding 90 days;

   d. as the holder of a licence which does not include a valid instrument rating (aeroplane), fly as pilot in command of an aeroplane carrying passengers at night unless during the previous 90 days at least one of the take-offs and landings required in sub-paragraph (b) has been carried out at night;

   e. unless his licence includes an instrument rating (aeroplane), fly any such aeroplane of which the maximum total weight authorised exceeds 2300 kg on any flight for the purpose of public transport, except a flight beginning and ending at the same aerodrome and not extending beyond 25 nautical miles from that aerodrome;

   f. fly such an aeroplane on a flight for the purpose of public transport unless it is certificated for single pilot operation;

   g. fly such an aeroplane on any flight for the purpose of public transport after he attains the age of 60 years unless the aeroplane is fitted with dual controls and carries a second pilot who has not attained the age of 60 years and who holds an appropriate licence under this Order entitling him to act as pilot in command or co-pilot of that aeroplane; or

   h. unless his licence includes an instrument rating (aeroplane), fly as pilot in command or co-pilot of such an aeroplane flying in Class A, B or C airspace in circumstances that require compliance with the Instrument Flight Rules.

4. Subject to sub-paragraph (5), he shall be entitled to fly as pilot in command of an aeroplane of a type or class specified in an instructor's rating included in the licence on a flight for the purpose of aerial work which consists of -

a. the giving of instruction in flying; or

b. the conducting of flying tests for the purposes of this Order;

in either case in an aeroplane owned, or operated under arrangements entered into, by a flying club of which the person giving the instruction or conducting the test and the person receiving the instruction or undergoing the test are both members.

5. He shall not be entitled to exercise privileges contained in paragraph (4) other than in an aeroplane which he is entitled to fly as pilot in command on a private flight, an aerial work flight or a public transport flight pursuant to the privileges set out in paragraph (1) or (2) of these privileges.

6. Subject to paragraph (7) he shall be entitled to fly as co-pilot of any aeroplane of a type specified in an aircraft rating included in the licence when the aeroplane is engaged on a flight for any purpose whatsoever.

7. He shall not at any time after he attains the age of 65 years act as pilot in command or co-pilot of any aeroplane on a flight for the purpose of public transport.

Airline Transport Pilot's Licence (Aeroplanes)

Minimum age - 21 years

Maximum period of validity - 10 years

Privileges:

The holder of an Airline Transport Pilot’s Licence (Aeroplanes) shall be entitled to exercise the privileges of a United Kingdom Commercial Pilot's Licence (Aeroplanes) except that sub-paragraph (3) (f) of those privileges shall not apply.

Sub-section 2
Helicopter and Gyroplane Pilots

Private Pilot's Licence (Helicopters)

Minimum Age - 17 years

No Maximum Period of Validity

Privileges:

1. Subject to paragraph (2), the holder of a Private Pilot’s Licence (Helicopters) shall be entitled to fly as pilot in command or co-pilot of any helicopter of a type specified in an aircraft rating included in the licence.

2. He shall not -

a) fly such a helicopter for the purpose of public transport or aerial work other than aerial work that consists of -

i. the giving of instruction in flying if his licence includes a flying instructor's rating, flight instructor rating or an assistant flying instructor's rating; or

ii. the conducting of flying tests for the purposes of this Order;

in either case in a helicopter owned, or operated under arrangements entered into, by a flying club of which the person giving the instruction or conducting the test and the person receiving the instruction or undergoing the test are both members.

b. receive any remuneration for his services as a pilot on a flight other than remuneration for the giving of such instruction or the conducting of such flying tests as are specified in sub-paragraph (a).

c. fly as pilot in command of such a helicopter at night unless his licence includes a night rating (helicopters) or a night qualification (helicopter);

d. unless his licence includes an instrument rating (helicopter) fly as pilot in command or co-pilot of such a helicopter flying in Class A, B or C airspace in circumstances that require compliance with the Instrument Flight Rules; or

e. fly as pilot in command of such a helicopter carrying passengers unless -

i. within the preceding 90 days he has made three circuits, each to include take-offs and landings as the sole manipulator of the controls of a helicopter of the same type; or

ii. if the privileges are to be exercised by night and his licence does not include an instrument rating, within the preceding 90 days he has made three circuits, each to include take-offs and landings by night as the sole manipulator of the controls of a helicopter of the same type.

Private Pilot's Licence (Gyroplanes)

Minimum age - 17 years

No maximum period of validity

Privileges:

1. Subject to paragraph (2), the holder of a Private Pilot's Licence (Gyroplanes) shall be entitled to fly as pilot in command or co-pilot of any gyroplane of a type specified in the aircraft rating included in the licence.

2. He shall not -

   a. fly such a gyroplane for the purpose of public transport or aerial work other than aerial work that consists of -

      i. the giving of instruction in flying if his licence includes a flying instructor's rating, flight instructor rating or an assistant flying instructor's rating; or

      ii. the conducting of flying tests for the purposes of this Order;

   in either case in a gyroplane owned, or operated under arrangements entered into, by a flying club of which the person giving the instruction or conducting the test and the person receiving the instruction or undergoing the test are both members.

   b. receive any remuneration for his services as a pilot on a flight other than remuneration for the giving of such instruction or the conducting of such flying tests as are specified in sub-paragraph (a).

   c. as pilot in command of such a gyroplane at night unless his licence includes a night rating (gyroplanes) and he has within the immediately preceding 13 months carried out as pilot in command not less than 5 take offs and five landings at a time when the depression of the centre of the sun was not less than 12° below the horizon.

Commercial Pilot's Licence (Helicopters and Gyroplanes)

Minimum age - 18 years

Maximum period of validity - 10 years

Privileges:

1. Subject to paragraphs (2) and (5) , the holder of a Commercial Pilot's Licence (Helicopters and Gyroplanes) shall be entitled -

   a. to exercise the privileges of a United Kingdom Private Pilot's Licence (Helicopters) or a United Kingdom Private Pilot's Licence (Gyroplanes) which includes respectively either a night rating (helicopters) or night qualification (helicopter) or a night rating (gyroplanes); and

   b. to fly as pilot in command of any helicopter or gyroplane on which he is so qualified and which is of a type specified in an aircraft rating included in the licence when the helicopter or gyroplane is engaged on a flight for any purpose whatsoever.

2. He shall not -

   a. unless his licence includes an instrument rating (helicopter) fly such a helicopter on any scheduled journey or on any flight for the purpose of public transport other than in visual meteorological conditions;

   b. fly such a helicopter on a flight for the purpose of public transport unless it is certificated for single pilot operation;

   c. fly such a helicopter on any flight for the purpose of public transport after he attains the age of 60 years unless the helicopter is fitted with dual controls and carries a second pilot who has not attained the age of 60 years and who holds an appropriate licence under this Order entitling him to act as pilot in command or co-pilot of that helicopter;

   d. unless his licence includes an instrument rating (helicopter) fly as pilot in command of such a helicopter flying in Class A, B or C airspace in circumstances that require compliance with the Instrument Flight Rules;

   e. fly as pilot in command of a helicopter carrying passengers unless he has carried out at least three circuits, each to include take-offs and landings, as pilot flying in a helicopter of the same type or a flight simulator of the helicopter type to be used, in the preceding 90 days;

   f. as the holder of a helicopter licence which does not include a valid instrument rating (helicopter) act as pilot in command of a helicopter carrying passengers at night unless during the previous 90 days at least one of the take-offs and landings required in sub-paragraph (e) above has been carried out at night;

   g. fly such a gyroplane on a flight for the purpose of public transport unless it is certificated for single pilot operation;

   h. fly such a gyroplane at night unless he has within the immediately preceding 13 months carried out as pilot in command not less than 5 take-offs and 5 landings at a time when the depression of the centre of the sun was not less than 12° below the horizon; or

i. fly such a gyroplane on any flight for the purpose of public transport after he attains the age of 60 years unless the gyroplane is fitted with dual controls and carries a second pilot who has not attained the age of 60 years and who holds an appropriate licence under this Order entitling him to act as pilot in command or co-pilot of that gyroplane.

3. Subject to paragraphs (4) and (5) he shall be entitled to fly as co-pilot of any helicopter or gyroplane of a type specified in an aircraft rating included in the licence when the helicopter or gyroplane is engaged on a flight for any purpose whatsoever.

4. He shall not -

a. unless his licence includes an instrument rating (helicopter) fly as co-pilot of a helicopter flying in Class A, B or C airspace in circumstances that require compliance with the Instrument Flight Rules;

b. as co-pilot serve at the flying controls in a helicopter carrying passengers during take-off and landing unless he has served as a pilot at the controls during take-off and landing in a helicopter of the same type or in a flight simulator of the helicopter type to be used, in the preceding 90 days; or

c. unless his licence includes an Instrument Rating (Helicopter) fly as co-pilot of a helicopter on any scheduled journey or on a flight or the purpose of public transport other than in visual meteorological conditions.

5. He shall not at any time after he attains the age of 65 years act as pilot in command or co-pilot of any helicopter or gyroplane on a flight for the purpose of public transport.

Airline Transport Pilot's Licence (Helicopters and Gyroplanes)

Minimum age - 21 years

Maximum period of validity - 10 years

Privileges:

The holder of an Airline Transport Pilot's Licence (Helicopters and Gyroplanes) shall be entitled to exercise the privileges of a United Kingdom Commercial Pilot's Licence (Helicopters and Gyroplanes) except that sub-paragraphs (2)(b) and (2)(g) of those privileges shall not apply.

Sub-section 3
Balloon and Airship Pilots

Private Pilot's Licence (Balloons and Airships)

Minimum age - 17 years

No maximum period of validity

Privileges:

1. Subject to paragraph (2), the holder of a Private Pilot's Licence (Balloons and Airships) shall be entitled to fly as pilot in command of any type of balloon or airship on which he is so qualified and which is specified in an aircraft rating in the licence and co-pilot of any type of balloon or airship specified in such a rating.

2. He shall not -

a. fly such a balloon or airship for the purpose of public transport or aerial work, other than aerial work which consists of the giving of instruction in flying or the conducting of flying tests in either case in a balloon or airship owned, or operated under arrangements entered into, by a flying club of which the person giving the instruction or conducting the test and the person receiving the instruction or undergoing the test are both members;

b. receive any remuneration for his services as a pilot on a flight other than remuneration for the giving of such instruction or the conducting of such flying tests as are specified in sub-paragraph (a); or

c. fly such a balloon unless he has within the immediately preceding 13 months carried out as pilot in command in a free balloon 5 flights each of not less than 5 minutes duration.

Commercial Pilot's Licence (Balloons)

Minimum age - 18 years

Maximum period of validity - 10 years

Privileges:

1. The holder of a Commercial Pilot's Licence (Balloons) shall be entitled to exercise the privileges of a United Kingdom Private Pilot's Licence (Balloons and Airships).

2. Subject to paragraph (3), he shall be entitled to fly, when the balloon is flying for any purpose whatsoever, as pilot in command or co-pilot of any type of balloon specified in the aircraft rating included in the licence.

3. He shall not act as pilot in command on a flight for the purpose of the public transport of passengers

unless he has within the immediately preceding 90 days carried out as pilot in command in a free balloon 3 flights each of not less than 5 minutes duration.

Commercial Pilot's Licence (Airships)

Minimum age - 18 years

Maximum period of validity - 10 years

Privileges:

1. The holder of a Commercial Pilot's Licence (Airships) shall be entitled to exercise the privileges of a United Kingdom Private Pilot's Licence (Balloons and Airships).

2. He shall be entitled to fly, when the airship is flying for any purpose whatsoever, as pilot in command of any type of airship on which he is so qualified and which is specified in an aircraft rating included in the licence and as co-pilot of any type of airship specified in such a rating.

Sub-section 4
Glider Pilots

Commercial Pilot's Licence (Gliders)

Minimum age - 18 years

Maximum period of validity - 10 years

Privileges:

The holder of a Commercial Pilot's Licence (Gliders) shall be entitled to fly for any purpose as pilot in command or co-pilot of -

a. any glider of which the maximum total weight authorised does not exceed 680 kg;

b. any glider of which the maximum total weight authorised exceeds 680 kg and which is of a type specified in the rating included in the licence.

Sub-section 5
Other Flight Crew

Flight Navigator's Licence

Minimum age - 21 years

Maximum period of validity - 10 years

Privileges:

The holder of a Flight Navigator's licence shall be entitled to act as flight navigator in any aircraft.

Flight Engineer's Licence

Minimum age - 21 years

Maximum period of validity - 10 years

Privileges:

The holder of a Flight Engineer's licence shall be entitled to act as flight engineer in any type of aircraft specified in an aircraft rating included in the licence.

Flight Radiotelephony Operator's Licence

Minimum age - 16 years

Maximum period of validity - 10 years

Privileges:

The holder of a Flight Radiotelephony Operator's licence shall be entitled to operate radiotelephony apparatus in any aircraft if the stability of the frequency radiated by the transmitter is maintained automatically but shall not be entitled to operate the transmitter, or to adjust its frequency, except by the use of external switching devices.

Sub-section 2
JAR-FCL Licences

Sub-section 1 - Aeroplane Pilots

Private Pilot Licence (Aeroplane)

Minimum age - 17 years

Maximum period of validity - 5 years

Privileges and conditions:

1. Subject to any conditions specified in respect of the licence, the privileges of the holder of a Private Pilot Licence (Aeroplane) are to act, but not for remuneration, as pilot in command or co-pilot of any aeroplane specified in a class or type rating included in Part XII of the licence engaged in non-revenue flights.

2. The licence is subject to the conditions and restrictions specified in paragraph 1.175 of JAR-FCL 1.

3. The holder shall not -

   a. unless his licence includes an instrument rating (aeroplane) or an instrument meteorological conditions rating (aeroplanes), fly as pilot in command of such an aeroplane -

      i. on a flight outside controlled airspace when the flight visibility is less than 3km;

      ii. on a special VFR flight in a control zone in a flight visibility of less than 10km except on a route or in an aerodrome traffic zone notified for the purpose of this sub-paragraph; or

      iii. out of sight of the surface.

   b. unless his licence includes an instrument meteorological conditions rating (aeroplanes), fly as pilot in command or co-pilot of such an aeroplane flying in Class D or E airspace in circumstances which require compliance with the Instrument Flight Rules.

c. fly as pilot in command of such an aeroplane at night unless his licence includes a night rating (aeroplanes) or a night qualification (aeroplane); or

d. fly as pilot in command of such an aeroplane carrying passengers unless within the preceding 90 days he has made at least three take-offs and three landings as the sole manipulator of the controls of an aeroplane of the same type or class and if such a flight is to be carried out at night and his licence does not include an instrument rating (aeroplanes) at least one of those take-offs and landing shall have been at night.

Commercial Pilot Licence (Aeroplane)

Minimum age - 18 years

Maximum period of validity - 5 years

Privileges and conditions:

1. Subject to any conditions specified in respect of the licence, the privileges of the holder of a Commercial Pilot Licence (Aeroplane) are to:

a. exercise all the privileges of the holder of a JAR-FCL Private Pilot Licence (Aeroplane) which includes a night qualification;

b. act as pilot in command or co-pilot of any aeroplane specified in a type or class rating included in Part XII of the licence on a flight other than a public transport flight;

c. act as pilot in command on a public transport flight of any aeroplane included in Part XII of the licence certificated for single pilot operation; and

d. act as co-pilot on a public transport flight of any aeroplane included in Part XII of the licence.

2. The licence is subject to the conditions and restrictions specified in paragraph 1.175 of JAR-FCL 1.

3. The holder shall not -

a. fly as pilot in command on a flight for the purpose of public transport unless he complies with the requirements of JAR-OPS 1.960(a)(1) and (2) of Section 1 of JAR-OPS 1;

b. unless his licence includes an instrument rating (aeroplane), fly such an aeroplane on any scheduled journey;

c. fly as pilot in command of an aeroplane carrying passengers unless he has carried out at least three take-offs and three landings as pilot flying in an aeroplane of the same type or class or in a flight simulator, approved for the purpose, of the aeroplane type or class to be used, in the preceding 90 days;

d. as co-pilot serve at the flying controls in an aeroplane carrying passengers during take-off and landing unless he has served as a pilot at the controls during take-off and landing in an aeroplane of the same type or in a flight simulator, approved for the purpose, of the aeroplane type to be used, in the preceding 90 days;

e. as the holder of a licence which does not include a valid instrument rating (aeroplane) act as pilot in command of an aeroplane carrying passengers at night unless during the previous 90 days at least one of the take-offs and landings required in sub-paragraph (c) above has been carried out at night; or

f. unless his licence includes an instrument rating (aeroplane), fly any such aeroplane of which the maximum total weight authorised exceeds 2300 kg on any flight for the purpose of public transport, except a flight beginning and ending at the same aerodrome and not extending beyond 25 nautical miles from that aerodrome.

4. The holder shall be entitled, subject to paragraph (5), to fly as pilot in command of an aeroplane of a type or class specified in any flying instructor's rating, class rating instructor rating, flight instructor rating or assistant flying instructor's rating included in the licence on a flight for the purpose of aerial work which consists of -

a. the giving of instruction in flying; or

b. the conducting of flying tests for the purposes of this Order;

in either case in an aeroplane owned, or operated under arrangements entered into, by a flying club of which the person giving the instruction or conducting the test and the person receiving the instruction or undergoing the test are both members.

5. The holder shall not be entitled to exercise privileges contained in paragraph (4) other than in an aeroplane which he is entitled to fly as pilot in command on a private flight, an aerial work

flight or a public transport flight pursuant to the privileges set out in paragraph (1) or (2) of these privileges.

Curtailment of privileges of licence holders aged 60 years or more

6. The holder of a licence who has attained the age of 60 years but not attained the age of 65 years shall not act as a pilot of an aeroplane on a public transport flight except where the holder is:

   a. a member of a multi-pilot crew;

   b. the only pilot in the flight crew who has attained the age of 60 years.

7. The holder of a licence who has attained the age of 65 years shall not act as a pilot of an aeroplane on a public transport flight.

Airline Transport Pilot Licence (Aeroplane)

Minimum age - 21 years

Maximum period of validity - 5 years

Privileges and conditions:

1. Subject to any conditions specified in respect of the licence, the privileges of the holder of an Airline Transport Pilot Licence (Aeroplane) are to -

   a. exercise all the privileges of the holder of a JAR-FCL Private Pilot Licence (Aeroplane), a JAR-FCL Commercial Pilot Licence (Aeroplane) and an instrument rating (aeroplane); and

   b. act as pilot in command or co-pilot of any aeroplane specified in a type rating included in Part XII of the licence on a public transport flight.

2. The licence is subject to the conditions and restrictions specified in paragraph 1.175 of JAR-FCL 1.

   Curtailment of privileges of licence holders aged 60 years or more

3. The holder of a licence who has attained the age of 60 years but not attained the age of 65 years shall not act as a pilot of an aeroplane on a public transport flight except where the holder is -

   a. a member of a multi-pilot crew;

   b. the only pilot in the flight crew who has attained the age of 60 years.

4. The holder of a licence who has attained the age of 65 years shall not act as a pilot of an aeroplane on a public transport flight.

Sub-section 2
Helicopter Pilots

Private Pilot Licence (Helicopter)

Minimum age - 17 years

Maximum period of validity - 5 years

Privileges and conditions:

1. Subject to any conditions specified in respect of the licence, the privileges of the holder of a Private Pilot Licence (Helicopter) are to act, but not for remuneration, as pilot in command or co-pilot of any helicopter included in a type rating in Part XII of the licence engaged in non-revenue flights.

2. The licence is subject to the conditions and restrictions specified in paragraph 2.175 of Section 1 of JAR-FCL 2.

3. The holder shall not -

   a. fly as pilot in command of such a helicopter at night unless his licence includes a night rating (helicopters) or a night qualification (helicopter); or

   b. fly as pilot in command of such a helicopter carrying passengers unless -

      i. within the preceding 90 days he has made three solo circuits, each to include take-offs and landings as the sole manipulator of the controls of a helicopter of the same type; or

      ii. if the privileges are to be exercised by night and his licence does not include an instrument rating, within the preceding 90 days he has made three circuits, each to include take-offs and landings by night as the sole manipulator of the controls of a helicopter of the same type.

Commercial Pilot Licence (Helicopter)

Minimum age - 18 years

Maximum period of validity - 5 years

Privileges and conditions:

1. Subject to any conditions specified in respect of the licence, the privileges of the holder of a Commercial Pilot Licence (Helicopter) are to -

a. exercise all the privileges of the holder of a JAR-FCL Private Pilot Licence (Helicopter);

b. act as pilot in command or co-pilot of any helicopter included in a type rating in Part XII of the licence on a flight other than a public transport flight;

c. act as pilot in command on a public transport flight of any helicopter certificated for single-pilot operation included in Part XII of the licence;

d. act as co-pilot on a public transport flight in any helicopter included in Part XII of the licence required to be operated with a co-pilot.

2. The licence is subject to the conditions and restrictions specified in paragraph 2.175 of Section 1 of JAR-FCL 2.

3. The holder shall not fly as pilot in command on a flight for the purpose of public transport unless he complies with the requirements of paragraph 3.960(a)(2) of Section 1 of JAR-OPS 3.

4. The holder shall not -

a. unless his licence includes an instrument rating (helicopter), fly such a helicopter on any scheduled journey or on any flight for the purpose of public transport other than in visual meteorological conditions;

b. fly as pilot in command of a helicopter carrying passengers unless he has carried out at least three circuits, each to include take-offs and landings, as pilot flying in a helicopter of the same type or a flight simulator of the helicopter type to be used, in the preceding 90 days; or

c. as the holder of a helicopter licence which does not include a valid instrument rating (helicopter) act as pilot in command of a helicopter carrying passengers at night unless during the previous 90 days at least one of the take-offs and landings required in sub-paragraph (a) above has been carried out at night.

Curtailment of privileges of licence holders aged 60 years or more

5. The holder of a licence who has attained the age of 60 years but not attained the age of 65 years shall not act as a pilot of a helicopter on a public transport flight except where the holder is -

a. a member of a multi-pilot crew;

b. the only pilot in the flight crew who has attained the age of 60 years.

6. The holder of a licence who has attained the age of 65 years shall not act as a pilot of a helicopter on a public transport flight.

Airline Transport Pilot Licence (Helicopter)

Minimum age - 21 years

Maximum period of validity - 5 years

Privileges and conditions:

1. Subject to any conditions specified in respect of the licence, the privileges of the holder of an Airline Transport Pilot Licence (Helicopter) are to:

a. exercise all the privileges of the holder of a JAR-FCL Private Pilot Licence (Helicopter) and a JAR-FCL Commercial Pilot Licence (Helicopter); and

b. subject to paragraph (2), act as pilot in command or co-pilot in any helicopter included in a type rating in Part XII of the licence on a public transport flight.

2. The holder shall not fly as pilot in command on a flight for the purpose of public transport unless he complies with the requirements of paragraph 3.960(a)(2) of Section 1 of JAR-OPS 3.

Curtailment of privileges of licence holders aged 60 years or more

3. The holder of a licence who has attained the age of 60 years but not attained the age of 65 years shall not act as a pilot of a helicopter on a public transport flight except where the holder is -

a. a member of a multi-pilot crew and provided that,

b. is the only pilot in the flight crew who has attained the age of 60 years.

4. The holder of a licence who has attained the age of 65 years shall not act as a pilot of a helicopter on a public transport flight.

Section 3
National Private Pilot's Licence (Aeroplanes)

National Private Pilot's Licence (Aeroplanes)

Minimum age – 17 years

No maximum period of validity

Privileges and conditions:

1. Subject to paragraphs (2), (3), (4), (5), (6) and (7) the holder of the licence shall be entitled to fly as pilot in command of any simple single engine aeroplane, microlight aeroplane or SLMG specified or otherwise falling within an aircraft rating included in the licence.

Flight outside the United Kingdom

2. He shall not fly -

   a. such a simple single engine aeroplane or a microlight aeroplane outside the United Kingdom except with the permission of the competent authority for the airspace in which he flies; or

   b. such a SLMG in or over the territory of a Contracting State other than the United Kingdom except in accordance with permission granted by the competent authority of that State provided that he may fly a SLMG outside the United Kingdom if his licence includes a SLMG rating and a medical certificate.

Flight for purpose of public transport and aerial work

3. He shall not fly any such aeroplane for the purpose of public transport or aerial work except in the circumstances specified in paragraph (4).

4. The circumstances referred to in paragraph (3) are that he flies such an aeroplane for the purpose of aerial work which consists of towing another aeroplane or glider in flight -

   a. in an aeroplane owned, or operated under arrangements entered into, by a flying club of which the holder of the licence and any person carried in the towing aeroplane or in any aeroplane or glider being towed are members; or

   b. in an aeroplane owned, or operated under arrangements entered into, by an organisation approved by the CAA for the purpose of this provision when -

      i. the holder of the licence is a member of an organisation approved by the CAA for the purpose of this provision; and

      ii. any person carried in the towing aeroplane or in any aeroplane or glider being towed is a member of an organisation approved by the CAA for the purpose of this provision.

Prohibitions on flight in specified conditions

5. He shall not fly -

   a. as pilot in command of such a simple single engine aeroplane on a flight outside controlled airspace when the flight visibility is less and 5 km;

   b. as pilot in command of such a SLMG or microlight aeroplane on a flight outside controlled airspace when the flight visibility is less than 3 km;

   c. as pilot in command of any such aeroplane -

      i. on a special VFR flight in a control zone in a flight visibility of less than 10 km;

      ii. out of sight of the surface; or

      iii. at night; or

   d. as pilot in command of any such aeroplane in circumstances which require compliance with the Instrument Flight Rules.

Carriage of persons

6. He shall not fly as pilot in command of any such aeroplane -

   a. when the total number of persons carried (including the pilot) exceeds four; or

   b. when carrying passengers unless within the preceding 90 days he has made at least three take-offs and three landings as the sole manipulator of the controls of an aeroplane of the same class as that being flown.

Differences training

7. He shall not fly -

   a. as pilot in command of such a simple single engine aeroplane where -

      i. the aeroplane is fitted with a tricycle undercarriage;

      ii. the aeroplane is fitted with a tailwheel;

      iii. the engine is fitted with either a supercharger or turbo-charger;

      iv. the engine is fitted with a variable pitch propeller;

      v. the landing gear is retractable;

vi. a cabin pressurisation system is fitted; or

vii. the aeroplane has a maximum continuous cruising speed in excess of 140 knots indicated airspeed; unless appropriate differences training has been completed and recorded in his personal flying logbook; or

b. as pilot in command of such a microlight aeroplane where -

i. the aeroplane has 3 axis controls and his previous training and experience has only been in an aeroplane with flexwing controls; or

ii. the aeroplane has flexwing controls and his previous training and experience has only been in an aeroplane with 3 axis controls;

unless appropriate differences training has been completed and recorded in his personal flying logbook.

PART B - RATINGS AND QUALIFICATIONS

The following ratings may be included in a pilot's licence granted under Part 4 and, subject to the provisions of this Order and of the licence, the inclusion of a rating in a licence shall have the consequences respectively specified as follows -

Aircraft rating: The licence shall entitle the holder to act as pilot of aircraft of the types and classes specified in an aircraft rating included in the licence and different types and classes of aircraft may be specified in respect of different privileges of a licence.

Instrument meteorological conditions rating (aeroplanes)

1. Subject to paragraph (2) the rating within the United Kingdom -

a. entitle the holder of a United Kingdom entitle the holder of a United Kingdom Private Pilot's Licence (Aeroplanes) or a United Kingdom Basic Commercial Pilot's Licence (Aeroplanes) to fly as pilot in command of an aeroplane without being subject to the restrictions contained respectively in paragraph (2)(c)or (f) of the privileges of the United Kingdom Private Pilot's Licence (Aeroplanes) or (3)(a) or (i) of the privileges of the United Kingdom Basic Commercial Pilot's Licence (Aeroplanes); and

b. entitle the holder of a JAR-FCL Private Pilot Licence (Aeroplane) to fly as pilot in command of an aeroplane in Class D or E airspace in circumstances that require compliance with the Instrument Flight Rules.

2. The rating shall not entitle the holder of the licence to fly -

a. on a special VFR flight in a control zone in a flight visibility of less than 3km; or

b. when the aeroplane is taking off or landing at any place if the flight visibility below cloud is less than 1,800 metres.

Instrument rating (aeroplane) shall entitle the holder of the licence to act as pilot in command or co-pilot of an aeroplane flying in controlled airspace in circumstances which require compliance with the Instrument Flight Rules.

Instrument rating (helicopter) shall entitle the holder of the licence to act as pilot in command or co-pilot of a helicopter flying in controlled airspace in circumstances which require compliance with the Instrument Flight Rules.

Microlight class rating shall, when included in the aircraft rating of a National Private Pilot's Licence (Aeroplanes) or a United Kingdom Private Pilot's Licence (Aeroplanes) and subject to the conditions of the licence in which it is included, entitle the holder to act as pilot in command of any microlight aeroplane.

Night rating (aeroplanes) shall entitle the holder of a United Kingdom Private Pilot's Licence (Aeroplanes) or a United Kingdom Basic Commercial Pilot's Licence (Aeroplanes) to act as pilot in command of an aeroplane at night.

Night qualification (aeroplane) shall entitle the holder of a United Kingdom Private Pilot's Licence (Aeroplanes), a JAR-FCL Private Pilot Licence (Aeroplane) or a United Kingdom Basic Commercial Pilot's Licence (Aeroplanes) to act as pilot in command of an aeroplane at night.

Night rating (helicopters) shall entitle the holder of a United Kingdom Private Pilot's Licence (Helicopters) to act as pilot in command of a helicopter at night.

Night qualification (helicopter) shall entitle the holder of either a United Kingdom Private Pilot's Licence (Helicopters) or a JAR-FCL Private Pilot Licence (Helicopter) to act as pilot in command of a helicopter at night.

Night rating (gyroplanes) shall entitle the holder of a United Kingdom Private Pilot's Licence (Gyroplanes) to act as pilot in command of a gyroplane at night.

Simple single engine aeroplane (NPPL) class rating shall, when included in the aircraft rating of a National Private Pilot's Licence (Aeroplanes) and subject to the conditions of that licence, entitle the holder to act as pilot in command of any simple single engine aeroplane with a maximum take off weight authorised not exceeding 2000 kg excluding any such aeroplane which is a self launching motor glider or a microlight aeroplane.

SLMG class rating shall, when included in the aircraft rating of a National Private Pilot's Licence (Aeroplanes) or a United Kingdom Private Pilot's Licence (Aeroplanes) and subject to the conditions of the licence in which it is included, entitle the holder to act as pilot in command of any SLMG.

Towing rating (flying machines) shall entitle the holder of the licence to act as pilot of a flying machine while towing a glider in flight for the purposes of public transport or aerial work.

Flying instructor's rating shall entitle the holder of the licence to give instruction in flying aircraft of such types and classes as may be specified in the rating for that purpose.

Assistant flying instructor's rating shall entitle the holder of the licence to give instruction in flying aircraft of such types and classes as may be specified in the rating for that purpose provided that -

a. such instruction shall only be given under the supervision of a person present during the take-off and landing at the aerodrome at which the instruction is to begin and end and holding a pilot's licence endorsed with a flying instructor's rating;

b. such a rating shall not entitle the holder of the licence to give directions to the person undergoing instruction in respect of the performance by that person of

   i. his first solo flight;

   ii. his first solo flight by night;

   iii. his first solo cross-country flight otherwise than by night; or

   iv) his first solo cross-country flight by night.

Flight instructor rating (aeroplane) shall entitle the holder of the licence to give instruction in flying aircraft of such types and classes as may be specified in the rating for that purpose subject to the restrictions specified below.

Flight instructor rating (aeroplane) - Restrictions

Restricted period

1. Until the holder of a flight instructor (aeroplane) rating has completed at least 100 hours flight instruction and, in addition, has supervised at least 25 solo flights by students, the privileges shall be restricted.

2. The restrictions shall be removed from the rating when the above requirements have been met and on the recommendation of the supervising flight instructor (aeroplane).

Restricted Privileges

3. The privileges shall be restricted to carrying out under the supervision of the holder of a flight instructor (aeroplane) rating approved for this purpose -

   a. flight instruction for the issue of the Private Pilot Licence (Aeroplane) or those parts of integrated courses at Private Pilot Licence (Aeroplane) level and class and type ratings for single-engine aeroplanes, excluding approval of first solo flights by day or by night and first solo cross country flights by day or by night; and

   b. night flying instruction.

Flight instructor rating (helicopter) shall entitle the holder of the licence to give instruction in flying helicopters of such types as may be specified in the rating for that purpose subject to the restrictions specified below.

Flight instructor rating (helicopter) - Restrictions

Restricted period

1. Until the holder of a flight instructor (helicopter) rating has completed at least 100 hours flight instruction and, in addition, has supervised at least 25 solo flights by students, the privileges of the rating shall be restricted.

2. The restrictions shall be removed from the rating when the above requirements have been met and on the recommendation of the supervising flight instructor (helicopter).

Restricted Privileges

3. The privileges shall be restricted to carrying out under the supervision of the holder of a flight instructor (helicopter) rating approved for this purpose -

   a. flight instruction for the issue of the Private Pilot Licence (Helicopter) or those parts of integrated courses at Private Pilot Licence (Helicopter) level and type ratings for single-engine helicopters, excluding approval of first solo flights by day or by night and first solo cross country flights by day or by night; and

b. night flying instruction.

Type rating instructor rating (multi-pilot aeroplane) shall entitle the holder to instruct licence holders for the issue of a multi-pilot aeroplane type rating, including the instruction required for multi-crew co-operation.

Type rating instructor rating (helicopter) shall entitle the holder to instruct licence holders for the issue of a type rating, including the instruction required for multi-crew co-operation as applicable.

Class rating instructor rating (single-pilot aeroplane) shall entitle the holder to instruct licence holders for the issue of a type or class rating for single-pilot aeroplanes.

Instrument rating instructor rating (aeroplane) shall entitle the holder to conduct flight instruction for the issue of an instrument rating (aeroplane) or an instrument meteorological conditions rating (aeroplanes).

Instrument rating instructor rating (helicopter) shall entitle the holder to conduct flight instruction for the issue of an instrument rating (helicopter).

An aircraft rating included in a flight engineer's licence shall entitle the holder of the licence to act as flight engineer only of aircraft of a type specified in the aircraft rating.

For the purposes of this Schedule:

'Day' means the time from half an hour before sunrise until half an hour after sunset (both times exclusive), sunset and sunrise being determined at surface level.

'Solo flight' means a flight on which the pilot of the aircraft is not accompanied by a person holding a pilot's licence granted or rendered valid under this Order.

'Cross-country flight' means any flight during the course of which the aircraft is more than 3 nautical miles from the aerodrome of departure.

PART C - MAINTENANCE OF LICENCE PRIVILEGES

Section 1 - Requirement for Certificate of Test or Experience

1. **Appropriateness of certificate**

a. A certificate of test or a certificate of experience required by article 28, 30 (2) or 31(1) of this Order shall not be appropriate to the functions to be performed on a flight unless it is a certificate appropriate to the description of the flight according to the following Table:

Case	Class of national licence	Description of Flight	Certificate required
A	Microlight Licence SLMG Licence Private Pilot's Licence (Gyroplanes)	Any flight within the privileges of the licence	Certificate of Test or Certificate of Experience
B	Commercial Pilot's Licence (Balloons) Commercial Pilot's Licence (Gliders) Commercial Pilot's Licence (Airships)	Carriage of passengers on a flight in respect of which the holder of the licence receives remuneration	Certificate of Test
C	Commercial Pilot's Licence (Balloons) Commercial Pilot's Licence (Gliders) Commercial Pilot's Licence (Airships)	For public transport	Certificate of Test
D	Commercial Pilot's Licence (Balloons) Commercial Pilot's Licence (Gliders) Commercial Pilot's Licence (Airships)	For aerial work	Certificate of Test or Certificate of Experience
E	Commercial Pilot's Licence (Balloons) Commercial Pilot's Licence (Gliders) Commercial Pilot's Licence (Airships)	Any flight within the privileges of a Private Pilot's Licence	Certificate of Test or Certificate of Experience
F	Flight Navigator's Licence	Flights to which article 25(9) applies.	Certificate of Experience

b. For the purposes of this Part of this Schedule, references to Cases are references to the Cases indicated in the first Column of the Table in paragraph 1(a) of this Part of this Schedule.

Certificate of test

2. A certificate of test required by article 28, 30(2) or 31(1) shall be signed by a person authorised by the CAA to sign certificates of this kind and shall certify the following particulars:

a. the functions to which the certificate relates;

b. that the person signing the certificate is satisfied that on a date specified in the certificate the holder of the licence or personal flying logbook of which the certificate forms a part, as the case may be, passed an appropriate test of his ability to perform the functions to which the certificate relates;

c. the type of aircraft or flight simulator in or by means of which the test was conducted; and

d. the date on which it was signed.

Nature of test

3. The appropriate test referred to in paragraph 2 above shall be -

a. in the case of a test which entitles the holder of the licence of which the certificate forms part to act as pilot in command or co-pilot (or both) of aircraft of the type, types or class specified in the certificate, a test of the pilot's competence to fly the aircraft as pilot in command or co-pilot (or both) and shall, where the CAA so specifies in respect of the whole or part of a test, be conducted in an aircraft in flight or by means of a flight simulator approved by the CAA;

b. in the case of a test which entitles the holder of the licence of which the certificate forms part to perform the functions to which a flying instructor's rating (gyroplanes), an assistant flying instructor's rating (gyroplanes) or an instrument meteorological conditions rating (aeroplanes) relates, a test of his ability to perform the functions to which the rating relates and shall, where the CAA so specifies in respect of the whole or part of the test, be conducted in an aircraft in flight.

Period of validity of certificate of test

4. A certificate of test -

a. required by article 28 in respect of a Commercial Pilot's Licence (Balloons) shall not be valid in relation to a flight made more than 13 months after the date of the test which it certifies and, required by article 28 or 30(2)in respect of any other licence, shall not be valid in relation to a flight made more than 13 months in Cases A, B and E or more than 6 months in Cases C and D after the date of the test which it certifies provided that in the case of Cases C and D, 2 certificates of test shall together be deemed to constitute a valid certificate of test if they certify flying tests conducted on 2 occasions within the period of 13 months preceding the flight on which the functions are to be performed, such occasions being separated by an interval of not less than 4 months, and if both certificates are appropriate to those functions.

b. required by article 31(1) in respect of an instrument meteorological conditions rating (aeroplanes) shall not be valid in relation to a flight made more than 25 months after the date of the test that it certifies.

c. required by article 31(1) in respect of an assistant flying instructor's rating (gyroplanes) and a flying instructor's rating (gyroplanes) shall not be valid in relation to a flight made more than 3 years after the date of the test that it certifies.

Certificate of experience

5. A certificate of experience required by article 28 or 30 (2) shall be signed by a person authorised by the CAA to sign such a certificate and shall certify the following particulars -

a. the functions to which the certificate relates;

b. in the case of a pilot, that on the date on which the certificate was signed the holder of the licence or personal flying log book of which it forms part, as the case may be, produced his personal flying log book to the person signing the certificate and satisfied him that he had appropriate experience in the capacity to which his licence relates within the appropriate period specified in paragraph 6 of this Part of this Schedule;

c. in the case of a flight navigator, that on the date on which the certificate was signed the holder of the licence of which it forms part produced his navigation logs, charts and workings of astronomical observations to the person signing the certificate and satisfied him that he had appropriate experience in the capacity to which the licence relates within the appropriate period specified in paragraph 6 of this Part of this Schedule;

d. in the case of a pilot or flight engineer, the type or types of aircraft in which the experience was gained;

e. the date on which it was signed.

Period of experience

6. A certificate of experience shall not be valid unless the experience was gained within the period of 13 months preceding the signing of the certificate in the case of Cases A, E and F, or 6 months preceding the signing of the certificate in the case of Case D.

Section A GENERAL INFORMATION
Section B
Section C
Section D
Section E
Section F
Section G
Section H
Section I
Section J
Section K
Index

Period of validity of certificate of experience

7. A certificate of experience in respect of a Commercial Pilot's Licence (Balloons) shall not be valid for more than 13 months after it was signed and in respect of any other licence shall not be valid for more than 6 months after it was signed for Case D nor for more than 13 months after it was signed for any other case.

Section 2
Requirement for certificate of revalidation

1. **Appropriate certificate of revalidation**

A certificate of revalidation required by article 29 or 31(2) of this Order shall not be appropriate to the exercise of the privileges of a flight crew licence unless it is a certificate which accords with this Section.

2. **Type and class ratings**

Aeroplane type and class ratings

a. Type ratings and multi-engine class ratings, aeroplane

i. Validity
Type ratings and multi-engine class ratings for aeroplanes are valid for one year beginning with the date of issue, or the date of expiry if revalidated within the period of three months preceding the date of expiry.

ii. Revalidation
For revalidation of type ratings and multi-engine class ratings, aeroplane, the applicant shall satisfy the requirements specified in paragraph 1.245(a) and (b) of Section 1 of JAR-FCL 1.

b. Single-pilot single-engine class ratings

i. Validity
Single-pilot single-engine class ratings are valid for two years from the date of issue, or the date of expiry if revalidated within the period of three months preceding the date of expiry.

ii. Revalidation of all single-engine piston aeroplane class ratings (land) and all touring motor glider ratings.

For revalidation of single-pilot single-engine piston aeroplane (land) class ratings or touring motor glider class ratings (or both) the applicant shall on single-engine piston aeroplanes (land) or touring motor gliders (as the case may be) satisfy the requirements specified in paragraph 1.245(c)(1) of Section 1 of JAR-FCL 1.

iii. Revalidation of single-engine turbo-prop aeroplanes (land) single-pilot .

For revalidation of single-engine turbo-prop (land) class ratings the applicant shall within the three months preceding the expiry date of the rating, pass a proficiency check with an authorised examiner on an aeroplane in the relevant class.

iv. Revalidation of single-engine piston aeroplanes (sea)

For revalidation of single pilot single engine piston aeroplane (sea) class ratings the applicant shall -

aa. within the three months preceding the expiry date of the rating, pass a proficiency check with an authorised examiner on a single-engine piston aeroplane (sea); or

bb. within the 12 months preceding the expiry of the rating complete at least 12 hours of flight time including 6 hours of pilot in command time on either a single engine piston aeroplane (sea) or a single engine piston aeroplane (land) and 12 water take-offs and 12 alightings on water; and either complete a training flight of at least 1 hour duration with a flight instructor or pass a proficiency check or skill test for any other class or type rating.

c. Expired ratings

i. If a type rating or multi-engine class rating has expired, the applicant shall meet the requirements in paragraph (b) above and meet any refresher training requirements as determined by the CAA and the rating will be valid from the date of completion of the renewal requirements.

ii. If a single-pilot single-engine class rating has expired, the applicant shall complete the skill test in accordance with the requirements specified at Appendix 3 to paragraph 1.240 of Section 1 of JAR-FCL 1.

Helicopter type ratings

a. Type ratings, helicopter - validity

Type ratings for helicopters are valid for one year beginning with the date of issue, or the date of expiry if revalidated within the period of three months preceding the date of expiry.

b. Type ratings, helicopter - revalidation

For revalidation of type ratings, helicopter, the applicant shall complete the requirements specified in paragraph 2.245(b) of Section 1 of JAR-FCL 2.

c. Expired ratings

If a type rating has expired, the applicant shall meet the requirements in paragraph (b) above and meet any refresher training requirements as determined by the CAA and the rating shall be valid for a period beginning with the date of completion of the renewal requirements.

Flight engineer type ratings

a. Type ratings - validity

Flight engineer type ratings are valid for one year beginning with the date of issue, or the date of expiry if revalidated within the period of three months preceding the date of expiry.

b. Type ratings - revalidation

For revalidation of flight engineer type ratings the applicant shall, within the three months preceding the expiry date of the rating, pass a proficiency check with an authorised examiner on the relevant type of aircraft.

3. Forms of certificate of revalidation

1. A certificate of revalidation required by article 29 or 31(2) of this Order shall be signed by a person authorised by the CAA to sign certificates of this kind and shall certify:

   a. the functions to which the certificate relates;

   b. that the person signing the certificate is satisfied that on a date specified in the certificate, the holder of the licence of which the certificate forms a part met the appropriate requirements for revalidation specified in respect of the rating, in the case of an aircraft rating in paragraph (2) and in the case of any other rating specified in the Table at sub-paragraph (2) below, to exercise the privileges of the licence or rating to which the certificate relates;

   c. the type of aircraft or flight simulator in or by means of which the test was conducted; and

   d. the date on which it was signed.

2. The requirements for revalidation of a rating are those set out in the following Table -

Rating	Paragraph in Section 1 of JAR-FCL 1 or 2
Instrument rating (aeroplane)	1.185
Instrument rating (helicopter)	2.185
Flight instructor (aeroplane) Flying instructor's rating (aeroplanes) Assistant flying instructor's rating (aeroplanes)	1.355
Flight Instructor (helicopter) Flying instructor's rating (helicopters) Assistant flying instructor's rating (helicopters)	2.355
Type rating instructor rating (multi-pilot aeroplane)	1.370
Type rating instructor rating (helicopter)	2.370
Class rating instructor rating (single pilot aeroplane)	1.385
Instrument rating instructor rating (aeroplane)	1.400
Instrument rating instructor rating (helicopter)	2.400

Section 3
Maintenance of Validity of National Private Pilot's Licence (Aeroplanes)

1. A simple single engine aeroplane (NPPL) class rating included in a National Private Pilot's Licence (Aeroplanes) shall not be valid for the purposes of article 30(1) unless the provisions of this Section have been complied with.

2. A simple single engine aeroplane (NPPL) class rating shall be valid if either:

   a. the holder has within the 12 months preceding the flight shown not less than six hours in an aeroplane falling within the simple single engine aeroplane (NPPL) class rating, four hours of which shall have been as pilot in command and he has carried out a training flight of at least 1 hour duration with a flying instructor within the previous 24 months; or

   b. he has within the three months preceding the expiry of the rating undertaken a simple single engine aeroplane (NPPL) General Skills Test.

APPENDIX G

FLIGHT INSTRUCTION & SKILL TESTING IN AEROPLANES/ HELICOPTERS - LIMITATIONS FOR HOLDERS OF CLASS 1 MEDICAL CERTIFICATE WITH OPERATIONAL MULTI-CREW LIMITATION (OML)

AEROPLANES

Instructing/Examining

A fixed-wing instructor or examiner who is subject to an OML may only conduct flight instruction or skill tests (subject to holding the relevant instructor rating or examiner authorisation) in aircraft fitted with dual controls, and under circumstances where the student has demonstrated, or is deemed competent, to act as pilot-in-command should the instructor or examiner suffer incapacitation, taking full account of the conditions under which the instruction or skill test is being carried out.

Generally, a student will be considered to have demonstrated, or be deemed competent, to act as pilot-in-command if he:

a. holds a current licence (UK or non-UK) which would entitle him to act as pilot-in-command of the aircraft if the flight were a private flight; or

b. was, within the period of six months immediately preceding the flight, serving as a qualified pilot of an aircraft in any of the naval, military or air forces of Her Majesty or of a foreign state, and holds a current medical certificate appropriate to the intended licence or rating; or

c. was, within the period of six months immediately preceding the flight, employed as a pilot by an airline operating aircraft registered in a Contracting State other than the United Kingdom, and holds a current medical certificate appropriate to the intended licence or rating; or

d. is undergoing an integrated course for the CPL(A) or CPL(A)/IR, approved by the CAA and has:

   i. completed Phase 2 of the integrated course for single-engine piston flying, or

   ii. completed the training and class/type rating skill test for multi-engine aeroplanes.

Tables 1 and 2 show a guidance matrix of the activities permissible.

Table 1

Flight instruction allowable by Instructors with a Class 1 medical certificate with OML

	Flight Instructor (FI)	Class Rating Instructor (CRI)	Type Rating Instructor (TRI)	Instrument Rating Instructor (IRI)
Ab-initio PPL instruction before first solo cross-country	No			
Ab-initio PPL instruction post first solo cross-country	Yes			
CPL instruction (Integrated course) - single-engine (before completion of Phase 2); multi-engine (before LST pass)	No			
CPL instruction (Integrated course - single-engine (post completion of Phase 2); multi-engine (post LST pass)	Yes			
CPL instruction (Modular course - non-current ICAO PPL holders)	No			
CPL instruction (Modular course - current ICAO PPL holders)	Yes (in VMC only)			
Instruction for issue of additional single-pilot type/class ratings	No	No		
Instruction for renewal of single-pilot type/class ratings	No	No		
Instruction for revalidation of SEP or TMG class ratings	Yes			
Differences training	Yes	Yes	Yes	
Instruction for issue of a Night Qualification	No			
Instruction to regain night flying currency for carriage of passengers	Yes			
Instruction for issue & renewal of an IMC rating	Yes (in VMC only)			Yes (in VMC only)
Instruction for issue & renewal of an IR	Yes (in VMC only)*			Yes (in VMC only)*
Instruction for issue of a multi-pilot type rating			No	
Instruction for renewal of multi-pilot type rating			No	

*Except where the student holds a current and valid IMC rating or a valid non-JAA UK CPL(A), when instruction may be given in airspace and meteorological conditions appropriate to the privileges of an IMC rating.

Table 2

Skill Testing allowable by Examiners with a Class 1 medical certificate with OML

	Flight Examiner (PPL)	Flight Examiner (CPL)	Class Rating Examiner (CRE)	Type Rating Examiner (TRE)	Flight Instructor Examiner (FIE)
PPL(A) Skill Test	Yes (in VMC only)	Yes (in VMC only)			Yes (in VMC only)
CPL(A) Skill Test		Yes (in VMC only)			
IMC Skill Test	Yes (in VMC only)	Yes (in VMC only)	Yes (in VMC only) (CRE(IRR) only)		Yes (in VMC only)
IMC Revalidation Test	Yes	Yes	Yes (CRE(IRR) only)		Yes
IMC Renewal Test	Yes (in VMC only)	Yes (in VMC only)	Yes (in VMC only) (CRE(IRR) only)		Yes (in VMC only)
IR Revalidation (SPA)			Yes (CRE(IRR) only)		
IR Renewal (SPA (under 5 years)			Yes (in VMC only) (CRE(IRR) only		
Skill Test (LST) for issue of an additional single-pilot type or class rating	No	No	No		No
Proficiency Check (LPC) for revalidation of a single-pilot type or class rating	Yes	Yes	Yes		Yes
Skill Test (LST) or Proficiency Check (LPC) (as appropriate) for renewal of a single-pilot type or class rating	No	No	No		No
Skill Test (LST) for issue of a multi-pilot type rating				No	
Proficiency Check (LPC) for revalidation of a multi-pilot type rating				Yes	
Proficiency Check (LPC for renewal of a multi-pilot type rating				No	

HELICOPTERS

Instructing/Examining

A helicopter instructor or examiner who is subject to an OML may only conduct flight instruction or skill tests (subject to holding the relevant instructor rating or examiner authorisation) in aircraft fitted with dual controls, and under circumstances where the student has demonstrated, or is deemed competent, to act as pilot-in-command should the instructor or examiner suffer incapacitation, taking full account of the conditions under which the instruction or skill test is being carried out.

Generally, a student will be considered to have demonstrated, or be deemed competent, to act as pilot-in-command if he:-

a. holds a current licence (UK or non-UK) which would entitle him to act as pilot-in-command of the aircraft if the flight were a private flight; or

b. was, within the period of six months immediately preceding the flight, serving as a qualified pilot of an aircraft in any of the naval, military or air forces of Her Majesty or of a foreign state, and holds a current medical certificate appropriate to the intended licence or rating; or

c. was, within the period of six months immediately preceding the flight, employed as a pilot by an airline operating aircraft registered in a Contracting State other than the United Kingdom, and holds a current medical certificate appropriate to the intended licence or rating; or

d. is undergoing an integrated course for the CPL(H) or CPL(H)IR, approved by the CAA and has completed Phase 1 of the integrated course.

Tables 3 and 4 show a guidance matrix of the activities permissible

Table 3

Flight instruction allowable by Instructors with a Class 1 medical certificate with OML

	Flight Instructor (FI)	Type Rating Instructor (TRI)	Instrument Rating Instructor (IRI)
Ab-initio PPL instruction before first solo cross-country	No		
Ab-initio PPL instruction post first solo cross-country	Yes		
CPL instruction (Integrated course) (before completion of Phase 1)	No		
CPL instruction (Integrated course) (post completion of Phase 1)	Yes		
CPL instruction (Modular course) - non-current or non-type rated ICAO PPL holders	No		
CPL instruction (Modular course) - current, type rated ICAO PPL holders	Yes (in VMC only)		
Instruction for issue of additional single-pilot type ratings	No	No	
Instruction for renewal of single-pilot type ratings	No	No	
Differences training	Yes	Yes	
Instruction for issue of a Night Qualification	No		
Instruction to regain night flying currency for carriage of passengers	Yes		
Instruction for issue & renewal of an IR rating	Yes (in VMC only)		Yes (in VMC only)
Instruction for issue of a multi-pilot type rating		No	
Instruction for renewal of multi-pilot type rating		No	

Table 4

Skill Testing allowable by Examiners with a Class 1 medical certificate with OML

	Flight Examiner (PPL)	**Flight Examiner (CPL)**	**Type Rating Examiner (TRE)**	**Flight Instructor Examiner (FIE)**
PPL(H) Skill Test	Yes (in VMC only)	Yes (in VMC only)		Yes (in VMC only)
CPL(H) Skill Test		Yes (in VMC only)		
IR Revalidation (SPH)			Yes (TRE(IRR) only)	
IR Renewal (SPH) (under 5 years)			Yes (in VMC only) (TRE(IRR) only)	
Skill Test (LST) for issue of an additional single-pilot type rating	No	No	No	No
Proficiency Check (LPC) for revalidation of a single-pilot type rating	Yes	Yes	Yes	Yes
Skill Test (LST) or Proficiency Check (LPC) (as appropriate) for renewal of a single-pilot type rating	No	No	No	No
Skill Test (LST) for issue of a multi-pilot type rating			No	
Proficiency Check (LPC) for revalidation of a multi-pilot type rating			Yes	
Proficiency Check (LPC) for renewal of a multi-pilot type rating			No	
Skill Test or Proficiency Check for issue, revalidation or renewal of a FI rating - non current or non-type rated candidates				No
Skill Test or Proficiency Check for issue, revalidation or renewal of a FI rating - current, type rated candidates				Yes

SECTION B

FLIGHT RADIO TELEPHONY OPERATOR'S LICENCE (FRTOL)

B1 FLIGHT RADIO TELEPHONY OPERATOR'S LICENCE

This Section offers information as a basic guide to obtaining a Flight Radio Telephony Operator's Licence (FRTOL) as follows:-

B1.1 FRTOL GENERAL INFORMATION

Requirement to hold a Flight Radiotelephony Operator's Licence (FRTOL)

The FRTOL is a flight crew licence that may be issued to existing flight crew members and other persons who have a requirement to operate Aircraft Radio Stations. It may be issued as a stand-alone licence, or in conjunction with another flight crew licence.

The requirement for flight crew to hold a FRTOL is detailed in the ANO, Article 26. In particular a number of exemptions are listed, including aircrew under training, and glider pilots when transmitting on frequencies specifically allocated for glider operation. The privileges of the FRTOL are detailed in Schedule 8 to the ANO (please refer to Section A, Appendix F).

The requirement for non-flight crew members to hold a FRTOL is detailed in the schedule to the Aircraft Radio Licence issued under the Wireless Telegraphy (WT) Acts of 1949 and 1998. This document forms part of the aircraft radio licence.

Holders of a PPL issued in accordance with ICAO Annex 1 may exercise the privileges of an ICAO FRTOL in UK registered aircraft, in accordance with the provisions of the UK ANO (Article 26) subject to certain provisions. They must hold a licence that includes radiotelephony privileges based on tests conducted in the English Language. Pilot Certificates issued by some States do not confer International privileges for the operation of an aircraft radio station. Pilots holding FAA Certificates must also hold an aircraft radio operator permit issued by the FCC. Applications should be made to the FCC using Form 605. http://wireless.fcc.gov/aviation/fctsht4.htm.

No person may operate an aircraft radio station in the air, or on the ground, unless they are in possession of a FRTOL, or are operating directly under the supervision of the holder of a FRTOL. The latter implies that the FRTOL holder is present in the aircraft. This applies equally to groundcrew and other persons who wish to operate radio-transmitting equipment licensed in accordance with, and operating on, frequencies listed in the Aircraft Radio Licence.

The FRTOL conveys no privileges in relation to the installation or establishment of a Radio Station; it is simply an operator's licence. The FRTOL does not entitle the holder to operate a radio station which is installed anywhere other than in an aircraft. All Aeronautical and Aircraft Radio Stations require a Radio Station Licence issued by the CAA in accordance with the Wireless Telegraphy Acts of 1949 and 1998. The holder of a FRTOL is responsible for ensuring that the aircraft radio station they operate has a valid radio station licence. Failure to do so will render them liable to prosecution under the WT Act.

The FRTOL issued by the CAA meets the requirements of the Flight Radiotelephony Operator's (Restricted) Licence defined in the General Radio Regulations to the International Telecommunications Union (ITU) (Article 37). The privileges of the FRTOL are limited to *VHF only* (frequencies above 60 MHz) where the holder has not passed an examination in HF radio theory. Holders of UK or JAA professional pilot licences do not have this limitation.

UK radiotelephony procedures are detailed in CAP 413 The Radiotelephony Manual. This document can be viewed on the CAA web site at www.caa.co.uk/docs/33/CAP413.pdf. This document is edited in parallel with CAP 493 The Manual of Air Traffic Services Part 1.

Minimum Age

An applicant for a Flight Radiotelephony Operators Licence shall be at least 16 years of age.

B1.2 FRTOL GROUND EXAMINATION REQUIREMENTS - VALIDITY

Applicants for the FRTOL will be required to pass a Radiotelephony (RTF) theoretical written examination and a practical Communications test. An additional (HF) written examination is available for candidates who wish to remove the *VHF only* limitation.

Authorised RTF Examiners at Regional Test Centres conduct examinations for the FRTOL. An authorised PPL ground examiner may also conduct the theoretical written examination when it forms part of the qualification for a PPL. Details of Examinations are published regularly by AIC (White). A list of RTF Examiners is located on the SRG web site at: www.caa.co.uk/docs/33/srg_fcl_RTF_examiners.pdf

Candidates for a JAR-FCL Private Pilot Licence are required to pass the written theoretical Communications examination prior to attempting the PPL Skill Test. This may either be the JAR-FCL Communications examination, or the UK Radiotelephony (Communications - PPL) written examination. Applicants for a JAR-FCL PPL should be aware that they must also pass the practical Communications test if they wish to apply for the additional FRTOL, which is a separate licence. Applicants for a FRTOL must complete Form SRG\1106, which must be signed by the examiner(s) conducting both written and practical tests.

Validity - The RTF written examinations and practical test for a stand-alone licence are valid for a period of 12 months for licence issue. Where a candidate completes the examinations for a FRTOL in conjunction with a course of training for a JAR-FCL private pilot licence, the validity of the radiotelephony examinations may be extended to 24 months from the date of passing the last PPL theoretical examination, provided that all examinations are passed within a 18 month period and that application for both licences is made concurrently. PPL holders who subsequently apply for a FRTOL will be required to meet the 12-month validity requirements for a stand-alone licence.

B1.3 FRTOL SYLLABUS OF TRAINING

The syllabus of training for the UK theoretical written examination (Communications – PPL), and practical Communications test, is based upon CAP 413 - Radiotelephony Manual, the UK AIP and the Air Navigation Order (ANO), and is detailed in Appendix A. The syllabus for the written JAR-FCL Communications examination differs slightly, and is detailed in JAR-FCL 1 and 2 under Subject 090.

B1.4 FRTOL EXAMINATION CREDITS

The International Telecommunications Union General Radio Regulations Article 37 details the requirements for the issue of a Flight Radiotelephone Operator Certificate. However, this leaves individual States responsible for deciding how to implement these requirements. Regardless of the test format, the UK is the only State to operate in accordance with CAP 413 The UK Radiotelephony Manual and it is essential to ensure that all UK professional pilots are familiar with the procedures contained in that document which is closely aligned with the Air Traffic Controllers phraseology manual. Pilots who are trained outside the UK and who hold a radiotelephony certificate or licence issued by another State are not likely to have the required experience of UK RTF procedures. For this reason the CAA has found it necessary to ensure that all applicants for professional licences and instrument ratings are suitably qualified for the issue of a UK FRTOL at the time of issuing a professional pilots licence or rating.

FTO's offering training for the UK issued JAA CPL and IR shall ensure that the applicant either holds a valid UK FRTOL or has qualified for the issue of a UK FRTOL prior to attempting the ATPL, CPL or IR Skill Tests. Candidates who do not have a valid FRTOL shall have a completed SRG\1106 (FCL 508) prior to taking the Skill Test.

Holders of a non-UK Flight Radiotelephony Operator's Licence, Qualified Service Pilots (QSP) and ATCOs may be exempt from the requirement to pass some or all of the UK FRTOL examinations. The following exemptions apply:

- A Qualified Service Pilot (QSP) in the UK Armed Forces, who is within 12 months of a flying appointment, is credited with the RTF practical Communications test. A QSP who has obtained a pass in the JAR-FCL Communications Examinations will be exempt the RTF written examination.
- Graduates of No.44 (or subsequent) DEFTS course, who are presented with a full accreditation course completion certificate (annotated with a green border), are credited with the practical Communications test. The RTF written examination will be taken as part of the full DEFTS course. Graduates presented with a partial accreditation course completion certificate (annotated with a yellow border) are credited the practical Communications test only.
- Holders of a valid pass in the JAR-FCL Communications Examinations in VFR and IFR Communications (Subject 90) are credited with the written theoretical examination.
- Holders of a valid UK ATCO licence are credited with the practical Communications test and theoretical written examination. Applications should be accompanied by form SRG\1162 which can be downloaded from the SRG web site: http://www.caa.co.uk/publicationdetails.asp?id=547.
- Holders of a JAR-FCL Pilot licence issued by another JAA State that includes an Instrument Rating are credited with the practical Communications test and theoretical written examination.

- The Holder of a valid CPL or ATPL with in excess of 1500 hours flight time engaged in International public transport flights who holds a Flight Radiotelephony Operator's Licence issued by any ICAO contracting State, in accordance with Article 37 of the ITU Radio Regulations, which has been issued on the basis of comparable tests and examinations to those required in the UK, will be credited with the practical Communications test and theoretical written examination, provided that the licence is valid and the tests were conducted using the English language. Article 37 requires that the licence itself contain a certificate indicating its compliance, letters of Authority are not acceptable.

- Holders of a PPL issued in accordance with ICAO Annex 1 seeking licence conversion to a UK issued PPL shall, in order to qualify for the issue of a UK FRTOL pass the RTF practical test in the 12 months prior to application.

- Holders of a JAA PPL issued by a State other than the UK shall be required to sit the UK RTF Practical test in order to qualify for the issue of a UK FRTOL.

Applicants who believe they fulfil the criteria for exam credits and licence conversion must submit the valid licence and provide logbook evidence of flights during which the privileges have been exercised. Applicants who hold licences in languages other than English must provide an English translation.

Holders of Flight Radiotelephony Licences and privileges issued by States in ITU Region 1 (North and South America) or where no tests or examinations have been required will <u>not</u> be credited. A number of States are known to issue FRTOL's with 'VFR only' privileges for use in National languages – holders of any such licence will not be credited. Students who are seeking to obtain a UK issued JAA professional pilots licence **or** Instrument rating will be required to provide evidence of either holding a valid UK FRTOL or of having passed the UK RTF practical test prior to attempting the CPL or IR Skill Test. (A student attempting both the CPL and IR Skill Test will be required to hold a valid UK FRTOL or passed the UK RTF practical test prior to attempting their first test, whichever comes first).

B1.5 FRTOL VALIDITY

A stand-alone FRTOL is issued for a period of 10 years; a fee as prescribed in the CAA Scheme of Charges is made for the issue of such licences.

Where a FRTOL is issued in conjunction with a flight crew licence the validity period of the FRTOL will be the same as the flight crew licence to which it is associated. For JAR-FCL licences, and some UK national licences, this validity period is 5 years; where a UK national licence has been issued with a lifetime validity, the FRTOL will be deemed to be valid as long as the associated flight crew licence is valid. Where the associated flight crew licence is allowed to expire, the FRTOL shall not be valid for a period greater than 10 years from the last renewal/revalidation of the flight crew licence.

Where a FRTOL is issued/renewed in conjunction with a UK flight crew licence, no charge is made for the issue of a FRTOL.

B1.6 FRTOL RE-VALIDATION/RENEWAL

A stand-alone FRTOL may be revalidated within the 6 months preceding the date of expiry, or renewed up to 12 months after the date of expiry, provided evidence that the FRTOL privileges have been exercised is submitted with the renewal application. The FRTOL is a flight crew licence, and for the purpose of revalidation a logbook must be kept in accordance with the ANO, Article 35. The logbook must show evidence of flights on which the FRTOL privileges were exercised (within the 36 months prior to application) on either UK registered aircraft (including gliders), flights conducted in the UK on non UK registered aircraft or International flights on public transport aircraft. Alternatively a certificate from an employer where FRTOL privileges have been exercised as part of his/her employment (e.g. Flight Test Observer/Groundcrew).

Where a FRTOL is held by a pilot who holds no other UK or JAA licences, and who does not fly in the UK or on International public transport flights, the applicant will be required to demonstrate current knowledge by passing the RTF practical and written tests. A fee is payable as defined in the CAA Scheme of Charges. Where FRTOL is attached to a flight crew licence, the FRTOL will be automatically re-issued when the flight crew licence is re-issued. No charge is made for the re-issue of the FRTOL when held in conjunction with another UK issued flight crew licence.

The holder of a FRTOL expired for more than 1 year but less than 10 years, will be required to pass the theoretical written examination. To renew a FRTOL that has expired by 10 years or more, applicants will be required to pass the practical Communications test and theoretical written examination.

The holder of a UK national flight crew licence with lifetime validity, who has not exercised the privileges of the FRTOL for a period exceeding 10 years, will be required to pass the practical Communications test and theoretical written examination in order to reactivate the FRTOL.

B1.7 FRTOL APPLICATION

A RTF training record form (SRG\1171), for licence applicants who are conducting PPL training, is available on the SRG web site at: http://www.caa.co.uk/docs/33/FORSRG1171.PDF

This record is designed to ensure applicants receive training in all aspects of communications that may be tested in both the written and practical examinations. The record may be used by the candidate to indicate to the RTF examiner that the recommended training for the FRTOL has been completed. SRG\1171 is not mandatory and should not be submitted to the CAA with the licence application.

The FRTOL is not a prerequisite for the issue of a PPL, neither is it automatically issued to applicants for a PPL.

Applicants for a FRTOL must ensure that they make application for licence issue using form SRG\1106.

Applicants who wish to claim credits against the FRTOL examinations must provide evidence to support their claim; where this takes the form of a FRTOL issued by another State, the original licence must be valid and submitted with the licence application.

APPENDIX TO SECTION B

APPENDIX A SYLLABUS OF TRAINING FOR THE FRTOL

1 Introduction

1.1 Applicants for the Flight Radiotelephony Operator's Licence (FRTOL) will be required to pass the theoretical written communications examination and pass a practical Communications test. The licence is normally issued with a **VHF only** limitation, which may be removed by passing an additional written examination in HF radio theory or the Radio Navigation theory examinations at CPL or ATPL level. The FRTOL may be issued to any person who does not also hold a flight crew licence. Privileges of the FRTOL are given at Schedule 8 to the Air Navigation Order 2005, Section 1 Sub-Section 5.

2 RTF Examinations

2.1 The written Communications examination may be conducted by an authorised RTF Examiner, or in the case of PPL students at a registered Facility or Flying Training Organisation where the flying training is conducted. The syllabus for the examination is detailed below:

2.2 Syllabus

2.2.1 **Pre-Flight**
Use of United Kingdom AIP.
General (GEN) 1.7, 2.4, 2.5, 3.3, 3.6;
En Route (ENR) 1.1, 1.2, 1.6, 2.2;
Aerodrome (AD) Individual aerodrome radio procedures.

The Air Navigation Order, Articles 20, 26, 27, 28, 29, 30, 31, 32, 33, 34, 35 and 55.

Familiarisation with aircraft radio equipment and (RA) aircraft radio licence.

Familiarisation with CAP413 Radiotelephony Manual,
Microphone technique and listening out,
Call signs and abbreviations,
Phonetic alphabet, standard words and phrases.

2.2.2 **Departure Procedures**
Radio Checks,
Taxi instructions/information and read back,
Pre-departure manoeuvring,
Departure clearance

2.2.3 **En Route Procedures**
Frequency changing,
Level reporting,
Position reporting,
Use of FIS,
Use of LARS,
Use of SSR,
MATZ Penetration,
SVFR Flight,
Flight in a control zone (CTR),
VDF procedures and terminology.

2.2.4 **Circuit Procedures**
Joining circuit,
Landing clearance,
Orbit, Extend, Touch-and-go,
Go around,
Vacating runway.

2.2.5 **Emergency Procedures**
Uncertainty of position,
Radio failure,
Degrees of Urgency,
Practice PAN,
MAYDAY (Not transmitted).

2.3 Practical Communication Test

The RTF Practical test may only be conducted by an authorised RTF Examiner, using approved testing equipment, at a location approved by the CAA. The candidate will be briefed individually to follow a route representative of a typical cross country flight in a light aircraft during which he/she must make all the appropriate communications in accordance with the published syllabus.
Note: the test may not be conducted with more than one candidate present, the test may not be conducted in an aircraft, or without the use of a CAA approved RTF simulator. The examiner may not delegate the conduct of the test to any other person.

2.4 HF Theory Written Examination

2.4.1 Candidates who wish to operate HF radiotelephony equipment (below 60 MHz) and who do not hold a CAA or JAR-FCL ATPL, CPL or Flight Navigator's licence, are required to pass the written HF examination with an RTF Examiner authorised to conduct the HF examination. Reference material includes *Ground Studies for Pilots Vol. 1*- R B Underdown - Blackwell Science. The syllabus is as follows:

2.4.2 **Electro magnetic radiation**
Speed of propagation,
Frequency/Wavelength,
Phase,
Frequency bands.

2.4.3 **Basic Radio Transmitter**
Signal generation,
Feeding and emission of RF signals,
Modulation, CW, AM, SSB,
Classification of Emissions.

2.4.4 **Wave Propagation**
Factors affecting range of ground, direct, and sky waves,
Height, and layers of the ionosphere.

2.4.5 **Radio Communication**
HF radio equipment and operation,
Frequency prediction charts,
HF R/T Networks,
SELCAL

SECTION C

PRIVATE PILOT LICENCE

The CAA currently issues the following classes of Private Pilot Licence (PPL).

Each section details the requirements to obtain each licence, including flying training, ground examinations and flight tests. Details of credits against training are also given.

C1 JAR-FCL PPL (AEROPLANE)

This section offers information as a basic guide to obtaining a JAR-FCL Private Pilot Licence (Aeroplanes) - JAR-FCL PPL(A) as follows:-

For full details you are advised to refer to **JAR-FCL 1 Subpart C**.

C1.1 JAR-FCL PPL(A) GENERAL INFORMATION

Privileges

Details of licence privileges can be found in Schedule 8 of the Air Navigation Order, (please also refer to Section A, Appendix F).

The holder of a UK JAR-FCL licence with SEP rating may also subject to completion of differences training with an appropriately qualified flying instructor, exercise the privileges of their licence on microlight aeroplanes and SLMG's in UK airspace only, without the necessity of obtaining a NPPL (the normal licence for such aeroplanes). However, any experience gained in microlight aeroplanes or SLMG's cannot be counted towards the flying experience necessary to revalidate the SEP rating.

Minimum Age

An applicant for a JAR-FCL PPL(A) shall be at least 17 years of age but some of the required qualifications for the grant of the licence may be gained earlier. Applicants should ensure that any qualifications gained earlier will still be valid at the time they plan to apply for the grant of the licence.

The validity periods of training, examinations and flight tests are covered in this section.

Student pilots may act as Pilot-in-Command from their 16th birthday provided they act only in accordance with instructions given by a flying instructor, hold a valid JAR-FCL Medical Certificate and, generally, fly only in UK territorial airspace. There is no minimum age for dual instruction, but any received before the age of 14 is not countable towards the experience requirements specified in this document.

Licence Validity

The JAR-FCL PPL(A) will be issued for a maximum period of 5 years.

C1.2 JAR-FCL PPL(A) FLYING TRAINING/ EXPERIENCE REQUIREMENTS

Training shall be conducted on aeroplanes having a certificate of airworthiness issued or accepted by a JAA member state and will enable an applicant to obtain a single-engine piston class rating for licence issue (Appendix 1 to JAR-FCL 1.125 refers). Training conducted on a touring motor glider certificated to JAR-22 will enable an applicant to obtain a touring motor glider class rating for licence issue.

Experience Requirements

An applicant for a JAR-FCL PPL(A) shall have completed at least **45** hours flight time as a pilot of aeroplanes or TMGs as appropriate. This must include the training requirements specified below. A maximum of **5** hours of these **45** hours may have been completed in a Basic Instrument Training Device (BITD - see App 1 to JAR-FCL 1.125), Flight & Navigation Procedures Trainer (FNPT) or a Flight Simulator. A FNPT or Flight Simulator used for this purpose must be device qualified **and** user approved.

Flying Training Requirements

An applicant for the PPL(A) shall complete at a FTO or an accepted registered facility the required instruction in accordance with the syllabus as set out in Appendix 1 to JAR-FCL 1.125. This must include:-

a. **25 hours*** Dual Instruction on aeroplanes

b. **10 hours** Supervised solo flight time on aeroplanes, must include (i);

i. **5 hours** Solo cross-country flight time, must include (ii);

ii. One cross-country flight of at least 270km (150nm), during which full stop landings at two different aerodromes different from the aerodrome of departure shall be made as per JAR-FCL 1.125.

* Reduced to not less than **20** hours where an applicant has been credited for Pilot-in-Command flight time on other aircraft.

Night Qualification

Training for a Night Qualification (Aeroplanes) may be completed and included within the 45 hours total flight time required for the JAR-FCL PPL(A), providing the minimum requirements at (a) and (b) have been met.

Credits from Flying Training

- Holders of pilot licences or equivalent privileges for Helicopters (including UK QSP(H) with no previous SEP aeroplane experience), Microlights having fixed wings and moveable aerodynamic control surfaces acting in all three dimensions, Gliders, Self-Sustaining Gliders or Self Launching sailplanes or gyroplanes, may be credited with 10% of their total flight time as Pilot-in-Command in such aircraft up to a maximum of **10** hours towards a JAR-FCL PPL(A).

- Any previous flying training gained during a PPL(A) course conducted in another JAA Member State (other than the UK) may be credited with such flight time towards the issue of a UK JAR-FCL PPL(A). Applicants who intend to continue with their training with a UK Registered Facility or Flying Training Organisation, must in the first instance contact the Authority of the Member State in which training was commenced. The applicant should confirm with that other State that they will allow them to continue their training with a UK training provider, and agree that the UK will be the 'State of Licence Issue'. If the other State agrees then the applicant will be required to obtain written confirmation to this effect in order for all previous PPL training to be recognised by the UK CAA. The applicant should also arrange with the other JAA State for any PPL training records to be forwarded onto the new Registered Facility or FTO. If the other State does not give agreement then the UK CAA will only recognise up to a maximum of 10 hours of the previous training towards the overall 45 hour requirement for licence issue. The applicant will in this case be required to complete the further 35 hours as specified in Flying Training Requirements.

- In circumstances where previous flying training towards an ICAO PPL(A) (non-JAR-FCL) has been completed but no licence has been issued, PLD will consider the crediting of such flight time towards the issue of a JAR-FCL PPL(A). In all cases, applicants must apply in writing to PLD enclosing appropriate training records and flying logbooks for the PPL training received. PLD will review the training records to establish a course of training and advise the applicant accordingly.

  In addition to any additional training required (where there is a shortfall of requirements), applicants will be required to complete One cross-country flight of at least 270km (150nm), during which full stop landings at two different aerodromes from the aerodrome of departure shall be made, pass all the JAR-FCL PPL(A) theoretical knowledge examinations and pass the PPL(A) skill test.

- Any previous flying experience gained in TMG aircraft (i.e. Vigilant) may be counted towards the 45 hour minima required for the grant of a JAR-FCL PPL(A) with TMG rating, however the specific requirements under JAR-FCL (25 hours dual instruction and 10 hours supervised solo-flight time) must be completed. Individuals who have already met the 45 hour experience requirement will be required to complete discretional flying training, at a Registered Facility or Approved FTO One cross-country flight of at least 270km (150nm), during which full stop landings at two different aerodromes different from the aerodrome of departure shall be made, and the PPL(A) Skill Test with a CAA Authorised TMG Examiner. Individuals who then wish to obtain the SEP rating will be required to complete an SEP Class Rating Skill Test.

  All hours must be properly logged and certified by the Chief Flying Instructor or Commanding Officer as appropriate. Applicants must ensure that each individual exercise requirement is met in full.

- The holder of a current and valid PPL(A)* issued by an ICAO Contracting State (not being a JAA Member State), who has flown a minimum of 100 hours as pilot of aeroplanes, is credited the JAR-FCL PPL(A) flying training/experience requirements, except the PPL(A) Skill Test.

- The holder of a current and valid PPL(A)* issued by an ICAO Contracting State (not being a JAA Member State), who has flown less than 100 hours as pilot of aeroplanes, but meets the JAR-FCL PPL(A) flying experience requirements (as per JAR-FCL 1.125(b) is credited the flying training, except the PPL(A) Skill Test.

* If the ICAO licence has expired and/or no valid aeroplane rating has been held for a period exceeding 5 years preceding application, applicants will be required to complete flying training at the discretion of the Head of Training of the approved training provider, and pass the PPL(A) Skill Test.

- The holder of a NPPL (SSEA) wishing to obtain a JAR-FCL PPL(A) should refer to Section C6.2 Upgrade to JAR-FCL PPL(A).

C1.3 JAR-FCL PPL(A)THEORETICAL KNOWLEDGE EXAMINATION REQUIREMENTS

An applicant for a JAR-FCL PPL(A) is required to pass theoretical knowledge examinations in the following subjects:

1. Aviation Law & Operational Procedures
2. Human Performance & Limitations
3. Navigation & Radio Aids
4. Meteorology
5. Aircraft (General) & Principles of Flight
6. Flight Performance & Planning
7. JAR-FCL Communications (PPL)

    - These examinations contain multiple-choice questions for the most part and are normally conducted under the auspices of a Flight Training Organisation or a Registered Facility. An applicant shall be deemed to have successfully completed the theoretical examinations for the JAR-FCL PPL(A) when awarded a pass in all of the above examinations within a period of 18 months counted from the end of the calendar month when the applicant first attempted the examination. A pass will be accepted for the grant of a JAR-FCL PPL(A) during the 24 months from the date of successfully completing all of the theoretical knowledge examinations.

Credits from Theoretical Knowledge Examinations

- The holder of a current and valid PPL(A)* issued by an ICAO Contracting State (not being a JAA Member State), who has flown a minimum of 100 hours as pilot of aeroplanes, will be required to pass written examinations in Air Law and Human Performance and Limitations. (If no valid aeroplane rating has been held in the 5 years preceding application, then all JAR theoretical knowledge exams would need to be passed). An applicant who also wishes to obtain a FRTOL will be required to pass the JAR-FCL PPL Communications (PPL) theoretical knowledge examination and practical communications test unless they qualify for credit as detailed in Section B1.4.

  *If the ICAO PPL(A) has expired then all JAR theoretical knowledge exams would need to be passed.

- The holder of a current and valid PPL(A) issued by an ICAO Contracting State (not being a JAA Member State), who has flown less than 100 hours as pilot of aeroplanes, will be required to pass all JAR theoretical knowledge examinations.

- The holder of a UK or JAR PPL(H), CPL(H) or ATPL(H) is credited the examinations in Aviation Law & Operational Procedures, Navigation & Radio Aids, Meteorology and Human Performance & Limitations and JAR-FCL Communications (PPL) (if already passed). *Please note*: If no helicopter rating has been held in the 10 years preceding application, then the applicant would be required to pass all the JAR ground exams.

- The holder of a valid pass in the former professional UK Navigation and Technical ground examinations (Aeroplanes) or the JAR-FCL CPL(A) or ATPL(A) examinations will be credited this requirement. (Applicants who have taken and passed the Flight Engineer examinations may not claim this credit).

- The holder of a NPPL(SSEA) who has previously passed the JAR-FCL PPL(A) Theoretical Knowledge Examinations IN ALL SUBJECTS will be credited this requirement.

- An applicant who has held a valid UK/JAA FRTOL within the 5 years preceding successful application for a PPL(A) will be exempt the JAR-FCL Communications (PPL) examination.

FULL DETAILS OF THE EXAMINATIONS ARE GIVEN IN APPENDIX 1 TO JAR-FCL 1.130 & 1.135.

C1.4 JAR-FCL PPL(A) SKILL TEST REQUIREMENTS

An applicant for a JAR-FCL PPL(A) is required to pass the PPL(A) Skill Test with a CAA Authorised Examiner. Examiners shall not test applicants to whom flight instruction has been given by them for that licence except with the express consent in writing of the Authority.(If the training has been completed in a TMG and the licence is to be opened with the TMG rating, the PPL(A) Skill Test must be conducted in a TMG with a CAA Examiner authorised for the TMG rating.)

- An applicant for a skill test for the PPL(A) shall have received instruction on the same class/type of aeroplane to be used for the skill test. The applicant shall be permitted to choose to take the test on a single-engine aeroplane or, subject to the experience requirement in JAR-FCL 1.255 or 1.260 of 70 hours flight time as pilot-in-command, on a multi-engine aeroplane. The aeroplane used for the skill test shall meet the requirements for training aeroplanes (see Appendix 1 to JAR-FCL 1.125).

- An applicant may not take the Skill Test until all of the associated theoretical knowledge examinations have been passed.

- Applicants must be in possession of a JAA Class 1 or Class 2 medical certificate at the time of the test. The medical certificate shall be shown to the examiner. If the certificate is out of date the examiner may still conduct the test, but the applicant should be aware that, regardless of the outcome, he will not be permitted to use his licence or rating until the certificate is revalidated.

- An applicant may not take the Skill Test until all required flying training has been completed.

- The Skill Test shall be taken within 6 months of completing the flight instruction. All sections of the Skill Test must be completed within 6 months. The Skill Test has a validity of 12 months for the purpose of licence issue.

- An applicant shall pass sections 1 through 5 of the skill test, and applicable items of Section 6. If any item in a section is failed, that section is failed. Failure in more than one section will require the applicant to take the entire test again. An applicant failing only one section shall take the failed section again, plus Section 1 of the Skill Test. Failure in any section of the re-test, including those sections that have been passed on a previous attempt, will require the applicant to take the entire test again. Further training may be recommended following the failure of one Section of the Skill Test. Further training will be required prior to any full re-test.

- All sections of the skill test shall be completed within six months.

- There is no limit to the number of Skill Tests that may be attempted.

FULL DETAILS ON THE JAR-FCL PPL(A) SKILL TEST ARE GIVEN IN APPENDIX 1 & 2 TO JAR-FCL 1.135.

Guidance for applicants taking the PPL(A) Skill Test can also be found in Standards Document 19(A) on the CAA web site at www.caa.co.uk.

C1.5 ALLOWANCES AGAINST TRAINING REQUIREMENTS FOR UK QUALIFIED AND NON-QUALIFIED SERVICE PILOTS TOWARDS THE JAR-FCL PPL(A)

For PPL(A) purposes only, where reference is made to a Service Pilot this is defined as being a UK Service Pilot (Aeroplanes) who has completed a recognised military course of flying training and has had the award of the flying badge confirmed in compliance with QR(RAF) J727*. In addition, the applicant must have been qualified to act as Pilot-in-Command of military registered aircraft.

* The term "flying badge" is used to include all badges worn by personnel who have successfully completed a prescribed course of flying training.

QSP should also note that the CAA makes a distinction between pilots who initially qualify on fixed-wing aircraft (QSP(A)), and those who initially qualify on helicopters (QSP(H)).

The terms given are based on Qualified Service Pilots in current military service and are defined as current.

Current in this context means a Qualified Service Pilot (Aeroplanes) who has flown a minimum of 12 hours as pilot of aeroplanes during the course of his service duties, including at least 6 hours as First Pilot, and at least 12 take-offs and landings, and one flight with a flight or UK military instructor pilot in the 12 month period preceding the date of application for licence issue.

UK QUALIFIED SERVICE PILOTS (AEROPLANES) (UK QSP(A))

Flying Training/Theoretical Knowledge Requirements

- A UK QSP(A) with previous military SEP aeroplane experience (Bulldog, Chipmunk,T67 Firefly or Grob 115 Tutor) will be credited all flying training requirements. A QSP(A) who has been current on any military aeroplane in the preceding 5 years will be credited the JAR-FCL PPL(A) examinations in Navigation & Radio Aids, Meteorology, Aircraft (General) & Principles of Flight and Flight performance & Planning. A QSP(A) who meets the eligibility criteria for any of the QSP accreditation schemes (as detailed in Sections D3 and D6) will additionally be credited the Human Performance & Limitations exam. A QSP(A) who has been current on any military aeroplane in the preceding 5 years will be credited Section 3 En-Route Procedures of the PPL(A) Skill Test. A QSP(A) who is current on SEP aeroplanes will be credited the PPL(A) Skill Test.

- A UK QSP(A) with jet experience only, who is/has been current on any military aeroplane in the preceding 5 years, will be required to complete a minimum of 15 hours flight instruction in SEP aeroplanes, including 10 hours dual instruction and 5 hours solo, and pass the PPL(A) skill test (but will be credited Section 3 (En-route procedures)). The examinations in Navigation & Radio Aids, Meteorology, Aircraft (General) & Principles of Flight and Flight Performance & Planning will be credited.

UK QUALIFIED SERVICE PILOTS (HELICOPTERS) (QSP(H))

- A current UK QSP(H) with previous SEP aeroplane experience will be required to meet the flying training/experience requirements as detailed in C1.2. However, a credit will be given for the 150 nm solo Qualifying Cross Country flight. In addition, a QSP(H) will also be required to pass the complete JAR-FCL PPL(A) Skill Test and pass the JAR-FCL PPL(A) Theoretical Knowledge Examinations in all subjects with the exception of Navigation & Radio Aids and Meteorology examinations that are credited.

  A QSP who meets the eligibility criteria for any of the QSP accreditation schemes (as detailed in Sections D3 and D6) will additionally be credited the Human Performance & Limitations exam.

No. 1 ELEMENTARY FLYING TRAINING SCHOOL SERVICE ELEMENTARY FLYING TRAINING COURSE/UAS FLYING COURSE

Flying Training/Theoretical Knowledge Requirements

Graduates from the Service Elementary Flying Training Course (commenced November 2000 onwards) will be presented with a Course Completion Certificate by, No. 1 Elementary Flying Training School, indicating **FULL** or **PARTIAL** accreditation towards the JAR-FCL PPL(A) requirements detailing either a fully completed accredited course or completed parts of an accredited course.

Graduates presented with a full accreditation course completion certificate (annotated with a Green Border) will be credited all the flying training and theoretical knowledge requirements. Graduates presented with a partial course completion certificate (annotated with a Yellow Border) will be credited only the elements completed during EFT training. Students will be required to complete the outstanding elements to qualify for licence issue. In both cases, credit for the PPL(A) skill test will be given for a period of 24 months from the date of the Final Handling Test.

Any previous flying experience in single-engine piston (Land) aeroplanes gained during any Service Elementary Flying Training Courses including the UAS Flying Course (that commenced prior to November 2000, or incomplete courses from any period of time) may be counted towards the requirements for the grant of a JAR-FCL PPL(A). Applicants wishing to claim credits against these requirements will be required to attend a registered facility or approved FTO and provide logbook evidence of their training (certified by their military course instructor) to the Chief Flying Instructor. The CFI will then establish a course of training taking into account previous experience to ensure that the specific requirements of C1.2 have been met.

In addition to any flying training required (where there is a shortfall of requirements), applicants will be required to complete one cross-country flight of at least 270km (150nm), during which full stop landings at two different aerodromes of departure shall be made, pass all JAR-FCL PPL(A) theoretical knowledge examinations* and pass the PPL(A) skill test.

*If the graduate is now a UK QSP(H) credits will be given for the Navigation & Radio Aids and Meteorology examinations.

C1.6 UK FLIGHT RADIOTELEPHONY OPERATOR'S LICENCE (FRTOL) REQUIREMENTS

Pilots who intend to operate radiotelephony equipment will require a FRTOL. It should be noted that whilst Radio Communication forms part of the JAR-FCL PPL(A) training syllabus, the FRTOL remains a UK national licence. Applicants for a JAR-FCL PPL should be aware that they will be tested in practical radio operation as part of the Licensing Skill Test. A JAR-FCL PPL(A) may be issued without an FRTOL, however individuals will still be required to pass the JAR-FCL Communications (PPL) theoretical knowledge examination for the issue of the JAR-FCL PPL(A). Applicants who wish to have radiotelephony privileges included with their PPL are also required to pass the RTF communications practical test and apply for a FRTOL using a separate application form (SRG\1106). The PPL and FRTOL are two separate licences under different legislation.

FULL DETAILS OF THE FRTOL REQUIREMENTS INCLUDING CREDITS AVAILABLE ARE CONTAINED IN SECTION B.

Section A
Section B
Section C PPL
Section D
Section E
Section F
Section G
Section H
Section I
Section J
Section K
Index

C1.7 JAR-FCL PPL(A) MEDICAL REQUIREMENTS

An applicant for a JAR-FCL PPL(A) shall hold a valid JAR-FCL Class 1 or Class 2 Medical Certificate. The reduced medical requirement to maintain an NPPL will not be acceptable irrespective of the class of aircraft being flown under the JAR-FCL SEP rating (e.g. microlights and SLMGs). **Full details of medical requirements are contained in JAR-FCL 3 and Section A5**.

C2 JAR-FCL PPL(HELICOPTER)

This section offers information as a basic guide to obtaining a JAR-FCL Private Pilot Licence (Helicopters) - JAR-FCL PPL(H) as follows:-

For full details you are advised to refer to **JAR-FCL 2 Subpart C.**

C2.1 JAR-PPL(H) GENERAL INFORMATION

Privileges

Details of licence privileges can be found in Schedule 8 of the Air Navigation Order, (please also refer to Section A, Appendix F).

Minimum Age

An applicant for a JAR-FCL PPL(H) shall be at least 17 years of age but some of the required qualifications for the grant of the licence may be gained earlier. Applicants should ensure that any qualifications gained earlier will still be valid at the time they plan to apply for the grant of the licence. The validity periods of training, examinations and flight tests are covered in this document.

Student pilots may act as Pilot-in-Command from their 16th birthday provided they act only in accordance with instructions given by a flying instructor, hold a valid JAR-FCL Medical Certificate and, generally, fly only in UK territorial airspace. There is no minimum age for dual instruction, but any received before the age of 14 is not countable towards the experience requirements specified in this document.

Licence Validity

The JAR-FCL PPL(H) will be issued for a maximum validity period of 5 years.

UK Qualified Service Pilots

Where reference is made to a 'Qualified Service Pilot' this is defined as being a UK Qualified Service Pilot (QSP) who has completed a recognised military course of flying training and has been awarded the pilot's flying badge in compliance with QR(RAF) J727*. In addition, the applicant must have been qualified to act as Pilot-in-Command of military registered aircraft.

* The term "flying badge" is used to include all badges worn by personnel who have successfully completed a prescribed course of flying training. The initial award of a flying badge is on a provisional basis. It is not deemed to be fully earned until the holder has successfully completed an operational conversion or equivalent course and has joined an operational or non-operational unit in the capacity for which the provisional badge has been awarded. Joining is defined for each service as follows:-

a. RN: on issue of the Certificate of Competence.

b. Army and RM: on award of the badge (and successful completion of conversion to type (CTT) course).

c. RAF: On successful attainment of an appropriate aircrew categorisation or qualification to undertake productive flying duties (C categorisation or above, B1 or above instructor category or CR status).

QSPs should also note that the CAA makes a distinction between pilots who qualify on helicopters (QSP(H)), and those who initially qualify on aeroplanes (QSP(A)).

The terms given within this section are based on Qualified Service Pilots who are defined as current. For pilots who are not current, then providing that they have been current in the last 5 years preceding date of application for licence issue, the credits given within this Section will also apply.

C2.2 JAR-FCL PPL(H) FLYING TRAINING/ EXPERIENCE REQUIREMENTS

The requirements detailed in this section assume that an applicant will apply for a JAR-FCL PPL(H) with a single-pilot, single-engine helicopter type rating. The training must be completed in a helicopter type listed in JAR-FCL 2 Subpart F.

Experience Requirements

An applicant for a JAR-FCL PPL(H) shall have completed at least **45** hours flight time as a pilot of helicopters. This must include the training requirements specified below. A total of **5** hours of these **45** hours may be completed in a Flight & Navigation Procedures Trainer (FNPT) or a Flight Simulator. A FNPT or Flight Simulator used for this purpose must be device qualified **and** user approved.

Flying Training Requirements

An applicant for a JAR-FCL PPL(H) shall have completed on **one** type of helicopter, having a certificate of airworthiness issued or accepted by a JAA Member State, the particular requirements specified in (a) and (b) below. Training for an additional helicopter type rating may be included within the PPL (H) training providing that the particular specified requirements in (a) and (b) and the PPL (H) Skill Test have completed on one helicopter type. Applicants must also complete a LST on the additional helicopter type to also be endorsed and theoretical knowledge examination.

An applicant for the PPL(H) shall complete at a FTO or an accepted registered facility the required instruction in accordance with the syllabus as set out in Appendix 1 to JAR-FCL 2.125. This must include:-

a. **25 hours*** Dual Instruction on Helicopters, must include (i);
   - i. **5 hours** Instrument dual instruction time

b. **10 hours** Supervised solo flight time on Helicopters, must include (i);
   - i. **5 hours** Solo cross-country flight time, must include (ii);
   - ii. One cross-country flight of at least 185km (100nm) as per JAR-FCL 2.125 (b)

* Reduced to not less than **20** hours where an applicant has been credited for Pilot-in-Command flight time on other aircraft.

Credits from Flying Training

- Holders of pilot licences or equivalent privileges for Aeroplanes (including UK QSP(A)), Microlights having fixed wings and moveable aerodynamic control surfaces acting in all three dimensions, Microlight Helicopters, Gyroplanes, Gliders, Self-Sustaining Gliders or Self Launching Gliders, may be credited with 10% of their total flight time as Pilot-in-Command in such aircraft up to a maximum of **6** hours towards a PPL(H).

- A current QSP(A) will be required to meet the flying training/experience requirements as detailed in C2.2, however a credit will be given from having to complete the 100 nm solo Qualifying Cross Country flight. In addition, a QSP(A) will be required to pass the complete JAR-FCL PPL(H) Skill Test and pass the JAR-FCL PPL(H) Examinations as detailed in C2.3.

- A current* Qualified Service Pilot (Helicopters) is credited all the JAR-FCL PPL(H) flying training/experience requirements **except** the PPL(H) Skill Test. However, a QSP who wishes to undertake the PPL(H) Skill Test on a helicopter type for which he is not qualified to fly in the UK Armed Forces, must undertake an approved type rating course for the type to be used on the skill test. *Current in this context means a UK Qualified Service Pilot (Helicopters) who has flown a minimum of 12 hours as pilot of helicopters during the course of his service duties, including at least 6 hours as First Pilot, and at least 12 take-offs and landings, and one flight with a flight or military instructor in the 12 month period preceding the date of application for licence issue.

- Any previous flying experience experience in helicopters gained during military DHFS training may be counted towards the requirements for the grant of a JAR-FCL PPL(H). Applicants wishing to claim credits against these requirements will be required to attend a registered facility of approved FTO and provide the following evidence of their training to the Chief Flying Instructor who will then establish a course of training taking into account previous experience to ensure that all the specific requirements of C2.2 have been met:-

  In addition to any flying training required (where there is a shortfall of requirements), applicants will be required to complete one cross-country flight of at least 185km (100nm), during which full stop landings at two different aerodromes of departure shall be made, pass all JAR-FCL PPL(H) theoretical knowledge examinations and pass the PPL(H) skill test.

  DHFS - applicants should submit actual logbook evidence.

Note: the training requirements specified in (a) and (b) above must all be completed in one type of helicopter as used on the PPL(H) Skill Test.

- Any previous flying training gained during a PPL(H) course conducted in another JAA Member State (other than the UK) may be credited with such flight time towards the issue of a UK JAR-FCL PPL(H). Applicants who intend to continue with their training with a UK Registered Facility or Flying Training Organisation, must in the first instance contact the Authority of the

Member State in which training was commenced. The applicant should confirm with that other State that they will allow them to continue their training with a UK training provider, and agree that the UK will be the 'State of Licence Issue'. If the other State agrees then the applicant will be required to obtain written confirmation to this effect in order for all previous PPL training to be recognised by the UK CAA. The applicant should also arrange with the other JAA State for any PPL training records to be forwarded onto the new Registered Facility or FTO. If the other State does not give agreement then the UK CAA will only recognise up to a maximum of 10 hours of the previous training towards the overall 45 hour requirement for licence issue. The applicant will in this case be required to complete the further 35 hours as specified in Flying Training Requirements.

- In circumstances where previous flying training towards an ICAO PPL(H) (non-JAR-FCL) has been completed but no licence has been issued, PLD will consider the crediting of such flight time towards the issue of a JAR-FCL PPL(H). In all cases, applicants must apply in writing to PLD enclosing appropriate training records and flying logbooks for the PPL training received. PLD will review the training records to establish a course of training and advise the applicant accordingly.
- The holder of a current and valid PPL(H)* issued by an ICAO Contracting State (not being a JAA Member State), who has flown a minimum of 100 hours and meets the JAR-FCL PPL(H) flying experience requirements (including 5 hours instrument instruction) as pilot of helicopters, is credited the JAR-FCL PPL(H) training requirements, however they will be required to undertake the PPL(H) Skill Test on a helicopter type for which he is qualified. Applicants wishing to take the PPL(H) Skill Test on a helicopter type on which they are not qualified will be required to complete the training requirements for an additional helicopter type as detailed in Section F8.
- The holder of a current and valid PPL(H)* issued by an ICAO Contracting State (not being a JAA Member State), who has flown <u>less than</u> 100 hours as pilot of helicopters, but meets the JAR-FCL PPL(H) flying experience requirements (including 5 hours instrument instruction) is credited the flying training, except the PPL(H) Skill Test. Applicants wishing to take the PPL(H) Skill Test on a helicopter type on which they are not qualified will be required to complete the training requirements for an additional helicopter type as detailed in Section F8.

* If the ICAO licence has expired and/or no valid helicopter rating has been held for a period exceeding 5 years preceding application, applicants will be required to complete flying training at the discretion of the Head of Training of the approved training provider, and pass the PPL(H) Skill Test.

FULL DETAILS OF THE EXPERIENCE/TRAINING REQUIREMENTS ARE GIVEN IN JAR-FCL 2 SUBPART C

C2.3 JAR-FCL PPL(H) THEORETICAL KNOWLEDGE EXAMINATION REQUIREMENTS

An applicant for a JAR-FCL PPL(H) is required to pass theoretical knowledge examinations in the following subjects:

1. Aviation Law & Operational Procedures
2. Human Performance & Limitations
3. Navigation & Radio Aids
4. Meteorology
5. Aircraft (General) & Principles of Flight
6. Flight Performance & Planning
7. Communications (PPL)

These examinations contain multiple-choice questions for the most part and are normally conducted under the auspices of a Registered Facility or Flight Training Organisation. An applicant shall be deemed to have successfully completed the theoretical examinations for the JAR-FCL PPL(H) when awarded a pass in all of the above examinations within a period of 18 months counted from the end of the calendar month when the applicant first attempted an examination. A pass will be accepted for the grant of a JAR-FCL PPL(H) during the 24 months from the date of successfully completing the theoretical knowledge examinations.

Credits from Theoretical Knowledge Examinations

- A current UK Qualified Service Pilot (Helicopters) is credited the examinations in Navigation & Radio Aids, Meteorology, Aircraft (General) & Principles of Flight and Flight Performance & Planning. A QSP who meets the eligibility criteria for <u>any</u> of the QSP accreditation schemes (as detailed in Sections D3 and D6) will additionally be credited the Human Performance & Limitations exam.
- A current UK Qualified Service Pilot (Aeroplanes) is credited the examinations in Navigation & Radio Aids and Meteorology. A QSP who meets the eligibility criteria for <u>any</u> of the QSP accreditation schemes (as detailed in Sections

D3 and D6) will additionally be credited the Human Performance & Limitations exam.

- The holder of a UK or JAR PPL(A), CPL(A) or ATPL(A) is credited the theoretical knowledge examinations in Aviation Law & Operational Procedures, Navigation & Radio Aids, Meteorology and Human Performance & Limitations and JAR-FCL Communications (PPL) if already passed. (Please note: If no aeroplane rating has been held in the 10 years preceding application, then the applicant would be required to pass all the JAR ground exams.
- The holder of a valid pass in the former professional UK Navigation and Technical ground examinations (Helicopters) or the JAR-FCL CPL(H) or ATPL(H) ground examinations will be credited this requirement.
- The holder of a current and valid PPL(H)* issued by an ICAO Contracting State (not being a JAA Member State), who has flown a minimum of 100 hours as pilot of helicopters, will be required to pass written examinations in Air Law and Human Performance and Limitations. (If no helicopter rating has been held in the 5 years preceding application, then all JAR theoretical knowledge examinations would need to be passed. An applicant who also wishes to obtain a FRTOL will be required to pass the JAR-FCL PPL Communications (PPL) theoretical knowledge examination and practical communications test unless they qualify for credit as detailed in Section B1.4.

  *If the ICAO PPL(H) has expired then all JAR theoretical knowledge exams would need to be passed.
- The holder of a current and valid PPL(H) issued by an ICAO Contracting State (not being a JAA Member State), who has flown less than the minimum of 100 hours as pilot of helicopters, will be required to pass all JAR theoretical knowledge examinations.
- An applicant who has held a valid UK/JAA FRTOL within the 5 years preceding successful application for a PPL(H) will be exempt the JAR-FCL Communications (PPL) examination.

FULL DETAILS OF THE EXAMINATIONS ARE GIVEN IN APPENDIX 1 TO JAR-FCL 2.130 & 2.135.

C2.4 JAR-FCL PPL(H) SKILL TEST REQUIREMENTS

An applicant for a JAR-FCL PPL(H) is required to pass the **PPL(H) Skill Test** with a CAA Authorised Examiner. Examiners shall not test applicants to whom flight instruction has been given by them for that licence except with the expressed consent in writing of the Authority.

- An applicant for a skill test for the PPL(H) shall have received instruction on the same type of helicopter to be used for the skill test. The applicant shall be permitted to choose to take the test on a single-engine helicopter or, subject to the experience requirement in JAR-FCL 2.255 of 70 hours flight time time as pilot-in-command, on a multi-engine helicopter. The helicopter used for the skill test shall meet the requirements for training helicopters (see Appendix 1 to JAR-FCL 2.125).
- An applicant may not take the Skill Test until all of the associated theoretical knowledge examinations have been passed.
- Applicants must be in possession of a JAA Class 1 or Class 2 medical certificate at the time of the test. The medical certificate shall be shown to the examiner. If the certificate is out of date the examiner may still conduct the test, but the applicant should be aware that, regardless of the outcome, he will not be permitted to use his licence or rating until the certificate is revalidated.
- An applicant may not take the Skill Test until all required flying training has been completed.
- The Skill Test shall be taken within 6 months of completing the flight instruction. All sections of the Skill Test must be completed within 6 months. The Skill Test has a validity of 12 months for the purpose of licence issue.
- An applicant shall pass sections 1 through 5 of the Skill Test. If any item in a section is failed, that section is failed. Failure in more than one section will require the applicant to take the entire test again. An applicant failing only one section shall take the failed section again, plus Section 1 and elements of Section 4 of the Skill Test. Failure in any items of the re-test and failure in any other items already passed, will require the applicant to take the entire test again. Further training may be required following any one failed skill test. Failure to achieve a pass in all sections of the test in two attempts will require further training as determined by the Authority.
- There is no limit to the number of Skill tests that may be attempted.

FULL DETAILS OF THE JAR-FCL PPL(H) SKILL TEST ARE GIVEN IN APPENDIX 1 & 2 TO JAR-FCL 2.135

Guidance for applicants taking the PPL(H) Skill Test can also be found in Standards Document 19(H) on the CAA web site at www.caa.co.uk.

C2.5 UK FLIGHT RADIOTELEPHONY OPERATOR'S LICENCE (FRTOL) REQUIREMENTS

Pilots who intend to operate radiotelephony equipment will require a FRTOL. It should be noted that whilst Radio Communication forms part of the JAR-FCL PPL(H) training syllabus, the FRTOL remains a UK national licence.

Applicants for a JAR-FCL PPL should be aware that they will be tested in practical radio operation as part of the Licensing Skill Test. A JAR-FCL PPL(H) may be issued without a FRTOL, however individuals will still be required to pass the JAR-FCL Communications (PPL) theoretical knowledge examination for the issue of the JAR-FCL PPL(H). Applicants who wish to have radiotelephony privileges included with their PPL are also required to pass the RTF communications practical test and apply for a FRTOL using a separate application form (SRG\1106). The PPL and FRTOL are two separate licences under different legislation.

FULL DETAILS OF THE FRTOL REQUIREMENTS INCLUDING CREDITS AVAILABLE ARE CONTAINED IN SECTION B.

C2.6 JAR-FCL PPL(H) MEDICAL REQUIREMENTS

An applicant for a JAR-FCL PPL(H) shall hold a valid JAR-FCL Class 1 or Class 2 Medical Certificate.

FULL DETAILS OF MEDICAL REQUIREMENTS ARE CONTAINED IN JAR-FCL 3 AND SECTION A5.

C3 UK PPL (GYROPLANE)

This section offers information as a basic guide to obtaining a UK Private Pilot Licence (Gyroplanes) - UK PPL (G) as follows:-

C3.1 UK PPL(G) GENERAL INFORMATION

Details of licence privileges can be found in Schedule 8 of the Air Navigation Order, (please also refer to Section A, Appendix F).

When a UK PPL(G) is issued, it will be endorsed with the following restriction:

"The holder of this licence is not permitted to fly gyroplanes:

a. out of sight of ground or water

b. by sole reference to instruments.

Minimum Age

The minimum age for an applicant for a UK PPL(G) is 17 years but some of the required qualifications for the grant of the licence may be gained earlier. Applicants should ensure that any qualifications gained earlier will still be valid at the time they plan to apply for the grant of the licence. The validity periods of training, examinations and flight tests are covered within this section.

Licence Validity

The UK PPL(G) will be issued with a lifetime validity but for the privileges conferred by it to be exercised the pilot must have a current Medical Certificate/Declaration and a valid Aircraft Rating.

Non-UK Licence Holders

The holder of a Non-UK Pilot's Licence or equivalent privileges for Gyroplanes who wishes to obtain a UK PPL(G) should apply in writing to PLD for an assessment of their flying experience. The Non-UK licence and all logbooks must be submitted for this purpose. A fee will be levied for this service. Any United Kingdom flight crew licences issued on conversion of foreign licences, will contain a statement on the licence to that effect. This is in order to comply with Article 6 of EC Directive 670/1991 effective from 1 June 1992. This statement will NOT be entered in UK licences issued on conversion from an EC Member State's licence.

C3.2 UK PPL(G) FLYING TRAINING/ EXPERIENCE REQUIREMENTS

An applicant for a UK PPL(G) shall produce evidence of having satisfactorily completed a course of training to a syllabus recognised by the CAA, at a Flying Club, Registered Facility or a Flight Training Organisation.

There is presently one recognised syllabus of training known as The British Rotorcraft Association Syllabus. This syllabus mandates a prescribed amount of dual and solo training in gyroplanes and for those students wishing to conduct some of the flight training on their own single seat gyroplane (subject to suitability and approval from the CAA for ab-initio flight training). The latter single seat training may be integrated into the course.

The flight training shall initially be completed on an approved 2 seat gyroplane with a Permit to Fly Certificate of Airworthiness (C of A) amended by the CAA to allow flight instruction on the aircraft. For persons owning or intending to fly single seat variants after licence issue, an approved single seat gyroplane with a valid Permit to Fly C of A may also be used on the course after a specified minimum of dual flight instruction.

In this case the requirement for 4 hours differences flight training, not including wheel balancing, for single seat gyroplanes must be met in addition to the PPL(G) syllabus requirements.

An applicant for a UK PPL(G) must produce logbook evidence of having flown a minimum of **40** hours as a Pilot of a flying machine. This flying must include the particular requirements specified below:-

a. **5 hours** dual flying training (P/UT) in Single-Engine Piston (Land) Aeroplanes, Helicopters, Self Launching Motor Gliders, gyroplanes;

b. **10 hours** dual flying training in gyroplanes;

   10 hours as Pilot in Command (PIC) of gyroplanes, must include;

   i. **3 hours** Solo cross-country flying, must include (ii);

   ii. Two cross-country flights of at least 25 nm during which full stop landings at two aerodromes different from the aerodrome of departure shall be made in the 9 months prior to the date of application.

Credits from Flying Training

- Holders of pilot licences for aeroplanes, microlights (both weight shift/flex wing and three axis aircraft), gliders (with BGA Silver C minimum qualification), self-sustaining gliders or self-launching gliders and current UK Qualified Service Pilots (Aeroplanes) may be credited with up to a maximum of 10 hours towards the flying training requirements, but are required to complete the minimum requirements specified in a) & b) above.
- Holders of pilot licences for helicopters and UK Qualified Service Pilots (Helicopters) may be credited with up to 20 hours, and are required to complete the minimum requirements specified in a) & b) above.
- Flight time in an authorised gyro glider with an Authorised Gyro glider Instructor or Flying Instructor Gyroplanes (PPL(G)) may be counted toward the dual flying requirement up to a maximum of 5 hours for an applicant on the 40 hour ab-initio course, and 3 hours for pilots converting from other aircraft types as specified above.

C3.3 UK PPL(G) GROUND EXAMINATION REQUIREMENTS

An applicant for a UK PPL(G) will be required to take and pass the Theoretical Knowledge Examinations at the same level as the National Private Pilot's Licence (Microlights):

a. Pass the written examinations in the following subjects:

   1. Aviation Law, Flight Rules & Procedures
   2. Human Performance & Limitations
   3. Navigation
   4. Meteorology

   - The examinations are written multiple-choice papers and are normally conducted under the auspices of a Gyroplane Examiner. The above examinations are valid for **12** months from the date of passing.
   - Applicants should arrange their training so that they pass the ground examinations in the following sequence:

   i. Aviation Law, Flight Rules & Procedures before the first solo flight.

   ii. Navigation, Meteorology and Human Performance & Limitations before the first solo cross-country flight.

b. Pass the technical examinations for the Aircraft (General) and Aircraft (Type) examination.

   - The Aircraft (General) and Aircraft (Type) examinations are currently conducted as an oral examination by the Gyroplane Examiner who conducts the Flight Test and will remain valid for 9 months from the date of passing. These examinations will in due course be a written multiple choice examination.

Credits from Ground Examinations

- The holder of a current and valid Pilot's Licence (Aeroplanes or Helicopters) issued by an ICAO Contracting State, current Flight Navigators and Qualified Service Pilots (Aeroplanes) and (Helicopters) will be credited the examinations in Navigation and Meteorology.
- The holder of a valid UK or JAR-FCL Pilot's Licence (**except Balloons**) will be credited with all of the ground examinations with the exception of the Aircraft General (Gyroplane) examination. Holders of a balloon licence and NPPL will be required to pass all UK PPL(G) ground examinations.

C3.4 UK PPL(G) FLIGHT TEST REQUIREMENTS

An applicant for a UK PPL(G) is required to pass a **Flight Test** in a two-seat gyroplane and additionally in a single seat gyroplane if integrating a single seat aircraft into the syllabus with, or supervised by, a CAA Authorised Gyroplane Examiner. The test shall be completed within six months of completing the flight instruction, and may be included as part of the overall flight time required for licence issue, but not towards the 10 hours flight time as Pilot-in-Command.

- The Flight Test will remain valid for **9** months from the date of passing.

The whole flight test shall be completed within a period of 28 days. An applicant who fails any part of the test may be required to undertake further flight training before being accepted for retest.

DETAILS OF THE PPL(G) FLIGHT TEST ARE GIVEN IN APPENDIX A.

C3.5 FLIGHT RADIOTELEPHONY OPERATOR'S LICENCE (FRTOL) REQUIREMENTS

Pilots who intend to operate radiotelephony equipment will require a FRTOL **(Section B refers).**

C3.6 UK PPL(G) MEDICAL REQUIREMENTS

An applicant for a UK PPL(G) shall hold a valid NPPL medical declaration (DVLA Group 1 or Group 2 Standard) or a JAR-FCL medical certificate. For full information regarding the medical requirements please refer to the CAA web site at www.caa.co.uk.

C3.7 UK PPL(G) RE-VALIDATION REQUIREMENTS

The minimum flying experience required to maintain the above ratings is 5 hours as pilot (3 hours as Pilot-in-Command) in an aircraft of the same class as the rating in the licence within the 13 months preceding the date of issue of the new C of E. The flying must be completed within the validity period of an existing C of E or C of T.

Of the 5 hours experience required 3 hours must have been as Pilot-in-Command. The remaining time may be made up of:

a. Pilot-in-Command under supervision (PIC U/S) flight time gained with a flying instructor on a successful check flight or with an authorised Examiner on a successful Flight Test for the grant or revalidation of a rating in a PPL.

b. Dual flying instruction flown with a flying instructor but only if, at the end of the dual flight or flights, the instructor considered the pilot was fit to fly as Pilot-in-Command and certifies the logbook to that effect.

C3.8 UK PPL(G) RENEWAL REQUIREMENTS

A pilot who has not met the appropriate flying experience to re-validate the appropriate rating, but wishes to qualify for a further 13 months flying must pass the Aircraft Rating Revalidation Flight Test. The Flight Test to revalidate aircraft rating privileges will require the pilot to demonstrate that he/she is competent to fly the aircraft as PIC and include the following items:

To revalidate a Gyroplane, all manoeuvres used in normal flight, including take-off and landing, and simulated forced landing.

For a period **exceeding 26 months but not more than 5 years** since the last flight flown as Pilot-in-Command a pilot must undergo the following training and Flight Test. The training and testing must be conducted in an aircraft included in the Aircraft Rating on the licence.

The Training Syllabus, which must be completed within the 9 months period preceding the date of issue of the Certificate of test, is:

1. **All Aircraft Ratings**

   Discussion in changes to regulations, procedures, etc., introduced since the pilot last flew as PIC, and revision of the Aviation Law and Flight Rules and Procedures syllabus for the PPL. Revision of the Human Performance and Limitations syllabus for the Aircraft rating being revalidated.

2. **For Gyroplanes**

   i. At least one hour's training in circuits, landings and general handling to include a 'power-off' approach and landing to touchdown, to a selected area under the direction of a flying instructor.

   ii. A Flight Test.

The Flight Test

A Flight Test with an authorised PPL(G) Examiner consisting of one flight in a gyroplane of the appropriate Type to include:

1. a General Flight Test to cover all items in the Flight Test for initial issue of the Aircraft rating, and

2. a cross-country flight to an aerodrome at least 30 minutes flight time from the aerodrome of departure, a circuit and landing at the destination, and a return flight to the aerodrome of departure; the preparation (Flight Planning) for each leg will form part of this test.

The flights are to be entered in the pilot's personal flying logbook and endorsed by the flying instructor who gave the dual instruction and/or directed the solo flying.

For a period **exceeding 5 years** since the last flight flown as Pilot-in-Command of **GYROPLANES,** applicants must apply to the CAA or an assessment of the training and subsequent testing required for the renewal of the Aircraft Rating.

C3.9 CARRIAGE OF PASSENGERS

The holder of a PPL(G) shall not act as Pilot-in-Command of a gyroplane carrying passengers unless within the preceding 90 days that person has made three take-offs and three landings as the sole manipulator of the controls in a gyroplane of the same type.

C3.10 ADDITIONAL MANUFACTURE TYPES

For the time being gyroplane PPL's are issued with the privilege to fly one type of gyroplane i.e. single engine gyroplane.

Pilots wishing to fly gyroplanes different from the specific manufactured type that they received flight training on, shall receive appropriate differences training from a gyroplane assistant flight instructor or flight instructor and have their log book endorsed by the instructor. In the case of single seat gyroplanes arrangements shall be made with an instructor for the differences to be covered and where necessary a flight demonstration by the pilot to confirm his/her competency: a logbook endorsement shall also be made.

Differences flight training shall consist of at least 4 hours of flight training which shall not include time spent on the wheel balancing exercises.

There may be occasions when the ownership of a rare single seat type of gyroplane is transferred or another pilot wishes to fly someone else's machine, and there is no instructor with the appropriate experience on the machine. If this is the case the qualified pilot on the specific type should arrange with an instructor for the supervision of such difference training and the log book endorsement to be made by the instructor.

In the interest of flight safety, it is imperative that the above differences training is carried out.

C4 UK PPL (BALLOON & AIRSHIP)

This section offers information as a basic guide to obtaining a UK Private Pilot Licence (Balloons and Airships) - UK PPL (BA) as follows:-

C4.1 UK PPL (BA) GENERAL INFORMATION

Privileges

Details of licence privileges can be found in Schedule 8 of the Air Navigation Order, (please also refer to Section A, Appendix F).

For this purpose, the types of balloon or airships are:

a. Hot-air Balloon

b. Gas-filled Balloon (solo only)

c. Gas Balloon

d. Combination Gas/Hot-air Balloon

e. Hot Air Airships – Pressurised (up to 160,000 CuFt/4550 CuM Volume)

f. Hot Air Airships – Un-pressurised (up to 160,000 CuFt/4550 CuM Volume)

g. Hot Air Airships – Un-pressurised and Pressurised (up to 160,000 CuFt/4550 CuM Volume)

h. Gas Airships – Pressurised (up to 160,000 CuFt/ 4550 CuM Volume)

When a UK PPL(BA) is issued, it will be endorsed with a **"Day Flying Only"** restriction. (For removal of this restriction, please refer to the Night Flying section). Airship ratings can only be obtained and endorsed onto an existing PPL(BA) licence. (Please refer to C4.7 for full details).

Minimum Age

The minimum age for an applicant for a UK PPL(BA) is 17 years but some of the required qualifications for the grant of the licence may be gained earlier. Applicants should ensure that any qualifications gained earlier will still be valid at the time they plan to apply for the grant of the licence. The validity periods of training, examinations and flight tests are covered in this document.

Student pilots may act as Pilot-in-Command from their 16th birthday provided they act only in accordance with instructions given by a flying instructor, hold a valid UK or JAR-FCL Medical Certificate or UK Medical Declaration and fly only in UK airspace.

Licence Validity

The UK PPL(BA) will be issued with a lifetime validity but for the privileges conferred by it to be exercised the pilot must have a current Medical Certificate/ Declaration and a valid Aircraft Rating.

Non-UK Licence Holders

Any credits or exemptions against training for holders of a non-UK Pilot's Licence or equivalent privileges for Balloons are indicated at the relevant section.

Applicants for conversion to a UK PPL(BA) must obtain a valid UK or JAR-FCL Medical Certificate or UK Declaration of Health certificate.

Any United Kingdom flight crew licences issued on conversion of foreign licences, will contain a statement on the licence to that effect. This is in order to comply with Article 6 of EC Directive 670/1991 effective from 1 June 1992. This statement will NOT be entered in UK licences issued on conversion from an EC Member State's licence

C4.2 UK PPL(BA) FLYING TRAINING/ EXPERIENCE REQUIREMENTS

An applicant for a UK PPL(BA) shall produce evidence of having satisfactorily completed a course of training to a syllabus recognised by the Authority, within the 24 months preceding the date of application for the licence.

Flying hours by day under instruction in balloons - must include:-

- not less than **16 hours** total flying time in Balloons to cover the syllabus of training detailed in Appendix B;
- **6** ascents by day under the instruction of a licensed Balloon pilot of which **4** ascents must be made under the instruction of a BBAC instructor.

In addition to the above, applicants must complete:-

- **1** solo ascent by day of not less than 30 minutes duration under the supervision of a CAA appointed examiner or delegated instructor (to be completed within the 6 months preceding licence application);
- **1** tethered flight.

Non-UK Licence Holders

Logbook evidence that the applicant has met the above minimum flying experience must be provided.

Night Flying

Where an applicant wishes to exercise the licence privileges by night, the following additional training must be completed: 2 night flights, each of which shall include a night take-off and subsequent night operation of not less than 1 hour's duration under the supervision of a licensed balloon pilot whose licence is not limited to day flying only.

C4.3 UK PPL(BA) GROUND EXAMINATION REQUIREMENTS

An applicant for a UK PPL(BA) is required to:

a. The study of syllabus for subjects 1), 3) and 4) is as for the former UK PPL(A), although the examination papers are moulded towards the special aspects of balloon and airship flying (please refer to Appendix C - UK PPL(BA) Syllabus of Ground Examinations).

   1. Aviation Law, Flight Rules & Procedures
   2. Human Performance & Limitations
   3. Navigation
   4. Meteorology
   5. Airmanship & Balloon Systems (for Hot-air Balloons only)
   6. Airmanship & Aerostatics (for Gas-filled Balloons only)

- The study of syllabus for subjects 1), 3) and 4) is as for the PPL(A), although the examination papers are moulded towards the special aspects of balloon and airship flying. The syllabus for subjects 5) and 6) are maintained by the BBAC, and a copy may be obtained from the club on request.
- The examinations are written multiple-choice papers and are normally conducted under the auspices of a Balloon or Airship Examiner. The above examinations are valid for 24 months from the date of passing. Candidates must obtain not less than 70% in each subject to pass.

Credits from Ground Examinations

- The holder of a valid UK or JAR-FCL Private or Professional Pilot's Licence is credited the examinations in Aviation Law, Flight Rules and Procedures, Navigation, Meteorology and Human Performance and Limitations if already passed.
- Holders of a valid non-UK Private or Professional Pilot's Licence (Balloons) may be exempt the examinations in Navigation, Meteorology, Airmanship and Balloon Systems.

C4.4 UK PPL(BA) FLIGHT TEST REQUIREMENTS

An applicant for a UK PPL(BA) is required to pass a Flight Test with, or supervised by, a CAA Authorised Balloon Examiner.

- The Flight Test will remain valid for **9** months from the date of passing.

Note: Where the balloon used can carry only one person, the Flight Test is carried out under the supervision of the Examiner. There is no requirement for a further solo flight. It is not essential to complete the test in one flight, but the whole test must be done within a 28 day period.

Credits from Flight Test

The holder of a non-UK balloon licence who has completed 5 ascents as pilot-in-command on a similar balloon type in the last 13 months will be credited with the flight test requirement.

DETAILS OF THE UK PPL(BA) FLIGHT TEST ARE GIVEN IN APPENDIX B.

C4.5 UK PPL(BA) MEDICAL REQUIREMENTS

An applicant for a UK PPL(BA) shall hold a valid National PPL (DVLA Group 1 or 2) medical declaration. For full details please refer to the CAA web site at www.caa.co.uk.

Applicants are strongly advised to ensure that they meet the appropriate medical standard before embarking on a course of training.

C4.6 UK PPL(BA) RE-VALIDATION REQUIREMENTS

The minimum flying experience required maintaining the above rating is 5 ascents as Pilot-in-Command within the previous 13 months, or satisfactorily passing the Flight Test as detailed in **Appendix B.**

A pilot who has not met the appropriate flying experience specified above but wishes to qualify for a further 13 months flying must pass a Balloon Flight test. For a period **exceeding 4 years** since the last flight flown as Pilot-in-Command must apply to the CAA through the British Balloon and Airship Club (BBAC) for an assessment of the amount of dual and solo flying to be undertaken, and the subsequent testing requirement necessary, before the Balloon Rating in the licence can be re-validated.

C4.7 ADDITIONAL BALLOON OR HOT-AIR AIRSHIP RATING

If the holder of a PPL(BA) wishes to add another Balloon Rating to his licence, the holder must pass a further Flight Test in the appropriate type of balloon and pass the additional Ground Examination.

The holder of a PPL(BA) wishing to obtain a Hot-Air Airship Rating will be required to meet/undertake the following flying experience/training requirements:-

a. Have achieved at least 5 hours experience as Pilot-in-Command of hot-air balloons.

b. Undergo at least 5 hours flying training on a hot-air airship to include at least 3 hours dual instruction, and one supervised solo flight.

c. Pass a Flight Test in a hot-air airship conducted by CAA Authorised Examiner, followed by a qualifying solo flight.

d. Pass the Aircraft Technical examination conducted by the authorised examiner. This takes the form of an oral test on the technical differences between the hot-air balloon and the hot-air airship.

C4.8 UK FLIGHT RADIOTELEPHONY OPERATOR'S LICENCE (FRTOL) REQUIREMENTS

Although a FRTOL is not a mandatory requirement for the issue of a UK PPL(BA), applicants who intend to operate radiotelephony equipment will require a FRTOL.

FULL DETAILS OF THE FRTOL REQUIREMENTS ARE CONTAINED IN SECTION B.

C5 LICENCE RE-ISSUE

C5.1 LICENCE RE-ISSUE

For a licence to be valid, a pilot must hold a current medical certificate appropriate to the licence held, and have a valid aircraft rating.

Note for UK BCPL(A) Holders

The medical certificate required for the re-issue of a UK BCPL(A) shall be a JAR-FCL Class 1 medical certificate.

60 DAY RULE

Applicants may apply for the re-issue of a licence within a period of 60 days prior to the expiry date of the licence.

Holders of a lifetime UK PPL should note that the licence itself is un-expiring, but the privileges conferred by it, and by any ratings in it, may only be exercised when the licence and the appropriate ratings are valid. Re-validation or renewal of the appropriate rating(s) is specified in Section F. Details to revalidate or renew a FRTOL (if held) are specified in Section B.

A UK National or JAR-FCL Pilot's Licence will be re-issued for a further period (5 or 10 year validity as appropriate to the licence held) subject to meeting the following:-

1. Hold a medical certificate appropriate to the licence being re-issued valid for the first day of issue of the new licence.

2. Have held a valid Certificate of Test, Certificate of Experience or Certificate of Revalidation for any type/class rating that has not expired by more than 5 years*.

*Applicants who are currently flying under the privileges of a non-UK ICAO licence and are currently flying an aircraft type endorsed <u>within</u> their UK or JAR-FCL licence, may have their licence re-issued by holding a valid medical certificate appropriate to the licence being re-issued. A QSP in current flying practice on <u>any</u> military aircraft type (aeroplane for re-issue of aeroplane licence and helicopter for re-issue of helicopter licence) may have their licence re-issued by holding a valid medical certificate appropriate to the licence being re-issued.

Applicants who are <u>not</u> flying an aircraft endorsed within their UK or JAR-FCL licence may <u>not</u> have their licence renewed until such time as an appropriate valid medical certificate and Certificate of Revalidation are obtained. Applicants may either renew an existing rating within their UK or JAR-FCL licence or may wish to transfer a type/class rating that he/she is currently flying under the privileges of their non-UK ICAO licence. Renewal of appropriate ratings or the transfer of type/class ratings is specified in Section F.

EXPIRED LICENCES

If the holder of an expired UK National or JAR-FCL pilot's licence has held a valid Certificate of Test, Certificate of Experience or Certificate of Revalidation for any type/class rating that has not expired by more than 5 years, then only the appropriate valid medical certificate must be obtained to re-issue the licence.

If the holder of a UK National or JAR-FCL pilot's licence has <u>not</u> held a valid Certificate of Test, Certificate of Experience or Certificate of Revalidation for any type/class rating that has expired by more than 5 years** they may <u>not</u> have their licence re-issued until such time as an appropriate valid medical certificate and Certificate of Revalidation are obtained. Applicants may either renew an existing rating within their UK or JAR-FCL licence or may wish to transfer a type/class rating that he/she is currently flying under the privileges of their non-UK ICAO licence. Renewal of appropriate ratings or the transfer of type/class ratings is specified in Section F.

**Where an applicant can show that he/she is currently flying under the privileges of a non-UK ICAO licence and are flying an aircraft endorsed <u>within</u> their UK or JAR-FCL licence, they may have their licence re-issued by holding a valid UK or JAR-FCL medical certificate as appropriate to the licence being re-issued. A QSP in current flying practice on <u>any</u> military aircraft type (aeroplane for re-issue of aeroplane licence and helicopter for re-issue of helicopter licence) may have their licence re-issued by holding a valid medical certificate appropriate to the licence being re-issued.

FRTOL RE-VALIDATION/RENEWAL

Details to revalidate or renew a FRTOL (if held) are specified in Section B.

C6 NPPL (SSEA/SLMG/MICROLIGHT AND POWERED PARACHUTE)

This section offers information as a basic guide to obtaining the National Private Pilot Licence (NPPL) as follows:-

C6.1 NPPL GENERAL INFORMATION

Introduction

The National Private Pilots Licence (NPPL) has been available since 30th July 2002, and comes under the auspices of the National Pilots Licensing Group Limited (NPLG). NPLG Ltd receives technical support from Popular Flying Association (PFA), Aircraft Owners and Pilots Association (AOPA), British Gliding Association (BGA) and British Microlight Aircraft Association (BMAA). Personnel Licensing Department is not responsible for dealing with any enquiries regarding this licence and associated ratings.

The responsibility for dealing with all NPPL SSEA/ SLMG/Microlight customer enquiries rests with the following representative bodies:-

For SSEA enquiries contact AOPA.
For SLMG enquiries contact BGA.
For Microlight and Powered Parachute enquiries contact BMAA.

Contact details can be found in Section A, Appendix E.

Further details can be found on their respective web sites:-

www.nppl.uk.com
www.aopa.co.uk
www.pfa.org.uk
www.bmaa.org
www.gliding.co.uk

The aim of the NPPL is to devolve the regulation of some recreational flying to these representative bodies. The licence has been specifically designed to meet the requirements of the recreational flyer and is easier to obtain than the standard JAR-PPL. Medically, this devolution means changing from an aviation medical examination system, using a network of specially qualified doctors, to a declaration of medical fitness by you, the pilot. To validate this declaration, and to prevent concealment of disease, it has to be endorsed by a doctor with access to your medical records, your General Practitioner (GP).

The holder of a NPPL (SSEA) may, subject to appropriate differences training, exercise the privileges of their licence on microlight aeroplanes and SLMG's.

In order to permit holders of NPPL's who wish to instruct on microlight aeroplanes and SLMG's upon application to the CAA and, providing evidence of having undergone the required training and experience is produced, the holder of a NPPL may be granted an Exemption from the requirements of the Air Navigation Order 2005 to permit the licence holder to provide instruction in microlight and SLMG's only. These Exemptions issued will be for a limited period to permit more permanent administrative procedures to be formulated by the CAA which will be incorporated into a future amendment to the ANO following the necessary consultative process.

Privileges

Details of licence and rating privileges can be found in Schedule 8 of the Air Navigation Order, (please also refer to Section A, Appendix F).

The NPPL is a sub-ICAO licence and therefore is restricted for use in G-registered aircraft within UK airspace. For flights outside of the United Kingdom please refer to Schedule 8, Part A, Section 3 of the Air Navigation Order or Section A, Appendix F of LASORS.

Important Note: **The following information is for guidance purposes only and has been supplied by the aforementioned organisations. Applicants wishing to obtain an NPPL should refer to the NPPL web site at www.nppl.uk.com to ensure that the information is still current and has not changed since publication of this document.**

C6.2 NPPL (SSEA/SLMG)

Minimum Age

An applicant for a NPPL(SEP/SLMG) shall be at least 17 years of age. The minimum age for the first solo flight is 16 years of age.

Licence Validity

The NPPL(SSEA/SLMG) will be issued with a lifetime validity.

At present ratings included in a NPPL are issued with a 12 month validity period. On reflection, it has been decided that applying such a date to the initial issue could cause confusion if the rating included in the licence is maintained by means of the experience method as detailed in Schedule 8 Section 3 of the Air Navigation Order 2005. Accordingly, in future the rating page of the NPPL will only show the date that a Skill Test was undertaken and a validity column will not now be included in the Certificate of Revalidation page.

Flying Training/Experience Requirements

An applicant for a NPPL (SSEA/SLMG) shall have completed at least **32** hours flight time as pilot of aeroplanes (excluding Navigation Skill Test and General Skill Test). NPPL(SSEA) training shall be completed at a Registered Facility or Flight Training Organisation, and training for the NPPL(SLMG) at an approved BGA site. This must include the following particular requirements:-

a. **22 hours** dual instruction (to include 1 hour instrument appreciation);

b. **10 hours** solo flight time (to include at least 4 hours of solo cross-country flight time, including one cross-country flight of at least 185km (100nm) in the course of which full stop landings at two aerodromes other than the aerodrome of departure shall be made;

c. **Navigation Skill Test (NST)** (minimum of 1 hour duration and to be taken prior to undertaking the qualifying solo cross-country flight);

d. **General Skill Test (GST)** (minimum of 1 hour duration)

Note

- An applicant may not take the General Skill Test until **all** associated flying training has been completed and the associated theoretical knowledge examinations have been passed.
- The General Skill Test shall be taken within 6 months of the completion of training and all sections of the test must be completed within 6 months of the first attempt. If the applicant does not pass all sections of the skill test at the first attempt, the section(s) that have been failed may be attempted in a further test(s).
- There is no limit to the number of tests that may be taken.

Credits from Flying Training

Allowances against training for the grant of a NPPL(SSEA/SLMG) may be given for holders of other licences (UK/JAR-FCL/NPPL or Non-UK), military flying experience and other qualifications. For full details, applicants should refer to the cross-crediting document within the licence allowances section on the NPPL web site at www.nppl.uk.com.

Theoretical Knowledge Examination Requirements

An applicant for a NPPL(SSEA/SLMG) is currently required to pass the JAR-FCL PPL(A) theoretical knowledge examinations as detailed in Section C1.3, and will be subject to the same pass standards and validity periods.

The requirement to pass the JAR-FCL PPL(A) theoretical knowledge examinations will be reconsidered after a suitable period of operation of the NPPL, with the intention of providing an option to take a simpler written examination, with theoretical knowledge syllabus and examinations reduced to a level consistent with the practical and relatively limited needs of the NPPL(SEP) holder.

Full details of the NPPL(SEP/SLMG) syllabi of flying training and Skill Tests and theoretical knowledge requirements can be found on the NPPL web site at www.nppl.uk.com.

Upgrade to JAR-FCL PPL(A)

The holder of a NPPL with SSEA aircraft rating wishing to obtain a JAR-FCL PPL(A) shall have completed on SEP Aeroplanes:-

a. At least 45 hours flight time, of which at least 35 hours must have been as a pilot of SEP aeroplanes. A maximum of 5 hours may be completed in an approved FNPT or flight simulator. This flight time must include:-

   1. **20hours** dual instruction of SEP aeroplanes with a JAR qualified instructor;

2. **10 hours** solo flight time on SEP aeroplanes which must include 5 hours solo cross country flight time including one cross country flight of at least 270 km (150 nm), during which full stop landings at two different aerodromes different from the aerodrome of departure shall be made as per JAR-FCL 1.125.

b. Have passed the JAR-FCL PPL(A) Theoretical Knowledge Examinations in all subjects.

c. Hold a valid JAR-FCL Class 1 or 2 medical certificate.

d. Pass the JAR-FCL PPL(A) Skill Test as detailed in Section C1.4.

C6.3 NPPL (MICROLIGHT AND POWERED PARACHUTE)

Minimum Age

An applicant for a NPPL(Microlight) shall be at least 17 years of age. The minimum age for the first solo flight is 16 years of age.

Licence Validity

The NPPL(Microlight) will be issued with a lifetime validity.

Flying Training/Experience Requirements

The training requirements for a NPPL(Microlight) remain unchanged from the former requirements for a UK PPL(A) Microlight. Applicants may obtain either an "unrestricted" licence or a "restricted" licence (which includes operational limitations).

NPPL(Microlight) - Restricted with Operational Limitations

Applicants shall be required to complete a minimum of **15 hours** training as pilot of microlight aeroplanes, including not less than **7 hours** as Pilot-in-Command in the 9 months prior to the date of application for licence issue. In addition, applicants will be required to pass a NPPL (Microlight) General Flight Test

When a NPPL(Microlight) is issued with operational limitations, it will impose the following constraints on the licence holder:-

Limitation 1:
The licence is valid only for flights within the United Kingdom, the Channel Islands and the Isle of Man; provided that it shall be valid for flights within the territory of other Contracting States with the prior written permission of the appropriate Authority of such States.

Limitation 2:
No person in addition to the pilot shall be carried in the aeroplane other than a qualified flying instructor in an aeroplane equipped with dual controls provided that where the pilot has gained not less than 25 hours experience on microlight aeroplanes, including not less than 10 hours as Pilot-in-Command and such experience has been entered in his/her personal flying log book and has been certified by a person authorised by the Authority in writing to sign Certificates of Test or Certificates of Experience in a Private Pilot's Licence, then this Limitation (numbered 2) shall cease to apply.

Limitation 3:
No flight shall commence or continue unless:

a. the surface wind speed is 15 knots or less, and

b. there is no cloud below 1000 feet above ground level over the take-off site and over the planned route including the landing site, and

c. the flight can be conducted in a flight visibility of not less than 10 kilometres.

Limitation 4:
The aeroplane shall not fly further than 8 nautical miles from the take-off site.

Limitation 5:
No flight shall commence or continue at night.

Limitation 6:
The aeroplane shall not fly over any congested area of a city, town or settlement.

Note: The Limitation No. 2 will cease to apply when the minimum flying experience quoted in the Limitation has been achieved.

Limitations No. 3 & 4 will be removed from the licence, upon recommendation to the CAA by the BMAA upon completion of at least 25 hours experience in microlights, including at least 5 hours training in flight navigation in microlights supervised by a flying instructor within the 9 months prior to the date of application for the removal of the limitations. This navigation training, which forms part of the BMAA syllabus shall include two solo 40nm cross-country flights, during each of which the applicant landed at least at one other site not less than 15nm from the take-off site at which the flight began. The two solo cross-country flights must be flown over different routes and to different sites.

NPPL(Microlight)-without Operational Limitations

Applicants shall be required to complete a minimum of **25 hours** training as pilot of microlight aeroplanes, including not less than **5 hours** navigation training (to include 3 hours solo cross-country and two 40nm cross-country flights during which the applicant landed at least at one other site not less than 15nm from the take-off site at which the flight began, and must be flown over different routes and to different sites) and **10 hours** as Pilot-in-Command of microlight aeroplanes within the 9 months prior to the date of application for licence issue. In addition applicants will be required to complete a NPPL(Microlight) General Flight Test.

Credits from Flying Training

Allowances against training for the grant of a NPPL(Microlight) may be given for holders of other licences (UK/JAR-FCL/NPPL or Non-UK), military flying experience and other qualifications. For full details, applicants should refer to the cross-crediting document within the licence allowances section on the NPPL web site.

Theoretical Knowledge Examination Requirements

An applicant for a NPPL(Microlight) is currently required to pass theoretical knowledge examinations in the following subjects:-

1. Aviation Law, Flight Rules & Procedures
2. Human Performance & Limitations
3. Navigation & Meteorology
4. Aircraft (General)
5. Aircraft (Type) (Oral as part of the NPPL Microlight GFT)

Full details of the NPPL(Microlight) syllabi of flying training, flight tests and theoretical knowledge requirements can be found on the NPPL web site.

Microlight pilots wishing to convert from weight shift to 3-axis control systems, or the reverse, should undertake adequate conversion training and pass the Additional Control System Test (ACST) conducted by an appropriately qualified microlight examiner.

POWERED PARACHUTE

All flying training must be carried out under the supervision of a flying instructor holding a valid AFI rating or a FI rating on the type of powered parachute on which the training is conducted. Solo flying may only be carried out when the flying instructor is present at the take-off site at which the flight commences.

Flight in any powered parachute is acceptable and should follow either the dual training system for a two seat aeroplane or the solo training system for a single seat aeroplane.

Applicants may obtain either an "unrestricted" licence or a "restricted" licence (which includes operational limitations).

With Operational Limitations

Applicants shall be required to produce evidence of having satisfactorily completed a course of training to a syllabus recognised by the CAA and pass a Flight Test. The syllabus of training must provide for a minimum of **4 hours** of flight time in a powered parachute including not less than **1 hour** as solo PIC and not less than **25** take-offs and full stop landings of which at least **6** must be as solo PIC in the 9 months prior to the date of application. In addition applicants will be required to pass a GFT. The Flight Test can be included in the minimum 4 hours of flight time.

The licence will impose the following constraints on the licence holder:-

Limitation 1:
The licence is valid only for flights within the United Kingdom, the Channel Islands and the Isle of Man; provided that it shall be valid for flights within the territory of other Contracting States with the prior written permission of the appropriate Authority of such States.

Limitation 2:
No person in addition to the pilot shall be carried in the aeroplane other than a qualified flying instructor in an aeroplane equipped with dual controls provided that where the pilot has gained not less than 15 hours experience on Powered Parachute aeroplanes, including not less than 6 hours as solo PIC and such experience has been entered in his personal flying log book and has been certified by a person authorised by the CAA in writing to sign Cs of T or Cs of E in a Private Pilot's Licence, then this Limitation (numbered 2) shall cease to apply.

Limitation 3:
No flight shall commence or continue unless:

a. the surface wind speed is 10 knots or less, and

b. there is no cloud below 1000 feet above ground level over the take-off site and over the planned route including the landing site, and

c. the flight can be conducted in a flight visibility of not less than 10 kilometres.

Limitation 4:
The aeroplane shall not fly further than 8 nautical miles from the take-off site.

Limitation 5:
No flight shall commence or continue at night.

Limitation 6:
The aeroplane shall not fly over any congested area of a city, town or settlement.

Note: The Limitation No. 2 will cease to apply without application to the Authority when the minimum flying experience quoted in the Limitation has been achieved.

Limitations No. 3 & 4 will be removed from the licence, free of charge, on application to the Authority when the holder of the licence has obtained at least 15 hours experience in Powered Parachutes, including at least 5 hours training in flight navigation in Powered Parachutes, supervised by a flying instructor, within the 9 months prior to the date of application for the removal of the limitations. This navigational shall include two 25 nm solo cross-country flights, during each of which the applicant landed at least at one other site not less than 10 nm from the take-off site at which the flight began. The two-solo cross-country flights must be flown over different routes and to different sites.

Without Operational Limitations

Applicants shall be required to produce evidence of having satisfactorily completed a course of training to a syllabus recognised by the CAA and pass a Flight Test. The syllabus of training must provide for a minimum of **15 hours** of flight time in a powered parachute supervised by a flying instructor in a powered parachute. The total must include not less than **6 hours** as solo PIC, not less than **25** take-offs and full stop landings of which at least **6** must be as solo PIC, not less than **5 hours** training in navigation during which at least **3 hours** must be as solo PIC and must include two solo 25nm cross-country flights during each of which the applicant landed at least at one other site not less than 10nm from the take-off site at which the flight began. The two solo cross-country flights must be flown over different routes and to different sites.

The hours laid down must be within the 9 months prior to the date of application. The Flight Test can be included in the minimum 15 hours of flight time.

Credits from Flying Training

Non-UK licence holders and military pilots who have previous experience on Powered Parachutes should contact the BMAA for details of any credits that may be given.

Theoretical Knowledge Examination Requirements

An applicant for a Powered Parachute licence is currently required to pass theoretical knowledge examinations in the following subjects:-

1. Aviation Law, Flight Rules & Procedures
2. Human Performance & Limitations
3. Navigation & Meteorology
4. Aircraft (General)
5. Aircraft (Type) (Oral as part of the GFT)

Examinations 1, 2 and 3 are common to Microlights and Powered Parachutes. The Aircraft (General) and Aircraft (Type) are specific to Powered Parachutes.

Credits from Examinations

- The holder of a valid Non-UK Pilot's licence (Aeroplanes) issued by another ICAO Contracting State may be credited the examinations in Navigation, Meteorology, Aircraft (General) and Aircraft (Type).
- A QSP in the UK Armed Forces may be credited the examinations in Navigation, Meteorology and Aircraft (General).
- A holder of a valid UK or another ICAO Contracting State's Flight Navigator's Licence and UK Military Navigators may be credited the examinations in Navigation and Meteorology.

Flight Test

Applicants are required to pass the General Flight Test conducted by a CAA authorised PPL Powered Parachute Examiner in a Powered Parachute.

C6.4 NPPL MEDICAL REQUIREMENTS

An applicant for a NPPL shall hold a valid NPPL medical declaration (DVLA Group 1 or Group 2 Standard) or a JAR-FCL medical certificate. For full information regarding the medical requirements please refer to the CAA web site at www.caa.co.uk.

C6.5 UK FLIGHT RADIOTELEPHONY OPERATOR'S LICENCE (FRTOL) REQUIREMENTS

Pilots who intend to operate radiotelephony equipment will require an FRTOL.

Full details of the FRTOL requirements are contained in Section B.

C6.6 RE-VALIDATION/RENEWAL OF A NPPL (SSEA)

Re-validation

Section 3 of Schedule 8 of the Air Navigation Order 2005 states that the SSEA rating included in a NPPL may be validated by means of a continuous experience process or by means of a skill test. The Order does not stipulate a validity period for the skill test so the CAA sets out below a clarification of its policy:-

For the SSEA rating to be valid so that a pilot is entitled to exercise its privileges on a flight, the licence holder must either:-

a. have completed 6 hours flight time in the 12 month period preceding the flight including not less than 4 hours as pilot in command and have completed an instructional flight of at least 1 hour in the preceding 24 months; or

b. undertaken and passed a Skill Test with an Authorised Examiner within the previous 12 months. The Examiner conducting the test will sign the Certificate of Revalidation Page of the NPPL and enter the date of the test but no expiry date will be shown in view of the fact that validation may, in the future be maintained via the experience route.

It is for the individual NPPL holder to ensure that the rating contained in the licence is valid pursuant to one of the above means before any flight is undertaken.

Renewal

Where a NPPL SSEA class rating has expired for not more than 5 years, applicants will be required to pass the NPPL GST and hold a valid NPPL medical certificate.

Where a NPPL SSEA class rating has expired by more than 5 years but less than 10 years, applicants will be required to undergo a course of training as specified by a flight instructor and pass the NPPL NST and GST, and hold a valid NPPL medical certificate.

Where a NPPL SSEA class rating has expired by more than 10 years, applicants will be required to undergo dual instruction at the discretion of a flight instructor which must include 2 hours of stall awareness/spin avoidance training. Also, as PIC of aeroplanes, he/she must include:-

a. 4 hours solo general handling exercises;

b. 4 hours solo cross-country flying, including the NPPL qualifying cross-country flight.

In addition, the applicant will be required to pass all the JAR-FCL PPL(A) theoretical knowledge examinations, the NPPL NST and GST, and hold a valid NPPL medical certificate.

C6.7 RE-VALIDATION/RENEWAL OF A NPPL(SLMG) AND NPPL(MICROLIGHT AND POWERED PARACHUTE)

Re-validation

The minimum flying experience required to maintain the above ratings is 5 hours as pilot (3 hours as Pilot-in-Command) in an aircraft of the same class as the rating in the licence within the 13 months preceding the date of issue of the new Certificate of Experience. The remaining time may be made up of:-

a. Pilot-in-Command under supervision (PIC U/S) flight time gained with a flying instructor on a successful check flight or with an authorised Examiner on a successful Flight Test for the grant or revalidation of a rating.

b. Dual flying instruction flown with a flying instructor but only if, at the end of the dual flight or flights, the instructor considered the pilot was fit to fly as Pilot-in-Command and certifies the logbook to that effect.

The flying must be completed within the existing validity period of the rating.

Renewal

NPPL(SLMG)

Where a NPPL SLMG class rating has expired for not more than 5 years, applicants will be required to pass the NPPL(SLMG) GST and hold a valid NPPL medical certificate.

Where a NPPL SLMG class rating has expired by more than 5 years but less than 10 years, applicants will be required to undergo a course of training as specified by a flight instructor and pass the NPPL(SLMG) NST and GST, and hold a valid NPPL medical certificate.

Where a NPPL SLMG class rating has expired by more than 10 years, applicants will be required to undergo dual instruction at the discretion of a flight instructor which must include 2 hours of stall awareness/spin avoidance training. Also, as PIC of aeroplanes, he/she must include;

a. 4 hours solo general handling exercises;

b. 4 hours solo cross-country flying, including the NPPL qualifying cross-country flight.

In addition, the applicant will be required to pass all the JAR-FCL PPL(A) theoretical knowledge examinations, the NPPL NST and GST, and hold a valid NPPL medical declaration.

NPPL Microlight

Where the holder of a NPPL(Microlight) licence or rating has not flown as pilot-in-command of an aircraft for up to a period of 5 years, he/she will be required to complete the following:-

a. Pass the NPPL(Microlight) GFT as appropriate;

b. Pass a Microlight Aeroplanes general (Part 2) oral examination conducted by a Microlight Flight Examiner, the examination to include pilot maintenance and conditions of the Permit to Fly;

c. Hold a valid NPPL medical declaration.

Where the holder of NPPL(Microlight) licence or rating has not flown as Pilot-in-Command of an aircraft for between 5 and 10 years, he/she will be required to complete the following:-

a. undergo a course of training as specified by a flight instructor and pass the NPPL(Microlight) GFT (and oral examination). The Flight Test must include a cross country flight to another airfield at least 30 minutes flight time from the aerodrome of departure, a join into the traffic pattern at that airfield, and landing with a return flight to the airfield of departure;

b. Pass the NPPL(Microlight) theoretical knowledge examination in Aviation Law;

c. Unless holding a lapsed license with Microlight rating, pass the NPPL(Microlight) theoretical knowledge examination in Aircraft General part 1;

d. Hold a valid NPPL medical declaration.

No credit is given for pilots who have not flown as PIC for a period of 10 years or more.

Powered Parachute

Applicants wishing to renew their Powered Parachute rating should contact the BMAA for details of the requirements.

APPENDICES TO SECTION C

- Appendix A UK PPL(G) FLIGHT TEST
- Appendix B UK PPL(BA) FLYING TRAINING EXERCISES AND FLIGHT TEST
- Appendix C UK PPL(BA) SYLLABUS OF GROUND EXAMINATIONS

APPENDIX A UK PPL(G) FLIGHT TEST

The syllabus lists all the items which should be covered during training and which may be examined during the Flight Test. The candidate will be required to demonstrate a satisfactory standard of knowledge and handling in all the items included in the Flight Test.

The Flight Test will consist of:

a. Pre-flight Inspection.

b. Starting procedure: running up.

c. Taxying.

d. Take-off and landing into wind.

e. Take-off and landing cross-wind, within the limitations of the type of gyroplane.

f. Straight and level flying at pre-determined power settings and airspeeds, including at the lowest possible speed to maintain level flight.

g. Climbing and descending turns.

h. Recovery, at a safe altitude, from a point where forward speed has been reduced below the minimum speed for the maintenance of level flight:

   1. by application of power, and

   2. without application of power.

i. Go-around from a baulked approach.

j. Flight into and out of a restricted landing area, the landing to achieve the lowest possible touch-down speed consistent with safety.

k. A 'power-off' approach and landing, to touch down as near as possible to a selected point.

l. Shut down procedure.

APPENDIX B UK PPL(BA) FLYING TRAINING EXERCISES AND FLIGHT TEST

1 FLYING TRAINING EXERCISES

The numbered exercises detailed below should be completed during the 16 hours flying training:

Exercise No.	Training Details
1.	Preparation for flight: explain met. forecast, selection of launch site, carry out flight planning (to include load chart calculations and navigation).
2.	Familiarisation: crew and passenger briefing.
3.	Assembly and layout.
4.	Inflation.
5.	Take-off in wind less than 8 knots.
6.	Take-off in wind less than 5 knots without shelter.
7.	Take-off in wind more than 8 knots.
8.	Climb to level flight.
9.	Level flight.
10.	Descent to level flight.
11.	Emergencies - systems.
12.	Emergencies - fire.
13.	Navigation.
14.	Fuel Management.
15.	Approach from low level.
16.	Approach from high level.
17.	Operating at low level.
18.	Landing in wind less than 8 knots.
19.	Landing in wind more than 8 knots.
20.	Tethered flight.

a. Notes on the required standard are in the BBAC Pilot Training Record.

b. Notes on the recommended training schedule for one-man balloons and for gas balloons are available from BBAC.

2. FLIGHT TEST

2.1 All the listed items should be carried out, subject to the Balloon's characteristics. Where an item is not appropriate, the Examiner should make this clear on the Test Report Form.

2.1.1 Preparation for Flight

Weather check, launch site check, flight planning, load calculation, fuel state check, crew briefing, passenger briefing.

2.1.2 Pre-inflation

Rigging envelope and burner, testing burner, equipment check.

2.1.3 Inflation

Safety and control, operation of burner, instructions to crew.

2.1.4 Take-off

Pre-take-off checks, assessment of wind.

2.1.5 Climb

Normal, fast

2.1.6 Straight and Level Flight

Maintenance

2.1.7 Descent

Normal, using parachute/vent

2.1.8 Navigation

Use of maps and recognition of features, position plotting, assessment of wind

2.1.9 Management Procedure

Procedure for tank change over and refuelling; tank arrangement

2.1.10 Approach for Landing

Choice of field, checks, choice of level

2.1.11 Other Emergencies (simulated)

Fire in the air and on the ground, pilot-light failure, procedure and checks for emergency lighting

2.1.12 Landing

Pre-landing checks, choice of field

2.1.13 Post Flight Actions

Checks, packing away, landowner consultation, recording of flight times

Section A
Section B
Section C PPL
Section D
Section E
Section F
Section G
Section H
Section I
Section J
Section K
Index

APPENDIX C **UK PPL(BA) SYLLABUS OF GROUND EXAMINATIONS**

1 AVIATION LAW, FLIGHT RULES AND PROCEDURES

1.1 The UK Aeronautical Information Publication, NOTAMs and Aeronautical Information Circulars.

A detailed knowledge of the operational provisions of:

1.1.1 *Aerodromes*

Limitations of use; customs facilities; identification beacons.

1.1.2 *Air Traffic Rules and Services*

Definitions: Visual Flight Rules, Instrument Flight Rules. Types of airspace and air traffic service units. The flight plan. Airprox reporting procedures. Altimeter setting procedures. Flight in various types of airspace, e.g. at aerodromes, within flight information regions, control zones and airways, on advisory routes and in advisory service areas. Airspace restrictions and hazards. Ground signals and lights. Marshalling signals.

1.1.3 *Meteorology*

Methods of obtaining flight forecasts (but not names of stations).

1.1.4 *Facilitation*

Arrival, departure and transit of civil aircraft on international flights. Private flights; documentary requirements and advance notice or permit requirements. Arrival, departure and transit of passengers and crew. Customs, public health and security requirements.

1.1.5 *Search and Rescue*

Organisation and Responsibility. Aircraft not equipped with radio. Visual distress and urgency signals.

1.1.6 Any information which may from time to time be added to the AIP, NOTAMs and AICs, and of which a private pilot should have a working knowledge.

1.2 The Air Navigation Order 2005

A general knowledge of the provisions, with particular reference to the following:

- Aircraft to be Registered Article 3
- Application for Registration Article 4 (6) (10) (11) (12) (13)
- Certificate of Airworthiness Article 8, 9 (2)
- Certificate of Maintenance Review Article 14 (1)
- Technical log Article 15 (1) (2)
- Inspection, overhaul, repair, replacement and modification Article 16 (1) (3) (4)
- Equipment to be carried Article 19 (1) (2)
- Radio Equipment Article 20 (1)
- Engine and Propeller log books Article 22
- Weight Schedule Article 23
- Composition of Crew Article 25 (1)
- Crew Licences Article 26 (1) (7)
- Personal Flying log books Article 35
- Flying Instruction Article 36
- Pilot to remain at Controls Article 50
- Duties of a Commander Article 52
- Passenger briefing by Commander Article 53
- Operation of Aircraft Radio Article 55 (1) (2) (3) (4) (5)
- Flight Data Recorders Article 62
- Towing of Gliders Article 63
- Picking up of articles or persons Article 65
- Dropping of Articles Article 66
- Dropping of Persons Article 67
- Carriage of Munitions Article 69
- Carriage of Dangerous Goods Article 70

- Carriage of Persons Article 71
- Endangering Safety of Aircraft Article 73
- Endangering Safety of Persons and Property Article 74
- Drunkenness in aircraft Article 75
- Smoking in aircraft Article76
- Authority of Commander Article 77
- Flying Displays Article 80
- Documents to be Carried Article 86
- Production of Documents Article 88 (1) (3) (4)
- Offences in Relation to Documents Article 94 (1) (2) and Records(3) (4)
- Rules of the Air Article 95 (2) (3) (4) (5)
- Power to Prohibit or Restrict Flying Article 96
- Balloons, Kites and Airships Article 97
- Licensed Aerodromes Article 128 (1)(2)
- Aviation Fuel Article 137 (3)(4)
- Penalties Article 148
- Interpretation Article 155
- Classification of Aircraft Schedule 2 (Part A)
- A and B Conditions Schedule 3
- Categories of Aircraft Schedule 3 (Part B)
- Aircraft Equipment Schedule 4
- Radio and Radio Navigation Equipment Schedule 5
- Privileges of Private Pilot's Licence (Aeroplanes) Schedule 8, Sub-Section 1
- Privileges of Private Pilot's Licence Schedule 8, (Helicopters/Gyroplanes) Sub-Section 2
- Privileges of Ratings Schedule 8, Part B
- Certificate of Test or Article 26 and Experience Schedule 8, Part C insofar as they relate to the Private Pilot's Licence

Note: Questions in the details in the schedules will not be asked except where specifically indicated above.

1.3 The Rules of the Air Regulations 1996

- Interpretation Section I
- General Section II
- Lights and Signals to be shown by aircraftSection III
- General Flight Rules Section IV
- Visual Flight Rules Section V
- Instrument Flight Rule Section VI
- Aerodrome Traffic Rules Section VII
- Special Rules Section VIII
- Aerodrome Signals and Markings:
- Visual and Aural Signals Section IX

1.4 The Civil Aviation (Investigation of Air Accidents) Regulations 1996

Notification of Accidents - Regulations 5 & 6

1.5 The Air Navigation (Investigation of Air Accidents involving Civil and Military Aircraft or Installations) Regulations 1996

Duty to furnish information relating to accidents - Regulations 5 & 6

Note 1: Publications may not be consulted during the examination

Note 2: Candidates will not be required to memorise details of geographical positions or of special procedures applicable to a particular aerodrome, flight information region, control zone or airway.

2 NAVIGATION

2.1 *Aeronautical Charts*

Practical use of the 1:500,000 (Lambert Conformal Conic), and the UK 1:250,000 topographical charts, including a knowledge of: representative fraction, methods of indicating relief, the principal ICAO chart symbols, isogonals, latitude and longitude, plotting positions, measuring tracks and distances.

2.2 Units of distance and height used in navigation, viz. nautical miles, statute miles, kilometres, metres and feet. Conversion from one unit to another.

2.3 Track, heading (true, magnetic and compass). Variation and deviation. airspeed (IAS, RAS, TAS), ground speed, wind velocity and drift.

2.4 The use of the navigational computer for the determination of heading, airspeed, groundspeed, wind velocity, track and drift angle. The use of the slide rule for solving simple fuel calculations. Methods of determining track error and corrections to heading by the 1 in 60 rule, and by 5 degree and 10 degree lines. Corrections to ETA. Flight Planning, CAA Form 48.

2.5 The direct reading magnetic compass; unreliability during turns and accelerations; the effect of metal objects placed in the vicinity of the compass.

3 METEOROLOGY

3.1 *Properties of the Atmosphere*

Relationship between temperature, pressure and density. International Standard Atmosphere.

3.2 *Wind*

Relationship between wind and isobars; gusts, squalls and turbulence; diurnal variation of wind; variation of wind with height; sea brezes; airflow in vicinity of high ground and low level wind shear.

3.3 *Clouds and Precipitation*

Clouds associated with different types of precipitation; flight conditions in and near clouds giving precipitation; cumulonimbus and thunderstorms and orographic effects.

3.4 *Visibility*

Fog, mist, haze and their differences; formation and clearance of radiation and advection fog (diurnal variations); hill fog, and vertifal and oblique visibility.

3.5 *Fronts and Pressure Systems*

Characteristics of warm and cold front and occlusions; and weather associated with depressions, anticyclones, cols and different air masses.

3.6 *Icing*

Airframe icing in relation to cloud types; hoar frost; rain ice, and engine icing.

3.7 *Altimetry*

Correction for variations in surface pressure; variation of pressure with height and QFE and QNH.

3.8 *Forecasts, Reports and Warnings*

Contents of and terms and symbols used in aviation forecast documents (including TAFs), in other forms of forecast service (including pre-recorded voice), and weather reports (including METARs), available to the private pilot, and SIGMETs and Aerodrome warnings.

SECTION D

COMMERCIAL PILOT LICENCE

The UK Civil Aviation Authority currently issues the following classes of Commercial Pilot Licence.

Each section details the requirements to obtain each licence, including flying training, ground examinations and flight tests. Details of credits against training are also given.

D1 JAR-FCL CPL (AEROPLANE)

This section offers information as a basic guide to obtaining a JAR-FCL Commercial Pilot Licence (Aeroplane) – JAR-FCL CPL(A) as follows:-

For full details you are advised to refer to **JAR-FCL 1 Subpart D.**

D1.1 JAR-FCL CPL(A) GENERAL INFORMATION

Privileges

Details of licence privileges can be found in Schedule 8 of the Air Navigation Order, (please refer also to Section A, Appendix F).

Minimum Age

An applicant for a JAR-FCL CPL(A) shall be at least 18 years of age.

Licence Validity

A JAR-FCL CPL(A) will be issued for a maximum period of 5 years.

UK BCPL(A) conversion to JAR-FCL CPL(A)

Although JAR-FCL includes provision for the issue of a JAR-FCL licence on the basis of an existing national licence, it does not provide for the conversion of a UK BCPL(A) to a JAR-FCL CPL(A). However, it has been agreed that a BCPL(A) holder who has passed the UK national examinations at BCPL, CPL or ATPL level, can apply for the issue of a JAR-FCL CPL(A) (Restricted) subject to satisfying specific criteria. Full details, including requirements and licence restrictions, can be found in Section D2.

D1.2 JAR-FCL CPL(A) COURSES

A JAR-FCL CPL(A) may be obtained by completing an approved Integrated Course or approved Modular Course of training. Applicants intending to train in another JAA Member State should refer to Section A8.

INTEGRATED COURSES

The Integrated Course is a full time course of ground and flying training run by a Flying Training Organisation approved to conduct such courses. There are three integrated courses available:

1 Commercial Pilot Licence (Aeroplane) Integrated Course

The aim of this course is to train pilots to the level of proficiency necessary for the issue of a CPL(A), excluding flight instructor training and instrument rating instruction. The course shall last for between 9 and 24 months.

This course consists of a minimum of 150 hours of flying training and 300 hours (reduced to 200 hours for PPL holders) of theoretical knowledge instruction. See **D1.2(A)** for details.

2 Commercial Pilot Licence (Aeroplane) with Instrument Rating (I/R) Integrated Course

The aim of this course is to train pilots to the level of proficiency necessary to operate single pilot, single-engine or multi-engine aeroplanes in commercial air transportation and to obtain the CPL(A)/IR. The course shall last between 9 and 30 months.

This course consists of a minimum of 180 hours of flying training and 500 hours of theoretical knowledge instruction. See **D1.2(B)** for details.

3 Airline Transport Pilot (Aeroplane) Integrated Course

The aim of this course is to train pilots to the level of proficiency necessary to enable them to operate as Co-Pilot on multi-pilot, multi-engine aeroplanes in commercial air transportation and to obtain the CPL(A)/IR. The course shall last between 12 and 36 months.

The course consists of a minimum of 195 hours of flying training and 750 hours of theoretical knowledge instruction. The course also includes training in multi-crew co-operation for the operation of multi-pilot aeroplanes. See **D1.2(C)** for details.

Modular Course

The aim of this course is to train a PPL(A) holder to the level of proficiency necessary for the issue of a CPL(A).

This course is designed for applicants who do not wish to undertake a full time course of integrated training or who wish to stagger their training by completing approved 'modules' of approved training over a period of time, i.e. instrument rating course, Multi-Crew Co-operation Course (MCC), ATPL theoretical knowledge instruction etc.

The course consists of a minimum of 25 hours of flying training and 200 hours of theoretical knowledge instruction for CPL(A) and 650 hours theoretical knowledge instruction for ATPL(A) (see **D1.2D** for details).

D1.2(A) JAR-FCL CPL(A) INTEGRATED COURSE FLYING TRAINING/ EXPERIENCE REQUIREMENTS

A graduate from an approved CPL(A) Integrated Course shall have completed a minimum of **150** hours of flight time, not including type rating training. This must include the particular requirements specified in **D1.2(A) a, b and c below**. Each of these requirements must be met in full but hours may be credited, where appropriate, towards more than one requirement except where stated otherwise.

a. i. **80 hours** dual instruction of which up to 5 hours may be instrument ground time;

ii. **70 hours** as Pilot-in-Command (PIC);

iii. **20 hours** cross country flight time as Pilot-in-Command, including, a VFR cross-country flight of at least 540km (300 nm) in the course of which full-stop landings at two aerodromes different from the aerodromes of departure shall be made;

iv. **5 hours** of the flight instruction shall be carried out in a complex type unless previously completed.

b. **5 hours** night flying as Pilot of Aeroplanes, comprising of at least **3 hours** dual instruction, including **1 hour** cross-country navigation. and **5** solo take-offs and 5 full-stop landings.

c. **10 hours** instrument flight instruction, of which up to **5 hours** may be instrument ground time in a FNPT I or II or a Flight Simulator.

D1.2(A) NOTES

An applicant may be admitted to training as an ab-initio entrant, or as a holder of a PPL(A) or PPL(H) (excluding NPPL) issued in accordance with ICAO Annex 1. In the case of a PPL(A) or PPL(H) entrant, 50% of the aircraft hours flown by the entrant prior to the course may be credited towards the required flight instruction up to a credit of 40 hours flying experience or 45 hours if an aeroplane night flying qualification has been obtained, of which up to 20 hours may be dual instruction. This credit for the hours shall be at the discretion of the FTO and entered into the applicant's training record, and is subject to confirmation by the FTO at the time of application. In the case of a student pilot who does not hold a pilot licence and with the approval of the Authority, a FTO may designate certain dual exercises (see AMC FCL 1.160 & 1.165(a)(3), phase 2 & 3) to be flown in a helicopter of a TMG up to a maximum of 20 hours.

An applicant failing or unable to complete the entire CPL(A) course may apply to the Authority for the theoretical knowledge examination and skill test for a lower licence.

An applicant wishing to transfer to another FTO during a course of training shall apply to the Authority for a formal assessment of the further hours of training required at another FTO.

D1.2(B) JAR-FCL CPL(A)/IR INTEGRATED COURSE FLYING TRAINING/ EXPERIENCE REQUIREMENTS

A graduate from an approved CPL(A)/IR Integrated Course must have completed a minimum of **180 hours** of flight time, not including type rating training. This must include the particular requirements specified in D1.2(B) a, b and c below. Each of these requirements must be met in full but hours may be credited, where appropriate, towards more than one requirement except where stated otherwise.

a. i. **80 hours** dual instruction of which up to 40 hours may be instrument ground time;

   ii. **100 hours** as Pilot-in-Command (PIC), including 50 hours VFR flight and 50 hours instrument flight time as Student Pilot-in-Command (SPIC). (SPIC time shall be credited as Pilot-in-Command time, unless the flight instructor had to influence or control any part of the flight. A ground de-briefing by the flight instructor does not affect the crediting as Pilot-in-Command time).

   iii. **50 hours** cross country flight time as Pilot-in-Command, including a VFR cross-country flight of at least 540km (300 nm) in the course of which full-stop landings at two aerodromes different from the aerodrome of departure shall be made.

b. **5 hours** night flying as Pilot of Aeroplanes, comprising of at least **3 hours** dual instruction, including **1 hour** Cross-Country navigation, and **5** solo take-offs and 5 full-stop landings.

c. i. **100 hours** instrument time comprising (ii) and (iii);

   ii. **50 hours** instrument flight instruction **25 hours (max)** instrument ground time (in a FNPT I), **or 40 hours (max)** (in a FNPT II or a Flight Simulator). With the agreement of the Authority not more than **10 hours** of FNPT II or flight simulator instrument ground time may be conducted in a FNPT I.

   iii. **50 hours** instrument flight as Student Pilot-in-Command (SPIC).

D1.2(B) NOTES

An applicant may be admitted to training as an ab-initio entrant, or as a holder of a PPL(A) or PPL(H) (excluding NPPL) issued in accordance with ICAO Annex 1. In the case of a PPL(A) or PPL(H) entrant, 50% of the aircraft hours flown by the entrant prior to the course may be credited towards the required flight instruction up to a credit of 40 hours flying experience or 45 hours if an aeroplane night flying qualification has been obtained, of which up to 20 hours may be dual instruction. This credit for the hours shall be at the discretion of the FTO and entered into the applicant's training record, and is subject to confirmation by the FTO at the time of application. In the case of a student pilot who does not hold a pilot licence and with the approval of the Authority, a FTO may designate certain dual exercises (see AMC FCL 1.160 & 1.165(a)(3), phase 2 & 3) to be flown in a helicopter of a TMG up to a maximum of 20 hours.

Where an applicant has completed a CPL(A) Skill Test on a SEP(Land) and a Licensing Skill Test on a MEP(Land) as part of an approved course of training, the licence is usually issued with the SEP(Land) endorsement as the CPL(A) Skill Test is completed on this aircraft. However, it has now been agreed that applicants may choose to open their licence with either the SEP(Land) or MEP(Land). If both ratings are to be endorsed an additional fee will be required. Both ratings will have a 12 month validity from the date of the skill test(s).

An applicant failing or unable to complete the entire CPL(A)/IR course may apply to the Authority for the theoretical knowledge examination and skill test for a lower licence.

An applicant wishing to transfer to another FTO during a course of training shall apply to the Authority for a formal assessment of the further hours of training required at another FTO.

D1.2(C) JAR-FCL ATPL(A) INTEGRATED COURSE FLYING TRAINING/ EXPERIENCE REQUIREMENTS

Training Requirements

A graduate from an approved ATPL(A) Integrated Course must have completed a minimum of **195 hours** of flight time, not including type rating training. This must include the particular requirements specified in **D1.2(C) a, b & c below**. Each of these requirements must be met in full but hours may be credited, where appropriate, towards more than one requirement except where stated otherwise.

a. i. **95 hours** Dual Instruction of which up to 55 hours may be instrument ground time;

   ii. **100 hours** Pilot-in-Command (PIC), including 50 hours VFR flight and 50 hours instrument flight time as Student Pilot-in-Command (SPIC). (SPIC time shall be credited as Pilot-in-Command time, unless the flight instructor had to influence or control any part of the flight. A ground de-briefing by the flight instructor does not affect the crediting as Pilot-in-Command time);

   iii. **50 hours** cross-country flight time as Pilot-in-Command, including a VFR cross-country flight of at least 540km (300 nm) in the course of which full-stop landings at two aerodromes different from the aerodrome of departure shall be made.

b. **5 hours** Night flying as Pilot of Aeroplanes, comprising of 3 hours dual instruction including at least 1 hour of cross-country navigation and 5 solo take-offs and 5 full stop landings.

c. i. **115 hours** Instrument time comprising:

ii. **50 hours** Instrument flight instruction of which up to **25 hours (max)** Instrument Ground Time in a FNPT I, **or 40 hours (max)** in a FNPT II or a Flight Simulator. With the agreement of the Authority not more than **10 hours** of FNPT II or flight simulator instrument ground time may be conducted in a FNPT I.

iii. **50 hours** Instrument flight as Student Pilot-in-Command (SPIC);

iv. **15 hours** Multi-Crew Co-Operation for which a flight simulator or FNPTII may be used.

D1.2(C) NOTES

An applicant may be admitted to training as an ab-initio entrant, or as a holder of a PPL(A) or PPL(H) (excluding NPPL) issued in accordance with ICAO Annex 1. In the case of a PPL(A) or PPL(H) entrant, 50% of the aircraft hours flown by the entrant prior to the course may be credited towards the required flight instruction up to a credit of 40 hours flying experience or 45 hours if an aeroplane night flying qualification has been obtained, of which up to 20 hours may be dual instruction. This credit for the hours shall be at the discretion of the FTO and entered into the applicant's training record, and is subject to confirmation by the FTO at the time of application. In the case of a student pilot who does not hold a pilot licence and with the approval of the Authority, a FTO may designate certain dual exercises (see AMC FCL 1.160 & 1.165(a)(3), phase 2 & 3) to be flown in a helicopter of a TMG up to a maximum of 20 hours.

An applicant failing or unable to complete the entire ATPL(A) course may apply to the Authority for the theoretical knowledge examination and skill test for a lower licence.

An applicant wishing to transfer to another FTO during a course of training shall apply to the Authority for a formal assessment of the further hours of training required at another FTO.

D1.2(D) JAR-FCL CPL(A) MODULAR COURSE FLYING TRAINING/ EXPERIENCE REQUIREMENTS

Training Requirements

The holder of a PPL(A) issued in accordance with ICAO Annex 1 (excluding the NPPL) with at least 150 hours flight time as a pilot, may commence an approved JAR CPL(A) Modular Course consisting of 25 hours dual flight instruction including 10 hours of instrument instruction (up to 5 hours may be instrument ground time in a BITD or a FNPT I or II or a flight simulator). At least 5 hours of the flight instruction shall be carried out in a complex aeroplane (certificated for the carriage of at least four persons and have a variable pitch propeller and retractable landing gear).

- Applicants with a valid JAR-FCL or ICAO Instrument Rating (Aeroplane) shall be given at least 15 hours dual visual flight instruction, and shall be fully credited towards the dual instrument instruction time. The same credit may be given to applicants who have completed an IR(A) modular course of training and passed IR(A) skill test but who have yet to apply for the issue of the IR(A), provided the IR(A) course and JAR CPL(A) modular course are conducted independent of each other, and that there is no training overlap between the two courses.

- Applicants with a valid JAR-FCL or ICAO Instrument rating (helicopter) or a QSP(H) who has held a 'Green' Instrument Rating within the preceding 5 years, may be credited up to 5 hours of the dual instrument instruction time, in which case at least 5 hours dual instrument instruction shall be given in an aeroplane.

- An applicant who does not already hold a Night Qualification/Rating (Aeroplane) shall be given additionally at least 5 hours night flight instruction.

Experience

Flying completed on the course may be counted towards meeting the flying experience requirements for licence issue as detailed below.

An applicant for a JAR-FCL CPL(A) must have completed a minimum of 200 hours of flight time, including the particular requirements specified in a, b and c below. These must be flown in aeroplanes irrespective of any credits applicable under D1.2(D) Notes below:-

a. i. **100** hours as Pilot-in-Command, or **70** hours as Pilot-in-Command if completed during a course of integrated flying training;

ii. **20** hours of VFR cross-country flight time as Pilot-in-Command, including a cross-country flight totalling at least 540 km (300 nm) in the course of which full-stop landings at two aerodromes different from the aerodromes of departure shall be made.

b. **10** hours of instrument dual instruction time (for applicants without an IR), of which not more that 5 hours is to be instrument ground time (in a FNPT I or II or a Flight Simulator).

c. **5** hours Night Flying comprising of at least 3 hours of dual instruction, including at least 1 hour of cross-country navigation, and 5 solo take-offs and full-stop landings.

D1.2(D) NOTES

The 200 hours flying experience may comprise flight time in any of the following capacities:

- Pilot-in-Command/Solo (PIC), counted in full.
- Pilot-under-Instruction (Dual), counted in full.

The following credits will apply towards the total 200 hours of flight time and not the specific requirements of (a)(i) and (ii), (b) or (c) above:

i. 30 hours as pilot-in-command holding a PPL(H) on helicopters; or

ii. 100 hours as pilot-in-command holding a CPL(H), or as a QSP(H), on helicopters; or

iii. 30 hours as pilot-in-command in touring motor gliders or gliders (including Vigilant).

JAR-FCL CPL(A) Modular Course - Multi Engine (ME) Training

As detailed earlier, the CPL(A) Modular Course comprises a minimum of 25 hours dual flight instruction, including 5 hours in a complex aeroplane and the CPL Skill Test.

The Skill Test may be completed in a multi-engine aeroplane, but to add a ME rating, a minimum of 6 hours dual flight instruction is necessary (see Section F3.2). This training is additional to the CPL(A) Modular course. If the minimum 6 hours ME training has been completed, the Skill Test in a ME aeroplane serves 2 purposes - for the CPL itself and for the MEP class rating.

It has been agreed that if the 5 hours training in a complex aeroplane, required in the CPL course, is flown in a ME aeroplane, we can amend the minimum CPL(A) Modular Course requirements as follows:

20 hours Single Engine training
8 hours Multi Engine training
CPL Skill Test in an MEP aeroplane

Prior to commencement of the course, the requirements of JAR-FCL 1.225 and 1.240 shall be complied with.

During the course, all mandatory training for the MEP class rating (in accordance with JAR-FCL 1.261(a) and (b)) must be covered, including theoretical knowledge instruction (and associated written test paper) in-flight engine shut down and asymmetric training. If a school wished to include more than 8 hours ME training, the SE element could be reduced accordingly.

D1.3 JAR-FCL CPL(A) THEORETICAL KNOWLEDGE EXAMINATION REQUIREMENTS

Candidates without a full pass in the UK national professional ground examinations

A candidate, who did not achieve a full pass in the UK National professional ground examinations, is required to pass the JAR-FCL theoretical knowledge examinations in all subjects. JAR-FCL additionally requires candidates to complete an approved theoretical knowledge course prior to attempting the examinations. However, a candidate who has previously passed at least one examination in the UK Navigation or Technical Group of examinations will not be required to complete the full theoretical knowledge course - the amount of theoretical knowledge instruction required will be at the discretion of the Head of Training of an approved training provider. This credit against the JAR-FCL theoretical knowledge course recognises the studies already completed by candidates who have passed national exams.

CPL(A) Integrated Courses

An applicant from either course must pass the nine **CPL(A) Theoretical Knowledge** examinations in the following subjects:

Air Law
Navigation
Aircraft General Knowledge
Operational Procedures
Flight Performance and Planning
Principles of Flight
Human Performance and Limitations
Communications (VFR)
Meteorology

CPL(A)/IR Integrated Course

An applicant from this course must pass the nine **CPL(A)** Theoretical Knowledge examinations **and** the seven **IR(A)** Theoretical Knowledge examinations in the following subjects:

CPL Theoretical Knowledge

Air Law
Aircraft General Knowledge
Flight Performance and Planning
Human Performance and Limitations
Meteorology
Navigation
Operational Procedures

Principles of Flight
Communications (VFR)

IR Theoretical Knowledge

Air Law/ Operational Procedures
Aircraft General Knowledge
Flight Performance and Planning
Human Performance and Limitations
Meteorology
Navigation
Communications (IFR)

ATPL(A) Integrated Course

An applicant from this course must pass the fourteen **ATPL(A) Theoretical Knowledge** examinations in the following subjects:

Air Law
Aircraft General Knowledge (2 papers)
Flight Performance and Planning (3 papers)
Human Performance and Limitations
Meteorology
Navigation (2 papers)
Operational Procedures
Principles of Flight
Communications (2 papers)

CPL(A) Modular Course

The theoretical examinations can be attempted before reaching 150 hours of flying experience.

An applicant on a CPL(A) Modular Course will be required to pass either the nine CPL(A) Theoretical Knowledge Examinations or the 14 ATPL(A) Theoretical Knowledge Examinations detailed previously. However, it should be noted that CPL(A) examinations will only be valid towards the issue of the JAR-FCL CPL(A) licence, and not an Instrument Rating (Aeroplanes). Therefore, applicants wishing to obtain a JAR-FCL CPL(A)/IR via the modular route will either be required to pass all CPL(A) and IR(A) examinations or the ATPL(A) examinations. Details of the ATPL(A) Modular Theoretical Knowledge Course can be found in Section G1.3

JAR-FCL Theoretical Knowledge Acceptance Period

Potential candidates for the JAR-FCL CPL(A) should first consider the implications of JAR-FCL 1.495 that relates to the Acceptance Period.

A pass in the theoretical knowledge examinations given in accordance with JAR-FCL 1.490 will be accepted for the grant of the CPL(A) or IR(A) during the 36 months from the end of the month of the date of gaining a pass in all the required examination papers*. Provided that an IR(A) is obtained in accordance with the above, a pass in the ATPL(A) theoretical knowledge examinations will remain valid for a period of 7 years from the last validity date of the IR(A) entered in the CPL(A) for the issuance of an ATPL(A).

*All requirements for the issue of the CPL(A) and IR(A) must be met and the applicant required to apply to PLD for issue within the 36 month validity period of the theoretical knowledge examinations.

Credits from JAR-FCL Theoretical Examinations

- An applicant who has previously passed the VFR Communications examination at CPL(A) level, and have been issued with a CPL(A) will not be re-examined in subject VFR Communications at ATPL(A) level.
- An applicant who has previously passed the IFR Communications examination at IR level, and have been issued with an IR(A) will not be re-examined in subject IFR Communications at ATPL(A) level.
- An applicant having passed the theoretical knowledge examination in Human Performance & Limitations for an IR(A)/(H) is credited with the theoretical knowledge requirement in subject Human Performance & Limitations for a CPL(A) according to the pass standards set out in JAR-FCL 1.490 and Section J1.5.
- The holder of a valid JAR-FCL CPL(H) will be required to complete the appropriate bridging examination requirements at CPL(A) level (see Section J1.9) or all examination papers at ATPL(A) level except VFR Communications.
- The holder of a valid JAR-FCL ATPL(H)/IR will be required to complete the bridging examination requirements appropriate to the level of examinations being taken (see Section J1.9)

DETAILS OF THE ABOVE EXAMINATIONS, PASS RULES, VALIDITY PERIODS, ETC, ARE GIVEN IN SECTION J and JAR-FCL 1, SUBPART J.

D1.4 JAR-FCL CPL(A)SKILL TEST REQUIREMENTS

An applicant for a JAR-FCL CPL(A) is required to:

1. Pass the **CPL Skill Test** with a CAA Flight Examiner.
    - An applicant for a skill test for the CPL(A) shall have satisfactorily completed all of the required training, including instruction on the

same type/class of aeroplane to be used in the skill test. The applicant shall be permitted to choose to take the test on a single-engine aeroplane or, subject to the experience requirement in JAR-FCL 1.255 or JAR-FCL 1.260 of 70 hours flight time as pilot-in-command, on a multi-engine aeroplane. The aeroplane used for the skill test shall meet the requirements for training aeroplanes set out in Appendix 1a to JAR-FCL 1.255 and shall be certificated for the carriage of at least four persons, have a variable pitch propeller and retractable landing gear.

- Before undertaking the Skill Test, the applicant shall have passed the associated theoretical knowledge examination (exceptions may be made by the CAA for applicants undergoing a course of integrated flying training), and completed all of the related flying training.

- Before undertaking the CPL(A) Skill Test an applicant must obtain a pre-entry form F170A. The applicant will also be required to provide evidence of either holding a valid UK FRTOL or of having passed the UK RTF practical test prior to undertaking the CPL(A) Skill Test.

- An applicant shall pass sections 1 through 5 of the skill test, and applicable items of Section 6. If any item in a section is failed, that section is failed. Failure in more than one section will require the applicant to take the entire test again. An applicant failing only one section shall take the failed section again. Failure in any section of the re-test, including those sections that have been passed on a previous attempt, will require the applicant to take the entire test again. Further training may be recommended following the failure of one Section of the Skill Test. Further training will be required prior to any full re-test.

- For the purpose of licence issue the skill test will remain valid for 12 months.

- There is no limit to the number of skill tests that may be attempted.

Instrument Rating IR(A) Skill Test

Students on an Integrated Course of Training for the CPL(A)/IR or ATPL(A) are also required to pass an IR(A) Skill Test with a CAA Flight Examiner.

- ATPL(A) Integrated Course students shall take the IR(A) Skill Test on a multi-engine aeroplane.

- CPL(A)/IR Integrated Course students shall take the IR(A) Skill Test on either a single-engine or multi-engine aeroplane.

- An applicant for a skill test for the IR(A) shall have received instruction on the same class or type of aeroplane to be used for the skill test. The aeroplane used for the skill test shall meet the requirements for training aeroplanes set out in Appendix 1a to JAR-FCL 1.055.

- Before undertaking the IR(A) Skill Test an applicant must pass a pre-entry form F170A flight check. The applicant will also be required to provide evidence of either holding a valid UK FRTOL or of having passed the UK RTF practical test prior to undertaking the IR(A) Skill Test.

- The format of the IR(A) Skill Test is laid down in Appendix 2 to JAR-FCL 1.210. An applicant shall pass Sections 1 through 5 of the test, and Section 6 if a multi-engine aeroplane is used. If any item in a section is failed that section is failed. Failure in more than one section will require the applicant to take the entire test again. An applicant failing only one section shall take the failed section again plus Section 1. Failure in any section of the re-test, including those sections that have been passed on a previous attempt, will require the applicant to take the entire test again. All sections of the skill test shall be completed within six months.

- Further training may be recommended following the failure of one Section of the Skill Test. Further training will be required prior to any full re-test. There is no limit to the number of skill tests that may be attempted.

- Before undertaking the Skill Test, the applicant shall have passed the associated theoretical knowledge examination (exceptions may be made by the CAA for applicants undergoing a course of integrated flying training) and completed all of the related flying training.

DETAILS OF THE CPL(A) SKILL TEST REQUIREMENTS ARE DETAILED IN APPENDICES 1 AND 2 TO JAR-FCL 1.170.

Guidance for applicants taking the CPL(A) Skill Test can also be found in Standards Document 03 on the CAA web site at www.caa.co.uk.

DETAILS OF THE IR(A) SKILL TEST REQUIREMENTS ARE DETAILED IN APPENDICES 1 AND 2 TO JAR-FCL 1.210.

Guidance for applicants taking the IR(A) Skill Test can also be found in Standards Document 01(A) on the CAA web site at www.caa.co.uk

D1.5 CONVERSION OF A NON-JAA PROFESSIONAL LICENCE TO A JAR-FCL CPL(A)

A licence issued by a non-JAA State may be converted to a JAR-FCL licence provided that an arrangement exists between the JAA and the non-JAA State. This arrangement shall be established on the basis of reciprocity of licence acceptance and shall ensure that an equivalent level of safety exists between the training and testing requirements of the JAA and non-JAA State. Until such arrangements exist, the following requirements have been agreed by the JAA and are now incorporated in JAR-FCL 1, paragraph 1.016.

Non-JAA CPL(A)

The holder of a **current and valid*** CPL(A) issued in accordance with ICAO Annex 1 by a non-JAA State may be issued with a JAR-FCL CPL(A) providing the experience requirements of JAR-FCL 1.155(b) and (c) have been met. Applicants must:

- Hold a valid JAR-FCL Class 1 medical certificate.
- Undertake CPL(A) theoretical knowledge instruction as determined by the Head of Training of an approved training provider and pass ALL of the JAR-FCL theoretical knowledge examinations at CPL(A) level. Applicants who wish to attempt examinations at a higher level (i.e. ATPL(A) level) must undertake the full 650 hour course of approved theoretical knowledge instruction and pass ALL of the JAR-FCL theoretical knowledge examinations at ATPL(A) level.
- Undertake flying training as determined by the Head of Training of a FTO approved to conduct CPL(A) modular flying training courses, sufficient to obtain the pre-entry Form 170A (to include 5 hours on a complex aeroplane type if this requirement has not been previously satisfied) and pass the CPL(A) skill test (in accordance with Appendices 1 and 2 to JAR-FCL 1.170) with a CAA Flight Examiner.
- Qualify for the issue of a UK Flight Radio Telephony Operator's Licence (FRTOL) - Section B refers.

* The holder of an ICAO CPL(A) that is not current and valid will be required to complete the full CPL(A) modular flying training course.

Non-JAA ATPL(A)

The holder of a **current and valid*** ICAO ATPL(A) who <u>does not</u> meet the experience requirements for the grant of a JAR-FCL ATPL(A) as detailed in Section G1.5, can still apply for a JAR-FCL CPL(A)/IR. Applicants must:

- Hold a valid JAR-FCL Class 1 medical certificate.
- Undertake CPL(A) <u>and</u> IR theoretical knowledge instruction as determined by the Head of Training of an approved training provider, and pass ALL of the JAR-FCL theoretical knowledge at CPL(A) <u>and</u> IR level. Applicants who wish to attempt examinations at a higher level (i.e. ATPL(A)) must undertake the full 650 hour course of approved theoretical knowledge instruction and pass ALL of the JAR-FCL theoretical knowledge examinations at ATPL(A) level.
- Undertake flying training as determined by the Head of Training of a Flight Training Organisation approved to conduct CPL(A) modular flying training courses, sufficient to obtain the pre-entry Form 170A (to include 5 hours on a complex aeroplane type if this requirement has not been previously satisfied), and pass the CPL(A) skill test (in accordance with Appendices 1 and 2 to JAR-FCL 1.170) with a CAA flight examiner.
- **for additional IR(A) training see non-JAA ICAO IR(A) below:**
- Qualify for the issue of a UK Flight Radio Telephony Operator's Licence (FRTOL) – Section B refers.

* The holder of an ICAO ATPL(A) that is not current and valid will be required to complete the full CPL(A) modular flying training course.

Non-JAA ICAO IR(A)

The holder of a **current and valid** Instrument Rating Aeroplane (issued in accordance with ICAO Annex 1 by a non-JAA State may be issued with a JAR-FCL IR(A). Full details of conversion requirements are contained in Section E1.2.

D1.6 UK FLIGHT RADIOTELEPHONY OPERATOR'S LICENCE (FRTOL) REQUIREMENTS

An applicant for a UK FRTOL is required to pass the Radiotelephony written examination and practical test with an authorised RTF Examiner. It should be noted that whilst Radio Communication forms part of the JAR-FCL CPL(A) training syllabus, the FRTOL remains a UK national licence.

FULL DETAILS OF THE FRTOL REQUIREMENTS INCLUDING CREDITS AVAILABLE ARE CONTAINED IN SECTION B.

D1.7 JAR-FCL CPL(A) MEDICAL REQUIREMENTS

An applicant for a JAR-FCL CPL(A) shall hold a valid JAR-FCL Class 1 Medical Certificate.

FULL DETAILS OF MEDICAL REQUIREMENTS ARE CONTAINED IN JAR-FCL 3 AND SECTION A5

D2 JAR-FCL CPL (AEROPLANE) RESTRICTED TO UK REGISTERED AIRCRAFT

This section offers information as a guide to obtaining a JAR-FCL Commercial Pilot Licence (Aeroplanes)(Restricted) – JAR-FCL CPL(A)(R) as follows:-

D2.1 JAR-CPL(A)(R) GENERAL INFORMATION

Privileges

Details of licence privileges can be found in Schedule 8 of the Air Navigation Order, (please also refer to Section A, Appendix F). (See **Licence Endorsement**)

Minimum Age

An applicant for a JAR-FCL CPL(A)(R) shall be at least 18 years of age.

Licence Validity

The JAR-FCL CPL(A)(R) will be issued for a maximum period of 5 years.

Licence Endorsement

As the JAR-FCL CPL(A)(R) does not fully comply with the requirements of the JAR-FCL, the holder is not entitled to the automatic recognition accorded to a JAR-FCL. The licence will be endorsed with the following statement;

"Valid for United Kingdom registered aircraft. As this licence does not fully comply with JAR-FCL the holder must have permission from any other JAA Member State prior to exercising the licence privileges in aircraft registered in that State".

The effect of this endorsement on the licence is to restrict its use, initially, to aeroplanes registered in the UK only. Prior to exercising the privileges of the licence in aircraft registered in another JAA Member State, permission must be sought from that State. The JAR-FCL CPL(A)(R) will be issued only where the applicant fulfils the provisions of the licensing requirements set out below.

D2.2 JAR-FCL CPL(A)(R) FLYING EXPERIENCE/TRAINING REQUIREMENTS)

Experience

The JAR-FCL CPL(A)(R) licence is only available to existing UK BCPL(A) licence holders having passed UK BCPL(A), CPL(A) or ATPL(A) level theoretical knowledge. Applicants for the JAR-FCL CPL (A)(R) shall meet all experience requirements for this issue of a JAR-FCL CPL(A) as specified in Section D1.2(D). The training requirements are as specified below. No credit from the flying hours requirement will be given for the holder of an IMC Rating, however, applicants can attach an IMC Rating to the JAR-FCL CPL(A)(R) by completing the 5 hours of applied dual instrument instruction and passing IMC rating flight test (see Section E3.4).

Training

- Complete or show logbook evidence of at least 5 hours flight instruction in an aeroplanes certificated for the carriage of at least four persons and having a variable pitch propeller and retractable landing gear ("complex type"). May be SE or ME aeroplane.
- Complete a Licensing Proficiency Check on that category of aeroplane within the 12 months prior to licence issue. (LPC SPA form shall be signed by an authorised examiner (FE(CPL)) certifying that the flight was conducted on a "complex type").
- Gain a Night Qualification in accordance with JAR-FCL 1. Apply for the JAR-FCL CPL(A)(R).
- A pass in the UK BCPL(A), CPL(A) or ATPL(A) level theoretical knowledge examinations will be accepted without time limit for the grant of the JAR-FCL CPL(A)(R). However, a pass in the UK CPL(A) or ATPL(A) level theoretical knowledge examinations were only accepted for the grant of

an IR(A) until 31 December 2004. Applicants should note that provided that the JAR-FCL CPL(A) (R) and IR(A) are obtained during the 36 months from the date of gaining a pass in the UK ATPL(A) theoretical knowledge examinations, this pass will remain valid for a period of 7 years from the last validity date of the IR(A) entered in the JAR-FCL CPL(A)(R) for the issuance on an ATPL(A) (JAR-FCL 1.495 refers).

D2.3 JAR-FCL CPL(A)(R) THEORETICAL KNOWLEDGE REQUIREMENTS

A full pass in the UK BCPL(A), CPL(A) or ATPL(A) theoretical knowledge examinations will be accepted for the issue of a JAR CPL(A)(R). Details of the theoretical knowledge acceptance period are specified in Section J1.7.

D2.4 REMOVAL OF THE (RESTRICTED) ENDORSEMENT

The holder of a JAR-FCL CPL(A)(R) may apply to have the (R) endorsement removed when;

a. They achieve 700 hours as pilot of flying machines, to include;

   i. 200 hours PIC of aeroplanes;

   ii. 50 hours cross country or overseas flying as PIC or PIC U/S of aeroplanes or helicopters, of which not less than 35 hours must be as PIC of aeroplanes;

or

b. Obtain a pass in the JAR-FCL CPL(A) or ATPL(A) examinations following an approved course of ground instruction.

On completion of D2.4 a) or b) the licence holder can apply to PLD (using Form SRG\1163) to have the restriction removed and paying the appropriate fee.

D2.5 UPGRADING TO JAR-FCL ATPL(A)

Pilots who have passed the UK ATPL(A) examinations, who hold a JAR-FCL CPL(A)(R) with Instrument Rating and a valid type rating on a multi-pilot aeroplane will be required to meet the following requirements for the issue of a JAR-FCL ATPL(A):

- Achieve 1500 hours as pilot of aeroplanes, to include;

  i. 500 hours on multi-pilot aeroplanes,

  ii. 250 hours PIC of which up to 150 hours may be PIC U/S,

  iii. 200 hours cross country flight of which 100 hours may be as P2 or PIC U/S,

  iv. 75 hours of instrument time of which not more than 30 hours may be instrument ground time,

  v. not more than 100 hours may be in a flight simulator.

D2.6 UK FLIGHT RADIO TELEPHONY OPERATOR'S LICENCE (FRTOL) REQUIREMENTS

An applicant for a UK FRTOL is required to pass the Radiotelephony written examination and practical test with an authorised RTF Examiner. It should be noted that whilst Radio Communications forms part of the JAR-FCL CPL(A) training syllabus, the FRTOL remains a UK national licence.

FULL DETAILS OF THE FRTOL REQUIREMENTS INCLUDING CREDITS AVAILABLE ARE CONTAINED IN SECTION B.

D2.7 JAR-FCL CPL(A)(R) MEDICAL REQUIREMENTS

An applicant for a JAR-FCL CPL(A)(R) shall hold a valid JAR-FCL Class 1 medical certificate.

FULL DETAILS ARE CONTAINED IN JAR-FCL 3 AND SECTION A5.

D3 JAR-FCL CPL (AEROPLANE) FOR UK QUALIFIED SERVICE PILOTS (AEROPLANES)

This section offers information as a basic guide to obtaining a JAR-FCL Commercial Pilot Licence (Aeroplane) – JAR-FCL CPL (A) – for UK Qualified Service Pilots (Aeroplanes).

D3.1 JAR-FCL CPL (A) GENERAL INFORMATION

Introduction

JAR-FCL permits the knowledge, experience and skill gained in military service to be credited towards the relevant requirements of JAR-FCL licences and ratings, at the discretion of each national authority. The CAA has worked closely with the MoD through the MoD/CAA Working Group (MCWG) to determine the scope and level of accreditation that can be applied to suitably experienced UK military pilots.

In particular, the MCWG sought to determine an agreed level of equivalence between the theoretical knowledge acquired by pilots throughout military flying training and subsequent operational experience, and those required at JAR-FCL ATPL (A) level.

Full details of the theoretical knowledge requirements, including credits and eligibility criteria, can be found in section D3.3.

It should be noted that a QSP(A) can still take advantage of any flying or skill test credits for which he qualifies even if he does not qualify for theoretical knowledge credits under D3.3. Similarly, a QSP (A) does not have to be in current military flying practice to take advantage of any theoretical knowledge credits for which he may be eligible.

Although not exclusive, a licensing flow diagram can be found at Appendix I to Section D, to demonstrate typical licensing routes for experienced military fixed-wing pilots.

Questions regarding the accreditation schemes should be directed in writing to: FT (Proj) 1, HQ TGDA, RAF Innsworth, Gloucester, GL3 1EZ or by e-mail to ftproj1@tgda.gov.uk.

Taxi-time allowances

For details of Recording of Military Flying Times-Taxi-time allowances please refer to Section A, Appendix B.

Privileges

Details of licence privileges can be found in Schedule 8 of the Air Navigation Order (please also refer to Section A, Appendix F).

Minimum Age

An applicant for a JAR-FCL CPL (A) shall be at least 18 years of age.

Licence Validity

A JAR-FCL CPL (A) will be issued for a maximum period of 5 years.

Definition of Qualified Service Pilot

To qualify for any of the credits detailed in Section D3, an applicant must be a UK Qualified Service Pilot (QSP).

A QSP is defined as a pilot who has completed a recognised military course of flying training and has been awarded a pilot's flying badge in full compliance with QR (RAF) J727.

The term "flying badge" is used to include all badges worn by personnel who have successfully completed a prescribed course of flying training. The initial award of a flying badge is on a provisional basis. It is not deemed to be fully earned until the holder has successfully completed an operational conversion or equivalent course and has joined an operational or non-operational unit in the capacity for which the provisional badge has been awarded. Joining is defined for each Service as follows:-

a. RN: on issue of the Certificate of Competence.

b. Army and RM: on award of the badge (and successful completion of conversion to type (CTT) course).

c. RAF: On successful attainment of an appropriate aircrew categorisation or qualification to undertake productive flying duties (C categorisation or above, B1 or above instructor category or CR status).

In addition, the applicant must have been qualified to act as pilot-in-command of military registered aircraft.

QSPs should also note that the CAA makes a distinction between pilots who initially qualify on fixed-wing aircraft (QSP (A)), and those who initially qualify on helicopters (QSP (H)). A QSP (H) will not qualify for credits under Section D3 unless he has subsequently undertaken a formal conversion to a fixed-wing type and completed a tour on that type e.g. QFI training and subsequent Instructor tour, or Army Islander conversion and operational tour. A QSP (H) who undertakes a fixed-wing conversion on an AEF, is NOT considered to be a QSP (A) and will NOT be eligible for credits under Section D3. Details of credits against CPL (A) requirements for a QSP (H) can be found in Section D1.2D.

Non-UK Military Pilots

Non-UK military pilots operating UK military aircraft through exchange programs etc., are **not** eligible for any credits afforded to UK military pilots - if a serving member of the Armed Forces of another JAA State, applicants should contact the National Aviation Authority of that State for details of any accreditation arrangements for its military personnel.

Ex-Qualified Service Pilots

An ex-QSP (A) can claim any credits for which he qualifies, for a period of one year from the last date of service.

An ex-QSP (A) employed by a Defence Contractor in flying-related duties, is deemed to be a QSP (A) for licensing purposes. He can claim any credits for which he qualifies, for a period of one year from the date of last flight in a military aeroplane.

A Volunteer Reservist or Full Time Reserve Service (FTRS) pilot is deemed to be a QSP (A) for licensing purposes. He can claim any credits for which he qualifies, for a period of one year from the date of last flight in a military aeroplane.

Definition of Current Flying Practice

In order to qualify for credit against the CPL (A) Skill Test (see D3.4), a QSP (A) shall be in current flying practice.

To be deemed to be in current flying practice, a QSP (A) shall have a minimum of 12 hours flying experience as a pilot in military or civil aeroplanes (or combination of both) in the 12 months preceding the date of application for licence issue. This experience shall include at least 6 hours as pilot-in-command (PIC) for this purpose, military 1st pilot hours may be counted towards the PIC requirement, one flight with a military instructor pilot or civil Flight Instructor, and 12 take-offs and landings; for this purpose, military 1st Pilot hours may be counted towards the 6 hours PIC requirement.

A QSP (A) on a ground tour can still achieve currency, either by flying on military (AEF) or civil aeroplanes. A QSP (A) not on an AEF can achieve currency on civil aircraft through a combination of solo flying (to meet the 6 hours PIC requirement) and training towards other licence requirements (i.e. IR and/or multi-engine training). A QSP (A) who does not already hold a valid PPL (A), can satisfy the 6 hours PIC requirement by flying solo at a PPL registered facility, under the authority of the CFI (in much the same way as an ab-initio PPL student would). The balance could be made up with an approved FTO during training for a class rating and/or IR (A).

D3.2 JAR-FCL CPL (A) FLYING TRAINING AND EXPERIENCE REQUIREMENTS

The CAA recognises all QSPs who have completed a course of military ground and flying training and who meet the definition of a QSP in D3.1. Provided such pilots remain in current flying practice (see D3.1) and meet the flying experience requirements of Section D1.2(D) they will be credited the approved CPL (A) Modular course of flying training.

D3.3 JAR-FCL CPL (A) THEORETICAL KNOWLEDGE EXAMINATION REQUIREMENTS

An applicant for a JAR-FCL CPL (A) is required to complete an approved course of theoretical knowledge instruction and pass theoretical knowledge examinations at CPL level, or if IR(A) privileges will be required, at CPL and IR or ATPL level.

However, as described in D3.1, the MCWG determined a level of equivalence between theoretical knowledge training and subsequent operational experience, and that required at JAR-ATPL (A) level. It should be recognised that the scope for accreditation was not the same for all military pilots, and that role training and experience ultimately determined the level of equivalence achieved. Accreditation schemes have been agreed, based on the level of equivalence found, for the following:

1. FW (ME) scheme for experienced fixed-wing pilots with a high level of multi-engine operational experience (see D3.3(A).

2. Scheme for experienced fixed-wing pilots with a primarily fast-jet or instructor background, or low levels of multi-engine operational experience (see D3.3(B)).

3. Scheme for experienced Army Islander pilots (see D3.3(C)).

A QSP (A), who does not meet the eligibility criteria of any accreditation scheme, will be required to demonstrate the appropriate level of theoretical knowledge by passing ALL of the theoretical knowledge examinations at the appropriate level. (i.e. CPL, CPL and IR or ATPL). However, credit will be given against the requirement to complete an approved course of theoretical knowledge instruction course prior to attempting the examinations. Applicants will be required to undertake theoretical knowledge instruction as determined by the Head of Training of an approved training provider.

D3.3(A) FW (ME) ACCREDITATION SCHEME

Eligibility

To qualify for theoretical knowledge examination credits under the FW (ME) accreditation scheme, a QSP(A) shall have completed:

1. A recognised ME OCU; **(BAe 125/146, C17, Hercules, Nimrod, Sentry, TriStar or VC10) (RN-Jetstream T2)**

2. A minimum of 2000 hours* flying experience on military aircraft, including at least 1500 hours** as 1st pilot (Captain)/1st pilot (Nimrod) P1 (can incl. max. 500 hours 1st pilot (non-Captain)/co-pilot P1/2nd pilot P1 (Nimrod)) on recognised multi-engine aeroplanes.

* as recorded in Service logbook i.e. excluding any taxi-time allowances.

** QSPs with a mix of military helicopter and multi-engine aeroplane experience may be permitted to enter the FW(ME) Accreditation Scheme, depending on their experience. Advice should be sought from PLD.

The following types in current military service are considered to be multi-engine aeroplanes for this purpose:

Andover	**Tristar**	**VC10**
BAe 125	**BAC 1-11**	
Beech 200	**BAe 146**	
Canberra	**C17**	
Hercules C1/C3	**Dominie**	
Islander	**Hercules C4/C5**	
Jetstream T3	**Jetstream T1/T2**	
PA31	**Nimrod**	
Sentry		

Applicants shall have had operational experience on one of the approved ME aeroplanes, within the 5 years preceding the date of application for licence issue.

Flying experience on military multi-engine aeroplanes not included in the above list i.e. types flown whilst on exchange duties with a foreign air arm, will be considered on a case-by-case basis. Flying experience on multi-engine aeroplanes no longer in UK military service can be credited towards the 2000 hours requirement, but not the 1500 hour PIC requirement - only flying experience on recognised ME aeroplanes listed above can be credited towards the PIC requirement.

Theoretical Knowledge Requirements

A QSP (A) who meets the eligibility criteria in full, is required to:

1. Pass the ATPL (A) examination in: -

   i. Air Law

DETAILS OF THE ABOVE EXAMINATION, PASS RULES, VALIDITY PERIODS, ETC, ARE GIVEN IN JAR-FCL 1, SUBPART J.

D3.3(B) FW (NON-ME) ACCREDITATION SCHEME

Eligibility

To qualify for theoretical knowledge examination credits under the FW (Non-ME) accreditation scheme, a QSP(A) shall have completed:

1. A minimum of 2000 hours* flying experience on military aircraft, including at least 1500 hours** as 1st pilot (Captain) 1st pilot (Nimrod) P1 (can incl.

max. 500 hours 1st pilot (non-Captain)/Co-pilot P1/2nd pilot P1 (Nimrod)) on aeroplanes.

* as recorded in Service logbook i.e. excluding any taxi-time allowances.

** QSPs with a mix of military helicopter and multi-engine aeroplane experience may be permitted to enter the FW(NON-ME) Accreditation Scheme, depending on their experience. Advice should be sought from PLD.

Theoretical Knowledge Requirements

A QSP (A) who meets the eligibility criteria in full, is required to:

1. Complete a FW Bridging Package with an approved training provider;

Note: In certain subject areas, military theoretical training does not meet the level of equivalency required at JAR ATPL (A) level. In order to secure credit from the source JAR examinations, it was agreed that these topics should form the basis of a FW Bridging Package. Further details, including a summary of the content of the FW Bridging Package, can be found at Appendix F to Section D.

2. Pass the ATPL (A) examinations in:

   i. Air Law

   ii. Mass & Balance

   iii. Performance

   iv. Operational Procedures

To prepare for the above examinations, a QSP (A) is required to undertake theoretical knowledge instruction as determined by the Head of Training of an approved training provider.

DETAILS OF THE ABOVE EXAMINATIONS, PASS RULES, VALIDITY PERIODS, ETC, ARE GIVEN IN JAR-FCL 1, SUBPART J.

D3.3(C) AAC ISLANDER ACCREDITATION SCHEME

Eligibility

To qualify for theoretical knowledge examination credits under the AAC Islander accreditation scheme, a QSP(A) shall have completed:

1. MELIN and Islander Conversion Course (including Islander Airways Course with procedural IR);

2. a minimum of 2000 hours flying experience on military aircraft, including at least 1250 hours as Pilot-in-Command (maximum 500 hours PIC/US) on ME aeroplanes.

Theoretical Knowledge Requirements

A QSP (A) who meets the eligibility criteria in full, is required to:

1. Complete an Islander Bridging Package with an approved training provider;

Note: In certain subject areas, military theoretical training does not meet the level of equivalency required at JAR ATPL (A) level. In order to secure credit from the source JAR examinations, it was agreed that these topics should form the basis of an Islander Bridging Package. Further details, including a summary of the content of the Islander Bridging Package, can be found at Appendix G to Section D.

2. Pass the ATPL (A) examinations in:

   i. Air Law

   ii. Performance

   iii. Operational Procedures

To prepare for the above examinations, a QSP (A) is required to undertake theoretical knowledge instruction as determined by the Head of Training of an approved training provider.

DETAILS OF THE ABOVE EXAMINATIONS, PASS RULES, VALIDITY PERIODS, ETC, ARE GIVEN IN JAR-FCL 1, SUBPART J.

D3.4 JAR-FCL CPL (A) SKILL TEST REQUIREMENTS

A QSP (A) in current flying practice as defined in D3.1 will be credited the CPL (A) Skill Test, and should refer to D3.5 for details of the type /class rating requirements for licence issue.

A QSP (A) not in current flying practice as defined in D3.1 will be required to pass the **CPL (A) Skill Test** with a CAA Flight Examiner.

- Before undertaking the Skill Test, applicants must complete CPL training at the discretion of the Head of Training of a FTO approved to conduct CPL (A) modular courses, sufficient to obtain the 170A Certificate of Competence.

- Before undertaking the Skill Test, the applicant shall have passed the required theoretical knowledge examinations.
- The Skill Test can be completed in a single-engine (SE) or multi-engine (ME) aeroplane. If a ME aeroplane is to be used, applicants shall also complete an approved course of training for a multi-engine piston class rating (see Section F3) in addition to the required CPL training.
- For the purpose of licence issue, the skill test is valid for 12 months.

D3.5 TYPE/CLASS RATING REQUIREMENTS

A QSP (A), who is required under D3.4 to pass the CPL (A) Skill Test, will qualify for a class rating appropriate to the class of aircraft used for the skill test.

A QSP (A) who is credited the CPL (A) Skill Test in D3.4, shall qualify for a type or class rating to open the licence.

The type/class rating requirements for ME pilots (including AAC Islander pilots) differ from those for non-ME pilots.

Non-ME Pilots

A non-ME QSP (A) is required to complete a class rating for a Single-pilot, SE or ME aeroplane in accordance with Section F.

Applicants should note that if an Instrument Rating is also required (see D3.6), the class rating must be completed on the same class of aeroplane as that to be used on the IR (A) Skill Test.

ME Pilots

Subject to currency on type, and completion of an IR(A) Skill Test on type (see D3.6), a military type rating can be issued for any of the following recognised military multi-engine aeroplane types:-

Multi-Pilot	Single-Pilot
Andover	**Dominie**
Hercules C4/C5 (C130J)	
Nimrod	
Sentry	
VC10	

Although the **Canberra and C17** are recognised as military multi-engine aeroplane types, it is not possible to complete the IR(A) skill test on either type. As a result, **Canberra and C17** pilots will be unable to obtain a type rating for their respective types, and should instead complete the type/class rating and IR(A) requirements applicable to Non-ME pilots.

Subject to currency on type and completion of an IR(A) skill test on type (see G2.6), a JAR-FCL type rating (in brackets) will be issued for any of the following recognised military multi-engine aeroplane types:-

Multi-Pilot	Single-Pilot
	Beech 200 (BE90/99/100/200)
BAC 1-11 (BAC 1-11)	
BAe 125 (HS 125)	**Islander** (BN2T)
Hercules C1/C3 (Hercules)	**Jetstream T1/T2** (Jetstream 200)
Jetstream T3 (Jetstream 31/32)	**PA31** (MEP)
TriStar (L1011)	

Currency Requirements

In order to qualify for a type rating credit for one of the above types, a QSP (A) must:

i. show a minimum of 500 hours flying experience on any ONE type;

ii. show evidence of a valid annual check (RAF - aircraft category renewal, RN - QFI check with NFSF(FW)) on the same type as (i) completed in the 12 months preceding the date of application for licence issue.

1. Islander pilots must additionally complete differences training for the operation of a retractable undercarriage. This will consist of a pre-flight brief and at least one hour of flight instruction with a JAA Flight Instructor or Class Rating Instructor, in SE or ME aeroplanes with a retractable undercarriage. Completion of this differences training is to be recorded in the pilot's civilian logbook and countersigned by the instructor.
2. Any QSP (A) who does not meet the above currency requirements in full, will be required to obtain a Class Rating for a Single-pilot, SE or ME aeroplane in accordance with Section F.

Applicants should note that if an Instrument Rating is also required (see D3.6), the class rating must be completed on the same class of aeroplane as that to be used on the IR (A) Skill Test.

D3.6 INSTRUMENT RATING REQUIREMENTS

It is not mandatory for a QSP (A) to obtain an Instrument Rating before being issued with a CPL (A), *unless* he is applying for a type rating for a multi-pilot type as listed in D3.5.

However, QSPs should be aware that to preserve the validity of ATPL theoretical knowledge credits for the subsequent issue of an ATPL (A), both a CPL (A) and IR (A) must be obtained within the 36 month Acceptance Period of the theoretical knowledge examinations. If a CPL (A) and IR (A) are not obtained within this period, the ATPL theory credit will expire and the examinations would have to be re-sat. It is therefore recommended that QSPs qualify for the issue of a CPL (A) and IR (A) at the same time.

IR (A) Skill Test Requirements

The IR (A) Skill Test arrangements for ME pilots differ from those for non-ME pilots.

ME Pilot - Multi-Pilot Types

A QSP (A) who meets the currency requirements for a Multi-pilot, Multi-engine type rating as detailed in D3.5, is required to:

1. Pass the IR (A) Skill Test on the Multi-pilot type, observed by a CAA Flight Examiner.

ME Pilot – Single Pilot Types

A QSP (A) who qualifies for a Single-pilot, Multi-engine type rating as detailed in D3.5, is required to:

1) Pass the IR (A) Skill Test on the Single-pilot type, with a CAA Flight Examiner.

C17/Canberra/Non-ME Pilot/Non-Current Pilot

A non-ME QSP (A), a QSP (A) who is required to pass the CPL (A) Skill Test under D3.4, or a QSP (A) who is required under D3.5 to obtain a Class Rating for a Single-pilot aeroplane (i.e. a Canberra/C17 pilot or a QSP (A) who does not meet the currency requirements), is required to:

1. Pass the IR (A) Skill Test with a CAA Flight Examiner.

   - Before undertaking the Skill Test, applicants must complete IR training at a FTO approved to conduct IR (A) modular courses. The amount of training required depends on the type of Service IR held. Please refer to Section E1.2 (credits from IR(A) training).

D3.7 UK FLIGHT RADIO TELEPHONY OPERATORS LICENCE (FRTOL)

An applicant for the JAR-FCL CPL (A) shall hold/qualify for a UK FRTOL.

A QSP (A), who meets the eligibility criteria for any of the accreditation schemes detailed in D3.3, will be credited with the written examination and practical communications test.

FULL DETAILS OF THE FRTOL REQUIREMENTS ARE CONTAINED IN SECTION B.

D3.8 JAR-FCL CPL (A) MEDICAL REQUIREMENTS

An applicant for a JAR-FCL CPL (A) shall hold a valid JAR-FCL Class One medical certificate.

FULL DETAILS OF MEDICAL REQUIREMENTS ARE CONTAINED IN JAR-FCL 3 AND SECTION A5

Section A Section B Section C Section D CPL Section E Section F Section G Section H Section I Section J Section K Index

D4 JAR-FCL CPL (HELICOPTER)

This section offers information as a basic guide to obtaining a JAR-FCL Commercial Pilot Licence (Helicopter) - CPL(H) as follows:-

For full details you are advised to refer to **JAR-FCL 2 Subpart D**.

D4.1 JAR-FCL CPL(H) GENERAL INFORMATION

Privileges

Details of licence privileges can be found in Schedule 8 of the Air Navigation Order, (please also refer to Section A, Appendix F).

Minimum Age

An applicant for a JAR-FCL CPL(H) shall be at least 18 years of age.

Licence Validity

The JAR-FCL CPL(H) will be issued for a maximum period of 5 years.

D4.2 JAR-FCL CPL(H) COURSES

A JAR-FCL CPL(H) may be obtained by completing an approved Integrated Course or approved Modular Course of training. Applicants intending to train in another JAA Member State should refer to Section A8.

Integrated Courses

The Integrated Course is a full time course of ground and flying training run by a Flying Training Organisation approved to conduct such courses. There are two Integrated courses available:

Commercial Pilot Licence (Helicopter) Integrated Course

The aim of this course is to train pilots to the level of proficiency necessary for the issue of a CPL(H) but not the Instrument Rating or any further specialisation (e.g. aerial work activities) The course shall last between 9 and 24 months.

This course consists of a minimum of 135 hours of flying training and 550 hours (reduced to 500 hours for PPL(H) holders) of theoretical knowledge instruction (see D4.2(A) for details).

Airline Transport Pilot (Helicopter) Integrated Course

The aim of this course is to train pilots to the level of proficiency necessary to enable them to operate as co-pilot on multi-pilot, multi-engine helicopters in commercial air transportation and to obtain the CPL(H)/IR but not any further specialisation (e.g. aerial work activities) The course shall last between 12 and 36 months.

The course consists of a minimum of 195 hours of flying training and 750 hours of theoretical knowledge instruction. The course also includes training in multi-crew co-operation for the operation of multi-pilot helicopters (see D4.2(B) for details).

CPL(H) Modular Course

The aim of this course is to train PPL(H) holders to the level of proficiency necessary for the issue of a CPL(H) but not the instrument rating or any further specialisation (e.g. aerial work activities).

This course is designed for applicants who do not wish to undertake a full time course of integrated training or who wish to stagger their training by completing approved 'modules' of approved training over a period of time i.e. instrument rating course, Multi-Crew Co-operation Course (MCC), ATPL theoretical knowledge instruction etc.

The course consists of a minimum of 30 hours of flying training and 500 hours of theoretical knowledge instruction, for CPL(H) and 650 hours theoretical knowledge instruction for ATPL(H) (see D4.2(C) for details).

D4.2(A) JAR-FCL CPL(H) Integrated Course Flying Training/Experience Requirements

A graduate from an approved CPL(H) Integrated Course must have completed a minimum of **135** hours of flight time. This must include the particular minimum requirements specified in **D1.2(A) a to g below**. Each of these requirements must be met in full but hours may be credited, where appropriate, towards more than one requirement except where stated otherwise.

a. **100 hours** dual instruction;

b. **35 h**ours as pilot-in-command, to include at least 14 hours solo day, 1 hour solo night and may include 20 hours as SPIC.

SPIC time shall be credited as pilot-in-command time, unless the flight instructor had to influence or control any part of the flight. A ground de-briefing by the flight instructor does not affect the crediting as pilot-in-command time;

c. **10** hours dual cross-country flying;

d. **10** hours of cross-country flight as pilot-in-command including a VFR cross-country flight totalling at least 185 km (100 nm) in the course of which full stop landings at two different aerodromes from the aerodrome of departure shall be made;

e. **5** hours flight time in helicopters shall be completed at night comprising 3 hours of dual instruction including at least 1 hour of cross-country navigation and 5 sold circuits. Each circuit shall include a take-off and landing;

f. **10** hours of instrument dual instruction time, including at least 5 hours in a helicopter;

g. Of the **100** hours of dual instruction up to:

i. **90** hours visual instruction may include:

1. **40** hours in a helicopter FS level C/D, or
2. **30** hours in a helicopter FNPT II/III, or
3. **20** hours in an aeroplane or TMG

ii. 10 hours instrument instruction, which may include 5 hours in at least an aeroplane FNPT I or helicopter FNPT I or an aeroplane.

If the helicopter used for the flying training is of a different type from the FS used for the visual training, the maximum credit shall be limited to that allocated for the FNPT II/III.

D4.2(B) JAR-FCL ATPL(H) Integrated Course Flying Training/Experience Requirements

A graduate from an approved ATPL(H) Integrated Course must have completed a minimum of **195** hours of flight time. This must include the particular requirements specified in **D4.2(B) a to g below**. Each of these requirements must be met in full but, hours may be credited, where appropriate, towards more than one requirement except where stated otherwise.

a. **125** hours of dual instruction;

b. **70** hours as pilot-in-command, to include at least **14** hours solo day, **1** hour solo night and may include **55** hours as SPIC.

SPIC time shall be credited as pilot-in-command time, unless the flight instructor had to influence or control any part of the flight. A ground debriefing by the flight instructor does not affect the crediting as pilot-in-command time.

c. **50** hours of cross-country flight, at least 10 hours of cross-country flight as student pilot-in-command including a VFR cross-country flight totalling at least 185 km (100 nm) in the course of which landings at two different aerodromes from the aerodrome of departure shall be made;

d. **5** hours flight time in helicopters shall be completed at night comprising 3 hours of dual instruction including at least 1 hour of cross-country navigation and 5 solo night circuits. Each circuit shall include a take-off and a landing; and

e. **50** hours of instrument time comprising:

i. **35** hours of instrument flight time instruction of which up to 10 hours may be instrument ground time in a FNPT I, or 20 hours if all the instrument ground training is conducted in an FNPT II or flight simulator;

ii. **15** hours as SPIC, and

f. **15** hours multi-crew co-operation;

g. of the **125** hours of dual instruction up to:

i. **75** hours visual instruction may include:

1. **30** hours in a helicopter FS level C/D, or

2. **20** hours in a helicopter FNPT II/III, or
3. **20** hours in an aeroplane or TMG.

ii. **35** hours instrument instruction may include:

1. up to **20** hours in a helicopter FNPT II/III or FS, or
2. **10** hours in at least a helicopter FNPT I or aeroplane FNPT I or an aeroplane.

iii. **15** hours multi-crew co-operation, for which a helicopter FS or helicopter FNPT I/III (MCC) may be used.

If the helicopter used for the flying training is of a different type from the helicopter FS used for the visual training, the maximum credit shall be limited to that allocated for the helicopter FNPT I/II.

D4.2(B) NOTES

The holder of a PPL(H) issued in accordance with ICAO Annex 1 may, at the discretion of the FTO, be credited with 50% of the helicopter hours flown prior to the course up to a credit of 40 hours flying experience of which up to 20 hours may be dual instruction, or 50 hours if a helicopter night flying qualification has been obtained of which, up to 25 hours may be dual instruction. Any credit given is subject to confirmation by the FTO at the time of application.

D4.2(C) JAR-FCL CPL(H) Modular Course Flying Training/Experience Requirements

Holders of a PPL(H) issued in accordance with ICAO Annex 1, with the minimum flying experience detailed below, may commence an **Approved JAR CPL(H) Modular Course** of training:

- 155 hours flight time as pilot of helicopters, including 50 hours as PIC of helicopters of which 10 hours shall be cross-country, or
- 135 hours as pilot of helicopters if holder of a PPL(A), including 30 hours as PIC of helicopters; or
- 105 hours as pilot of helicopters if holder of a CPL(A).
- have complied with JAR-FCL 2.225 and 2.240 if a multi-engine helicopter is to be used on the skill test.
- Applicants with a valid JAR-FCL or ICAO Instrument Rating (H) shall be given at least 20 hours dual visual flight instruction and shall be fully credited towards the dual instrument instruction time. The same credit may be given to applicants who have completed an IR(H) modular course of training and passed the IR(H) skill test but have not applied for the IR(H) licence endorsement **providing** that the IR(H) course and JAR CPL(H) modular course are conducted totally separately from each other, and that there is no training overlap between the two courses.
- Applicants with a valid JAR-FCL or ICAO Instrument Rating (A) or a QSP(A) with Green Instrument Rating shall be given at least 20 hours dual visual flight instruction and 5 hours helicopter dual instrument training.
- Applicants without a Night Qualification (Helicopter) shall additionally complete a minimum of 5 hours night flight instruction.

The Modular Course consists of 30 hours dual instruction time, up to 20 hours visual instruction may include 5 hours in a helicopter FNPT II/III or FS, and 10 hours instrument instruction, which may include 5 hours in at least an aeroplane FNPT I or helicopter FNPT I or an aeroplane. Flying completed on the course may be counted towards meeting the flying experience requirements for licence issue as detailed below.

An applicant for a JAR-FCL CPL(H) must have completed a minimum of 185 hours of flight time (see D4.2(C) Notes). This must include the particular requirements specified in D4.2(c) a, b and c below as pilot of helicopters:-

a. **50** hours as Pilot-in-Command, or **35** hours as Pilot-in-Command if completed during a course of integrated flying training;

   10 hours of cross-country flight time as Pilot-in-Command, including a cross-country flight totalling at least 185 km (100 nm) in the course of which full-stop landings at two aerodromes different from the aerodromes of departure shall be made.

b. **10** hours of instrument dual instruction time (for applicants without an IR), of which not more than 5 hours is to be instrument ground time (in a FNPT I or II or a Flight Simulator).

c. **5** hours Night flying (for applicants without a PPL(H) NQ) comprising of at least 3 hours of dual instruction, including at least 1 hour of cross-country navigation, and 5 solo take-offs and full-stop landings, each to include one circuit.

D4.2(C) Notes

The 185 hours flying experience may comprise flight time in any of the following capacities:

- Pilot-in-Command/Solo (PIC), counted in full;

- Pilot-under-Instruction (Dual), counted in full;

Crediting from the 185 hours of flight time:

i. 20 hours as pilot-in-command holding a PPL(A); or

ii. 50 hours as pilot-in-command holding a CPL(A) may have been completed in aeroplanes; or

iii. 10 hours as pilot-in-command in touring motor gliders or gliders.

D4.3 JAR-FCL CPL(H) THEORETICAL KNOWLEDGE EXAMINATION REQUIREMENTS

Candidates with national CPL/H theoretical passes

Candidates who failed to achieve a full pass in the former UK national CPL(H) theoretical knowledge examinations will be required to pass all the JAR-FCL theoretical knowledge examinations. However, provided they have a pass in at least one of the former UK national theoretical knowledge subjects, the amount of ground instruction needed to prepare them for the JAR examinations will be at the discretion of the approved training provider.

CPL(H) Modular and CPL(H) Integrated Courses

An applicant from either course must pass the nine **CPL(H) Theoretical Knowledge** examination in the following subjects:

Air Law
Aircraft General Knowledge
Flight Performance and Planning
Human Performance and Limitations
Meteorology
Navigation
Operational Procedures
Principles of Flight
Communications (VFR)

ATPL(H) Integrated Course

An applicant from this course must pass the fourteen **ATPL(H) Theoretical Knowledge** examination in the following subjects:

Air Law
Aircraft General Knowledge (2 papers)
Flight Performance and Planning (3 papers)
Human Performance and Limitations
Meteorology
Navigation (2 papers)
Operational Procedures
Principles of Flight
Communications (2 papers)

JAR-FCL theoretical knowledge acceptance period – *warning*

Potential candidates for the JAR-FCL CPL(H) should first consider the implications of JAR-FCL 2.495 that relates to the Acceptance Period.

A pass in the theoretical knowledge examinations given in accordance with JAR-FCL 2.490 will be accepted for the grant of the CPL(H) or IR(H) during the 36 months from the end of the month of the date of gaining a pass in all the required examination papers*. Provided that an IR(H) is obtained in accordance with the above, a pass in the ATPL(H) theoretical knowledge examination will remain valid for a period of 7 years from the last validity date of the IR(H) entered in the CPL(H) for the issuance of an ATPL(H).

* All requirements for the issue of the CPL(H) and IR(H) must be met and the applicant required to apply to PLD for issue within the 36 month validity period of the theoretical knowledge examinations.

Credits from JAR-FCL Theoretical Examinations

- An applicant who has previously passed the VFR Communications examination at CPL(H) level, and have been issued with a CPL(H) will not be re-examined in subject VFR Communications at ATPL(H) level.

- An applicant who has previously passed the IFR Communications examination at IR level, and have been issued with an IR(H) will not be re-examined in subject IFR Communications at ATPL(H) level.

- The holder of a valid JAR-FCL CPL(A) will be required to complete the appropriate bridging examinations at CPL(H) level (see Section J1.9) or all the examinations at ATPL(H) level.

- The holder of a valid JAR-FCL ATPL(A) will be required to complete the bridging examination requirements appropriate to the level of examinations being taken (see Section J1.9).

DETAILS OF THE ABOVE EXAMINATIONS, PASS RULES, VALIDITY PERIODS, ETC, ARE GIVEN IN JAR-FCL 2, SUBPART J.

D4.4 JAR-FCL CPL(H) SKILL TEST REQUIREMENTS

An applicant for a JAR-FCL CPL(H) is required to:

1. Pass the **CPL Skill Test** with a CAA Flight Examiner.

   - An applicant for a skill test for the CPL(H) shall have satisfactorily completed all of the required training, including instruction on the same type of helicopter to be used in the test. An applicant graduating from an ATP(H) integrated course shall take the test on a multi-engine helicopter. An applicant graduating from a CPL(H) integrated course, or a CPL(H) modular course, may take the test on either a single-engine helicopter or, subject to the experience requirement set out in JAR-FCL 2.255(a) to have 70 hours as pilot-in-command of helicopters, a multi-engine helicopter. The helicopter used for the skill test shall meet the requirements for training helicopters set out in Appendix 1 to JAR-FCL 2.055. For the purpose of licence issue the skill test is valid for 12 months.
   - An applicant shall pass sections 1 through 5 of the skill test. Failure in more than one section will require the applicant to take the entire test again. If any item in a section is failed, that section is failed. An applicant failing only one section shall take the failed section again. Failure in any items of the re-test and failure in any other items already passed, will require the applicant to take the entire test again. All sections of the skill test shall be completed within six months.
   - Further training may be required following any failed skill test. Failure to achieve a pass in all sections of the test in two attempts shall require further training as determined by the Authority. There is no limit to the number of skill tests that may be attempted.
   - Before undertaking the Skill Test, the applicant shall have passed the associated theoretical knowledge examination (exceptions may be made by the Authority for applicants undergoing a course of integrated flying training) and completed all of the related flying training.
   - Before undertaking the CPL(H) Skill Test an applicant must obtain a pre-entry form F170A. The applicant will also be required to provide evidence of either holding a valid UK FRTOL or having passed the UK RTF practical test prior to undertaking the CPL(H) Skill Test.

Instrument Rating IR(H) Skill Test

Students on an Integrated Course of Training for the ATPL(H) are also required to pass an IR(H) Skill Test with a CAA Flight Examiner.

- An applicant for a skill test for the IR(H) shall have received instruction on the same type of helicopter to be used for the skill test. The helicopter used for the skill test shall meet the requirements for training helicopters set out in Appendix 1 to JAR-FCL 2.055.
- An applicant shall pass all sections of the skill test. Failure in more than one section will require the applicant to take the entire test again. An applicant failing only one section shall take the failed section again. Failure in any section of the re-test, including those sections that have been passed on a previous attempt, will require the applicant to take the entire test again. All sections of the skill test shall be completed within six months.
- Further training may be required following any failed skill test. Failure to achieve a pass in all sections of the test in two attempts shall require further training as determined by the Authority. There is no limit to the number of skill tests that may be attempted.
- The IR(H) Skill Test must be completed on a multi-engine helicopter.
- Before undertaking the Skill Test, the applicant shall have passed the associated theoretical knowledge examination (exceptions may be made by the Authority for applicants undergoing a course of integrated flying training) and completed all of the related flying training.
- Before undertaking the IR(H) Skill Test an applicant must obtain a pre-entry form F170A. The applicant will also be required to provide evidence of either holding a valid UK FRTOL or having passed the UK RTF practical test prior to undertaking the IR(H) Skill Test.

DETAILS OF THE CPL(H) SKILL TEST REQUIREMENTS ARE DETAILED IN APPENDICES 1 AND 2 TO JAR-FCL 2.170.

Guidance for applicants taking the CPL(H) Skill Test can also be found in Standards Document 03(H) on the CAA web site at www.caa.co.uk.

DETAILS OF THE IR(H) SKILL TEST REQUIREMENTS ARE DETAILED IN APPENDICES 1 AND 2 TO JAR-FCL 2.210.

Guidance for applicants taking the IR(H) Skill Test can also be found in Standards Document 01(H) on the CAA web site at www.caa.co.uk.

D4.5 CONVERSION OF A NON-JAA PROFESSIONAL LICENCE TO A JAR-FCL CPL(H)

A licence issued by a non-JAA State may be converted to a JAR-FCL licence provided that an arrangement exists between the JAA and the non-JAA State. This arrangement shall be established on the basis of reciprocity of licence acceptance and shall ensure that an equivalent level of safety exists between the training and testing requirements of the JAA and non-JAA State. Until such arrangements exist, the following requirements have been agreed by the JAA and are now incorporated in JAR-FCL 2, paragraph 2.016;

Non-JAA CPL(H)

The holder of a **current and valid*** CPL(H) issued in accordance with ICAO Annex 1 by a non-JAA State may be issued with a JAR-FCL CPL(H) providing the experience requirements of JAR-FCL 2.155(b) and (c) have been met. Applicants' must:

- Hold a valid JAR-FCL Class 1 medical certificate.
- Undertake CPL(H) theoretical knowledge instruction as determined by the Head of Training of an approved training provider and pass ALL of the JAR-FCL theoretical knowledge examinations at CPL(H) level. Applicants who wish to attempt examinations at a higher level (i.e. ATPL(H) level) must undertake the full 650 hour course of approved theoretical knowledge instruction and pass ALL of the JAR-FCL theoretical knowledge examinations at ATPL (H) level.
- Undertake flying training as determined by the Head of Training of a Flight Training Organisation approved to conduct CPL(H) modular flying training courses, sufficient to obtain the pre-entry Form 170A and pass the CPL(H) Skill Test (in accordance with Appendices 1 and 2 to JAR-FCL 2.170) with a CAA Flight Examiner;
- Qualify for the issue of a UK Flight Radio Telephony Operator's Licence – Section B refers.

* The holder of an ICAO CPL(H) that is not current and valid will be required to complete the full CPL(H) modular flying training course.

Non-JAA ATPL(H) Licence

The holder of a **current and valid*** ICAO ATPL(H) who does not meet the experience requirements for the grant of a JAR-FCL ATPL(H) as detailed in Section G3.5, can still apply for a JAR-FCL CPL(H)/IR. Applicants' must:

- Hold a valid JAR-FCL Class 1 medical certificate.
- Undertake CPL(H) and IR theoretical knowledge instruction as determined by the Head of Training of an approved training provider, and pass ALL of the JAR-FCL theoretical knowledge at CPL and IR level. Applicants who wish to attempt examinations at a higher level (i.e. ATPL(H)) must undertake the full 650 hour course of approved theoretical knowledge instruction and pass ALL of the JAR-FCL theoretical knowledge examinations at ATPL(H) level.
- Undertake flying training as determined by the Head of Training of a Flight Training Organisation approved to conduct CPL(H) modular flying training courses, sufficient to obtain the pre-entry Form 170A, and pass the CPL(H) skill test (in accordance with Appendices 1 and 2 to JAR-FCL 2.170) with a CAA Flight Examiner.
- Qualify for the issue of a UK Flight Radio Telephony Operator's Licence (FRTOL) – Section B refers.

* The holder of an ICAO ATPL(H) that is not current and valid will be required to complete the full CPL(H) modular flying training course.

Non-JAA (ICAO) IR(H)

The holder of a **current and valid** Instrument Rating Helicopter IR(H) issued in accordance with ICAO Annex 1 by a non-JAA State may be issued with a JAR-FCL IR(H). (Please refer to Section E2.2).

D4.6 UK FLIGHT RADIOTELEPHONY OPERATOR'S LICENCE (FRTOL) REQUIREMENTS

An applicant for a UK FRTOL is required to pass the Radiotelephony written examination and practical test with an authorised RTF Examiner. It should be noted that whilst Radio Communication forms part of the JAR-FCL CPL(H) training syllabus, the FRTOL remains a UK national licence.

FULL DETAILS OF THE FRTOL REQUIREMENTS INCLUDING CREDITS AVAILABLE ARE CONTAINED IN SECTION B.

D4.7 JAR-FCL CPL(H) MEDICAL REQUIREMENTS

An applicant for a JAR-FCL CPL(H) shall hold a valid JAR-FCL Class 1 Medical Certificate.

FULL DETAILS ARE CONTAINED IN JAR-FCL 3 AND SECTION A5

D5 JAR-FCL CPL (HELICOPTER) RESTRICTED TO UK REGISTERED AIRCRAFT

This section offers information on the JAR-FCL Commercial Pilot Licence (Helicopters)(Restricted) – JAR-FCL(H)(R) as follows:-

D5.1 JAR-FCL CPL(H)(R) GENERAL INFORMATION

The JAR-FCL CPL(H)(R) licence can no longer be issued. This section does however provide information for existing JAR-FCL CPL(H)(R) licence holders to remove the restricted endorsement from the licence and upgrade to a JAR-FCL ATPL(H).

Privileges

Details of licence privileges can be found in Schedule 8 of the Air Navigation Order, (please also refer to Section A, Appendix F). (See **Licence Endorsement**).

Minimum Age

An applicant for the JAR-FCL CPL(H)(R) shall be at least 18 years of age.

Licence Validity

The JAR-FCL CPL(H)(R) will be issued for a maximum period of 5 years.

Licence Endorsement

As the JAR-FCL CPL(H)(R) does not fully comply with the requirements of the JAR-FCL, the holder is not entitled to the automatic recognition accorded to a JAR-FCL. The licence will be endorsed with the following statement;

"Valid for United Kingdom registered aircraft. As this licence does not fully comply with JAR-FCL the holder must have permission from any other JAA Member State prior to exercising the licence privileges in aircraft registered in that State".

The effect of this endorsement on the licence is to restrict its use, initially, to aircraft/helicopters registered in the UK only. Prior to exercising the privileges of the licence in aircraft registered in another JAA Member State, permission must be sought from that State.

D5.2 REMOVAL OF THE (RESTRICTED) ENDORSEMENT

The holder of a JAR-FCL CPL(H)(R) may have the endorsement removed when:

a. They achieve 700 hours as pilot of flying machines, to include;

   200 hours PIC of helicopters;

   50 hours cross country or overseas flying as PIC or PIC U/S of helicopters or aeroplanes of which not less than 35 hours must be as PIC of helicopters;

   OR

b. Obtain a pass in the JAR-FCL CPL(H) or ATPL(H) examinations following an approved course of ground instruction.

On completion of D5.4 a or b the licence holder can apply to PLD (using Form SRG\1163) to have the restriction removed and pay the appropriate fee.

D5.3 UPGRADING TO JAR-FCL ATPL(H)

Holders of a JAR-FCL CPL(H)(R) wishing to obtain a JAR-FCL ATPL(H) should refer to the requirements in Section G3.

D6 JAR-FCL CPL (HELICOPTER) FOR UK QUALIFIED SERVICE PILOTS (HELICOPTERS)

This section offers information as a basic guide to obtaining a JAR-FCL Commercial Pilot Licence (Helicopter) – JAR-FCL CPL (H) – for a UK Qualified Service Pilot (Helicopters)

D6.1 JAR-FCL CPL (H) GENERAL INFORMATION

Introduction

JAR-FCL permits the knowledge, experience and skill gained in military service to be credited towards the relevant requirements of JAR-FCL licences and ratings at the discretion of each national authority. The CAA has worked closely with the MoD through the MoD/CAA Working Group (MCWG) to determine the scope and level of accreditation that can be applied to suitably experienced UK military pilots.

In particular, the MCWG sought to determine an agreed level of equivalence between the theoretical knowledge acquired by pilots throughout military flying training and subsequent operational experience, and those required at JAR-FCL ATPL (H) level.

Full details of the theoretical knowledge requirements, including credits and eligibility criteria, can be found in section D6.3. It should be noted that a QSP (H) can still take advantage of any flying or skill test credits for he qualifies even if he does not qualify for theoretical knowledge credits under D6.3. Similarly, a QSP (H) does not have to be in current military flying practice to take advantage of any theoretical knowledge credits for which he may be eligible.

Although not exclusive, a licensing flow diagram can be found at Appendix I to Section D, to demonstrate typical licensing routes for experienced military helicopter pilots.

Questions regarding this scheme should be directed in writing to: FT (Proj) 1, HQ TGDA, RAF Innsworth, Gloucester, GL3 1EZ or by e-mail to ftproj1@tgda.gov.uk.

Taxi-time allowances

For details of Recording of Military Flying Times-Taxi-time allowances please refer to Section A, Appendix B.

Privileges

Details of licence privileges can be found in Schedule 8 of the Air Navigation Order (please also refer to Section A, Appendix F).

Minimum Age

An applicant for a JAR-FCL CPL (H) shall be at least 18 years of age.

Licence Validity

A JAR-FCL CPL (H) will be issued for a maximum period of 5 years.

Definition of Qualified Service Pilot

To qualify for any of the credits detailed in Section D6, an applicant must be a UK Qualified Service Pilot (QSP). A QSP defined as a pilot who has completed a recognised military course of flying training and has been awarded a pilot's flying badge in full compliance with QR (RAF) J727. This is deemed to be:

The term "flying badge" is used to include all badges worn by personnel who have successfully completed a prescribed course of flying training. The initial award of a flying badge is on a provisional basis. It is not deemed to be fully earned until the holder has successfully completed an operational conversion or equivalent course and has joined an operational or non-operational unit in the capacity for which the provisional badge has been awarded. Joining is defined for each Service as follows:

a. RN: on issue of the Certificate of Competence.

b. Army and RM: on award of the badge (and successful completion of conversion to type (CTT) course).

c. RAF: on successful attainment of an appropriate aircrew categorisation or qualification to undertake productive flying duties (C categorisation or above, B1 or above instructor category or CR status).

Non-UK Military Pilots

Non-UK military pilots operating UK military aircraft through exchange programs etc., are not eligible for any of the credits afforded to UK military pilots - if a serving member of the Armed Forces of another JAA State, applicants should contact the National Aviation Authority of that State for details of any accreditation arrangements for its military personnel.

Ex-Qualified Service Pilots

An ex-QSP (H) can claim any credits for which he qualifies, for a period of one year from the last date of service.

An ex-QSP (H) employed by a Defence Contractor in flying-related duties, is deemed to be a QSP (H) for licensing purposes. He can claim any credits for which he qualifies, for a period of one year from the date of last flight in a military helicopter.

Definition of Current Flying Practice

In order to qualify for credit against the CPL (H) Skill Test (see D6.4), a QSP (H) shall be in current flying practice.

To be deemed to be in current flying practice, a QSP(H) shall have a minimum of 12 hours flying experience as a pilot in military or civil helicopters (or combination of both) in the 12 months preceding the date of application for licence issue. This experience shall include at least 6 hours as pilot-in-command (PIC) - for this purpose, military 1st pilot hours may be counted towards the PIC requirement, one flight with a military instructor pilot or JAA Flight Instructor, and 12 take-offs and landings.

A QSP(H) on a ground tour can still achieve currency, by flying on civil helicopters. A QSP(H) who does not already hold a valid PPL(H) can satisfy the 6 hours PIC requirement by flying solo at a PPL registered facility, under the authority of the Chief Flight Instructor (in much the same way as an ab-initio PPL student would). The balance could be made up with dual training for a JAA type rating and/or IR(H).

D6.2 JAR-FCL CPL (H) FLYING TRAINING AND EXPERIENCE REQUIREMENTS

The CAA recognises all QSPs who have completed a course of military ground and flying training and who meet the definition of a QSP in D6.1. Provided such pilots remain in current flying practice (see D6.1), and meet the flying experience requirements of Section D4.2(c)), they will be credited the approved CPL (H) modular course of flying training.

D6.3 JAR-FCL CPL (H) THEORETICAL KNOWLEDGE EXAMINATION REQUIREMENTS

An applicant for a JAR-FCL CPL (H) is required to complete an approved course of theoretical knowledge instruction, and pass theoretical knowledge examinations at CPL level, or if IR(H) privileges will be required, at CPL and IR level or ATPL level.

However, as described in D6.1, the MCWG determined a level of equivalence between theoretical knowledge training and subsequent operational experience, and that required at ATPL(H) level. It should be recognised that the scope for accreditation was not the same for all military pilots, and that role training and experience ultimately determined the level of equivalence achieved. A Rotary accreditation scheme has been agreed, based on the level of equivalence found.

A QSP (H), who does not meet the eligibility criteria, will be required to demonstrate the appropriate level of theoretical knowledge by passing ALL of the theoretical knowledge examinations at the appropriate level (i.e. CPL, CPL and IR or ATPL). However, credit will be given against the requirement to complete and approved course or theoretical knowledge instruction course prior to attempting the examinations. Applicants will be required to undertake theoretical knowledge instruction as determined by the Head of Training of an approved training provider.

D6.3(A) ROTARY ACCREDITATION SCHEME

Eligibility

To qualify for theoretical knowledge examination credits under the Rotary accreditation scheme, a QSP(H) shall have completed:

1. A minimum of 2000 hours* flying experience on military aircraft, including at least 1500 hours** as 1st pilot of helicopters (can incl. max. 500 hours under supervision, as P2 or in a flight simulator).

* As recorded in service logbook i.e. excluding any taxi-time allowances.

** QSPs with a mix of military helicopter and aeroplane experience may be permitted to enter the Rotary Accreditation Scheme, depending on their experience. Advice should be sought from PLD.

Theoretical Knowledge Requirements

A QSP (H) who meets the eligibility criteria in full, is required to:

1. Complete a Rotary Bridging Package with an approved training provider.

In certain subject areas, military theoretical training does not meet the level of equivalency required at JAR ATPL (H) level. In order to secure credit from the source JAR examinations, it was agreed that these topics should form the basis of a Rotary Bridging Package. Further details, including a summary of the content of the Rotary Bridging Package, can be found at Appendix H to Section D.

2. Pass the ATPL (H) examinations in:

    i. Air Law

    ii. Performance

    iii. Operational Procedures

To prepare for the above examinations, a QSP (H) is required to undertake theoretical knowledge instruction as determined by the Head of Training of an approved training provider.

Due to a delay in the introduction of the JAR-FCL ATPL (H) examinations, interim arrangements are in place until further notice. Applicants will sit the equivalent ATPL (A) examinations in Air Law and Operational Procedures. A temporary exemption exists against the Performance examination until such time as this examination becomes available.

DETAILS OF THE ABOVE EXAMINATIONS, PASS RULES, VALIDITY PERIODS, ETC, ARE GIVEN IN JAR-FCL 2, SUBPART J.

D6.4 JAR-FCL CPL (H) SKILL TEST REQUIREMENTS

A QSP (H) in current flying practice as defined in D6.1 will be credited the CPL (H) Skill Test, and should refer to D6.5 for details of the JAA type rating requirements for licence issue.

A QSP (H) not in current flying practice as defined in D6.1 will be required to pass the **CPL (H) Skill Test** with a CAA Flight Examiner.

- Before undertaking the Skill Test, applicants must complete CPL training at the discretion of the Head of Training of a FTO approved to conduct CPL (H) modular courses, sufficient to obtain the 170A Certificate of Competence.

It may also be necessary to complete an approved type rating conversion course for the helicopter type to be used for the skill test. This will be the case for a QSP (H) who has not flown the type to be used for the Skill Test before, or has less than 500 hours flying experience on the type (the minimum experience to qualify for exemption from the approved type conversion course).

- Before undertaking the Skill Test, the applicant shall have passed the required theoretical knowledge examinations.

- The Skill Test can be completed in a single-engine (SE) or multi-engine (ME) helicopter.

- For the purpose of licence issue, the skill test is valid for 12 months.

D6.5 TYPE RATING REQUIREMENTS

A QSP (H), who is required under D6.4 to pass the CPL (H) Skill Test, will qualify for a type rating appropriate to the helicopter used for the skill test.

A QSP (H) who is credited the CPL (H) Skill Test under D6.4, shall qualify for a type rating to open the licence.

Subject to currency on a type, a military rating will be issued for any of the following helicopter types in military service:

Apache	**Chinook**
Lynx	**Merlin**
SeaKing	**Wessex**

Subject to currency on type, a JAR-FCL type rating will be issued for any of the following helicopter types:-

Agusta* A109A (A109/109K/109E
Bell 212* (Bell 212/412)
Gazelle* (SA341/342)
Puma* (SA330)
Squirrel* (AS350/350B3)

Currency Requirements

In order to qualify for a type rating credit, a QSP (H) must:

i. show a minimum of 500 hours flying experience on any ONE type;

ii. show evidence of a valid annual check (AAC - Standards check, RN - QHI check with NFSF(RW) RAF - QHI check) on the same type as (i) completed in the 12 months preceding the date of application for licence issue.

Notes:

1. A QSP (H), who meets the requirement of (i) but not (ii) on a type indicated by '*', may apply for a 'one-off 'authorisation for a CFS Agent to conduct a type rating skill test (LST-SPH) on the type

2. A QSP (H) who does not meet the above currency requirements in full, will be required to obtain a type rating for a Single-pilot, SE or ME helicopter in accordance with Section F.

D6.6 INSTRUMENT RATING REQUIREMENTS

It is not mandatory for a QSP (H) to complete an Instrument Rating before being issued with a CPL(H).

An applicant for an IR (H) is required to complete the requirements in accordance with Section E.

QSPs should note that JAR-FCL 2 requires both a CPL (H) and IR (H) to be obtained within the 36 month Acceptance Period of the ATPL (H) examinations to maintain ATPL (H) theory credit for the subsequent issue of an ATPL (H). However, it has been agreed that a QSP (H) will not be subject to this requirement. Whilst the 36 months Acceptance Period will still apply to the issue of a CPL (H), an IR (H) can be obtained at any time up to 3 years from the date of the last flight in a military helicopter, and still retain ATPL (H) theory credit.

D6.7 UK FLIGHT RADIO TELEPHONY OPERATORS LICENCE (FRTOL)

An applicant for the JAR-FCL CPL (H) shall hold/qualify for a UK FRTOL.

A QSP (H), who meets the eligibility criteria for the accreditation scheme detailed in D6.3, will be credited with the written examination and practical communications test.

FULL DETAILS OF THE FRTOL REQUIREMENTS ARE CONTAINED IN SECTION B.

D6.8 JAR-FCL CPL (H) MEDICAL REQUIREMENTS

An applicant for a JAR-FCL CPL (H) shall hold a valid JAR-FCL Class One medical certificate.

FULL DETAILS OF MEDICAL REQUIREMENTS ARE CONTAINED IN JAR-FCL 3 AND SECTION A5.

D7 UK CPL (BALLOONS)

This section offers information as a basic guide to obtaining a UK Commercial Pilot Licence (Balloons) - UK CPL(B)

D7.1 UK CPL(B) GENERAL INFORMATION

Privileges

Details of licence privileges can be found in Schedule 8 of the Air Navigation Order, (please also refer to Section A, Appendix F).

Minimum age

The minimum age for the grant of a UK CPL(B) is 18 years, but some of the required qualifications for the grant of the licence may be gained earlier. Applicants should ensure that any qualifications gained earlier would still be valid at the time they plan to apply for the grant of the licence. The validity periods of training, examinations and flight tests are covered in this document.

Licence validity

The UK CPL(B) will be issued with a maximum period of validity of 10 years.

Non-UK licence holders

Any credits or exemptions against training for holders of a non-UK Pilot's Licence or equivalent privileges for Balloons are indicated at the relevant section.

Applicants for conversion to a UK CPL(B) must obtain a valid UK or JAR-FCL Medical Certificate (see D7.7).

Any United Kingdom flight crew licences issued on conversion of foreign licences will contain a statement on the licence to that effect. This is in order to comply with Article 6 of EC Directive 670/1991 effective from 1 June 1992. This statement will NOT be entered in UK licences issued on conversion from an EC Member State's licence.

D7.2 UK CPL(B) FLYING EXPERIENCE REQUIREMENTS

CPL(B) (Restricted privileges)

An applicant for a CPL(B) with privileges restricted to aerial work and private flying must have completed at least **35 hours flight time as pilot of balloons** including the requirements of **D7.2 a & b** below.

a. **15 hours** of instruction in flying as pilot of balloons, including:

   i. **4 free flights**, one of which must be an ascent to at least 5000 ft above the elevation of the place of departure;

   ii. **2 tethered flights.**

b. **20 hours** as PIC, including:

   i. **16 free flights**, including one cross-country flight with a landing made at a place not less than 20 km from the point of departure;

   ii. **2 tethered flights**.

D7.2 Notes:

1. The candidate will be required to obtain a PPL(B) licence before completing the PIC requirement.
2. A free flight means a flight in a free balloon of at least 5 minutes.
3. A tethered flight means a flight in a captive balloon of at least 5 minutes.
4. The instructional hours at D7.2A (a) must be to a syllabus recognised by the CAA and conducted by a person approved by the CAA for the purpose.

UK CPL(B) (Unrestricted Privileges)

An applicant for a CPL(B) must have a minimum of:

a. **75 hours** as pilot of balloons (including experience requirements of **D7.2** a) & b) and;

b. **60 Hours** as PIC of balloons.

D7.3 UK CPL(B) GENERAL FLIGHT TEST REQUIREMENTS

Unless qualifying for exemption as detailed below, applicants for a CPL(B) will be required to pass a General Flight Test (GFT), conducted by an examiner authorised for the purpose by the CAA, in the first type of balloon to be included in the Aircraft Rating of the licence.

The details of the GFT are given in Appendix C.

D7.3 Note

Holders of a professional balloon pilot's licence issued by another ICAO Contracting State who are in regular flying practice and meet the experience requirements given in D7 2, may be exempted from having to take the GFT for a period of 12 months from the date when they last exercised the professional pilot privileges of their non-UK licence as PIC.

However, candidates qualifying for such an exemption will be required to pass an appropriate aircraft rating flight test with a CAA Flight Examiner (see D7.2 and Section D, Appendix C).

D7.4 UK CPL(B) GROUND EXAMINATION REQUIREMENTS

Unless qualifying for exemptions as detailed below, applicants for a UK CPL(B) are required to pass ground examinations in:

1. Aviation Law, Flight Rules & Procedures
2. Human Performance & Limitations
3. Navigation
4. Meteorology
5. Aircraft (General) Balloons

The syllabus for the examinations is given in Appendix D.

Exemptions from Ground Examinations

- The holder of a valid UK or JAR-FCL professional pilot's licence will normally be exempt from having to take:

  Aviation Law, Flight Rules and Procedures
  Navigation
  Meteorology
  Human Performance and Limitations (if already passed).

- The holder of a valid professional pilot's licence (Balloons) issued by another ICAO Contracting State who can show that he was examined to CPL(A), CPL(H) or higher standard will normally be exempt from having to take:

  Navigation
  Meteorology

D7.4 Note

Failure to pass any of the required papers in a maximum of four attempts will lead to withdrawal of any ground examination credits that have been granted on the basis of a non-UK licence.

Examination Conditions

A candidate is required to complete all examination papers within a period of eighteen months from the end of the calendar month when an initial sitting took place. A maximum 6 sittings is allowed to complete the group with a maximum of 4 attempts per paper. The candidate may attempt the papers in any order and may opt for a schedule to meet their own training requirements.

DETAILS OF PASS RULES, VALIDITY PERIODS ETC, ARE GIVEN IN JAR-FCL 1, SUBPART J.

Examination arrangements

Written examinations for the CPL(B) are conducted by the CAA at an examination centre. Details of examination dates and closing dates for applications to take the examinations are published in Aeronautical Information Circulars (AICs).

The examination in Aircraft (Type) may take the form of an oral test conducted by the authorised examiner who carries out the Aircraft Rating flight test.

Examination Validities

The Ground examinations are valid for a period of **36 months** from the final pass.

D7.5 UK CPL(B) AIRCRAFT RATING REQUIREMENTS

The privileges of a professional pilot's licence may be exercised only in aircraft specified in the Aircraft Rating included in the licence and in respect of which the licence contains a valid Certificate of Test (C of T) or Certificate of Experience (C of E).

FULL DETAILS OF THE AIRCRAFT RATING REQUIREMENTS ARE CONTAILED IN SECTION D APPENDIX E.

D7.6 FLIGHT RADIOTELEPHONY OPERATOR'S LICENCE (FRTOL)

Although an FRTOL is not a mandatory requirement for the issue of a CPL(B) holders, applicants intending to operate radio equipment capable of receiving and transmitting messages on frequencies within the Aeronautical Mobile Band will require a FRTOL.

FULL DETAILS OF THE FRTOL ARE CONTAINED IN SECTION B

D7.7 UK CPL(B) MEDICAL REQUIREMENTS

An applicant for a UK CPL(B) restricted licence (aerial work) shall hold a valid National PPL (DVLA Group 2) medical declaration.

An applicant for a UK CPL(B) unrestricted licence shall hold a valid JAR Class 2 medical certificate.

Applicants are strongly advised to ensure that they meet the appropriate medical standard before embarking on a course of training. For full details please refer to the CAA web site www.caa.co.uk

D8 UK CPL (AIRSHIPS)

This section offers information as a basic guide to obtaining a Commercial Pilot's Licence (Airships) - UK CPL(AS) as follows:-

D8.1 UK CPL(AS) GENERAL INFORMATION

Privileges

Details of licence privileges can be found in Schedule 8 of the Air Navigation Order, (please also refer to Section A, Appendix F).

Minimum age

The minimum age for the grant of a CPL(AS) is 18 years.

Approved training

Persons wishing to obtain a CPL(AS) will be required to undergo an approved course of full time flight and ground training. Such a course will comprise of not less than 50 hours flight training on airships and 600 hours ground training.

Credits towards this approved course of training for grant of a CPL(AS), in the form of reduced flying and ground training requirements, will normally be granted to applicants holding a valid UK or JAR-FCL professional pilot's licence for any other category of aircraft. Consideration for reduced approved training will also be considered for applicants holding valid non-UK/JAR-FCL professional pilot licences. Applicants holding valid non-UK professional airship pilot licences will normally be exempt from the requirement for approved training for a UK CPL(AS) and terms for the conversion of their licences to the UK equivalent will be provided upon application to the Personnel Licensing Department.

D8.2 UK CPL(AS) FLYING TRAINING/ EXPERIENCE REQUIREMENTS

Flying experience requirements Approved Course Graduates

The minimum flying experience for the grant of a CPL(AS) in the case of a graduate from an approved course of training is a minimum of 150 hours as pilot of power driven aircraft, of which the following must be completed in helium filled airships:-

a. 50 hours total experience as pilot of helium filled airships, which must include (b) & (c) below;

b. 20 hours Cross-country or overseas flying, to include (i) & (ii) below;

   i. 10 hours PIC, including (ii);

   ii. 2 hours PIC flight **by day***;

   iii. 2 cross-country flights **at night** as PIC or PIC U/S*;

c. 10 hours Night flying as PIC or P/UT, including **5** take-offs and landings without assistance (may include b(iii))

d. 5 hours Instrument flying appreciation in power driven aircraft, to include the following minimum;

   i. 1 hour instrument familiarisation in helium filled airships;

* Cross-country flights require the airship to land at a site not less than 50 nm from the point of departure by day, and not less than 30 nm from the point of departure by night. The airship is required to come to rest in the hands of the airship ground party.

The remaining flight time to complete the 150 hour minimum may be completed in airships, aeroplanes or helicopters, and may include flight time logged prior to commencement of the course of approved training for the CPL(AS).

As there are no airships currently certificated in the UK for instrument flying, the CPL(AS) privileges will therefore be initially limited to day and night operations in VMC. Requirements for instrument flying training/ testing to remove this limitation will be developed in due course.

D8.3 UK CPL(AS) SYLLABUS FOR APPROVED COURSE OF FLYING TRAINING

The approved course of flying training must include:-

a. **15 hours** of initial flying training to reach 'solo' standard;
   This will cover effects of controls, circuits, take-offs and landings, height changes and emergency procedures. These should include operations covering extremes of permitted lightness and heaviness;

b. **10 hours** of night flying to include the minimum requirements for licence issue as stated above;
   Night circuits should include operations covering a significant spectrum of the lightness and heaviness range;

c. **20 hours** of cross-country navigation training;
   To include the cross-country licence issue flying experience minima as stated above.

The remaining flight time may be used at the discretion of the approved training provider for revision, flight to pressure altitude, maximum rate descents etc.

D8.4 THEORETICAL KNOWLEDGE EXAMINATION REQUIREMENTS

Unless qualifying for credits by virtue of holding a current UK or JAR-FCL professional aeroplane or helicopter pilot's licence, applicants for a CPL(AS) will be required to pass ground examinations in:

Aviation Law, Flight Rules and Procedures
Flight Planning and Navigation Procedures
Flight Instruments and Radio Aids
Meteorology
Signals
Aircraft (General) (Airships) (Including Loading)
Radiotelephony
Human Performance & Limitations

General examination information

Before being permitted entry for any required ground examinations, applicants must:-

- have embarked on an approved course of training, or;
- be exempt from having to undergo an approved course of training by virtue of existing professional licence qualification and flying experience

All papers, with the exception of signals, will be in multiple-choice format, with up to four alternative answers to each question.

Simple scientific calculators will be permitted in all examinations (with the exception of Signals), but <u>those which are programmable or which have triangle of velocities functions will not be permitted.</u>

Credits from the theoretical knowledge examination

Credits from having to take certain of the ground examinations may be given as follows to:-

- Holders of a valid UK PPL with Instrument Rating will normally be credited with the examinations in Signals and Radiotelephony;
- Holders of a valid UK CPL(A), ATPL(A), CPL(H) or ATPL(H) will normally be credited with the theoretical knowledge examinations for the grant of a CPL(AS) *other than*;

  i. Aircraft (General) (Airships) (Including Loading)

  ii. Human Performance & Limitations (if not already passed)

- Holders of a valid BCPL(A) who have previously passed the Navigation Group of examinations for this licence at BCPL(A) level only (as distinct from having completed examinations at CPL(A) or ATPL(A) level) will be required to sit all of the ground examinations for the grant of a CPL(AS) *other than*:

  i. Aviation Law, Flight Rules & Procedures

  ii. Meteorology

  iii. Signals

  vi. Human Performance & limitations (if already passed for BCPL)

The theoretical knowledge examination syllabus may found in Appendix A to Section D.

D8.5 UK CPL(AS) SKILL TEST REQUIREMENTS

All applicants for a CPL(AS) will be required to pass a Skill Test conducted by a CAA Staff Flight Examiner comprising Basic Aircraft Handling by day and night.

The Skill Test syllabus may be found at Appendix B to Section D.

D8.6 UK CPL(AS) AIRCRAFT TYPE RATING REQUIREMENTS

All single pilot certificated airship will be covered by an appropriate Class Rating as specified below:-

a. Single engine, fixed line thrust;

b. Multi engine, fixed line thrust;

c. Vectored thrust.

Satisfactory completion of a CPL(AS) Skill Test with a CAA Staff Flight Examiner will satisfy the requirement for this Class Rating.

All 2 pilot certificated airships will require individual specific type ratings, with all training and testing being completed through an approved Type Rating Training Organisation.

D8.7 UK CPL(AS) VALIDITY OF RATINGS

The privileges of a Commercial Pilot's Licence (Airships) may only be exercised in airships specified in the Aircraft Rating and in respect of which the licence also contains a valid **Certificate of Test or Certificate of Experience**, as appropriate, on the type/class for which the privileges are to be exercised:-

a. Public Transport Flights - Certificate of Test required;

b. Aerial Work Flights - Certificate of Test or Certificate of Experience;

c. Flight within Private Privileges - Certificate of Test or Certificate of Experience.

A **Certificate of Test** will be endorsed in the licence on completion of a Flight Test on the required type or class with an authorised Examiner (valid for 6 months from date of test).

A **Certificate of Experience** will be endorsed in the licence on providing evidence to an authorised Examiner that the applicant has completed 5 ascents and landings as Pilot-in-Command within the preceding 13 months on the required type or class (valid for 13 months from date of endorsement).

D8.8 FLIGHT RADIO TELEPHONY OPERATOR'S LICENCE (FRTOL) REQUIREMENTS

An applicant for a UK FRTOL is required to pass the Radiotelephony written examination and practical test with an authorised RTF Examiner.

FULL DETAILS OF THE FRTOL REQUIREMENTS INCLUDING CREDITS AVAILABLE ARE CONTAINED IN SECTION B.

D8.9 UK CPL(AS) MEDICAL REQUIREMENTS

An applicant for a UK CPL(AS) shall hold a valid JAR-Class 2 medical certificate.

Applicants are strongly advised to ensure that they meet the appropriate medical standard before embarking on a course of training. For full details please refer to the CAA web site www.caa.co.uk.

D9 LICENCE RE-ISSUE

For a licence to be valid, a pilot must hold a current medical certificate appropriate to the licence held, and have a valid aircraft rating.

Note for UK BCPL(A) Holders

The medical certificate required for the re-issue of a UK BCPL(A) shall be a JAR-FCL Class 1 medical certificate.

Note for Professional Licence Holders

The holder of a professional licence who only intends to fly privately, may continue to have their professional licence re-issued, but will be required to hold a valid medical certificate appropriate to the licence held. The licence cannot be re-issued with a lower class of medical. Alternatively, to take advantage of the lower class of medical, a Private Pilot Licence may be obtained.

60 Day Rule

Applicants may apply for the re-issue of a licence within a period of 60 days prior to the expiry date of the licence.

Holders of a lifetime UK PPL should note that the licence itself is unexpiring, but the privileges conferred by it, and by any ratings in it, may only be exercised when the licence and the appropriate ratings are valid. Re-validation or renewal of the appropriate rating(s) is specified in **Section F.** Details to revalidate or renew a FRTOL (if held) are specified in Section B.

A UK National or JAR-FCL Pilot's Licence will be re-issued for a further period (5 or 10 year validity as appropriate to the licence held) subject to meeting the following:-

1. hold a medical certificate appropriate to the licence being re-issued valid for the first day of issue of the new licence.

2. have held a valid Certificate of Test, Certificate of Experience or Certificate of Revalidation for any type/class rating that has not expired by more than 5 years*.

* Applicants who are currently flying under the privileges of a non-UK ICAO licence and are flying an aircraft type endorsed within their UK or JAR-FCL licence, may have their licence renewed by holding a valid medical certificate appropriate to the licence being re-issued. A QSP in current flying practice on any military aircraft type (aeroplane for re-issue of aeroplane licence and helicopter for re-issue of helicopter licence) may have their licence re-issued by holding a valid medical certificate appropriate to the licence being re-issued.

Applicants who are not flying an aircraft endorsed within their UK or JAR-FCL licence may not have their licence renewed until such time as an appropriate valid medical certificate and Certificate of Revalidation are obtained.

Applicants may either renew an existing rating within their UK or JAR-FCL licence or may wish to transfer a type/class that he/she is currently flying under the privileges of their non-UK ICAO licence. Renewal of appropriate rating(s) or the transfer of type/class ratings is specified in Section F.

Expired Licences

If the holder of an expired UK National or JAR-FCL pilot's licence has held a valid Certificate of Test, Certificate of Experience or Certificate of Revalidation for any type/class rating that has not expired by more than 5 years, then only the appropriate valid medical certificate must be obtained to re-issue the licence.

If the holder of a UK National or JAR-FCL pilot's licence has not held a valid Certificate of Test, Certificate of Experience or Certificate of Revalidation for any type/class rating that has expired by more than 5 years** they may not have their licence re-issued until such time as an appropriate valid medical certificate and Certificate of Revalidation are obtained. Applicants may either renew an existing rating within their UK or JAR-FCL licence or may wish to transfer a type/class that he/she is currently flying under the privileges of their non-UK ICAO licence. Renewal of appropriate rating(s) or the transfer of type/class ratings is specified in Section F.

** Where an applicant can show that he/she is currently flying under the privileges of a non-UK ICAO licence. and are flying an aircraft type endorsed within their UK or JAR-FCL licence, they may have their licence re-issued by holding a valid UK or JAR-FCL medical certificate as appropriate to the licence. A QSP in current flying practice on any military aircraft type (aeroplane for re-issue of aeroplane licence and helicopter for re-issue of helicopter licence) may have their licence re-issued by holding a valid medical certificate appropriate to the licence being re-issued.

FRTOL Re-validation/Renewal

Details to revalidate or renew a FRTOL (if held) are specified in Section B.

APPENDICES TO SECTION D

APPENDIX A **UK CPL(AS) THEORETICAL KNOWLEDGE EXAMINATION SYLLABUS**

AVIATION LAW, FLIGHT RULES AND PROCEDURES

This paper will consist of thirty questions to be answered within thirty minutes.

Questions will derive from:

The Air Navigation Order

Any part of the Order relating to the operation of airships, including:

- Flight Crew Licence Requirements and Privileges
- Public Transport and Aerial Work
- Definitions
- Documentation
- Maintenance

The Rules of the Air and Air Traffic Control

Any part of the Rules including:

- Definitions
- General Flight Rules
- Visual Flight Rules
- Instrument Flight Rules
- Avoidance of collision
- Lights to be displayed
- Aerodrome traffic rule
- Aerodrome signals and markings
- Distress, urgency and safety signals
- Warning signals

The Air Navigation (General) Regulations

Any part relevant to airships

The Civil Aviation (Investigation of Air Accidents) Regulations

- Definitions
- Duty to furnish information relating to accidents

The AIP (Air Pilot)

Any part relevant to airship operation including:

- Safety procedures and reporting of airproxes and hazardous conditions
- Prohibited areas, danger areas and regulated airspace including MATZ and special rules
- Procedures for distress and difficulty in the air
- Aerodrome procedures
- Airways procedures relevant to airship operation
- Navigation obstructions
- Aerodrome beacons

Aeronautical Information Circulars (AIC's)

Any information of an operational or safety nature relevant to airship operation.

AIRCRAFT (GENERAL) AIRSHIPS

This paper will consist of fifty questions to be answered within 45 minutes.

Topics will include:

Definitions - relating to airship components and operation

Aerostatics and Airship Buoyancy:

- Dalton's Law/Combined Gas Laws
- Lifting gas
- Factors affecting density of air and lifting gas - affect on lift
- Causes and effects of superheat and super-pressure
- Construction and components of envelope
- Control of pressure within the envelope and ballonets
- Purpose and operation of the ballonets

- Handling of lifting gas
- Flight Controls - Aerodynamics
- Static trimming
- Static buoyancy
- Motion and stability about the three major axes
- Factors affecting aerodynamic lift
- Pressure distribution about an aerofoil
- Effects of aerodynamic controls
- Aerodynamic and mass balance of aerodynamic controls
- Methods of positioning aerodynamic controls
- Aerodynamic trimming
- Duplicate inspection of controls by pilots

Piston engines and turbo-charging

- Principles of the four-stroke engine and its operation
- Engine cooling
- Principles of the magneto
- Principles and function of the carburettor and fuel injection
- Mixture control and fuel consumption
- Engine oil system
- Fuel handling
- Starter operation
- Purpose and function of superchargers (including turbo)
- Components and operation of turbo-chargers

DC Electrics

- Relationship between potential difference, resistance, current, power
- Purpose and function of battery cut-out, voltage regulator, generator, warning light, fuses and circuit-breakers
- Use and care of batteries
- Purposes and methods of electrical bonding

Propellers and vectoring

- Principles of conversion of engine torque into thrust
- Pitch and blade angle
- Forces acting on propellers
- Principles and function of constant speed units
- Propeller icing
- Advantages, principles and operation of vector and ducted control systems

Loading

- Affect of varying load on centre of gravity position

Flight Instruments and Radio Aids

This paper will consist of thirty questions to be answered within sixty minutes.

Flight Instruments

- Elementary principles, use, limitations, errors and pre-flight checks of altimeter, airspeed indicator, vertical speed indicator
- The gyroscope and its properties
- Elementary principles, use, limitations, errors and pre-flight checks of direction indicator, artificial horizon, turn and slip indicator
- Magnetic compasses - variation and deviation, tests for serviceability, when compasses should be swung, turning and acceleration errors, remote reading compass.

Radio Aids

- Elementary principles, use, limitations, errors and pre-flight checks of SSR. ILS, VOR, DME, VDF and ADF (and associated NDBs) including the use of RMI, RBI, OBS, CDI and GPS.

Signals

- Ability to identify radio aids by their Morse characters

Meteorology

This paper will consist of forty questions to be answered within ninety minutes

Definitions

- Properties of the atmosphere
- Temperature, radiation, conduction and convection, variation of temperature near the earth's surface and with height, lapse rates, troposphere, tropopause pressure, variation horizontally and vertically
- Air Density, factors affecting
- Relationship between temperature, density, pressure and humidity, the international standard atmosphere

Wind

- Relationship between wind and isobars, geostrophic and gradient winds
- Variation of wind with height
- Local variation of wind with topography, diurnal variation, anabatic and katabatic winds, Fohn effect, land and sea breezes
- Airflow over mountains, standing waves
- Gusts, squalls, turbulence, low-level wind-shear

Clouds and precipitation

- Stability and instability in the atmosphere
- Types of clouds, methods of formation, height of base vertical extent
- Thunderstorms
- Precipitation associated with different types of cloud
- Operating hazards associated with various types of cloud and precipitation

Visibility

- Fog, mist, haze and their differences
- Formation of radiation and advection fog, diurnal and seasonal variation
- Vertical and Oblique visibility, RVR, IRVR

Ice accretion

- Forms of airframe icing and relationship to types of cloud
- Flight in icing conditions
- Power Plant icing

Air masses and fronts

- Classification and characteristics of air masses
- Warm and cold fronts and occlusions
- Depressions, anticyclones, cols, their associated weather

The weather map

- Interpretation of symbols and figures used on weather charts
- The development and movement of simple pressure systems and fronts
- Elementary forecasting

Observations

- The Q code groups QFE, QNE, QNH, QFF
- Comprehension and interpretation of flight forecast documents, significant weather and spot wind charts in particular
- Decoding TAF and METAR

AIP MET Section

- A knowledge of the relevant information contained in CAP32 MET
- Sources of meteorological information available to a pilot in the UK

Practical

- The practical application of the material contained herein, using specimen charts and data

Flight Planning and Navigation Procedures

This examination will consist of 40 questions to be completed within 75 minutes.

For this examination the following maps will be provided:

ICAO Aeronautical Chart 1:500000 topographical
Radio Navigation Chart by Aerad or Jeppesen

Use of navigation computer

- Resolution of the triangle of velocities to produce any vector

Use of Charts

- Measurement of tracks, distances, bearings
- Establishment of geographical position by any method
- Transfer of position between two charts
- Selection of suitable routes using the charts provided
- Extraction of aeronautical information from the charts provided

Flight Planning

- Completion of a flight plan given a route and the relevant data (including flight times, headings, fuel consumption, relevant ATC data and procedures)
- Calculation of fuel reserves, critical points and PNRs (including off route)
- Completion of CA48 (ATC flight plan form)

Plotting

- Plotting of bearings to establish position on a chart
- By means of plotting on a chart to establish desired track, track made good, drift angle, W/V being experienced and revised ETA
- Determine position by use of topographical pinpoints and bearings

Conversion

- Conversion of units Imp gallons, US gallons, litres, pounds, kilograms, statute miles, nautical miles, kilometres, feet metres.

Human Performance and Limitations

This syllabus is divided into four main topic areas:

Basic Aviation Physiology and Health Maintenance
Basic Aviation Psychology
Stress, Fatigue and their Management
The Social Psychology and Ergonomics of the Flight Deck

Basic Aviation Physiology and Health Maintenance

Basic Physiology and the Effects of Flight

- Anatomy and physiology of the eye, ear, vestibular, circulatory, and respiratory systems
- Composition of the atmosphere, gas laws and the nature of the human requirement of oxygen
- Effects of reduced ambient pressure and of sudden decompression; times of useful consciousness
- Recognising and coping with hypoxia and hyperventilation
- Entrapped gases and barotrauma
- Diving and flying
- Effects of acceleration (+/–G) on circulatory system, vision and consciousness
- Mechanism, Effects and management of motion sickness

Flying and Health

- Noise and age-induced hearing loss
- Visual defects and their correction
- Arterial disease and coronary risk factors, ECG, blood pressure, stroke
- Diet, exercise, obesity
- Fits, faints and the EEG
- Psychiatric diseases; drug dependence and alcoholism
- Tropical diseases and their prophylaxis, hepatitis and sexually transmitted diseases
- Common ailments and fitness to fly; gastro-enteritis, colds, use of common drugs and their side effects
- Toxic hazards
- Causes and management of in-flight incapacitation

Section A Section B Section C Section D CPL Section E Section F Section G Section H Section I Section J Section K Index

Basic Aviation Psychology

- Basic plan of human information processing, including the concepts of sensation, attention, memory, central decision-making and the creation of mental models.
- Limitations of central decision channel and mental workload
- Function of attention is selecting information sources, attention-getting stimuli
- Types of memory; peripheral or sensory memory, long term (semantic and episodic) memory, short term or working memory, motor memory (skills)
- Memory limitations and failures
- Perception, the integration of sensory information to form a mental model
- Effects of experience and expectation on perception
- Erroneous mental models; visual, vestibular and other illusions
- Recognising and managing spatial disorientation
- Use of visual cues in landing
- Eye movements, visual search techniques, mid-air collisions
- Skill-, rule- and knowledge-based behaviours
- The nature of skill acquisition, the exercise of skill, conscious and automatic behaviour, errors of skill
- Rule-based behaviour, procedures, simulator training, failures in rule-based behaviour
- Knowledge-based behaviour, problem solving and decision making, inference formation, failures in knowledge-based behaviour
- Maintaining accurate mental models, situational awareness, conformation bias

Stress and Stress Management

Models and Effects of Stress

- Definitions, concepts and models of stress
- Arousal; concepts of over- and under-arousal
- Environmental stresses and their effects; heat, noise, vibration, low humidity
- Domestic stress, home relationships, bereavement, financial and time commitments
- Work stress, relationships with colleagues and management
- Effects of stress on attention, motivation and performance
- Life stress and health, other clinical effects of stress
- Defence mechanisms, identifying stress and stress management
- *Sleep and Fatigue*
- Biological clocks and circadian rhythms, sleep/ wakefulness and temperature rhythms, 'zeitgebers'
- Sleep stages, sleep at abnormal times of day, required quantity of sleep
- Work-induced fatigue
- Shift work
- Time zone crossing, circadian disrhythmia, re-synchronisation
- Rostering problems, sleep management and naps
- Sleep hygiene
- Management of sleep with drugs

Social Psychology and Ergonomics of the Flight Deck

Individual Differences, Social Psychology and Flight Deck Management

- Individual differences, definitions of intelligence and personality
- Assessing personality
- Main dimensions of personality; extroversion and anxiety. Other important traits: warmth and sociability, impulsivity, tough-mindedness, dominance, stability and boldness.
- Goal-directed, person-directed types of behaviour
- Autocratic and democratic leadership styles
- Individual personality related problems of flying, especially risk-taking

- Personality interaction on the flight deck, and the interaction of personality with status or seniority, role (e.g. handling/non-handling) and perceived ability of crew members
- Concepts of conformity, compliance and risky shift. Implications of these concepts for the flight deck with regard to effects of crew size (especially 2 v 3 crew)
- Communication, verbal and non-verbal communication, one and two way communication, different communication styles
- Methods of maximising crew effectiveness and improving flight deck, or cockpit resource, management
- Interacting with cabin crew, air traffic services, maintenance personnel and passengers

The Design of Flight Decks, Documentation and Procedures

- Basic principles of control, display and workspace design
- Eye datum, anthropometry and workspace constraints, external vision requirements, reach, comfort and posture
- Display size, legibility, scale design, colour and illumination. Common errors in display interpretation
- Control size, loading, location and compatibility of controls with displays
- The presentation of warning information and misinterpretation of warnings
- The design and appropriate use of checklists and manuals
- Effects of automation and the 'glass cockpit'. Integration of information from many data sources on one display, and automatic selection of displayed information. Mode and status representation
- Machine intelligence and relationship between aircraft decisions and pilot decisions
- The avoidance of complacency and boredom, and maintaining situational awareness. Maintaining basic flying skills

Judgement

- Making decisions
- Assessing risk

APPENDIX B UK CPL(AS) SKILL TEST SYLLABUS

The Skill Test Syllabus for Airships

1 Section 1 Basic Aircraft Handling

1.1 Off Masting and Ground Manoeuvring.
1.2 Pre take-off Weigh-off and Completion of Load-sheet.
1.3 Normal take-off/Transition to Climb.
1.4 Climbing, descending and turns.
1.5 Action in the event of Fire.
1.6 Weigh-off and estimation of Static and Trim.
1.7 Normal approach and landing.
1.8 Simulated emergency take-off and subsequent weigh-off.
1.9 Simulated complete engine failure and free ballooning.
1.10 Landing at equilibrium.
1.11 Statically light take-off and landing.
1.12 Statically heavy take-off and landing.
1.13 Simulated engine failure after take-off.
1.14 Simulated single-engine approach and go-around.
1.15 Simulated single-engine landing.
1.16 Nominated Emergencies specific to airship type, such as rudder failure, ballonet fans inoperative, engine vector system inoperative etc.
1.17 After landing, ground manoeuvring and masting.
1.18 Shutdown procedure.
1.19 Flight Deck Management/Airmanship.

2 Section 2 Instrument Flying

To be detailed when applicable.

3 Section 3 Night Flying

3.1 Off masting and ground manoeuvring.
3.2 Pre take-off weigh-off and completion of Load Sheet.
3.3 Normal take-off and transition to climb (heavy).
3.4 Weigh-off.
3.5 Normal approach and go-around.
3.6 Approach and landing (heavy).
3.7 Normal take-off and transition to climb (light).
3.8 Approach and landing (light).
3.9 Take-off with engine failure immediately after take-off followed by single-engine approach and landing.
3.10 Approach and landing with landing lights inoperative.
3.11 After landing, ground manoeuvring and masting.

4 Section 4 Preparation for Flight

4.1 Self-briefing.
4.2 Attention to Weather Minima.
4.3 Document checking.
4.4 Preliminary and external checks.
4.5 Preparation of load-sheet.
4.6 Checks before starting.
4.7 Starting procedure.
4.8 Checks after starting including instruments/radio.
4.9 Power check.
4.10 Trimming prior to unmasting.
4.11 ATC liaison and compliance.

APPENDIX C

UK CPL(B) THE GENERAL FLIGHT TEST

1 Syllabus and Conditions for the Test For Balloons

This appendix sets out the content of the General Flight Test (Day) (GFT) for the grant of the Commercial Pilot's Licence (Balloons) (CPL(B)), the flight test pass conditions, the validity period of a successful flight test results and the flight test arrangements.

2 General Flight Test (Day) Content

2.1 The content of the GFT has been expanded in detail to give applicants guidance as to the skills and knowledge they will be expected to demonstrate during the test.

2.2 In addition to the specific items detailed, applicants will be required to demonstrate their knowledge of, and adherence to the guidelines for balloon flying agreed with the National Farmers Union (NFU). Whilst these guidelines do not form part of the test, the examiner, as pilot-in-command of the balloon during the test, is overall responsible for the conduct of the flight and may curtail the test at his discretion unless the NFU guidelines are being followed without just cause, i.e. in an emergency.

3 Flight Test Pass Conditions

3.1 A fail in any one section of Sections 1, 2, 3 and 4 will require a re-test of that section except that in all re-tests Section 1 will be re-assessed whether or not it was a re-test item. Also, in the event of a failure in Section 3 or Section 4 then both sections will be re-assessed. A failure in Section 2 and in Section 3 or Section 4 will require a re-test of all four sections.

3.2 A failure to obtain a pass in all four sections within a series of 3 attempts will invalidate that series and all four sections will have to be taken at the next attempt as for the initial test.

4 General Flight Test Results. Period of Validity

A pass in all four sections of the GFT within a series must be obtained within the 6 months immediately preceding the date of receipt by CAA of the licence application.

5 Flight Test Arrangements

5.1 The flight test will be conducted by a Flight Examiner employed by the CAA or by an examiner recommended by the British Balloon and Airship Club and who has been approved for the purpose by the CAA.

5.2 Applicants will be required to make their own arrangements for the flight test. The applicant will be required to provide a suitable balloon for the flight test.

5.3 Where the flight test is conducted by an examiner employed by the CAA, the statutory charge published in the Air Navigation Order or on the SRG web site www.srg.caa.co.uk must be paid in advance by post or in person to the CAA, PLD at Aviation House, Gatwick or, by agreement at the time of making the arrangements for the test, to the examiner.

5.4 Where the flight test is conducted by an examiner approved for the purpose by the CAA, the payment and scale of charges must be agreed between the examiner and the applicant.

6 General Flying Test (Day)

6.1 **Section 1**

1.0	Pre-flight
1.1	Preparation for flight
1.2	Pre-inflation
1.3	Inflation

6.2 **Section 2**

2.0	Tethered Flight
2.1	Pre-inflation
2.2	Inflation
2.3	Tethered flight
2.4	Emergencies
2.5	Fuel Management

6.3 **Section 3**

3.0	General Handling
3.1	Take off
3.2	Level Flight
3.3	Climb
3.4	Descent
3.5	Approaches
3.6	Emergencies
3.7	Landing
3.8	Action after flight
3.9	Fuel Management
3.10	ATC liaison

6.4 **Section 4**

4.0	Navigation
4.1	Weather assessment
4.2	Use of maps, charts etc.
4.3	ATC Liaison
4.4	Position Fixing
4.5	Fuel Planning
4.6	Airmanship

7 Expanded Syllabus

7.1 Section 1 – Pre-Flight

7.1.1 Preparation For Flight

a. Documentation

i. Aircraft logbook
ii. C of A
iii. C of R
iv. C of M Review
v. Medical Certificate
vi. Crew Licence (where applicable)
vii. Radio Licence (where applicable)
viii. Aircraft Flight Manual
ix. Load Sheet

b. Weather

i. Weather Limitations
ii. Meteorological actual and forecast conditions for proposed flight
iii. Weather Suitability

c. Selection of Launch Site

i. Hazards to inflation
ii. Field conditions
iii. Downwind obstructions

d. Equipment Check

i. Maps, charts
ii. Pencil, scale, etc.
iii. Timepiece
iv. Means to assess track angles
v. Gloves
vi. Sources of Ignition (Matches, Striker etc.)

e. Load Calculations

i. Load calculations as specified in Aircraft Flight Manual
ii. Load Sheet

f. Flight Planning

i. Pre-Flight Planning and Map Preparation
ii. Airspace information (Danger, Prohibited, Restricted areas, ATZ, SRZ etc.)
iii. Endurance
iv. Altimeter settings (Actual and Forecast QNH)
v. ATS frequencies (where applicable)
vi. Retrieve information
vii. Fuel Calculations

7.1.2 **Pre-Inflation**

a. Layout Considerations

i. Position of balloon
ii. Position of vehicle
iii. Launch Tether

b. Basket Preparation & Inspection

i. Assembly of burner frame, basket wires, fuel hoses and karabiners
ii. Assembly of burner frame support rods and covers (where fitted)
iii. Location and securing of fuel cylinders

c. Burner Preparation & Inspection

i. Inspection and connection of vapour and liquid hoses
ii. Leak Test
iii. Operation of pilot light and valves
iv. Operation of main burner and valves

d. Envelope Preparation & Inspection

i. Connection of flying wires to burner frame

ii. Attachment of Quick Release/ Restraint (where fitted)
iii. Layout

e. Equipment Preparation, Inspection and Checks

i. Altimeter
ii. Variometer, thermistor (if fitted)
iii. Radio (if fitted)
iv. Navigation equipment stowed
v. Handling line stowed
vi. Fire Extinguisher

f. Crew & Passenger Briefing

i. Commander's supervision and direction of crew and passengers

g. Airmanship

7.1.3 Inflation

a. Operation of Fan

i. Position of fan
ii. Precautions

b. Deflation System

i. Parachute type
ii. Velcro type
iii. Combination type
iv. Turn Vents (where fitted)

c. Control of Crew during Inflation of Envelope

i. Envelope and fan
ii. Crown Line
iii. Basket

(b. and c. above: In accordance with Flight Manual)

d. Operation of Burner

i. Control
ii. Safety precautions

e. Pre-take off Checks

i. In accordance with Flight Manual

f. Airmanship

g. Emergencies

i. Action in event of fire
ii. Action in event of equipment failure
iii. Action in event of gusting conditions

7.2 Section 2 – Tethered Flight

7.2.1 Pre-Inflation

a. Layout Consideration

i. Position of tether points (vehicles, trees etc.)
ii. Position of balloon
iii. Position of tether lines
iv. Tether height calculations
v. Safety requirements
vi. Compliance with the Air Navigation Order and Rules of the Air

b. Basket Preparation and Inspection
In accordance with 7.1.2 (b)
(Pre-inflation)

c. Burner Preparation and Inspection
In accordance with 7.1.2 (c)
(Pre-inflation)

d. Envelope Preparation and Inspection
In accordance with 7.1.2 (d)
(Pre-inflation)

e. Equipment Preparation, Inspection and Checks

i. Attachment of tether lines to tether points in accordance
ii. Attachment of tether lines to balloon (i) and (ii) in accordance with Flight Manual)
iii. Thermistor (if fitted)
iv. Fire Extinguisher

f. Crew and Passenger Briefing

i. Supervision and direction of crew
ii. Procedure for supervision of passenger transfer
iii. Directions to advise pilot of any changes in conditions
vi. Actions in event of emergency

g. Crowd Control

h. Airmanship

7.2.2 Inflation

i. In accordance with 7.1.3 (Inflation)

7.2.3 Tethered Flight

i. Application of and reaction to changes in weather conditions
ii. Climb to achieve level flight at a height nominated by the examiner
iii. Maintenance of level flight for a minimum of five minutes at a height of between 10 feet and 50 feet agl.
iv. Descent to land
v. Procedures for transfer of passengers (Discussion)

7.2.4 Emergencies

i. Action in event of Fire
ii. Actions in event of equipment failure
iii. Actions in event of gusting conditions

7.2.5 Fuel Management

i. Fuel calculations
ii. Fuel transfer precautions

7.3 **Section 3 – General Handling**

7.3.1 Take-off

i. Obtaining equilibrium
ii. Operation of quick release (where fitted.
iii. Awareness of false lift
iv. Awareness of downwind obstructions
v. Establish climb rate to clear downwind obstructions
vi. Climb to achieve level flight

7.3.2 Level flight

i. Maintain level flight for a minimum of 5 minutes to within ±50 ft of required altitude

7.3.3 Climb and transition to level flight

i. Maintain steady rate of climb to a briefed height
(minimum height of 500 ft agl ROC not to exceed Flight Manual limits)
ii. Round out for level flight

7.3.4 Descent and transition to level flight

i. Achieve a steady rate of descent to a new briefed minimum height of 500 ft agl (ROD not to exceed Flight Manual Limits)
ii. Round out for level flight

7.3.5 Approach and overshoot

i. Airspace considerations
ii. Site selection and assessment of wind
iii. Pre-landing checks
iv. Use of controls
v. Airmanship

a. High level

i. An approach to land procedure starting at a minimum height of 1000 ft agl
ii. Stabilised descent at 400 fpm ±100 fpm to a point from which a landing could be made
iii. Round out at 75 ft agl ±25 ft
iv. Initiate and establish a normal climb

b. Low level

i. An approach to land procedure starting at a maximum height of 500 ft agl
ii. Stabilised descent at a ROD not exceeding 200 fpm to a point from which a landing could be made
iii. Round out at 50 ft agl ±25 ft
iv. Initiate and establish a normal climb

7.3.6 Emergencies

i. Envelope overheat
ii. Fire in the Air
iii. Contact with power lines
iv. Contact with obstacles
v. Loss of main burner
vi. Loss of pilot light
vii. Emergency Landing
viii. Parachute/Velcro Malfunction
ix. Approach with simulated failure of one burner

7.3.7 Landing

i. Site selection
ii. Pre-landing checks – in accordance with Flight Manual
iii. Passenger briefing
iv. Use of controls to achieve desired ROD (touchdown final velocity not to exceed 50 feet per minute)
v. Deflation
vi. Burner shutdown
vii. Passenger transfer (where applicable)

7.3.8 Action after flight

i. Safety actions
ii. Passenger off-load
iii. Re-seal velcro (if appropriate)
iv. Pack away envelope
v. De-rig burner
vi. Landowner consultation
vii. Recording of flight details in appropriate logbooks

7.3.9 Fuel management

i. Minimum requirements in accordance with Flight Manual
ii. Checks
iii. Calculations
iv. Transfer of hoses
v. Refuelling procedures and appropriate safety precautions

7.3.10 ATC liaison

i. Communications with the appropriate Air Traffic Services by radiotelephony, telephone etc. as appropriate (the use of cellular telephones in flight is not permitted).

7.4 **Section 4 – Navigation**

7.4.1 Weather

i. Awareness and usage of variations in wind direction and speed at different altitudes
ii. Prediction of potential hazards – curlover, turbulence, thermals etc.
iii. Anticipation of conditions in landing area
iv. Assessment of low level and surface wind speed, and direction using smoke, trees, water, crops etc.

7.4.2 Use of maps and charts

i. Scales and units. Conversion between units
ii. Computation of safety altitudes and selection of altitudes for flight
iii. Transfer of information from various types and projections of maps and charts
iv. Amendments to flight plan, and flight log (map)
v. Position of balloon in relation to potential hazards and restrictions

7.4.3 ATC Liaison

i. Recognition of and compliance with visual signals
ii. RT communications (where applicable)
iii. Traffic avoidance
iv. SAR requirements and signals
v. Airmiss procedure
vi. Urgency and distress signals, and procedures
vii. Altimeter setting requirements
viii. Observance of air traffic control regulations and Rules of the Air

7.4.4 Position Fixing

i. Fixing position within 500 metres of actual position (minimum of three fixes at intervals of not less than 5 minutes)
ii. Determine track made good and ground speed
iii. Projection of track and calculation of ETA, to within ±3 minutes, to overhead a position nominated by the examiner
iv. Calculation of a forecast ground position. Position to be 30 minutes ahead and based upon TMG and G/S

7.4.5 Fuel management

i. Calculations of fuel used
ii. Revision of endurance based upon variations in fuel consumption
iii. Calculation of point from which a landing could be made aiming to land with 20% usable fuel remaining

APPENDIX D

UK CPL(B) GROUND EXAMINATION SYLLABUS

Commercial Pilot's Licence (Balloons)

1. Questions based on the contents of current Aeronautical Information Circulars (AICs) may be asked under an appropriate subject heading.

2. A simple electronic calculator and three figure trigonometrical tables are provided for use in the examinations (except Navigation).

1 Aviation Law, Flight Rules and Procedures

1. Publications may NOT be consulted during the examinations.

2. Candidates will not be required to memorise details of geographical positions, or of special procedures applicable to any particular aerodrome, Flight Information Region, Control Zone or Airway.

1.1 The UK Aeronautical Information Publication, NOTAM and Aeronautical Information Circulars. A general knowledge of the operational provisions with a more detailed knowledge of the following:

1.1.1 **Aerodromes**

Definitions; conditions of availability; customs and health airports; use of military aerodromes; aeronautical ground lights.

1.1.2 **Communications**

The aeronautical mobile service; the aeronautical radio navigation service.

1.1.3 **Meteorology**

Types of service provided; observing systems and operating procedures; application of METAR, TAF, TREND and AIREP codes; runway visual range; aircraft meteorological observations and reports.

1.1.4 **Air Traffic Rules and Services**

Definitions. Visual flight rules, instrument flight rules and general air traffic control procedures. Types of airspace and air traffic service units. Separation standards. Carriage of radio equipment and communication failure procedures. 'Airprox' reporting procedures. Altimeter setting procedures. Use of radar in air traffic services. Control areas. Advisory airspace. Flight information service. Airspace restrictions. Signals for aerodrome traffic.

1.1.5 **Search and Rescue**

Responsible authority. Communications. Distress frequencies. Aircraft not equipped with radio. Procedure for pilot-in-command requiring SAR escort facilities. Procedure for pilot-in-command observing an accident or intercepting a distress call (or message) and for guiding surface craft to the scene of a ditching. Flight in areas where search and rescue operations are in progress. Action by survivors. Ground/air visual signal code for use by survivors.

1.1.6 **Additional matters**

Any information of an operational nature that may, from time to time, be added to the UK AIP, NOTAM and Aeronautical Information Circulars. (It should be noted that questions based on the contents of current pink (Safety) Aeronautical Information Circulars may also be asked under an appropriate subject heading).

1.2 **The Air Navigation Order 2005**

A general knowledge of the provisions, with particular reference to the following:

Article 3	Aircraft to be registered
Article 4	Registration of aircraft in the United Kingdom
Article 8	Certificate of airworthiness to be in force
Article 9	Issue, renewal, etc. of certificates of airworthiness
Article 14	Certificate of maintenance review
Article 15	Technical log
Article 16	Inspection, overhaul, repair, replacement and modification.
Article 19	Equipment of aircraft
Article 20	Radio equipment of aircraft
Article 25	Composition of crew of aircraft
Article 26	Members of flight crew – requirements of licences
Article 27	Grant, renewal and effect of flight crew licences
Article 34	Validation of licences
Article 35	Personal flying logbook
Article 36	Instruction in flying
Article 38	Operations Manual
Article 40	Training Manual
Article 42	Public transport – operator's responsibilities

Article 44 & 45	Public transport – operating conditions
Article 52	Pre-flight action by commander of aircraft
Article 54	Public transport of passengers – additional duties of commander
Article 55	Operation of radio in aircraft
Article 65	Towing, picking up and raising of persons and articles
Article 66	Dropping of articles and animals
Article 67	Dropping of persons
Article 69	Carriage of weapons and munitions of war
Article 70	Carriage of dangerous goods
Article 71	Method of carriage of persons
Article 72	Exits and break-in marking
Article 74	Endangering safety of any person or property
Article 75	Drunkenness in aircraft
Article 77	Authority of commander and members of the crew of aircraft
Article 81	Application and interpretation of Part VI
Article 82	Fatigue of crew – operator's responsibilities
Article 84	Flight times: responsibilities of flight crew
Article 86	Documents to be carried
Article 88	Production of documents and records
Article 94	Offences in relation to documents and records
Article 95	Rules of the air
Article 96	Power to prohibit or restrict flying
Article 97	Balloons, kites, airships, gliders and parascending parachutes.
Article 142	Mandatory reporting
Article 148	Penalties
Article 155 & 156	Interpretation

Schedule 2	Part A Table of General Classification of Aircraft.
Schedule 3	A and B conditions.
Schedule 4	Categories of Aircraft.
Schedule 5	Radio equipment to be carried in aircraft.
Schedule 8	Flight Crew of Aircraft: Licences and Ratings.
Schedule 11	Documents to be carried by Aircraft Registered in the United Kingdom

Questions will not be asked on the details of the Schedules except where specifically indicated above.

1.3 **The Air Navigation (General) Regulations 1993 (as amended)**

Load sheets	Regulation 4
Mandatory reporting	Regulations 17

1.4 **The Rules of the Air Regulations 1996 (as amended)**

Interpretation	Section I
General	Section II
Lights and other signals to be shown by aircraft	Section III
General Flight Rules	Section IV
Visual Flight Rules	Section V
Instrument Flight Rules	Section VI
Aerodrome Traffic Rules	Section VII
Aerodrome signals and markings:	Section IX

aural and visual signals (excluding dimensions), marshalling signals, distress, urgency and safety signals

1.5 **The Civil Aviation (Investigation of Air Accidents and Incidents) Regulations 1996 (as amended)**

Duty to furnish information relating to accidents and incidents Regulation 5-6

1.6 **The Air Navigation (Dangerous Goods) Regulations 1994 (as amended)**

2 Navigation

2.1 Maps

2.1.1 The interpretation and use of the ICAO 1:500,000 chart and the Ordnance Survey 1:50,000 map; methods of indicating scale and relief; interpretation of chart symbols.

2.1.2 Position on the earth in latitude and longitude, grid reference and in bearing and distance from a prominent point.

2.1.3 Measurement of distance and bearings.

2.1.4 Determination of spot elevation from the Ordnance Survey 1:50,000 map.

2.1.5 Transfer of data from the ICAO 1:500,000 chart to the O/S 1:50,000 map and vice versa, especially the boundaries of controlled and special rules airspace and prohibited, danger and restricted areas.

2.2 **Instruments**

2.2.1 The principles of operation and the errors of the pressure altimeter; the meaning and uses of QNH, QFE, standard pressure setting, altitude, transition altitude, transition level, elevation, height, pressure altitude.

2.2.2 The principles of operation and the errors of the magnetic compass.

2.2.3 The principles of operation of the vertical speed indicator.

2.3 **Practical navigation**

2.3.1 Track (true, magnetic, compass), wind velocity, groundspeed/distance/time/gas consumption calculations.

2.3.2 Conversion of units: nautical miles, statute miles, feet, inches, kilometres, metres, centimetres.

2.3.3 Determination of distance by scale calculation.

2.3.4 Given the relevant flight information and charts, predict a probable flight path with elapsed times/ ETAs for prominent points, and extract significant features from the charts including topographical and aeronautical data.

2.3.5 Given the relevant information, determine position by the use of topographical pinpoints and bearings, including simple VOR bearings.

3 Meteorology

3.1 **Properties of the atmosphere**

3.1.1 Temperature: radiation, conduction and convection; variation of temperature near the earth's surface; variation of temperature with height; lapse rates, temperature inversions, troposphere, tropopause.

3.1.2 Pressure: definition; variation horizontally and vertically.

3.1.3 Air density: variation at surface and with height.

3.1.4 Humidity: dew point; latent heat and change of state; evaporation, condensation, sublimation.

3.1.5 Relationship between density, pressure, temperature and humidity; the International Standard Atmosphere.

3.2 **Wind**

3.2.1 Relationship between wind and isobars; geostrophic wind, gradient wind.

3.2.2 Variation of wind with height; elementary knowledge of thermal winds.

3.2.3 Local variation of wind with topography; diurnal; anabatic and katabatic effects, Fohn effect; land and sea breezes.

3.2.4 Airflow over mountains; standing waves.

3.2.5 Gusts, squalls, turbulence; low-level wind shear.

3.3 **Clouds and precipitation**

3.3.1 Stability and instability in the atmosphere.

3.3.2 Types of cloud; methods of formation; height of base and vertical extent.

3.3.3 Turbulence cloud; orographic cloud; convection cloud.

3.3.4 Thunderstorms.

3.3.5 Precipitation associated with different types of cloud: drizzle, rain, snow, hail.

3.3.6 Operating hazards associated with various types of cloud and precipitation.

3.4 **Visibility**

3.4.1 Fog, mist, haze and their differences.

3.4.2 Formation of radiation fog and advection fog, diurnal and seasonal variation.

3.4.3 Vertical and oblique visibility; runway visual range.

3.5 **Ice Accretion**

3.5.1 Flight procedure in icing conditions.

3.6 **Air masses and fronts**

3.6.1 Classification and characteristics of air masses.

3.6.2 Characteristics of warm and cold fronts and occlusions.

3.6.3 Depressions, anticyclones, cols: associated weather.

3.7 **The Weather Map**

3.7.1 interpretation of symbols and figures used on weather charts.

3.7.2 The development and movement of simple pressure systems and fronts.

3.7.3 Elementary forecasting.

3.8 **Observations**

3.8.1 Knowledge of standard methods of measuring pressure, temperature, humidity, cloud height, visibility, surface wind, upper wind.

3.9 Sources of meteorological information and its presentation

3.9.1 Weathercall and special arrangements for balloon operators.

3.9.2 Volmet.

3.9.3 Decoding of TAF and METAR.

3.9.4 Comprehension and interpretation of flight forecast documents (significant weather and low level wind charts in particular).

4 Aircraft (General) (Balloons)

4.1 This written examination is based on the knowledge areas specified in this section.

4.2 **Systems**

4.2.1 **Fuel systems and burners**

a. Main components, the purpose of each component and the safety features of the system;

b. The principles of operation of the system;

c. The care and maintenance of the system;

d. Burner rating;

e. The symptoms of fuel exhaustion and the use of an emergency (or back-up) system, if fitted;

f. Icing;

g. Leaks;

h. Cylinder position.

4.2.2 **Propane**:

a. Properties

i. specific gravity in liquid gaseous form;
ii. effect of altitude on burner pressure;
iii. effect of temperature on tank pressure and burner pressure;

b. Fuel quantity measurement with reference to a percentage fuel gauge;

c. The reasons for, and the method of, heating tanks;

d. The precautions to be observed.

i. for the prevention of fire;
ii. during refuelling;

e. The action required in the event of a propane fire.

4.2.3 **Deflation**

a. The operation of the deflation system, the function of the main components.

b. Main advantages and disadvantages of the system.

c. Safety checks.

d. Routine checks and limitations.

4.2.4 Equipment and instruments – altimeter, vertical speed indicator (vario), thermistor, their construction, principles of operation, limitations, presentation, adjustments and serviceability checks.

4.3 **Balloon performance**

4.3.1 Factors that may affect fuel consumption, burner output (pressure and ambient temperature). Use of nitrogen pressure systems.

4.3.2 Knowledge of the terms: equilibrium, inertia, momentum, false lift, terminal velocity, curlover, lift, weighing off.

4.3.3 Operational limitations, loading and limitations and the reasons for imposing those limits (to include normal and maximum rates of climb and descent, envelope temperature maximum and continuous).

4.3.4 The factors to be considered in preparation for, and the execution of:

a. high wind landing;

b. high vertical speed landing;

c. landing in thermic conditions;

d. landing in gusty/turbulent conditions;

e. tethering for display purposes;

f. tethering for passenger rides;

g. take-off in varying conditions.

4.3.5 Factors that may affect performance: altitude, wind, terrain.

4.4 Balloon maintenance: qualifications, C of A requirements, routine maintenance, minor repairs, inspection schedules, fabric overheating, deflation system, fire extinguisher.

4.5 Flight characteristics.

4.6 Accidents and incidents.

4.7 Documents.

4.8 Aero medical.

4.8.1 Basic knowledge of first aid and use of generally available kits.

4.8.2 Physiological factors: the senses, spatial disorientation and sensory illusions.

4.8.3 Effects of colds, alcohol and drugs.

4.8.4 Recognition of the effects of hypoxia and carbon monoxide, and knowledge of their dangers.

5 Aircraft (Type) (Balloons)

5.1 This is an examination, conducted by an authorised examiner and confined to the type of balloon upon which the candidate is being flight-tested.

5.2 Flight Manual

a. Emergency procedure: fire on the ground and in the air.

b. In-flight system failures.

c. Limitations.

d. Use of the load system specified in the Flight Manual, and determination of the maximum payload for a given pressure height and outside air temperature.

5.3 Balloon systems specific to type used during flight test.

6 Human Performance and Limitations Syllabus (Balloons)

6.1 This syllabus is divided into four main topic areas:

a. Basic Aviation Physiology and Health Maintenance.

b. Basic Aviation Psychology.

c. Stress, Fatigue and their Management.

d. Social Psychology.

6.2 **Basic Aviation Physiology and Health Maintenance**

6.2.1 *Basic Physiology and the Effects of Flight*

Anatomy and physiology of the eye, ear, vestibular, circulatory and respiratory systems.
Composition of the atmosphere, gas laws and the nature of the human requirement for oxygen.
Effects of reduced ambient pressure.
Recognising and coping with hypoxia and hyperventilation.
Entrapped gases and barotrauma.
Motion sickness.
Diving and flying.

6.2.2 *Flying and Health*

Noise and age-induced hearing loss.
Visual defects and their correction.
Arterial disease and coronary risk factors, ECG, blood pressure, stroke.
Diet, exercise, obesity.
Fits, faints and the EEG.
Psychiatric diseases; drug dependence and alcoholism.
Common ailments and fitness to fly; gastro-enteritis, colds, use of common drugs and their side effects.

6.3 **Basic Aviation Psychology**

Basic plan of human information processing, including the concepts of sensation, attention, memory, central decision-making and the creation of mental models.

Limitation of central decision channel and mental workload.

Function of attention in selecting information sources, attention getting stimuli.

Effects of experience and expectation on perception.

Erroneous mental models; visual, vestibular and other illusions.

Use of visual cues in landing.

Eye movements, visual search techniques, mid-air collisions.

Skill-, rule- and knowledge-based behaviour.

The nature of skill acquisition, the exercise of skill, conscious and automatic behaviour errors of skill.

Rule-based behaviour, procedures, failures of rule-based behaviour.

Knowledge-based behaviour, problem solving and decision-making, inference formation, failures in knowledge-based behaviour.

Maintaining accurate mental models, situational awareness, confirmation bias.

6.4 **Stress and Stress Management**

6.4.1 *Models and Effects of Stress*

Definitions, concepts and models of stress.

Arousal; concepts of over- and under-arousal. Environmental stresses and their effects; heat, noise.

Domestic stress, home relationships, bereavement, financial and time commitments.

Work stress, relationship with colleagues.

Effects of stress on attention, motivation and performance.

Life stress and health, other clinical effects of stress.

Defence mechanisms, identifying stress and stress management.

6.4.2 *Sleep and Fatigue*

Work-induced fatigue.

Shift work.

Rostering problems, sleep management and naps.

Sleep hygiene.

6.5 **Social Psychology**

6.5.1 *Individual Differences, Social Psychology and Interaction with Others*

Individual differences, definitions of intelligence and personality.

Assessing personality.

Main dimensions of personality: extroversion and anxiety. Other important traits; warmth and sociability, impulsivity, tough-mindedness, dominance, stability and boldness.

Goal-directed, person-directed types of behaviour.

Individual personality related problems of flying, especially risk-taking.

Communication, verbal and non-verbal communication, one and two-way communication, different communication styles.

Interacting with crew, air traffic services, ground handling personnel and passengers.

6.5.2 *Judgement*

Making decisions.

Assessing risk.

APPENDIX E UK CPL(B) - THE AIRCRAFT RATING REQUIREMENTS

In the case of the CPL(B), Aircraft Ratings are issued in the Free Balloon category, and are related to the class and size of the balloon in which the Pilot wishes to exercise the licence privileges. Class is specified by reference to lifting agency. There are 4 such classes, each being further divided into 3 Groups based upon envelope capacity, as follows:

Classes: Hot air
Gas filled
Pressurised
Combination gas and hot air
A - not exceeding 3,000 cubic metres' volume (105,600 cubic feet)
B - exceeding 3,000 cubic metres but not exceeding 9,000 cubic metres (316,800 cubic feet)
C - exceeding 9,000 cubic metres

A licence holder with a valid Aircraft Rating for a Class and Group of balloon may fly any balloon within the same Class and Group.

Flight tests

Aircraft Rating flight tests are conducted by Type Rating Examiners (TRE) authorised by the CAA to conduct such tests and to sign a C of T or C of E in respect of the Aircraft Rating. Information concerning the availability of such examiners is obtainable from the CAA (Personnel Licensing). The arrangements and payment for conduct of an Aircraft Rating flight test are a matter between the applicant and the TRE concerned. Where the TRE is an employee of the Authority the charge will be in accordance with the current statutory list of charges.

The test requires that the applicant demonstrates to the examiner his competence in carrying out normal and emergency manoeuvres and drills appropriate to the aircraft type in question. The detailed content of the test is specified in the application form for the inclusion of an aircraft type in the rating (Form CA1179).

On application for grant of the CPL(B) the applicant should forward the completed CA1179 in which the examiner has certified the completion of the required test items. Provided that it is satisfactory, and that the other licensing requirements have been met, the CAA will issue the licence with the appropriate class and group entered in the Aircraft Rating. The Aircraft Rating flight test for the issue of a CPL(B) must be satisfactorily completed within the 12-month period immediately preceding the date of receipt by the CAA of the licence application.

Additional class/group

An additional Class/Group of balloon will be included in the Aircraft Rating following a successful flight test and Aircraft (Type) examination in a balloon representative of the Class/Group, conducted by an examiner authorised for the purpose by the CAA.

Exemption from the Aircraft Rating flight test

The holder of a professional balloon pilot's licence issued by another ICAO Contracting State, and which includes a specific balloon type, may have the appropriate Class/Group entered in the Aircraft Rating of the UK licence without having to take the Aircraft Rating flight test, provided that he has not less than 100 hours experience as PIC of such a balloon.

Certificates of test and experience

An Aircraft Rating C of T is valid for a period of 13 months from the date of the initial successful flight test. Thereafter the validity of the Aircraft Rating must be maintained by either a C of T or a C of E as follows:

Flight for the purpose of public transport

A C of T is required for public transport flights. The Certificate is valid for 13 months. The test must have been carried out in a balloon of the Class and Group in which the public transport flight is to be conducted, except that a test in a Group B balloon will also be valid for Group A balloons of the same Class, or a test in a Group C balloon will also be valid for Group A and Group B balloons of the same Class. The individual type used for the test must be within a Class and Group included in the Aircraft Rating. In addition, the pilot is required to have carried out in the 90 days preceding the public transport flight not less than 3 free flights, each of at least 5 minutes' duration, for any purpose, as PIC of a balloon in a free balloon.

Flight for the purpose of aerial work

A C of E or a C of T is required for aerial work flights. The C of E is valid for 13 months, and will be entered in the licence by an examiner appointed or employed by the CAA on production of logbook evidence that the pilot has, within the preceding 13 months, carried out as pilot at least 3 hours free flight in a class and group entered in the Aircraft Rating of the licence, including at least 5 flights. At least one tethered flight must also have been made in the period. Of the 3 hours free flight experience required, at least 2 hours and 3 flights must have been as PIC. The remainder of the time may be made up of:

a. free flight as PIC U/S gained with an authorised examiner on a successful flight test for the grant or revalidation of a licence or Aircraft Rating;

b. dual flying instruction flown with a person authorised by the CAA provided that, at the completion of the free flight or flights, the authorised person considered the pilot fit to fly as PIC, and so certified in the pilot's personal flying logbook.

A pilot with more than one balloon class/group included in the Aircraft Rating of his licence, wishing to revalidate each Aircraft Rating, must include at least one free flight as PIC in a balloon in the class or group as part of the overall minimum 3 hours.

Expiry of Cs of T and Cs of E by more than five years

If a period of more than 5 years has elapsed since the validity of the most recent C of T and the most recent C of E for the type of balloon on which the licence holder wishes to exercise the licence privileges, then before the C of T may be revalidated in respect of that type an assessment of training and testing requirements must be obtained from the CAA (Licensing Services).

APPENDIX F OUTLINE FW (NON-ME) QSP(A) BRIDGING PACKAGE

Approved training providers will provide the bridging package via correspondence or attendance course. The CAA publishes a list of approved training providers on a monthly basis, a copy of which can also be found on the CAA web site at www.caa.co.uk/docs/33/srg_fcl_approvedftos.pdf.

Testing of subject matter will usually be undertaken by the training provider, but may be delegated to a Station Education Centre. The training provider will notify the CAA when a pass is achieved.

TOPIC	JAR-FCL SUBJECT REF. No	SOURCE JAR EXAMINATION
Emergency Equipment	021 04 00 00	Paper 2 – Airframes/Systems/ Powerplant
Automatic Flight Control Systems	022 02 00 00	Paper 3 – Instruments/Electronics
Warning & Recording Equipment	022 03 00 00	Paper 3 – Instruments/Electronics
Microwave Landing Systems	062 01 06 00	Paper 10 – Radio Navigation
Airborne Weather Radar	062 02 03 00	Paper 10 – Radio Navigation
Area Navigation Systems	062 05 00 00	Paper 10 – Radio Navigation
Self-contained & external referenced Navigation Systems	062 06 00 00	Paper 10 – Radio Navigation
Asymmetric Thrust	081 08 02 00	Paper 12 – Principles of Flight

APPENDIX G OUTLINE AAC ISLANDER BRIDGING PACKAGE

Approved training providers will provide the bridging package via correspondence or attendance course. The CAA publishes a list of approved training providers on a monthly basis, a copy of which can also be found on the CAA web site at www.caa.co.uk/docs/33/srg_fcl_approvedftos.pdf

Testing of subject matter will usually be undertaken by the training provider, but may be delegated to a Station Education Centre. The training provider will notify the CAA when a pass is achieved.

Topic	JAR-FCL Subject Ref. No	Source JAR Examination
Stabilising Surfaces	021 01 04 00	Paper 2 – Airframes/Systems/ Powerplant
Landing Gear	021 01 05 00	Paper 2 – Airframes/Systems/ Powerplant
Secondary Controls	021 01 06 02	Paper 2 – Airframes/Systems/ Powerplant
Air Driven Systems	021 01 08 00/ 021 01 09 00	Paper 2 – Airframes/Systems/ Powerplant
Fuel Dumping System	021 01 11 03	Paper 2 – Airframes/Systems/ Powerplant
Jet Pipe	021 03 03 06	Paper 2 – Airframes/Systems/ Powerplant
Reverse Thrust	021 03 03 08	Paper 2 – Airframes/Systems/ Powerplant
Performance & Thrust Augmentation	021 03 03 09	Paper 2 – Airframes/Systems/ Powerplant
Ram Air Turbine	021 03 05 02	Paper 2 – Airframes/Systems/ Powerplant
Emergency Equipment	021 04 00 00	Paper 2 – Airframes/Systems/ Powerplant
Mach Meter	022 01 01 04	Paper 3 – Instruments/Electronics
Electronic Flight Instrument System	022 01 05 00	Paper 3 – Instruments/Electronics
Flight Management System	022 01 06 00	Paper 3 – Instruments/Electronics
Automatic Flight Control Systems	022 02 00 00	Paper 3 – Instruments/Electronics
Warning & Recording Equipment	022 03 00 00	Paper 3 – Instruments/Electronics
Inertial Navigation Systems	061 06 00 00	Paper 9 – General Navigation
Microwave Landing Systems	062 01 06 00	Paper 10 – Radio Navigation
Loran-C	062 06 03 00	Paper 10 – Radio Navigation
Transonic Aerodynamics	081 02 00 00	Paper 12 – Principles of Flight
Supersonic Aerodynamics	081 03 00 00	Paper 12 – Principles of Flight

APPENDIX H OUTLINE ROTARY BRIDGING PACKAGE

Approved training providers will provide the bridging package via correspondence or attendance course. The CAA publishes a list of approved training providers on a monthly basis, a copy of which can also be found on the CAA web site at www.caa.co.uk/docs/33/srg_fcl_approvedftos.pdf

Testing of subject matter will usually be undertaken by the training provider, but may be delegated to a Station Education Centre. The training provider will notify the CAA when a pass is achieved.

Topic	JAR-FCL Subject Ref. No.	Source JAR Examination
Emergency Equipment	021 04 00 00	Paper 2 – Airframes/Systems/ Powerplant
Air Conditioning	021 05 10 02	Paper 2 – Airframes/Systems/ Powerplant
Electronic Flight Instrument System	022 01 05 00	Paper 3 – Instruments/Electronics
Flight Management System	022 01 06 00	Paper 3 – Instruments/Electronics
Warning & Recording Equipment	022 03 00 00	Paper 3 – Instruments/Electronics
IFR (Airways) Flight Planning	033 04 00 00	Paper 6 – Flight Planning & Monitoring
Inertial Navigation Systems	061 06 00 00	Paper 9 – General Navigation
Radio Aids	062 01 00 00	Paper 10 – Radio Navigation
Airborne Weather Radar	062 02 03 00	Paper 10 – Radio Navigation
Area Navigation Systems	062 05 00 00	Paper 10 – Radio Navigation
Self-contained & external referenced Navigation Systems	062 06 00 00	Paper 10 – Radio Navigation
IFR Communications	092 00 00 00	Paper 14 – IFR Communications

APPENDIX I LICENSING FLOW DIAGRAMS

FW QSP(A) LICENSING FLOW

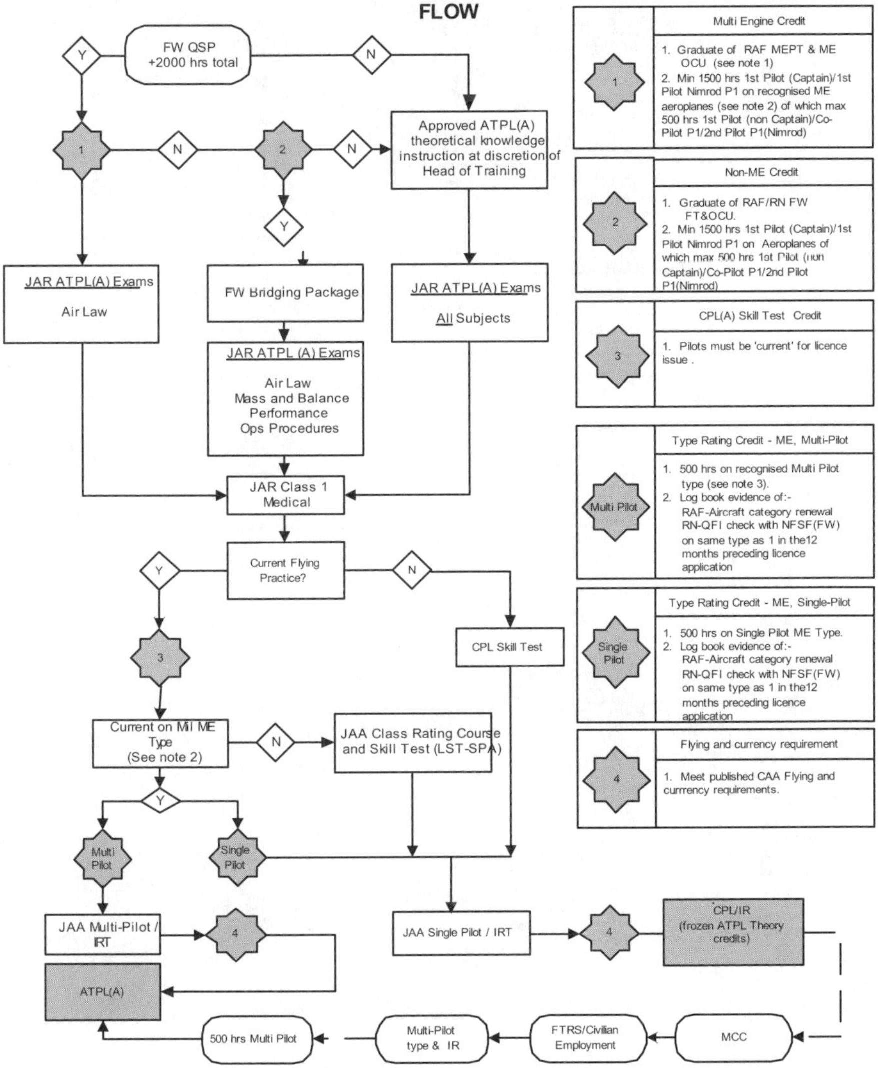

NOTES:

1. Recognised Multi-Engine OCU's: BAE 125/146, C17, Hercules, Nimrod, Sentry, Tristar and VC10 (RN - Jetstream T2).
2. Recognised Multi-Engine aircraft : Andover, BAC1-11, Bae125/146, B200 C17*, Canberra, Dominie, Hercules (all variants), Islander, Jetstream (all variants), Nimrod, PA31, Sentry, Tristar and VC10.
3. Recognised Multi Pilot aircraft: Andover, BAC 1-11, Bae125/146, Hercules C1/C3, Hercules C4/C5, Jetstream T3, Nimrod, Sentry, Tristar and VC10.

*Whilst it is not possible for C17 pilots to obtain a JAR-FCL ATPL(A) through this scheme (as the IR(A) Skill Test cannot be completed in this aircraft type), pilots may still qualify for ATPL theory credits as a ME pilot.

AAC ISLANDER LICENSING FLOW

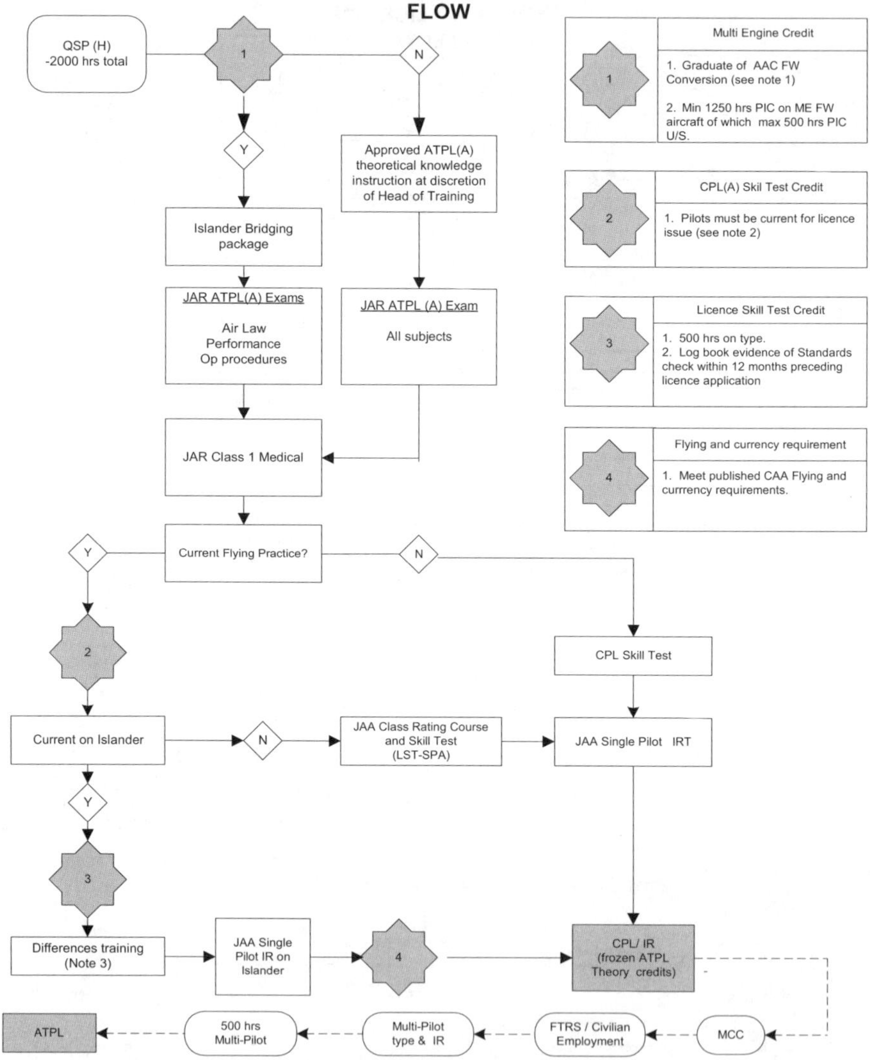

NOTES:

1. Graduate of MELIN and Islander conversion course (including Islander Airways course with proc IR.
2. To be deemed 'current', pilots shall have a minimum of 12 hours flying experience as a pilot in military or civil aeroplanes (or combination of both) in the 12 months preceding the date of application for licence issue. This experience shall include at least 6 hours as PIC - for this purpose military 1st Pilot hours may be counted towards the PIC requirement, one flight with a military instructor pilot or JAA Flight Instructor, and 12 take offs and landing. A QSP(A) on a ground tour can still achieve currency by flying on civil aeroplanes.
3. Differences training (undercarriage) - to consist of pre-flight brief plus one hour flight instruction in SE/ME aircraft with retractable undercarriage.

RW QSP(H) LICENSING FLOW

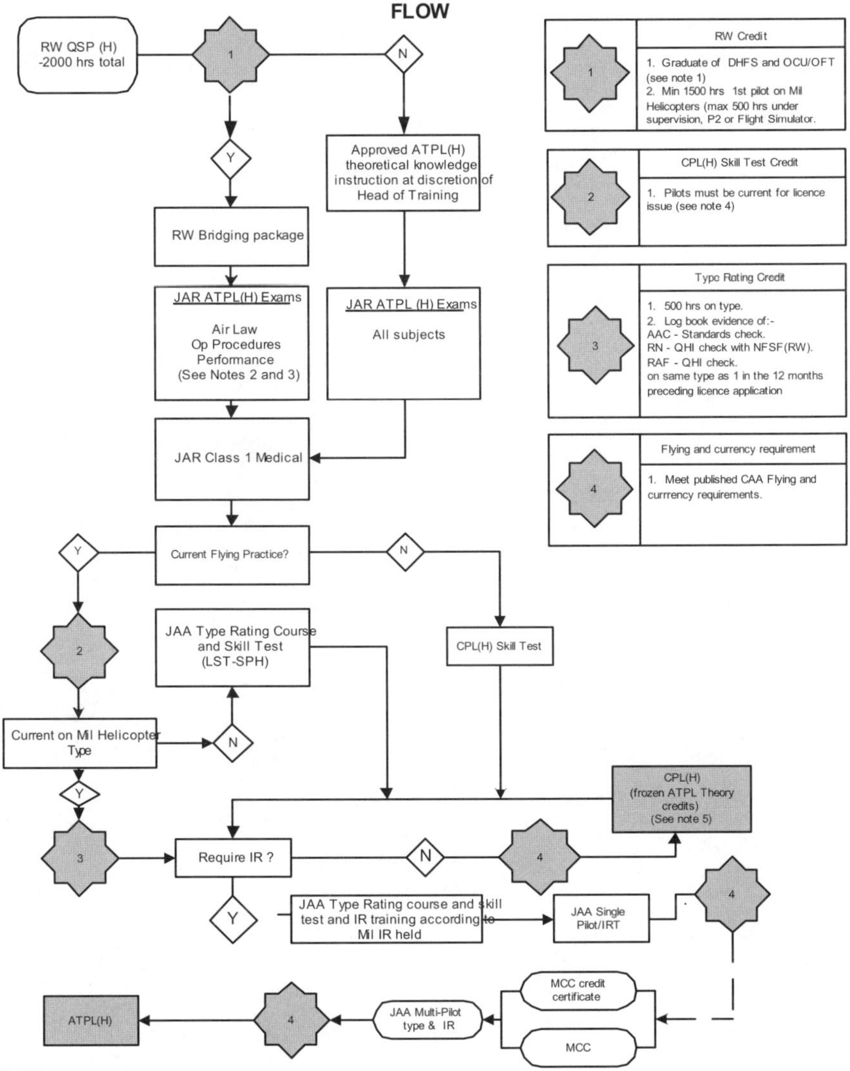

NOTES:

1. Or single Service equivalents.
2. A temporary exemption exists against the Performance examination until such time as this examination becomes available.
3. Equivalent ATPL(A) exams being used as an interim measure until ATPL(H) exams become available.
4. To be deemed 'current', pilots shall have a minimum of 12 hours flying experience as a pilot in military or civil helicopters (or combination of both) in the 12 months preceding the date of application for licence issue. This experience shall include at least 6 hours as PIC - for this purpose military 1st Pilot hours may be counted towards the PIC requirement, one flight with a military instructor pilot or JAA Flight Instructor, and 12 take offs and landing. A QSP(H) on a ground tour can still achieve currency by flying on civil helicopters.
5. CAA will apply a 3 year validity on IR theory element of exam credit from date of last flight in Mil helicopter, or date of passing last ATPL(H) exam, whichever is <u>later</u>. When IR obtained, ATPL(H) theory is banked.

SECTION E

INSTRUMENT RATING, INSTRUMENT METEOROLOGICAL CONDITIONS RATING AND NIGHT QUALIFICATION

E1 THE INSTRUMENT RATING (AEROPLANE)

This section offers information as a basic guide to obtaining and maintaining a JAR-FCL Instrument Rating (Aeroplane) – IR(A) as follows:-

E1.1 IR(A) GENERAL INFORMATION

Privileges

Details of rating privileges can be found in Schedule 8 of the Air Navigation Order (please also refer to Section A, Appendix F).

Medical Fitness

An applicant for an IR(A) shall be medically fit in accordance with JAR-FCL 3.355(b)

E1.2 IR(A) FLYING TRAINING/ EXPERIENCE REQUIREMENTS

An applicant for a modular IR(A) course shall be the holder of a PPL(A) or a CPL(A), either licence to include the privileges to fly by night, issued in accordance with ICAO Annex 1. In addition, applicants must hold a Flight Radio Telephony Operator's Licence.

Experience Requirements

When applying for an IR(A) you must produce evidence of having met the following flying requirements:-

50 hours cross-country flight time as PIC in aeroplanes or helicopters, of which at least **10 hours** shall be in aeroplanes.

Flying Training

An applicant for an IR(A) shall complete an approved modular course of training at a JAA Approved Flying Training Organisation (FTO).

IR(A) Training conducted in other JAA States

In accordance with JAR-FCL 1.065(c), training and testing for an IR(A) may be undertaken at a JAA Approved FTO in another JAA Member State. Applicants will be required to complete the full modular course of training and the IR(A) Skill Test in that State as detailed below. Applicants who qualify for the conversion requirements detailed below must also complete the applicable course and IR(A) Skill Test in that State. (A list of JAA Member States recommended by the JAA for mutual recognition can be found in Section A2).

Applicants should be aware of the UK CAA's policy with regards applicants who have already commenced IR(A) training and wish to then transfer to another JAA State. The policy is as follows:

- Applicants who have commenced IR(A) training with a UK Approved FTO will not be permitted to complete the remainder of their flying training and testing in another JAA Member State. Applicants will be required to complete the remainder of their IR(A) course and Skill Test with the UK Approved FTO, or, complete an entire course of IR(A) training and Skill Test in the other JAA Member State.

- Applicants who have commenced IR(A) training in a JAA Member State other than the UK will not be permitted to complete the remainder of their flying training and testing in the UK or with another JAA Member State. Applicants will be required to complete the remainder of their IR(A) course and Skill Test with the existing JAA State or, complete an entire course of IR(A) training and Skill Test in the UK or another JAA Member State.

- Applicants who have completed a course of IR(A) training and testing with a UK Approved FTO and are required to complete remedial training following failure of their IR(A) Skill test(s) must complete their training and IR(A) Skill Test with their existing UK Approved FTO. Alternatively, the applicant can complete another entire course of IR(A) training and Skill Test in another JAA Member State.

For IR restricted to Single-Engine (SE) aeroplanes

A single-engine IR(A) course shall comprise of at least:-

a. **50 hours** instrument time under instruction, which may include (b) or (c).

b. **20 hours** (maximum) in FNPT 1 if approved by CAA;

c. **35 hours** (maximum) in FNPT II or Flight Simulator if approved by CAA. With the agreement of the approving Authority not more than 10 hours of FNPT II or flight simulator instrument ground time may be conducted in a FNPT I.

For Multi-Engine (ME) aeroplanes

A multi-engine IR(A) course shall comprise of at least:-

a. **55 hours** instrument time under instruction, which may include (b) or (c) and must include (d);

b. **25 hours** (maximum) in FNPT 1 if approved by CAA.

c. **40 hours** (maximum) in FNPT II or Flight Simulator if approved by CAA. With the agreement of the approving Authority not more than 10 hours of FNPT II or flight simulator instrument ground time may be conducted in a FNPT I.

d. **15 hours** in ME aeroplanes.

Note: An applicant for a multi-engine IR(A) course who does not hold a multi-engine aeroplane class or type rating shall have completed the multi-engine training specified in JAR-FCL 1.261(b)(2) (see Section F3.2) prior to commencing the flight training for the IR(A) course.

SE IR(A) to ME IR(A)*

a. **5 hours** instrument time under instruction in ME aeroplanes, which may include (b);

b. **3 hours** in FNPT II or Flight Simulator if approved by CAA**;**

c. Pass a ME IR(A) Skill Test with a UK CAA Staff Flight Examiner.

* The holder of a SE IR(A) wishing to upgrade to ME IR(A) shall either hold a multi-engine type/class rating, or have at least completed an approved course of training for the ME class rating.

Credits from IR(A) Training

- Holders of a CPL(A) or ATPL(A) issued in accordance with ICAO are eligible for a 5 hour reduction in training in accordance with Appendix 1 to JAR-FCL 1.205. The same credit can be applied to applicants who have completed a JAR CPL(A) modular course of training and passed the CPL(A) skill test (and have met <u>all</u> requirements for CPL(A) licence issue prior to commencement of the IR(A) modular course), but have yet to apply for licence issue provided that the JAR CPL(A) modular course and IR(A) modular course are conducted totally separately from each other, and that there is no training overlap between the two courses.

- A QSP (A) who has held an AAC (unlimited) or Unrestricted* Green (or Master Green) aeroplane instrument rating within the 5 years preceding the date of application for the IR(A), will be required to complete flight instruction at the discretion of the Head of Training or an approved FTO.

- A QSP(A) who has held an AAC (limited) or restricted* Green (or Master Green) aeroplane instrument rating within the 5 years preceding the date of application for the IR(A), is required to complete a minimum of 15 hours IR training at an approved FTO, of which 5 hours may be in a FNPT1, or 10 hours in a FNPT2 or flight simulator.

- A QSP(H) who has held an AAC (unlimited) or unrestricted* Green (or Master Green) helicopter instrument rating within the 5 years preceding the date of application for the IR(A), is required to complete a minimum of 15 hours IR training at an approved FTO, of which 5 hours may be in a FNPT1, or 10 hours in a FNPT2 or flight simulator.

- A QSP(H) who has held an AAC (limited) or restricted* Green (or Master Green) helicopter instrument rating within the 5 years preceding the date of application for the IR(A), is required to complete a minimum of 25 hours IR training at an approved FTO, of which 5 hours may be in a FNPT 1, or 10 hours in a FNPT2 or flight simulator.

- A QSP(A)/(H) who has <u>not</u> held a Green instrument rating in the 5 years preceding the date of application for the IR(A) is required to complete the full IR(A) course.

* The terms "restricted" and "unrestricted" apply as used in MOD documents referring to the Pilot Instrument Rating Scheme. Thus "unrestricted" is the privilege to operate as GAT or OAT in all classes of airspace; "restricted" refers to any restrictions applied by Commands/Groups according to the experience of the pilot or limitations of the aircraft/helicopter type.

In all cases the applicant is required to obtain a 170A Certificate of Training and Competence from an authorised 170A signatory. Upon application for the grant of an IR(A), a QSP claiming credit on the basis of holding an unrestricted or unlimited Green Instrument Rating (aeroplane or helicopter) will be required to submit a certified copy of the MOD Form 166 or AAC Form 4 as appropriate, relating to the most recent issue/renewal of such an instrument rating.

Conversion Requirements

These arrangements will provide a route to a JAR-FCL IR(A) qualification for the following holders of a **current and valid*** IR issued in accordance with ICAO Annex 1.

ICAO IR(A) holder to JAR-FCL IR(A)
ICAO IR(H) holder to JAR-FCL IR(A)
JAR-FCL IR(H) holder to JAR-FCL IR(A)

* The holder of an ICAO IR(A)/(H) that is not current and valid will be required to complete the full IR(A) course.

Table 1 details the IR training requirements for holders of an existing valid Instrument Rating wishing to obtain a JAR-FCL IR **equivalent** qualification (i.e. ICAO SE IR(A) to JAR-FCL SE IR(A)). Table 1 notes should also be read in conjunction with this table (see below).

Table 1

	IR Required
IR Held	JAR IR(A)
ICAO IR(A)	1, 2, 5, 6
ICAO IR(H)	1, 4, 5, 6
JAR IR(H)	3, 6

Table 1 Key

IR Training Requirements

1. Undertake JAR-IR(A) theoretical knowledge instruction as determined by the Head of Training of an approved training provider and pass all JAR-FCL theoretical knowledge examinations at IR level. Applicants who wish to attempt the ATPL(A) examinations must undertake the full 650 hour course of approved theoretical knowledge instruction and pass all JAR-FCL ATPL(A) examinations.

2. Complete a minimum of 15 hours instrument time under instruction (including 170A flight test) of which 5 hours may be in a FNPT 1 or 10 hours in a FNPT 2 or Flight Simulator.

3. Complete a minimum of 10 hours IR flight instruction (including 170A flight test) as per JAR-FCL 1.205 in Aeroplanes.

4. Complete a minimum of 25 hours instrument flight time under instruction (including 170A flight test) of which 5 hours may be in a FNPT 1 or 10 hours in a FNPT 2 or Flight Simulator. Note D may apply.

5. Additional IR training considered necessary by the Head of Training of an approved FTO.

6. Pass the JAR IR(A) Skill Test.

Table 1 Notes

a. ICAO CPL holders may not claim a further 5 hour reduction as per Appendix 1 to JAR-FCL 1.205 or 2.205 as appropriate.

b. Synthetic Training Devices (FNPT1, FNPT 2, Flight Simulator) shall be appropriately approved.

c. Holder of an ATPL(A) with IR issued in accordance with ICAO Annex 1 who meets the 1500 hours flying experience requirements on multi-pilot aeroplanes as PIC or co-pilot of Appendix 1 to JAR-FCL 1.015 may be exempted from the requirements to undergo approved IR training prior to undertaking the theoretical knowledge examinations and the skill test, if that licence contains a valid multi-pilot type rating for the aeroplane to be used for the ATPL(A) skill test, or will be undertaking a JAA Approved Type Rating Course for a multi-pilot type rating.

d. Other exceptional cases should continue to be referred to the CAA.

e. These credits shall remain subject to review in discussion with the JAA and representatives of UK Training Organisations.

f. Candidates for an IR(A) shall meet the experience requirements as per JAR-FCL 1.190.

g. Holders of an ICAO SE IR(A) wishing to obtain a JAR-FCL ME IR(A) will be required to attend an approved IR(A) training provider. There are currently 3 alternative approved courses of training to obtain the JAR-FCL ME IR(A). Applicants should consult with the IR training provider as to which course of training they have been approved to conduct:-

Option 1: Complete a minimum of 15 hours SE IR flight instruction, of which 5 hours may be in a FNPT 1 or 10 hours in a FNPT 2 or Flight Simulator. In addition, applicants must hold a multi-engine class rating and complete an additional 5 hours instrument flying instruction in multi-engine aeroplanes, of which 3 hours may be in a Flight Simulator or FNPT 2 and pass a ME IR(A) Skill Test; or

Option 2: Complete a minimum of 13 hours ME IR flight instruction in a ME FNPT 2. In addition, applicants must hold a multi-engine class rating and complete at least 7 hours instrument flying instruction in multi-engine aeroplanes; or

Option 3: Complete a minimum of 15 hours ME IR instruction in a multi-engine aeroplane (no instructional time will be allowed in a FNPT or Flight Simulator).

E1.3 IR(A) THEORETICAL KNOWLEDGE EXAMINATION REQUIREMENTS

Applicants for a JAR-FCL IR(A) will be required to pass the IR(A) theoretical knowledge examinations in the following subjects:-

a. Air Law/Operational Procedures

b. Aircraft General Knowledge

c. Flight Performance & Planning

d. Human Performance & Limitations

e. Meteorology

f. Navigation

g. Communications (IFR)

The course of theoretical knowledge instruction shall be completed within 18 months. The acceptance period of these examinations towards the issuance of the IR(A) can be found in Section J1.7. Applicants must apply to PLD for the issue of the IR(A) within this acceptance period.

Credits from JAR-FCL Examinations

- The holder of an IR(H) will be exempted from the theoretical knowledge instruction and examinations for an IR(A).
- An applicant having passed the theoretical knowledge examination in subject Human Performance for a CPL(A)/(H) is credited with the theoretical knowledge requirement in subject Human Performance for an IR(A) according to the pass standards set out in JAR-FCL 1.490 and Section J1.5.
- An applicant who has passed the JAR-FCL ATPL(A) theoretical knowledge examinations is credited with the theoretical knowledge requirements for an IR(A). The acceptance period of these examinations for the issuance of the IR(A) can be found in Section J1.7.

E1.4 IR(A) SKILL TEST REQUIREMENTS

An applicant for an IR(A) shall complete a Skill Test with a UK CAA Staff Flight Examiner in order to demonstrate the ability to perform the procedures and manoeuvres as set out in **Appendices 1 & 2 to JAR-FCL 1.210**, with a degree of competency appropriate to the privileges granted to the holder of an IR(A).

- ME Aeroplanes - for a ME aeroplane Instrument Rating, the test shall be taken in a ME aeroplane;
- SE Aeroplanes - for a SE aeroplane Instrument Rating, the test shall be taken in a SE aeroplane. A ME centreline thrust aeroplane shall be considered a SE aeroplane for the purposes of a SE aeroplane IR.
- If the IR(A) skill test is completed in a multi-pilot aeroplane, the privileges of the IR(A) will be restricted to multi-crew only. The restriction may be lifted by completing approved IR(A) training in a single-pilot, single/multi-engine aeroplane, sufficient to obtain a 170A, and pass a further IR(A) skill test with a CAA Flight Examiner.
- An applicant for the IR(A) Skill Test shall have received instruction and obtained a 170A on the same class or type of aeroplane to be used for the Skill Test. Before undertaking the Skill Test the applicant shall have passed the associated theoretical knowledge examinations (exceptions may be made by the CAA for applicants undergoing a course of Integrated flying training) and completed all of the related flying training.
- An applicant is required to provide evidence of either holding a valid FRTOL or of having passed the UK RTF practical test prior to attempting the IR(A) Skill Test.
- An applicant shall pass sections 1 through 5 of the test/check and applicable items of section 6. If any item in a section is failed, that section is failed. Failure in more than one section will require the applicant to take the entire test again. An applicant failing only one section shall take the failed section again and Section 1. Failure in any section of the re-test, including those sections that have been passed on a previous attempt, will require the applicant to take the entire test again.
- All sections of the skill test shall be completed within six months. For the purpose of IR(A) issue, the skill test will remain valid for 12 months.
- Further training may be recommended following the failure of one Section of the Skill Test. Further training will be required to any full re-test.

DETAILS OF THE IR(A) SKILL TEST REQUIREMENTS ARE DETAILED IN APPENDICES 1 AND 2 TO JAR-FCL 1.210.

Guidance for applicants taking the IR(A) Skill Test can also be found in Standards Document 01(A) on the CAA web site at www.caa.co.uk.

E1.5 IR(A) RE-VALIDATION AND RENEWAL

Validity

An IR(A) is valid for a period of one year from the date of issue or renewal, or from the expiry date of a current IR(A) if revalidated in accordance with JAR-FCL 1.246(a).

Re-validation of an IR (A)

An IR(A) shall be revalidated within the three months immediately preceding the expiry date of the rating. Whenever possible, revalidation of an IR(A) shall be combined with the proficiency check for revalidation of a type or class rating.

An applicant for the revalidation of an IR(A) when combined with a class rating or a type rating shall complete a proficiency check in accordance with Appendix 1 and 2 to JAR-FCL 1.240 & 1.295 or Appendix 3 to JAR-FCL 1.240. In this case the instrument rating will be valid for the same period as the class or type rating, except in the case of a single-engine aeroplane class rating revalidation where the validity period of the instrument rating will be 12 months.

Where a proficiency check including IR is performed, cross-credits may be given towards the IR part of a proficiency check single pilot single/multi-engine aeroplanes. Such cross-credits shall be given in accordance with Appendix 1 to JAR-FCL 1.246 (see Section E Appendix C).

An applicant for the revalidation of an IR(A) when not combined with the revalidation of a class or type rating shall:-

i. complete 3b of Appendix 3 to JAR-FCL 1.240;

ii. and those parts of Section 1 relevant to the intended flight;

iii. and for multi-engine aeroplane, Section 6 of Appendix 3 to JAR-FCL 1.240 as a proficiency check by sole reference to instruments.

An FNPT II or Flight Simulator may be used but at least each alternate proficiency check for the revalidation of an IR(A) in these circumstances shall be performed in an aeroplane.

An applicant who fails to achieve a pass in the relevant section of an IR(A) proficiency check in accordance with JAR-FCL 1.246(a) (1) or (a) (2), before the expiry date of an instrument rating shall not exercise the IR(A) privileges until the proficiency check has successfully been completed.

Important Note

- Single-Pilot Aeroplane (SPA) and Multi-Pilot Aeroplane (MPA) Instrument Rating (IR) privileges are separate and must be re-validated separately;
- MPA IR privileges are type specific - the IR re-validation is an integral part of the LPC/LST for a MPA Type;
- SPA IR privileges are not type or class specific - the holder of more than one SPA type or class rating is required to re-validate the IR on only one SPA type or class (usually the most complex one). However, the holder of a ME IR must revalidate on a ME class or type. An IR SPA ME will confer SPA SE IR privileges whereas an IR SPA SE does not confer SPA ME IR privileges.

Renewal of an IR (A)

The requirements to renew an IR(A) are based on the period of time elapsed since the rating expired i.e. calculated from the date of expiry of the most recent IR(A) proficiency check entered in the licence. However, where IR privileges have been exercised in another category of aircraft (i.e. UK/JAR IR(H)) or under the privileges of an ICAO licence (Aeroplanes and Helicopters) or under a UK military IR qualification (fixed-wing or rotary), the renewal requirements will be based on the expiry date of that IR.

- To renew an IR(A) that has expired by less than 5 years, applicants must complete Section 3b of Appendix 3 to JAR-FCL 1.240 including the flight preparation as a Skill Test with an authorised examiner.
- To renew an IR(A) that has expired by more than 5 years but less and 7 years, applicants must: **For single-pilot aircraft** complete Section 3b of Appendix 3 to JAR-FCL 1.240 including the flight preparation as a Skill Test in an aeroplane with a UK CAA Staff Flight Examiner. **For multi-pilot aircraft** pass a type rating skill test with or observed by a UK CAA Flight Operations Training Inspector.
- To renew an IR(A) that has expired by more than 7 years, applicants must: **For single-pilot aircraft** pass an IR(A) skill test in an aeroplane with a UK CAA Staff Flight Examiner. **For multi-pilot aircraft** pass a type rating skill test with or observed by a UK CAA Flight Operations Training Inspector. Applicants will also be required to retake the IR(A) theoretical knowledge examinations.

Section A
Section B
Section C
Section D
Section E IR, IMC, NIGHT
Section F
Section G
Section H
Section I
Section J
Section K
Index

E2 THE INSTRUMENT RATING (HELICOPTER)

This section offers information as a basic guide to obtaining and maintaining a JAR-FCL Instrument Rating (Helicopter) – IR (H) as follows:-

E2.1 IR (H) GENERAL INFORMATION

Privileges

Details of the rating privileges can be found in Schedule 8 of the Air Navigation Order (please also refer to Section A, Appendix F).

Medical Fitness

An applicant for an IR(H) shall be medically fit in accordance with JAR-FCL 3.355(b).

E2.2 IR (H) FLYING TRAINING/ EXPERIENCE REQUIREMENTS

An applicant for a modular IR(H) course shall be the holder of a PPL(H) with a night qualification issued in accordance with Appendix 4 to JAR-FCL 2.125, or a CPL(H) issued in accordance with ICAO Annex 1. Prior to commencing the IR(H) course, the applicant shall be the holder of the helicopter type rating used for the IR(H) skill test, or have completed approved type rating training on that type.

In addition, applicants must hold a Flight Radio Telephony Operator's Licence.

Experience Requirements

When applying for the issue of an IR (H), applicants must produce evidence of having met the following flying requirements:

50 hours cross-country flight time as PIC, in aeroplanes or helicopters, of which at least **10 hours** must be in helicopters.

Flying Training

An applicant for an IR(H) shall complete an approved modular course of training at a JAA Approved Flying Training Organisation (FTO).

IR(H) Training conducted in other JAA States

In accordance with JAR-FCL 2.065(c), training and testing for an IR(H) may be undertaken at a JAA Approved FTO in another JAA Member State. Applicants will be required to complete the full modular course of training and the IR(H) Skill Test in that State as detailed below. Applicants who qualify for the conversion requirements detailed below must also complete the applicable course and IR(H) Skill Test in that State. (A list of JAA Member States recommended by the JAA for mutual recognition can be found in Section A2).

Applicants should be aware of the UK CAA's policy with regards applicants who have already commenced IR(H) training and wish to then transfer to another JAA State. The policy is as follows:

- Applicants who have commenced IR(H) training with a UK Approved FTO will not be permitted to complete the remainder of their flying training and testing in another JAA Member State. Applicants will be required to complete the remainder of their IR(H) course and Skill Test with the UK Approved FTO, or, complete an entire course of IR(H) training and Skill Test in the other JAA Member State.

- Applicants who have commenced IR(H) training in a JAA Member State other than the UK will not be permitted to complete the remainder of their flying training and testing in the UK or with another JAA Member State. Applicants will be required to complete the remainder of their IR(H) course and Skill Test with the existing JAA State or, complete an entire course of IR(H) training and Skill Test in the UK or another JAA Member State.

- Applicants who have completed a course of IR(H) training and testing with a UK Approved FTO and are required to complete remedial training following failure of their IR(H) Skill test(s) must complete their training and IR(H) Skill Test with their existing UK Approved FTO. Alternatively, the applicant can complete another entire course of IR(H) training and Skill Test in another JAA Member State.

For IR restricted to Single-Engine (SE) helicopters

a. **50 hours** instrument time under instruction of which may include (b) or (c);

b. **20** hours (maximum) may be instrument ground time in a FNPT I (H) or (A). These 20 hours instruction time in FNPT I (H) or (A) may be substituted by 20 hours instruction time for IR(H) in an aeroplane, approved for this course

c. **35 hours** (maximum) may be instrument ground time in a helicopter FNPT II/III or FS.

The instrument flight instruction shall include at least 10 hours in an IFR certificated helicopter.

For Multi-Engine (ME) helicopter

a. **55 hours** instrument time under instruction which may include (b) or (c) and must include (d);

b. **20 hours** (maximum) may be instrument ground time in a FNPT I (H) or (A). These 20 hours instruction time in FNPT I (H) or (A) may be substituted by 20 hours instruction time for IR(H) in an aeroplane, approved for this course, or

c. **40 hours** (maximum) may be instrument ground time in a helicopter FNPT II/III or FS.

d. The instrument flight instruction shall include at least 10 hours in an IFR certificated multi-engine helicopter.

SE IR (H) to ME IR(H)*

a. **5 hours** instrument time under instruction in ME Helicopters;

b. Pass a ME IR(H) Skill Test.

* The holder of a SE IR(H) wishing to upgrade to ME IR(H) will be required to hold a multi-engine type rating.

Credits against IR (H) Training

- Holders of a PPL(H) with a night qualification issued in accordance with Appendix 4 to JAR-FCL 2.125, or a CPL (H) or ATPL (H) issued in accordance with ICAO (including the JAR CPL (H)(R)) are eligible for a 5 hour reduction in training in accordance with Appendix 1 to JAR-FCL 2.205. The same credit can be applied to applicants who have completed a JAR CPL (H) modular course of training and passed the CPL(H) skill test (and have met all requirements for CPL(H) licence issue prior to commencement of the IR(H) modular course) but have yet to apply for licence issue **provided** that the JAR CPL (H) modular course and IR (H) modular courses are conducted independent of each other, and that there is no training overlap between the two courses.

Credits for QSPs

Applicants should note that the IR (H) is type specific. In most cases, IR training at an approved FTO will be undertaken on a helicopter type not operated by HM Forces. In this instance, applicants will additionally be required to complete an approved type rating course for the type to be used for the IR (H) Skill Test.

- A QSP(H) who has held an AAC (unlimited) or Unrestricted* Green (or Master Green) helicopter instrument rating within the 5 years preceding the date of application for the IR(H), will be required to complete flight instruction at the discretion of the Head of Training of an approved FTO.

- A QSP(H) who has held a AAC (limited) or a restricted* Green (or Master Green) helicopter instrument rating within the 5 years preceding the date of application for the IR(H), is required to complete a minimum of 15 hours IR training at an approved FTO, of which 5 hours may be in a FNPT 1 or 10 hours in a FNPT 2 or flight simulator.

- A QSP(A) who has held an AAC (unlimited) or unrestricted* Green (or Master Green) aeroplane instrument rating within the 5 years preceding the date of application for the IR(H), is required to complete a minimum of 10 hours IR training at an approved FTO, of which 5 hours may be in a FNPT 1, FNPT 2 or flight simulator.

- A QSP(A) who has held a AAC (limited) or restricted* Green (or Master Green) aeroplane instrument rating within the 5 years preceding the date of application for the IR(H), is required to complete a minimum of 25 hours IR training at an approved FTO, of which 5 hours may be in a FNPT 1, or 10 hours in a FNPT 2 or flight simulator.

- A QSP(H)/(A) who has not held a Green instrument rating in the 5 years preceding the date of application for the IR(H) is required to complete the full IR(H) course.

* The terms "restricted" and "unrestricted" apply as used in MOD documents referring to the pilot Instrument Rating Scheme. Thus "unrestricted" is the privilege to operate as GAT or OAT in all classes of airspace; "restricted" refers to any restrictions applied

by Commands/Groups according to the experience of the pilot or limitations of the aircraft/helicopter type.

In all cases the applicant is required to obtain a 170A Certificate of Training and Competence from an authorised 170A signatory. Upon application for the grant of an IR(H), a QSP claiming credit on the basis of holding an unrestricted or unlimited Green Instrument Rating (aeroplane or helicopter) will be required to submit a certified copy of the MOD Form 166 or AAC Form 4 as appropriate, relating to the most recent issue/renewal of such an Instrument Rating.

IR Conversion Requirements

These arrangements will provide a route to JAR-FCL IR(H) qualification for the following holders of a **current and valid*** IR issued in accordance with ICAO Annex 1:

ICAO IR (H) holder to JAR-FCL IR (H)
ICAO IR (A) holder to JAR-FCL IR (H)
JAR-FCL IR (A) holder to JAR-FCL IR (H)

* The holder of an ICAO IR(H)/(A) that is not current and valid will be required to complete the full IR(H) course.

Table 1 details the IR training requirements for holders of an existing valid IR to obtain an **equivalent** IR under JAR-FCL (i.e. ICAO SE IR(H) to JAR-FCL SE IR(H)).

Table 1

	IR Required
IR Held	JAR IR (H)
ICAO IR (H)	1, 2, 5, 6
ICAO IR (A)	1, 4, 5, 6
JAR IR (A)	3, 6

Table 1 Key

1. Undertake IR theoretical knowledge instruction as determined by the Head of Training of an approved provider and pass all JAR-FCL theoretical knowledge examinations at IR level. Applicants who wish to attempt the ATPL(H) examinations must undertake the full 650 hour course of approved theoretical knowledge instruction and pass all JAR-ATPL(H) examinations.

2. Complete a minimum of 15 hours instrument flight under instruction (including 170A Flight Test) of which 5 hours may be in a FNPT 1, or 10 hours in a FNPT 2 or Flight Simulator.

3. Complete a minimum of 10 hours IR flight instruction (including 170A flight test) as per JAR-FCL 2.205 in helicopters.

4. Complete a minimum of 25 hours instrument flight time under instruction (including 170A flight test). Note D may apply.

5. Additional IR training as considered necessary by the Head of Training of an approved FTO.

6. Pass the JAR IR (H) Skill Test.

Notes:

a. ICAO CPL holders may not claim a further 5 hour reduction as per Appendix 1 to JAR-FCL 2.205.

b. Synthetic Training Devices (FNPT 1, FNPT 2, Flight Simulator) shall be appropriately approved.

c. Holder of an ATPL(H) with IR issued in accordance with ICAO Annex 1 who meets the 1000 hours flying experience requirements on multi-pilot helicopters as PIC or co-pilot of Appendix 1 to JAR-FCL 2.015 may be exempted from the requirements to undergo approved IR training prior to undertaking the theoretical knowledge examinations and the skill test, if that licence contains a valid multi-pilot type rating with IR(H) privileges for the helicopter to be used for the ATPL (H) skill test in accordance with JAR-FCL 2.295.

d. Other exceptional cases should continue to be referred to the CAA.

e. These credits shall remain subject to review in discussion with the JAA and representatives of UK Training Organisations.

f. Candidates for an IR (H) shall meet the experience requirements as per JAR-FCL 2.190.

g. Holders of an ICAO SE IR (H) wishing to obtain a JAR-FCL ME IR(H) will be required to complete a minimum of 15 hours SE IR flight instruction, of which 5 hours may be in a FNPT 1 or 10 hours in a FNPT 2 or Flight Simulator. In addition, applicants must hold a multi-engine type rating, complete at least 5 hours instruction in instrument flying in multi-engine helicopters, of which 3 hours may be in a flight simulator or FNPT 2, and pass a ME IR Skill Test. Alternatively, applicants shall complete 15 hours ME IR flight instruction and pass a ME IR Skill Test in a multi-engine helicopter (no instructional time will be allowed in a FNPT or Flight Simulator).

E2.3 IR(H) THEORETICAL KNOWLEDGE EXAMINATION REQUIREMENTS

Applicants for an IR (H) will be required to pass the IR (H) theoretical knowledge examinations in the following subjects:

a. Air Law/Operational Procedures
b. Aircraft General Knowledge
c. Flight Performance & Planning
d. Human Performance &Limitations
e. Meteorology
f. Navigation
g. Communications (IFR)

The course of theoretical knowledge instruction shall be completed within 18 months. The acceptance period of these examinations towards the issuance of the IR(H) can be found in Section J1.7. Applicants must apply to PLD for the issue of the IR(H) within this acceptance period.

Credits from JAR-FCL Examinations

- The holder of an IR(A) will be exempted from the theoretical knowledge instruction and examinations for an IR(H).
- The holder of a JAR-FCL ATPL(H) issued on the conversion from the previous UK National Helicopter licence will be exempted from the theoretical knowledge instruction and examinations for an IR(H).
- An applicant who has passed the JAR-FCL ATPL(H) theoretical knowledge examinations is credited with the theoretical knowledge requirements for an IR(H). The acceptance period of these examinations for the issuance of the IR(H) can be found in Section J1.7.

E2.4 IR(H) SKILL TEST

An applicant for an IR (H) shall complete a Skill Test in order to demonstrate the ability to perform the procedures and manoeuvres as set out in **Appendices 1 & 2 to JAR-FCL 2.210**, with a degree of competency appropriate to the privileges granted to the holder of an IR (H).

- ME Helicopters - for a ME helicopter Instrument Rating, the test shall be taken in a ME helicopter.
- SE Helicopters - for a SE helicopter Instrument Rating, the test shall be taken in a SE helicopter.
- An applicant for the IR (H) Skill Test shall have received instruction, and obtained a 170A on the same type of helicopter to be used for the Skill Test. Before undertaking the skill test, the applicant shall have passed the associated theoretical knowledge examination (exceptions may be made by the CAA for applicants undergoing a course of Integrated flying training) and completed all of the related flying training.
- An applicant is required to provide evidence of either holding a valid FRTOL or of having passed the UK RTF practical test prior to attempting the IR(H) Skill Test.
- An applicant shall pass all sections of the skill test. Failure in more than one section will require the applicant to take the entire test again. An applicant failing only one section shall take the failed section again. Failure in any section of the re-test, including those sections that have been passed on a previous attempt, will require the applicant to take the entire test again.
- All sections of the skill test shall be completed within six months. For the purpose of IR (H) issue the Skill Test will remain valid for 12 months.
- Further training may be required following any failed test/check. Failure to achieve a pass in all sections of the test in two attempts shall require further training as determined by the Authority. There is no limit to the number of skill tests that may be attempted.

Note: the IR (H) will be restricted to Multi-Pilot helicopter if the initial Skill Test was completed with a co-pilot onboard. This restriction may be lifted by completing an IR Skill Test in a ME helicopter as a single-pilot.

DETAILS OF THE IR(H) SKILL TEST REQUIREMENTS ARE DETAILED IN APPENDICES 1 AND 2 TO JAR-FCL 2.210.

Guidance for applicants taking the IR(H) Skill Test can also be found in Standards Document 01(H) on the CAA web site at www.caa.co.uk.

E2.5 IR(H) RE-VALIDATION AND RENEWAL

Validity

An Instrument Rating (Helicopters) is valid for a period of 12 months

Re-Validation of an IR(H)

A Helicopter Instrument Rating if held, will normally be combined with the relevant type rating re-validation requirements by proficiency check.

Important Note

- Single Pilot Helicopter (SPH) and Multi-Pilot Helicopter (MPH) Instrument Rating (IR) privileges are separate and must be re-validated separately;
- Helicopter IR privileges are type specific - the IR re-validation is an integral part of the LPC;
- MPH IR privileges do not carry over to single pilot helicopters - the holder of both MPH and SPH ratings has to complete a separate SPH IR re-validation to maintain IR privileges on single pilot helicopters;
- Some helicopters are certified single pilot, but are required to be operated multi-pilot for public transport purposes. If a pilot completes a multi-pilot LPC (including Instrument Rating re-validation) in such a helicopter, then this does not confer SPH IR privileges.

Renewal

The requirements to renew an IR(H) are based on the period of time elapsed since the rating expired i.e. calculated from the date of expiry of the most recent IR(H) proficiency check entered in the licence. However, where IR privileges have been exercised in another category of aircraft (i.e. UK/JAR IR(A)) or under the privileges of an ICAO licence (aeroplanes or helicopters) or under a UK military IR qualification (fixed-wing or rotary), the renewal requirements will be based on the expiry date of that IR.

- To renew an IR(H) that has expired by less than 5 years, applicants must pass an IR(A) proficiency check with an authorised examiner.
- To renew an IR(H) that has expired by more than 5 years but less than 7 years, applicants must: **For single-pilot aircraft** pass an IR(H) proficiency check with a UK CAA Staff Flight Examiner. **For multi-pilot aircraft** pass a type rating skill test with or observed by a UK CAA Flight Operations Training Inspector.
- To renew an IR(H) that has expired by more than 7 years, applicants must: **For single-pilot aircraft** pass an IR(H) skill test with a UK CAA Staff Flight Examiner. **For multi-pilot aircraft** pass a type rating skill test with or observed by a UK CAA Flight Operations Training Inspector. Applicants will also be required to re-take the IR(H) theoretical knowledge examinations.

E3 THE UK INSTRUMENT METEOROLOGICAL CONDITIONS RATING

This section offers information as a basic guide to obtaining and maintaining a UK Instrument Meteorological Conditions (IMC) Rating as follows:-

E3.1 UK IMC RATING GENERAL INFORMATION

The IMC Rating is a national rating. The CAA will only add an IMC Rating to a UK issued pilot licence. When you are training for the issue of a UK Instrument Meteorological Conditions (IMC) you must follow a syllabus recognised by the Civil Aviation Authority. Training for the IMC rating is permitted outside the UK in a non-JAA state provided that the flying training is conducted by an organisation that is fully approved by the UK Civil Aviation Authority for such purposes. Instruction on the course may only be given by instructors with ratings unrestricted with regard to instrument flying restrictions.

Privileges

Details of rating privileges can be found in Schedule 8 of the Air Navigation Order (please also refer to Section A, Appendix F). The privileges of the IMC Rating may be exercised in UK territorial airspace. The IMC Rating may not be used in the airspace of any other Country unless permission to do so has been given by the appropriate authority of that Country.

E3.2 UK IMC FLYING TRAINING/ EXPERIENCE REQUIREMENTS

When applying for an IMC Rating you must produce logbook evidence of having met the following flying requirements:-

a. **25 hours** total experience as pilot of aeroplanes following PPL issue and which must include (b), (c), (d) & (e) below;

b. **10 hours** as Pilot in Command of aeroplanes to include (c) below.

c. **5 hours** as Pilot in Command of aeroplanes on cross-country flights.

d. **15 hours** as Pilot under Training in instrument flying with an instructor in a dual controlled aeroplane (during IMC course). Up to 2 hours in a device qualified BITD, FNPT 1, FNPT 2 or in other STDs recognised by the Authority.

e. **10 hours** total flight time by sole reference to instruments (during IMC course).

These minimum course requirements assume that the applicant has completed the 4 hours of dual instruction in instrument flying previously required for the issue of a UK PPL(A). An applicant who has not had these 4 hours training, must satisfy the training provider that he has reached an equivalent standard of ability before starting the course.

Where an applicant wishes to be tested for the IMC Rating on a single-pilot multi-engine aeroplane the flying training must ensure that in simulated instrument flight conditions you can maintain stable flight after an engine failure at climb power, then climb at the recommended speed and execute the normal range of flight manoeuvres under asymmetric power.

Requirement for a Flight Radio Telephony Operator's Licence

Applicants for the IMC Rating must hold a valid UK issued Flight Radiotelephony Operator's Licence. Details on how to obtain the FRTOL can be found in Section B.

E3.3 UK IMC RATING GROUND EXAMINATIONS

Unless exempted for the reasons stated below you are required to pass a written ground examination covering subjects drawn from the IMC Rating course syllabus and the PPL(A) syllabus including questions on the planning and execution of a typical flight under IFR outside controlled airspace. The syllabus may be found in **Appendix A**. The pass mark for the IMC ground examination is 72%.

E3.4 UK IMC RATING FLIGHT TEST

Unless exempted for reasons stated below, an applicant for the rating must complete the required training before taking a Flight Test conducted by an Examiner authorised by the CAA. The test includes full and limited panel instrument flying, use of radio navigation aids whilst flying by sole reference to instruments, instrument approach procedures, bad weather circuits and landings. In the case of a multi-engine aeroplane it includes flight with asymmetric power. Detailed contents of the test are in **Appendix B**.

Initial, revalidation and renewal Flight Tests may be completed in more than one flight but not more than three and must be completed in a period of 28 days. Failure in any part of the test will require the candidate to take the full test again. Where a candidate chooses not to continue with a test for reasons considered inadequate by the examiner, that test will be regarded as a failure with regard to the items not attempted. There is no limit on the number of cycles of attempts that can be made to pass the flight test.

Validities

The Flight Test and Ground Examination required for the inclusion of an IMC Rating in an aeroplane pilot licence must be completed (and application for rating submitted) within the time period shown below:

Ground Examination	**12 months**
Flight Test	**9 months**

The IMC Rating is valid for a period of 25 months from the date of the successful flight test.

Details of the requirements to renew a rating that has expired may be found in **Section E3.5**.

Exemptions and Credits

- An applicant who has held an ICAO or military green aeroplane Instrument Rating or a UK professional pilots licence aeroplanes at some time in the 10 years before the date of application for the IMC Rating will be exempt from the requirement to undergo a formal course of flight or ground training but will need to pass the ground examination and initial IMC Rating flight test. Applicants who have held a military amber or white aeroplane Instrument Rating will be required to complete discretional IMC training to cover the IMC syllabus, pass the initial IMC flight test and ground examination.

- An applicant who has held an ICAO or military green aeroplane Instrument Rating or a UK professional pilot licence aeroplanes or a valid Aircraft Owners and Pilots Association (AOPA) Ground Instructors Certificate at some time in the 5 years before the date of application for the IMC Rating will be exempt from taking the ground examination.

- An applicant who holds an ICAO IR or military green Instrument Rating (Aeroplanes) and have passed an IR test in the 24 months preceding the date of application for the IMC Rating will be exempt from taking the initial IMC Flight Test and written examination. Applicants will be required to apply for the issue of the IMC rating within this period, and the IMC granted will be based from the date the last IR test was passed.

- An applicant with a PPL(A) which includes a Night Rating (**not** Night Qualification) may be exempt from 3 hours of the flying instruction, including not more than 2 hours by sole reference to instruments*.

- An applicant who has qualified for the AOPA Radio Navigation Certificates may be exempt from up to 5 hours instrument training of the Applied Stage of the IMC course*.

- The holder of a valid ICAO or military IR(H) who wishes to add an IMC Rating to a pilot licence (aeroplanes) will be required to:

  a. have not less than 50 hours as a pilot of aeroplanes, including 15 hours as PIC;

  b. have received dual instruction in instrument flying in aeroplanes including not less than 5 hours flight time by sole reference to instruments gained in aeroplanes since the grant of a PPL(A);

  c. pass the initial IMC Rating Flight Test in aeroplanes.

Note: * The reduction in hours referred to here are not cumulative. The maximum reduction in flying training allowed is 5 hours.

- The holder of a Professional Pilot's Licence (Helicopters) will be exempt from taking the Ground Examination.

- An applicant who has achieved a full pass in the former UK National Professional Ground Exams will be exempt from taking the IMC Ground Exam.

- An applicant who has achieved a full pass in the JAR-FCL IR(A), JAR-FCL CPL(A) or JAR-FCL ATPL(A) theoretical knowledge exams will be exempt from taking the IMC Ground Exam.

UK National Professional Aeroplane Licence Holders

IMC Rating privileges are contained within UK CPL(A) and ATPL(A) licences therefore providing the licence remains valid there is no requirement for a separate IMC Certificate of Test.

JAR-FCL Professional Aeroplane Licence Holders

JAR-FCL CPL(A) and ATPL(A) licences **does not** have in-built IMC privileges. The holder of a JAR-FCL professional aeroplane licence **without** a valid IR(A) who wishes to obtain an IMC Rating must complete the following:

i. 5 hours of applied dual instrument instruction in accordance with the IMC Rating syllabus and;

ii. pass an initial IMC Rating Flight Test.

The holder of a UK issued JAR-FCL professional aeroplane licence with a valid single-pilot IR(A) does not require a separate IMC Rating endorsement as the privileges are included within the IR(A) privileges. If, however, you wish to obtain an IMC Rating you will need to apply to PLD for endorsement. The normal IMC rating issue fee will apply unless application is made in conjunction with an Instrument Rating (IR). In this case, the IMC Rating will be valid for a period of 25 months from the date of the IR(A) skill test and will not need to be revalidated if the IR(A) remains valid. If the IR(A) lapses an IMC revalidation flight test is required.

The holder of a JAR-FCL professional aeroplane licence with a valid multi-pilot IR(A) is not automatically entitled to fly using the privileges of an IMC Rating in single-pilot aeroplanes. They will be required to pass a IMC Flight Test and apply to PLD for a separate IMC Rating endorsement.

E3.5 IMC RATING (RE-VALIDATION AND RENEWAL)

The privileges of an IMC Rating may not be exercised unless your UK issued aeroplane pilot licence contains a valid IMC rating C of T. The period of validity of the C of T is 25 months from the date of the last satisfactory flight test (recorded in the National Ratings Certificate of Revalidation). Note however that holders of a UK national CPL(A) or ATPL(A) need only maintain a valid licence, medical certificate and aircraft rating.

Re-validation

The IMC Rating will be re-validated by revalidation Flight Test details of which can be found at Appendix B.

The candidate is also to show logbook evidence that, in the period between initial and/or re-validation flight tests, he has successfully completed a let-down and approach to DH/MDH, a go-around and a missed approach procedure, using an aid of a different type from that used during item (b) of the test. This shall be accomplished to the satisfaction of an instructor qualified to give instrument flying instruction. Alternatively, the candidate may carry out two approach procedures using different aids during the re-validation flight test.

Renewal

For a period not exceeding 5 years from the expiry date of the rating, the re-validation terms will apply to renew the IMC rating.

For a period exceeding 5 years from the expiry date of the rating, a candidate will be required to carry out dual instruction, at the CFI's discretion, covering the IMC rating Course with an IMC rating instructor, and pass the Initial IMC Rating Test with an IMC rating examiner in a suitably equipped aircraft. If the rating has expired by more than 10 years, then successful completion of the IMC Ground Examination will also be required.

Holders of a Non-JAA ICAO or Military Green IR(A)

An IMC rating may be revalidated/renewed for a further period by the CAA, on the basis of the most recent Non-JAA IR(A) flight test or military Green (IR(A) flight test. A fee is payable if the C of T is signed up by the CAA.

Section A Section B Section C Section D Section E IR, IMC, NIGHT Section F Section G Section H Section I Section J Section K Index

E4 THE NIGHT QUALIFICATION (AEROPLANE)

This section offers information as a basic guide to obtaining a JAR-FCL Night Qualification (Aeroplane) Rating as follows:-

E4.1 NIGHT QUALIFICATION (AEROPLANE) GENERAL INFORMATION

Training for the Night Qualification must be in accordance with JAR-FCL 1. Training may be undertaken in a non-JAA state provided that the organisation is fully approved in accordance with JAR-FCL 1 by the UK Civil Aviation Authority.

Training for the Night Qualification (Aeroplanes) may be completed during the training for a JAR-FCL PPL(A) providing the specific requirements of JAR-FCL 1.125(b) have been met (see Section C1.2).

Privileges

Details of rating privileges can be found in Schedule 8 of the Air Navigation Order (please also refer to Section A, Appendix F).

E4.2 NIGHT QUALIFICATION (AEROPLANE) FLYING TRAINING/EXPERIENCE REQUIREMENTS

When applying for a Night Qualification you must produce evidence of having met the following flying requirements:-

a. **5 hours** overall night training in aeroplanes to include b) and c),

b. i. **3 hours** dual night training to include ii);

   ii. **1 hour** dual night navigation;

c. **5** Take-off and full stop landings at night as PIC of aeroplanes.

Validity

The holder of a licence that does not include a valid instrument rating (aeroplane) shall not act as pilot-in-command of an aeroplane carrying passengers at night unless, during the previous 90 days, at least one take-off and landing has been completed at night.

E4.3 TRANSFERRING NIGHT RATINGS/ QUALIFICATIONS (AEROPLANE) FROM NON-JAR-FCL LICENCES

Any previous night flying training completed in an ICAO Contracting State may be credited towards the JAR-FCL Night Qualification (Aeroplane) flying training requirements.

Where an applicant holds a night rating/qualification (or a logbook entry if that is the method of endorsement required by the National Aviation Authority) issued by an ICAO Contracting State, they may apply for the Night Qualification (Aeroplane) endorsement onto their UK or JAR-FCL licence providing the requirements of E4.2 have been met. Logbook evidence of the night flying training completed will be required together with evidence of licence/logbook endorsement.

Where an applicant has completed night training towards a night rating/qualification in an ICAO Contracting State and has met the requirements of E4.2 but do not hold any licence/logbook endorsement from the National Aviation Authority, they will be required to complete discretional night training with a JAA Registered Facility or Approved FTO.

Where an applicant has only completed partial night flying training towards a night rating/qualification in an ICAO Contracting State but does not meet the requirements of E4.2, they will be required to complete sufficient training with a JAA Registered Facility or Approved FTO and meet the minimum requirements.

Qualified Service Pilots (QSP)

For the issue of a night qualification (aeroplanes), a QSP who is qualified on aeroplanes is required to submit logbook evidence that he meets the experience requirements as per the full night rating syllabus.

A QSP on helicopters is required to complete the full night qualification syllabus on aeroplanes - night flying in helicopters may not be counted towards the experience requirements.

E5 THE NIGHT QUALIFICATION (HELICOPTER)

This section offers information as a basic guide to obtaining a JAR-FCL Night Qualification (Helicopter) Rating as follows:-

E5.1 NIGHT QUALIFICATION (HELICOPTER) GENERAL INFORMATION

Training for the Night Qualification must be in accordance with JAR-FCL 2. Training may be undertaken in a non-JAA state provided that the organisation is fully approved in accordance with JAR-FCL 2 by the UK Civil Aviation Authority.

In order to fly as Pilot-in-Command (PIC) at night, with or without passengers, you must have a Night Qualification. For this purpose 'night' means the time between half-an-hour after sunset and half-an-hour before sunrise, sunset and sunrise being determined at surface level.

Privileges

Details of rating privileges can be found in Schedule 8 of the Air Navigation Order (please also refer to Section A, Appendix F).

E5.2 NIGHT QUALIFICATION (HELICOPTER) FLYING TRAINING/ EXPERIENCE REQUIREMENTS

Applicants applying for a Night Qualification you must produce evidence of having met the following flying requirements:

- **100 hours** of flight time as pilot of helicopters after the issue of the PPL(H), including:
  - **60 hours** as Pilot in Command of helicopters; and
  - **20 hours** cross-country flight.

The main features of the PPL(H) Night Qualification Course are:

- **5 hours** theoretical knowledge instruction;
- **10 hours** dual helicopter instrument instruction - this is in addition to any instrument instruction completed prior to the course. The holder of an IR(A) is credited 5 hours of this training;
- **5 hours** helicopter night training, including 3 hours dual instruction and 5 solo night circuits. Each circuit shall include a take-off and landing.
- The course must be completed within 6 months.

Validity

The holder of a licence that does not include a valid instrument rating (helicopter) shall not act as pilot-in-command of a helicopter carrying passengers at night unless, during the previous 90 days, at least three take-offs and landings have been carried out by night.

E5.3 TRANSFERRING NIGHT RATINGS/ QUALIFICATIONS (HELICOPTER) FROM NON-JAR-FCL LICENCES

Any previous night flying training completed in an ICAO Contracting State may be credited towards the JAR-FCL Night Qualification (Helicopter) flying training requirements.

Where an applicant holds a night rating/qualification (or a logbook entry if that is the method of endorsement required by the National Aviation Authority) issued by an ICAO Contracting State, they may apply for the Night Qualification (Helicopter) endorsement onto their UK or JAR-FCL licence providing the requirements of E5.2 have been met. Logbook evidence of the night flying training completed will be required together with evidence of licence/logbook endorsement.

Where an applicant has completed night training towards a night rating/qualification in an ICAO Contracting State and has met the requirements of E5.2 but do not hold any licence/logbook endorsement from the National Aviation Authority, they will be required to complete discretional night training with a JAA Registered Facility or Approved FTO.

Where an applicant has only completed partial night flying training towards a night rating/qualification in an ICAO Contracting State but does not meet the requirements of E5.2, they will be required to complete sufficient training with a JAA Registered Facility or Approved FTO and meet the minimum requirements.

Qualified Service Pilots (QSP)

For the issue of a night qualification (helicopters), a QSP who is qualified on helicopters is required to submit logbook evidence that he meets the experience requirements as per the full night qualification syllabus.

A QSP on aeroplanes is required to complete the full night qualification syllabus on helicopters - night flying in aeroplanes may not be counted towards the experience requirements.

APPENDICES TO SECTION E

APPENDIX A UK IMC RATING - GROUND EXAMINATION SYLLABUS

1 GROUND EXAMINATION SYLLABUS

This examination will be essentially practical and will cover the planning and execution of a typical flight under Instrument Flight Rules outside controlled airspace notified for the purposes of Schedule 8 to the ANO. It will include the use of Aeronautical Information Publications and, in particular, the extraction and interpretation of the Recommended Aerodrome Operating Minima applicable to IMC Rating holders. In preparing for the examination, the student's aptitude and previous experience must be taken into account when determining the amount of instructional time allotted to each particular item. It is likely that, under average conditions, a minimum of 20 hours study will be required.

1.1 **Physiological Factors**

The senses, spatial disorientation, sensory illusions.

1.2 **Flight Instruments**

Principles of operation, pre-flight and in-flight checks, errors and limitations, system failures associated with the pressure altimeter, airspeed indicator, direct reading magnetic compass, directional gyro indicator, turn and slip indicator, artificial horizon and vertical speed indicator.

1.3 **Aeronautical Information Service**

1.3.1 *Notams Class 1 and 2*

1.3.2 *UKAIP*

a. *Rules of the Air and Air Traffic Services*

Visual flight rules and instrument flight rules, flight plans and ATS messages, use of radar in air traffic services, radio failure procedures, special VFR, Class D airspace, control zones and terminal control areas, control areas, advisory airspace, radar advisory service, airspace restrictions and hazards, royal flights, holding and approach to land procedures.

The last item listed includes: recommended aerodrome operating minima for non-public transport flights, pilot-interpreted approach procedures, radar approach procedures, VDF procedures, missed approach procedures, and visual manoeuvring after an instrument approach.

b. *Communications*

Types of service, extracting data for radio aids from UKAIP.

c. *Aeronautical Charts*

General description of chart series available, symbols used, topographical charts, instrument approach and landing charts, system for chart amendment and revision.

1.3.3 AICs

Contents of current circulars of an operational nature.

1.4 **Flight Planning**

1.4.1 General

Objectives of flight planning, preparation of flight plan/log, choice of routes and levels, factors affecting aircraft and engine performance, selection of alternate aerodromes.

1.4.2 Meteorology

Contents of terms and symbols used in aviation forecasts, documents (including TAFS), in other forms of present service (including pre-recorded voice), and weather reports (including METARs), available to the private pilot and SIGMET messages, the route forecast, operational significance of information given (including icing, turbulence and visibility).

1.4.3 Altimetry

Definitions (transition altitude, transition level, flight level, standard pressure setting, QFE, QNH, regional pressure setting), setting procedures (pre-flight check, take-off and climb, en-route, approach and landing, missed approach).

1.4.4 Terrain Clearance

Minimum safe en-route altitude, aerodrome minimum sector altitudes and visual manoeuvring heights, obstacle clearance limits, decision height, minimum descent height.

1.4.5 Radio Aids

Selection and use of Radio aids including VDF, VOR, ADF, DME, ILS, marker receiver, transponder: Principles of operation, pre-flight checks, range and accuracy, identification (morse code).

1.4.6 Radar Approach Procedures

Accuracy and limitations of equipment, operational use.

1.5 **Privileges of IMC Rating**

A detailed knowledge of the privileges of the IMC Rating, its period of validity and revalidation procedure.

APPENDIX B

UK IMC RATING - FLYING TRAINING & FLIGHT TEST REQUIREMENTS

1 FLYING TRAINING

1.1 The flying training for the initial issue of the IMC Rating must include a minimum of 15 hours training in instrument flying of which up to 2 hours in a device qualified BITD, FNPT 1, FNPT 2 or in other STDs recognised by the Authority. The remaining training must be completed in a suitably equipped dual control aeroplane. The go-around procedure is to be carried out in an aeroplane. The course must cover the items detailed below.

1.2 Instruction on the course may only be given by instructors with ratings unrestricted with regard to instrument flying instruction.

1.3 When the applicant wishes to be trained and tested for an IMC Rating on a multi-engine aeroplane, the training must include sufficient instruction to enable the pilot to maintain stable flight following the failure of one engine at climbing power, to climb at the recommended speed, and to carry out normal flight manoeuvres during asymmetric flight in simulated instrument flight conditions.

1.4 A student's ability and experience may be taken into account in deciding how much time should be allotted to each of the following items but the course must cover all of them.

2 BASIC STAGE

2.1 **Full Panel**

a. *Instrument Attitude Flight*

Pitch indications, bank and direction indications, effect of power variations and aircraft configuration, instrument limitations, selective radial scan.

b. *Basic Flight Manoeuvres*

Straight and level in various configurations, climbing, descending, standard rate turns (level, climbing and descending, compass/ timed).

c. *Intermediate Flight Manoeuvres*

Turns at various rates, transfer to instruments after take-off (full panel only), recovery from unusual attitudes (incipient stall, steep bank, spiral dive).

2.2 **Limited Panel**

Simulated loss of gyroscopic pitch and bank indicator and gyroscopic direction indicator.

2.3 **Partial Panel**

Simulated loss of pitot/static pressure: recognition of loss of pitot/static pressure, maintenance of attitude and safe airspeed, straight and level and turning flight.

3 APPLIED STAGE

3.1 **Pre-Flight Planning**

Published procedures, operating minima applicable to IMC Rating holders.

3.2 **Departure and En Route**

Aircraft equipment checks, radio aid selection and identification appropriate to the planned departure, ATC liaison and compliance with RT procedures, use of lower airspace radar services, operation of radio aids for the establishment of planned track, track keeping by interception and maintenance of pre-selected bearings/radials to and from a facility, use of bearing information from off-track radio aids for position finding, en route holding procedures. The candidate to be trained in the use of at least 2 from VOR, VDF or ADF to carry out these procedures.

3.3 **Approach and Let-Down**

Use of approach charts, Decision Height/ Minimum Descent Height calculations using the recommended minima for the IMC Rated pilot given in the UK AIP forming a mental picture of the approach, initial homing, achieving the overhead/approach fix, holding procedures, achieving the horizontal and vertical patterns, calculation of rate of descent, go-around, missed approach procedure. Candidates are to be trained in at least 2 instrument approach procedures using VOR, ADF, ILS, radar or VDF of which at least one must be pilot interpreted. Completion of a recognised civil or military instrument approach procedure, during training, is to be certified in the flying log book.

3.4 **Bad Weather Circuits and Landings**

Low cloud with good visibility, low cloud with poor visibility.

4 FLIGHT TEST SYLLABUS

The Flight Test for the initial issue of the IMC Rating will take approximately 1.5 hours chock to chock time and a candidate must demonstrate satisfactory manual instrument flying capability in the following:

a. *Full Panel Instrument Flying*

Straight and level flight at given speeds, turns at a given rate, turns onto given headings, climbing and descending including turns, recovery from unusual attitudes.

b. *Limited Panel Instrument Flying*

assuming failure of the gyroscopic pitch and bank indicator and gyroscopic direction indicator): Straight and level flight, climbing and descending, turns onto given headings, recovery from unusual attitudes.

c. *Radio Navigation Aids*

Use of Radio Navigation Aids for position-finding using one or more aids (to include VOR or ADF), maintenance of a given track based on a pilot-interpreted aid for 10 minutes.

d. *Let-down and Approach Procedures*

Let-down and approach to Decision Height, Minimum Descent Height and missed approach procedure using a pilot-interpreted aid, carry out a recognised instrument approach procedure to Decision Height, Minimum Descent Height hence the appropriate go-around and missed approach procedure.

e. *Bad Weather Circuits*

Bad weather circuit and landing following item (d), position the aircraft in the circuit at the direction of the Examiner, to carry out a visual bad weather circuit and landing under specified simulated weather conditions.

f. *Flight with Asymmetric Power*

Control of the aeroplane and maintenance of a given heading and asymmetric climb speed, following the failure of one engine in the climbing configuration at normal climb power.

Identification of the failed engine and the completion of all essential drills and checks.

Climbing and level turns in asymmetric flight as directed by the Examiner.

Throughout item f) of the test, the Examiner will be responsible for navigation and ATC liaison. On resumption of normal flight the candidate will be told the position of the aeroplane. Feathering will be simulated by the Examiner on completion of the correct touch drills by the candidate.

5 TOLERANCES

To qualify for a pass, a candidate must demonstrate his ability to fly safely in smooth air to the limits specified in the following table (these limits should not be achieved at the expense of smoothness and good co-ordination (due allowance will be made for turbulent conditions).

TOLERANCES			
Flight Condition	Normal Flight	Limited Panel Flight	Asymmetric Power Flight (Full Panel)
Height in Level Flight	± 100 ft	± 200 ft	± 200 ft
Height for initiating missed Approach Procedure from Decision Height or Minimum Descent Height	0 ft +50 ft	N/A	N/A
Tracking (on Radio Aids)	± 5° (VOR) ± 10° (ADF)	N/A	N/A
Heading	± 10°	15°	± 10°
Speed	± 10 kt	± 20 kt	± 10 kt
	(but not below threshold speed)		
ILS Procedure - Final Approach	½ scale deflection on Localiser and Glidepath		

6 REVALIDATION FLIGHT TEST

6.1 The Flight Test required after initial qualification for the purpose of revalidating the Rating will comprise items (b), (d) and (e) of the initial Flight Test (see paragraph 4). The type of approach aid used must be entered in the log book. A revalidation Flight Test that is a first multi-engine test must include (f) at paragraph 4.

6.1.1 The candidate is also to show log book evidence that, in the period between initial and/or re-validation flight tests, he has successfully completed a let-down and approach to DH/MDH, a go-around and a missed approach procedure, using an aid of a different type from that used during item d) of the test. This shall be accomplished to the satisfaction of an instructor qualified to give instrument flying instruction. Alternatively the candidate may carry out two approach procedures using different aids during the re-validation flight test.

6.1.2 Item f) at paragraph 4 is required in multi-engine aeroplanes only. The Examiner will be responsible for navigation and ATC liaison. On resumption of normal flight, the candidate will be told the position of the aeroplane. Feathering will be simulated by the Examiner on completion of the correct touch drills by the candidate.

APPENDIX C CROSS CREDITING OF THE IR PART OF A TYPE OR CLASS RATING PROFICIENCY CHECK

Credits shall be granted only when the holder is revalidating IR privileges for single engine and single pilot multi engine aeroplanes as appropriate -

When a proficiency check including IR is performed, and the holder has a valid:	Credit is valid towards the IR part in a proficiency check for:	
(1)	(2)	
MP type rating	a. SE class * and b. SE type rating *, and c. SP ME class and type rating, only credits for Section 3b of Appendix 3 to JAR-FCL 1.240	(a)
SP ME type rating, operated as single pilot	a. SP ME class , and b. SE class and type rating	(b)
SP ME type rating, restricted to MP operation	a. SP ME class * , and b. SE class and type rating *	(c)
SP ME class rating, operated as single pilot	a. SE class and type rating, and b. SP ME type rating	(d)
SP ME class rating, restricted to MP operation	a. SE class and type rating * , and b. SP ME type rating *	(e)
SP SE class rating	SE class and type rating	(f)
SP SE type rating	SE class and type rating	(g)

*** Provided within the previous 12 months at least 3 IFR departures and approaches have been performed on a SP class or type of aeroplane in a single pilot operation**

SECTION F

TYPE AND CLASS RATINGS (AEROPLANES AND HELICOPTERS)

Each section details the requirements to obtaining and maintaining each additional type/class rating, including flying training, ground examinations and flight tests. Details of re-validation and renewal requirements to maintain each rating are also given. Unless otherwise stated, all requirements specified in this Section pertain to holders of UK or JAR-FCL Licences (not NPPL, PPL(A) SLMG or PPL(A) Microlight Licences).

For full details of JAR-FCL aircraft ratings you are advised to refer to JAR-FCL 1 or 2 Subpart F.

Section A
Section B
Section C
Section D
Section E
Section F TYPE CLASS RATINGS
Section G
Section H
Section I
Section J
Section K
Index

GENERAL INFORMATION

Training

Aeroplane Class Rating

An applicant for a class rating for aeroplanes shall comply with the requirements set out in JAR-FCL 1.260, 1.261(a), (b) and (c) and 1.262 (a), and if applicable 1.251.

High Performance Aeroplanes (HPA)

In accordance with JAR-FCL 1.251 an applicant for a first type or class rating for a single pilot aeroplane classed as high performance is required to undergo additional theoretical knowledge training as a pre-requisite to attending the type/class rating course.

Aim of Course

The aim of the theoretical knowledge course is to provide the applicant with sufficient knowledge of those aspects of the operation of aeroplanes capable of operating at high speeds and altitudes and the aircraft systems necessary for such operation.

Course Providers

Theoretical knowledge instruction for the HPA may be provided by a Flying Training Organisation (FTO) approved to conduct theoretical knowledge training for the ATPL(A). Type Rating Training Organisations (TRTO's) may also provide courses providing they have obtained specific approval. Course providers will be required to certify completion of the training and demonstration of knowledge by the applicant as a pre-requisite for training for an initial type or class rating for aeroplanes designated as high performance.

Course Syllabus and Examination

There is no minimum or maximum duration of the theoretical knowledge instruction but the syllabus, as set out in Appendix 1 to JAR-FCL 1.251, must be covered. On completion of the training a written examination set by the training provider must be passed. The written examination should consist of not less than 60 multi-choice questions, and the pass mark is 75%. A successful pass in the examination will result in the issuance of a certificate indicating that the course and examination have been completed and passed. The certificate will represent a "once only" qualification and will satisfy the requirement for the addition of all future HPA to the holder's licence. The certificate will be valid indefinitely and must be submitted to PLD with the application for the first HPA type/class rating.

Note: A pass in any of the theoretical knowledge subjects as part of the HPA course will not be credited against future theoretical knowledge requirements for the issue of a CPL(A), IR(A) or ATPL(A).

Pre-requisite to training for first HPA

An applicant for a first type/class rating for a single-pilot HPA shall have at least 200 hours total flying experience to include at least 70 hours Pilot-in-Command of aeroplanes and hold a certificate of satisfactory completion of a pre-entry approved course by a FTO or TRTO.

Exemption from HPA Course

In order to be exempt the requirement to attend a HPA course the applicant must meet one of the following requirements:-

a. Have passed the ATPL(A) theoretical knowledge examinations in accordance with JAR-FCL or UK ATPL(A) theory examinations;

or

b. Hold a valid ICAO ATPL(A) or CPL(A)/IR with theoretical knowledge credit for ATPL(A);

or

c. Have a valid HPA endorsed onto the licence held. (If an applicant wishes to add an additional type to his/her licence but has low experience on previous HPA types and has not passed the HPA course or ATPL(A) exams previously, the Authority recommends that the HPA course is completed;

or

d. When the holder of a licence, issued by a JAA Member State under National arrangements, which contains a single-pilot HPA class/type rating, converts to a JAR-FCL licence, the holder will be credited with the theoretical knowledge requirement.

For details of aircraft classified as HPA please refer to Section F, Appendix B.

Single-Pilot Aeroplane/Helicopter Type Training

An applicant for a type rating for a single-pilot type of aeroplane/helicopter shall comply with the requirements set out in JAR-FCL 1.255/2.255, 1.261(a), (b) and (c)/2.261, 1.262(a)/2.262 as appropriate. An applicant wishing to add the first High Performance Aeroplane (HPA) class rating (please refer to Section F, Appendix B) is required to undergo additional theoretical knowledge training as a pre-requisite to attending the type rating course (JAR-FCL 1.251 refers).

PA 46 Type Rating

At present the PA46 Malibu (Piston-Engine) and the PA46 Malibu Turbine rating are classified as a High Performance Aeroplane. However, it has been decided that an applicant for the PA46 type rating who trains on the piston engine variant will not be required to hold a certificate of proof of having undergone HPA training as a pre-requisite for adding the type to a UK issued licence. Whilst it will not be necessary to comply with the HPA theoretical knowledge requirement as detailed earlier, applicants will still be required to meet the 200 hours total flying experience pre-requisite. This policy only refers to the PA46 Malibu (Piston-Engine) variant, the PA46 Malibu Turbine requires the HPA theoretical knowledge requirement.

A pilot who has trained on the piston engine variant who then wishes to fly the turbine engine variant will only be required to complete differences training as per Appendix 1 to JAR-FCL 1.220. It will be for the instructor giving the differences training to ensure it is suited to the purpose.

Holders of a Private or Commercial Pilot Licence for whom the PA46 (piston-engine) rating is the first type rating for an aeroplane which according to JAR-FCL required HPA knowledge, are **not** entitled to the HPA knowledge credit for subsequent types requiring HPA knowledge unless the HPA knowledge training was actually completed as a pre-requisite for the endorsement of the PA46 type rating.

Multi-Pilot Aeroplane/Helicopter Type Rating

An applicant for a multi-pilot aeroplane/helicopter type rating shall comply with the requirements for type ratings set out in JAR-FCL 1.250/2.250, 1.261/2.261 and 1.262/2.262 as appropriate.

Knowledge of Aeroplane Performance

Applicants for additional type ratings to professional licences are required to have demonstrated knowledge of aeroplane performance appropriate to that type (please refer to Section F4 - Knowledge of Aeroplane Performance).

Piloting of Ex-military Aircraft (Aeroplanes and Helicopters

General - Ex-military aircraft on the UK register may be piloted by either private or professional licence holders. A pilot must hold a current civil licence with current civil class/type rating appropriate to the ex-military type being flown or, where no civil rating exists, and Exemption from the need to hold such a rating.

An ex-military aircraft with a Permit to Fly having a Maximum Total Weight Authorised (MTWA) in excess of 2730 kg must also be operated in accordance with CAP 632 - Operation of 'Permit to Fly' ex-military aircraft on the UK Register. This CAP requires the operator to compile an Organisational Control Manual (OCM) which among other things must contain information about pilot qualification on the type being flown.

The following general requirements are applicable to ex-military aircraft:

Single Engine Piston (SEP) Aeroplanes - All ex-military SEP aeroplanes can be flown on a current SEP Class Rating with appropriate differences training having been completed if necessary (for retractable undercarriage, variable pitch propellers etc.). The OCM will detail the minimum experience levels and training requirements for pilots converting to the type.

Multi-engine Piston (MEP), Single Pilot Aeroplanes All ex-military MEP, single pilot aeroplanes can be flown on a current MEP Class Rating with appropriate differences training having been completed if necessary (for retractable undercarriage variable pitch propellers etc.). The OCM will detail the minimum experience levels and training requirements for pilots converting to the type.

Multi-engine Piston (MEP), Multi-pilot Aeroplanes- To fly any multi-pilot aeroplane the pilots require to hold a type rating or, where no type rating exists, and Exemption from the need to hold a type rating. For details of obtaining an Exemption, please refer to Exemptions for Training/Full Exemptions paragraphs below.

Any Turbine Powered Aeroplane - To fly an ex-military turbine powered aeroplane a pilot must hold an Exemption from the need to hold a type rating. For details of obtaining an Exemption, please refer to Exemptions for Training/Full Exemptions paragraphs below.

Any Helicopter - To fly any ex-military helicopter a pilot requires a type rating or, where no type rating exists, an Exemption from the need to hold a type rating. For details of obtaining an Exemption, please refer to Exemptions for Training/Full Exemptions paragraphs below.

Licence Type Rating Exemptions

Exemptions for Training - Prior to the start of training pilots are to agree with CAA PLD (Policy) the training syllabus appropriate to their experience levels and the name(s) of the person(s) responsible for training;

normally the Chief Pilot of the aircraft operating organisation. PLD will issue an Exemption for training which will specify the period of the training and the name of the person(s) responsible for the conduct of the training.

Full Exemptions - After suitable training and testing and on the recommendation of the Chief Pilot of the organisation, an Exemption against the requirement to hold an appropriate aircraft type rating will be issued by PLD. This Exemption will be renewed annually on production of evidence that no fewer than five separate flights as pilot-in-command have been completed on the type itself or a similar agreed type in the immediately preceding 12 months. However on a case-by-case basis where a pilot is current and experienced on a number of similar types (e.g. a test pilot), this requirement may be relaxed with the approval of the CAA Flight Ops Inspectorate (General Aviation).

Queries about requirements to fly ex-military aircraft should be addressed to PLD.

Medical Requirements

You are strongly advised to ensure you meet the relevant Medical requirements before embarking on a course of training.

Rating Privileges

Full details of rating privileges, operational limitations, test arrangements and validities can be found in JAR-FCL 1 (aeroplanes), JAR-FCL 2 (helicopters) or Schedule 8 of the Air Navigation Order, (please refer to Section A, Appendix F). The rating privileges are re-validated by means of Certificate of Test, Certificate of Experience or Certificate of Re-validation as appropriate to the re-validation/renewal requirements of the rating, and signed by an authorised examiner. There is no JAR-FCL limit to the number of ratings that may be held at one time. JAR-OPS however, may restrict the number of ratings that can be exercised at any one time.

Upon issue of your pilot's licence you will be issued with a Certificate of Test (C of T) or a Certificate of Experience (C of E) or Certificate of Revalidation (C of R) to validate your licence and the Rating. The validity of the licence is determined by the validity of the ratings contained therein and the medical certificate. Without a current C of T, C of E or C of R your rating is not valid.

Validity Periods of Ratings

Under JAR-FCL, type and class ratings are valid for one year (2 years for single-pilot, single engine class ratings) from the date of issue, or the date of expiry if re-validated within the validity period. Therefore, a rating issued on, say, 15th August 2006 will remain valid until 14th August 2007. For AOC holders, this is at variance to the provisions of JAR-OPS, which in the above example would allow the rating to remain valid until 31st August 2007 (i.e. until the end of the calendar month in which the rating falls due). To resolve this anomaly, the CAA's Flight Operations Department has granted certain AOC operators exemptions that extend the validity of ratings to the end of the month, in line with JAR-OPS. Where a licence holder is affected by such an exemption, the date of the next re-validation will run from the end of the month in which the previous rating was due to expire. Ratings are revalidated/renewed exclusively, with no cross-over unless otherwise stated.

Re-validation

Re-validation is the administrative action taken **within the validity period of a rating** that allows the holder to continue to exercise the privileges of a rating for a further specified period (provided certain, specified requirements are met).

Renewal

Renewal is the administrative action taken after a rating has lapsed which renews the privileges of the rating for a further specified period (provided certain, specified requirements are met).

Forfeiture of an Existing Rating Validity Period

JAR-FCL outlines the rating revalidation criteria period prior to expiry of the existing rating (i.e. last 3 months for type ratings, 12 months for SEP (Land)). Individuals meeting the appropriate revalidation requirements will have their rating extended for a further period, the validity calculated from the date of expiry of the previous rating.

Where an individual has several ratings/authorisations within their licence this can often mean they have differing rating expiry dates. There are occasions where, for reasons of efficiency and cost effectiveness, pilots require ratings to run concurrently with other ratings/authorisations (e.g. Instructor, Examiner, IMC etc).

It has been agreed that where a licence holder wishes to revalidate early, thereby forfeiting the remaining validity period of their existing rating, this should be permitted. Any such revalidation would, of course run from the date of the new revalidation and not the original expiry date. Such permission would also assume that all other experience and test validities are in order.

Aircraft Ratings – JAR-FCL1 & 2		Validity
SE Piston (Land)	**(single pilot)**	24 Months
ME Piston (Land)	**(single pilot)**	12 Months
SE Piston (Sea)	**(single pilot)**	24 Months
ME Piston (Sea)	**(single pilot)**	12 Months
Touring Motor Gliders	**(single pilot)**	24 Months
SE Turbo prop (Land)	**(single pilot)**	24 Months
SE Turbo prop (Sea)	**(single pilot)**	24 Months
ME Turbo prop (Land)	**(single pilot)**	12 Months
SE single pilot type rating	**(single pilot)**	12 Months
ME Turbo prop (Sea)	**(single pilot)**	12 Months
ME Turbo-Jet (Land)	**(single pilot)**	12 Months
Multi-pilot type ratings	**(multi-pilot)**	12 Months
Helicopter Type ratings	**(single and multi-pilot)**	12 Months
Simple Single-engine Aeroplane		12 Months
Airships		13 Months

Aircraft Ratings – Not covered by JAR-FCL1 & 2	
Self Launching Motor Gliders (SLMG)	13 Months
Microlights	13 Months
Powered Parachutes	13 Months
Gyroplanes	13 Months
Balloons	13 Months

Endorsement of a Certificate of Test, Certificate of Experience or Certificate of Re-validation

When a rating has been revalidated/renewed, an entry will need to be endorsed within the Certificate of Test/ Experience or Revalidation page within the UK licence as detailed below:-

For UK national licence holders

For UK national ratings within a UK issued licence, a UK Authorised Examiner **only** can sign the certificate.

For JAR-FCL ratings within a UK national licence, a UK JAR Authorised Examiner **only** can sign the certificate.

JAR-FCL Licence holders

For JAR-FCL ratings within a UK JAR-FCL licence, any JAR Authorised Examiner (in the UK or another fully compliant JAA Member State) can sign the certificate.

An Examiner shall make no endorsement when a rating has expired by more than 5 years, the appropriate paperwork should be submitted to PLD for endorsement together with the current fee as per the Scheme of Charges.

Where a test is to be conducted by either a non-UK or non-JAR-FCL Examiner, prior to the test the Examiner will be required to seek permission from the UK CAA and obtain a "one-off" Authorisation to conduct the test.

Type/Class Rating Training conducted in Other JAA States

Training conducted in other JAA states for type/class ratings is acceptable to the CAA provided the relevant state has been accepted by JAA as having fully implemented JAR-FCL and is approved to issue JAR-FCL licences and ratings.

Applicants must ensure all the necessary information is presented to the CAA, with particular attention to the following:

a. Course Completion Certificate;

b. MCC certificate (if required);

c. Evidence of ATPL examination knowledge (if required);

d. proof that training organisation has JAR-FCL approval for the type required;

e. proof that the examiner who conducted the LST has JAR-FCL approval for the type required.

Skill Test

Before a skill test for the issue of a licence or rating is taken, the applicant shall have passed the associated theoretical knowledge examination and have completed all the required instruction. The type/class rating course, including theoretical knowledge, shall be completed within the 6 months preceding the skill test. Each applicable item in the appropriate skill test shall be satisfactorily completed within the six months immediately preceding the date of receipt of the application for the rating.

Carriage of Passengers

Pilots not operating in accordance with JAR-OPS 1 or 3 are required to meet recent experience criteria to carry passengers. A pilot shall not operate an aeroplane or helicopter carrying passengers as pilot-in-command or co-pilot unless that pilot has carried out at least three take-offs and three landings as pilot flying (sole manipulator of the controls) in an aeroplane or helicopter of the same type/class or flight simulator of the aeroplane type/class or helicopter type to be used in the preceding 90 days. If the flight is to be carried out in an aeroplane at night, one of these take-offs and landings must have been at night, unless a valid instrument rating is held. If the flight is to be carried out in a helicopter at night, 3 take-offs and landings must have been at night, unless a valid instrument rating (helicopters) is held.

A pilot who has not met the experience criteria above will be required to complete the above requirements either as Pilot-in-Command of aeroplanes/helicopters as appropriate or with a flight instructor, providing that the instructor does not influence the controls at any time. The carriage of a safety pilot is not permitted to satisfy this requirement.

Differences Training

Introduction

The purpose of these notes is to provide guidance to instructors and pilots of Single-Pilot Aeroplanes in the application of Differences and Familiarisation Training, in accordance with JAR-FCL 1.215, 1.220 and 1.235.

Requirements

In order to change to a different type or variant of aeroplane, within the same class rating, or another variant within the same type rating, Differences or Familiarisation Training is required. Differences Training must be done with an appropriately qualified Type or Class Rating Instructor or Flight Instructor.

Note: This material does not cover the additional training required for those pilots without theoretical knowledge credit at ATPL(A) level when converting to aeroplanes designated as High Performance Aeroplanes (HPA) in Appendix 1 to JAR-FCL 1.215 and Appendix 1 to JAR-FCL 1.220.

Definitions

Differences Training requires both theoretical knowledge instruction and training on an aeroplane or appropriate training device.

Familiarisation Training merely requires the acquisition of additional knowledge, relevant to the new type or variant. This may be achieved with the assistance of an instructor, another pilot experienced on type, or by self-study. Familiarisation Training is only sufficient where Differences Training is not required.

It should be noted that when changing to different types, or variants of types, that fall within the single-pilot single-engine piston (SEP) class rating, the Differences Training is specifically required to encompass particular 'complex' features with which the new type or variant may be equipped. These features are:-

- Variable Pitch (VP) Propellers
- Retractable Undercarriage
- Turbo/Super-charged Engines
- Cabin Pressurisation
- Tail-Wheel

For MEP Class aeroplanes, differences training with a FI or CRI is always required when converting to another type or variant within the class. However, some common sense must be applied; the amount of training will depend on the similarity of the new MEP type to those already being flown. The training must be sufficient to ensure that the pilot can operate the aeroplane systems and operate the aeroplane safely.

Differences Training in these features when first completed in such aeroplanes NEGATES the need for equivalent Differences Training to be completed again, in aeroplanes that fall within the SEP class rating.

Differences Training completed within the SEP class rating DOES NOT count towards the requirement for Differences Training within the MEP class rating or any single pilot type rating.

Syllabus

It is not possible to produce comprehensive guidance for every situation.The material at Section F Appendix E is intended as an aide-memoire for instructors who are fully conversant with the aeroplane to be flown. Pilots engaging in Familiarisation Training are recommended to refer to Section F Appendix E for guidance on areas for study. The Appendix should not be considered in isolation nor should it be considered as a comprehensive guide to the necessary training. It remains the instructor's responsibility to create a training programme, which is suitable for the particular pilot's experience and the aeroplane to be flown.

The primary reference for any Differences Training (or Familiarisation Training) should be the manufacturers' Aircraft Flight Manual (including UK and other supplements). Where there is no Flight Manual available for the type, the Pilots Operating Handbook or Pilots Notes, should be the primary reference. When considering what to include in the training, Instructors must consider, carefully, the experience of the student, and check in their logbook for any previous differences training which is claimed.

Differences & Familiarisation Training on SEP Aeroplanes for Holders of a MEP Class Rating or Single-Pilot Type Rating (Piston Types only)

Many pilots with a MEP class or type rating may only have had experience on SEP aeroplanes with Fixed pitch propellers. Where a Constant Speed Unit (CSU) is fitted to a 'single', some of the MEP training will be of value, but comparison should be made of the effect of the propeller, on performance and handling between types and variants within the SEP class.

The handling of a non-feathering VP propeller, on a SEP aeroplane, during an emergency, may also be quite different from the technique used in a single pilot ME aeroplane. For example, not all VP propellers in SEP aeroplanes have counterweights in the hub, so the failsafe propeller pitch may be either fine or course, and the effect on glide performance, may vary considerably from type to type.

Where Differences Training on a particular feature has been completed within the MEP class, these differences may be covered, for SEP aeroplanes, by Familiarisation. It is recommended, however, that some flying training be carried out on the SE type, to demonstrate these differences.

Validity

Differences Training in aeroplanes within the SEP class rating is valid indefinitely. If a type, or variant of a type, within the SEP class rating, has not been flown for some time, pilots must use their judgement to decide if refresher training is warranted. However, it is recommended that such re-training be undertaken when the lay-off is more than two years.

If a type or variant, within any other class or type rating, has not been flown within the preceding two years, further Differences Training, recorded again in the pilots logbook or a proficiency check, on that type or variant, is required.

Instructors must consider the contents of Section F Appendix E, as appropriate to type, in the light of the pilot's previous experience and current knowledge, when deciding how to conduct this recurrent training.

Experience on SEP aeroplanes does not satisfy the two year recency requirement for variants or types, within other class or type ratings.

Differences or Familiarisation Training alone does not, in itself, take the place of the proficiency check required for revalidation of the original rating. For full details please refer to Section F, Appendix E.

Administration

Satisfactory completion of Differences Training is to be recorded in the pilot's logbook, and countersigned by the instructor. This certification must include details of the features covered and the type or class within which the training was carried out.

Self-adhesive logbook labels, providing the format for this certification, are available from CAA, Personnel Licensing Department, Aviation House, Gatwick Airport South Area, Gatwick, West Sussex, RH6 OYR.

Differences Training in Single Pilot Piston-engined Aeroplanes with Single Power Lever Controls (SPLC Aeroplanes)

The advance of new technology has brought some significant changes to single pilot aircraft. Some piston engine aeroplanes are now fitted with a single lever, automated power control, that combines electronically all the functions of an engine and propeller - sometimes known as Full Authority Digital Engine Control (FADEC) - including control of turbochargers, superchargers and auto-feather systems where fitted. These new systems require additional knowledge and skill from the pilot. For the purposes of this publication, these aircraft will be referred to as aeroplanes with Single Power Lever Controls (SPLC aeroplanes).

There is a proposal with the JAA formally to identify SPLC aeroplanes as requiring differences training. Until this proposal is adopted in JAR-FCL 1, pilots are strongly advised to follow these recommendations.

Differences Training requires both theoretical knowledge instruction and training on an appropriate training device or the aeroplane. The instructors and training providers who may give the training are described below. Pilots converting **either to or from** a SPLC Aeroplane for the first time are strongly advised to complete Differences Training to the satisfaction of an appropriately qualified Class Rating Instructor or Flight Instructor.

Notwithstanding that these systems may be largely automatic, it remains important that the pilot understands how the systems work and how to use them correctly in all normal, abnormal and emergency operations.

Pilots trained in a SPLC Aeroplane **as their first type or variant within the licence or a Type/Class Rating** (single or multi-engine), should complete Differences Training when converting, for the first time, to an aeroplane in the same Type/Class rating that is equipped with independent, manual engine and/or propeller controls.

This includes conversion to aeroplanes with manually controlled variable pitch propellers and/or turbo/superchargers, notwithstanding that the pilot may have experience of these features within the systems of a SPLC aeroplane. Converting to independent manual control of these systems requires a full understanding by the pilot of how each system works and its operation. Detailed guidance on Differences Training in the operation of manually controlled variable pitch propellers and/or turbo/superchargers can be found in Section F, Appendix E.

Differences Training should be conducted by the holder of an appropriate instructor rating who meets the following requirements:

a. hold a valid Flight Instructor or Class Rating Instructor qualification (SPA) for the aircraft on which the training is to be carried out.

b. hold a valid Type/Class Rating applicable to the particular aircraft to be flown.

c. Have completed their own Differences Training to fly the particular aircraft on their own licence, including full familiarity with SPLC Aeroplanes or Manual Engine Controls, as applicable.

The range of differences between single-pilot aeroplane types or variants is such that specific requirements for training cannot be set. The primary reference for any Differences Training should be the Manufacturers' and/or Aircraft Flight Manual (including UK and other supplements). It is the responsibility of the instructor to ensure that such training includes all relevant aspects of the particular aircraft or feature, taking into account the experience and qualification of the pilot undergoing training.

Upon completion of Differences Training, and when the instructor is satisfied that an acceptable level of competency has been achieved, the pilot's logbook or equivalent document should be annotated to show successful completion and signed by the instructor who conducted the training (see **Administration** mentioned above).

Differences Training in Single Pilot Aircraft with Electronic ('Glass') Flight Instruments

Increasingly, single-pilot aircraft are being fitted with digital Electronic Flight Instrumentation Systems (EFIS) consisting of electronic 'glass instruments' and integrated digital avionics displays of widely varying complexity and capability. These systems present a significant change from conventional, mechanical flight instruments in the way the information is presented and the interpretation of these systems requires a thorough understanding by the pilot.

There is a proposal with the JAA formally to identify integrated electronic digital avionics displays as requiring Differences Training. Until this proposal is adopted in JAR-FCL 1 and 2, pilots are strongly advised to follow these recommendations.

Differences Training requires both theoretical knowledge and training on an appropriate training device or the aircraft. The instructors and training providers who may give the training are detailed below.

Pilots should obtain Differences Training before exercising the privileges of a Single Pilot Type or Class Rating in an aircraft equipped with an Integrated EFIS display. For the purpose of this publication, an Integrated EFIS display is an all glass, primary flight deck display that presents gyroscopic instruments, pressure instruments and navigation information in an integrated electronic display of the primary flight instruments.

Pilots converting to an Integrated EFIS display for the first time, should complete Differences Training to the satisfaction of a Flight Instructor or Class/Type Rating

Instructor, qualified as detailed below.

Alternatively, satisfactory training may be obtained from a training provider specialising in training on the particular equipment to be used. This training should be carried out with an appropriate Part Task Trainer or FNPT. Actual flying of the aircraft, should follow such training, **with an instructor or safety pilot**, until full familiarity with the equipment is achieved.

Pilots converting to any other Integrated EFIS display should obtain further Differences Training, whether or not the same manufacturer produces the new system. Familiarisation training should be sufficient for FIs or CRI/TRIs who are fully qualified to teach all applied instrument flying and who are already trained on another Integrated EFIS system.

Differences Training for an Integrated EFIS display, for holders of an Instrument or IMC Rating, should include all normal, abnormal and emergency operations in IMC and under IFR, including instrument approaches.

Pilots trained in using Integrated EFIS Displays but not trained on individual mechanical flight instruments, are likely to have established a scan pattern quite different from the techniques required by a conventional, mechanical instrument layout. These pilots are strongly advised to obtain Differences Training on conventional instruments, including selective radial scan techniques, before flying aircraft without an Integrated EFIS Display.

EFIS can provide very precise information, which requires little interpretation, as opposed to conventional instrument displays, which require considerable interpretation and different scan techniques. A key element in this type of training, on whatever system, is ensuring the pilot fully understands what information is available, what is being displayed and how to interpret the display correctly.

Airborne training in the use of Integrated EFIS demands considerable attention of both instructor and pilot, often at the expense of lookout and flight safety. It is recommended, therefore, that this training be carried out with an appropriate Part Task Trainer or FNPT. In any event maximum use should be made of any available video's, manufacturers' or agents' computer based training aids and programmes.

F1 SINGLE-ENGINE PISTON (LAND) CLASS RATING

This section offers information as a basic guide to obtaining and maintaining a JAR-FCL Single-Engine Piston (Land) Class Rating – SEP (Land). Individuals wishing to obtain the NPPL (SEP) licence or rating should contact AOPA, please refer to Section A Appendix E for contact details.

F1.1 INTRODUCTION

In order to fly as pilot-in-command (PIC) of an aeroplane in the SEP (Land) class you must have an SEP (Land) Rating endorsed on your licence.

The holder of a UK/JAR-FCL licence with valid SEP rating and appropriate JAR-FCL medical certificate may, subject to completion of appropriate differences training, exercise the privileges of the JAR-FCL licence on microlight aeroplanes and SLMG's in UK airspace only. For microlight privileges this training must be with a microlight instructor, for SLMG privileges this training must be with a Flight Instructor holding a TMG rating or Motor Glider Instructor Rating. However, any experience gained in microlight aeroplanes or SLMG's cannot be counted towards the flying experience requirements to maintain the SEP rating.

F1.2 REQUIREMENTS FOR THE ADDITION OF AN SEP (LAND) CLASS RATING

For rating issue you must:-

a. Provide evidence of having completed a course of training in accordance with JAR-FCL for the purposes of the rating.

b. Pass a class rating skill test (LST) conducted by a JAR authorised Class Rating Examiner (CRE) or Flight Examiner (FE).

c. Pass a theoretical knowledge exam (oral as part of the LST).

The class rating course, including theoretical knowledge shall be completed within the 6 months preceding the skill test. Each applicable item of the skill test shall be satisfactorily completed within the 6 months immediately preceding the date of receipt of the application for the rating.

JAR-FCL1.261/1.262 refers.

F1.3 CONVERTING FROM UK PPL(A) SLMG TO JAR-FCL PPL(A) WITH SEP (LAND) CLASS RATING

There is no direct conversion of a UK motor glider licence to the JAR-FCL PPL(A) with SEP (Land) Class rating. The holder of a UK PPL(A) SLMG has 2 options to a JAR PPL with SEP (Land) class rating:

Option 1: Obtain a JAR-FCL PPL(A) with TMG class rating in accordance with the criteria stated in F5.3 and then complete the requirements of F1.2 to add a SEP (land) class rating.

Option 2: Complete the 45 hour PPL(A) course at a JAR-FCL Registered Facility or Flight Training Organisation. A credit of up to 10 hours could be applicable in accordance with JAR-FCL 1.120, in respect of flight as pilot of *self-launching gliders.* No additional credit will be given in respect of flight time in SLMGs that meet the JAR-FCL definition of a TMG.

F1.4 RE-VALIDATION OF SINGLE-ENGINE PISTON – SEP (LAND) OR TMG CLASS RATINGS

Revalidation by Proficiency Check

A SEP (Land) and/or TMG rating may be revalidated by passing a **Proficiency Check** (LPC) with a JAR authorised Flight Examiner (FE(A)) or Class Rating Examiner (CRE(A)). If completed within the three months preceding the expiry date of the rating(s), no loss of rating validity will be incurred - the new rating expiry date will be calculated from the preceding rating expiry date, not from the date of the Proficiency Check,

or,

Revalidation by flying experience

A SEP (Land) and/or TMG class rating can be revalidated by flying experience by producing logbook evidence to an appropriately authorised JAR-FCL Examiner, before the rating expiry date has passed, of the following flying experience completed within the 12 months preceding the rating expiry date.

12 hours of flight time in SEP or TMG aircraft as appropriate to include;

i. **6 hours** as pilot-in-command;

ii. **12** take-offs and landings;

iii. a training flight of at least **1 hour's** duration with a FI(A) or CRI(A)* who must countersign the appropriate logbook entry (see full details below).

*The instructor must be authorised in accordance with JAR-FCL to instruct for the JAR-FCL TMG or SEP(Land) rating as appropriate. UK QSP only may undertake the instructional flight with a UK Military instructor. This training flight may be replaced by any other aeroplane proficiency check or skill test for an instrument, class or type rating (as defined by JAR-FCL) with a JAA qualified Examiner, or by a flight test for the issue/revalidation or renewal of a UK IMC rating.

- If revalidating by flying experience, and providing the examiner signs the Certificate of Revalidation page within the 3 months prior to the rating expiry, the validity of the revalidated rating will be calculated from the date of expiry of the preceding rating.

- If the licence contains both SEP (Land) and TMG ratings, revalidation requirements of both classes may be satisfied by completing the above requirements in EITHER a TMG or a SEP (Land) aeroplane (or a combination of both).

Important Note: **If intending to revalidate by flying experience, the Certificate of Revalidation must be signed before the expiry date of the previous rating has passed, otherwise the SEP/TMG rating renewal requirements of F1.5 will apply.**

The Training Flight

The FI should make the purpose of the training flight clear at the outset. His function is to ascertain the applicant's knowledge and skills, and interject if necessary to improve on these. If the primary purpose of the flight was for some other training then the FI must select suitable items of general handling to fulfil the purpose of the JAR-FCL requirement and brief how these will fit into the profile for the purpose of the applicant's revalidation request.

Where the aim is achieved the FI will sign the applicants logbook, append his/her licence number and identify the 'Training Flight' for the examiners purpose.

For revalidation of an IR(A) if held please refer to Section E1.5.

PA 46 (Piston-engine) Malibu Type Rating Re-Validation

The JAR-FCL Committee has agreed that the Proficiency Check required to re-validate the stand alone PA 46 type rating could also serve to re-validate a Single-Engine Piston (SEP) Class Rating. Also, as single-engine aeroplane Instrument Ratings (IR) are not class or type specific, an IR re-validated on any single engine aeroplane will be valid for use in a PA 46. By combining the IR re-validation with the PA 46 re-validation every year, a pilot could keep an IR, a PA 46 type rating and an SEP (Land) class rating valid, all on the basis of one combined flight test, providing that the examiner conducting the test was authorised for the purpose of both the PA 46 type rating and IR proficiency checks.

F1.5 RENEWAL OF SINGLE-ENGINE PISTON – SEP (LAND), TMG CLASS RATINGS

Where licence holders have been unable to renew a SEP (Land) or TMG Class Rating for a period **not exceeding 5 years** from the date of expiry, they will be required to complete the following requirements:

i. The CAA will require no mandatory additional training. Applicants should complete training at their own discretion sufficient to pass the Skill Test.

ii. Complete the Skill Test in accordance with Appendices 1 & 3 to JAR-FCL 1.240 with a JAR Authorised Examiner. For renewal of an instrument rating if held, please refer to Section E1.5.

iii. Pass an oral theoretical knowledge examination conducted by the Examiner as part of the skill test.

iv. A UK Authorised Examiner can sign the Certificate of Revalidation page (FCL150CJAR) within a UK national pilot's licence. An Examiner qualified in accordance with JAR-FCL (in any fully compliant JAA Member State) can sign a Certificate of Revalidation page within a JAR-FCL licence. The LST/LPC form, completed as a renewal, should be sent to CAA PLD.

v. The CAA will charge no fee provided that the Examiner signs the Certificate of Revalidation.

Where licence holders have been unable to renew a SEP (Land) or TMG Class Rating for a period **exceeding 5 years** from the date of expiry*, they will be required to complete the following requirements:

i. Complete the Skill Test in accordance with Appendices 1 & 3 to JAR-FCL 1.240 with a JAR Authorised Examiner.

ii. Pass an oral theoretical knowledge examination conducted by the Examiner as part of the Skill Test.

iii. The LST/LPC form, completed as a renewal, should be sent to CAA PLD for endorsement, together with the appropriate fee as per the Scheme of Charges.

iv. The Examiner should make no licence entry.

For renewal of an Instrument rating, if held, please refer to Section E1.5.

* Where an applicant can show that they are currently flying under the privileges of an ICAO licence, and are flying the same aircraft type/class within their UK or JAR-FCL licence, the renewal requirements will be based on the expiry date of the rating currently being exercised.

F2 SINGLE-ENGINE TURBOPROP (LAND) CLASS RATING

This section offers information as a basic guide to obtaining and maintaining a Single-Engine Turboprop Class Rating – SET (Land) as follows:-

F2.1 INTRODUCTION

To fly as pilot-in-command (PIC) of an aeroplane in the SET (Land) class you must have an appropriate SET (Land) Class Rating endorsed onto your licence.

F2.2 REQUIREMENTS FOR THE ADDITION OF AN SET (LAND) CLASS RATING

For rating issue you must:-

a. Provide evidence of having completed a course of training in accordance with JAR-FCL for the purposes of the rating.

b. Pass a Licensing Skills Test (LST) conducted by a JAR authorised Class Rating Examiner (CRE) or FE.

c. Pass a theoretical knowledge exam (oral as part of the LST).

JAR-FCL1.261/1.262 refers.

F2.3 REVALIDATION OF SINGLE-ENGINE TURBOPROP (LAND) CLASS RATING

To revalidate a SET (Land) Class Rating, applicants are required to complete the following requirements:

i. Complete a Proficiency Check with a JAR Authorised Examiner within the 3 months preceding the date of expiry, without loss of validity period. For revalidation of an instrument rating if held, please refer to Section E1.5.

ii. A UK Authorised Examiner can sign the Certificate of Revalidation page (FCL150CJAR) within a UK national pilot's licence. An Examiner qualified in accordance with JAR-FCL (in any fully compliant JAA Member State) can sign a Certificate of Revalidation page within a JAR-FCL licence. The LST/LPC form completed as a revalidation, should be sent to CAA PLD.

iii. The CAA will charge no fee provided that the Examiner signs the Certificate of Revalidation.

F2.4 RENEWAL OF SINGLE-ENGINE TURBOPROP (LAND) CLASS RATING

Where licence holders have been unable to renew a SET (Land) Class Rating for a period **not exceeding 5 years** from the date of expiry, they will be required to complete the following requirements:

i. The CAA will require no mandatory additional training. Applicants should complete training at their own discretion sufficient to pass the Skill Test.

ii. Complete the Skill Test in accordance with Appendices 1 & 3 to JAR-FCL 1.240 with a JAR Authorised Examiner. The renewal of a SE instrument rating, if held, should be combined with the Skill Test. For renewal of a SE instrument rating if held, please refer to Section E1.5.

iii. A UK Authorised Examiner can sign the Certificate of Revalidation page (FCL150CJAR) within a UK national pilot's licence. An Examiner qualified in accordance with JAR-FCL (in any fully compliant JAA Member State) can sign a Certificate of Revalidation page within a JAR-FCL licence. The LST/LPC form, completed as a renewal, should be sent to CAA PLD.

iv. The CAA will charge no fee provided that the Examiner signs the Certificate of Revalidation.

Where licence holders have been unable to renew a SET (Land) Class Rating for a period **exceeding 5 years** from the date of expiry*, they will be required to complete the following requirements:

i. Complete the Skill Test in accordance with Appendices 1 & 3 to JAR-FCL 1.240 with a JAR Authorised Examiner.

ii. Pass an oral theoretical knowledge examination conducted by the Examiner as part of the Skill Test.

iii. The LST/LPC form, completed as a renewal, should be sent to CAA PLD for endorsement, together with the appropriate fee as per the Scheme of Charges.

iv. The Examiner should make no licence entry.

For renewal of an Instrument Rating, if held, please refer to Section E1.5.

* Where an applicant can show that they are currently flying under the privileges of an ICAO licence, and are flying the same aircraft type/class within their UK or JAR-FCL licence, the renewal requirements will be based on the expiry date of the rating currently being exercised.

F3 MULTI-ENGINE PISTON (LAND) CLASS RATING (SINGLE-PILOT) AND MULTI-ENGINE CENTRE-LINE THRUST PRIVILEGES

This section offers information as a basic guide to obtaining and maintaining a Multi-Engine Piston Class Rating (Single-Pilot) and Multi-Engine Centre-Line Thrust Privileges as follows:-

F3.1 INTRODUCTION

To fly as pilot-in-command (PIC) of an aeroplane in the MEP (Land) Class Rating you must have a MEP (Land) Class Rating endorsed onto your licence.

F3.2 REQUIREMENTS FOR THE ADDITION OF AN MEP (LAND) CLASS RATING

An applicant for a class rating for a single-pilot MEP (Land) aeroplane rating must produce evidence of having completed a minimum of **70 hours as pilot-in-command of aeroplanes.**

Training Requirements

For rating issue you must:-

a. provide evidence of having completed a course of training at an approved FTO or Type Rating Training Organisation (TRTO), following a syllabus recognised by the JAA, including the following:-

   i. flying training consisting of not less than **2 hrs. 30 min.** dual instruction under normal conditions of multi-engine operation, and not less than **3 hrs. 30 min.** dual instruction in engine failure procedures and asymmetric flight techniques;

   ii. a course of instruction consisting of a minimum of **7 hours** theoretical knowledge instruction in multi-engine aeroplane operation;

b. pass a theoretical knowledge written examination as part of the approved course. The pass mark is 75%.

c. pass a Licensing Skills Test (LST) conducted by an authorised Class Rating Examiner (CRE) or Flight Examiner (FE);

JAR-FCL1.261/1.262 refers.

The class rating course, including theoretical knowledge shall be completed within the 6 months preceding the skill test. Each applicable item of the skill test shall be satisfactorily completed within the 6 months immediately preceding the date of receipt of the application for the rating.

Credit against training for QSPs

A UK QSP(A) who holds/has held a qualification to fly any of the recognised military multi-engine aeroplane types listed below, and has a minimum of 7 hours flying experience as 1st pilot will qualify for a reduced course of approved training to qualify for a JAR-FCL multi-engine piston (Land) class rating:

Andover	**BAC 1-11**
BAe 125	**BAe 146**
Bassett	**Beech 200**
C17	**Canberra**
Dominie	**Hercules (all variants)**
Islander	**Jetstream (all variants)**
Nimrod	**PA31**
Sentry	**Tristar**
VC10	

Eligible pilots will be required to attend a FTO and complete an approved course of training at the discretion of the Head of Training, pass the written theoretical knowledge examination and pass the licensing skill test (LST) on a MEP aeroplane.

Flying experience on other types (e.g. those flown on exchange tours and those no longer in UK military service) will be considered on a case-by-case basis.

F3.3 RE-VALIDATION OF MULTI-ENGINE PISTON (LAND) CLASS RATING

Revalidation of Multi-Engine Piston (Land) class ratings requires a proficiency check with a JAR Authorised Examiner within the 3 months preceding the expiry date of the rating*. In addition to this, there is also a minimum flying experience requirement of at least 10 route sectors within the validity of the rating. The experience requirement may be substituted by 1 route sector flown with an authorised examiner that may be undertaken as part of the proficiency check. A route sector is defined as a flight comprising take-off, cruise of not less than 15 minutes, arrival, approach and landing.

* Provided this check is flown within the 3 month period, the new rating 12 month validity period will run from the date the old one was due to expire. For revalidation of an instrument rating if held, please refer to Section E1.5.

A UK Authorised Examiner can sign the Certificate of Revalidation page (FCL150CJAR) within a UK national pilot's licence. An Examiner qualified in accordance with JAR-FCL (in any fully compliant JAA Member State) can sign a Certificate of Revalidation page within a JAR-FCL licence. The LST/LPC form, completed as a revalidation, should be sent to CAA PLD.

The CAA will charge no fee provided that the Examiner signs the Certificate of Revalidation.

F3.4 RENEWAL OF MULTI-ENGINE PISTON (LAND) CLASS RATING

Where licence holders have been unable to renew a MEP (Land) Class rating for a period **not exceeding 5 years** from the date of expiry, they will be required to complete the following requirements:

i. The CAA will require no mandatory additional training. Applicants should complete training at their own discretion sufficient to pass the proficiency check.

ii. Pass a proficiency check in accordance with Appendix 1 to JAR-FCL 1.240 with a JAR Authorised Examiner. For renewal of an instrument rating if held, please refer to Section E1.5.

iii. A UK Authorised Examiner can sign the Certificate of Revalidation page (FCL150CJAR) within a UK national pilot's licence. An Examiner qualified in accordance with JAR-FCL (in any fully compliant JAA Member State) can sign a Certificate of Revalidation page within a JAR licence. The LST/LPC form, completed as a renewal, should be sent to CAA PLD.

iv. The CAA will charge no fee provided that the Examiner signs the C of R.

Where licence holders have been unable to renew a MEP (Land) Class Rating for a period **exceeding 5 years** from the date of expiry*, they will be required to complete the following requirements:

i. Complete type technical training and obtain a pass in the ground examination in accordance with the TRTO/FTO approval.

ii. Complete flying/simulator training at the discretion of the Head of Training of the TRTO/FTO.

iii. Pass a proficiency check in accordance with Appendices 1 to JAR-FCL 1.240 with a JAR Authorised Examiner. The course completion certificate gives the TRTO/FTO the opportunity to indicate what refresher training has been completed.

iv. The completed form should be sent to CAA PLD for endorsement together with the appropriate fee as per the Scheme of Charges.

v. The Examiner should make no licence entry.

For renewal of an instrument rating, if held, please refer to Section E1. 5.

* Where an applicant can show that they are currently flying under the privileges of an ICAO licence, and are flying the same aircraft class within their UK or JAR-FCL licence, the renewal requirements will be based on the expiry date of the rating currently being exercised.

F3.5 EXTENSION OF LICENCE PRIVILEGES TO INCLUDE MULTI-ENGINE CENTRE-LINE THRUST AEROPLANES

Multi-engine centre-line thrust aeroplanes may be flown using the privileges of an existing valid MEP (Land) Class Rating. However, differences training must be carried out on the appropriate centre-line thrust type before exercising the privileges on such an aeroplane.

Holders of licences without a MEP (Land) Class Rating who wish to obtain centre-line thrust privileges may:-

a. Obtain a MEP (Land) Class Rating by meeting the requirements of F3.2, followed by differences training on a centre-line thrust aeroplane;

or

b. Complete 4 hours dual instruction on a Multi-Engine Centre-Line Thrust aeroplane. The course shall include a minimum of 1 hour of training in single engine operations.

The rating endorsement will be restricted to centre-line thrust aircraft only. Applicants then wishing to obtain the MEP (Land) Class Rating will be required to complete 3 hours 30 minutes dual instruction in asymmetric training, theoretical knowledge examination and Skill Test as detailed in Section F3.2.

F3.6 RE-VALIDATION/RENEWAL OF MULTI-ENGINE CENTRE-LINE THRUST PRIVILEGES

Privileges may be maintained by revalidation or renewal of the MEP class rating as per F3.3 and F3.4 respectively.

Alternatively, individuals who wish to revalidate or renew the rating on centre-line thrust aircraft should also meet the requirements as per F3.3 and F3.4 respectively, however it should be noted that the rating will be restricted to centre-line thrust aircraft only.

F4 MULTI-PILOT AEROPLANE TYPE RATING

This section offers information as a basic guide to obtaining and maintaining a Multi-Pilot Aeroplane (MPA) Type Rating as follows:-

A list of MPA type ratings can be found in Appendix 1 to JAR-FCL 1.220(b).

F4.1 INTRODUCTION

To fly as pilot-in-command (PIC) or co-pilot of a multi-pilot aeroplane you must have the appropriate type rating endorsed onto your licence. In order to add a type rating to the licence you are required to complete training at a Type Rating Training Organisation (TRTO) or Flight Training Organisation (FTO). An up-to-date list of JAR-FCL approved training providers can be found on the CAA-SRG web site – www.caa.co.uk.

Pre-requisite conditions for training

An applicant for the first type rating course for a MPA shall provide evidence that the following requirements have been met:-

a. have completed at least 100 hours as pilot-in-command of aeroplanes;

b. hold a **current and valid** multi-engine Instrument Rating (Aeroplanes). This is only a requirement for an initial MPA type rating and not subsequent type ratings. A UK QSP(A) who has held a Green Instrument Rating within the preceding 5 years is deemed to hold a 'valid' Instrument Rating.

c. hold a certificate of satisfactory completion of a multi-crew co-operation (MCC) course (this requirement is not applicable to those who have attended a TRTO course which includes MCC). For full details on the MCC Course and MCC credits can be found at **Section F10.**

d. have a valid pass in the professional flight crew examinations at ATPL level.

Knowledge of Aeroplane Performance

Applicants for additional type ratings to Professional Licences are required to have demonstrated knowledge of aeroplane performance appropriate to that type.

a. Licence holders who have passed the CPL level JAR-FCL performance examination are deemed to have demonstrated the appropriate knowledge for single and light twin-engine aeroplanes (approximating to Performance Groups C, D and E as per established aircraft certification practice).

b. Licence holders who have passed the ATPL level JAR-FCL performance examination are deemed to have demonstrated the appropriate knowledge for multi-engine turbine aircraft (approximating to Performance Groups A and C), in addition to those stated at (a).

c. A QSP(A) with a minimum of 2000 hours flying experience on military aircraft, including at least 1500 hours as Pilot-in-Command (maximum 500 hours PIC/US or Co-pilot P1) on recognised ME aeroplanes. **(Andover, BAC 1-11, BAe 125/146, C17, Canberra, Dominie, Hercules, Islander, Jetstream (all Mks), Nimrod, PA31, Sentry, TriStar or VC10)** is credited the JAR-FCL performance examination at ATPL level. Credit for experience on multi-pilot aeroplanes not included in the above list i.e. types that are no longer in UK military service, or types flown whilst on exchange duties with a foreign air arm, will be considered on a case-by-case basis.

d. Licence holders who have previously passed national examinations in **Performance Group A** will be deemed to have satisfied the appropriate aeroplane performance knowledge for the addition of any aeroplane type or class rating.

e. Licence holders not meeting the criteria at (c) and who are required to demonstrate knowledge of aeroplane performance for an additional type rating, are required to sit the JAR-FCL aeroplane performance paper at the level appropriate to the aeroplane type or class to be added to the licence. Applicants without a previous pass in the national Performance Group A examination who elect to take the JAR-FCL performance paper at CPL level will be required to pass the examination at ATPL level if they subsequently wish to add an aeroplane rating classed as Performance Group A or B.

F4.2 REQUIREMENTS FOR THE ADDITION OF A MPA TYPE RATING

For rating issue you must:-

a. Provide evidence of having completed a course of training at an authorised Type Rating Training Organisation (TRTO), following a syllabus recognised by the JAA, including the following:-

b. Pass a Licensing Skills Test (LST) conducted by an authorised JAR Type Rating Examiner (TRE);

c. Pass a theoretical knowledge written exam as part of the TRTO course.

JAR-FCL1.261/1.262 refers.

The type rating course, including theoretical knowledge shall be completed within the 6 months preceding the skill test. Each applicable item of the skill test shall be satisfactorily completed within the 6 months immediately preceding the date of receipt of the application for the rating.

Any application made to PLD outside of this 6 month period will require the applicant to complete further discretional flying/ground training at the TRTO. In addition, the applicant will be required to re-take and pass the theoretical knowledge examination, Licensing Skill Test and complete the required take-offs and landings as specified below.

Flight Training Minima

Aeroplane (with flight simulator):

With the exception of courses approved for Zero Flight Time Training, certain training exercises normally involving take-off and landing in various configurations will need to be completed in the aeroplane rather than an approved Flight Simulator.

Upon completion of simulator training and the simulator based Licence Skill Test (LST) at an approved TRTO, flying in the relevant aircraft is required. This must be accomplished before an application is submitted for rating endorsement to PLD, (in accordance with JAR-FCL 1, AMC1.261(c)(2) para 11).

The requirement is for **six** landings to be completed, including at least one full stop landing. In the case of an application for a multi-pilot aeroplane; an applicant who has logged more than 500 hours experience on multi-pilot aeroplanes of similar size and performance, this requirement may be reduced to a minimum of **four** landings in the aircraft. As such it is reasonable to assume that aircraft falling into the following groupings are considered similar:-

All turboprops with a MTOM of less than 10 tons and a passenger configuration of less than 19;

All turbojets/fans with a MTOM of less than 10 tons and a passenger configuration of less than 19;

All turboprops with a MTOM greater than 10 tons and a passenger configuration of 19 or more;

All turbojets/fans with a MTOM greater than 10 tons and a passenger configuration of 19 or more.

It should be noted that the commander of the aircraft should hold either a valid instructor rating for the type (CRI/TRI) or hold a valid examiner authorisation for the type (CRE/TRE). In specific cases where it is not possible to obtain the services of a suitably qualified aircraft commander or there is any doubt as to the acceptability of Instructor or Examiner qualifications (e.g. if they do not hold JAA licences), the trainee should make written application to the Authority requesting permission for the pilot to conduct the exercise and receive consent, prior to the flight taking place.

As mentioned previously, the LST has a 6 month validity from the date of test and the landings and rating application must be made to PLD within that time period.

Aeroplane (without flight simulator):

Where an aeroplane is used for training, the amount of flight time should be adequate for completion of the skills test; this must be a minimum of **8 hours** for turbo-jet and turbo-prop aeroplanes.
AMC FCL 1.261(c)(2) refers.

F4.3 RE-VALIDATION OF TYPE RATINGS (AEROPLANES)

Revalidation of type ratings requires a proficiency check within the 3 months preceding the expiry date of the rating*. In addition to this, there is also a minimum flying experience requirement of at least 10 route sectors within the validity of the rating. The experience requirement may be substituted by 1 route sector flown with an authorised examiner that may be undertaken as part of the proficiency check. A route sector is defined as a flight comprising take-off, cruise of not less than 15 minutes, arrival, approach and landing.

*Provided this check is flown within the 3 month period, the new rating 12 month validity period will run from the date the old one was <u>due</u> to expire. For revalidation of an instrument rating, please refer to Section E1.5.

A UK Authorised Examiner can sign the Certificate of Revalidation page (FCL150CJAR) within a UK national pilot's licence. An Examiner qualified in accordance with JAR-FCL (in any fully compliant JAA Member State) can sign a Certificate of Revalidation page within a JAR-FCL licence. The LST/LPC form, completed as a revalidation, should be sent to CAA PLD.

The CAA will charge no fee provided that the Examiner signs the Certificate of Revalidation.

Qualified Service Pilots

Qualified Service Pilots wishing to revalidate a civil rating on the basis of an annual military check should refer to Section F9.3.

F4.4 RENEWAL OF TYPE RATINGS (AEROPLANES)

Where licence holders have been unable to renew a MPA Type Rating for a period **not exceeding 5 years** from the date of expiry, they will be required to complete the following requirements:

i. The CAA will require no mandatory additional training. Applicants should complete training at their own discretion sufficient to pass the proficiency check.

ii. Complete a Proficiency Check in accordance with Appendix to JAR-FCL 1.240. For renewal of an instrument rating, please refer to Section E1.5.

iii. A UK Authorised Examiner can sign the Certificate of Revalidation page (FCL150CJAR) within a UK national pilot's licence. An Examiner qualified in accordance with JAR-FCL (in any fully compliant JAA Member State) can sign a Certificate of Revalidation page within a JAR licence. The LST/LPC form, completed as a renewal, should be sent to CAA PLD.

iv. The CAA will charge no fee provided that the Examiner signs the C of R.

Where licence holders have been unable to renew a MPA Type Rating for a period **exceeding 5 years** from the date of expiry*, they will be required to complete the following requirements:

i. Complete type technical training and obtain a pass the ground exam in accordance with the TRTO/FTO approval.

ii. Complete flying/simulator training at the discretion of the Head of Training of the TRTO/FTO.

iii. A minimum of 3 take-offs and landings must be completed in flight unless the training is ZFT approved.

iv. Complete the Proficiency Check in accordance with Appendices 1 & 2 or 3 to JAR-FCL 1.240 and 1.295. The course completion certificate gives the TRTO/FTO the opportunity to indicate what refresher training has been completed.

v. The completed form should be sent to CAA PLD together with the appropriate fee as per the Scheme of Charges.

vi. The Examiner should make no licence entry.

For renewal of an instrument rating, if held, please refer to Section E1.5.

* Where an applicant can show that they are currently flying under the privileges of an ICAO licence, and are flying the same aircraft type/class within their UK or JAR-FCL licence, the renewal requirements will be based on the expiry date of the rating currently being exercised.

Qualified Service Pilots

Qualified Service Pilots wishing to renew a civil rating on the basis of an annual military check should refer to Section F9.3.

F5 SELF LAUNCHING MOTOR GLIDER AND TOURING MOTOR GLIDER RATINGS

This section offers information as a basic guide to obtaining and maintaining the Self Launching Motor Glider (SLMG) and Touring Motor Glider (TMG) Ratings as follows:-

F5.1 INTRODUCTION

With effect from 30 July 2002 requirements for the endorsement of the former SLMG rating came under the auspices of NPLG Ltd. and is now known as the NPPL (SLMG) rating. Applicants wishing to obtain the NPPL (SLMG) should refer to Section C6.2 or contact the British Gliding Association (BGA), please refer to Section A Appendix E for contact details.

Further details can be found on the NPPL web site www.nppl.uk.com.

Alternatively, the holder of a UK JAR-FCL licence with SEP rating may, subject to differences training, exercise the privileges of their licence on SLMG's. However, any experience gained in SLMG's cannot be counted towards the flying experience necessary to maintain the full SEP privileges in the UK/JAR licence.

F5.2 RE-VALIDATION AND RENEWAL OF AN EXISTING SLMG RATING

Applicants wishing to revalidate or renew their NPPL (SLMG) rating or former SLMG rating should refer to Section C6.7 or contact the BGA for details of the requirements to maintain the rating.

F5.3 REQUIREMENTS FOR THE ENDORSEMENT OF A TMG RATING

As a licence issued under national regulations, no additional ratings may be endorsed on a UK PPL(A)SLMG. The holder of a UK PPL(A)SLMG who wishes to obtain a TMG class rating, must obtain a JAR-FCL PPL(A). Conversion to the JAR-FCL PPL(A) with TMG class rating is possible subject to the following criteria:

a. complete a minimum of 75 hours as pilot of aircraft that meet the JAR-FCL definition of TMG and hold a current Certificate of Test or Experience for such aircraft;

b. hold a JAR-FCL Class 2 medical certificate;

c. demonstrate to the satisfaction of the UK CAA that a knowledge of the relevant parts of JAA requirements has been acquired (may be satisfied by signing a declaration contained in application form);

d. appropriate licence issue fee.

Existing SEP class rating holders

The holder of a UK or JAA licence with SEP class rating (excluding NPPL) may add a TMG class rating by passing the JAR-FCL TMG class rating Licence Skill Test with a Flight Examiner (FE) authorised in accordance with JAR-FCL for the purposes of the TMG class rating.

However, a holder of a UK/JAR-FCL PPL(A) with SLMG rating and a valid Certificate of Test/ Experience for SLMG's and has flown 75 hours as pilot of aeroplanes (including motor gliders which meet the JAR definition of TMG) can apply for the TMG rating without passing the TMG LST.

Without a TMG class rating, the holder of a JAR-FCL SEP rating may not count hours flown under national SLMG privileges (even in an aircraft which meets the JAR definition of TMG) towards the re-validation of the SEP rating.

Please note: In UK airspace, the holder of a TMG rating may fly any UK registered motor glider, including those outside the definition of a TMG. In this case, there is no requirement to maintain a national SLMG rating. Likewise the national SLMG rating confers the privilege to fly any motor glider, including those which meet the JAR-FCL definition of a TMG. However, there are some motor gliders that do not meet the JAR-FCL definition of TMG, therefore if you intend to fly such aircraft outside UK airspace you should contact the appropriate National Aviation Authority to ascertain if this is acceptable or not. (For details of motor gliders defined as SLMGs and/or TMGs please refer to Section F, Appendix D).

F5.4 RE-VALIDATION OF A TMG RATING

A TMG Rating may be re-validated by meeting the requirements as stated earlier in **Section F1.4.**

F5.5 RENEWAL OF A TMG RATING

A TMG Rating may be renewed by meeting the requirements as stated earlier in **Section F1.5**

F6 MICROLIGHT AEROPLANE RATING

This section offers information as a basic guide to obtaining and maintaining the Microlight Aeroplane Rating as follows:-

F6.1 INTRODUCTION

With effect from 30 July 2002 requirements for the endorsement of the former microlight rating came under the auspices of BMAA and became known as NPPL (Microlight) rating. Applicants wishing to obtain the NPPL (Microlight) rating should contact the British Microlight Aircraft Association (BMAA), see Section A Appendix E for contact details.

Alternatively, the holder of a UK/JAR-FCL licence with SEP rating, may, subject to differences training, exercise the privileges of their licence on microlight aeroplanes. However, any experience gained in microlight aeroplanes cannot be counted towards the flying experience necessary to maintain the full SEP privileges of their UK/JAR licence.

Further details can be found on the NPPL web site www.nppl.uk.com.

F6.2 RE-VALIDATION/RENEWAL OF A MICROLIGHT RATING

Applicants wishing to revalidate or renew their NPPL (Microlight) rating or former Microlight rating should refer to Section C6.7 or contact the BMAA for details of the requirements to maintain the rating.

Section A
Section B
Section C
Section D
Section E
Section F TYPE, CLASS RATINGS
Section G
Section H
Section I
Section J
Section K
Index

F7 SEAPLANE RATING

This section offers information as a basic guide to obtaining and maintaining a Seaplane Rating as follows:-

F7.1 SEAPLANE RATING GENERAL INFORMATION

When a seaplane is to be flown solely from land aerodromes in the manner of a landplane, it may be flown under the privileges of an Aeroplane (Land) rating covering the appropriate class (or type). If, however, the seaplane is to be operated from water, an Aeroplane (Sea) class (or type) rating for the appropriate class (or type) is required.

At present there are very limited facilities within the JAA that would allow students to receive ab-initio training for the grant of a PPL (Seaplanes). Thus when you are training for a SEP (Sea) you are required to hold at least a UK or JAR-FCL PPL(A) with SEP (Land) privileges. You should also ensure that you hold a valid JAR Class 1 or 2 medical certificate as appropriate.

F7.2 TRAINING AND TESTING FOR A MICROLIGHT SEAPLANE RATING

At present the exact requirements for the addition of this rating are being formulated. Once the requirements have been determined an amendment to this document will be issued.

F7.3 TRAINING AND TESTING FOR A SINGLE-ENGINE PISTON (SEA) CLASS RATING

Flight Training

The SEP (Sea) Class Rating requirements currently call for a minimum of **5 hours** dual instruction in SEP (Sea) aircraft with a suitably qualified JAR FI or CRI covering all elements appropriate to the Class Rating Skill Test.

Ground Training

The applicant must have gained a pass in the **UK Seamanship** examination (at Private or Professional level* as appropriate to the privileges required) within the 12 months prior to rating application. A guide to the examination and the syllabus is given in **Appendix A.**

* The UK Seamanship Examination at Professional level is undertaken at a CAA Examination venue and bookings are made through the Personnel Licensing Department.

The applicant for the rating must have a valid pass in the relevant Theoretical Knowledge examination (an oral examination as part of the Skill Test).

Skill Test

Upon completion of the training mentioned previously the applicant will be required to pass the SEP (Sea) Class Rating Skill Test with a suitably authorised JAA examiner.

The aim of the skill test is for the applicant to demonstrate his/her knowledge of the procedures and ability to handle a seaplane on water, land (if conducted on an amphibian) and in flight.

An applicant for SEP (Sea) class rating skill test shall have satisfactorily completed all of the required flight and ground training on the same class/type of aeroplane to be used for the test.

The training flights in the applicants logbook shall be clearly identified and certified correct by the instructor who carried out the training.

A skill test consists of a group of up to two attempts. All sections must be passed in the two attempts and completed within the six months immediately preceding the date of application for the rating to PLD. The oral is not considered as a section for this assessment.

The applicant shall pass all sections of the skill test. If any item in a section is failed, that section is failed. Failure in more than one section will require the applicant to take the entire test again. Any applicant failing only one section (often referred to as a "partial pass") shall take the failed section again. Failure in any section of the re-test including those items that have been passed at a previous attempt will require the applicant to take the entire test again.

Following a partial pass the examiner may recommend additional training. Though not mandatory, applicants are strongly advised to follow the examiner's recommendation. After a Failed test the examiner may prescribe a minimum of 1 hour and a maximum of 3 hours retraining. Retraining prescribed after a Failed test is to be entered on the Form 252 (SRG\1159) and is mandatory. The applicant may elect to fly more than the recommended or mandatory training.

The result of the Skill Test is valid for a period of 12 months only and application for the rating shall be made within this time period.

The examiner should certify the applicants logbook on successful completion of the skill test.

Should an applicant choose to terminate a skill test for reasons considered inadequate by the examiner the applicant shall retake the entire skill test. If the test is terminated for reasons considered adequate by the examiner, only those items not completed shall be tested in a further flight.

The examiner may terminate the test at any stage if it is considered that the applicant's demonstration of flying skills requires a re-test.

FOR FULL DETAILS OF THE SKILL TEST, PLEASE REFER TO SECTION F, APPENDIX G.

F7.4 RE-VALIDATION OF A SINGLE-ENGINE PISTON (SEA) CLASS RATING

The privileges of a SEP (Sea) may be revalidated **within the current validity of a rating** by passing a proficiency check with an authorised Flight Examiner (FE(A)) or Class Rating Examiner (CRE(A)) within the three months preceding the expiry date of the rating without loss of validity period. Alternatively, they may be revalidated on flying experience by producing logbook evidence to an authorised examiner of having in the 12 calendar months preceding the expiry date of the rating completed **12 hours** of flight time in SEP (Land or Sea) including **6 hours** as pilot-in-command and at least **12 take-offs and alightings on water**.

Provided the examiner signs the Certificate of Revalidation page within the 3 months prior to the rating expiry, the revalidated rating will run from the date the existing rating would have expired. This experience must include a **single** flight of at least one hour with an instructor (authorised in accordance with JAR-FCL to instruct for the JAR-FCL SEP rating) for which the appropriate log book entry has been countersigned by the flight instructor. This instructional flight may be replaced by successfully undertaking any other skill test or proficiency check for a class or type rating.

If a SEP (Sea) and SEP (Land) rating are to be re-validated concurrently the above experience requirements must include 12 take-offs and landings on land and 12 take-offs and alightings on water. At least 1 hour of the pilot-in-command time must be completed on each class.

F7.5 RENEWAL OF A SINGLE-ENGINE PISTON (SEA) CLASS RATING

An SEP (Sea) Class Rating may be renewed by meeting the requirements as stated earlier in **Section F1.5**

F7.6 TRAINING AND TESTING FOR A SINGLE-PILOT MEP (SEA) CLASS RATING

Flight Training

The MEP (Sea) Class Rating requirements currently call for a minimum of **6 hours** dual instruction in an MEP (Sea) aeroplane with a JAA authorised Flying Training Organisation (FTO), covering all elements appropriate to the Class Rating Skill Test.

The above flying training must consist of not less than **2 hrs. 30 min.** dual instruction under normal conditions of MEP (Sea) aeroplane operation and not less than **3 hrs. 30 min.** dual instruction in engine failure procedures and asymmetric flight techniques;

In addition, the applicant must have completed a minimum of **70 hours** as Pilot-in-Command of aeroplanes (SE or ME).

Ground Training

The applicant must have gained a pass in the **UK Seamanship** examination (at Private or Professional level as appropriate to the privileges required) within the 12 months prior to rating application. A guide to the examination and the syllabus is given in **Appendix A.**

The applicant for the rating must have a valid pass in the relevant Theoretical knowledge examination (an oral examination as part of the Skill Test).

Skill Test

Upon completion of the training mentioned previously the applicant will be required to pass the MEP (Sea) Class Rating Skill Test with a suitably authorised JAA examiner.

F7.7 RE-VALIDATION OF A SINGLE-PILOT MEP (SEA) CLASS RATING

A Single-Pilot MEP (Sea) Class rating may be re-validated by meeting the requirements as stated earlier in **Section F3.3.**

F7.8 RENEWAL OF A SINGLE-PILOT MEP (SEA) CLASS RATING

A Single-Pilot MEP (Sea) Class Rating may be renewed by meeting the requirements as stated earlier in Section **F3.4**.

F7.9 CONVERTING A NON-UK SEAPLANE RATING

Many pilots wishing to obtain the rating travel abroad to complete the training and have a Seaplane Rating endorsed on a non-UK licence. When they return to the UK they will then attempt to "convert" this rating onto their CAA or JAR-FCL Pilot's Licence. Anyone wishing to gain a UK seaplane rating on the basis of a foreign endorsement is advised to check with Licensing Services to ensure that their flying is satisfactory. However, generally speaking the following requirements must be met:-

SEP (Sea)

1. Provide logbook evidence of having completed the minimum hour requirements as per **Section F7.3** for the SEP (Sea) Class Rating.

2. i. Provide logbook evidence of having successfully passed a flight test in appropriate seaplane with a JAR-FCL authorised examiner.

   or

   ii. Provide logbook evidence of having completed at least **12 hours** of flight time in SEP aeroplanes (Land or Sea) in the preceding 12 months, of which **6** are as pilot-in-command. This experience must include at least one hour with a flight instructor and one flight as pilot in command of an appropriate seaplane.

3. The experience at 2 ii) must include **12 take-offs and alightings on water as** pilot-in-command or in a dual capacity.

4. Pass the **UK Seamanship** examination.

Single Pilot MEP (Sea) Class Rating

1. Provide logbook evidence of having completed the minimum hour requirements as per **Section F7.6** for the Single Pilot MEP (Sea) Class Rating.

2. Provide logbook evidence of having completed at least **70 hours** as pilot-in-command of aeroplanes (Land or Sea).

3. Complete training as required by an authorised JAA Flying Training Organisation followed by the appropriate Class Rating Skills Test.

4. Pass the **UK Seamanship** examination.

F8 HELICOPTER TYPE RATINGS (SINGLE AND MULTI-PILOT)

This section offers information as a basic guide to obtaining and maintaining a Helicopter Type Rating (Single and Multi-Pilot) as follows:-

F8.1 INTRODUCTION

In order to add a specific type to the licence you are required to complete training at a Type Rating Training Organisation (TRTO) or Flight Training Organisation (FTO). An up-to-date list of JAR-FCL Approved Course providers can be found on the CAA web site – www.caa.co.uk

F8.2 REQUIREMENTS FOR THE ENDORSEMENT OF A SINGLE-PILOT HELICOPTER TYPE RATING

Pre-requisite Conditions for training

An applicant for a type rating for single-engine or multi-engine helicopters shall complete a course of flight instruction related to the type rating skill test (please refer to Section F, Appendix F).

An applicant for the issue of a first type rating for a multi-engine helicopter shall:

a. hold a certificate of satisfactory completion of a pre-entry approved course in accordance with Appendix 1 to JAR-FCL 2.255 to be conducted by a FTO or TRTO or have passed at least the CPL(H) theoretical knowledge examinations in accordance with JAR-FCL 2.470; and

b. have completed at least 70 hours as pilot-in-command of helicopters in accordance with Appendices 1 and 3 to JAR-FCL 2.240.

c. The possession of a certificate of satisfactory completion of the pre-entry approved courses in accordance with Appendix 1 to JAR-FCL 1.155 shall not be a substitute for showing compliance with JAR-FCL 2.160(b) for the grant of a CPL(H).

JAR-FCL 2.261/2.262 refers.

F8.3 REQUIREMENTS FOR THE ENDORSEMENT OF A MULTI-PILOT HELICOPTER TYPE RATING

Pre-requisite Conditions for training

An applicant for the first type rating for a MPH shall provide evidence that the following requirements have been met:-

a. Have completed at least 70 hours as pilot-in-command of helicopters except that an applicant for a multi-pilot type rating graduating from a CPL(H) integrated course who has less than 70 hours as pilot-in-command of helicopters shall have the type rating issued limited to co-pilot privileges only. To remove this limitation, an applicant shall:

   i. have completed 70 hours as pilot-in-command or PIC US of helicopters; and

   ii. have passed the multi-pilot skill test on the applicable helicopter type as pilot-in-command in accordance with JAR-FCL 2.262(b)

.b. hold a certificate of satisfactory completion of MCC (unless this is part of the TRTO course or the applicant is exempt as detailed in **Section F10**);

c. i. for a VFR type rating have completed the course and passed the examination in accordance with JAR-FCL 2.160 (a) and (b); or

   ii. for a type rating including IR(H) privileges hold a CPL(H) and IR(H) or meet the requirements of JAR-FCL 2.285 and hold an IR(H).

Training Requirements

For rating issue you must:-

a. Provide evidence of having completed a course of training at an authorised Type Rating Training Organisation (TRTO), following a syllabus recognised by the JAA (see Section F, Appendix F).

b. Pass a Licensing Skills Test (LST) conducted by an authorised Type Rating Examiner (TRE),

c. Pass a theoretical knowledge written exam as part of the TRTO course.

JAR-FCL 2.261/2.262 refers.

The type rating course, including theoretical knowledge shall be completed within the 6 months preceding the skill test. Each applicable item of the skill test shall be satisfactorily completed within the 6 months immediately preceding the date of receipt of the application for the rating.

Any application made to PLD outside of this 6 month period will require the applicant to complete further discretional flying/ground training at the TRTO. In addition, the applicant will be required to re-take and pass the theoretical knowledge examination, Licensing Skill Test and complete the required circuits and landings as specified below.

Flight Training Minima

Helicopter (with flight simulator)

With the exception of courses approved for zero flight time, the amount of flight time in a helicopter should be adequate for completion of the skills test.

A pilot with **less** than **300 hours** flight time on similar types, or less than **1000 hours** total flight time, must complete at least **6** full circuits each including full-stop landings.

A pilot with **more** than **300 hours** flight time on similar types, or more than **1000 hours** total flight time must complete at least **4** full circuits each including full-stop landings.

Helicopter (without flight simulator)

Whenever a helicopter is used for training the amount of flight time practical training should be adequate for the completion of the skill test. This should be at least **5** hours for single-pilot single engine, **8** hours for single-pilot multi-engine and **10** hours for multi-pilot helicopters.

The amount of flight training will depend on the complexity of the helicopter type involved and, to some extent, on the previous experience of the applicant. Holders of an IR(H) wishing to extend the **IR**(H) to a **further type** should have an additional **5** hours flight training on type according to **IFR**.

F8.4 RE-VALIDATION OF HELICOPTER TYPE RATINGS

Revalidation of a helicopter type rating requires a proficiency check in the relevant type of helicopter within the 3 months immediately preceding the expiry date of the rating, and at least 2 hours (including the proficiency check) as pilot of the relevant helicopter within the validity period of the rating.

For single-engine piston helicopters as listed below (Appendix 1 to JAR-FCL 2.245(b)(3) refers), an applicant shall complete at least the proficiency check in accordance with JAR-FCL 2.245(b)(1) on one of the applicable types held provided that the applicant has fulfilled at least 2 hours pilot-in-command flight time on the other type(s) during the validity period which that revalidation proficiency check shall carry across. The type ratings for this purpose are:-

Bell 47, Brantley B2, Hughes 269, Enstrom ENF28 and Hiller UH12

For single-engine turbine helicopters with a maximum gross weight of less than 3175 kg, the proficiency check in accordance with JAR-FCL 2.245(b)(1) is only required on one of the applicable types held, provided that the applicant has:-

i. completed at least 300 hours as pilot in command of helicopters; and

ii. completed 15 hours as pilot on each of the type(s) to which that revalidation proficiency check shall carry across, and

iii. completed at least 2 hours as pilot-in-command flight time on each of the other type(s) during the validity period to which that revalidation proficiency check shall carry across;

iv. performed consecutive revalidation on different types.

Qualified Service Pilots

Qualified Service Pilots wishing to revalidate a civil rating on the basis of an annual military check should refer to Section F9.3.

F8.5 RENEWAL OF HELICOPTER TYPE RATINGS

Where licence holders have been unable to renew a helicopter type rating for a period **not exceeding 5 years** from the date of expiry, they will be required to complete the following requirements:

i. Applicants that have no helicopter flight time i.e. the minimum of 2 hours as pilot of the relevant helicopter type during the previous 12 months, shall complete refresher training at the discretion of the Head of Training or CFI of an Approved FTO and for single pilot single-engine helicopters, may be completed at a Registered Facility to include at least 2 hours refresher flight training on type. The latter does not include the LPC.

ii. Complete a Licensing Proficiency Check (LPC) in accordance with Appendix 1 to JAR-FCL 2.240. The renewal of an Instrument Rating, if held should be combined with the LPC if the type is certified for IFR.

iii. A UK Authorised Examiner can sign the Certificate of Revalidation page (FCL150CJAR) within a UK national pilot's licence. An Examiner qualified in accordance with JAR-FCL (in any fully compliant JAA Member State) can sign a Certificate of Revalidation page within a JAR licence. The LST/LPC form, completed as a renewal, should be sent to CAA PLD.

iv. The CAA will charge no fee provided the Examiner signs the C of R.

Where licence holders have been unable to renew a helicopter type rating for a period **exceeding 5 years** from the date of expiry*, they will be required to complete the following requirements:

i. Type technical training and a pass in the ground examination in accordance with the TRTO/FTO approval.

ii. Complete at least 2 hours of flight training on type.

iii. Complete a Proficiency Check in accordance with Appendix 1 to JAR-FCL 2.240. The LST/LPC form gives the TRTO/FTO opportunity to indicate what refresher training has been completed.

iv. The completed form should be sent to CAA PLD together with the appropriate fee as per the Scheme of Charges.

v. The Examiner should make no licence entry. For renewal of an Instrument Rating, if held, please refer to Section E2.5.

* Where an applicant can show that they are currently flying under the privileges of an ICAO licence, and are flying a helicopter type within their UK or JAR-FCL licence, the renewal requirements will be based on the expiry date of the rating currently being exercised.

Qualified Service Pilots

Qualified Service Pilots wishing to renew a civil rating on the basis of an annual military check should refer to Section F9.3.

F9 TRANSFER OF TYPE/CLASS RATINGS (INCLUDING MILITARY)

This section offers information as a basic guide to transferring type/class ratings from a non-JAA State licence to a UK or JAR-FCL equivalent, and transferring UK Military type ratings.

F9.1 TRANSFER OF TYPE/CLASS RATINGS FROM A NON-JAA STATE LICENCE

Type Ratings

(Aeroplane/Helicopter)

A type rating endorsement on a licence issued by a non-JAA State may be transferred to a UK issued pilot's licence, subject to:-

i. 500 hours flying experience as pilot on type, operating as P1 or P2 appropriate to the rating required (PUT time may not be counted).

ii. Operational experience as pilot on type within the preceding 5 years.

iii. Pass a Proficiency Check on type with a JAA Authorised Examiner.

iv. Have met the requirements of JAR-FCL 1.250/2.250, 1.251 and 2.255 as applicable, including knowledge of aeroplane performance appropriate to that type (please refer to Section F4 - Knowledge of Aeroplane Performance).

Applicants who hold a type rating but do not meet the experience requirements above will be required to complete a course of training at an approved TRTO. The CAA may consider a reduction in the amount of training required to take account of previous experience on type, subject to a recommendation in writing by the Head of Training. Applicants will be required to pass the written theoretical knowledge examination and a Licensing Skill Test (LST).

Class Ratings

(Aeroplanes)

A class rating endorsed on a licence issued by a non-JAA State may be transferred to a UK issued pilot's licence, subject to:-

i. 100 hours flying experience on the class.

ii. Operational experience as pilot on the class within the preceding 5 years.

iii. Pass a Proficiency Check with a JAA Authorised Examiner.

iv. have flown at least 70 hours as pilot-in-command of aeroplanes. (ME aeroplanes only) in accordance with JAR-FCL 1.260.

v. In the case of a HPA meet the requirements of JAR-FCL 1.251.

Applicants wishing to gain a SE Class Rating who hold a valid non-JAA SE Class Rating but do not meet the requirements in items i) or ii) above will be required to undergo flying training and theoretical knowledge instruction given by a suitably qualified CRI or FI before passing the Skill Test.

Applicants wishing to gain a MEP Class Rating who hold a valid non-JAA MEP Class Rating but who do not meet the experience requirements in items i) or ii) above will be required to attend an approved FTO and complete training at the discretion of the Head of Training. Applicants will be required to pass a written theoretical knowledge examination and a Skill Test as well as meeting the experience requirement of item iv) and the requirements of item v) if applicable.

F9.2 TRANSFER OF CO-PILOT ONLY MULTI-PILOT TYPE RATINGS TO PILOT-IN-COMMAND RATINGS

It is UK policy that all new multi-pilot type ratings included in a UK issued licence will be unrestricted Pilot-in-Command ratings. This is based on the fact that all pilots are trained and tested in the role of Pilot-in-Command.

Therefore, applicants wishing to transfer their Co-Pilot rating to a UK issued licence will be required to meet the following requirements:-

Case 1: Transfer of co-pilot rating from non-JAR-FCL licence

The applicant must:

1. Produce evidence of having a valid co-pilot rating within non-JAR-FCL licence.

2. Meet the requirements of JAR-FCL 1.250/2.250.

3. Complete the type rating training at the discretion of the Head of Training at a JAA Approved TRTO.

4. Pass the course based theoretical knowledge examination.

5. Pass the skill test.

Case 2: Transfer of co-pilot rating from JAR-FCL licence (on Transfer of State of Licence Issue)

The applicant must:-

1. Produce evidence of a valid co-pilot rating within non-UK JAR-FCL licence.

2. Produce written evidence from National Aviation Authority to confirm that all training and testing for the **initial grant** of the rating including skill test and subsequent proficiency checks have been carried out in the role of pilot-in-command.

[If these conditions are not fulfilled, the applicant must meet the requirements set out in Case 1].

Alternatively, the applicant may wish to go back to the State of Licence issue to meet their requirements to remove the co-pilot restriction.

Case 3: Transfer of a co-pilot rating from UK National Licence to UK issue JAR-FCL licence

The applicant must:

1. Hold a valid co-pilot rating within their UK licence.

2. The co-pilot rating may be extended to pilot-in-command rating by passing a Licensing Skill Test on the aircraft type in the role as pilot-in-command.

F9.3 TRANSFER OF MILITARY TYPE/CLASS RATINGS AND SUBSEQUENT REVALIDATIONS/RENEWALS

A UK QSP can apply for a JAR-FCL type/class rating to be endorsed on an existing UK/JAR-FCL pilot's licence, on the basis of an equivalent military qualification. The only aircraft types in military service that are considered to have an equivalent JAR-FCL type/class rating are:-

Aeroplanes

BAC 1-11 (BAC 1-11)
BAe 125 (HS125)
BAe 146 (Avro RJ/BAe 146)
Beagle Bassett (multi-engine piston class)
Beech 200 (BE 90/99/100/200)
Hercules C1/C3 (Hercules)
Jetstream T1/T2 (Jetstream 200)
Islander (BN2T)
Jetstream T3 (Jetstream 31/32)
PA31 (Multi-engine Piston Class)
TriStar (L1011)

UK military type conversion training is not JAA approved. In order to transfer a military qualification for any of the above types, a UK QSP shall produce certified logbook evidence of the following:-

a. **500 hours** as pilot on type (**100 hours** as pilot for PA31 and Beagle Bassett)

b. Operational experience as pilot on type within the preceding 5 years.

c. A valid annual check (RAF - aircraft category renewal, RN - QFI check with NFSF(FW) on type within the 12 months preceding the date of application for the rating. A QSP who does not meet the experience requirement in a) will be required to attend a FTO and complete an approved course of training at the discretion of the Head of Training, pass the theoretical knowledge examination and the Licensing Skill Test (LST).

d. A QSP(A) who meets the requirement of a) but not c) on a type listed above may apply for a 'one-off' authorisation for a CFS Agent to conduct a LST on the type.

e. A QSP who is qualified on one of the types listed but does not meet the experience requirements of (a) above, will be required to attend an approved FTO/TRTO and complete training at the discretion of the Head of Training, pass a written theoretical knowledge examination and a Licensing Skill Test.

Revalidation/Renewal

A QSP who holds a civil type/class rating for any of the types listed above can revalidate or renew their civil rating on the basis of meeting the military annual check requirements of (c) above.

Helicopters

Agusta A109 A (A109/109K/109E)
Agusta A109 Power (A109/109K/109E)
Bell 212 (Bell 212/412)
Griffin (Bell 212/412)
Gazelle (SA341/342)
Puma (SA330)
Squirrel (AS350/350B3)
Twin Squirrel (A5355/355N)

UK military type conversion training is not JAA approved. In order to transfer a military qualification for any of the above types, a UK QSP shall produce certified logbook evidence of the following:-

a. **500 hours** as pilot on type

b. Operational experience as pilot on type within the preceding 5 years.

c. A valid annual check (AAC - Standards check, RN - QHI check with NFSF(RW), RAF - QHI check) on type within the 12 months preceding the date of application for the rating.

d. A QSP(H) who is qualified on one of the types listed but does not meet the experience requirements of (a) above, will be required to attend an approved FTO/TRTO and complete training at the discretion of the Head of Training, pass a written theoretical knowledge examination and a Licensing Skill Test.

Note for SeaKing Pilots

The SeaKing is not considered to be a direct equivalent of the civil S61 for licensing purposes. A SeaKing pilot wishing to obtain a civil S61 Type Rating will be required to complete an approved TRTO course for the type. However, the Head of Training may recommend in writing to PLD a reduction in the amount of training required on the course, to take account of previous experience on the SeaKing.

Revalidation/Renewal

A QSP who holds a civil type rating for any of the types listed above can revalidate or renew their civil rating on the basis of meeting the military annual check requirements of (c) above.

F10 MULTI-CREW CO-OPERATION COURSE

JAR-FCL requires aeroplane and helicopter pilots to complete an approved Multi-Crew Co-operation Course (MCC before adding the first multi-pilot aircraft (MPA) rating to a licence.

The MCC Course

JAR-FCL 1.261/2.261 states the following:-

The MCC course shall comprise of:

- A minimum of 25 hours of theoretical knowledge instruction and exercises.
- A minimum of 20 hours of MCC training.

Students attending an ATP integrated course may have the practical training reduced by 5 hours.

Wherever possible, the MCC training should be combined with the initial type rating training for a multi-pilot aeroplane/helicopter, in which case the practical MCC training may be reduced to not less than 10 hours if the same flight simulator is used for both the MCC and type rating training.

The MCC training must be completed within 6 months, under the supervision of either the Head of Training of an approved FTO, an approved TRTO or an approved training course conducted by an operator.

Claiming a MCC Credit

Applicants who have a minimum of not less than 500 hours experience as a pilot of a multi pilot aeroplane/ helicopter may be credited with the MCC requirement (see Eligibility for Credits). In accordance with JAR-FCL 1.250/2.250, completion of MCC or credit from this requirement is a pre-requisite for training for the first type rating for a multi-pilot type. Prior to commencement of such training, the TRTO will need to be satisfied that the trainee is eligible for MCC credit. Therefore, applicants who believe that they qualify for such a credit should apply to PLD for written confirmation of entitlement prior to undertaking the type rating training for their first multi-pilot type rating.

Multi-pilot helicopter experience is allowable in respect of a first multi-pilot aeroplane rating and vice versa.

Applicants who meet the following criteria shall ensure that they complete and submit Application Form SRG\1164, together with the appropriate fee as per the Scheme of Charges, and supply full documentary evidence as stated on the application, including actual flying logbooks in all cases. Failure to do so will result in a delay in the processing of the application. Upon satisfactory assessment, PLD will then provide written confirmation of credit entitlement to the applicant.

Eligibility for Credits

Holders of JAR-FCL or UK national licences who already have an MPA type rating endorsement will be credited with the MCC Course requirement. The following applicants will also be credited the MCC Course:-

Jet Orientation Courses

Graduates from the Jet Orientation Courses at BAe Prestwick (45 hours), the ATP Academy (40 hours or more) and Oxford Air Training School (40 or 60 hours) **are** considered to have met the MCC requirements. However, CRM and LOFT courses are **not** adequate for this purpose.

UK Qualified Service Pilots (QSPS)

QSPs who have completed an operational conversion unit course on a **multi-pilot** aeroplane type, and have not less than 600 hours operational experience as a pilot on such a type, will be credited the MCC course. For this purpose, the following types are deemed to be Multi-pilot aeroplanes.

Andover	**BAC 1-11**
BAe 125 (not Dominie)	**C17**
BAe 146	**Jetstream T3**
Hercules	**Sentry**
Nimrod	**VC10**
TriStar	

Experience on multi-pilot aeroplanes not included in the above list i.e. types that are no longer in UK military service, or types flown whilst on exchange duties with a foreign air arm, will be considered on a case-by-case basis.

We are aware that some military helicopter types are operated exclusively by 2 pilots in certain theatres of operation. Therefore, if an applicant can show evidence of 500 hours of genuine 2-pilot operation, an MCC credit will be allowed.

The evidence to be supplied must include logbooks detailing the 500 hours claimed, together with a letter from a commanding officer confirming the following:

- All the hours claimed were flown with 2 pilots, qualified on type, at the controls (and not with a navigator, air crewman, air loadmaster or observer in one of the pilots' seats).
- The hours claimed were in respect of true 2-pilot operation (and not flights on which one of the pilots was acting as an instructor or an examiner).
- A QSP who qualifies for an ATPL(A) through the CAA/MOD FW(ME) Accreditation arrangements does not need to apply for MCC credit.

Multi-Pilot Experience Gained With Foreign Military Forces

Multi-pilot experience (minimum 500 hours) gained by UK QSPs when on exchange duty with foreign military forces and non-UK QSPs may be considered for an MCC credit on an individual basis.

Other Multi-Pilot Experience

Requests for MCC credit will be considered from applicants who have logged 500 hours as pilot in multi-pilot public transport operations, even if that flying took place in single-pilot certified aircraft. Where an applicant has accrued such experience exercising the privileges of a non-UK licence, in addition to the actual logbook record of those hours, we will require documentary evidence from both the operator and the national aviation authority concerned confirming that the aircraft was required to be operated *exclusively* by 2 pilots qualified on type - even on non-revenue and positioning flights. The organisation(s) under whose Air Operator's Certificate the operations were carried out must be clearly identified. A copy of the non-UK ICAO licence and AOC will also be required.

Commercial Helicopter Pilots

MCC credit will also be allowed for applicants who have logged 500 hours as pilot in multi-pilot IFR public transport operations on S61, S76, AS332 or AS365 helicopters or on other helicopter types which are required to be operated *exclusively* by 2 pilots qualified on type - even for non-revenue and positioning purposes. Written confirmation by the operator is required.

Flight Engineers and Military FE

The holder of an ATPL(A) or CPL(A) or military Air Engineers with a minimum of 1500 hours of flight experience whilst operating as a Flight Engineer or RAF Air Engineer are not required to complete an MCC course before adding the first multi-pilot aircraft rating to his licence.

APPENDICES TO SECTION F

APPENDIX A GUIDE TO STUDYING FOR THE SEAMANSHIP EXAMINATION

Seamanship Ground Examination Syllabus:-

(The examination syllabus is common to Professional and Private Pilot ratings)

Symbols and abbreviations used in Admiralty charts and plans that are of importance to seaplane and amphibian pilots;

The regulations for preventing collisions at sea; lights and shapes to be carried by ships and aeroplanes; sound and light signals of distress (ships);

International Association of Lighthouse Authorities Maritime Buoyage System A;

Knowledge of tides and tidal definitions in general use.

Examination:

Professional: Approximately 30 multiple-choice questions without penalty marking

Time allowed:	1 hour
Pass Mark	75%
Venue:	Gatwick

Private: Approximately 20 multiple-choice questions without penalty marking

Time allowed:	40 minutes
Pass Mark	75%
Venue:	As arranged by examiner

References:

Chart 5011 (November 1991; Symbols and abbreviations used on Admiralty charts and plans.) (Available from Admiralty Agents)

International Association of Lighthouse Authorities (IALA)

Maritime Buoyage System ANP 735 (Edition 3 1982) (Available from Admiralty Agents)

Statutory Instrument 1996 No. 75 MERCHANT SHIPPING Safety "The Merchant Shipping" (Distress Signals and Prevention of Collisions) Regulations 1996"
(Available from HMSO)

Statutory Instrument 1990 No. 251 MERCHANT SHIPPING Safety "The Collision Regulations (Seaplanes) Order 1990"
(Available from HMSO)

ICAO Annex 2	"Rules of the Air", Chapter 3 Paragraph 3.2.6, Water Operations
ICAO Annex 6	Parts One and Two, "Operations of Aircraft" Chapter 6
Equipment	Appendix to Chapter 6, Lights to be displayed by Aircraft.

Other Publications:

International Regulations for Preventing Collisions at Sea
(Available from: Royal Yachting Association)

Reeds Nautical Almanac
(Thomas Reed Publications Ltd.)

The Macmillan and Silk Cut Nautical Almanac (Macmillan Press Ltd., Houndmills, Basingstoke, Hants, RG21 2XS)

APPENDIX B LIST OF CLASS/TYPE OF AEROPLANE

Class of Aeroplane

Explanation of Table

a. the symbol (D) in column 3 indicates that differences training is required when moving between variants or other types of aeroplane which are separated by the use of a line in column 2.

b. Although the licence endorsement (column 4) contains all aeroplanes listed in column 2, the required familiarisation or differences training has still to be completed (details of differences training can be found at the front of this section).

c. The specific variant on which the skill test for the class rating has been completed will be recorded according to JAR-FCL 1.080.

d. The symbol HPA (High Performance Aeroplane) in column 3 indicates that additional knowledge instruction is required for this type of aeroplane if the applicant for the type rating is not the holder of an ATPL(A) or has no theoretical knowledge credit at ATPL(A) level.

Aeroplanes not listed may be entered into a JAR-FCL licence, but the rating privileges are restricted to aeroplanes on the register of the 'State of licence issue'.

This list has been compiled from the JAA list of aeroplanes and is correct as at end October 2006. Please refer to the JAA web site at www.jaa.nl to ensure that the information is still current and has not changed since publication of this document.

1. Single/multi engine piston aeroplane (land/sea) - Single-pilot (SP) (A)

Manufacturer 1	Aeroplanes 2	3	Licence Endorsement 4
All manufacturers	Single-engine piston (land)	(D)	SEP (land)
	Single-engine piston (land) with Variable pitch propellers (VP)		
	Single-engine piston (land) with Retractable undercarriage (RU)		
	Single-engine piston (land) with Turbo/super charged engines (T)		
	Single-engine piston (land) with Cabin pressurisation (P)		
	Single-engine piston (land) with Tail Wheel (TW)		
	Single-engine piston (sea)	(D)	SEP (sea)
	Single-engine piston (sea) with Variable pitch propellers (VP)		
	Single-engine piston (sea) with Turbo/super charged engines (T)		
	Single-engine piston (sea) with Cabin pressurisation (P)		
All manufacturers	Multi -engine piston (land)	(D)	MEP (land)
	Multi-engine piston (sea)	(D)	MEP (sea)

2. Single-engine turboprop (land) - Single-pilot

Manufacturer 1	Aeroplanes 2	3	Licence Endorsement 4
Aerospatiale (Socata)	TBM 700	(HPA)	Aerospatiale SET
Aero Vodochody a.s.	Ae 270	(HPA)	Aero Vodochody SET
Snow/Rockwell/ Ayres	S2R turbo thrush		Snow/Ayres SET
Cessna	206 A/T Soloy 207 A/T Soloy	(D)	Cessna SET
	208		
De Havilland (Air Tech Canada) (Bombardier)	DHC-3 Turbo-Otter		DHC3
	DHC-2 Turbo-Beaver		DHC2
Gulfstream	Am.G-164D		Gulfstream SET
Pilatus	PC-6series PC6 B2H2	(D)	Pilatus SET
	PC-7		
Rhein Flugzeugbau	FT 600		Rhein Flugzeugbau SET

3. Single-engine piston touring motor gliders (land) - Single-pilot

Manufacturer 1	Aeroplanes 2	3	Licence Endorsement 4
All manufacturers	All Touring Motor Gliders having an integrally mounted, non-retractable engine and a non-retractable propeller		TMG

Type of aeroplane

This Appendix includes aeroplanes type certificated in JAA Member States and does not include:

i. aeroplanes not type certificated in accordance with FAR/JAR 23, FAR/JAR 23 Commuter Category, FAR/JAR 25, BCAR or AIR 2051;

ii. aeroplanes type certificated in a JAA Member State under special registration such as military, ex-military, experimental or vintage aeroplanes;

Aeroplanes not listed may be entered into a JAR-FCL licence, but the rating privileges are restricted to aeroplanes on the register of the State of rating issue.

Explanation of table refer to JAR-FCL 1.235(c).

a. the symbol (D) in column 3 indicates that differences training is required when moving between variants or other types of aeroplane which are separated by the use of a line in column 2;

b. although the licence endorsement (column 4) contains all aeroplanes listed in column 2, the required familiarisation or differences training has still to be completed;

c. the specific variant on which the skill test for the type rating has been completed will be recorded according to JAR-FCL 1.080.

d. the symbol HPA (High Performance Aeroplane) in column 3 indicates that additional knowledge instruction is required for this type of aeroplane if the applicant for the type rating is not the holder of an ATPL(A) or has no theoretical knowledge credit at ATPL(A) level.

e. SP* means Single Pilot certificated in some JAA Member States.

A. Single-pilot aeroplanes
1. Multi-engine turboprop aeroplane (land): single-pilot (SP) (A)

Manufacturer 1	Aeroplanes 2	3	Licence Endorsement 4
Asta GAF	Nomad - 22B - 24A		AstaMET
Beechcraft	90 series	(HPA) (D)	BE90/99/100/200
	99 series		
	100 series		
	200 series		
	300 series	(HPA) (D)	BE300/1900
	1900 series		

A. Single-pilot aeroplanes
1. Multi-engine turboprop aeroplane (land): single-pilot (SP) (A)

Manufacturer 1	Aeroplanes 2	3	Licence Endorsement 4
Cessna/Reims Aviation	F406 425	(HPA)	C406/425
	441	(HPA)	C441
De Havilland - Canada (Bombardier)	DHC6 series		DHC6
Dornier	DO 128-6		D128
	Do 228 series		D228
Embraer	Bandeirante EMB 110		EMB110
Grumman	Tracker S2FT		S2FT
Mitsubishi	MU 2B series	(HPA)	MU2B
Piaggio	P166		Piaggio 166
	P180	(HPA)	Piaggio 180
Pilatus Britten	BN2T Turbine Islander	(D)	BN2T
	BN2T-4R MSSA BN2T-4S Defender		
Piper	PA31 series Cheyenne I/II	(HPA) (D)	PA31/42
	PA42 series Cheyenne III		
Rockwell	AC 680 T AC 690 series AC 900 series	(HPA)	Rockwell MET
Short (Bombardier)	SC7Skyvan		SC7Skyvan
Swearingen/Fairchild	226 T 226 T (B)	(HPA) (D)	SA226/227
	226AT 226TC		
	227TT		
	227 AC 227 AT 227 BC		

2. Single engine - single-pilot

Manufacturer 1	Aeroplanes 2	3	Licence Endorsement 4
Pilatus	PC-7MkII PC-9P C-9 (M)	(HPA)	PC9/PC7MkII
	PC-12 series	(HPA)	PC12
Piper	PA-46 Malibu	(HPA) (D)	PA46
	PA-46 Malibu Turbine		
Walter Extra	Extra 400	(HPA)	Extra400

3. Multi-engine turbo-prop (sea) - single-pilot

Manufacturer 1	Aeroplanes 2	3	Licence Endorsement 4
Canadair (Bombardier)	CL215T		CL215T

4. Multi-engine turbo-jet (land) - single-pilot (SP)

Manufacturer 1	Aeroplanes 2	3	Licence Endorsement 4
Aerospatiale	MS 760 Paris	(HPA)	S760
Cessna	C501/500SP*	(HPA) (D)	C501/551
	C551/500SP*		
	C525	(HPA)	C525

B. Multi-Pilot Aeroplanes

Manufacturer 1	Aeroplanes 2	3	Licence Endorsement 4
	SN601 Corvette		SN601
Aerospatiale/Sud Aviation	SE210III IIIR VIN	(D)	SE210/10B3/11/12
	SE 10B3		
	SE 11		
	SE 12		
Aerospatiale/BAC	Concorde		Concorde

B. Multi-Pilot Aeroplanes

Manufacturer 1	Aeroplanes 2	3	Licence Endorsement 4
Aerospatiale/Nord Aviation	Nordatlas 2501		ND25
	C160 P Transall		ND16
	260A Nord 262 A-B-C Nord		ND26
Aero Spaceline	377 SGTF Super Guppy		Super Guppy
Airbus	A300-B1 -B2series -B4 series -C4-200 series -F4-200 series		A300
	A300-FFCC		A300FFCC
	A310-200 series -300 series A300-B4600 series -C4 600 series -F4 600 series		A310/300-600
	A318-100 series A319-100 series A320-100 series -200 series A321-100 series -200 series		A320
	A330-300 series -200 series		A330
	A340-200 series -300 series -500 series -600 series		A340
	A300-600ST/Beluga		A300-600ST
ATR	ATR 42 (not PEC* equipped)	(D)	ATR42/72
	ATR 42 (PEC* equipped) ATR 72 (not PEC* equipped) ATR 72 (PEC* equipped) *Propeller Electronic Control		
Mitsubishi/Beech/ Raytheon	Beechjet 400 series MU 300		Beech400/MU300

Manufacturer 1	Aeroplanes 2	3	Licence Endorsement 4
Boeing	B707 -100 series -300 series	(D)	B707/720
	B720		
	B717 series		B717
	B727 -100 series -200 series		B727
	B737-100 series -200 series		B737 100-200
	B737 -300 series -400 series -500 series	(D)	B737 300-900
	-600 series -700 series -800 series -900 series		
	B747 -100 series -200 series -300 series	(D)	B747 100-300
	B747-SP		
	B747 -400 series		B747 400
	B757 -200 series -300 series	(D)	B757/767
	B767 -200 series -300 series		
	B767 -400 ER *		
	B777 -200 series -300 series		B777
* The differences training course is valid from the B757/767 'classic' to the B767-400ER for crew members previously qualified on the B757/767 'classic variants. The 767-400ER to B757/767 'classic' differences training shall be evaluated or the full type rating training shall be accomplished.			
Bombardier	Global Express 1-A-10 1-A-11		BD700
British Aerospace/AVRO	ATP Jetstream 61		BAe/ATP/Jetstream 61
	AVRO RJ series 146-100 series -200 series -300 series		AVRO RJ/Bae146
British Aerospace/AVRO	BAC 1-11-200 series -400 series -500 series		BAC1-11
Hawker Siddeley/BAe/ Raytheon	HS125 series	(D)	HS125
	Bae 125-800 series -1000 series		
	HS 748 series		HS748
Hawker Siddeley/Bae	Jetstream 3100 series 3200 series		Jetstream31/32

Manufacturer 1	Aeroplanes 2	3	Licence Endorsement 4
Bae/Avro	Jetstream 41		Jetstream41
Canadair (Bombardier)	CL 30		CL 30
	CL 415		CL 415
	(Challenger series) CL 600 CL 601-1A CL 601-3A		CL600/601
	(Challenger) CL 604		CL604
	(Regional Jet series) CRJ -100 -200	(D)	CRJ 100
	-700 -900		
Casa	C212 series		C212
	CN-235		CN235
Cessna	C 500	(D)	C500/550/560
	C 550 CS 550		
	CS 550 Bravo		
	C 560 Encore		
	C 560XL		C560XL
	C650 Citation III Citation VI Citation VII		C650
	C680 Sovereign		C680
	C750 Citation X		C750
Consolidated Vultee Aircraft	CV 240-4	(D)	CV240/340/440
	CV 340 CV 440		
	CV 580		CV580

Manufacturer 1	Aeroplanes 2	3	Licence Endorsement 4
Dassault	Falcon 10	(D)	Falcon 10/100
	Falcon 100		
	Falcon 20 series	(D)	Falcon 20/200
	Falcon 200		
	Falcon 50	(D)	Falcon 50/900
	Falcon 900		
	Falcon 900 EX		
	Falcon 900 EX EASy		Falcon 900 EX EASy
	Falcon 2000 EX EASy		Falcon 2000 EX EASy
	Falcon 2000	(D)	Falcon 2000/2000 EX
	(2) Falcon 2000 EX		
(2) The differences training course is valid from the Falcon 2000 to the Falcon 2000EX for crew members previously qualified on the Falcon 2000. The Falcon 2000EX to the Falcon 2000 differences training shall be evaluated or the full type rating training shall be accomplished.			
De Havilland - Canada (Bombardier)	DHC7		DHC7
	DHC8 -100 series -200 series -300 series	(D)	DHC8
	DHC8 -400 series		
Dornier	DO328-100		DO328-100
	DO328-300		DO328-300
McDonnel-Douglas	Douglas A-26B		DCA26
	Douglas -3A-SIC3G		DC3
	DC4		DC4
	DC6 series		DC6
	DC7C		DC7
McDonnel-Douglas / Boeing	DC8-33 -50, 60, 70 series		DC8
	DC9 10-50 series		DC9 10-50
	DC9 80 series	(D)	DC980/MD88/MD90
	MD88 series MD90 series		
	DC10 series		DC10
	MD11		MD11

Manufacturer 1	Aeroplanes 2	3	Licence Endorsement 4
Embraer	EMB 120 Brasilia		EMB120
	EMB 145 - 135 145 series		EMB 135/145
	ERJ 170 -100 ERJ 170 -200 ERJ 190 -100		EMB 170
Fokker/Fairchild	FH227 F27A/F/J F27 series		F27
	F28 series		F28
	F50		F50
	F70 F100		F70/100
Grumman Gulfstream	Grumman G-159		Gulfstream I
	Grumman G-1159	(D)	Gulfstream II/III
	Grumman G-1159A		
	Gulfstream 1159C Gulfstream IV (G300/G400)		Gulfstream IV
	Gulfstream V	(D)	G-V
	G V-SP (G500/G550)		
	GIV-X (G350/G450)		
Handley Page	Herald series		Herald
Israel Aircraft Industry	IAI -1121 Jetcommander -1123 Commodore Jet -1124 Westwind		IAI1121/23/24
	IAI - 1125 Astra		IAI1125
Junkers	Junkers 52		JU52
Lockheed	L188 Electra series A	(D)	L188 Electra
	L188 Electra series C		
	L382 G (C 130)		Hercules
	L1011 series		L1011
	L1329		Jetstar

Manufacturer 1	Aeroplanes 2	3	Licence Endorsement 4
Learjet (Bombardier)	Learjet-20 series - 30 series	(D)	Learjet20/30
	Learjet-45 series		Learjet45
	Learjet-55 series		Learjet55
	Learjet-60 series		Learjet60
Leteckee	L410 UVP		LetL410
MBB	HFB 320		HFB320
	VFW 614		VFW-614
PT Industry	IPTN CN 235-110		IPTNCN235
Rockwell International	NA-265 series		NA265
Saab	SAAB SF340 series		SAAB340
	SAAB 2000		SAAB2000
Short Brothers (Bombardier)	SD3-30 -60	(D)	SD3-30/60
	SC5 Belfast		Belfast
Vickers-Armstrong	Vanguard		Vanguard
	Viscount		Viscount

APPENDIX C LIST OF TYPE OF HELICOPTER

This Appendix includes helicopters type certificated in JAA Member States and does not include:

i. helicopters not type certificated in accordance with FAR/JAR-27, FAR/JAR-27 or BCAR;

ii. helicopters type certificated in a JAA Member State under special registration such as military, ex-military, experimental or vintage helicopters.

Helicopters not listed may be entered into a JAR-FCL licence, but the rating privileges are restricted to helicopters on the register of the State of rating issue.

Explanation of Table

a. if a dividing line exists in column 2, this indicates a variant;

b. the symbol (D) between variants of types of helicopter used in column 3 indicates that differences training is required;

c. although the licence endorsement (column 4) contains all helicopters listed in column 2, the required familiarisation or differences training has still to be completed (details of differences training can be found at the front of this section);

d. the specific variant on which the skill test for the type rating has been completed will be recorded according to JAR-FCL 2.080.

Manufacturer 1	Helicopter 2	3	Licence Endorsement 4
Agusta			
- SE Turbine -	A 119 Koala		A119
- ME Turbine -	A 109A A 109A II A 109C	(D)	A109/109K/109E
	A 109K		
	A 109E		
Agusta-Bell			
- SE Piston -	Agusta Bell 47G-2 Agusta Bell 47G-2A-1 Agusta Bell 47G-3B-1 Agusta Bell 47G-4 Agusta Bell 47G-4A Agusta Bell 47J Agusta Bell 47J-2 Agusta Bell 47J-3		Bell 47
- SE Turbine -	Agusta Bell 206A Agusta Bell 206B	(D)	Bell206/206L
	Agusta Bell 206L		
	Agusta Bell 204	(D)	Bell204/205/UH-1D
	Agusta Bell 205		
- ME Turbine -	Agusta Bell 212		Bell212/412
	Agusta Bell 412		
	Agusta Bell 412 SP		
Agusta Sikorsky			

Manufacturer 1	Helicopter 2	3	Licence Endorsement 4
- ME Turbine -	Agusta S-61N1		SK-61
Bell Helicopters			
- SE Piston -	Bell 47D Bell 47G Bell 47G-1 Bell 47G-2 Bell 47G-3 B-1 Bell 47G-4 Bell 47G-4A Bell 47G-5 Bell 47H-1 Bell 47J Bell 47J-2 Bell 47J-2A		Bell 47
- SE Turbine -	Bell 47T		Bell47T
	Bell 47TA		
	Bell 204		Bell204/205/UH-1D
	UH-1D		
	Bell 206 A Bell 206 B Bell 206 B 2 Bell 206 B 3	(D)	Bell206/206L
	Bell 206 L		
	Bell 206 L-1		
	Bell 206 L-3		
	Bell 206 L-4		
	Bell 214 B Bell 214 B 1		Bell214
	Bell 407		Bell407

Manufacturer 1	Helicopter 2	3	Licence Endorsement 4
- ME Turbine -	Bell 206 LT Twinranger		Bell206LT
	Bell 212	(D)	Bell212/412
	Bell 412 Bell 412 SP Bell 412 HP Bell 412 EP		
	Bell 214 ST		Bell214ST
	Bell 222 Bell 222 A Bell 222 B Bell 222 UT Bell 222 SP	(D)	Bell222/230/430
	Bell 230		
	Bell 430		
	Bell 427		Bell427
Boeing-Vertol			
- ME Turbine -	Boeing 234LR		BV234
Bristol Aircraft			
- SE Piston -	B-171-B		Bristol 171B
Brantley			
- SE Piston -	B-2 B-2 B		Brantley B2
Breda Nardi			
- SE Piston -	Breda Nardi 269		HU269
- SE Turbine -	Breda Nardi 369		HU369
EH Industries			
- ME Turbine -	EH101		EH101
Enstrom			
- SE Piston -	F28 A-D F28 C 2 F28 F F280C F280F F280FX F280D		ENF28
- SE Turbine -	F480		ENF480

Manufacturer 1	Helicopter 2	3	Licence Endorsement 4
Eurocopter			
- SE Turbine -	AS350B AS350B 1 AS350B 2 AS350D AS350B A AS350B B	(D)	AS350/350B3
	AS350B 3		
	EC130B 4		EC130B4
	EC120		EC120
	SA341 G SA342 J		SA341/342
	SA3180 SA318 B SA318 C SE3130 SE313 B		SA318/SE313
	SE3160 SA316 B SA316 C	(D)	SA316/319/315
	SA319 B		
	SA315 B		
	SA360		SA360
	SO1221		SO1221
- ME Turbine -	AS332 C AS332 C 1 AS332 L AS332 L1	(D)	AS332/332L2
	AS332 L 2		
	EC 225 L P		EC 225LP
	AS355 E AS355 F AS355 F 1 AS355 F 2	(D)	AS355/355N
	AS355 N		

Manufacturer 1	Helicopter 2	3	Licence Endorsement 4
	BO105 A BO105 C BO105 D BO105 LS A-1 BO105 LS A-3 BO105 S BO105 CBS		BO105/105LS/105CBS
	EC135 T1 CDS EC135 P1 CDS	(D)	EC135
	EC135 T1 CPDS EC135 P1 CPDS EC135 T2 CPDS EC135 P2 CPDS		
	MBB-BK 117 A-1 MBB-BK 117 A-3 MBB-BK 117 A-4 MBB-BK 117 B-1 MBB-BK 117 B-2	(D)	BK117
	MBB-BK 117 C-1		
	MBB-BK 117 C-2		
	SA330 F SA330 G SA330 J		SA330
	SA365 SA365 C 1 SA365 C 2 SA365 C 3	(D)	SA365/365N
	SA365 N SA365 N 1 SA365 N 2		
	SA365 N 3		
	EC155		EC155
Hiller			
- SE Piston -	UH12 A UH12 B UH12 E		UH12
Hughes/Schweitzer			
- SE Piston -	269 A 269 B 269 C 300 C 300 CB		HU269
- SE Turbine -	330SP		SC330
Kaman			
- SE Turbine -	Kaman K 1200		K1200

Manufacturer 1	Helicopter 2	3	Licence Endorsement 4
McDonnell Douglas Helicopters			
- SE Turbine -	Hughes 369 D Hughes 369 E Hughes 369 HE Hughes 369 HS	(D)	HU369/MD500N/600
	MD500 N (NOTAR) MD520 N		
	MD600		
- ME Turbine -	MD900	(D)	MD900/902
	MD902		
Robinson			
- SE Piston -	R22 R22 A R22 B		R22
	R44		R44
Silvercraft			
- SE Piston -	SV 4		SV4
Sikorsky			
- SE Piston -	S55		SK55
	S58		SK58
- ME Turbine -	S58T		SK58T
	S76 A S76 A+ S76 A ++	(D)	SK76/76B/76C/76C+
	S76 B		
	S76 C		
	S76 C+		
	S-61 N S-61 S		SK61
Westland			
- SE Piston -	Westland Bell 47 G3 B-1		Bell47
Westland Helicopters			
- SE Piston -	Westland S55 Series 1	(D)	WHS55
- SE Turbine -	Westland S55 Series 3		
Ministry of Aviation Industry of Russia			
- ME Piston -	Kamov KA26 D		KA26D

Manufacturer 1	Helicopter 2	3	Licence Endorsement 4
- ME Turbine -	Kamov KA32 A		KA32
	MIL Mi-8 MIL Mi 17 MIL Mi 171 MIL Mi 172		Mi8
P.Z.L Swidnik, Poland			
- ME Turbine -	MIL Mi-2		Mi-2
	PZL KANIA		KANIA
	PZL W-3	(D)	W-3SOKOL
	PZL W-34		

APPENDIX D LIST OF MOTOR GLIDERS (SLMG AND/OR TMG)

In the UK for licensing purposes there is no distinction between SLMG and TMG aircraft. UK issued licence holders with a valid SLMG or TMG rating can fly any motor glider (SLMG and TMG). Below is a list of Motor Gliders which are classified as either SLMG only or SLMG/TMG. Please note that this list is not definitive.

SLMG

'an aircraft with the characteristics of a non power driven glider and which is fitted with one or more power units which is designed or intended to take off under its own power'

TMG

'a motor glider having a certificate of airworthiness issued or accepted by a JAA Member State having an integrally mounted, non retractable engine and a non retractable propeller plus those listed in Appendix 1 to JAR-FCL 1.215.

Motor Gliders Classed as SLMG and TMG

Aeromot AMT-200	
Super Ximango	Scheibe SF23A
ASK 14	Scheibe SF24A/B
ASK 16	Scheibe SF25A
	Scheibe SF25B Falke
Cadet Motor Glider	Scheibe SF25C
	Falke 87
Cadet III Motor Glider	Scheibe SF25E
	Super Falke
	Scheibe SF28A/B Tandem Falke
Diamond HK 36 TC/TTS	Scheibe SF36
Fournier RF3	Slingsby T29B
Fournier RF4D	Slingsby T31 Motor Cadet III
Fournier RF5	Slingsby T61A
Fournier RF5B	Slingsby T61C
Fournier RF7	Slingsby T61F Venture T Mk 2
Fournier RF9	Slingsby T61G
Grob 109 series	Sportavia RF5B
Hoffman H36 Dimona	SZD-25A
Hoffman H36R Super Dimona	SZD-50-3
IAR Brasov IS 28M2A	Taifun 17E II

Motor Gliders Classed as SLMG Only

Glaser Dirks DG-400 Series	Pik 20E
Glaser Dirks DG-500M	Pik 30
Glaser Dirks DG-600/18M	
Glaser Dirks DG-800A/B	Scheibe SF27M series
Janus CM	Schleicher ASH 26E
	Schleicher ASW 20 TOP
Nimbus 3DM	
Nimbus 4DM	Stemme S10 Series
	Ventus 2CM

Section A Section B Section C Section D Section E Section F TYPE, CLASS RATINGS Section G Section H Section I Section J Section K Index

APPENDIX E **GUIDANCE ON DIFFERENCES TRAINING**

Section 1 Variable Pitch (VP) Propellers (all propeller aeroplanes)

These systems make a significant difference to performance in all phases of flight. Mostly, the instruction in this section will be given to pilots converting from SEP aeroplanes with fixed pitch propellers to SEP or MEP aeroplanes with VP propellers and constant speed units (CSU). The system on some older types may not include a CSU and instructors must ensure that all of the system differences and handling techniques, introduced by the new type, are properly covered in the training given.

Differences Training completed, for this section, on a SEP aeroplane, does <u>not</u> provide equivalent qualification on MEP aeroplanes.

All Aeroplanes

Principle of operation and effect on performance;

System construction & function;

Propeller system limitations;

Engine limitations and instrumentation.

Operation of throttle, mixture and propeller controls, including pre-flight checks and normal handling during:-

- Start up and taxying;
- Take-off & climb;
- Cruise at various power settings & speeds;
- Low speed handling and stall/spin recovery;
- Approach and go-around;
- Landing & shut down.

In-flight failures, within the propeller system, including:-

- Loss of oil pressure;
- Loss of governor control;
- Overspeed;
- Underspeed.

Emergency handling, during:-

- Engine failure after take-off/go-around;
- Engine failure during other phases of flight, including approach and landing;
- Effect of engine failure on glide performance.

Emergency Handling Considerations for Multi-Engine Aeroplanes

Engine failures after take-off including propeller feathering and effect of wind-mill drag;

Circuit and approach with one or more engines inoperative;

Go-around with one or more engines inoperative;

Landing with one or more engines inoperative.

Note: See also LASORS (ORS section) Practical Guidance - Handling sense in Multi-Engine (Twin) Piston Aeroplanes.

Section 2 Retractable Undercarriage

Differences Training completed, for this section, on a SEP aeroplane, does <u>not</u> provide equivalent qualification on MEP Aeroplanes:-

- Principle and effect on performance;
- System construction & function;
- Limitations - raising, lowering & extended.

Operation including pre-flight checks and normal handling:-

- After take-off;
- On approach/go-around & landing.

In-flight system failures and emergency lowering.

Operation of undercarriage during:-

- Engine failure after take-off/go-around (Emergency raising - as applicable to type);
- Engine failure during other phases of flight, including approach and landing.
- Effect on glide performance.

Considerations for MEP Aeroplanes:-

- Effect on performance - one or more engines inoperative.

- Handling during approach and landing/go-around with one or more engines inoperative.
- Effect on engine out allowance & landing committal height.

Note: See also LASORS (ORS section) Practical Guidance - Handling sense in Multi-Engine (Twin) Piston Aeroplanes

Section 3 Turbo/Supercharged Engine(s)

Differences Training completed, for this section, on a SEP aeroplane, does not provide equivalent qualification on MEP Aeroplanes:-

- Principle and effect on performance, including cruise altitude;
- System construction & function;
- Engine limitations and instrumentation.

Engine handling including pre-flight checks and normal operation during:-

- Start up and taxying;
- Take-off & climb;
- Cruise at various power settings & speeds;
- Low speed handling and stall/spin recovery;
- Approach and go-around;
- Landing & shut down.
- In-flight failures and emergency handling;
- Single-Engine Stabilising Altitude (ME only).

Section 4 Cabin Pressurisation and Oxygen Systems

Differences Training completed, for this section, on a SEP aeroplane, does not provide equivalent qualification on MEP Aeroplanes:-

- Principle and effect on performance;
- Construction;
- System function including associated environmental heating and air conditioning systems;
- Oxygen system - storage capacity, pre-flight checks, system function (passengers & crew);
- Systems Limitations;
- Human Limitations including hypoxia and period of useful consciousness.

Operations at high altitude including:-

- Airspace classification;
- Licence & rating privileges;
- Rules of the Air;
- Weather;
- Air Navigation (BR Nav).

Normal operation including pre-flight checks, setting & monitoring during:-

- Take-off & climb;
- Cruise;
- Descent;
- Approach & Landing.
- In-flight failures and emergency handling including:-
- Use of oxygen;
- Emergency descent including terrain & ATC considerations;
- Single Engine Stabilising Altitude (ME only).

Section 5 Tail Wheel

Differences Training completed, for this section, on a SEP aeroplane, does not provide equivalent qualification on MEP aeroplanes:-

- Physical differences;
- Loading and Effect of CG Position.
- Dynamic differences and handling during:-
- Ground handling;
- Starting & taxying;
- Taking-off;
- Engine failure during take-off;
- Landings including 2-point "Wheelers" & 3-point landings (as applicable to type);

- Crosswind operations;
- Parking & mooring.
- Landing and ground handling with one or more engines inoperative (ME only).

Variants within a Type Rating

- Weight & loading - normal, utility and aerobatic load categories;
- Take-off and climb performance;
- Cruise performance;
- Landing performance;
- Speeds for normal operation;
- Speeds for emergency operation;
- Airframe limitations;
- Manoeuvre imitations and aerobatics;
- Spinning;
- Stall/Spin warning for protection systems;
- Fuel system;
- Engine systems & instrumentation;
- Undercarriage system;
- Electrical system (DC & AC);
- Cabin and environmental system (including pressurisation);
- Cockpit & cabin oxygen systems;
- Caution & warning annunciator system;
- Flight instrumentation;
- EFIS & navigation systems;
- Autopilot and trim system including pre-flight checks;
- Other systems including pneumatic, vacuum and hydraulic;
- Aerodynamic controls & handling characteristics;
- Engine handling;
- Flaps & lift/drag augmentation;
- Other systems particular to type;
- Emergency procedures.

APPENDIX F FLIGHT INSTRUCTION REQUIREMENTS FOR TYPE RATING COURSES (HELICOPTERS)

1. The amount of flight instruction required will depend on:

   i. complexity of the helicopter type, handling characteristics, level of technology

   ii. category of helicopter (SEP, SET, MET and MPH)

   iii. previous experience of the applicant

   iv. the availability of FSTDs (The level of qualification and the complexity of the type will determine the amount of practical training that may be accomplished in FSTDs, including completion of the skill test)

2. Initial issue – the **minimum** flight instruction **excluding the test** shall comprise a total of at least:

Helicopter Types	In Helicopter	In Helicopter & FSTD training credits
SEP (H)	5 hrs	Using F/S C/D: at least 2 hrs helicopter & at least 6 hrs total Using FTD 2/3: at least 4 hrs helicopter & at least 6 hrs total
SET (H) <3175kg MTOW	5 hrs	As above
SET (H) at or over 3175kg MTOW	8 hrs	Using FS C/D: at least 2 hrs helicopter & at least 10 hrs total Using FTD 2/3: at least 4 hrs helicopter & at least 10 hrs total
SPH MET (H) JAR/FAR 27 & 29	8 hrs	As above
MPH	10 hrs	Using FS C/D: at least 2 hrs helicopter & at least 12 hrs total Using FTD 2/3: at least 4 hrs helicopter & at least 12 hrs total

3. Additional types – the **minimum** flight instruction **excluding the test** shall comprise a total of at least:

Helicopter Types	In Helicopter	In Helicopter & FSTD training credits
SEP (H) TO SEP (H)	3 hrs	Using FS C/D: at least 1 hr helicopter & at least 4 hrs total Using FTD 2/3: at least 1 hr helicopter & at least 5 hrs total
SET (H) TO SET (H)	3 hrs	As above
SE & ME <3175kgs Differences Trg	1 hr	Not applicable
MET (H) to MET (H)	5 hrs	Using FS C/D: at least 1 hr helicopter & at least 6 hrs total Using FTD 2/3: at least 2 hrs helicopter & at least 7 hrs total
ME >3175kgs Differences Trg	3 hrs	Using FS C/D: at least 1 hr helicopter & at least 4 hrs total Using FTD 2/3: at least 2 hrs helicopter & at least 6 hrs total
MPH to MPH	5 hrs	Using FS C/D: at least 1 hr helicopter & at least 6 hrs total Using FTD 2/3: at least 2 hrs helicopter & at least 7 hrs total

Notes:

a. Holders of ME IR(H) wishing to extend the IR(H) to further ME types shall have an additional 2 hours flight training on type according to IFR which may be conducted in a FS level C/D or FTD level 2/3.

b. Prior to undertaking the skill test, a student shall demonstrate competency in the skill test items during the practical training.

c. On completion of the related flying training the applicant shall take the type rating skill test in accordance with Appendix 2 or 3 to JAR-FCL 2.240.

d. TRTO's wishing to reduce the duration of Type rating Courses in accordance with this Long Term Exemption no longer need to apply for individual agreement from Approvals Support, PLD.

APPENDIX G SEP (SEA) CLASS RATING SKILL TEST SCHEDULE

Section 1 Departure

- Pre-flight including:
  - Documentation - Pilot and Aircraft
  - Mass & Balance and Performance
  - LSJ, Anchor, Sea Anchor and Ropes
  - Weather briefing
- Pre-start checks - External & Internal
  - Water rudders
  - Float or hull inspection
  - Float or hull bilging
- Engine Starting - Normal & Malfunctions
  - Positioning of seaplane
  - Area check
  - Control of seaplane after start
- Taxiing
  - Assessment of wind and water conditions
  - Displacement, Plow and Step taxi and turns
  - Turn from upwind to downwind
  - Turn from downwind to upwind
  - Crosswind taxi
  - Sailing
- Pre-departure checks - Engine run-up
- Take-off procedure
  - Normal, Rough, Glassy, Crosswind and Restricted Area (Simulated)
  - Recovery from porpoising
  - Landing gear selection (Amphibian only)
- Climbing (Vx / Vy - turns onto headings, level off)
- ATC liaison - Compliance, R/T procedure
- Seamanship
  - Lookout and manoeuvring on the water
  - Water discipline and rights of way

Section 2 Airwork (VFR)

- Straight and level flight at various airspeeds including flight at critically low airspeed with and without flaps
- Steep turns (360° left and right at 45° bank)
- Stalls and recovery
  - Clean stall
  - Approach to stall in descending turn with bank, approach configuration and power
  - Approach to stall in landing configuration and power
  - Approach to stall, climbing turn with take-off flap and climb power
- Handling using autopilot and flight director (if applicable)
- ATC liaison - Compliance, R/T procedure

Section 3 En-route Procedures (VFR)

- Flight plan, dead reckoning and map reading
- Maintenance of altitude, heading and speed
- Orientation, timing and revision of ETAs
- Use of radio navigation aids (if applicable)
- Flight management (flight log, routine checks including fuel, systems and icing)
- ATC liaison - Compliance, R/T procedure

Section 4 Arrival and Landings

- Arrival procedure
  - Aerial inspection of landing area
  - Assessment of surface wind
- Landing
  - Normal, Glassy and Rough water
  - Flapless and Crosswind
  - Landing gear selection (Amphibian only)
  - After alighting checks
- Approach and landing from up to 2000' above the landing area
- Go-around from minimum height
- Mooring/Buoying and Buoy identification, Anchoring, Beaching and Ramping
- Docking - Normal and Sailing techniques
- ATC liaison - Compliance, R/T procedure
- Seamanship
  - Lookout and manoeuvring on the water
  - Water discipline and rights of way

Section 5 Abnormal and Emergency Procedures (may be combined with Sections 1 to 4)

- Rejected take-off (at a reasonable speed) on water
- Simulated engine failure after take-off
- Simulated forced landing without power
- Simulated emergencies
  - Engine fire in flight and on the water
  - Cabin fire in the flight
  - Damaged float landing
  - En-route engine failure over water and land
  - Engine failure whilst on the water
  - Systems malfunctions as appropriate
- ATC liaison - Compliance, R/T procedure
- Seamanship
  - Lookout and manoeuvring on the water
  - Water discipline and rights of way

Oral Examination

- The applicant shall be asked questions on subjects associated seaplane operations

SECTION G

AIRLINE TRANSPORT PILOT LICENCE

The UK Civil Aviation Authority currently issues the following classes of Airline Transport Pilot Licence.

Each section details the requirements to obtain each licence, including flying training, ground examinations and flight tests. Details of credits against training are also given.

- **G1** **JAR-FCL ATPL (Aeroplane)**
- **G2** **JAR-FCL ATPL (Aeroplane) for UK Qualified Service Pilots (Aeroplanes)**
- **G3** **JAR-FCL ATPL (Helicopter)**
- **G4** **JAR-FCL ATPL (Helicopter) for UK Qualified Service Pilots (Helicopters)**
- **G5** **Licence Re-issue**

G1 JAR-FCL ATPL (AEROPLANE)

This section offers information as a basic guide to obtaining a JAR-FCL Airline Transport Pilot Licence (Aeroplane) – JAR-FCL ATPL (A) as follows:-

For full details you are advised to refer to JAR-FCL 1 Subpart G.

G1.1 JAR-FCL ATPL (A) GENERAL INFORMATION

Privileges

Details of licence privileges can be found in Schedule 8 of the Air Navigation Order, (please also refer to Section A, Appendix F).

Minimum Age

An applicant for a JAR-FCL ATPL(A) shall be at least 21 years of age.

Licence Validity

The JAR-FCL ATPL(A) will be issued for a maximum period of 5 years.

G1.2 FLYING EXPERIENCE REQUIREMENTS FOR JAR-FCL ATPL(A)

The holder of a UK national CPL(A) should refer to Section A10.1 for details of the requirements to 'upgrade' to a JAR-FCL ATPL (A).

An applicant for a JAR-FCL ATPL(A) shall have completed as a pilot of aeroplanes at least **1500** hours of flight time **(see G1.2 Notes)**. This must include the particular requirements specified in **a, b, c, d & e below**. Each of these requirements must be met in full but, hours may be credited, where appropriate, towards more than one requirement except where stated otherwise.

a. 500 hours Multi-Pilot operations on aeroplanes type certificated in accordance with the **JAR/FAR-25** Transport Category or the **JAR/FAR-23** Commuter Category or equivalent code, or single-pilot aeroplanes operated by 2-pilots according to operational requirements.

b. i. 250 hours Pilot-in-Command (PIC) of Aeroplanes, can include (ii);

ii. 150 hours (max) Co-Pilot performing under the supervision of the Pilot-in-Command the duties and functions of a Pilot-in-Command (PIC/US). (see Notes below).

c. i. 200 hours Cross-country flight time, must include;

ii. 100 hours Pilot-in-Command (PIC) **or** Co-Pilot performing under the supervision of the Pilot-in-Command the duties and functions of a Pilot-in-Command (PIC U/S) of Aeroplanes.

d. i. 75 hours Instrument time, can include (ii);

ii. 30 hours (max) Instrument Ground Time.

e. 100 hours Night flight as Pilot-in-Command (PIC) or as Co-Pilot (PIC/US or P2)

G1.2 Notes

JAR-FCL 1.050 sets out the way in which flight time will be credited for a licence.

The 1500 hours flying experience may comprise flight time in any of the following capacities:

- as Pilot-in-Command/Solo (PIC), counted in full;
- as Pilot-under-Instruction (Dual), counted in full;
- as Co-Pilot performing under the supervision of the Pilot-in-Command the functions and duties of a Pilot-in-Command (PIC U/S) counted in full. For licence issue, confirmation of such flight time will be required. This can either take the form of a letter from the operating company or certification of each flight within the pilot's logbook by the Pilot-in-Command.

- as Co-Pilot (P2), counted in full;
- as Student Pilot-in-Command (SPIC) counted in full up to a maximum of **50** hours towards the Pilot-in-Command time required for the issue of a ATPL(A).
- A maximum of 100 hours may have been completed in an aeroplane Flight Simulator and FNPT of which a maximum of 25 hours may have been completed in FNPT.
- Up to 50% of the 1500 hours **and** each of the requirements specified in **G1.2 a, b, c, d & e above** may be completed in helicopters.
- Holders of a Flight Engineer Licence will be credited with 50% of the flight engineer time up to a maximum credit of **250** hours. This 250 hours may be credited against the 1500 hours experience requirement and the 500 hours requirement of **a** of **G1.2 above** provided that the total credit given against any of the above does not exceed 250 hours.
- A maximum of 30 hours flight time in Touring Motor Gliders or Gliders may be counted towards the 1500 hours experience requirement.

G1.3 JAR-FCL ATPL(A) THEORETICAL KNOWLEDGE EXAMINATION REQUIREMENTS

An applicant for a JAR-FCL ATPL(A) is required to:

1. Pass the fourteen **ATPL(A) Theoretical Knowledge** examinations in the following subjects:

Air Law	
Aircraft General Knowledge	(2 papers)
Flight Performance and Planning	(3 papers)
Human Performance and Limitations	
Meteorology	
Navigation	(2 papers)
Operational Procedures	
Principles of Flight	
Communications	(2 papers)

ATPL(A) Modular Theoretical Knowledge Course

The aim of this course is to train pilots who have not yet received the theoretical knowledge instruction during an integrated course, to the level of theoretical knowledge required for the ATPL(A). Applicants will be required to complete 650 hours of ATPL theoretical knowledge instruction at an Approved FTO within a period of 18 months. An applicant shall be the holder of a PPL(A) (excluding NPPL) issued in accordance with ICAO Annex 1.

Candidates without a full pass in the UK national professional ground examinations

A candidate who did not achieve a full pass in the UK National professional ground examinations, is required to pass the JAR-FCL theoretical knowledge examinations in all subjects. JAR-FCL additionally requires candidates to complete an approved theoretical knowledge course prior to attempting the examinations. However, a candidate who has previously passed at least one examination in the UK Navigation or technical Group of examinations will not be required to complete the full theoretical knowledge course - the amount of theoretical knowledge instruction required will be at the discretion of the Head of Training of an approved training provider. This credit against JAR-FCL theoretical knowledge course recognises the studies already completed by candidates who have passed national exams.

Credits from the ATPL(A) Theoretical Knowledge Examinations

- Holders of a CPL(A) may have the theoretical instruction reduced by 200 hours and holders of an IR may have the theoretical instruction hours reduced by 200 hours.
- An applicant who has previously passed the VFR Communications examination at CPL(A) level, and have been issued with a CPL(A) will not be re-examined in subject VFR Communications at ATPL(A) level.
- An applicant who has previously passed the IFR Communications examination at IR level, and have been issued with an IR(A) will not be re-examined in subject IFR Communications at ATPL(A) level.
- The holder of a valid JAR-FCL ATPL(H)/IR will be required to complete the appropriate bridging examination requirements (see Section J1.9).
- The holder of a valid JAR-FCL CPL(A)/IR with JAR-FCL ATPL Theory credit will be credited the JAR-FCL ATPL(A) Theoretical knowledge examination for a period of 7 years from the last validity date of the IR(A) entered in the CPL(A).
- A UK QSP(H) holding a valid JAR-FCL CPL(H) with valid ATPL(H) theory credit will be required to complete the appropriate bridging examination requirements (see Section J1.9).

- The holder of a valid JAR-FCL CPL(A)/IR may have the minimum ATPL theoretical instruction hours reduced by 350 hours.

FULL DETAILS OF THE ABOVE EXAMINATIONS, PASS RULES, VALIDITY PERIODS ETC, ARE GIVEN IN SECTION J and JAR-FCL 1, SUBPART J.

2. Complete an **Approved Multi-Crew Co-operation Course.**

    - Completion of this course is **only** required by CPL(A)/IR holders who have not graduated from an ATP(A) Integrated course but who wish to obtain an initial type rating on a multi-pilot aeroplane.

    - Holders of a non-UK Professional Pilot's Licence who have at least **500** hours flying experience on aeroplanes or helicopters certificated for operation by a minimum crew of two pilots, can be credited this requirement.

    Note: Experience gained in single-pilot certificated aeroplanes that are operated with a crew of two or more will **not** normally be accepted towards the 500 hour requirement but **may** be considered in certain circumstances (i.e. where national law requires such operation).

FULL DETAILS OF MCC ARE GIVEN IN JAR-FCL 1.261 AND SECTION F10.

G1.4 JAR-FCL ATPL(A) SKILL TEST REQUIREMENTS

An applicant for a JAR-FCL ATPL(A) is required to:

- Pass the **ATPL(A) Skill Test** with an authorised Type Rating Examiner.

- The applicant shall demonstrate the ability to perform as Pilot-in-Command of an aeroplane type certificated for a minimum of two pilots under IFR, the procedures and manoeuvres required with a degree of competency appropriate to the privileges granted to the holder of an ATPL(A).

- The Skill Test may serve as a skill test for the issue of the licence **and** a proficiency check for the revalidation of the type rating for the aeroplane used in the test, and may be combined with the skill test for the issue of a multi-pilot type rating.

- The Skill Test may not be taken until **all** of the flying experience requirements for the grant of the licence have been met together with the necessary theoretical knowledge examinations.

DETAILS OF THE ATPL(A) SKILL TEST ARE DETAILED IN APPENDICES 1 & 2 TO JAR-FCL 1.240 & 1.295.

G1.5 JAR-FCL ATPL(A) CONVERSION OF A NON-JAA PROFESSIONAL LICENCE

A professional pilot licence issued by a non-JAA State may be converted to a JAR-FCL licence provided that an arrangement exists between the JAA and the non-JAA State. This arrangement shall be established on the basis of reciprocity of licence acceptance and shall ensure that an equivalent level of safety exists between the training and testing requirements of the JAA and non-JAA State. Until such arrangements exist, the following requirements have been agreed by the JAA and are now incorporated in JAR-FCL 1.016.

Non-JAA ATPL(A)

The holder of **a current and valid** ATPL(A) issued in accordance with ICAO Annex 1 by a non-JAA State may be issued with a JAR-FCL ATPL(A) providing the experience requirements of JAR-FCL 1.280 have been met. Applicants' must:-

- hold a valid JAR-FCL Class 1 medical certificate;

- Undertake ATPL(A) theoretical knowledge instruction as determined by the Head of Training of an approved training provider, and pass ALL of the JAR-FCL theoretical knowledge examinations at ATPL(A) level;

- Qualify for the issue of a UK Flight Radio Telephony Operator's Licence (FRTOL) -Section B refers;

- Undertake a multi-pilot aeroplane type rating course at an approved TRTO (see Section F, Appendix B for a list of types);

- pass the ATPL(A) skill test in accordance with Appendices 1 and 2 to JAR-FCL 1.240 and 1.295 with, or observed by, a CAA Flight Operations Training Inspector.

G1.5 Note 1

ATPL(A) holders who have a minimum of 1500 hours flying experience as PIC or Co-pilot on multi-pilot aeroplanes (or single-pilot aeroplanes operated by 2-pilots according to operational requirements) and hold a valid multi-pilot type rating for the aeroplane to be used for the ATPL(A) skill test and have at least 500 hours experience as pilot on that type, will be exempted from the requirements to complete an approved TRTO course or undergo approved training prior to undertaking the theoretical knowledge examinations and the skill test.

The ATPL(A) Skill Test in this case will have a 12 month validity for the purpose of licence issue.

Section A Section B Section C Section D Section E Section F Section G ATPL Section H Section I Section J Section K Index

Pilots who meet the 1500 hours flying experience (as detailed above), with less than 500 hours experience as pilot on the type to be used for the ATPL(A) Skill Test, or do not hold a multi-pilot type rating will be exempted from the requirements to undergo approved ground and flying training prior to undertaking the theoretical knowledge examinations. In both cases, they will be required to complete an approved JAA type rating course and if applicable, the course may be reduced to take into account any previous experience on the same type upon recommendation by the Head of Training of the TRTO to PLD. An ATPL(A) Skill Test with, or observed by a CAA Flight Operations Training Inspector will be required at the end of the TRTO course. The ATPL(A) Skill Test in this case will have a 6 month validity for the purpose of licence issue.

G1.5 Note 2

Different terms apply to ATPL(A) holders with a minimum of 3,000 hours flying experience as pilot of public transport aircraft over 30,000kgs MTWA on scheduled international or similar routes, **including** a minimum of 1,500 hours as Pilot-in-Command (Captain). Applicants who believe they qualify should apply to PLD for a formal written assessment using form SRG\1103 and enclosing the appropriate fee, actual logbooks and non-UK licence (with validating medical certificate if separate).

Applicants who qualify under these terms will be eligible to complete reduced requirements for the issue of a JAR-FCL ATPL(A). With regards to the theoretical knowledge examinations requirement, a credit will be given towards the JAR-FCL ATPL(A) examinations, with the exception of Air Law and Human Performance and Limitations examinations which will need to be passed. An applicant who completes the reduced requirements will be issued with a JAR-FCL ATPL(A) however, as this licence does not fully comply with the requirements of JAR-FCL, the holder is not entitled to automatic recognition accorded to JAR-FCL. The licence will therefore be issued with the following statement:

Valid for United Kingdom registered aircraft. As this licence does not fully comply with JAR-FCL the holder must have permission from any other JAA Member State prior to exercising the licence privileges in aircraft registered in that State.

This endorsement may be removed by obtaining a pass in all JAR-FCL ATPL(A) theoretical knowledge examinations. (The 12 remaining JAR-FCL ATPL(A) examinations will be classed as a new set and attempt and will be subject to the pass standards as detailed in Section J1.5).

The holder of a current and valid ATPL(A) who does not meet the experience requirements for the grant of a JAR-FCL ATPL(A) can still apply for a JAR-FCL CPL(A)/IR. Details can be found in Section D1.5.

G1.6 JAR-FCL ATPL(A) FLIGHT RADIOTELEPHONY OPERATOR'S LICENCE (FRTOL) REQUIREMENTS

An applicant for a UK FRTOL is required to pass the Radiotelephony written examination and practical test with an authorised RTF Examiner. It should be noted that whilst Radio Communication forms part of the JAR-FCL ATPL(A) training syllabus, the FRTOL remains a UK national licence.

FULL DETAILS OF THE FRTOL REQUIREMENTS INCLUDING CREDITS AVAILABLE ARE CONTAINED IN SECTION B.

G1.7 MEDICAL REQUIREMENTS

An applicant for a JAR-FCL ATPL(A) shall hold a valid JAR-FCL Class 1 Medical Certificate.

FULL DETAILS OF THE MEDICAL REQUIREMENTS ARE CONTAINED IN JAR-FCL 3 AND SECTION A6.

G2 JAR-FCL ATPL (AEROPLANE) FOR UK QUALIFIED SERVICE PILOTS (AEROPLANES)

This section offers information as a basic guide to obtaining a JAR-FCL Airline Transport Pilot Licence (Aeroplane) – JAR-FCL ATPL(A) – for a UK Qualified Service Pilot (Aeroplanes).(see definition in G2.1)

G2.1 JAR-FCL ATPL (A) GENERAL INFORMATION

Introduction

JAR-FCL permits the knowledge, experience and skill gained in military service to be credited towards the relevant requirements of JAR-FCL licences and ratings at the discretion of each national authority. The CAA has worked closely with the MoD through the MoD/CAA Working Group (MCWG) to determine the scope and level of accreditation that can be applied to suitably experienced UK military pilots.

In particular, the MCWG sought to determine an agreed level of equivalence between the theoretical knowledge acquired by pilots throughout military flying training and subsequent operational experience, and those required at JAR-FCL ATPL (A) level.

Full details of the theoretical knowledge requirements, including credits and eligibility criteria, can be found in section G2.3. It should be noted that a QSP (A) can still take advantage of any flying or skill test credits that he may qualify for, even if he does not qualify for theoretical knowledge credits under G2.3.

Important Note: In order to qualify for a JAR-FCL ATPL(A), a QSP(A) is required to show a minimum of 500 hours flying experience on ONE type of military multi-pilot aeroplane (MPA), and pass an IR(A) skill test on that same type. The following types in current military service are considered to be multi-pilot aeroplanes for this purpose:

Andover	**BAC 1-11**
BAe 125	**BAe 146**
Jetstream T3	**Hercules** (C1/C3 and C4/C5 variants)
Sentry	**Nimrod**
VC10	**Tristar**

Note: Although the C17 is recognised as a military multi-pilot aeroplane type, an RAF limitation on asymmetric flying in the aircraft prevents all necessary items of the IR(A) skill test from being completed on this aircraft. As a result C17 pilots will be unable to obtain a JAR-FCL ATPL(A), and should refer to Section D3 for details of how to qualify for a JAR-FCL CPL(A)/IR with 'frozen' ATPL theory credit.

A QSP (A) without 500 hours flying experience on any ONE of the above types, or who has in excess of 500 hours on any ONE type but is unable (for whatever reason) to complete an IR skill test on that same type, will be <u>unable</u> to qualify for a JAR-FCL ATPL(A) and should refer to Section D3 for details of how to qualify for a JAR-FCL CPL(A)/IR with 'frozen' ATPL theory credit.

Although not exclusive, a licensing flow diagram can be found at Appendix I to Section D, to demonstrate typical licensing routes for experienced military fixed-wing pilots.

Questions regarding this scheme should be directed in writing to: FT (Proj) 1, HQ TGDA, RAF Innsworth, Gloucester, GL3 1EZ or by e-mail to ftproj1@tgda.gov.uk.

Privileges

Details of licence privileges can be found in Schedule 8 of the Air Navigation Order (please also refer to Section A, Appendix F).

Minimum Age

An applicant for a JAR-FCL ATPL (A) shall be at least 21 years of age.

Licence Validity

A JAR-FCL ATPL (A) will be issued for a maximum period of 5 years.

Definition of Qualified Service Pilot

To qualify for any of the credits detailed in Section G2, an applicant must be a UK Qualified Service Pilot (QSP).

A QSP is defined as a pilot who has completed a recognised military course of flying training and has been awarded a pilot's flying badge in full compliance with QR (RAF) J727.

The term "flying badge" is used to include all badges worn by personnel who have successfully completed a prescribed course of flying training. The initial award of a flying badge is on a provisional basis. It is not deemed to be fully earned until the holder has successfully completed an operational conversation or equivalent course and has joined an operational or non-operational unit in the capacity for which the provisional badge has been awarded. Joining is defined for each Service as follows:-

a. RN: on issue of the Certificate of Competence.

b. Army and RM: on award of the badge (and successful completion of conversation to type (CTT) course.

c. RAF: On successful attainment of an appropriate aircrew categorisation or qualification to undertake productive flying duties (C categorisation or above, B1 or above instructor category or CR status.

Non-UK Military Pilots

Non-UK military pilots operating UK military aircraft through exchange programs etc. are **not** eligible for any of the credits afforded to UK military pilots - if a serving member of the Armed Forces of another JAA State, applicants should contact the National Aviation Authority of that State for details of any accreditation arrangements for its military personnel.

Ex-Qualified Service Pilots

An ex-QSP (A) can claim any credits for which he qualifies, for a period of one year from the last date of service.

An ex-QSP (A) employed by a Defence Contractor in flying-related duties, is deemed to be a QSP (A) for licensing purposes. He can claim any credits for which he qualifies, for a period of one year from the date of last flight in a military aeroplane.

A Volunteer Reservist or Full Time Reserve Service (FTRS) pilot is deemed to be a QSP (A) for licensing purposes. He can claim any credits for which he qualifies, for a period of one year from the date of last flight in a military aeroplane.

Definition of Current Flying Practice

In order to qualify for credit against the ATPL (A) Skill Test (see G2.4), a QSP (A) shall be in current flying practice.

To be deemed to be in current flying practice, a QSP (A) shall have a minimum of 12 hours flying experience as a pilot in military or civil aeroplanes (or combination of both) in the 12 months preceding the date of application for licence issue. This experience shall include at least 6 hours as pilot-in-command (PIC) - for this purpose military 1st pilot hours may be counted towards the PIC requirement, one flight with a military instructor pilot or JAA Flight Instructor, and 12 take-offs and landings; for this purpose, military 1st Pilot hours may be counted towards the 6 hours PIC requirement.

A QSP (A) on a ground tour can still achieve currency, either by flying on military (AEF) or civil aeroplanes. A QSP (A) not on an AEF can achieve currency on civil aircraft through a combination of dual and solo flying. A QSP (A) who does not already hold a valid PPL (A), can satisfy the 6 hours PIC requirement by flying solo hours at a PPL Registered Facility, under the authority of the CFI (in much the same way as an ab-initio PPL student would).

G2.2 JAR-FCL ATPL (A) FLYING EXPERIENCE REQUIREMENTS

An applicant for a JAR-FCL ATPL (A) shall meet the flying experience requirements detailed in Section G1.2.

G2.3 JAR-FCL ATPL (A) THEORETICAL KNOWLEDGE EXAMINATION REQUIREMENTS

An applicant for a JAR-FCL ATPL (A) is required to complete an approved course theoretical knowledge instruction and pass theoretical knowledge examinations at ATPL level.

However, as described in G2.1, the MCWG determined a level of equivalence between military theoretical knowledge training and subsequent operational experience, and that required at ATPL (A) level. It should be recognised that the scope for accreditation was not the same for all military pilots, and that role training and experience ultimately determined the level of equivalence achieved.

Subject to meeting the appropriate eligibility criteria, a QSP(A) with at least 500 hours multi-pilot aeroplane experience can take advantage of either of two fixed-wing accreditation schemes to satisfy JAR ATPL(A) theoretical knowledge requirements; the FW(ME) scheme (see G2.3(A)) for experienced pilots with a high level of multi-engine operational experience, OR the FW (Non-ME) scheme (see G2.3(B)) for experienced pilots with a primarily fast-jet or instructor background, or low levels of multi-engine operational experience, OR he can pass the JAR ATPL(A) exams in all 14 subjects (see G2.3(C)).

G2.3(A) FW (ME) ACCREDITATION SCHEME

Eligibility

To qualify for theoretical knowledge exam credits under the FW (ME) accreditation scheme, a QSP(A) shall have completed:

1. A recognised ME OCU; **(BAe 125/146, C17, Hercules, Nimrod, Sentry, TriStar or VC10) (RN - Jetstream T2).**

2. A minimum of 2000 hours flying experience* on military aircraft, including at least 1500 hours as 1st Pilot (Captain)/1st Pilot (Nimrod) P1 (can incl. max. 500 hours 1st Pilot (non-Captain) Co-pilot P1 /2nd Pilot (Nimrod) on aeroplanes on recognised multi-engine aeroplanes. The following types in current military service are considered to be multi-engine aeroplanes for this purpose:-

* as recorded in Service logbook i.e. excluding any taxi-time allowances.

Andover*	**BAC 1-11***
BAe 125*	**BAe 146***
Beagle Bassett	**C17**
Beech 200	**Dominie**
Canberra	**Hercules C4/c5***
Hercules C1/C3*	**Jetstream T1/T2**
Islander	**Nimrod***
Jetstream T3*	**Sentry***
PA31	**VX10***
Tristar*	

Applicants shall also have operational experience on one of the approved ME aeroplanes, within the 5 years preceding the date of application for licence issue.

* denotes this type is also a recognised MPA for the purposes of obtaining a JAR-ATPL(A).

Flying experience on military multi-engine aeroplanes not included in the above list i.e. types flown whilst on exchange duties with a foreign air arm, will be considered on a case-by-case basis. Flying experience on multi-engine aeroplanes no longer in UK military service can be credited towards the 2000 hours requirement, but not the 1500 hour PIC requirement - only flying experience on recognised ME aeroplanes listed above can be credited towards the PIC requirement.

Theoretical Knowledge Requirements

A QSP (A) who meets the eligibility criteria in full, is required to:

1. Pass the ATPL (A) examination in:

    i. Air Law

DETAILS OF THE ABOVE EXAMINATION, PASS RULES, VALIDITY PERIODS, ETC, ARE GIVEN IN JAR-FCL 1, SUBPART J.

G2.3(B) QSPs INELIGIBLE FOR ACCREDITATION SCHEMES

A QSP(A) who does not meet the eligibility criteria of either accreditation scheme, will be required to demonstrate the appropriate level of theoretical knowledge by passing ALL of the theoretical knowledge examinations at ATPL level. However, credit will be given against the requirement to complete an approved course of theoretical knowledge instruction prior to attempting the examinations. Applicants will be required to undertake theoretical knowledge instruction as determined by the Head of Training of an approved training provider.

G2.4 JAR-FCL ATPL (A) SKILL TEST REQUIREMENTS

A QSP (A) in current flying practice as defined in G2.1 and who meets the multi-pilot type rating requirements detailed in G2.5 will be credited the ATPL (A) Skill Test.

G2.5 TYPE RATING REQUIREMENTS

Subject to currency on type and completion of an IR(A) skill test on type (see G2.6), a military type rating will be issued for any of the following recognised military multi-pilot aeroplane types:

Section A Section B Section C Section D Section E Section F Section G ATPL Section H Section I Section J Section K Index

Andover	**Hercules C4/C5** (C130J)
Nimrod	**Sentry**
VC10	

Subject to currency on type and completion of an IR(A) skill test on type (see G2.6), a JAR-FCL type rating (in brackets) will be issued for any of the following recognised military multi-pilot aeroplane types:-

BAC 1-11 (BAC 1-11)	**BAe 125** (HS 125)
BAe 146 (AVRORJ/BAe 146)	**Hercules C1/C3** (Hercules)
Jetstream T3 (Jetstream 31/32)	**Tristar** (L1011)

Currency Requirements

In order to qualify for a type rating credit for one of the above types, a QSP (A) must:

i. Show a minimum of 500 hours flying experience on any ONE type;

ii. Show evidence of a valid annual check (RAF - aircraft category renewal, RN - QFI check with NFSF(FW) on the SAME type (i) completed in the 12 months preceding the date of application for licence issue.

iii. Where the requirement of (i) has been met on one of the types listed above that qualify for a JAR-FCL type ratings pass on ATPL(A) skill test on an approved simulator, observed by a CAA Flight Operations Training Inspector (this would also serve as the IR(A) skill test.

Note:

1. A QSP (A) who does not meet the above currency requirements in full, will not qualify for a multi-pilot type rating credit, and will not qualify for a JAR-FCL ATPL (A). In this case, a QSP (A) should refer to Section D3 for details on how to qualify for a JAR-FCL CPL (A)/IR with 'frozen' ATPL theory credit.

However, where a QSP (A) meets the requirement of i) on one of the types indicated by '*', but not ii), he may still qualify for a JAR-FCL ATPL (A) by

a. completing the ATPL (A) Skill Test through an approved Type Rating Training Organisation (TRTO), observed by a CAA Flight Operations Training Inspector (this would also serve as the IR (A) Skill Test),

G2.6 INSTRUMENT RATING REQUIREMENTS

IR(A) Skill Test Requirements

A QSP (A) who qualifies for a Multi-pilot type rating as detailed in G2.5, is required to:

1. Pass the IR (A) Skill Test on the Multi-pilot type, observed by a CAA Flight Examiner.
   - Before undertaking the Skill Test, applicants shall have passed the associated theoretical knowledge examinations.

G2.7 UK FLIGHT RADIO TELEPHONY OPERATORS LICENCE (FRTOL)

An applicant for the JAR-FCL ATPL (A) shall hold/ qualify a UK FRTOL.

A QSP (A), who meets the eligibility criteria for either of the the accreditation schemes detailed in G2.3(A) or G2.3(B) will be credited with the written examination and practical communications test.

FULL DETAILS OF THE FRTOL REQUIREMENTS ARE CONTAINED IN SECTION B.

G2.8 JAR-FCL ATPL (A) MEDICAL REQUIREMENTS

An applicant for a JAR-FCL ATPL (A) shall hold a valid JAR-FCL Class One medical certificate.

FULL DETAILS OF MEDICAL REQUIREMENTS ARE CONTAINED IN JAR-FCL 3 AND SECTION A5

G3 JAR-FCL ATPL (HELICOPTER)

This section offers information as a basic guide to obtaining a JAR-FCL Airline Transport Pilot Licence (Helicopter) – JAR-FCL ATPL (H).

For full details you are advised to refer to JAR-FCL 2 Subpart G.

G3.1 JAR-FCL ATPL (H) GENERAL INFORMATION

Privileges

Details of licence privileges can be found in Schedule 8 of the Air Navigation Order, (please also refer to Section A, Appendix F).

Minimum Age

An applicant for a JAR-FCL ATPL (H) shall be at least 21 years of age.

Licence Validity

The JAR-FCL ATPL (H) will be issued for a maximum period of 5 years.

G3.2 JAR-FCL ATPL (H) FLYING TRAINING/ EXPERIENCE REQUIREMENTS

The holder of a UK national CPL(H) should refer to Section A10.2 for details of the requirements to 'upgrade' to a JAR-FCL ATPL (H).

An applicant for a JAR-FCL ATPL (H) shall have completed as a pilot of helicopters at least **1000** hours of flight time **(see G3.2 Notes)**. This must include the particular requirements specified in **G3.2 a, b, c, d & e below**. Each of these requirements must be met in full but, hours may be credited, where appropriate, towards more than one requirement except where stated otherwise.

a. 350 hours Multi-Pilot operations on helicopters type certificated in accordance with the **JAR/ FAR-27 and JAR/FAR-29** Helicopter Category or equivalent code or in helicopters required to be operated by two pilots under JAR-OPS.

b. i. 250 hours Pilot-in-Command (PIC) of Helicopters, can include (ii);

   ii. 150 hours (max) Co-Pilot performing under the supervision of the Pilot-in-Command the duties and functions of a Pilot-in-Command (PIC/US).

c. i. 200 hours Cross-country flight time, must include;

   ii. 70 hours Pilot-in Command (PIC) **or** Co-Pilot performing under the supervision of the Pilot-in-Command the duties and functions of a Pilot-in-Command (PIC U/S) of Helicopters.

d. i. 70 hours Instrument time, can include (ii);

   ii. 30 hours (max) Instrument Ground Time.

e. 100 hours Night flight as Pilot-in-Command (PIC) or as Co-Pilot (PIC/US or P2).

G3.2 Notes

JAR-FCL 2.050 sets out the way in which flight time will be credited for a licence.

The 1000 hours flying experience may comprise flight time in any of the following capacities:

- as Pilot-in-Command/Solo (PIC), counted in full;
- as Pilot-under-Instruction (Dual), counted in full;
- as Co-Pilot performing under the supervision of the Pilot-in-Command the functions and duties of a Pilot-in-Command (PIC U/S) counted in full. For licence issue, confirmation of such flight time will be required. This can either take the form of a letter from the operating company or certification of each flight within the pilot's logbook by the Pilot-in-Command.

- as Co-Pilot (P2), counted in full;
- as Student Pilot-in-Command (SPIC) counted in full up to a maximum of **50** hours towards the Pilot-in-Command time required for the issue of a ATPL(H).
- A maximum of 100 hours may have been completed in a helicopter STD if which not more than 25 hours in a FNPT.
- Up to 50% of each of the requirements specified in **G3.2 a, b, c, d & e** may be completed in aeroplanes.

G3.3 JAR-FCL ATPL (H) THEORETICAL KNOWLEDGE EXAMINATION REQUIREMENTS

An applicant for a JAR-FCL ATPL (H) is required to:

1. Pass the fourteen **ATPL (H) Theoretical Knowledge** examination in the following subjects:

Air Law	
Aircraft General Knowledge	(2 papers)
Flight Performance and Planning	(3 papers)
Human Performance and Limitations	
Meteorology	
Navigation	(2 papers)
Operational Procedures	
Principles of Flight	
Communications	(2 papers)

ATPL(H) Modular Theoretical Knowledge Course

The aim of this course is to train pilots who have not yet received the theoretical knowledge instruction during an integrated course, to the level of theoretical knowledge required for the ATPL(H). Applicants will be required to complete 650 hours of ATPL theoretical knowledge instruction at an Approved FTO within a period of 18 months. An applicant shall be the holder of a PPL(H) issued in accordance with ICAO Annex 1.

Credits from the ATPL(H) Theoretical Knowledge Examination

- Holders of an IR(H) may have the theoretical instruction hours reduced by 200 hours.
- The holder of a JAR-FCL CPL(H) and IR(H) satisfies the knowledge requirements for the issue of an ATPL(H). (Holders of a UK CPL(H) and IR(H) will be required to convert to a JAR-FCL licence)
- An applicant who has previously passed the VFR Communications examination at CPL(H) level, and have been issued with a CPL(H) will not be re-examined in subject VFR Communications at ATPL(H) level.
- An applicant who has previously passed the IFR Communications examination at IR level, and have been issued with an IR(H) will not be re-examined in subject IFR Communications at ATPL(H) level.
- The holder of a valid JAR-FCL CPL(A) with valid ATPL(A) theory credit/ATPL (A)/IR will be required to complete the appropriate bridging examination requirements (see J1.9).
- The holder of a valid JAR-FCL CPL (H)/IR with JAR-FCL ATPL Theory credit will be credited the JAR-FCL ATPL (H) Theoretical knowledge examination for a period of 7 years from the last validity date of the IR (H) entered in the CPL (H).

FULL DETAILS OF THE ABOVE EXAMINATIONS, PASS RULES, VALIDITY PERIODS ETC, ARE GIVEN IN JAR-FCL 2, SUBPART J.

2. Complete an **Approved Multi-Crew Co-operation Course**.

   - Completion of this course is **only** required by CPL(H)/IR holders who have not graduated from an ATPL(H) Integrated course but who wish to obtain an initial type rating on a multi-pilot helicopter.

FULL DETAILS OF MCC ARE GIVEN IN JAR-FCL 2.261 & SECTION F10.

G3.4 JAR-FCL ATPL (H) SKILL TEST REQUIREMENTS

An applicant for a JAR-FCL ATPL (H) is required to:

1. Pass the **ATPL (H) Skill Test** with an authorised Type Rating Examiner.

   - The applicant shall demonstrate the ability to perform as Pilot-in-Command of a helicopter type certificated for a minimum of two pilots under IFR, the procedures and manoeuvres required with a degree of competency appropriate to the privileges granted to the holder of an ATPL (H).
   - The Skill Test may serve as a skill test for the issue of the licence **and** a proficiency check for the revalidation of the type rating for the helicopter used in the test, and may be combined with the skill test for the issue of a multi-pilot type rating

- The Skill Test may not be taken until **all** of the flying experience requirements for the grant of the licence have been met together with the required theoretical knowledge.

FULL DETAILS OF THE ATPL (H) SKILL TEST ARE DETAILED IN APPENDICES 1 & 2 TO JAR-FCL 2.240 & 2.295.

G3.5 JAR-FCL ATPL (H) CONVERSION OF A NON-JAA PROFESSIONAL LICENCE

A licence issued by a non-JAA State may be converted to a JAR-FCL licence provided that an arrangement exists between the JAA and the non-JAA State. This arrangement shall be established on the basis of reciprocity of licence acceptance and shall ensure that an equivalent level of safety exists between the training and testing requirements of the JAA and non-JAA State. Until such arrangements exist, the following requirements have been agreed by the JAA and are now incorporated in JAR-FCL 2, paragraph 2.016;

The holder of a **current and valid** ATPL (H) issued in accordance with ICAO Annex 1 by a non-JAA State may be with a JAR-FCL ATPL (H) providing the experience requirements of JAR-FCL 2.280 have been met. Applicants must:

- Hold a valid JAR-FCL Class 1 medical certificate;
- Undertake ATPL (H) theoretical knowledge instruction as determined by the Head of Training of an approved training provider, and pass ALL of the JAR-FCL theoretical knowledge examinations at ATPL (H) level;
- Qualify for the issue of a UK Flight Radio Telephony Operator's Licence (FRTOL) – **Section B** refers.
- Undertake a multi-pilot helicopter type rating course at an approved TRTO for a helicopter type certificated for a minimum crew of two pilots under IFR in accordance with FAR/JAR 27 and 29 helicopter category; or equivalent code; or helicopter required to be operated by two pilots under JAR-OPS.
- Pass the ATPL (H) skill test in accordance with Appendices 1 and 2 to JAR-FCL 2.240 and 2.295 with, or observed by, a CAA Flight Operations Training Inspector.

Note: ATPL (H) holders who have a minimum of 1000 hours flying experience as PIC or Co-pilot on multi-pilot helicopters and hold a valid multi-pilot type rating for the helicopter to be used for the ATPL (H) skill test <u>and</u> have at least 500 hours experience as pilot on that type, will be exempted from the requirements to complete an approved TRTO course or undergo approved training prior to undertaking the theoretical knowledge examinations, and the skill test. Pilots with less than 500 hours experience as pilot on the type to be used for the ATPL (H) skill test will be exempted from the requirements to undergo approved training prior to undertaking the theoretical knowledge examinations but will still be required to complete an approved type rating course. However, the course may be reduced to take account of previous experience on the same type upon recommendation by the TRTO to PLD.

The holder of a current and valid ATPL (H) **who does not qualify for the grant of a JAR-FCL ATPL (H)**, as detailed above, can still apply for a JAR-FCL CPL (H)/IR, details can be found in Section D4.5.

G3.6 JAR-FCL ATPL (H) UK FLIGHT RADIOTELEPHONY OPERATOR'S LICENCE (FRTOL) REQUIREMENTS

An applicant for a UK FRTOL is required to pass the Radiotelephony written examination and practical test with an authorised RTF Examiner. It should be noted that whilst Radio Communication forms part of the JAR-FCL ATPL (H) training syllabus, the FRTOL remains a UK national licence.

FULL DETAILS OF THE FRTOL REQUIREMENTS INCLUDING CREDITS AVAILABLE ARE CONTAINED IN SECTION B.

G3.7 JAR-FCL ATPL (H) MEDICAL REQUIREMENTS

An applicant for a JAR-FCL ATPL (H) shall hold a valid JAR-FCL Class 1 Medical Certificate.

FULL DETAILS OF THE MEDICAL REQUIREMENTS ARE CONTAINED IN JAR-FCL 3 AND SECTION A6.

G4 JAR-FCL ATPL (HELICOPTER) FOR UK QUALIFIED SERVICE PILOTS (HELICOPTERS)

There is no direct route to a JAR-FCL ATPL (H) for a QSP (H).

In order to qualify for a JAR-FCL ATPL(H), applicants must also qualify for a JAR-FCL IR(H) and a JAR-FCL multi-pilot helicopter type rating (i.e. certificated for a minimum of two pilots under IFR, or required to be operated by two pilots under JAR-OPS).

Full details of the JAR-FCL ATPL (H) requirements, including credits available, are detailed in Section G3.

A QSP (H) should refer to Section D6 for details of the requirements to obtain a JAR-FCL CPL (H).

G5 LICENCE RE-ISSUE

G5.1 LICENCE RE-ISSUE

For a licence to be valid, a pilot must hold a current medical certificate appropriate to the licence held, and have a valid aircraft rating.

Note for UK BCPL(A) Holders

The medical certificate required for the re-issue of a UK BCPL(A) shall be a JAR-FCL Class 1 medical certificate.

Note for Professional Licence Holders

The holder of a professional licence who only intends to fly privately, may continue to have their professional licence re-issued, but will be required to hold a valid medical certificate appropriate to the licence held. The licence cannot be re-issued with a lower class of medical. Alternatively, to take advantage of the lower class of medical, a Private Pilot Licence may be obtained.

60 Day Rule

Applicants may apply for the re-issue of a licence within a period of 60 days prior to the expiry date of the licence.

Holders of a lifetime UK PPL should note that the licence itself is un-expiring, but the privileges conferred by it, and by any ratings in it, may only be exercised when the licence and the appropriate ratings are valid. Re-validation or renewal of the appropriate rating(s) is specified in **Section F.** Details to revalidate or renew a FRTOL (if held) are specified in Section B.

A UK National or JAR-FCL Pilot's Licence will be re-issued for a further period (5 or 10 year validity as appropriate to the licence held) subject to meeting the following:-

1. hold a medical certificate appropriate to the licence being re-issued valid for the first day of issue of the new licence.

2. have held a valid Certificate of Test, Certificate of Experience or Certificate of Revalidation for any type/class rating that has not expired by more than 5 years*.

*Applicants who are currently flying under the privileges of a non-UK ICAO licence and are currently flying an aircraft type endorsed within their UK or JAR-FCL licence, may have their licence re-issued by holding a valid medical certificate appropriate to the licence being re-issued. A QSP in current flying practice on any military aircraft type (aeroplane for re-issue of aeroplane licence and helicopter re-issue of helicopter licence) may have their licence re-issued by holding a valid medical certificate appropriate to the licence being re-issue.

Applicants who are not flying an aircraft endorsed within their UK or JAR-FCL licence may not have their licence renewed until such time as an appropriate valid medical certificate and Certificate of revalidation are obtained. Applicants may either renew an existing rating within their UK or JAR-FCL licence or may wish to transfer a type/class rating that he/she is currently flying under the privileges of their non-UK ICAO licence. Renewal of appropriate ratings or the transfer of type/class ratings is specified in Section F.

Expired Licences

If the holder of an expired UK National or JAR-FCL pilot's licence has held a valid Certificate of Test, Certificate of Experience or Certificate of Revalidation for any type/class rating that has not expired by more than 5 years, then only the appropriate valid medical certificate must be obtained to re-issue the licence.

If the holder of a UK National or JAR-FCL pilot's licence has not held a valid Certificate of Test, Certificate of Experience or Certificate of Revalidation for any type/class rating that has expired by more than 5 years** they may not have their licence re-issued until such time as an appropriate valid medical certificate and Certificate of Revalidation are obtained. Applicants may either renew an existing rating within their UK or JAR-FCL licence or may wish to transfer a type/class rating that he/she is currently flying under the privileges of their non-UK ICAO licence. Renewal of appropriate ratings or the transfer of type/class ratings is specified in Section F.

** Where an applicant can show that he/she is currently flying under the privileges of a non-UK ICAO licence and are flying an aircraft endorsed within their UK or JAR-FCL licence, they may have their licence re-issued by holding a valid UK or JAR-FCL medical certificate as appropriate to the licence being re-issued. A QSP in current flying practice on any military aircraft type (aeroplane for re-issue of aeroplane licence and helicopter re-issue of helicopter licence) may have their licence re-issued by holding a valid medical certificate appropriate to the licence being re-issue.

FRTOL Re-validation/renewal

Details to revalidate or renew a FRTOL (if held) are specified in Section B.

SECTION H

INSTRUCTOR RATINGS

The UK Civil Aviation Authority currently issues the following categories of Instructor Ratings.

Each section details the requirements to obtain each and maintain each rating, including flying training, ground examinations and flight tests.

H1 JAR FCL FI(A) & FI(H) RATINGS

This section offers information as a basic guide to obtaining an Instructor Rating (Aeroplane), (Helicopter) and (Flight Engineer).

H1.1 GENERAL INFORMATION

The circumstances under which an Instructor Rating is required are set out in Article 36 of the Air Navigation Order 2005. In general, a valid Instructor Rating is required if flying instruction is given for the purposes of a person becoming qualified for the grant of a licence or for the inclusion or variation of any rating in a licence.

Pre-requisites

All instructors shall unless specified otherwise:

i. hold at least the licence, rating and qualification for which instruction is being given, and

ii. have at least 15 hours experience as pilot on the type or class of aeroplane on which instruction is being given, and

iii. shall be entitled to act as pilot-in-command of the aircraft during such training.

JAA Instructor Ratings are issued in accordance with the requirements of JAR-FCL 1, 2 and 4 Subpart H. JAR-FCL 1.305 specifies the following categories of instructor (Aeroplanes):

a. Flight Instructor – Aeroplane (FI (A))

b. Type Rating Instructor – Aeroplane (TRI (A))

c. Class Rating Instructor – Aeroplane (CRI (A))

d. Instrument Rating Instructor – (IRI (A))

e. Synthetic Flight Instructor – Aeroplane (SFI (A))

f. Multi Crew Co-operation Instructor Authorisation Aeroplanes (MCCI(A))

g. Synthetic Training Instructor - (STI(A))

JAR-FCL 2.305 specifies the following categories of instructor (Helicopters):

a. Flight Instructor – Helicopter (FI (H))

b. Type Rating Instructor – Helicopter (TRI (H))

c. Instrument Rating Instructor – Helicopter (IRI (H))

d. Synthetic Flight Instructor (SFI (H))

JAR-FCL 4.305 specifies the following categories of instructor (Flight Engineer):

a. Flight Engineer Instructor Rating - TRI(E)

b. Synthetic Flight Engineer Instructor - SFI(E)

The restricted rating does not confer privileges for Night, Applied Instrument, Aerobatic or Multi-Engine instruction without additional training and the formal removal of a limitation imposed when the rating is issued. A Flight instructor may add the privileges of the IRI and CRI to the basic FI rating without need for an additional instructor rating, provided additional training and authorisation is completed. The IRI and CRI ratings may be regarded as standalone ratings for instructors without basic FI privileges.

Holders of JAR-FCL licences which contain appropriate Instructor Ratings (and Examiner Authorisations) may exercise the privileges of the ratings/authorisations included in their licences on Microlight aeroplanes and SLMG's but shall first undertake any necessary differences training. Also, for the SLMG there is a single type of Instructor Rating known as the Restricted Flying Instructors Rating (SLMG) (usually known as the MGIR-Motor Glider Instructors Rating). Assistant Flying Instructor (AFI) and Flying Instructor (FI) Ratings are issued for microlight aeroplanes (for further details, please refer to Sections H8 and H9.

Remuneration

In order to receive payment for flight instruction, an instructor must hold a valid professional pilots licence and valid JAR-FCL Class 1 Medical Certificate. Instructors who hold valid private pilot licences and valid JAR-FCL Class 2 Medical Certificate are entitled to instruct but cannot receive payment for this service*.

* This does not apply to the holder of a UK PPL(H) who qualified prior to 1 January 2000 under national arrangements.

Minimum Age

An applicant for a Flight Instructor Rating shall be at least 18 years of age.

Validities

All instructor ratings issued in accordance with JAR-FCL are valid for three years from the date of passing the Skill Test.

H1.2 FI(A) RATING

Restricted Privileges

Subject to any other conditions specified in JARs, the holder of a JAR-FCL FI(A) will be restricted to the following, carried out under the supervision of FI(A) authorised for the purpose:

a. Flight instruction for the issue of the JAR-FCL PPL(A) or those parts of a CPL or ATPL(A) integrated course at PPL(A) level. Class and Type ratings for single engine aeroplanes, excluding approval of first solo flights by day or by night and first solo navigation flights by day or by night; and

b. Night flying instruction, provided a night qualification or rating is held (if applicable), the ability to instruct at night has been demonstrated to a FI(A) authorised to conduct FI(A) training in accordance with JAR-FCL 1.330(f) and the night currency requirement of JAR-FCL 1.026 is satisfied.

JAR-FCL 1.325 refers.

For removal of the supervisory restriction, please refer to Section H1.4.

FI(A) Privileges and Requirements

The privileges of the holder of a FI(A) rating (for restrictions refer to Restricted Privileges above) are to conduct flight instruction for:-

a. the issue of the PPL(A) and class and type ratings for single-engine aeroplanes;

b. the issue of a CPL(A), provided that the FI(A) has completed at least 500 hours of flight time as pilot of aeroplanes including at least 200 hours of flight instruction;

c. night flying, provided a night qualification is held, the ability to instruct at night has been demonstrated to an FI(A) authorised to conduct FI(A) training (see Section H1.4 - Removal of No Night Instruction Restriction) and the night currency requirement of JAR-FCL 1.026 is satisfied;

d. the issue of an IR(A) provided that the instructor has met the requirements as detailed in Section H1.4 - Removal of No Applied Instrument Restriction;

e. the issue of single-pilot multi-engine type or class rating, provided that the instructor meets the requirements of JAR-FCL 1.380(a)(see Section H1.4 - Addition of Single Pilot Multi-Engine Privileges);

f. the issue of a FI(A) rating, provided that the instructor:

   i. has completed at least 500 hours of instruction in aeroplanes, and

   ii. has demonstrated to a FI(A) examiner the ability to instruct a FI(A) during a Skill Test conducted in accordance with JAR-FCL Appendix 1 to JAR-FCL 1.330 & 1.345, and

   iii. is authorised by the Authority for this purpose.

Pre-requisite flight and theoretical requirements

Before commencing an approved Flight Instructors Course (FIC) an applicant must satisfy the course pre-entry requirements as per JAR-FCL 1.335: -

a. Hold either a valid UK CAA or JAR-FCL aeroplane pilots licence, which includes a valid Single Engine Piston (Land) Class or single pilot, Single Engine Type Rating.

b. Meet the knowledge requirements for the grant of a JAR-FCL Commercial Pilot Licence (Aeroplanes) as per Appendix 1 to JAR-FCL 1.470.

c. Have at least a CPL(A) or completed at least 200 hours of flight time of which 150 hours as Pilot-in-Command if holding a PPL(A).

   i. Completed at least 30 hours on single engine piston powered aeroplanes of which at least 5 hours shall be in the six months preceding the pre-entry flight test.

   ii. Completed at least 10 hours instrument flight instruction in aeroplanes of which not more than 5 hours may be instrument ground time in a FNPT or a flight simulator.

   iii. Completed at least 20 hours of cross-country flight as PIC of aeroplanes, including a cross-country flight of at least 540km (300 nm) in the course of which full-stop landings at two aerodromes different from the aerodromes of departure shall be made.

   iv. Pass a specific pre-entry flight test with a FI qualified as per JAR-FCL 1.330(f) based upon the proficiency check as per JAR-FCL 1.240(b), **within the six months preceding the start of the course. ***

*The pre-entry flight test will assess the ability of the applicant to undertake the course.

Flight Instructor flight and theoretical training requirements - FI(A) Course

An applicant for the FI(A) rating shall have completed an approved course of both flight and theoretical knowledge instruction training at an approved FTO. The course is intended to train the applicant to give instruction on single engine aeroplanes up to PPL(A) standard. This must include the particular requirements specified below and each of these requirements must be met in full.

a. The flight instruction shall comprise at least 30 hours of flight training of which:

   i. 25 hours must be dual instruction;

   ii. 5 hours may be as mutual flying with another FI applicant.

b. 125 hours of theoretical knowledge instruction, to include:

   i. 40 hours tuition;

   ii. 78 hours teaching practise;

   iii. 7 hours progress tests.

Note:

- 5 hours of the dual instruction requirement may be conducted in a flight simulator or FNPT approved for the purpose by the Authority.
- The above course can also include the training requirements to allow night instruction, as detailed below.

Refer to JAR-FCL 1.340

Credits from JAR-FCL FI Theoretical Training

Holders of other valid instructor ratings issued in accordance with JAR-FCL will be credited the teaching and learning element of the theoretical knowledge training.

H1.3 FI(A) SKILL TEST REQUIREMENTS

An applicant for a FI rating shall demonstrate to an examiner, notified by the Authority for this purpose, the ability to instruct a student pilot to the level required for the issue of a PPL(A), including pre-flight, post-flight and theoretical knowledge instruction. The Skill Test is additional to the flight training course.

H1.4 FI(A) RATING FLIGHT AND THEORETICAL TRAINING REQUIREMENTS TO REMOVE FLIGHT INSTRUCTOR RESTRICTIONS

Removal of Supervisory Restriction

a. The Supervisory Restriction can be removed on the recommendation of the supervising FI(A) once the applicant has at least 100 hours flight instruction and, in addition, has supervised at least 25 student solo flights.

It should be noted that supervision of a students PPL(A) qualifying cross country flight is counted as one flight only*. Approval of first solo flights by day or night and first solo navigation flights by day or night are excluded.

*For the supervision of other multi-leg non-qualifying cross-country flights, each leg will be counted as an individual flight provided they are entered as such on the application for removal of this restriction.

Removal of No Night Instruction Restriction

a. Hold either a Night Qualification or Night Rating (Aeroplanes) and be in current flying practice.

b. Complete at least 1 hour of flight training at night and a minimum of 2 hours of theoretical training. All training to be conducted by an FIC Instructor at an approved FIC Flight Training Organisation (FTO). Obtain recommendation from FIC Instructor for the removal of the restriction.

Removal of No Applied Instrument Restriction

a. Hold either a valid single pilot, Instrument Rating (IR(A)) or Instrument Meteorological Conditions (IMC) Rating.

b. Hold a valid FI(A) with Supervisory Restriction removed.

c. Have flown at least 200 hours flight time in accordance with Instrument Flight Rules (IFR), of which up to 50 hours may be instrument ground time in an approved flight simulator or FNPT II. Where pilots have recorded flight by sole reference to instruments and not under IFR then 1 hour of flight by sole reference to instruments may be counted as 4 hours flight by IFR. Where pilots wish solely to instruct for the IMC Rating a reduced experience level of 10 hours flight time by sole reference to instruments is applicable and;

d. Complete an approved course comprising at least 5 hours dual flight training on instruments in an aeroplane, flight simulator or FNPT 2 and 10 hours of theoretical training. All training to be conducted by FIC Instructor qualified to conduct instrument training at an approved FIC FTO.

e. Pass the relevant elements of a FI Skill Test in a single pilot aeroplane with a suitably qualified FIE(A).

In addition, for the issue of an IR(A) multi-engine aeroplanes the instructor shall meet the requirements of JAR-FCL 1.380(a) (see Section H3.3)

Removal of No Aerobatics Restriction (UK CAA issued restriction)

Meet the requirements as specified below.

a. Hold a valid FI(A) rating.

b. To qualify for the removal of the restriction on aerobatics flight instruction from the FI(A) rating, the holder will be required to complete training specified in c) below at an approved FIC FTO under a FIC Instructor qualified to conduct aerobatics training.

c. Training must consist of at least 5 hours of aerobatics flight training and 8 hours of theoretical training in accordance with a recognised syllabus.

d. Obtain recommendation from FIC Instructor for the removal of the restriction.

Addition of Single Pilot Multi-Engine Privileges to FI(A)

a. Hold a valid single pilot Multi-Engine Piston (Land) Class or single pilot Multi-Engine Type Rating.

b. Hold a valid FI(A) with Supervisory Restriction removed.

c. Have flown at least 500 hours flight time as pilot of aeroplanes.

d. Have flown at least 30 hours as Pilot in Command (PIC) on the applicable type or class of aeroplane prior to commencing the course. It should be noted that ME SPIC time is not allowable towards this 30 hours requirement.

e. Complete an approved course at an approved FTO or TRTO including at least 10 hours of theoretical training and 5 hours flight instruction on the aeroplane or a flight simulator given by an instructor approved for this purpose (see Appendix 1 to JAR-FCL 1.380 and AMC FCL 1.380).

f. Pass the relevant elements of a FI Skill Test in a single pilot, multi-engine aeroplane with a suitably qualified FIE(A)

Addition of Aeroplane (Sea) (not Microlights) Privileges to FI(A)

Note: The holder of a FI(A) rating who wishes to extend the privileges to Seaplanes should refer to Section H6.

H1.5 FI(H) RATING

Restricted Privileges

Subject to any other conditions, specified in JARs, the holder of a JAR-FCL FI(H) will be restricted to the following carried out under the supervision of a FI(H) authorised for the purpose:

a. Flight instruction for the issue of a JAR-FCL PPL(H) or those parts of a CPL(H) or ATPL(H) integrated course at PPL(H) level and type ratings for single pilot, single engine helicopters, excluding approval of first solo flight by day or by night and first solo navigation flight by day or by night; and

b. Night flying instruction, provided a helicopter night qualification or rating is held (as applicable), the ability to instruct at night has been demonstrated to a FI(H) training in accordance with JAR-FCL 2.330 (f) and the night currency requirement of JAR-FCL 2.026 is satisfied.

FI(H) Privileges and Requirements

Provided that in the preceding 12 months the FI(H) has completed not less than 15 hours of flight instruction (which may include skill testing/proficiency checking) on single-pilot helicopters, or passed, as a proficiency check, the skill test set out in Appendices 1 & 2 to JAR-FCL 2.330 & 2.345, the privileges of the holder of a FI(H) rating (for restrictions refer to Restricted Privileges above) are to conduct flight instruction for the issue of:-

a. a PPL(H);

b. a CPL(H), provided that the FI(H) has completed at least 500 hours of flight time as a pilot of helicopters including at least 200 hours of flight instruction;

c. type ratings for single-pilot single engine helicopters;

d. a helicopter night qualification, provided the FI(H) has met the requirements as detailed in Section H1.7 - Removal of No Night Instruction Restriction;

e. an instrument rating, provided that the FI(H) has:

   i. at least 200 hours of instrument flight time in helicopters of which up to 50 hours may be instrument ground time in a flight simulator or FNPT II; and

   ii. completed as a student an approved course comprising of at least 5 hours of flight instruction in a helicopter, flight simulator or FNPT II (see Appendix 1 to JAR-FCL 2.395 and AMC FCL 2.395) and have passed the appropriate skill test as set out in Appendix 1 to JAR-FCL 2.330 and 2.345;

f. single-pilot multi-engine type rating, provided the FI(H) meets the requirements of JAR-FCL 2.365(a), (b), (d) and (f); and has:

   i. at least 50 hours as pilot-in-command of single-pilot multi-engine helicopters, including at least 5 hours flight time on the same type of helicopter to be used for the skill test;

   ii. completed as a student an approved course of at least 5 hours of flight instruction on the helicopter or a flight simulator of the helicopter type concerned (see Appendix 1 to JAR-FCL 2.365 and AMC FCL 2.365; and

   iii. passed a skill test for the initial issue of a single-pilot multi-engine FI(H) rating as set out in Appendix 1 to JAR-FCL 2.330 and 2.345.

g. A FI(H) rating, provided the FI(H) has:-

   i. completed at least 500 hours of flight instruction in helicopters;

   ii. demonstrated to a FIE(H) the ability to instruct a FI(H) during a skill test in accordance with Appendix 1 to JAR-FCL 2.330 and 2.345; and

   iii. is authorised by the Authority for this purpose.

Pre-requisite flight and theoretical knowledge requirements

Before commencing an approved Flight Instructors Course an applicant must satisfy all of the following course pre-entry requirements:

a. Hold either a valid UK CAA or JAR-FCL Pilot Licence that includes a valid type rating on the specific type to be used in the FI Skill Test.

b. Meet the knowledge requirements for the grant of a JAR-FCL CPL(H) as per Appendix 2 to JAR-FCL 2.470.

c. Completed at least 250 hours of flight time of which at least 100 hours shall be as Pilot-in-Command if holding a ATPL(H) or

CPL(H) or 200 hours as Pilot-in-Command if holding a PPL(H);

i. Received at least 10 hours instrument flight instruction of which not more than 5 hours may be instrument ground time in a FNPT II or flight simulator;

ii. Completed at least 20 hours of cross-country flight as PIC of helicopters;

iii. Pass a specific pre-entry flight test with a FI qualified as per JAR-FCL 2.330(f) based upon the proficiency check as per JAR-FCL 2.240(b), **within the six months preceding the start of the course***.

* The pre-entry flight test will assess the ability of the applicant to undertake the course.

Flight and Theoretical Training Requirements - FI(H) Course

An applicant for the FI(H) rating shall have completed an approved course of both flight and theoretical knowledge instruction training at an approved FTO. The course is intended to train the applicant to give instruction on single engine helicopters up to PPL(H) standard. This must include the particular requirements specified below and each of these requirements must be met in full.

a. The flight instruction shall comprise at least 30 hours of flight training of which:

   i. 25 hours must be dual instruction.

   ii. 5 hours may be as mutual flying with another FI applicant.

b. 125 hours of theoretical knowledge instruction to include:

   i. 40 hours tuition;

   ii. 78 hours teaching practice;

   iii. 7 hours progress tests

   - 5 hours of the dual instruction requirement may be conducted in a flight simulator or FNPT approved for the purpose by the Authority.

   - The above course can also include the training requirements to allow night instruction.

Credits from JAR-FCL FI Theoretical Training

- Holders of a valid instructor rating will be credited the teaching and learning element of the theoretical knowledge training.

H1.6 FI(H) SKILL TEST REQUIREMENTS

An applicant for a FI(H) rating shall demonstrate to an examiner, notified by the Authority for this purpose, the ability to instruct a student pilot to the level required for the issue of a PPL(H), including pre-flight, post flight and theoretical knowledge instruction. The skill test is additional to the flight training course.

H1.7 FI(H) RATING FLIGHT AND THEORETICAL TRAINING REQUIREMENTS TO EXTEND PRIVILEGES OR REMOVE FLIGHT INSTRUCTOR RESTRICTIONS

Addition of other single pilot, single engine helicopter type to FI(H) providing that the FI(H) has completed not less than 15 flight hours on that specific type in the preceding 12 months.

Removal of Supervisory Restriction

The Supervisory Restriction can be removed on the recommendation of the supervising FI(H) once the applicant has at least 100 hours flight instruction and, in addition, has supervised at least 25 student solo flight air exercises.

It should be noted that supervision of a students PPL(H) qualifying cross country flight is counted as one flight only. Approval of first solo flights by day or night and first solo navigation flights by day or night are excluded.

UK AFI(H) holders who are also required to upgrade to FI(H) using the same procedure as above, either before or at the same time as upgrading, must also remove the No Instrument instruction restriction as detailed below.

Removal of No Night Instruction Restriction

a. Hold either a Night Qualification or Night Rating (Helicopter) and be in current flying practice.

b. Complete at least 1 hour of flight training at night and 5 hours of theoretical training. All training to be conducted by a FIC Instructor at an approved FIC Flight Training Organisation (FTO). This flight training should include a night navigation instructional exercise and night emergencies in addition to circuit and landing work. Obtain recommendation from the FIC Instructor for the removal of the restriction.

Removal of No Instrument Instruction Restriction (for UK AFI or UK FI(H) holders only) - for PPL(H) Instrument Instructors

a. For holders of a UK PPL(H) the "out of sight of ground or water" restriction will need to be removed before training for the removal of the No Instrument instruction restriction is commenced. To remove the restriction, a licence holder must produce evidence of at least 5 hours instruction in instrument flying in a helicopter with a helicopter flying instructor and be certified as competent to fly a helicopter by sole reference to instruments.

b. Hold a current AFI or FI(H).

c. Complete at least 5 hours dual flight training by sole reference to instruments in a helicopter and 7 hours of theoretical training related to instruments. All training to be conducted by a FIC Instructor qualified to conduct instrument training.

d. Complete the ground and flight elements of Exercise 27 of the JAR-FCL 2 FI(H) syllabus with a FIC/FIE. The final flight and pre-flight brief are to be conducted as a FI Skill Test with a suitably qualified FIE(H)

An AFI(H) or FI(H) who does not meet the requirements to remove the restrictions as set out above, shall not hold the privilege to instruct a PPL(H) student in flight by sole reference to instruments.

To instruct for an Instrument Rating, the requirements of JAR-FCL 2.330(e) will need to be met (see FI(H) - Privileges and Requirements - Section H1.7).

H1.8 MILITARY CONCESSIONS FOR ISSUE OF A FI(A)

Credit is available only to holders of a CFS QFI category. The holder of any other military instructor qualification will not qualify for any credit against the FI(A) rating requirements.

a. The following terms are for holders of a valid CFS QFI category who has completed a CFS standardisation check (with a CFS Agent, and been granted a Certificate to Instruct) on single-pilot, single engine piston powered aeroplanes, within the 12 months preceding the date of receipt of the FI(A) application. The holder of a valid CFS QFI category who does not meet this requirement should refer to paragraph (b) of this section. The holder of a non-valid CFS QFI category, including ex-QSPs, should refer to paragraph (c).

b. The holder of a valid CFS QFI category who, in the 12 months has not completed a CFS standardisation check (and/or been granted a Certificate to Instruct) on single-pilot, single engine piston powered aeroplanes, will be required to complete training at the discretion of the Head of Training of a FTO approved to conduct Flight Instructor (Aeroplane) Courses, and pass a FI(A) skill test with an authorised examiner.

c. The holder of a lapsed QFI category including ex QSPs will be required to apply to PLD for an assessment.

Privileges

a. CFS Category B2 will equate to a FI(A) with all restrictions as per JAR-FCL 1.325. For details of these restrictions and their removal please refer to Section H1.4.

b. CFS Category B1, with at least 200 hours flight instruction, will equate to a FI(A) without the Supervisory Restriction. All other restrictions will be endorsed and to remove the restrictions please refer to Section H1.4.

c. CFS Categories A1 and A2 will equate to a FI(A) with no restrictions other than single pilot, single engine aeroplanes.

Pre-requisite Flight and Theoretical Requirements

a. Hold either a valid UK CAA or JAR-FCL Pilots Licence that includes a valid Single Engine Piston (Land) Class or Single Pilot, Single Engine Type Rating, and a FRTO licence.

b. CFS Standardisation Check in the last 12 months preceding the application.

c. Meet the knowledge requirements for the grant of a JAR-FCL Commercial Pilot Licence (Aeroplanes) as per AMC FCL 1.470(b). Alternatively have taken advantage of the Military Accreditation scheme towards a JAR-FCL ATPL(A).

d. Have at least 200 hours of flight time of which:

   i. PPL(A) holder shall have at least 150 hours as PIC or

   ii. CPL/ATPL(A) holder shall have at least 100 hours as PIC.

e. PPL/CPL/ATPL(A) holder shall have at least:

i. At least 30 hours on Single Engine Piston powered aeroplanes of **which at least 5 hours shall be in the 12 months preceding application.**

ii. At least 10 hours instrument flight instruction of which not more than 5 hours may be instrument ground time in a FNPT or a flight simulator.

iii. At least 20 hours of cross-country flight as PIC, including a cross-country flight of at least 540km (300 nm) in the course of which full-stop landings at two aerodromes different from the aerodrome of departure shall be made.

H1.9 MILITARY CONCESSIONS FOR ISSUE OF FI(H)

Credit is available only to holders of a CFS QHI category. The holder of any other military instructor qualification will not qualify for any credit against the FI(H) rating requirements.

a. The following terms are for holders of a valid CFS QHI category who has completed a CFS standardisation check (with a CFS Agent, and been granted a Certificate to Instruct) on single-pilot, single engine helicopters, within the 12 months preceding the date of receipt of the FI(H) application. The holder of a valid CFS QHI category who does not meet this requirement should refer to paragraph (b) of this section. The holder of a non-valid CFS QHI category, including ex-QSPs, should refer to paragraph (c).

b. The holder of a valid CFS QHI category who, in the 12 months has not completed a CFS standardisation check (and/or been granted a Certificate to Instruct) on single-pilot, single engine helicopters, will be required to complete training at the discretion of the Head of Training of a FTO approved to conduct Flight Instructor (Helicopter) Courses, and pass a FI(H) skill test with an authorised examiner.

c. The holder of a lapsed QHI category including ex QSPs will be required to apply to PLD for an assessment.

Privileges

a. CFS Category B2 will equate to a FI(H) with all restrictions.

b. CFS Category B1 with at least 200 hours flight instruction will equate to a FI(H) without the Supervisory Restrictions on any SP SE helicopter.

c. CFS Categories A1 and A2 will equate to a FI(H) with no restrictions endorsed other than single pilot, single engine helicopters.

Pre-requisite Flight and Theoretical Requirements

Before commencing a Flight Instructors Course (FIC) an applicant must satisfy the course pre-entry requirements as per JAR-FCL 2.335:

a. Hold either a valid UK CAA or JAR-FCL Pilots Licence, which includes a valid type rating on the specific type to be used in the FI Skill Test.

b. CFS Standardisation Check in the last 12 months preceding application (see below).

c. Meet the knowledge requirements for the grant of a JAR-FCL Commercial Pilot Licence (Helicopters) as per AMC FCL 2.470(b). Alternatively have taken advantage of the Military Accreditation scheme towards a JAR-FCL ATPL(A).

d. Have at least 250 hours of flight time in helicopters of which:

i. PPL(H) holder shall have at least 200 hours as PIC or.

ii. CPL/ATPL(H) holder shall have at least 100 hours as PIC.

e. PPL/CPL/ATPL(H) holder shall have completed:

i. At least 10 hours instrument flight instruction of which not more than 5 hours may be instrument ground time in a FNPT or a flight simulator.

ii. At least 20 hours of cross-country flight as PIC of helicopters.

iii. At least 15 hours on single pilot, single engine helicopters in the preceding 12 months.

H1.10 TRANSFERRING A FI(A) RATING FROM A NON-JAA STATE LICENCE

The UK CAA has aligned the training and testing for the grant of flight instructor ratings (aeroplanes) with JAR-FCL 1. Licences and ratings issued by a full Joint Aviation Authority (JAA) Member State in accordance with provisions of JAR-FCL are to be accepted without formality by all other full JAA Member States. **Therefore, the requirements set out in this part are**

only applicable to pilots seeking to convert a flight instructor rating (aeroplanes) issued by a non-JAA State.

This section also applies only to converting basic flight instructor privileges and restrictions similar to those issued to a full course JAR-FCL FI(A).

Pre-requisites flight and theoretical requirements

Before commencing a Flight Instructors Course (FIC) an applicant must satisfy the course pre-entry requirements:

a. Hold either a valid UK CAA or JAR-FCL aeroplane pilot's licence, which includes a valid Single Engine Piston (Land) Class or single pilot, Single Engine Type Rating.

b. Meet the knowledge requirements for the grant of a JAR-FCL Commercial Pilot Licence (Aeroplanes), as per Appendix 1 to JAR-FCL 1.470.

c. Have at least a CPL(A) or completed at least 200 hours of flight time of which 150 hours as Pilot-in-Command if holding a PPL(A).

d. i. Completed at least 30 hours on single engine piston aeroplanes of which at least 5 hours shall be in the six months preceding the pre-entry flight test.

ii. Completed at least 10 hours instrument flight instruction in aeroplanes of which not more than 5 hours may be instrument ground time in a FNPT or a flight simulator.

iii. Completed at least 20 hours of cross-country flight as PIC of aeroplanes, including a cross-country flight of at least 540km (300 nm) in the course of which full-stop landings at two aerodromes different from the aerodrome of departure shall be made.

iv. Pass a specific pre-entry flight test with a FI qualified as per JAR-FCL 1.330(f) based upon the proficiency check as per JAR-FCL 1.240(b), within the six months preceding the start of the course.*

* The pre-entry flight test will assess the ability of the applicant to undertake the course. FIC Flight and Theoretical Training Requirements

An applicant for the FI(A) rating shall have completed an approved course of both flight and theoretical knowledge instruction training at an approved FTO. The course is intended to train the applicant to give instruction on single engine aeroplanes up to PPL(A) standard.

a. This must include at least 15 hours of dual flight training and 30 hours of theoretical knowledge instruction.

Skill Test Requirement

a. Pass the relevant elements of a FI Skill Test in a single pilot, single engine aeroplane with a suitably qualified FIE(A).

Flight and Theoretical Training Requirements to Remove Instructional Restrictions

To remove any of the restrictions endorsed, please see Section H1.4.

Specific Authorisation (JAR-FCL 1.300 (a)(2))

Applicants who hold a specific authorisation issued by the UK CAA in accordance with Appendix 1 to JAR-FCL 1.300 who also complies with the requirements of JAR-FCL 1.355 and hold a JAR-FCL licence will be deemed to have fulfilled the requirements for the issue of a FI(A) rating, subject to the initial restrictions set out in JAR-FCL 1.325 (see H1.4). For full details please refer to Appendix 1 to JAR-FCL 1.300.

H1.11 TRANSFERRING A FI(H) RATING FROM A NON-JAA STATE LICENCE

Licences and ratings issued by one full Joint Aviation Authority (JAA) Member State in accordance with provisions of JAR-FCL are required to be accepted, without formality, by all other full JAA Member States. Therefore, the requirements set out in this part are only applicable to pilots seeking to convert a flight instructor rating (helicopters). A rating issued by a non-JAA State may be transferred to a UK or JAR-FCL licence provided that an arrangement exists between the JAA and the non-JAA State. This arrangement shall be established on the basis of reciprocity of licence acceptance and shall ensure that an equivalent level of safety exists between the training and testing requirements of the JAA and non-JAA State. Until such arrangements exist, the following requirements have been agreed by the JAA.

This section also applies only to converting basic flight instructor privileges and restrictions similar to those issued to a full course.

Pre-requisite Flight and Theoretical Requirements

Before commencing a Flight Instructors Course an applicant must satisfy the course pre-entry requirements:

a. Hold either a valid UK CAA or JAR-FCL Pilots Licence, which includes a valid type rating on the specific type to be used in the FI Skill Test.

b. Meet the knowledge requirements for the grant of a JAR-FCL Commercial Pilot Licence (Helicopters) as per Appendix 1 to JAR-FCL 2.470.

c. Completed at least 250 hours of flight time in helicopters of which at least 100 hours shall be as Pilot-in-Command if holding a ATPL(H) or CPL(H) or 200 hours as Pilot-in-Command if holding a PPL(H);

d. i. Received at least 10 hours instrument flight instruction of which not more than 5 hours may be instrument ground time in a FNPT II or a flight simulator.

ii. Completed at least 20 hours of cross-country flight as PIC of helicopters.

iii. Pass a specific pre-entry flight test with a FI qualified as per JAR-FCL 2.330(f) based upon the proficiency check as per JAR-FCL 2.240(b), **within the six months preceding the start of the course.***

*The pre-entry flight test will assess the ability of the applicant to undertake the course.

FIC Flight and Theoretical Training Requirements

An applicant for the FI(H) rating shall have completed an approved course of both flight and theoretical knowledge instruction training at an approved FTO. The course is intended to train the applicant to give instruction on single pilot, single engine helicopters up to PPL(H) standard.

a. This must include at least 15 hours of dual flight training and 30 hours of theoretical knowledge instruction.

Skill Test Requirement

a. Pass the relevant elements of a FI Skill Test with a suitably qualified FIE(H) as per JAR-FCL 2.345.

Flight and Theoretical Training Requirements to Remove Instructional Restrictions

To remove any of the restrictions imposed, please see Section H1.7.

The above course can also include the training requirements to allow night instruction, as detailed in Section H1.7.

Specific Authorisation (JAR-FCL 2.300(a)(2))

Applicants who hold a specific authorisation issued by the UK CAA in accordance with Appendix 1 to JAR-FCL 2.300 who also complies with the requirements of JAR-FCL 2.355 and hold a JAR-FCL licence will be deemed to have fulfilled the requirements for the issue of a FI(A) rating, subject to the initial restrictions set out in JAR-FCL 2.325 (see H1.7). For full details please refer to Appendix 1 to JAR-FCL 2.300.

H1.12 MEDICAL REQUIREMENTS

An applicant for a JAR-FCL FI(A) or FI(H) shall hold a valid JAR-FCL Medical Certificate appropriate to the licence held and the privileges being exercised.

FULL DETAILS OF THE MEDICAL REQUIREMENTS ARE CONTAINED IN JAR-FCL 3 AND SECTION A5

H1.13 REVALIDATION AND RENEWAL

FI(A) Revalidation

For the holder of a FI(A) to revalidate the rating they must complete 2 of the following requirements:

a. Complete at least 100 hours of flight instruction on aeroplanes as FI, CRI, IRI or as Examiner during the period of validity of the rating. To include at least 30 hours of flight instruction within the 12 months preceding the expiry date of the FI rating, 10 hours of this shall be instruction for an IR if the privileges to instruct for an IR are to be revalidated.

b. Attend a FI refresher seminar approved by the Authority within the validity period of the FI rating.

c. Pass a FI (A) proficiency check within the 12 months preceding the expiry of the FI rating. For CFS Category Instructors, a CFS Standardisation check on a single-engine piston aeroplane completed within the 12 months preceding the expiry date of the FI rating, will be accepted in lieu of a FI(A) proficiency check.

d. For at least each alternate revalidation of a FI(A) rating the holder shall pass a proficiency check.

The first revalidation after initial issue of the rating shall include a proficiency check as one of the requirements. Thereafter, a proficiency check shall be included as one of the requirements at least every alternate revalidation.

FI(A) Renewal

For the holder of a FI(A) to renew the rating they shall complete items b) & c) as for revalidation within the last 12 months before renewal.

For a FI(A) rating that has expired by more than 5 years, application should be sent to PLD for endorsement together with the appropriate fee as per Scheme of Charges. In addition, applicants will also be required to submit completed form SRG\1153 to demonstrate to the satisfaction of the Authority that knowledge of the relevant parts of JAR-FCL and JAR-OPS has been acquired.

An existing FI who has not previously passed CPL level examinations whose FI rating has expired by more than 5 years will be required to pass the JAR-CPL theoretical knowledge examination before the FI rating can be renewed.

FI(H) Revalidation

For the holder of a FI(H) to revalidate their rating they must complete 2 of the following requirements:

a. Complete at least 100 hours of flight instruction in helicopters as FI, IRI or as Examiner during the period of validity of the rating. To include at least 30 hours of flight instruction (which may include skill testing/proficiency checking) within the 12 months preceding expiry of the FI(H) rating.

b. Attend a FI(H) refresher seminar as approved by the Authority within the validity period of the FI rating.

c. Pass a FI(H) proficiency check within the 12 months preceding expiry of the rating. For CFS Category Instructors, a CFS Standardisation check on a single-pilot, single-engine helicopter completed within the 12 months preceding the expiry date of the FI rating will be accepted in lieu of an FI(H) proficiency check.

d. For at least each alternate revalidation of a FI(H) rating the holder shall pass, as a proficiency check, the skill test set out in Appendices 1 and 2 to JAR-FCL 2.330 & 2.345 as one of the two requirements to be fulfilled.

The first revalidation after initial issue of the rating shall include a proficiency check as one of the requirements. Thereafter, a proficiency check shall be included as one of the requirements at least every alternate revalidation.

FI(H) Renewal

For the holder of a FI(H) to renew the rating they shall complete items b) & c) as for revalidation within the last 12 months before renewal.

For a FI(H) expired by less than 5 years the Examiner will sign a Certificate of Revalidation following the proficiency check.

For a FI(H) rating that has expired by more than 5 years, application should be sent to PLD for endorsement together with the appropriate fee as per Scheme of Charges. In addition, applicants will also be required to submit completed form SRG\1153 to demonstrate to the satisfaction of the Authority that knowledge of the relevant parts of JAR-FCL and JAR-OPS has been acquired.

An existing FI who has not previously passed CPL level examinations whose FI rating has expired by more than 5 years will be required to pass the JAR-CPL theoretical knowledge examination before the FI rating can be renewed.

H2 JAR-FCL IRI(A) & IRI(H)

This section offers a basic guide to obtaining an Instrument Rating (Aeroplane) and (Helicopter).

H2.1 INSTRUMENT RATING INSTRUCTOR (AEROPLANE) (IRI(A))

Privileges

The privileges of the holder of an IRI(A) rating are limited to conduct flight instruction for:

a. The issue of an IR(A) single-engine aeroplanes;

b. The issue of an IR(A) multi-engine aeroplanes, provided that the instructor meets the requirements of JAR-FCL 1.380(a).

Requirements

a. The applicant for an IRI(A) shall hold a valid IR(A).

b. Have completed at least 800 hours of flight time under IFR of which at least 400 shall be in aeroplanes. Where pilots have recorded flight by sole reference to instruments and not under IFR, then 1 hour sole reference to instruments may be counted as 4 hours flight by IFR.

c. Successfully completed at an approved FTO and approved course (see Appendix 1 to JAR-FCL 1.395 and AMC FCL 1.395) comprising theoretical knowledge instruction and at least ten hours of flight instruction on an aeroplane, flight simulator or FNPT II; and.

d. Pass the relevant elements of a FI Skill Test in a single pilot aeroplane with a suitably qualified FIE(A).

e. IRI(A)'s who wish to conduct training for a ME IR are also required to have met the qualifications for a ME CRI. Where both courses are conducted together, the teaching and learning element is common to both CRI and IRI courses. Candidates qualifying for the teaching and learning exemption in accordance with Appendix 1 to JAR-FCL 1.395(2) who combine both ME CRI and IRI qualifications on one course will be required to complete a minimum of 15 hours theoretical training before attempting the ME CRI and IRI Skill Tests. The IRI(A) rating is designed to train instructors to teach for the JAA IR within an approved FTO. In the UK, the same (IRI) qualification course is also used to qualify instructors to teach for the UK National IMC rating. The entry requirements for the IRI course to teach solely for the UK IMC rating are detailed in Section H1.4 (Removal of No Applied Instrument Restriction). The theoretical ground training requirements shall be the same as those required for the IRI qualification.

H2.2 INSTRUMENT RATING INSTRUCTOR (HELICOPTER) (IRI(H))

Privileges

Holders of an IRI(H) rating are limited to instructing licence holders for the issue, revalidation and renewal of an Instrument Rating (IR(H)).

Requirements

a. An applicant for an IRI(H) shall hold a valid IR(H).

b. Have at least 500 hours of flight time under IFR of which at least 250 hours shall be in helicopters. Where pilots have recorded flight by sole reference to instrument and not under IFR, then 1 hour sole reference to instruments may be counted as 4 hours flight by IFR.

c. Successfully completed an approved course at an approved FTO (see Appendix 1 to JAR-FCL 2.395 and AMC FCL 2.395) comprising theoretical knowledge instruction and at least ten hours of flight instruction on a helicopter, flight simulator or FNPT II; and

d. Pass the relevant elements of a FI Skill Test with a suitably qualified FIE(H).

H2.3 MEDICAL REQUIREMENTS

An applicant for a JAR-FCL IRI(A) or IRI(H) shall hold a valid JAR-FCL Medical Certificate appropriate to the licence held and the privileges being exercised.

FULL DETAILS OF THE MEDICAL REQUIREMENTS ARE CONTAINED IN JAR-FCL 3 AND SECTION A5

H2.4 IRI(A)/(H) REVALIDATION AND RENEWAL

IRI(A) Revalidation

For the holder of an IRI(A) to revalidate the rating they must complete 2 of the following requirements:

a. Complete at least 100 hours of flight instruction on aeroplanes as FI, CRI, IRI or as Examiner during the period of validity of the rating. To include at least 30 of flight instruction within the 12 months preceding the expiry date of the IRI(A) rating, 10 hours of this shall be instruction for an IR.

b. Attend a FI refresher seminar approved by the Authority within the validity period of the IRI(A) rating.

c. Pass a FI proficiency check within the 12 months preceding the expiry of the IRI(A) rating.

IRI(A) Renewal

For the holder of an IRI(A) to renew the rating they shall complete items b) & c) as for revalidation within the last 12 months before renewal.

For an IRI(A) rating, expired by less than 5 years, the Examiner will sign a Certificate of Revalidation following the proficiency check. For a rating that has expired by more than 5 years application should be made to PLD, together with the appropriate fee.

IRI(H) Revalidation

For the holder of an IRI(H) to revalidate the rating they must complete 2 of the following requirements:

a. Complete at least 100 hours of flight instruction on aeroplanes as FI, CRI, IRI or as Examiner during the period of validity of the rating. To include at least 30 hours of flight instruction (which may include skill testing/proficiency checking) within the 12 months preceding the expiry date of the IRI(H) rating, 10 hours of this shall be instruction for an IR.

b. Attend a FI refresher seminar approved by the Authority within the validity period of the IRI(H) rating.

c. Pass a FI proficiency check within the 12 months preceding the expiry of the IRI(H) rating.

IRI(H) Renewal

For the holder of an IRI(H) to renew the rating they shall complete items b) & c) as for revalidation within the preceding 12 months before renewal.

For an IRI(H) rating, expired by less than 5 years, the Examiner will sign a Certificate of Revalidation following the proficiency check. For a rating that has expired by more than 5 years application should be made to PLD, together with the appropriate fee.

H3 JAR-FCL CLASS RATING INSTRUCTOR (SPA)

This section offers a basic guide to obtaining a Class Rating Instructor (SPA).

H3.1 CRI(SPA) PRIVILEGES

The holder of a CRI(SPA) rating can instruct licence holders for the issue of a type or class rating for single-pilot aeroplanes. The holder may instruct on single pilot single-engine or multi-engine aeroplanes, subject to being appropriately qualified, as per JAR-FCL 1.310(a).

H3.2 CRI(SPA) COURSE FOR SINGLE-ENGINE CLASS RATING

An applicant for the issue of a CRI(SPA) rating for single-engine aeroplanes shall have:

a. A valid SEP (Land), SET (Land), TMG Class Rating or a Single-Pilot Single-Engine Type Rating.

b. Completed at least 300 hours flight time as pilot of aeroplanes.

c. Completed at least 30 hours as PIC on the applicable type or class of aeroplane prior to commencing the course.

d. Completed an approved course at an approved FTO or TRTO of at least three hours flight instruction on the aeroplane or a flight simulator given by an instructor approved for this purpose (see Appendix 2 to JAR-FCL 1.380); and 25 hours* teaching and learning theoretical knowledge training.

e. Passed the relevant elements of a FI Skill Test in a single pilot, single engine aeroplane with a suitably qualified FIE(A)

* Holders of existing flight instructor ratings, who have already completed the teaching and learning syllabus, are exempt from completing this part of the CRI course (Appendix 1 and 2 to JAR-FCL 1.380 (2) refers). At first sight, this might appear to indicate that no additional theoretical knowledge training is mandated; however, it would be unrealistic to expect an instructor to gain additional instructional qualifications without the associated theoretical knowledge training. Instructors who qualify for the exemption to the teaching and learning element, will be required to complete a minimum of 10 hours theoretical knowledge training prior to attempting the rating skill test.

H3.3 CRI(SPA) COURSE FOR MULTI-ENGINE CLASS RATING

An applicant for the issue of a CRI(SPA) rating for multi-engine aeroplanes shall have:

a. A valid Multi-Engine Piston (Land) Class or Single Pilot Multi-Engine Type Rating.

b. Completed at least 500 hours flight time as pilot of aeroplanes.

c. Completed at least 30 hours as PIC on the applicable type or class of aeroplane prior to commencing the course. It should be noted that ME SPIC time is not allowable towards this 30 hours requirement.

d. Completed an approved course at an approved FTO or TRTO including at least five hours flight instruction on the aeroplane or a flight simulator given by an instructor approved for this purpose (see Appendix 1 to JAR-FCL 1.380 and AMC FCL 1.380); and 25 hours* teaching and learning theoretical knowledge training.

e. Passed the relevant elements of a FI Skill Test in a single pilot, multi-engine aeroplane with a suitably qualified FIE(A).

* Holders of existing flight instructor ratings, who have already completed the teaching and learning syllabus, are exempt from completing this part of the CRI course (Appendix 1 and 2 to JAR-FCL 1.380 (2) refers). At first sight, this might appear to indicate that no additional theoretical knowledge training is mandated; however, it would be unrealistic to expect an instructor to gain additional instructional qualifications without the associated theoretical knowledge training. Instructors who qualify for the exemption to the teaching and learning element, will be required to complete a minimum of 10 hours theoretical knowledge training prior to attempting the rating skill test.

Before the privileges of the rating are extended to another type or class of aeroplane, the holder shall within the past 12 months have completed at least

10 hours flight time in aeroplanes of the applicable type or class. For an extension of a CRI(A) from SE to ME aeroplanes the requirements of JAR-FCL 1.380(a) shall be met.

H3.4 MEDICAL REQUIREMENTS

An applicant for a JAR-FCL CRI(A) shall hold a valid JAR-FCL Medical Certificate appropriate to the licence held and the privileges being exercised.

FULL DETAILS OF THE MEDICAL REQUIREMENTS ARE CONTAINED IN JAR-FCL 3 AND SECTION A6

H3.5 CRI(SPA) RE-VALIDATION/RENEWAL

CRI(SPA) Revalidation

For revalidation of a CRI(SPA) rating the holder shall complete one of the following within 12 months preceding the expiry of the rating:

a. Conduct at least 10 hours flight instruction in the role of CRI(SPA); and if the applicant has CRI(SPA) privileges on both SE and ME aeroplanes, conduct at least 5 hours on SE aeroplanes and 5 hours on ME aeroplanes within the 10 hours of flight instruction required in the role, or

b. Conduct refresher training to the satisfaction of the Authority.

c. Receive refresher training as a CRI(A).

CRI(SPA) Renewal

The holder of a lapsed rating shall, in the 12 months preceding application:

a. Receive refresher training as a CRI(A) to the satisfaction of the Authority.

b. Pass, as a proficiency check, the relevant part of the skill test set out in Appendix 1 & 2 to JAR-FCL 1.330 & 1.345.

H4 JAR-FCL TYPE RATING INSTRUCTOR (A) (H) & (E)

This section offers a basic guide to obtaining a Type Rating Instructor (Aeroplane), (Helicopter) and Flight Engineer Instructor Rating.

H4.1 TYPE RATING INSTRUCTOR (MPA)

Privileges

The holder of a TRI(MPA) rating can instruct licence holders for the issue of a MPA type rating and give instruction required for multi-crew co-operation.

Requirements

An applicant for the initial issue of a TRI(MPA) rating shall have:

a. Successfully completed an approved TRI(MPA) course at an approved FTO or TRTO.

b. Completed at least 1500 hours flight time as a pilot of multi-pilot aeroplanes.

c. Completed, within the 12 months preceding the application for the rating, at least 30 route sectors to include take-offs and landings as PIC or P2 on the applicable aeroplane type or a similar type as agreed by the Authority. Not more than 15 sectors may be completed in a flight simulator.

d. Conducted, on a complete type rating course, at least 3 hours of flight instruction related to the duties of a TRI(MPA) on the applicable type of aeroplane under the supervision and to the satisfaction of a TRI(MPA) authorised by the Authority for this purpose.

The requirements above are fulfilled if the applicant holds a JAR-FCL licence, have been issued a specific authorisation in accordance with Appendix 1 to JAR-FCL 1.300 and complies with JAR-FCL 1.370.

Notes for extension of TRI(MPA) privileges

Before the privileges are extended to further MPA types, the holder shall have:

a. A valid type rating on the specific type of aeroplane.

b. Completed, within the 12 months preceding the application for the rating, at least 15 route sectors to include take-offs and landings as PIC or P2 on the applicable aeroplane type or a similar type as agreed by the Authority. Not more than 7 sectors may be completed in a flight simulator.

c. Successfully completed the relevant technical training content of an approved TRI(MPA) course at an approved FTO or TRTO.

d. Conducted in a complete type rating course at least 3 hours of flight instruction related to the duties of a TRI(MPA) on the applicable type of aeroplane and/or flight simulator under the supervision and to the satisfaction of a TRI(MPA) authorised by the Authority for the purpose.

H4.2 Type Rating Instructor (Helicopter)

Privileges

Provided that in the preceding 12 months the TRI(H) has completed not less than 15 hours of type rating instruction (which may include skill testing/proficiency checking) on helicopters, or meets the requirements of JAR-FCL 2.370(a)(2), the privileges of the holder of a TRI(H) rating are to instruct licence holders for the issue of a type rating, and the instruction required for multi-crew co-operation as applicable (as per JAR-FCL 2.261(d), Appendix 1 to JAR-FCL 2.261(d) and AMC FCL 2.261(d)).

Requirements for Single Pilot, Single and Multi Engine

a. Hold a valid Type Rating on the applicable type to instruct on.

b. Have at least 500 hours flight time as pilot of helicopters.

c. Completed, within the 12 months preceding the application, at least 30 hours flight time, to include 10 take-offs and landings as either PIC or P2 on the applicable type, of which not more than 15 hours may be completed in a flight simulator.

d. Successfully complete a TRI(H) course of at least 3 hours of flight instruction related to the duties of a TRI(H) on the applicable type of helicopter or flight simulator under the supervision and to the satisfaction of a TRI(H) authorised by the Authority for this purpose. All training to be conducted at an approved FTO or TRTO, approved for the applicable type of helicopter.

Multi-Pilot, Single or Multi Engine

a. Hold a valid Multi-Pilot Type Rating on the applicable type to instruct on.

b. Have at least 1000 hours flight time as pilot of helicopters of which at least 350 hours as pilot of multi-pilot helicopters.

c. Completed, within the 12 months preceding the application, at least 30 hours flight time to include 10 take-offs and landings as either PIC or P2 on the applicable type, of which not more than 15 hours may be completed in a flight simulator.

d. Successfully complete a TRI course of at least 3 hours of flight instruction related to the duties of a TRI(H) on the applicable type of helicopter or flight simulator under the supervision and to the satisfaction of a TRI(H) authorised by the Authority for this purpose. All training to be conducted at an approved FTO or TRTO, approved for the applicable type of helicopter.

Notes for extension of TRI(H) privileges

Before TRI(H) privileges are extended to further types of helicopter, the holder shall have:

a. A valid type rating on the specific type of helicopter.

b. Completed, within 12 months preceding the application, at least 15 hours flight time, to include 10 take-offs and landings as PIC or P2 on a similar class of helicopter type, i.e. single engine, single pilot etc. Not more than 7 hours may be completed in a flight simulator.

c. Successfully completed the relevant technical training content of an approved TRI course.

d. Successfully completed a TRI(H) course of at least 3 hours of flight instruction related to the duties of a TRI(H) on the applicable type of helicopter or flight simulator under the supervision, and to the satisfaction of, a TRI(H) authorised by the Authority for this purpose. All training to be conducted at an approved FTO or TRTO, approved for the applicable type of helicopter.

H4.3 FLIGHT ENGINEER INSTRUCTOR RATING (TRI(E))

Privileges

The holder of a TRI(E) may instruct for the issue of a FE licence and type ratings. Additionally, the training required for FE MCC.

Requirements

For initial issue of a TRI(E) the applicant shall have:

a. Successfully completed an approved TRI(E) course at an approved FTO or TRTO.

b. Completed at least 1500 hours flight time as a FE.

c. Completed, within the 12 months preceding application for the rating, at least 30 route sectors to include take-offs and landings as a FE on the applicable aeroplane type. A maximum 15 sectors may be completed in an approved flight simulator.

d. Conducted on a complete type rating course of at least 3 hours of flight instruction related to the duties of a TRI(E) on the applicable type of aeroplane and/or flight simulator under the supervision and to the satisfaction of a TRI(E) notified by the Authority for the purpose.

Notes for extension of TRI(E) privileges

Before TRI(E) privileges are extended to further aeroplane types, the holder shall have:

a. Completed, within the 12 months preceding the application, at least 15 route sectors as FE on the applicable type of aeroplane of which a maximum 7 sectors may be completed in a flight simulator.

b. Satisfactorily completed the relevant technical training content of an approved TRI(E) course.

c. Conducted, on a complete type rating course, at least 3 hours of flight instruction related to the duties of a TRI(E) on the applicable type of aeroplane and/or flight simulator under the supervision and to the satisfaction of a TRI(E) notified by the Authority for the purpose.

H4.4 MEDICAL REQUIREMENTS

An applicant for a JAR-FCL TRI(MPA) or TRI(H) shall hold a valid JAR-FCL Medical Certificate appropriate to the licence held and the privileges being exercised.

FULL DETAILS OF THE MEDICAL REQUIREMENTS ARE CONTAINED IN JAR-FCL 3 AND SECTION A6

H4.5 TRI REVALIDATION/RENEWAL

TRI(MPA) Revalidation

For revalidation of a TRI(MPA) rating, the applicant shall, within the last 12 months preceding the expiry date of the rating:

a. Conduct one of the following parts of a complete type rating/refresher/ recurrent training course:

   i. one simulator session of at least 3 hours; or

   ii. one air exercise of at least 1 hour comprising a minimum of 2 take offs and landings

or

b. Receive TRI(A) refresher training acceptable to the Authority.

TRI(MPA) Renewal

If the TRI(MPA) lapses the holder must complete the following before exercising the privileges of the rating:

a. Within 12 months, preceding application for renewal, at least 30 route sectors to include take-offs and landings as PIC or P2 on the applicable aeroplane type or similar, as agreed by the Authority, of which not more than 15 sectors may be completed in a flight simulator.

b. The relevant parts of an approved TRI(MPA) course, agreed by the Authority, taking into account the recent experience of the applicant.

c. Conduct, on a complete type rating course, at least 3 hours of flight instruction related to the duties of a TRI(MPA) on the applicable type of aeroplane and/or flight simulator under the supervision and to the satisfaction of a TRI(A) authorised by the Authority for the purpose.

TRI(H) Revalidation

For revalidation of a TRI(H) rating the applicant shall, within 12 months preceding the expiry date:

a. Conduct one of the following parts of a complete type rating/refresher/ recurrent training course:

   i. one flight simulator session of at least 3 hours; or

   ii. one air exercise of at least 1 hour comprising a minimum of 2 take-offs and landings.

or

b. Receive TRI(H) refresher training acceptable to the Authority.

TRI(H) Renewal

If the rating has lapsed the applicant shall have:

a. Completed, within the 12 months preceding renewal application, at least 30 hours flight time, to include take-offs and landings as PIC or P2 on the applicable helicopter type or similar as agreed by the Authority of which no more than 15 hours may be completed in a flight simulator.

b. Successfully completed the relevant parts of an approved TRI(H) course taking into account the recent experience of the rating holder.

c. Conducted, on a complete type rating course, at least 3 hours of flight instruction related to the duties of a TRI(H) on the applicable type of helicopter or flight simulator under the supervision of a TRI authorised by the Authority for the purpose.

TRI(E) Revalidation

For the holder of a TRI(E) to revalidate their rating they must, within the 12 months preceding the expiry date:

a. Conduct one of the following parts of an approved type rating/refresher/recurrent training course.

   i. one simulator session of at least 3 hours, or

   ii. one flight exercise of at least 1 hour including 2 take-offs and landings

or

b. Receive TRI(E) refresher training acceptable to the Authority.

TRI(E) Renewal

In order to renew a lapsed rating the applicant shall have:

a. Completed, within the 12 months preceding renewal, at least 30 route sectors to include take-offs and landings as FE on the applicable aeroplane type. A maximum 15 sectors may be completed in a flight simulator.

b. Successfully completed the relevant parts of an approved TRI(E) course taking into account the recent experience of the applicant.

c. Conducted, on a complete type rating course, at least 3 hours of flight training related to the duties of a TRI(E) on the applicable type of aeroplane and/or flight simulator under the supervision and to the satisfaction of a TRI(E) notified by the Authority for the purpose.

H5 JAR-FCL SYNTHETIC FLIGHT INSTRUCTOR (A), (H) & (E), MCCI(A) AND STI(A))

This section offers a basic guide to obtaining a Synthetic Flight Instructor Rating (Aeroplane), (Helicopter) and (Flight Engineer), Multi Crew Co-operation Course Instructor Authorisation (Aeroplane) and Synthetic Training Instructor Authorisation (Aeroplane)

H5.1 SYNTHETIC FLIGHT INSTRUCTOR AEROPLANE (SFI(A))

Privileges

The holder of a SFI(A) can carry out synthetic flight instruction for type ratings and multi-crew co-operation.

Requirements

An applicant for the initial issue of a SFI(A) rating shall:

a. Hold or have held a professional pilot licence issued by a JAA Member State or a non-JAR professional licence acceptable to the Authority.

b. Have completed the simulator content of the applicable type rating course at an approved FTO or TRTO.

c. Have at least 1500 hours flying experience as pilot on multi-pilot aeroplanes.

d. Have completed an approved TRI(A) course.

e. Have conducted, on a complete type rating course, at least 3 hours of flight instruction related to the duties of a TRI(A) on the applicable type of aeroplane under the supervision and to the satisfaction of a TRI(A) authorised by the Authority for this purpose.

f. Have completed, within a period of 12 months preceding application for the rating, a proficiency check on a flight simulator or the applicable type.

g. Have completed, within a period of 12 months preceding application for the rating, at least 3 route sectors as an observer on the flight deck of the applicable type or similar type as agreed by the Authority, or

h. have completed within a period of 12 months preceding the application, at least 2 LOFT based simulator sessions conducted by qualified flight crew as an observer on the flight deck of the applicable type or similar type as agreed by the Authority. These simulator sessions shall include:

   i. flight between 2 different airports of at least 2 hours duration each, and

   ii. associated pre-flight planning and de-briefing.

The requirements are fulfilled if the applicant has been issued a specific authorisation in accordance with Appendix 1 to JAR-FCL 1.300 and comply with the requirements of JAR-FCL 1.415.

Notes for extension of SFI(A) privileges

Before SFI(A) privileges are extended to further MPA the holder shall have:

a. Successfully completed the simulator content of the relevant type rating course.

b. Conducted, on a complete type rating course, at least 3 hours of flight instruction related to the duties of a TRI(A) on the applicable type of aeroplane under the supervision and to the satisfaction of a TRI(A) authorised by the Authority for this purpose.

H5.2 SYNTHETIC FLIGHT INSTRUCTOR HELICOPTER (SFI(H))

Privileges

The holder of a SFI(H) may carry out synthetic flight instruction for type ratings and multi-crew co-operation.

Requirements

An applicant for a SFI(H) rating shall:

a. Hold or have held a professional pilot licence issued by a JAA Member State or a non-JAA professional licence acceptable to the Authority.

b. Have completed the flight simulator content of the applicable type rating course at an approved FTO or TRTO.

c. Have at least 1000 hours flying experience as a pilot on MPH.

d. Have completed an approved TRI(H) course.

e. Have conducted, on a complete type rating course, at least one flight simulator session of at least 3 hours related to the duties of a TRI(H) on the applicable type of helicopter under the supervision and to the satisfaction of a TRI(H) authorised by the Authority for this purpose.

f. Have completed, within a period of 12 months preceding application for the rating, a proficiency check on a flight simulator of the applicable type.

g. Have completed, within a period of 12 months preceding the application for the rating, at least 1 hour flight time as an observer on the flight deck of the applicable type.

Notes for extension of SFI(H) privileges

Before SFI(H) privileges are extended to further types of MPH the holder shall have:

a. Successfully completed the flight simulator content of the relevant type rating course.

b. Conducted, on a complete type rating course, at least one flight simulator session of at least 3 hours related to the duties of a TRI(H) on the applicable type of helicopter under the supervision of a TRI(H) authorised by the Authority for this purpose.

H5.3 SYNTHETIC FLIGHT INSTRUCTOR (ENGINEER)

Privileges

The holder of a SFI(E) may carry out synthetic flight instruction for type ratings and multi-crew co-operation.

Requirements

An applicant for the initial issue of a SFI(E) authorisation shall:

a. Hold or have held a FE licence issued by a JAA Member State or a non JAR-FCL FE licence acceptable to the Authority.

b. Have completed the simulator content of the applicable type rating course at an approved FTO or TRTO.

c. Have at least 1500 hours flying experience as FE.

d. Have completed an approved TRI(E) course.

e. Have conducted, on a complete type rating course, at least 3 hours of synthetic flight instruction related to the duties of a TRI(E) on a flight simulator for the applicable type of aeroplane under the supervision and to the satisfaction of a TRI(E) notified by the Authority for the purpose.

f. Have completed, within 12 months preceding application, a proficiency check on a flight simulator for the applicable type.

g. Have completed, within 12 months preceding application, at least 3 route sectors as an observer on the flight deck for the applicable type.

Notes for extension of SFI(E) privileges

Before SFI(E) privileges are extended to further aeroplane types the holder shall:

a. Have satisfactorily completed the simulator content of the relevant type rating course.

b. Have conducted, on a complete type rating course, at least 3 hours synthetic flight instruction related to the duties of a TRI(E) on a flight simulator, for the applicable aeroplane type, under the supervision of a TRI(E) notified by the Authority for the purpose.

H5.4 SFI REVALIDATION AND RENEWAL

SFI(A) Revalidation

For revalidation of a SFI(A) rating the holder shall, within the last 12 months preceding expiry:

a. Conduct one simulator session of at least 3 hours as part of a complete type rating/refresher/ recurrent training course.

b. Have completed a proficiency check as set out in Appendix 1 & 2 to JAR-FCL 1.240 on a flight simulator of the appropriate type.

SFI(A) Renewal

If the SFI(A) rating has lapsed the holder shall have:

a. Completed the simulator content of the applicable type rating course.

b. Successfully completed an approved TRI(A) course.

c. Conducted, on a complete type rating course, at least 3 hours of flight instruction related to the duties of a TRI(A) on the applicable type of aeroplane under the supervision and to the satisfaction of a TRI(A) authorised by the Authority for this purpose.

d. Completed a proficiency check on a flight simulator for the appropriate type.

SFI(H) Revalidation

Within 12 months of the expiry the SFI(H) the privileges may be revalidated by:

a. Conducting one simulator session of at least 3 hours as part of a complete type rating/refresher/ recurrent training course.

or

b. Completing a proficiency check on a flight simulator for the applicable type.

SFI(H) Renewal

In order to renew a SFI(H) the holder shall:

a. Complete the flight simulator content of the applicable type rating course.

b. Successfully complete an approved TRI(H) course.

c. Conduct, on a complete type rating course, at least one flight simulator session of at least 3 hours related to the duties of a TRI(H) on the applicable type under the supervision and to the satisfaction of a TRI(H) notified by the Authority for the purpose.

SFI(E) Revalidation

For revalidation of a SFI(E) authorisation the holder shall, within 12 months preceding expiry date,

a. Conduct one simulator session of at least 3 hours as part of a complete type rating/refresher/ recurrent training course.

b. Have completed a proficiency check on a flight simulator for the appropriate type.

SFI(E) Renewal

If the authorisation has lapsed the holder shall have:

a. Completed the simulator content of the applicable type rating course.

b. Successfully completed an approved TRI(E) course according to the requirements of the Authority.

c. Conducted, on a complete type rating course, at least 3 hours of synthetic flight instruction related to the duties of a TRI(E) on a simulator for the applicable type under the supervision and to the satisfaction of a TRI(E) notified by the Authority for the purpose.

H5.5 MULTI CREW CO-OPERATION COURSE INSTRUCTOR AUTHORISATION (AEROPLANE) (MCCI(A)

Privileges

The privileges of the holder of a MCCI(A) are to carry out instruction for the practical part of MCC courses when not combined with type rating training.

Requirements

An applicant for a MCCI(A) authorisation shall:

a. Hold or have held a professional pilot licence issued by a JAA Member State or non-JAR-FCL professional licence acceptable to the Authority.

b. Have at least 1500 hours flying experience as pilot on multi-pilot aeroplanes.

c. Have completed on a FNPT II or a flight simulator an approved MCCI Course (AMC FCL 1.417 refers).

d. Have conducted on a complete MCC course at least 3 hours of flight instruction/MCC instruction on the relevant FNPT II or flight simulator under the supervision and to the satisfaction of a TRI(A), SFI(A) or MCCI(A) notified by the Authority for this purpose.

If the privileges are to be extended to another type of FNPT II or flight simulator the holder shall complete d) above on that type of FNPT II or FS.

H5.6 MCCI(A) REVALIDATION/RENEWAL

MCCI(A) Revalidation

For revalidation of a MCCI(A) authorisation of the applicant shall within the last 12 months of the validity period of authorisation:

Have conducted on a complete MCC course at least 3 hours of flight instruction/MCC instruction on the relevant FNPT II or flight simulator under the supervision and to the satisfaction of a TRI(A), SFI(A), or MCCI(A) notified by the Authority for this purpose.

MCCI(A) Renewal

If the MCCI(A) authorisation has lapsed the applicant shall:-

a. Meet any requirement for refresher training at the discretion of the Authority; and

b. Have conducted on a complete MCC course at least 3 hours of flight instruction/MCC instruction on the relevant FNPT II or flight simulator under the supervision and to the satisfaction of a TRI(A), SFI(A) or MCCI(A) notified by the Authority for this purpose.

H5.7 SYNTHETIC TRAINING INSTRUCTOR AUTHORISATION (AEROPLANE) STI(A)

Privileges

The privileges of the holder of a STI(A) authorisation are to carry out synthetic flight instruction for issue of a licence, instrument rating and class or type rating for single-pilot aeroplanes.

Requirements

An applicant for a STI(A) authorisation shall:-

a. Hold or have held within the previous 3 years a pilot licence containing an instructional qualification appropriate to the courses on which instruction is intended or a non-JAA licence acceptable to the Authority.

b. Have conducted in a flight simulator or FNPT II at least 3 hours of flight instruction related to the duties of a STI(A) under the supervision and to the satisfaction of a FIE(A) notified by the Authority for this purpose, or

  i. for a STI(A) wishing to instruct on a BITD only, have completed on a BITD at least 3 hours of flight instruction under the supervision and to the satisfaction of an FIE(A) notified by the Authority for this purpose.

c. Have completed within a period of 12 months preceding the application a proficiency check in accordance with Appendix 3 to JAR-FCL 1.240 in an FNPT of the class or type of aeroplane appropriate to the instruction intended. or

  i. for an STI(A) wishing to instruct on BITDs only, have completed within a period of 12 months preceding the application a proficiency check covering only those exercises listed in Appendix 1 to JAR-FCL 1.125.

H5.8 STI(A) REVALIDATION/RENEWAL

STI(A) Revalidation

For revalidation of a STI(A) authorisation the applicant shall within the last 12 months of the validity period of the authorisation:-

a. Have conducted at least 3 hours of instruction in a flight simulator or FNPT II or BITD where applicable as part of a complete CPL, IR, PPL or class or type rating course, and

b. Have completed Section 3B of the proficiency check set out in Appendix 3 to JAR-FCL 1.240 for the appropriate type or class of aeroplane in a flight simulator or FNPT II on which instruction is routinely conducted, or

c. for an STI(A) instructing on BITDs only, have completed a proficiency check covering those exercises listed in Appendix 1 to JAR-FCL 1.125.

STI(A) Renewal

If the STI(A) authorisation has lapsed the applicant shall:-

a. Have completed at least 3 hours refresher training in a flight simulator or FNPT II, or

b. Have conducted on a complete CPL, IR, PPL or class or type rating course at least 3 hours instruction under the supervision and to the satisfaction of a FIE(A), FI(A), CRI(A), IRI(A),

Section A
Section B
Section C
Section D
Section E
Section F
Section G
Section H INSTRUCTOR
Section I
Section J
Section K
Index

TRI(A) or SFI(A) notified by the Authority for this purpose. At least one hour instruction shall be supervised and to the satisfaction of a FIE(A).

c. Have completed Section 3B of the proficiency check set out in Appendix 3 to JAR-FCL 1.240 for the appropriate type or class of aeroplane in a flight simulator or FNPT II on which instruction is routinely conducted, or

i. for an STI(A) instructing BITDs only, have completed a proficiency check covering those exercises listed in Appendix 1 to JAR-FCL 1.125.

H6 FI RATINGS - AEROPLANE (SEA) - NOT MICROLIGHTS

This section offers a basic guide to obtaining a Flying Instructor Rating (Aeroplane) (Sea) - Not Microlights.

H6.1 General Information

At the present time, since there are no approved Seaplane FIC training facilities in the United Kingdom, other than for Microlight seaplanes, Flight Instructors wishing to instruct on aeroplanes (Sea) shall meet the following requirements.

H6.2 Additional Requirements

a. Hold or have held a valid FI(A) (Land) Instructors Rating within the previous 3 years for either SEP or MEP aeroplanes.

b. Pass the Professional Seamanship Examination;

c. Hold a valid class or type rating for an aeroplane (Sea) with a minimum of 5 hours PIC on the class or type in the 12 months preceding rating issue.

d. Pass a theoretical and Skill Test with a FIE (Sea) in an Aeroplane (Sea) of the Class to be included in the Rating.

e. Having completed the required training and FI Skill Test, an entry should be made in the pilots logbook and a certified endorsement made by the FIE. The FI Skill Test form (FCL685) should be submitted to PLD for record purposes.

H6.3 Skill Test and Theoretical Examination

There are no facilities to issue an initial FI(R) Rating on the basis of an aeroplane (Sea) Class rating. An applicant with a valid FI(A) (Land) Rating will be required to complete a Skill Test which includes those items detailed in the Aeroplanes (Seaplanes) Skill Test, Section H and Form FCL 674.

For the inclusion of an Aeroplane (Sea) Class or Type, an applicant with an expired FI(A) (Land) Rating will be required to complete the full Instructors Revalidation Test in a seaplane, to include all the test items and subjects normally in an Aeroplane (Land) Instructors Revalidation Test, and attend a FI refresher Seminar in the previous 12 months. Satisfactory completion of this Test will revalidate the FI(A) Rating for those classes or types of aeroplane for which a valid class or type rating is held

H7 AFI RATING AEROPLANE (LAND, SEA) MICROLIGHT

This section offers a basic guide to obtaining an Assistant flight Instructor Rating (Land, Sea) Microlight.

H7.1 Pre-requisite Requirements

To qualify for the grant of an AFI Rating (Aeroplanes) Microlight the applicant will be required to produce satisfactory evidence **before** starting his Assistant Flying Instructors Course of having:

a. At least a valid UK issued PPL with a current aircraft rating for microlight aeroplanes (without operational limitations if the licence is rated for microlights only) in a minimum period of 8 months before starting the AFI course, or be the holder of a valid UK issued licence with SEP rating who has been exercising the privileges of their licence on microlight aeroplanes.

b. 100 hours as PIC of which 60 hours are to be on microlights including 5 hours as PIC on the type to be used on the AFI course. The 100 hour requirement may be reduced to 70 hours in the case of holders of BHGA Full and Senior Flying Instructors Certificates.

c. Passed a pre-entry written examination and a Flight Test conducted by a Microlight FIE or a Microlight FIC Instructor in the 6 months immediately preceding the date of commencement of the course.

An AFI Rating (Aeroplanes) Microlight cannot be included in a NPPL.

Holders of JAR-FCL licences which contain appropriate Instructor Ratings (and Examiner Authorisations) may exercise the privileges of the ratings included in their licences on Microlight aeroplanes and SLMGs but should first undertake any necessary differences training.

In order to permit holders of NPPL's who wish to instruct on microlight aeroplanes and SLMGs, upon application to the CAA and, providing evidence of having undergone the required training and experience is produced, the holder of a NPPL may be granted an Exemption from the requirements of the Air Navigation Order 2005 to permit the licence holder to provide instruction in microlight and SLMGs only. The Exemptions issued will be for a limited period to permit more permanent administrative procedures to be formulated by the CAA which will be incorporated into a future amendment to the ANO following the necessary consultative process.

H7.2 Approved Course of Training

The minimum course of approved training for the AFI Rating Aeroplanes (Landplanes) Microlight comprises not less than 40 hours ground training and 15 hours flight training conducted by an instructor authorised by the CAA to conduct AFI Rating Courses (FIC Instructor) at FTOs approved for this purpose. Up to 2 hours of the course may be "mutual" flying with another AFIC student.

Flight Test and Ground Examination

The approved course of training for the AFI rating (Aeroplanes) Microlights and the AFI Rating Flight Test must be satisfactorily completed within a period of 12 months from the date on which the training is started. The applicant will be required to pass an AFI Rating Flight Test and Ground Examination conducted by a FIE (Microlight) authorised by the CAA to conduct such tests.

The candidate will be responsible for providing a suitable microlight aeroplane of the type and category he wishes to have endorsed in the rating. In this context, type refers to the design of the microlight: weight shift or three axis. Category refers to landplanes or seaplanes.

H7.3 Endorsement of Aeroplane Types

An AFI Rating holder wishing to instruct on an additional microlight type (i.e. weight shift or 3-axis) must have completed at least 5 hours as PIC on the type concerned. He must also have passed a Flight Test and Ground Examination on the type conducted by either a FIE (Microlight) or an instructor authorised to conduct Microlight AFI Courses.

H7.4 Rating Limitations

The syllabus for the AFI Course for microlights includes those items that form part of the syllabus of the Flight Test and Ground Examination for the Microlight PPL. It does not include instruction in night flying, instrument flying or aerobatics and a FI or AFI Rating for Microlights will be endorsed with limitations in respect of such instruction. Additional requirements will be specified for the removal of these limitations, if, in due course, microlights are suitably equipped and certificated to fly at night or in IMC or to perform aerobatics.

A microlight flying instructor qualified on landplanes and wishing to instruct on seaplanes must first attain the additional aircraft rating, and carry out sufficient ground and flight training with an appropriately qualified FIC instructor to enable him to pass a test with an FIE (microlights, seaplanes).

H8 FI RATING AEROPLANE (LAND, SEA) MICROLIGHTS

This section offers a basic guide to obtaining a Flight Instructor Rating (Land, Sea) Microlights

H8.1 FI(A) (Land, Sea) Microlights Experience/Requirements

To qualify for the grant of an FI Rating Microlight, the applicant will be required to:

a. Have gained not less than 250 hours experience as PIC of aeroplanes of which at least 200 hours must be on microlights (160 hours on microlights in the case of holders of the BHGA Full or Senior Flying Instructors Certificate);

b. Have held an AFI rating valid for microlights for at least 10 months and have 100 hours experience instructing on microlights;

c. have then passed a Flight Test and Ground Examination conducted by a FIE (Microlight), arrangements for which are as described in F6.

H8.2 Rating Limitations

As per H7.

H9 MOTOR GLIDER INSTRUCTORS RATING (MGIR)

This sections offers a basic guide to obtaining a Motor Glider Instructor Rating (MGIR)

H9.1 MGIR GENERAL INFORMATION

Much of the instructing which is given in motor gliders is for the training of glider pilots and the instructor is not required to teach aeroplane exercises. The qualification required for gliding exercises only is a certification issued by the BGA. It has no legal standing and is a BGA qualification.

For an instructor to teach students for the NPPL(A) SLMG he must hold a rating issued by the CAA, known as the (Restricted) Flying Instructor Rating SLMG (MGIR). This rating carries a restriction stating that the privileges may only be exercised under conditions laid down by the BGA. Alternatively, instruction for the NPPL SLMG licence or rating can also be given by the holder of a FI(A) with TMG rating or a FI(A) who has undergone differences training onto SLMG aircraft.

The fundamental difference between an Instructors Rating (MGIR), and the equivalent SEP or TMG Class Rating is that there is no Flying Instructors Course (FIC) for the SLMG.

In order to permit holders of NPPLs who wish to instruct on microlight aeroplanes and SLMGs, upon application to the CAA and, providing evidence of having undergone the required training and experience is produced, the holder of a NPPL may be granted an Exemption from the requirements of the Air Navigation Order 2005 to permit the licence holder to provide instruction in microlight and SLMGs only. The Exemptions issued will be for a limited period to permit more permanent administrative procedures to be formulated by the CAA which will be incorporated into a future amendment to the ANO following the necessary consultative process.

H9.2 MGIR QUALIFYING REQUIREMENTS

The qualifying requirements for the instructor rating issued by the CAA are that the applicant must:

a. Hold at least a UK Class 2 Medical Certificate.

b. Hold either a valid PPL(A) SLMG or a valid Professional Pilot's Licence (A) with the SLMG endorsement, or a valid JAR-FCL aeroplane pilot licence with either a TMG rating or certified completion of SLMG differences training.

c. Hold a current Full Gliding Instructors Rating issued by the BGA.

d. Pass a competency Flight Test with an approved Examiner. The approved Examiner must have CAA authorisation, i.e. hold a Flying Instructor Examiner Authorisation (SLMGs).

e. Have a minimum of 25 hours flying experience as PIC on SLMGs.

The qualifications required to train students for gliding exercise only, i.e. the certification issued by the BGA, are that the applicant must:

a. Hold at least a UK Class 2 Medical Certificate.

b. Hold either a valid UK PPL SLMG or a valid Professional Pilot's Licence (A) with the SLMG endorsement or a valid JAR-FCL aeroplane pilot licence with either a TMG rating or certified completion of SLMG differences training and;

c. Obtain such other qualifications and experience that the BGA require.

Full details will be made available, on request, by the BGA.

For the BGA certification, a nominated BGA Examiner may conduct the test.

There is no formal course of training for the conversion of Full Gliding Instructors Rating to MGIR: applicants are nominated by the CFI of the gliding organisation and tested by a BGA Panel Examiner on their ability to teach aeroplane exercises as opposed to gliding exercises.

There is no requirement to hold a Motor Glider Instructors Certification (gliding exercises only) before attaining a MGIR. Furthermore, since all applicants must hold a Full Gliding Instructors Rating, with its associated instructional experience, there is only one grade of Motor Glider Instructor (i.e. there is no Assistant Instructor category).

H9.3 MGIR RATING LIMITATIONS

There is no requirement for MGIR to hold IMC Ratings or have any experience in instrument flying. The Instructors Rating will be issued with the limitation that no night flying or instrument flying instruction will be given. The rating will also include a limitation precluding aerobatic instruction.

H9.4 REVALIDATION/RENEWAL OF RATING

The MGIR must be revalidated/renewed at least every 25 months by completing a Flight and Ground Test with a BGA Panel Examiner.

H10 AFI RATING AEROPLANES (LANDPLANES) POWERED PARACHUTES

This section offers a basic guide to obtaining an Assistant Flight Instructor Rating (AFI(A)) - Powered Parachutes.

H10.1 AFI Rating (Landplanes) Powered Parachutes General Information

H10.1 AFI Rating (Landplanes) Powered Parachutes General Information

To qualify for the grant of an AFI Rating (Aeroplanes) Powered Parachute, the applicant will be required to produce satisfactory evidence before starting his Assistant Flying Instructors Course of having:

a. Held at least a valid PPL with an Aircraft SEP Class Rating Microlight or Powered Parachute for a minimum period of 8 months and a PPL Powered Parachute without operational limitations before starting the AFI course.

b. 30 hours as Pilot-in-Command (PIC) on Powered Parachute including 2 hours as PIC on the type to be used on the AFI course.

c. Passed a pre-entry written examination and a Flight Test conducted by Powered Parachute Flight Instructor Examiner (FIE) or a Powered Parachute Flight Instructor Course (FIC) Instructor in the 6 months immediately preceding the date of the commencement of the course.

The minimum course of approved training for the AFI Rating Aeroplanes Powered Parachute comprises not less than 25 hours ground training and 4 hours flight training conducted by an instructor authorised by the CAA to conduct AFI Rating Courses (FIC Instructor) at FTOs approved for this purpose.

Flight Test and Ground Examination

On completion of the approved course of training, the applicant will be required to pass an AFI Rating Flight Test and Ground Examination conducted by a FIE (Powered Parachute) authorised by the CAA to conduct such tests.

Arrangements have been made for the BMAA to process applications for instructor tests for the issue, revalidation or extension of flying instructors ratings valid only on Powered Parachutes. Applications should be made direct to BMAA, who will then forward the application to the CAA for final action.

The approved course of training for the AFI Rating (Aeroplanes) Powered Parachute and the AFI Rating Flight Test must be satisfactorily completed within a period of 6 months from the date on which the training started.

Endorsement of Aeroplane Types

An AFI Rating Holder wishing to instruct an additional Powered Parachute type must have completed at least 2 hours as PIC on type concerned and have passed a Flight Test and Ground Examination on the type conducted by either an FIE (Powered Parachute) or an instructor authorised to conduct Powered Parachute AFI Courses.

H11 FI RATING AEROPLANE (LANDPLANES) POWERED PARACHUTES

This section offers a basic guide to obtaining a Flight Instructor Rating (Aeroplane) Powered Parachute

H11.1 FI Rating Aeroplane (Landplanes) Powered Parachutes General Information

H11.1General Information

To qualify for the grant of a FI Rating Powered Parachute (PP) the applicant will be required to complete 60 hours flying instruction under the supervision of a FI(PP) which must include instructing a minimum of one ab-initio student for the complete syllabus of training for the PPL(PP).

The applicant must also obtain from the holder of a FI(PP) Rating a certificate that the requirements have been complied with and that the FI(PP) considers the applicant competent to instruct unsupervised.

Flight Test and General Examination

Applicants for the FI(PP) Rating will be required to pass a Flight Test and oral Ground Examination conducted by a FIE(PP).

Endorsement of Powered Parachute Types

The holder of a FI(PP) rating is permitted to give flying instruction in any type of Powered Parachute for which the rating is endorsed. He must have at least 2 hours PIC on each type endorsed.

Application for Rating

On confirmation that the requirements laid down have been met, and on receipt from the applicant the licence, Medical Certificate, certified logbook and prescribed charge, the CAA (PLD) will issue a full FI(PP) Rating.

H12 AFI RATING (GYROPLANES) AFI(G)

This section offers a basic guide to obtaining an Assistant Flight Instructor Rating (AFI(G)) - Gyroplanes.

H12.1 AFI Rating (Gyroplanes) AFI(G) General Information

H12.1General Information

To qualify for the grant of an AFI Rating Gyroplanes the applicant will be required to have at least a minimum level of flying experience, undergo a course of training for the rating conducted by a FIC(G) Instructor and pass an AFI Rating Flight Test and Ground Examination conducted by an authorised Gyroplane Flying Instructor Examiner (FIE(G)).

Before being permitted to enter a course of training for the AFI(G)) Rating, applicants will be required to:

a. hold a valid PPL(G) with valid C or E;

b. have gained at least 100 hours flying experience on gyroplanes since the issue of a PPL(G), to include at least 15 hours on cross-country flights;

c. have at least 150 hours as pilot of flying machines;

d. pass a pre-entry exam, conducted by a FIC(G) Instructor.

The AFI Rating test will consist of a Flight Test and Ground Examination conducted by a FIE(G), which will include a pre-flight briefing, a long briefing and selected air exercises.

H13 FI RATING (GYROPLANES) FI(G)

This section offers a basic guide to obtaining a Flight Instructor Rating (FI(G)) - Gyroplanes.

H13.1General Information

To qualify for the grant of a FI Rating (Gyroplanes) the applicant will be required to complete 100 hours flying instruction under the supervision of a FI(G) which must include instructing a minimum of one ab-initio student for the complete syllabus of training for the PPL(G). The applicant must also obtain from the holder of a FI(G) Rating a certificate that this requirement has been complied with and that the FI(G) considers the applicant to be competent to instruct unsupervised.

Flight Test and General Examination

Applicants for the FI(G) Rating will be required to pass a Flight Test and oral Ground Examination conducted by a FIE(G).

Endorsement of Gyroplane Types

The holder of a FI(G) Rating is permitted to give flying instruction in any type of gyroplane for which the rating is endorsed. He must have at least 5 hours PIC on each type endorsed.

SECTION I

EXAMINER AUTHORISATIONS

The CAA currently issues the following types of Examiner Authorisations.

Each section details the requirements to obtain each authorisation, including flying training, ground examinations and flight tests.

I1 EXAMINER AUTHORISATIONS

For full details you are advised to refer to JAR-FCL 1 and 2 Subpart I.

I1.1 GENERAL INFORMATION

Examiners are authorised pursuant to Article 33(3) (b) of the Air Navigation Order (as amended) upon satisfactory completion of the requirements as published in JAR-FCL 1, 2 and 4 as appropriate, supported by further clarification published in CAA Standards Documents 21 and 11.

JAR-FCL 1.420 recognises six flight examiner (aeroplane) roles:

1. Flight Examiner (FE)
2. Class Rating Examiner (CRE)
3. Flight Instructor Examiner (FIE)
4. Type Rating Examiner (TRE)
5. Instrument Rating Examiner (IRE)
6. Synthetic Flight Examiner (SFE)

JAR-FCL 2.420 recognises five flight examiner (helicopter) roles:

1. Flight Examiner (FE)
2. Type Rating Examiner (TRE)
3. Instrument Rating Examiner (IRE)
4. Flight Instructor Examiner (FIE)
5. Synthetic Flight Examiner (SFE)

JAR-FCL 4.425 recognises one flight examiner (engineer) role:

1. Type Rating Examiner (TRE)

Provided they meet the qualification and experience requirements for each role undertaken, examiners are not confined to a single role.

Additionally, in the UK, examiners are appointed to conduct ground examinations for the PPL and to sign Certificates of Revalidation by experience.

Examiners shall hold a licence and rating at least equal to the licence or rating for which they are authorised to conduct skill tests or proficiency checks and, unless specified otherwise, the privilege to instruct for this licence or rating.

Examiners shall be qualified to act as pilot-in-command of the aircraft during a skill test or proficiency check, unless otherwise specified, and shall meet the applicable requirements set out in JAR-FCL 1.435 through 1.460. Where no qualified examiner is available and, at the discretion of the Authority, examiners/inspectors may be authorised without meeting the relevant instructor/type/class rating requirements as mentioned above.

Validities

All examiner authorisations are valid for a period of not more than 3 years and are re-authorised at the discretion of the Authority.

I1.2 FLIGHT EXAMINER (AEROPLANE)

FE(A) Privileges & Requirements

The privileges of a FE(A) are to conduct:

a. Skill tests for the issue of a PPL(A) and skill test/ proficiency checks for the associated single pilot class/type rating provided he has completed not less than 1000 hours flight time as a pilot of aeroplanes. This is to include a minimum 250 hours flight instruction.

b. Skill tests for the issue of a CPL(A) and skill test/ proficiency checks for the associated single-pilot class/type ratings provided he has completed not less than 2000 hours flight time as pilot of aeroplanes. To include a minimum of 250 hours flight instruction.

c. IMC Rating tests (if authorised).

Flight Examiners are <u>not</u> permitted to conduct theoretical knowledge examinations, unless authorised separately for this role.

I1.3 FLIGHT EXAMINER (HELICOPTER)

FE(H) Privileges & Requirements

The privileges of a FE(H) are to conduct:

a. Skill tests for the issue of a PPL(H) and skill test/ proficiency checks for the helicopter single-pilot type rating provided he has completed not less than 1000 hours flight time as a pilot of helicopters. This is to include a minimum of 250 hours flight instruction.

b. Skill tests for the issue of a CPL(H) and skill tests/ proficiency checks for the helicopter single-pilot type ratings provided he has completed not less than 2000 hours flight time as pilot of helicopters. This is to include a minimum 250 hours flight instruction.

Flight Examiners are <u>not</u> permitted to conduct theoretical knowledge examinations, unless authorised separately for this role.

I1.4 TYPE RATING EXAMINER (AEROPLANE)

TRE(A) Privileges & Requirements

The privileges of a TRE(A) are to conduct:

a. Skill tests for the issue of type ratings for multi-pilot aeroplanes.

b. Proficiency checks for -revalidation or renewal of multi-pilot type and instrument ratings.

c. Skill tests for issue of an ATPL(A).

The requirements for the issue of a TRE(A) are:

a. A minimum 1500 hours flight time as pilot of multi-pilot aeroplanes of which 500 hours are PIC.

b. To hold or have held a TRI(A) rating or authorisation.

I1.5 TYPE RATING EXAMINER (HELICOPTER)

TRE(H) Privileges & Requirements

The privileges of a TRE(H)(MPH) are to conduct:

a. Skill tests for the issue of type ratings.

b. Proficiency checks for revalidation or renewal of multi-pilot type ratings.

c. Proficiency checks for revalidation or renewal of instruments ratings provided the TRE(H) holds a valid IR(H).

d. Skill tests for ATPL(H) issue.

The requirements for the issue of a TRE(H)(MPH) are:

a. A minimum 1500 hours as pilot of multi-pilot helicopters of which 500 hours are PIC.

b. To hold or have held a TRI(H) rating or authorisation.

The privileges of a TRE(H)(SPH) are to conduct:

a. Skill tests for the issue of type ratings.

b. Proficiency checks for revalidation or renewal of single-pilot helicopter type and instrument ratings.

The requirements for issue of a TRE(H)(SPH) are:

a. A minimum 750 hours as pilot of helicopters.

b. To hold a professional helicopter licence with (if applicable) a valid IR(H).

I1.6 TYPE RATING EXAMINER (FLIGHT ENGINEER)

TRE(E) Privileges & Requirements

The privileges of a TRE(E) are to conduct:

a. Skill tests for the issue of FE licence and type ratings.

b. Proficiency checks for revalidation or renewal of a type rating.

The requirements for issue of a TRE(E) are:

a. A minimum 1500 hours flight time as a FE on MPA.

b. Hold a TRI(E) authorisation.

I1.7 CLASS RATING EXAMINER (AEROPLANE)

CRE(A) Privileges & Requirements

The privileges of a CRE(A) are to conduct:

a. Skill tests for the issue of class and type ratings for single-pilot aeroplanes.

b. Proficiency checks for revalidation or renewal of class and type ratings for single-pilot aeroplanes and revalidation or renewal, where specifically authorised by the Authority of instrument ratings.

The requirements for issue of a CRE(A) are:

a. A minimum 500 hours as pilot of aeroplanes.

b. To hold or have held a professional pilot aeroplane licence and holds a PPL(A).

c. To hold a current FI(A) or CRI rating on the appropriate class.

I1.8 INSTRUMENT RATING EXAMINER (AEROPLANE)

IRE(A) Privileges & Requirements

The privileges of an IRE(A) are to conduct:

a. Skill tests for initial issue of an instrument rating.

b. Proficiency checks for revalidation or renewal of an instrument rating.

The requirements for issue of an IRE(A) are:

a. A minimum 2000 hours as pilot of aeroplanes.

b. Not less than 450 hours flight time under IFR of which 250 hours as a flight instructor.

I1.9 INSTRUMENT RATING EXAMINER (HELICOPTER)

IRE(H) Privileges & Requirements

The privileges of an IRE(H) are to conduct:

a. Skill test for initial issue of an IR(H).

b. Proficiency checks for the revalidation or renewal of an IR(H).

The requirements for issue of an IRE(H) are:

a. A minimum 2000 hours as pilot of helicopters.

b. Not less than 300 hours flight time under IFR to include 200 hours as a flight instructor.

I1.10 SYNTHETIC FLIGHT EXAMINER (AEROPLANE)

SFE(A) Privileges & Requirements

The privileges of a SFE(A) are to conduct in a flight simulator:

a. skill tests for the issue of type ratings for multi-pilot aeroplanes;

b. proficiency checks for revalidation or renewal of multi-pilot type and instrument ratings.

Provided that the examiner holds an ATPL(A), has completed not less than 1500 hours of flight time as pilot of multi-pilot aeroplanes and is entitled to exercise the privileges of a SFI(A) and for the purpose of a) above holds a valid type rating on the applicable aeroplane type (see JAR-FCL 1.405).

I1.11 SYNTHETIC FLIGHT EXAMINER (HELICOPTER)

SFE(H) Privileges & Requirements

The privileges of a SFE(H) are to conduct type and instrument proficiency checks on MPH in a flight simulator.

The requirements for issue of a SFE(H) are:

a. To have a minimum 1000 hours flight time in MPH.

b. Hold an ATPL(H).

c. To be entitled to exercise the privileges of a SFI(H)

I1.12 FLIGHT INSTRUCTOR EXAMINER (AEROPLANE)

FIE(A) Privileges & Requirements

The privileges of an FIE(A) are to conduct skills test and proficiency checks or renewals for the issue and revalidation of flight instructor ratings.

The requirements for issue of the FIE(A) are that the applicant must have a minimum 2000 hours as pilot of aeroplanes including not less than 100 hours flight time instructing applicants for a FI(A) rating.

I1.13 FLIGHT INSTRUCTOR EXAMINER (HELICOPTER)

FIE(H) Privileges & Requirements

The privileges of a FIE(H) are to conduct skill tests and proficiency checks for the issue and revalidation or renewal of flight instructor ratings.

The requirements for issue of the FIE(H) are a minimum of 2000 hours as pilot of helicopters to include not less than 100 hours flight time instructing applicants for FI(H).

Further information on authorisation and re-authorisation are contained in the following documents:-

Standards Document 21 – Authorisation of Examiners for the Conduct of Skill Tests and Proficiency Checks in Single-Pilot Aeroplanes.

SECTION J

JAR-FCL THEORETICAL KNOWLEDGE EXAMINATION REQUIREMENTS

This section offers information as a basic guide to the requirements and procedures for the conduct of JAR-FCL theoretical knowledge examinations for a professional pilot licence, flight engineer licence and instrument rating.

J1 JAR-FCL THEORETICAL KNOWLEDGE EXAMINATION REQUIREMENTS

J1.1 GENERAL INFORMATION

An applicant for a professional pilot licence, or an instrument rating, shall demonstrate a level of knowledge appropriate to the privileges of the licence or rating for which application is made by passing theoretical knowledge examinations in accordance with the procedures set out in **JAR-FCL 1.470 to 1.495 or 2.470 to 2.495 inclusive.**

Questions appropriate to the syllabi will be held in a JAA Central Question Bank (CQB). The examinations will be provided in English, using abbreviations where applicable and compiled by a computer in multiple-choice format. Sample questions are available from the JAA web site www.jaa.nl. A list of common abbreviations used in the examinations can be found in JAA Administrative and Guidance Material Section 5, Part 2, Chapter 10, Attachment 3.

Candidates without a full pass in the UK national professional ground examinations

A candidate, who did not achieve a full pass in the UK National professional ground examinations, is required to pass the JAR-FCL theoretical knowledge examinations in all subjects. JAR-FCL additionally requires candidates to complete an approved theoretical knowledge course prior to attempting the examinations. However, a candidate who has previously passed at least one examination in the UK Navigation or Technical Group of examinations will not be required to complete the full theoretical knowledge course - the amount of theoretical knowledge instruction required will be at the discretion of the Head of Training of an approved training provider. This credit against the JAR-FCL theoretical knowledge course recognises the studies already completed by candidates who have passed national exams.

Examination Booking Procedure

In order to make an examination booking:-

Theoretical Knowledge Examination Bookings

All applications for a booking for any ATPL, CPL or IR examination (including re-sits) must be recommended and countersigned by the Chief Ground Instructor (or authorised signatory) of an approved training provider. A candidate who qualifies for exemption from approved theoretical knowledge training (i.e. some non-JAA ATPL conversions) will not be subject to this requirement.

- Candidates should apply in writing (either by post or fax) using the appropriate application forms (available from PLD or on our web site www.srg.caa.co.uk.) No bookings can be made by telephone, and all bookings are made on a first come, first served basis.
- Candidates should indicate on the application form their first and second preference venue choices and the date they wish to sit the examinations. Personnel Licensing Department will contact applicants where dates requested cannot be met and in the case of a venue being fully booked an alternative will be offered. The Authority reserves the right to change any venue to satisfy demand and does not guarantee a candidate a specific venue or examination date.
- Examination fees must be sent with the application form. Bookings will not be made unless the correct fees have been received.
- Once a booking has been made, candidates will receive an examination booking confirmation by post.
- The time between the closing date for applications and the examination sittings is two weeks. PLD will endeavour to send booking confirmations, venue details and examination timetables to reach candidates within 2 days of the booking and, in any case, at least 1 week prior to the sitting.

Examination Timetable

Details of the scheduled examination dates can be found at Appendix A.

Venue Details

Detailed venue maps can be found on the CAA (SRG) web site at www.caa.co.uk/publications

Facilities for lunchtime meals and/or snacks will be provided at all venues wherever possible on a payment basis.

Amending Examination Bookings

Examination bookings cannot be amended in the five clear working days prior to Day One of the examination week that the examination booking is contained within. Cancellations/transfers will only be accepted if received in writing at least five clear working days before Day One of the examination week, if accompanied by the cancellation/transfer fee as specified in the current Personnel Licensing Scheme of Charges. Cancellations/transfers requested within these five clear working days are subject to the loss of the subject fee(s). Refund of examination fees for emergency cancellations or non-attendance will only be given if a valid medical certificate (original) is provided, together with a letter of explanation.

Note: For CAA purposes, working days are Monday to Friday (excluding public holidays).

A fee applies to any amendment (except venue changes) to an existing booking and must accompany the written amendment request. Please refer to our current Scheme of Charges on our web site at www.caa.co.uk.

Money will only be debited from a debit/credit card or from money that is held in credit for that individual with prior authorisation from the card/account holder.

Where a candidate does not show for a booked examination(s), the fee for those subjects will be non-refundable and non-transferable. For any subjects not attempted within a sitting, when having attempted at least one subject, the fee(s) and attempt(s) are non-refundable and non-transferable.

On occasions when there is a possibility of disruption to public services, for whatever reason, candidates are expected to make alternative arrangements for attendance or if appropriate to give formal notice of their inability to attend.

Attendance at the Examination

Candidates should be present at the examination centre with photographic proof of identity* at least 20 minutes before the scheduled time for the commencement of each examination. A candidate who fails to provide authorised identification will not be permitted to sit and will be subject to forfeit the fee and attempt for that subject. The sitting number may also be affected. Candidates may enter the examination room only after invitation by the Invigilator, during the 10 minutes preceding the start of the examination to prepare examination material. Candidates must not remain in the examination room after the finish of the examination period.

*acceptable forms of photographic ID are: valid passport, UK Forces ID, photographic Driving Licence, School passes and Company ID. **All forms of ID must be photographic.**

On occasions when there is a possibility of disruption to public transport services, for whatever reason, candidates are expected to make alternative arrangements for attendance or, if appropriate, to give formal notice of their inability to attend.

Personal coats, bags, briefcases, etc. may be placed at the front/rear of the examination room, under the direction of the invigilating officer. Any bags etc. could be removed if left unattended outside the examination room. **Note:** the CAA accepts no responsibility for items of personal equipment a candidate brings into the examination hall and which he/she is not permitted to retain during the examination.

Whilst every attempt is made to ensure reasonable comfort in examination halls, the CAA cannot be held responsible for extraneous noise or for any breakdown or fluctuation in heating, lighting or ventilation facilities in examination halls which are operated on hire or lease arrangements and over which the CAA, as a result, has no direct control. Candidates are also advised that, at all examination centres, a 'no smoking rule' must be observed.

Please note you are not permitted to take any photographs at CAA examination venues.

Materials for the Examination

When necessary the following reference books and tables will be supplied to each candidate but they must not be marked in any way or removed from the examination room:

a. CAP 696 Loading Manual
b. CAP 697 Flight Planning Manual
c. CAP 698 Performance Manual

Candidates **may** bring the following materials to the following examination:

General Navigation ATPL, Navigation CPL and IR - E(LO) 1/2 and E(LO) 1A Jeppesen Chart.

Candidates **must** bring the following materials to the following examination:

Flight Planning - candidates must provide their own Jeppesen Training Route Manual. These are subject to random checks by the CAA Invigilators.

Candidates are required to provide themselves with all the necessary drawing and calculating instruments, e.g. dividers, compasses, protractors, parallel rules, slide rules and navigational computers and a scientific, non-programmable, non-alphanumeric calculator without aviation functions. Candidates may use their own pens, pencils, highlighters etc. on the rough working paper provided and/on their own documents. Documents provided by the CAA must not be marked in any permanent way (if pencils are used in CAA manuals, all marks must be erased before they are collected by the invigilator). **No pencil boxes, containers or instrument cases are permitted on tables**.

The use of slide rules or instruments containing printed information on critical point, point of no return, distance to the horizon, convergency, conversion angle, dep/d'long, conversion factors, etc. are not permitted.

Examination Briefing

Before the start of the examinations, the invigilator will give a briefing regarding the examination, details of which can be found in **Appendix B.**

Regulations which will be applied to the conduct of examinations

- Candidates are not allowed to use any loose paper other than that provided at the examination by the CAA. All papers issued and documents provided by the CAA are to be returned with the answer sheet to the Invigilator on completion. Failure to comply with this rule may result in disciplinary action being taken

- Answer sheets must be completed using the pencil provided. Candidates may use other writing implements on the rough working paper or on their own documents.

- Candidates must ensure that all answers have been transferred onto their answer sheet by the end of the examination. Candidates failing to do this will not be given any extra time.

- Silence is to be observed in the examination room at **all times.** Alarms from wristwatches and key rings are not permitted. Mobile telephones, pagers etc. must be switched off and left in the candidates personal belongings and **must not** be on your person.

- If a candidate wishes to speak to an invigilating officer, they should remain seated and raise their hand. *It should be noted that the invigilating officer will consider only those questions from candidates which relate to the general conduct of the examinations and they will not enter into discussion on the interpretation of words or questions contained in the examination papers.*

- A candidate may leave the room only with the permission of the invigilating officer if they have finished an examination before time, except during the last 5 minutes (after the warning is given) before the end of any paper. Candidates are to stop work and put pencils down immediately when so directed and must remain seated and quiet until all answer material has been collected. Failure to comply with this rule may result in disciplinary action being taken.

  If a candidate chooses to ignore any of the above regulations, they may be asked to leave the examination room.

- Any candidate who attempts to remove unauthorised examination materials from the room will be liable to disqualification from those examinations that have been taken and may be subject to special arrangements for future examinations.

Failure to comply with examination regulations

Any infringement of examination regulations may result in the candidate being disqualified in any subject that has been taken and barred from further participation in future examinations.

Immediate removal from the examination room may be imposed if a candidate chooses to ignore any of these regulations.

Examination Results

Candidates should not telephone in as we always endeavour to work to the timescales below and the results despatch enquiries before the published despatch date only serve to delay the process.

In normal circumstances results will be despatched by first class post or air mail within ten working days after the Friday of the examination week. Results will not be despatched until any outstanding payments have been received. It is not possible to collect your results on the day of despatch, simply because one candidate could enjoy a time advantage over another.

Please note that examination results cannot be e-mailed or advised via the telephone.

In the event of non-receipt of a result notification, arrangements can be made (on receipt of a written request) for repeat notifications to be sent by post, however an allowance should be made for possible postal delays before requesting a repeat notification.

The CAA cannot enter into discussion or correspondence with candidates on the subject of their examination results, but candidates may apply for any paper to be re-marked on payment of the fee as stated in the CAA Scheme of Charges, together with a written request.

Note:

Candidates for Professional Pilot and Flight Engineer Licences are advised to consult:-

a. JAR-FCL 1 and JAR-OPS 1 for aeroplane examinations

b. JAR-FCL 2 and JAR-OPS 3 for helicopter examinations

c. JAR-FCL 3 for relevant medical regulations

d. JAR-FCL 4 for flight engineer examinations

e. JAA Learning Objectives (LOs) at appropriate level.

All candidates are reminded that Aeronautical Information Circulars (White) published by the CAA are the means of conveying early warnings of, and short notice changes to, any of the examination requirements or timetables.

Re-sits

Candidates cannot apply to re-sit examinations, which they believe they may have failed, until they have received the official result notification.

J1.2 JAR-FCL ATPL(A)/(H) THEORETICAL KNOWLEDGE EXAMINATION REQUIREMENTS

Theoretical knowledge examination subjects for **ATPL** level * (see note regarding JAR Helicopter Exams) are available over a four day period as shown below.

Day One

Principles of Flight	0930-1030
Airframes/Systems	1045-1245
Mass & Balance	1400-1500
Performance	1515-1615
Daily Total	5 hours

Day Two

Instrumentation	0900-1030
Operational Procedures	1100-1220
Flight Planning	1300-1600
Daily Total	5 hours 50 min.

Day Three

General Navigation	0900-1100
Radio Navigation	1115-1245
Meteorology	1345-1615
Daily Total	6 hours

Day Four

Air Law	0900-1040
Human Performance & Limitations	1100-1200
VFR Communications	1300-1330
IFR Communications	1345-1415
Daily Total	3 hours 40 min.

*Currently the Helicopter Learning objectives have not been formalised by the JAA, and the Central Question Bank contains insufficient questions both in number and topic distribution in some subjects. Consequently, the CAA has decided not to proceed with the introduction of the JAR-FCL 2 examinations as previously intended. Until such time as the JAR-FCL helicopter examinations are introduced, the CAA have authorised interim arrangements using a combination of equivalent JAR-FCL aeroplane and JAR-FCL helicopter examinations as detailed below:

Instead of sitting the normal range of ATPL(H) as detailed previously, candidates may sit the following combination of JAR-FCL ATPL(H) and ATPL(A) papers. These interim arrangements for helicopter examinations will continue until further notice:-

ATPL(H) Papers

Airframes/Systems (subject to an agreement with the CAA), FTOs may substitute the ATPL(A) paper for this subject.

Principles of Flight (H)

ATPL(A) Papers

Air Law
Instruments/electronics
Mass and Balance
Flight Planning and Monitoring
Human Performance & Limitations
Meteorology
General Navigation
Radio Navigation
Operational Procedures
VFR Communications
IFR Communications

Candidates taking the exams under the interim arrangements should check their booking confirmation for exam start and finish times as they may differ from above. '

J1.3 JAR-FCL CPL (A)/(H) THEORETICAL KNOWLEDGE EXAMINATION REQUIREMENTS

Theoretical knowledge examination subjects for **CPL*** (see note regarding JAR Helicopter Exams) level are available over a two day period as shown below.

JAR-FCL CPL(A) Examinations

Day One

Principles of Flight Aircraft General	0900-0945
Knowledge	1000-1230
Flight Performance and Planning	1330-1630
Daily Total	6 hours 15 mins

Day Two

Navigation	0900-1030
Meteorology	1100-1230
Operational Procedures	1330-1415
Air Law	1430-1515
Human Performance & Limitations	1530-1600
VFR Communications	1615-1645
Daily Total	5 hours 30 mins

JAR-FCL CPL(H) Examinations

Day One

Principles of Flight	0900-1000
Aircraft General Knowledge	1015-1245
Flight Performance and Planning	1330-1700
Daily Total	7 hours

Day Two

Navigation	0900-1030
Meteorology	1045-1145
Operational Procedures	1200-1320
Air Law	1430-1530
Human Performance & Limitations	1545-1615
VFR Communications	1630-1700
Daily Total	5 hours 50 mins

*Currently the Helicopter Learning objectives have not been formalised by the JAA, and the Central Question Bank contains insufficient questions both in number and topic distribution in some subjects. Consequently, the CAA has decided not to proceed with the introduction of the JAR-FCL 2 examinations as previously intended. Until such time as the JAR-FCL helicopter examinations are introduced, the CAA have authorised interim arrangements using a combination of equivalent JAR-FCL aeroplane and JAR-FCL helicopter examinations as detailed below:

Instead of sitting the normal range of CPL(H) as detailed previously, candidates may sit the following combination of JAR-FCL CPL(H) and CPL(A) papers. These interim arrangements for helicopter examinations will continue until further notice:-

CPL(H) Papers

Principles of Flight (H)

CPL(A) Papers

Air Law
Aircraft General Knowledge
Flight Performance and Planning
Human Performance and limitations
Meteorology
Navigation
Operational Procedures
VFR Communications

Candidates taking the exams under the interim arrangements should check their booking confirmation for exam start and finish times as they may differ from above.

J1.4 JAR-FCL IR THEORETICAL KNOWLEDGE EXAMINATION REQUIREMENTS

Theoretical knowledge examination subjects for **IR** level are available over a two day period and are in the order as stated below.

Day One

Aircraft General	0900-1015
Flight Performance & Planning	1030-1230
Navigation	1330-1530
Human Performance & Limitations	1600-1630
Daily Total	5 hours 45 mins

Day Two

Meteorology	0900-1030
Air Law & ATC Procedures	1100-1200
IFR Communications	1230-1300
Daily Total	3 hours

J1.5 JAR-FCL THEORETICAL KNOWLEDGE EXAMINATION PASS STANDARDS

A candidate must complete all required written examination papers within 18 months of their first sitting, using a maximum of 6 sittings and no more than 4 attempts at an individual paper within the 6 sittings. The papers can be attempted in any order. A Pass in an examination paper will be awarded to a candidate achieving at least 75% of the marks allocated to that paper.

Failure to comply with Pass Standards

An applicant failing to pass all of the relevant examinations within the time limits (imposed by JAR-FCL 1.490/2.490) will be required to re-enter the examinations as though for an initial attempt.

An applicant will be required to complete the minimum approved theoretical knowledge training specified below prior to re-entering the examinations:

- Integrated or modular IR theory course = minimum 20 hours theoretical knowledge instruction.
- Integrated or modular CPL theory course = minimum 20 hours theoretical knowledge instruction.
- Integrated or modular ATPL theory course = minimum 60 hours theoretical instruction. A candidate who received a reduction in the ATPL theoretical instruction hours i.e. where an IR, CPL or CPL/IR was already held, will be required to complete further theoretical knowledge instruction equivalent to a minimum 10% of the original course completed.

A candidate who only completed ATPL, CPL and/or IR theoretical knowledge instruction at the discretion of an approved training provider i.e. conversion from a non-JAA qualification, will be required to complete further theoretical knowledge instruction at the discretion of an approved training provider.

All applications for resits must be countersigned by the Chief Ground Instructor (or authorised signatory) of an approved training provider. A candidate who qualifies for exemption from approved theoretical knowledge training (i.e. some non-JAA ATPL conversions) is not subject to this requirement.

J1.6 JAR-FCL THEORETICAL KNOWLEDGE EXAMINATION CREDITS

Details of JAR-FCL Theoretical Examination Credits can be found within the appropriate section for the licence being sought.

J1.7 JAR-FCL THEORETICAL KNOWLEDGE EXAMINATION ACCEPTANCE PERIOD

Potential candidates for the JAR-FCL ATPL theoretical knowledge examinations should first consider the implications of JAR-FCL 1.495 or 2.495 that relates to the Acceptance Period.

A pass in the ATPL theory examinations will be accepted for the issue of a CPL or IR during the 36 months from the end of the month of the date of the final pass in the examinations*. Provided that an IR is obtained during this period, a pass in the ATPL theoretical knowledge examinations will remain valid (for the purpose of ATPL issue) for a period of 7 years from the validity date of the most recent renewal IR entered in the CPL.

* All requirements for the issue of the CPL and IR must be met and the applicant required to apply to PLD for issue within the 36 month validity period of the theoretical knowledge examination.

Failure to comply with Acceptance Period

If a CPL and IR are not granted within the 36 month acceptance period then the ATPL theory credit will lapse. Candidates will be required to re-pass all ATPL theoretical knowledge examinations to regain ATPL theory credit. However, it has been agreed that where a candidate has previously passed all ATPL theoretical knowledge examinations but were not granted a CPL/IR within the 36 month acceptance period, the amount of ATPL theoretical knowledge instruction will be at the discretion of the Head of Training of the Approved FTO.

J1.8 CREDIT OF ATPL EXAMINATION PASSES AGAINST CPL EXAMINATION

In some circumstances a candidate who has previously attempted some ATPL theoretical knowledge examinations may wish to consider attempting examinations at a lower level (i.e. CPL and/or IR). A candidate who has failed to obtain a pass in any subject at ATPL level will be required to enter for the CPL and/or IR examinations as though for an initial sitting. A candidate who has previously completed an approved ATPL theoretical knowledge course may be credited with the CPL and/or IR theoretical knowledge course. Candidates will be required to enter for these theoretical knowledge examinations via an approved CPL FTO. A candidate who has passed at least one subject at ATPL level may be credited the equivalent subject at CPL and/or IR level as detailed below:-

a. a candidate who has passed any of the "common" subjects (Air Law, Human Performance and Limitations, Meteorology, Operational Procedures*, Principles of Flight, VFR Communications** and IFR Communications**) at ATPL level may be credited the equivalent examination at CPL and/or IR level;

b. the remaining subjects at CPL and/or IR level (Aircraft General Knowledge, Flight Performance and Planning, and Navigation) are associated with more than one examination at ATPL level. A candidate may be credited any of the remaining subjects only where he has passed all associated examinations for that subject at ATPL level, as set out in the table below;

c. candidates should note that where credit is given in accordance with (a) or (b) above, all sittings, attempts and time limits will be calculated from the initial attempt at the ATPL examinations.

* A candidate may only be credited the Air Law/Operational Procedures examination at IR level where they have passed both the Air Law and Operational Procedures examinations at ATPL level.

** A candidate who has previously passed either or both of the examinations in VFR and IFR Communications will be credited the examination in the appropriate subject(s) at CPL and/or IR level.

CPL or IR Examinations	Associated ATPL Examination
Aircraft General Knowledge	Airframe/Systems/Power-plant Instruments/Electronics
Flight Performance and Planning	Mass and Balance Performance Flight Planning and Monitoring
Navigation	General Navigation Radio Navigation

J1.9 CREDITING OF THEORETICAL KNOWLEDGE (BRIDGE INSTRUCTION)

Introduction

JAR-FCL 1.050(b)/2.050(b) provides for theoretical knowledge credits for the holder of a specific aeroplane licence wishing to obtain a helicopter licence and vice versa. Theoretical knowledge exam credits are subject to the completion of specific bridge instruction and examinations. The theoretical knowledge requirements set out in this section replicate those set out in Appendix 1 to JAR-FCL 1.050/2.050, and are broken down into topics within a particular subject.

The terms are applicable to bridge between JAR-FCL licences only. A UK national licence holder will be required to convert to an equivalent JAR-FCL licence in accordance with Appendix 1 to 1.005/2.005 (see A10) in order to take advantage of any of the credits available.

Bridge Instruction/examination Requirements

This section is separated into six parts:-

Part 1 Bridge instruction/examination requirements for holders of a JAR-FCL ATPL(H)/IR to obtain ATPL(A) theory credit

Part 1 Bridge instruction/examination requirements for holders of a JAR-FCL ATPL(H)/IR to obtain ATPL(A) theory credit

In order to satisfy the theoretical knowledge requirements for the JAR-FCL ATPL(A), the holder of a JAR-FCL ATPL(H)/IR is required to complete approved bridge instruction **(see Note 1)** for the subjects/topics detailed in Appendix 1 to JAR-FCL 1.050. In addition, a pass in the following ATPL(A) examinations must be obtained, in accordance with JAR-FCL 1.490:- Performance; Operational Procedures; Principles of Flight (A) and the Composite ATPL(A) bridge examination **(see Note 2)**.

Part 2 Bridge instruction/examination requirements for holders of a JAR-FCL ATPL(A) or CPL(A) with valid ATPL(A) theory credit, to obtain ATPL(H) theory credit

In order to satisfy the theoretical knowledge requirements for the JAR-FCL ATPL(H), the holder of a JAR-FCL ATPL(A), or CPL(A) with valid* ATPL(A) theory credit, is required to complete approved bridge instruction for the subjects/topics detailed in Appendix 1 to JAR-FCL 2.050. In addition, a pass in the following ATPL(H) examinations must be obtained, in accordance with JAR-FCL 2.490:- Performance; Operational Procedures; Principles of Flight (H) and the Composite ATPL(H) bridge examination **(see Note 2)**.

** valid in accordance with JAR-FCL 1.495(a) or (b)*

Part 3 Bridge instruction/examination requirements for holders of a JAR-FCL ATPL(H) or CPL(H) to obtain CPL(A) theory credit

In order to satisfy the theoretical knowledge requirements for the JAR-FCL CPL(A), the holder of a JAR-FCL ATPL(H) or CPL(H) is required to complete approved bridge instruction **(see Note 1)** for the subjects/topics detailed in Appendix 1 to JAR-FCL 1.050. In addition, a pass in the following CPL(A) examinations must be obtained, in accordance with JAR-FCL 1.490:- Performance*; Operational Procedures; Principles of Flight (A) and the Composite CPL(A) bridge examination **(see Note 2)**.

** At CPL(A) level, this subject forms part of the Flight Performance & Planning examination. For bridging purposes, a specific examination paper for CPL(A) Performance will be produced.*

Part 4 Bridge instruction/examination requirements for holders of a JAR-FCL ATPL(A) or CPL(A) with valid ATPL(A) theory credit, to obtain CPL(H) theory credit

As the JAA's Administrative & Guidance Material does not provide details of the distribution of questions for the Composite CPL(H) examination, the UK CAA will continue with interim bridging arrangements until further notice.

In order to satisfy the theoretical knowledge requirements for the JAR-FCL CPL(H), the holder of a JAR-FCL ATPL(A), or JAR-FCL CPL(A) with valid* ATPL(A) theory credit, is required to pass the following CPL(H) examinations, in accordance with JAR-FCL 2.490:- Principles of Flight (H).

** valid in accordance with JAR-FCL 1.495(a) or (b)*

Part 5 Bridge instruction/examination requirements for UK Qualified Service Pilot (Helicopters) holding a JAR-FCL CPL(H) with valid JAR-FCL ATPL(H) theory credit, to obtain ATPL(A) theory credit

In order to satisfy the theoretical knowledge requirements for the JAR-FCL ATPL(A), a UK QSP(H) holding a JAR-FCL CPL(H) with valid* ATPL(H) theory credit is required to complete approved bridge instruction **(see Note 1)** for the subjects/topics detailed in Appendix 1 to JAR-FCL 1.050. In addition, a pass in the following ATPL(A) examinations must be obtained, in accordance with JAR-FCL 1.490:- Performance;

Operational Procedures; Principles of Flight (A) and the Composite ATPL(A) bridge examination **(see Note 2)**.

** valid in accordance with JAR-FCL 2.495(a), or holding a JAR-FCL CPL(H) obtained via the UK QSP(H) Accreditation Scheme (no IR required as ATPL(H) theory is 'frozen' as long as the applicant maintains a valid military green IR(H))*

Part 6 Examination arrangements

All examination booking application forms for the bridging examinations (including re-sits), must be countersigned by the Chief Ground Instructor (or authorised signatory) of an approved training provider.

The Composite bridging examination for ATPL(A)/(H) will be scheduled for 13.00 on Day 2 of the published examination timetable i.e. together with candidates for the Flight Planning & Monitoring examination. The Composite bridging examination for CPL(A) will be scheduled for 10.00 on Day 1 of the published examination timetable i.e. together with candidates for the Aircraft General Knowledge examination.

Note 1

In circumstances where an approved bridge instruction course is not available, PLD will permit candidates to complete theoretical knowledge instruction, at the appropriate level, at the discretion of the Head of Training of an approved training provider.

However, candidates should consider carefully that in this circumstance, preparation for the Composite bridge examination may be affected, as the training provider may not have produced mock/final examination papers for this examination. The alternative, would be to pass the requisite examination for each subject in which at least one topic is detailed in the syllabus for the bridge examination (10 examinations at ATPL level; 7 examinations at CPL level).

Note 2

Under current arrangements, some UK approved helicopter theoretical knowledge training providers are continuing to utilise the interim arrangement of candidates sitting the equivalent JAR-FCL aeroplane examinations plus the necessary helicopter examinations to ensure all JAR CPL(H) or ATPL(H) syllabus subjects are covered.

A candidate with valid JAR ATPL(H) theory credit obtained under the interim arrangement, who wishes to obtain JAR CPL(A) or ATPL(A) theory credit, will be awarded a credit for those subjects in which the equivalent ATPL(A) examinations were passed - this may particularly be the case for Operational Procedures, Composite CPL(A) or ATPL(A) bridging exam*, and in some cases, Performance. **Important:** a candidate who qualifies for one or more exam credits should note that for the purposes of JAR-FCL 1.495, the validity of JAR CPL(A) or ATPL(A) theory credit will be calculated as **36** months from the date of gaining a pass in the JAR ATPL(H) theory examinations, NOT from the date of completing the CPL(A) or ATPL(A) bridging requirements.

* the syllabus for the Composite CPL(A) & ATPL(A) bridging exams comprises topics in Air Law & ATC Procedures, Airframe/Systems/Powerplant, Instruments/Electronics, Mass & Balance, Flight Planning & Monitoring, Meteorology and General Navigation. Credit for either Composite exam will only be given to a candidate who has passed the ATPL(A) examinations in ALL of the subjects listed above.

Similarly, until such time as the aforementioned interim arrangement for helicopter theoretical knowledge ceases, a candidate with valid JAR ATPL(A) theory credit who wishes to obtain JAR ATPL(H) theory credit through an approved training provider currently using the interim arrangement, will be awarded a credit for those subjects in which the equivalent ATPL(A) examinations are sat. **Important:** a candidate who qualifies for one or more exam credits should note that for the purposes of JAR-FCL 2.490, the validity of JAR ATPL(H) theory credit will be calculated as **36** months from the date of gaining a pass in the JAR ATPL(A) theory examinations, NOT from the date of completing the ATPL(H) bridging requirements.

APPENDICES TO SECTION J

APPENDIX A EXAMINATION TIMETABLE FOR 2007

JAR-FCL ATPL(A)/(H) - The examination centres for the JAR-ATPL(A) and (H) are Gatwick, Oxford, Silsoe and Glasgow.

Month	Dates	Papers	Closing Date
Jan	Mon 8	Principles of Flight, Airframes, Mass and Balance, Performance	15 Dec 2006
	Tue 9	Instrumentation, Operational Procedures, Flight Planning	
	Wed 10	General Navigation, Radio Navigation, Meteorology	
	Thur 11	Air Law, Human Performance, VFR Communications, IFR Communications	
Feb	Mon 5	Principles of Flight, Airframes, Mass and Balance, Performance	22 Jan 2007
	Tue 6	Instrumentation, Operational Procedures, Flight Planning	
	Wed 7	General Navigation, Radio Navigation, Meteorology	
	Thur 8	Air Law, Human Performance, VFR Communications, IFR Communications	
Mar	Mon 5	Principles of Flight, Airframes, Mass and Balance, Performance	19 Feb 2007
	Tue 6	Instrumentation, Operational Procedures, Flight Planning	
	Wed 7	General Navigation, Radio Navigation, Meteorology	
	Thur 8	Air Law, Human Performance, VFR Communications, IFR Communications	
Apr	Mon 2	Principles of Flight, Airframes, Mass and Balance, Performance	19 Mar 2007
	Tue 3	Instrumentation, Operational Procedures, Flight Planning	
	Wed 4	General Navigation, Radio Navigation, Meteorology	
	Thur 5	Air Law, Human Performance, VFR Communications, IFR Communications	
April	Mon 30	Principles of Flight, Airframes, Mass and Balance, Performance	16 Apr 2007
May	Tue 1	Instrumentation, Operational Procedures, Flight Planning	
	Wed 2	General Navigation, Radio Navigation, Meteorology	
	Thur 3	Air Law, Human Performance, VFR Communications, IFR Communications	

Jun	Mon 4	Principles of Flight, Airframes, Mass and Balance, Performance	18 May 2007
	Tue 5	Instrumentation, Operational Procedures, Flight Planning	
	Wed 7	General Navigation, Radio Navigation, Meteorology	
	Thur 8	Air Law, Human Performance, VFR Communications, IFR Communications	
Jul	Mon 2	Principles of Flight, Airframes, Mass and Balance, Performance	18 Jun 2007
	Tue 3	Instrumentation, Operational Procedures, Flight Planning	
	Wed 4	General Navigation, Radio Navigation, Meteorology	
	Thur 5	Air Law, Human Performance, VFR Communications, IFR Communications	
Aug	Mon 6	Principles of Flight, Airframes, Mass and Balance, Performance	23 Jul 2007
	Tue 7	Instrumentation, Operational Procedures, Flight Planning	
	Wed 8	General Navigation, Radio Navigation, Meteorology	
	Thur 9	Air Law, Human Performance, VFR Communications, IFR Communications	
Sep	Mon 3	Principles of Flight, Airframes, Mass and Balance, Performance	17 Aug 2007
	Tue 4	Instrumentation, Operational Procedures, Flight Planning	
	Wed 5	General Navigation, Radio Navigation, Meteorology	
	Thur 6	Air Law, Human Performance, VFR Communications, IFR Communications	
Oct	Mon 1	Principles of Flight, Airframes, Mass and Balance, Performance	17 Sep 2007
	Tue 2	Instrumentation, Operational Procedures, Flight Planning	
	Wed 3	General Navigation, Radio Navigation, Meteorology	
	Thur 4	Air Law, Human Performance, VFR Communications, IFR Communications	

Nov	Mon 5	Principles of Flight, Airframes, Mass and Balance, Performance	22 Oct 2007
	Tue 6	Instrumentation, Operational Procedures, Flight Planning	
	Wed 7	General Navigation, Radio Navigation, Meteorology	
	Thur 8	Air Law, Human Performance, VFR Communications, IFR Communications	
Dec	Mon 3	Principles of Flight, Airframes, Mass and Balance, Performance	19 Nov 2007
	Tue 4	Instrumentation, Operational Procedures, Flight Planning	
	Wed 5	General Navigation, Radio Navigation, Meteorology	
	Thur 6	Air Law, Human Performance, VFR Communications, IFR Communications	

JAR-FCL CPL(A) – These examinations will only be held at Gatwick

Month	Dates	Papers	Closing Date
Jan	Mon 15	Principles of Flight, Aircraft General, Performance and Planning	2 Jan 2007
	Tue16	Navigation, Meteorology, Operational Procedures, Air Law, Human Performance, VFR Communications	
Mar	Mon 12	Principles of Flight, Aircraft General, Performance and Planning	26 Feb 2007
	Tue 13	Navigation, Meteorology, Operational Procedures, Air Law, Human Performance, VFR Communications	
May	Mon 8	Principles of Flight, Aircraft General, Performance and Planning	25 Apr 2007
	Tue 9	Navigation, Meteorology, Operational Procedures, Air Law, Human Performance, VFR Communications	
Jul	Mon 9	Principles of Flight, Aircraft General, Performance and Planning	25 Jun 2007
	Tue 10	Navigation, Meteorology, Operational Procedures, Air Law, Human Performance, VFR Communications	
Sep	Mon 10	Principles of Flight, Aircraft General, Performance and Planning	28 Aug 2007
	Tue 11	Navigation, Meteorology, Operational Procedures, Air Law, Human Performance, VFR Communications	

Nov	Mon 12	Principles of Flight, Aircraft General, Performance and Planning	29 Oct 2007
	Tue 13	Navigation, Meteorology, Operational Procedures, Air Law, Human Performance, VFR Communications	

JAR-FCL CPL(H) – These examinations will only be held at Gatwick.

Month	Dates	Papers	Closing Date
Jan	Wed 17	Principles of Flight, Aircraft General, Performance and Planning	3 Jan 2007
	Thu 18	Navigation, Meteorology, Operational Procedures, Air Law, Human Performance, VFR Communications	
Mar	Wed 14	Principles of Flight, Aircraft General, Performance and Planning	28 Feb 2007
	Thu 15	Navigation, Meteorology, Operational Procedures, Air Law, Human Performance, VFR Communications	
May	Wed 10	Principles of Flight, Aircraft General, Performance and Planning	26 Apr 2007
	Thu 11	Navigation, Meteorology, Operational Procedures, Air Law, Human Performance, VFR Communications	
Jul	Wed 11	Principles of Flight, Aircraft General, Performance and Planning	27 Jun 2007
	Thu 12	Navigation, Meteorology, Operational Procedures, Air Law, Human Performance, VFR Communications	
Sep	Wed 12	Principles of Flight, Aircraft General, Performance and Planning	29 Aug 2007
	Thu 13	Navigation, Meteorology, Operational Procedures, Air Law, Human Performance, VFR Communications	
Nov	Wed 14	Principles of Flight, Aircraft General, Performance and Planning	31 Oct 2007
	Thu 15	Navigation, Meteorology, Operational Procedures, Air Law, Human Performance, VFR Communications	

JAR-FCL IR(A), (H) These examinations will only be held at Gatwick

Month	Dates	Papers	Closing Date
Feb	Mon 12	Aircraft General, Performance and Planning, Navigation, Human Performance	29 Jan 2007
	Tue 13	Meteorology, Air Law/Operational Procedures, IFR Communications	

Apr	Mon 10	Aircraft General, Performance and Planning, Navigation, Human Performance	27 Mar 2007
	Tue 11	Meteorology, Air Law/Operational Procedures, IFR Communications	
Jun	Mon 11	Aircraft General, Performance and Planning, Navigation, Human Performance	25 May 2007
	Tue 12	Meteorology, Air Law/Operational Procedures, IFR Communications	
Aug	Mon 13	Aircraft General, Performance and Planning, Navigation, Human Performance	30 Jul 2007
	Tue 14	Meteorology, Air Law/Operational Procedures, IFR Communications	
Oct	Mon 8	Aircraft General, Performance and Planning, Navigation, Human Performance	24 Sep 2007
	Tue 9	Meteorology, Air Law/Operational Procedures, IFR Communications	
Dec	Mon 10	Aircraft General, Performance and Planning, Navigation, Human Performance	26 Nov 2007
	Tue 11	Meteorology, Air Law/Operational Procedures, IFR Communications	

APPENDIX B EXAMINATION BRIEFING

- Bags and coats are to be placed at the rear/front of the exam room, or separate area if provided. Please remove all headwear and place on the floor. Check that phones and watch alarms are switched off and that mobile phones are away from your person (i.e. in a bag, etc.).
- Photo ID must be placed on the desk and will be checked during every exam. ID must be a passport or UK Forces ID. School passes and Company ID with a photo are acceptable.
- Please note the fire exits in the exam room. If the fire alarm sounds please leave all personal belongings and paperwork on the desk and leave the room quickly. Once the 'all clear' has been given the exam will restart.
- All pencil cases, CRP cases and confirmation notifications are to be placed on the floor. Only mandatory items i.e. charts, calculator, CRP, one highlighter pen, exam question and answer sheets are allowed on the desk. Random checks may be made on equipment during the exams.
- Candidates are to use only the pencil provided for completion of the answer sheet.
- Only non-programmable, non-alphanumeric calculators are permitted in the exams.
- Check the details are correct on the cover sheet and enter postal address if different. The cover sheet must stay on desk at all times, please note the start times for your exams and be available 10 minutes prior to each start time.
- Workings out must be done on the rough working paper provided. Do not write on any other paper except the answer sheet and rough working paper.
- Start and finish times will be put on the board and times are taken from the clock in the exam room.
- Any writing before the start of the exam, other than details requested on the examination paperwork will not be tolerated.
- Check the exam paperwork on your desk. Once you are satisfied that it is correct, including appendices, sign and date the exam paper. Read the instructions on the top left hand corner regarding how to fill out the answer sheet. Encode the exam and candidate number in pencil only. Do not make any other marks on the sheet apart from your answers.
- Be aware of the 5 minute warning which will be given before the end of the exam.
- Pencils must be put down immediately when time is called, otherwise disciplinary action will be taken. Answers must be transferred during the examination time.
- No extra time will be given after the exam has finished for candidates to write comments or queries. This must be done during the exam.
- During the exam only general questions may be answered. You will not be given meanings or explanations of words used in the question papers.
- At the end of the exam please remain seated until all paperwork is collected.
- If you finish your exam early please raise your hand and remain silent. Remain seated until your paperwork is collected and checked, then you may leave the exam room quietly. Be considerate of others still working.
- Appendices can be detached and handed in with the exam paperwork. Each separated appendix must have your name or initials on it.
- The exam room will be locked during lunchtimes and personal items may be left in the room. Personal items left anywhere are your own responsibility.
- Silence is to be observed in the examination room at all times. If you wish to speak with the Invigilator remain seated and raise your hand.

SECTION K

FLIGHT ENGINEER LICENCE

The UK Civil Aviation Authority currently issues UK Flight Engineer Licences.

K1 FLIGHT ENGINEER LICENCE

This section offers information as a basic guide to obtaining a UK Flight Engineer's Licence - UK F/EL as follows:-

Important Note: **The UK CAA has not yet adopted the requirements of JAR-FCL 4 - Flight Engineer Licence. Therefore, the requirements detailed within this Section are for the issue of a UK Flight Engineer's Licence (UK F/EL)**

K1.1 UK F/EL GENERAL INFORMATION

Privileges

Details of licence privileges can be found in Schedule 8 of the Air Navigation Order, (please refer to Section A, Appendix F).

Minimum Age

An applicant for a UK F/EL is 21 years.

Licence Validity

The UK F/EL will be issued for a maximum period of validity of 10 years.

Eligibility

The following persons may be eligible to qualify for the issue of a UK F/EL:

1. Experienced Aeronautical Ground Engineers who hold a valid Aircraft Maintenance Engineer's Licence (can be a 'Licence without Type Rating),

or

Have at least **three** years general aeronautical engineering maintenance experience.

2. Royal Air Force Air Engineers with at least **400** hours flying experience as an Air Engineer.

3. Holders of a **valid** Non-UK Flight Engineer's Licence.

4. Holders of a **valid** Professional Pilot's Licence (Aeroplanes).

A UK F/EL must contain a Type Rating that allows the holder to exercise the privileges of the licence.

Type Ratings are issued for the following aircraft:

Airbus A300
Boeing 707
Boeing 727
Boeing 747-100/200/300/S.P
DC-6
DC-8
DC-10
L382G (Hercules)
L1011 Tri-Star
L188 Electra
Shorts Belfast

The Royal Air Force (RAF) uses Flight Engineers (known as Air Engineers) on the following aircraft:

C130 Hercules
L1011 Tri-Star
Nimrod
Sentry (B707)
VC-10

Non-UK Licence Holders

Any United Kingdom flight crew licences issued on conversion of foreign licences, will contain a statement on the licence to that effect. This is in order to comply with Article 6 of EC Directive 670/1991 effective from 1 June 1992. This statement will NOT be entered in UK licences issued on conversion from an EC Member State's licence.

K1.2 UK F/EL FLYING TRAINING REQUIREMENTS

An applicant for a UK F/EL must undertake **100** hours of supervised Flight Engineer training on the first aircraft type to be included in the licence. This must include the particular requirements specified in a) below. All Flight Engineer training must be completed within the 12 months preceding the date of application for licence issue.

a. **100 hours*** Supervised Flight Engineer Training on Type, can include (i);

   i. **50 hours* (Maximum)** training in a CAA Approved Flight Simulator of the same type

*Royal Air Force Air Engineers are credited with **50** hours of the 100 hours supervised Flight Engineer training required in (a). Of the remaining **50** hours required on type, up to **25** hours may be completed in a CAA Approved Flight Simulator of the same type. Air Engineers who have more than 100 hours experience in a Service aircraft for which a type rating is issued (e.g. L1011 Tri-Star), will only be required to complete the Aircraft Rating Flight Test on that type.

b. Complete a **CAA Approved Type Rating Conversion Course**

K1.3 UK F/EL THEORETICAL KNOWLEDGE EXAMINATION REQUIREMENTS

An applicant for a UK F/EL is required to:

1. Pass the **JAR-FCL ATPL(A) Theoretical Knowledge Examinations** in the following subjects:

   Principles of Flight
   Airframes/Systems
   Mass & Balance
   Instrumentation
   Operational Procedures
   Human Performance and Limitations

Note: These theoretical knowledge examinations replace the former UK Flight Engineer Technical Group of Examinations.

Credits from Ground Examinations

- The holder of a valid Non-UK Flight Engineer's Licence with **more** than 3000 hours experience as a Flight Engineer will be credited the Principles of Flight, Airframes/Systems, Mass & Balance and Instrumentation examinations.

- A current UK Military Air Engineer will be credited the Airframes/Systems and Instrumentation examinations.

FULL DETAILS OF THE JAR-FCL-ATPL (A) THEORETICAL KNOWLEDGE EXMINATIONS, PASS RULES, VALIDITY PERIODS ETC ARE GIVEN IN SECTION J and JAR-FCL 1, SUBPART J.

Note for RAF Air Engineers

It has been agreed that qualified Air Engineers having passed the theoretical knowledge examinations may retain this pass for as long as they remain in current flying practice as appropriately categorised Air Engineers in the RAF. Once they leave the RAF, the 36 month acceptance period for licence issue will be calculated from the date of their last flight as Air Engineer in a military aeroplane.

K1.4 UK F/EL SKILL TEST REQUIREMENTS

An applicant for a UK F/EL is required to pass a Flight Engineer Skill Test on the aircraft type to be included in the licence with a CAA Authorised Flight Engineer Type Rating Examiner.

- For further details of Flight Engineer Type Rating Examiners, please contact the CAA Flight Operations Department, Tel: 01293 573496

- Holders of a valid Non-UK Flight Engineer's Licence which includes a specific aeroplane type, may have that type endorsed in the UK Licence without having to take an Aircraft Rating Flight Test on the type, provided that:

  i. The applicant has **more** than **3000** hours experience as a Flight Engineer including at least **100** hours experience as Flight Engineer on the type; and

  ii. The holder can produce logbook evidence of having acted as Flight Engineer on the type in the five years preceding date of application for licence issue.

Applicants who are eligible for this credit should note that a Flight Engineer Skill Test must be completed with a Flight Engineer Type Rating Examiner before the privileges of the licence are to be exercised.

K1.5 FLIGHT RADIOTELEPHONY OPERATOR'S LICENCE (FRTOL) REQUIREMENTS

Although a UK FRTOL is not a requirement for the issue of a Flight Engineer's Licence, applicants who intend to operate radiotelephony equipment will require an FRTOL **(Section B refers).**

K1.7 UK F/EL MEDICAL REQUIREMENTS

An applicant for a UK F/EL must hold a valid UK Class 1 or a JAR-FCL Class 1 Medical Certificate.

SECTION 2 - ORS

AICS PINK & YELLOW

1 AERONAUTICAL INFORMATION CIRCULARS (AICs) - GENERAL

1.1 This section is incorporated in LASORS as a ready reference to the Yellow AICs (Operational matters including ATS facilities and requirements) and Pink AICs (Safety related topics) that are considered to be most relevant to GA/single pilot operations. The content of White AICs (Administrative matters) is dealt with in LAS. Owing to the annual publication cycle of this document, it is not appropriate to reproduce the content of Mauve and Green AICs here.

1.2 The AICs are listed according to key subject content and, where applicable, an introductory paragraph is included (in italic) to indicate the scope of the AIC.

1.3 For a complete check list of all current AICs refer to the latest blue AIC cover sheet, AIC 30 2001(Index) or the AIS Web site **(http://www.ais.org.uk).**

1.4 Readers are reminded that any communication regarding content of AICs should be made to the 'Content' telephone number given in the heading of the original Circular.

AERONAUTICAL INFORMATION CIRCULARS

- Aerodromes and Airports
- Aerial Activities and Conduct of Flight
- Aircraft Handling and Performance
- Airspace
- Airspace Restrictions and Restriction of Flying Regulations
- Collision Avoidance
- Common Frequency
- Danger Areas
- Flight Crew Training, Testing and Licensing
- Flight Planning
- Helicopters
- Icing
- ILS
- Insurance Requirements
- Medical
- Meteorological
- Navigation
- Radiotelephony
- Safety
- SSR Mode S
- VFR
- VHF RTF Channels and Services

A1 AERODROMES AND AIRPORTS

AIC 56(P34)/02-Hazards in Using Disused and Partially used Aerodromes

[Advice to pilots regarding the hazards faced when attempting to land at disused or partially used aerodromes.]

A2 AERIAL ACTIVITIES AND CONDUCT OF FLIGHT

(see also under 'SAFETY')

AIC 95(Y117)/03 - Foot Launched Powered Flying Machines:

(Powered Paragliders and Hang Gliders)

[Advice to all airspace users on the possibility of encountering powered paragliders and hang gliders, the limitations of such machines and recommended avoidance procedures.]

AIC 94(P9)/00 - Level Busts

[Results of a safety review on the subject of level busts, analysis and identification of common causal and contributory factors.]

A3 AIRCRAFT HANDLING AND PERFORMANCE

AIC 4(P46)/03 - Piloting Old Aircraft and Their Replicas

[Advice to pilots of old aircraft and/or replica aircraft, particularly with regard to low speed stability, controllability and stall qualities and landing.]

AIC 67(P36)/02 - Take-off, Climb and Landing Performance of Light Aeroplanes

A4 AIRSPACE

(see also under 'AERIAL ACTIVITIES AND CONDUCT OF FLIGHT')

AIC 53(Y138)/04 - Airspace Speed Limits

[Amplification of the 250kt airspace speed limit for aircraft below FL100 in Class D, E, F and G airspace and for VFR flights in Class C airspace.]

AIC 9(Y39)/01 - Military Aerodrome Traffic Zones

[Description of and procedures for penetrating MATZ.]

A5 AIRSPACE RESTRICTIONS AND RESTRICTION OF FLYING REGULATIONS

AIC 103(P44)/02 - Helicopter Flights in Restricted (Emergency/Incident/Accident) airspace

[Advice to helicopter pilots flying in the vicinity of emergency/incident/accident sites.]

AIC 47(P31)/02 - Stansted Control Zone/Control Area Airspace Infringements

[Reminder to pilots of the dimensions of the dimensions of the Stansted CTZ/CTR and advice for pilots flying in the vicinity.]

A6 COLLISION AVOIDANCE

AIC 87(P39)/02 - AIRPROX Reporting - UK and Foreign Airspace

[Advice for pilots on the procedure for AIRPROX reports within UK, Shanwick Oceanic, Channel Islands and Foreign Regulated Airspace.]

AIC 112(P76)/04 - 'Avoiding Action' - What this Instruction should mean to Pilots

[Advice for pilots on the meaning and implications of the term "Avoiding Action".]

AIC 7(P79)/05 - Absolute Minima

[Clarification of absolute instrument approach minima and the role of ATC in warning pilots thereof.]

A7 COMMON FREQUENCY

AIC 103(Y153)/04 - Common Frequency Use at UK Aerodromes without a Notified Frequency.

[Details on a common frequency available to assist pilots to avoid potential collisions between arriving and departing aircraft].

A8 DANGER AREAS

AIC 99(Y93)/02 - Danger Areas (Temporary) within the United Kingdom Flight Information Regions - Identification of EG D701E Hebrides Notifiable Danger Area

A9 FLIGHT CREW TRAINING, TESTING AND LICENSING

AIC 22(P19)/01 - Newly Appointed Flying Instructors at Registered Facilities

[Recommendation for newly appointed flying instructors to undertake a flight with the CFI at a registered facility.]

AIC 52(P193)/99 - Simulation of Engine Failure in Aeroplanes - Guidance to Training Captains

[Advice for training captains on turbojet, turboprop and piston engined aircraft, including preparation for flight, in-flight procedures, performance considerations and techniques for simulating engine failure.]

A10 FLIGHT PLANNING

AIC 71(Y87)/02 - Cross Channel Flight Planning

[Advice for all agencies on the relevant procedures for cross channel flight planning.]

AIC 55(Y109)/03 - Instructions for the Completion of the ICAO Flight Plan Form specifically to comply with North Atlantic requirements

AIC 72(Y88)/2002 - Flight Planning in Remote Areas

[Advice regarding the importance of flight planning in remote areas and the safety aspects that are associated with notifying search and rescue services in good time.]

A11 HELICOPTERS

AIC 70(P5)/00 - Flight Safety

[*Recommendation that all helicopter pilots receive regular, appropriate flight and theoretical knowledge training.*]

A12 ICING

AIC 98(P200)/99 - Icing Induced Stalls - Turbo-prop and other Propeller Driven Aeroplanes

[An alert to pilots of the possibility of loss of control as a result of icing-induced wing stall, advice on recognition and appropriate recovery actions.]

AIC 145(P161)/97 - Induction System Icing on Piston Engines as fitted to Aeroplanes, Helicopters and Airships

A13 ILS

AIC 34(P141)/97 - The Use of ILS Facilities in the United Kingdom

[Advice on the operating parameters and use of ILS facilities in the UK.]

A14 INSURANCE REQUIREMENTS

AIC 46(Y170)/05 - Insurance Requirements for Air Carriers and Aircraft Operators - Regulation (EC) No. 785/2004.

[Details of minimum insurance requirements for air carriers and aircraft operators in respect of passengers, baggage, cargo and third parties].

A15 MEDICAL

AIC 97(P70)/04 - Blood, Plasma and Bone Marrow Donation - Flying and Air Traffic Control

[Aircrew recommended to refrain from donating blood or plasma within 24 hours of flying, or to refrain from donating bone marrow within 48 hours of flying.]

AIC 97(P10)/00 - Malaria

[Advice to raise awareness amongst aircrew of the importance of malaria and to reinforce "anti-bite" precautions.]

AIC 82(P85)/05 - Medical Emergencies

[Advice to pilots concerning situations where passengers become ill.]

AIC 99(P72)/04 - Medication, Alcohol and Flying

AIC 7(P49)/03 - Post Traumatic Stress

[*Recommendation for individuals involved in critical incidents to consider seeking professional assistance.*]

AIC 96(P69)/04 - Modern Medical Practice and Flight Safety

[A circular intended to draw the attention of licence holders to the need for aeromedical advice to be sought when determining fitness to operate after a medical condition or treatment.]

A16 METEOROLOGICAL

AIC 106(P74)/04 - Frost, Ice and Snow on Aircraft

AIC 5(P47)/03 - Instrument Pressure Settings in Conditions of Abnormally Low Atmospheric Pressure

[Recommended procedures to follow in instances of atmospheric pressure below the lowest available altimeter pressure setting (generally 950mb).]

AIC 61(P195)/99 - Runway Operations - Risks and Factors Associated with Contamination from Snow, Slush or Water

[Operations from contaminated runways, by all classes of aeroplane, should be avoided whenever possible.

This AIC outlines the risks and considers operational factors, reporting phraseology, take-off and landing considerations and performance.]

AIC 81(P66)/04 - Thunderstorms and Associated Turbulence on Aircraft Operations - The effect of navigation

[Warnings and advice regarding the hazards that thunderstorms and turbulence associated with thunderstorms can present to flight operations.]

AIC 19(P28)/02 - Low Altitude Windshear

[Information regarding the nature of windshear and an appreciation of it's dangers.]

A17 NAVIGATION

AIC 93(P41)/02 - UK Policy for the use of the United States Navstar Global Positioning System (GPS)

[Description of the GPS system, limitations of the GPS constellation and equipment, CAA policy for the use of GPS.]

AIC 18(Y129)/04 - Visual Reference Points (VRP) - Use of

[Advice for pilots and ATC controllers on the use of VRPs to manage traffic in the vicinity of aerodromes.]

A18 RADIOTELEPHONY

AIC 140(P205)/99 - RT Discipline

[The importance of using correct and precise standard RT phraseology and techniques.]

AIC 93(P68)/04 - VHF Radiotelephony Emergency Communications

[Advice for pilots regarding emergency communications, procedures and the use of air traffic services.]

A19 SAFETY

(see also under 'AERIAL ACTIVITIES AND CONDUCT OF FLIGHT')

AIC 97(P43)/02 - Aircraft Accidents and Serious Incidents - Duty to Report

AIC 57(P55)/03 - Coding and Registration of UK 406 MHz ELTs

[Guidance on the options available when coding, and the method of registering, 406MHz ELTs when installed in UK registered aircraft.]

AIC 6(P48)/03 Flight Over and in the Vicinity of High Ground

[Reminder of the basic theory of airflow over high ground, the effects of the airflow on aircraft in flight and advice on avoiding or minimising the various hazards that may be encountered.]

AIC 101(P175)/98 - Head Protection During Certain Aviation Operations in Light Aircraft and Balloons

AIC 110(P15)/00 - Mandatory Occurrence Reporting Scheme (MORS)

AIC 92(P89)/05 - Occurrence Reporting

[Objectives of, and procedures for, occurrence reporting.]

AIC 8(P50)/03 - Reporting of Birdstrikes on Aircraft

AIC 1(P62)/04 - Portable Electronic Games, Calculators etc. - Use of in Aircraft

AIC 100(P90)/05 - Propeller Feathering on Twin Piston Engined Aircraft

AIC 111(P75)/04 - Risk Avoidance - Controlled Flight into Terrain (CFIT)

[Advice to pilots and aircraft operators on actions that can be taken to minimise the risk of CFIT accidents.]

AIC 2(P78)/05 - Vortex Rings

[A reminder to helicopter pilots of the ever present danger and insidious nature of vortex ring conditions.]

AIC 17(P188)/99 - Wake Turbulence

A20 SSR MODE S

AIC 49(Y171)/05 - SSR Mode S - Transition Arrangements.

[Details of the transition arrangements for the carriage and operation of Mode S airborne equipment, as agreed by Eurocontrol and implementing State authorities].

A21 VFR

AIC 48(Y17)/00 - Clearances

[Pilots responsibility with regard to determining flight visibility and the acceptance of ATC clearances. Special VFR Clearances.]

AIC 99(Y120)/03 - Flight in UK Airspace - Guidance Material

[Publication of a VFR flight guide on the AIS web site http://www.ais.org.uk]

AIC 4(Y316)/99 - Recommended VFR Route between the Solent CTA and the Cherbourg Peninsula/Channel Islands

A22 VHF RTF CHANNELS AND SERVICES

(see also under 'RADIOTELEPHONY')

AIC 87(P7)/00 - Aeronautical VHF Services - FM Immunity Protection Requirements for ILS/VOR and VHF Communication Receivers

[Reminder of FM immunity protection requirements.]

AIC 43(P1)/00 - Malicious Interference to VHF Communications Services

[Identification of malicious transmissions and action to be taken if illegal transmissions are suspected.]

AIC 55(P2)/00 - VHF Aeronautical Voice Communication Channels - Problems Created by Simultaneous or Continuous Transmissions

LASORS

2007

SAFETY SENSE LEAFLETS GENERAL AVIATION

INDEX

HANDLING SENSE LEAFLETS

SAFETY SENSE 1
GENERAL AVIATION

GOOD AIRMANSHIP GUIDE

1 INTRODUCTION

a. Although this guide is mainly intended for Private Pilots of fixed wing aircraft, much of the advice will be relevant to all pilots, whatever their experience or the type of aircraft they fly. However, there are specific leaflets giving more detailed advice for helicopter (no 17) and balloon (no 16) pilots.

b. Any review of General Aviation Accidents shows that most should not have happened. They are a result of a combination of the following:

- use of incorrect techniques
- lack of preparation before flight
- being out of practice
- lack of appreciation of weather
- overconfidence
- flying illegally or outside licence privileges
- failing to maintain control
- a complacent attitude
- the 'it will be alright' syndrome.

c. Comprehensive Knowledge, careful Preparation and frequent flying Practice are key elements in developing 'Good Airmanship' which is the best insurance against appearing as an accident statistic.

2 KNOWLEDGE - REPORTING

a. "Learn from the mistakes of others; you might not live long enough to make all of them yourself".

b. Share your knowledge and experience with others, preferably by reporting to the CAA* (BMAA, BGA etc.) anything from which you think others could learn. Your report could prevent someone else's accident. Photographs often help to illustrate a problem.

c. Improve your knowledge by reading the CAA's GASIL, published every quarter, the Air Accident Investigation Branch's monthly Bulletin*, the General Aviation Safety Council's quarterly Bulletin* and the Confidential Human Factors Incident Reporting Programme's GA Feedback leaflet.

Details of reported light aircraft occurrences are held by the CAA's Safety Investigation & Data Department*, and available for safety purposes.

d.) More specific information is available in other Safety Sense Leaflets, in Aeronautical Information Circulars (available by subscription or free from the ais web site)* particularly the pink Safety ones, and in other publications.

3 STATISTICS

a. There is an average of one fatal GA accident a month in the United Kingdom.

b. The main fatal accident causes during the last 20 years have been:

- continued flight into bad weather, including impact with high ground and loss of control in IMC
- loss of control in visual met conditions, including stall/spin
- low aerobatics and low flying

- mid-air collisions (sometimes each pilot knew the other was there)
- runway too short for the aircraft's weight or performance
- colliding with obstacles, perhaps being too low on the approach

c. A high proportion of stall/spin fatal accident pilots were not in good flying practice.

d. Loss of control in flight is the major cause of fatal accidents in gliding and microlighting.

e. The main causes of twin-engined aircraft fatal accidents were:

- pressing on into bad weather (often to aerodromes with limited navigational facilities) resulting in controlled flight into terrain or loss of control IMC
- loss of control VFR particularly following engine failure

4 REFRESHER TRAINING

Revise your basic knowledge and skills by having a regular flight, at least every year, with an instructor which includes:

- steep turns
- slow flight and stalls (clean and with flap) so that you recognise buffet, pitch attitude, control loads etc.

Note: in a level 60° banked turn, the stall speed increases by about 42%, - a 50kt straight & level stall becomes 71kts.

Practise at a safe height,

- if the aircraft is aerobatic or cleared for spinning, practise full spins as well as incipient spin recovery from a safe height. Aim to recover by 3000 feet above ground.
- practise forced landing procedures
- instrument flying and cloud avoidance
- take-offs and landings, including normal, cross-wind, flapless and short
- if you fly a twin, practise engine out procedures and power off stalls. Manufacturers quote a minimum safe speed for flight with one engine inoperative, V_{MCA}. Age and modifications may increase this for your aircraft

5 LIMITATIONS

a. You must know the aircraft's limitations and **HEED THEM**. If it is placarded 'NO AEROBATICS', it means it!

b. **Know your own limitations**; if you do not have a valid Instrument or IMC Rating, then you must fly clear of cloud, in sight of the surface and with a flight visibility of 3000 metres. If not in practice, you are not as good as you were!

6 PREPARATION

a. Make sure that your personal paperwork (licence/rating, Certificate of Test/ Experience and medical), is up to date. Also check that the aircraft's documents, including Certificates of Airworthiness/ Permit to Fly, Maintenance Release and Insurance are current.

b. Make sure that the Check List you use conforms to the Flight Manual of that aircraft.

7 UNFAMILIAR AIRCRAFT

a. Before you fly a new aircraft type, ensure any 'Differences Training' is completed.

b. Before you fly either a new aircraft type, one you have not flown for a while or one you do not fly often, study the Pilot's Operating Handbook/Flight Manual and be thoroughly familiar with:-

- airframe and engine limitations
- normal and **emergency** procedures
- operating, stall and best glide speeds
- weight and balance calculation
- take-off, cruise and landing performance.

c. Familiarise yourself with the external and ground checks, cockpit layout and fuel system, e.g. don't confuse the carb heat control with the mixture control.

d. Even if not legally required, try to have one or more thorough check flight with an instructor, particularly if converting to a tail wheel type. (In the case of a single seat aircraft, make thoroughly pre-briefed exploratory flights.) Include the items in para 4, Refresher Training.

e. If you have not flown the type in the last six months, treat it as 'new'. Many clubs require a check-flight if you have not flown the type in the last 28 days.

8 WEATHER

a. Get an aviation weather forecast, heed what it says and make a carefully reasoned GO/ NO–GO decision. Do not let 'Get-there/ home–itis' affect your judgement and do not worry about 'disappointing' your passenger(s). Establish clearly in your mind the current en-route conditions, the forecast and the 'escape route' to good weather. Plan an alternative route if you intend to fly over high ground where cloud is likely to lower and thicken.

b. Note the freezing level. Don't forget to check on crosswind at the destination.

c. The various methods of obtaining aviation weather, (including codes) are described in the booklet '**GET MET**', available free from the Met Office*. Aerodrome and area forecasts and reports are freely available on the met office web site www.meto.gov.uk .

d. Know the conditions that lead to the formation of carburettor or engine icing and stay alert for this hazard. Do a carb heat check at top of climb and periodically use it in the cruise and with the first indication of a loss of power due to icing; once formed it may take more than 15 seconds of heat to melt the ice. In the circuit, check carb heat during pre-landing checks and use carb heat at low power settings as directed in the Pilot's Operating Handbook/ Flight Manual. (*See SafetySense Leaflet 14 'Piston Engine Icing'*.)

9 VFR NAVIGATION

a. Use appropriate current aeronautical charts. (*See SafetySense Leaflet 5 'VFR Navigation'*.) Amendments to charts are available on the web site www.caa.co.uk/dap

b. Check NOTAMs, Temporary Navigation Warnings, AICs etc. for changes issued since your chart was printed or which are of a temporary nature, such as a closed runway, an air display, navaid or ATC frequency change. These are available on the AIS web site at www.ais.org.uk Refer to the GASIL 'changes' sheet.

c. Information on Temporary Restricted or Controlled Airspace, Red Arrows displays and Emergency Restrictions is available on Freephone 0500 354 802, updated daily.

d. Prepare your Route Plan thoroughly, with particular reference to minimum flying altitude and suitable diversions. Familiarise yourself with the geographical features, time points, airspace en-route and frequencies.

e. Note masts and other obstructions in planning your minimum flying altitude; note Maximum Elevation Figures (MEF) printed on the charts.

f. Allow extra height over hilly terrain, particularly in windy conditions, to minimise turbulence and the effects of down draughts.

g. Plan to reach your destination at least one hour before sunset unless qualified and prepared for night flight. Note aerodrome operating hours.

h. In any aircraft, the minimum height over a congested (i.e. built- up) area is not less than 1000ft above the highest object within 600 metres. In any aircraft other than a helicopter, you must not fly over congested areas without sufficient height to safely alight clear of the area in the event of engine failure. This could be higher than 1000ft (note: Permit to Fly aircraft may not be allowed over congested areas).

i. Do not plan to fly below 1000ft agl, (where most military low flying takes place –see SafetySense Leaflet 18 'Military Low Flying), unless necessary. If your engine fails you may need time to select a safe landing field.

j. Know the procedure if you get lost, see para 25.

k. If you use GPS to back up your visual navigation, double check any way-points when working them out and entering them. Progress **must** be monitored by map reading and not by implicitly trusting the GPS. *(See SafetySense leaflet 25)*

10 RADIO

a. Know what to do in the event of radio failure, including when flying Special VFR in controlled airspace. Know your way round your radio switches.

b. Note all useful radio frequencies, including destination and diversion aerodromes, VOLMET, LARS, Danger Area Crossing Service etc.

c. Note the frequencies and morse ident of radio NAVAIDs for back-up to the visual navigation.

d. Remind yourself about radio procedures, phraseology etc. (*See CAP 413 'Radiotelephony Manual' and SafetySense leaflet 22*).

11 WEIGHT AND BALANCE

a. Use the **actual** empty weight and CG from the latest Weight and Balance Schedule of the specific aircraft you are flying. Aircraft get heavier due to extra equipment, coats of paint etc. Use people's actual weights, too.

b. Check that the aircraft maximum weight is complied with. If too heavy, you must reduce the weight by off- loading passengers, baggage or fuel.

c. Check that the CG is within limits for take-off and throughout the flight. If your calculations show that it will not stay within the approved range, including the restricted range for spinning or aerobatics, you must make some changes.

d. **Never** attempt to fly an aircraft which is outside the permitted weight/CG range and performance limitations. It is extremely dangerous (sudden loss of control likely), as well as illegal, invalidates the C of A and almost certainly your insurance. (*See Safety Sense Leaflet 9 'Weight and Balance'.*)

12 PERFORMANCE

a. Make sure that the runways you are going to operate from are long enough for take-off and landing. Use the Pilot's Operating Handbook/ Flight Manual to calculate the distances that you need. Check for any CAA Supplements that may downgrade the performance.

b. Note that any factors given for elevation, temperature, slope, grass, snow, tail wind etc. are all cumulative and must be **multiplied**, e.g. 1.3 x 1.2 etc.

c. The performance figures given in the Handbook/Manual were obtained by a test pilot on a new aircraft, so in addition to the published factors, **apply a safety factor** of 1.33 for take-off and 1.43 for landing. These give acceptable safety margins, and will offset an out-of-practice pilot/tired engine. On a few aircraft these may have been included in the manufacturers information as 'factored' data.

(*See SafetySense Leaflet 7 'Aeroplane Performance*')

d. Short wet grass is slippery and may need a factor of up to 1.6!

13 FUEL PLANNING

a. Always plan to land by the time the tank(s) are down to the greater of ¼ tank or 45 minutes cruise flight, but don't rely solely on gauge(s) which may be unreliable. Remember, headwinds may be stronger than forecast and frequent use of carb heat will reduce range.

b. Understand the operation and limitations of the fuel system, gauges, pumps, mixture control, unusable fuel etc. and remember to lean the mixture if it is permitted.

c. Don't assume you can achieve the Handbook/ Manual fuel consumption. As a rule of thumb, due to service and wear, expect to use 20% more fuel than the 'book' figures.

14 DESTINATION

a. Check for any special procedures and activities at your destination such as gliding, parachuting, or microlighting. Update the UK Aeronautical Information Publication (UK AIP) or other Flight Guides with NOTAMs from the AIS web site at www.ais.org.uk or their fax pollback numbers

b. If your destination is a strip, remember that the environment may be very different from the licensed aerodrome at which you learnt to fly, or from which you normally operate. There may be hard to see cables or other obstructions on the approach path, or hills, trees and buildings close to the strip giving wind shear and/ or unusual air currents.

c. Before going to a strip, it is suggested that you are checked out by an instructor or someone who knows the strip well. If you can't arrange either, go by road and have a look at the potential problems for different wind/surface conditions. Assess the slope; it may be visually deceptive. (*See SafetySense leaflet 12 'Strip Sense'*).

d. You **must** obtain permission by telephone (unless otherwise notified) if the destination is "Prior Permission Required (PPR)". Even if permission is not required, if flying non-radio, always phone to find out the procedures.

e. Prepare a Flight Plan for filing on the day if you are going over a sparsely populated area, or more than 10nm from the UK coast. . (*See UK AIP Enroute [ENR] 1.10 and Safety Sense leaflet 20*)

15 FLYING ABROAD

a. Make sure you are conversant with the aeronautical (and customs) regulations, charts (including scale and units, e.g. feet or metres), airspace restrictions etc. for each country you are flying over. Their individual AIS web site may help. Remember, an IMC rating is not valid outside the UK.

b. Ensure you know how to find weather forecasts and reports for your return flight.

c. Take the aircraft documents, your licence, and a copy of 'Interception Procedures' (AIP ENR 1.12 and Safety Sense leaflet 11).

d. Before crossing an international FIR boundary you must file a Flight Plan. Check that it has been accepted and the DEParture message sent once you are airborne. (*See SafetySense leaflet 20 'VFR Flight Plans'*)

e. Check the Terrorism Act's restrictions on flights to & from Ireland, Channel Isles and Isle of Man (UK AIP GEN 1.2.1).

f. Ensure you have informed Customs and Immigration if you are returning from an EU country and not using a Customs aerodrome. See AIP GEN 1.2.1.2 (1.2.1.3 covers flight from non-EU countries).

g. In some countries, e.g. Germany and France, it is a legal requirement to have a 760 channel radio which can transmit and receive on frequencies between 118 and 137 MHz.

16 FLIGHT OVER WATER

a. The weather over the sea can often be very different from the land, e.g. sea fog.

b. When flying over water, everyone in a single-engined aircraft should, as a minimum, wear life jackets. In the event of an emergency there will be neither time nor space to put it on.

c. The water around the UK coast is very cold in winter and cold in summer. Survival time in normal clothing may be as low as 15 minutes (about the time needed to scramble an SAR helicopter but not for it to reach you). A good quality insulated survival suit, with the hood up and well sealed, should provide over 3 hours survival time. In water, the body loses heat 100 times faster than in cold air.

d. In addition, take a life-raft; it's heavy, so re-check weight and balance. A life-raft is much easier to see and will help rescuers find you. It should be properly secured in the aircraft, but easily accessible, you will not have much time.

e. Make sure that life jackets, survival suits and life-raft have been tested recently by an approved organisation – they **must be serviceable** when needed.

f. You are strongly urged to carry an approved Emergency Locator Transmitter and flares.

g. Remain in contact with an appropriate aeronautical radio station.

h. Know the ditching procedure.

i. Pilots and passengers who regularly fly over water are advised to attend an underwater escape training and Sea Survival Course. (*See SafetySense Leaflet 21 'Ditching'*.)

17 PILOT FITNESS

a. Don't fly when unfit – it is better to cancel a flight than to wreck an aircraft or hurt yourself! (*See Safety Sense leaflet 24 'Pilot Health'*) Are you fit to fly? – Check against the 'I'm Safe" list below.

I Illness (any symptom)
M Medication (your family doctor may not know you are a pilot)
S Stress (upset following an argument?)
A Alcohol/ Drugs
F Fatigue (good night's sleep etc.)
E Eating (food keeps blood-sugar correct).

b. Plan to use oxygen when flying above 10,000ft. Use it at lower altitude when flying at night or if you are a smoker (more carbon monoxide in the blood). **Do not smoke** when using oxygen.

c. If you need to wear spectacles or contact lenses for flying, make sure that the required spare pair of glasses is readily accessible.

d. Wear clothes that cover the limbs and will give some protection in the event of fire. Avoid synthetic material which melts into the skin. In winter, take additional warm clothing in case of heater failure or a forced landing.

e. Use the seat belts/harnesses provided for everyone's protection. Wear a helmet in open-cockpit aircraft.

18 PRACTICE- PREFLIGHT INSPECTION

a. Remove tie-downs, control locks, pitot cover and tow bar, then complete a thorough pre-flight inspection. Use the Check List unless you are very familiar with the aircraft.

b Remember, magnetos are live unless properly earthed. Any damaged wiring may result in the engine suddenly bursting into life unexpectedly, especially if the propeller is moved. Take precautions such as closing the throttle, tightening the friction, and chocking the wheels before touching a propeller if you have to – and keep fingers away from the edges.

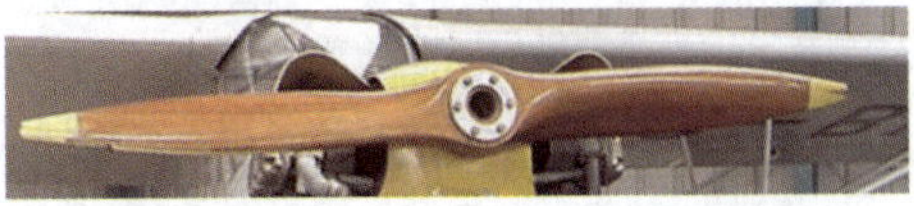

c. Determine **visually** that you have enough fuel of the right type. If necessary, use a dip-stick to check fuel levels. Personally supervise re-fuelling. Don't let anyone confuse AVGAS and AVTUR. Make sure the filler caps are properly secured. With the fuel selector ON, check fuel drains for water and other contamination. Be aware of the danger of static electricity during re-fuelling.

d. Check engine oil level and if necessary top up with the correct grade; do not over-fill.

e. Remove **all** ice, frost, and snow from the aircraft. Even frost spoils the airflow over aerofoil surfaces resulting in loss of lift and abnormal control effects. Beware of re-freezing. Use only authorised de-icing fluids. (*See SafetySense leaflet 3 'Winter Flying'*).

f. If you find anything with which you are unhappy, seek further advice.

g. Check **visually** that the flying control surfaces move in the correct sense in response to control inputs.

h. Properly secure any baggage so that nothing can foul the flying controls. Beware of loose items, e.g. passengers' cameras

i. The law requires you **must brief** passengers on location and use of doors, emergency exits and equipment, as well as procedures to be followed in the event of an emergency. Personally secure doors and luggage hatches. (*See Safety Sense Leaflet 2 'Care of Passengers'.*)

j. Confirm all seats are upright for takeoff and properly locked in place.

19 STARTING ENGINE

a. Know where to find and how to use the aircraft's fire extinguisher, as well as the location of any others in the vicinity.

b. **Never** attempt to hand swing a propeller (or allow anyone else to swing your propeller) unless you know the proper, safe procedure for your aircraft and situation, and there is a suitably briefed person at the controls, the brakes are ON and/or the wheels are chocked. Check that the area behind the aircraft is clear.

c. Use a Check List which details the correct sequence for starting the engine. Make sure the brakes are ON (or chocks in place) and that avionics are OFF before starting engine(s).

20 TAKE-OFF

a. Never attempt to take-off unless you are sure the surface and length available are suitable.

b. Visually check the approach and runway are clear before lining up and taking-off.

c. Choose an acceleration check point from which you can stop if the aircraft hasn't achieved a safe speed. If you haven't reached for example 2/3 of your rotate speed by 1/3 of the way along the runway, abandon the take-off!

d. In the event of engine failure after take-off, if the runway remaining is long enough, re-land and if not, **never** attempt to turn back. Use areas ahead of you and go for the best site. It is a question of knowing your aircraft, your level of experience and practice and working out beforehand your best option at the aerodrome in use. (One day, at a safe height, and well away from the circuit, try a 180° turn at idle rpm and see how much height you lose!)

21 LOOK OUT

a. Always keep a good look-out (and listen-out) for other aircraft, particularly over radio beacons and in the vicinity of aerodromes and Visual Reference Points.

b. The most hazardous conflicts are those aircraft with the least relative movement to your own. These are the ones that are difficult to see and the ones you are most likely to hit. Beware of blind spots and move your head or the aircraft to uncover these areas. Scan effectively. (*See SafetySense Leaflet 13 'Collision Avoidance'.*)

c. Remember the Rules of the Air, which include flying on the right side of line features and giving way to traffic on your right.

d. If the aircraft has strobe lights, use them in the air. Especially in a crowded circuit, use landing lights as well.

e. Spend as little time as possible with your head 'in the office'.

f. If you have a transponder, select and transmit the conspicuity code 7000 with Mode C (altitude reporting) unless another is appropriate or ATC advise.

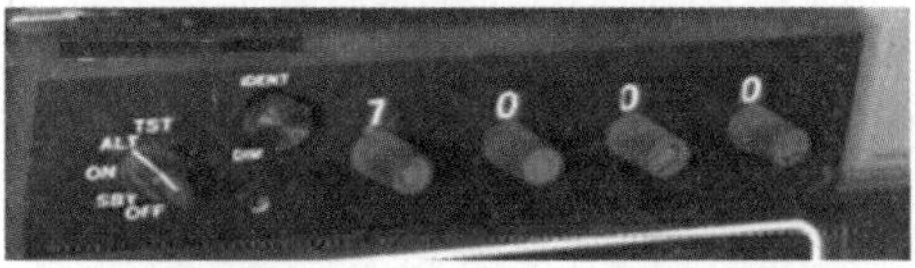

22 AIRSPACE

a. Do not enter controlled airspace unless **properly authorised**. At times, you might have to orbit and wait for permission. Keep out of Restricted Airspace including Danger Areas. Don't forget the Danger Area Crossing and Information Services.

b. Use the Lower Airspace Radar Service (LARS), available from many aerodromes, particularly on week days. It may prevent you from getting a nasty fright from military or other aircraft. (*See SafetySense Leaflet 8 'Air Traffic Services Outside Controlled Airspace'.*)

c. Radar Advisory Service (RAS) can tell you about conflicting aircraft and offer advice to avoid. Radar Information Service (RIS) can give you details of conflicting aircraft, but you have to decide if avoiding action is necessary. Make sure you know which service you are receiving. **Pilots are always responsible for their own terrain and obstacle clearance.**

d. Allocation of a transponder code does not mean that you are receiving a service.

23 EN-ROUTE

a. If you encounter deteriorating weather, turn back or divert before you are caught in cloud. A 180° turn in cloud will not be as easy as in the skills test!

b. Do not attempt to fly between lowering cloud and rising ground. Many pilots have come to grief because a lowering cloud base has forced them lower and lower into the hills. You MUST avoid 'scud running'.

c. If forced into or above cloud, do not fly below your planned Safety Altitude.

d. Don't overlook en-route checks such as **FREDA** – **f**uel, **r**adio, **e**ngine, **DI** and **a**ltimeter. 'Engine' should include a carb heat check.

24 DIVERSION

a. Unless you have a valid IMC or Instrument Rating, and are flying a suitably equipped aircraft, you must remain in sight of the surface. Before take-off, make plans for a retreat or diversion to an alternative aerodrome in the event of encountering lowering cloud base or deteriorating visibility,. If cloud base lowers to your calculated minimum flying altitude, or in flight visibility drops to 3 km, carry out these plans **immediately**. Turn back before entering cloud. Don't fly above clouds unless they are widely scattered and you can remain in sight of the surface.

b. Divert to the nearest aerodrome if the periodic fuel check indicates you won't have your planned fuel reserve at destination.

c. An occasional weather check from VOLMET is always worthwhile.

25 LOST

a. If you become unsure of your position, then **tell someone**. Transmit first on your working frequency. If you have lost contact on that frequency or they cannot help you, then change to 121.5 MHz and use Training Fix, PAN or MAYDAY, whichever is appropriate (*See CAP 413 'Radiotelephony Manual'*). If you have a transponder, you may wish to select the emergency code, which is 7700. It will instantly alert a radar controller.

b. Few pilots like to admit a problem on the radio. However, if any 2 of the items below apply to you, you should call for assistance quickly, **'HELP ME'**:

H High ground/ obstructions – are you near any?
E Entering controlled airspace – are you close?
L Limited experience, low time or student pilot (let them know)
P Position uncertain, get a 'Training Fix' in good time; don't leave it too late
M MET conditions; is the weather deteriorating?
E Endurance – fuel remaining; is it getting short?

c. As a last resort, make an early decision to land in a field while you have the fuel and daylight to do so. Choose a field with care by making a careful reconnaissance. Do not take off again without obtaining a weather update or further advice.

26 SPEED CONTROL

a. Good airspeed control can prevent inadvertent stalling or spinning, a major killer in aviation.

b. When landing, aim for the flight handbook speed, or 1.3 times the stall speed with flap, over the threshold and reduce speed in the round-out. If it is turbulent or gusty, add a margin of, say, 5kts or half the gust factor, whichever is the greater. If your speed is high, the landing distance required is likely to be more than you calculated.

c. A spin occurs when an aircraft is 'out of balance' at the stall, so always practise keeping the ball in the centre.

d. If you have not practised slow flight for some time, get an instructor to accompany you while you do so (at a safe altitude).

e. Do not exceed the limiting speeds for your aircraft. That includes maximum manoeuvring speed Va.

f. Do not apply extreme control movements at any time.

g. In aeroplanes with fixed pitch propellers, beware of maximum rpm.

27 ENVIRONMENTAL

a. Many people don't like aircraft noise and several aerodromes are under threat of closure due to this, so it is vital to be a good neighbour.

b. Adhere to noise abatement procedures and do NOT fly over published or briefed noise sensitive areas near aerodromes.

c. Select sites for practice forced landings or aerobatics very carefully. HASELL includes 'LOCATION'.

d. When en-route, fly at a height/ power setting to minimise noise nuisance, in addition to complying with Rule 5 'Low Flying'.

e. When flying a variable pitch propeller aircraft, change pitch slowly to avoid excessive noise. When flying twins, synchronise the engines to avoid 'beats'.

f. Select engine run-up areas to minimise disturbance to people, animals etc.

g. NEVER be tempted to fly low or 'beat up' the countryside.

28 WIND & WAKE TURBULENCE

a. Know the maximum demonstrated cross-wind for the aircraft type you are flying and factor this for your experience and recency.

b. Remember, that was obtained by a test pilot! If the wind approaches what you have decided is your own limit, be ready to divert. You may retain better control on landing by not using full flap.

c. Use the 'Sixth Sense' rule to work out the cross-wind component.

10° off runway = 1/ 6 of the wind
20° off runway = 2/ 6 wind
30° off runway = 3/ 6 wind etc.

d. If there is a cross-wind, the reduced head-wind component will cause the take-off and landing runs to be longer.

e. If another runway which is more into wind is available, use it (after **asking** Air Traffic Control if there is one). You may have to wait a few minutes to fit in with other traffic.

f. When winds or gusts exceed 66% of the aircraft's stall speed (50% for taildraggers), in general, don't go flying! If you have to, use outside assistance for taxiing such as a wing walker. Taxi very slowly when winds exceed 30% of the stall speed (unless the POH specifies otherwise) , and be VERY careful when the wind is from your rear.

g. On the ground, stay 1000ft clear of the 'blast' end of powerful aircraft.

h. Beware of wake turbulence behind heavier aircraft on take-off, during the approach or on landing. You should remain 8nm, or 4 minutes or more, behind large aircraft. Note that wake turbulence lingers **when wind conditions are very light.** These very powerful vortices are invisible. Heed Air Traffic warnings. (*SafetySense Leaflet 15 'Wake Turbulence'*.)

29 CIRCUIT PROCEDURES

a. When joining or re-joining, make your radio call early and keep radio transmissions to the point. If non-radio (or your radio has failed), know the procedures. (*See CAP 413 and SafetySense Leaflet 6 'Aerodrome Sense'*.)

b. Check that the change from QNH to QFE reduces the altimeter reading by the aerodrome elevation. If landing using QNH, e.g. at a strip, don't forget to add aerodrome elevation to your planned circuit height.

c. Use the correct joining procedures for your destination aerodrome. Unless otherwise published, make a standard join from the overhead (*See CAP 413 & poster "Standard Overhead Join*"). Check circuit height and direction. Look out for other aviation activity such as gliding, parachuting.

d. Check windsock/signals square or nearby smoke to ensure you land in the right direction. Be very sure of the wind direction and strength before committing yourself to an approach at a non-radio aerodrome.

e. Make radio calls in the circuit at the proper places and listen and look for other circuit traffic. Don't forget pre- landing checks, which are easily forgotten if you make a straight-in approach.

f. Be aware of optical illusions at unfamiliar aerodromes with sloping runway or terrain, or with very long, or very wide runways.

g. Take care at aerodromes where the runways can be confused, e.g. 02 and 20. Make sure you know whether the circuit is left- hand or right- hand, as this will determine the dead side. If in doubt – **ASK**.

h. In most piston engined aircraft, apply full carb heat BEFORE reducing power. You may decide to cancel carb heat at 200ft or so above the ground.

30 LANDING

a. A good landing is a result of a good approach. If your approach is bad, make an early decision and go- around. Don't try to scrape in.

b. Plan to touch down at the right speed, close to the runway threshold, unless the field length allows otherwise. Use any approach guidance (PAPI/ VASI) to cross-check your descent.

c. Go-around if not solidly 'on' in the first third of the runway, or the first quarter if the runway is wet grass. However, if the runway is very long, plan your landing to minimise runway occupancy – think of the next user.

d. Wait until you are clear of the active runway, then stop to carry out the after landing checks. Double check the lever you intend moving is the flaps and NOT the landing gear.

e. If the clearance between the propeller and the ground is small, or grass is long and hiding obstructions, be especially watchful to prevent taxiing accidents.

f. If you are changing passengers, shut down the engine. Do not do 'running changes'; propellers are **very** dangerous.

g. Remember, the flight isn't over until the engine(s) are shutdown and all checks completed.

h. 'Book in' and close any Flight Plan.

31 SUMMARY

- Keep in current flying practice, have an annual check-out with particular emphasis on stall recognition and asymmetric practice in twins.
- Get an aviation weather forecast.
- Prepare a thorough Route Plan using the latest charts, check on NOTAMs, Temporary Nav warnings etc.
- Know the aircraft thoroughly.
- Don't over-load the aircraft.
- Make sure the runway is long enough in the conditions.
- Over water in a single- engined aircraft, wear a life jacket (perhaps also an immersion suit), carry an accessible life-raft.
- Pre-flight properly with special emphasis on fuel/oil contents and flying controls.
- In a single-engined aircraft, bear in mind the consequences of engine failure.
- Maintain a good look- out, scan effectively.
- If the weather deteriorates, or night approaches, make the decision to divert or return early
- Don't end up in weather outside your ability or licence privileges.
- NEVER descend below your Safety Altitude in IMC.
- Request help early if lost or have other problems, e.g. fuel shortage.
- Keep out of controlled airspace unless you have clearance.
- Make regular cruise checks including fuel contents/selection and carb heat.
- Maintain flying speed, avoid inadvertent stall/ spin, don't fly low and slow.
- Always treat propellers as "live".
- Don't do anything stupid - become an old pilot, NOT a bold pilot.

Finally -

- Pilots exercising GOOD AIRMANSHIP never sit there 'doing nothing', they always think 15 to 20 miles ahead.

SAFETY SENSE 2
GENERAL AVIATION

PASSENGERS

1 INTRODUCTION

a. The Commander of an aircraft is responsible for the safety and well- being of his passengers and the law requires a pre- flight safety briefing in any UK registered aircraft. This applies to **ALL** aircraft, including gliders, balloons, microlights and helicopters, as well as ‘conventional’ aeroplanes.

b. Article 44 of the Air Navigation Order (ANO) 2000 requires the Commander of an aircraft registered in the UK to take all reasonable steps to ensure that before take- off all passengers are familiar with the position and method of use of emergency exits, safety belts and harnesses, life jackets and other emergency equipment. He/ she must also ensure that passengers are instructed on the actions to take in an emergency.

c. Although the guidance in this Leaflet is comprehensive and too long to be used on every flight, it is up to the pilot to decide what is appropriate on each occasion. He/she should use **simple** language, as some words (e.g. leading edge, trailing edge, port and starboard) may not be understood by all passengers. Remember, three quarters of the UK population have never flown.

d. Passengers in light aircraft may find it helpful to have a pre-flight discussion on the differences from larger aircraft (see para 6).

2 PRE-FLIGHT PREPARATION

The pilot must:

a. Comply with any airworthiness requirements such as having controls removed from passenger seats. Even if not required, consider this if permitted. While not a requirement, it is useful to place sick bags in easily accessible places without making it obvious to the passengers.

b. Ensure luggage is not so heavy that it adversely affects the weight and balance. The same applies to the passengers themselves. A set of scales (checked for accuracy) are useful to have available- many people are unsure of their weight and often under-estimate it. *See Safety Sense leaflet 9.*

c. Check that luggage is properly secured and does **not** contain hazardous items, such as:

- flammable liquids and solids, e.g. matches, fire- lighters, paint
- explosives, e.g. fireworks, toy gun caps
- magnetic materials, e.g. loudspeakers
- corrosives, e.g. acids, alkalis, car batteries.
- compressed gases, e.g. camping gas, aqualung cylinders
- active mobile telephones or other electronic devices

d. Advise passengers of the restrictions on smoking in or near the aircraft.

e. Suggest that passengers wear sensible shoes and clothing. Bare limbs are at risk and thin nylon melts if there is a fire. In winter, warm clothing should be available in case of heater failure, diversion or forced landing; walking down a Scottish hillside in winter would be no fun in shirt-sleeves and sandals!

f. Tell passengers it is best not to fly if they are unwell or even recovering from a cold.

g. **NOT** take passengers who are under the influence of alcohol (or anything worse). They could hazard the flight. Drunkenness in an aircraft is an offence under ANO Art 65.

h. Tell passengers not to distract the pilot at critical times when he/ she is busy, by asking questions in the middle of radio calls, when carrying out the Vital Actions or by interrupting the pilot's navigation/ monitoring of the flight. (Don't be distracted by an airsick or frightened passenger. FLY THE AIRCRAFT.)

3 BEFORE BOARDING

a. Check **personally** that external baggage doors are closed and locked, don't leave it to others.

b. Escort passengers when going to and from the aircraft.

c. Point out that propellers and helicopter rotors are extremely hazardous and should be avoided at all times, even when stationary. Rotating propellers and rotors (particularly helicopter tail rotors) may be hard to see, especially from the side or at night. The hazard may not be noticed if nearby aircraft have engines running.

d. **Always** shut down the engine(s) when passengers are boarding or leaving, avoid 'running changes', or passengers approaching the aircraft while a propeller/rotor is turning, unless they are escorted by properly briefed helpers.

e. Advise passengers that when going to and from a propeller- driven aeroplane, they must approach/depart from *behind* the wing. The only exceptions are a small number of types with pusher propellers or entry doors forward of the wing. With these aeroplanes the engine(s) must always be stopped when passengers are boarding or leaving.

f. Ensure that even if the engine is stopped passengers do not step forward off the wing leading edge towards a propeller.

g. If flying a helicopter, refer to Leaflet No 17 'Helicopter Airmanship', para 4.2, covering safe conduct of passengers with rotors running.

h. Arrange that someone is in charge of children, particularly small ones, both in flight and when going to and from the aircraft. It is safest to hold their hands.

i. Ensure everyone is aware of hazards under the wings of high-winged aircraft, e.g. struts, pitot tubes.

j. Show passengers the location of any steps or handholds, if there are wing walk-ways, show passengers where they can step to prevent holed fabric or dented skin.

k. Help passengers with external door catches and locks. A door, caught by a gust of wind, can injure passengers or pilots and cause damage to the door hinges.

l. For balloons, gliders, microlights etc. explain any additional specific instructions.

4 ON BOARD BEFORE STARTING ENGINE(S)

- The pilot must brief passengers so that they:
- know how to adjust and lock their seats/ seat backs securely in position.
- know how to fasten, unfasten and adjust seat belts/harnesses. Strongly suggest they keep them fastened through the flight in case of unexpected turbulence etc.

- know how to unlock and open doors or canopy noting that some aircraft have a double locking system. Locks and handles should be left alone once the doors are closed. **Personally** supervise the closure and locking of doors etc., don't be rushed.

- do not obstruct the controls with objects such as cameras, handbags, knees or feet.
- do not put metallic or magnetic objects near the compass.
- switch OFF all mobile telephones and electronic devices before flight.
- do not interfere with the controls in flight.
- know how to use the headsets.
- can use the intercom, if fitted, and know how to communicate if there is no intercom.
- know where to find the sick- bags.
- know the emergency procedures detailed below.

5 EMERGENCIES

a) Before flight, the pilot must brief passengers on how to brace themselves if a forced landing or ditching appears likely. There are two main reasons for this:

- to reduce injury due to striking objects inside the aircraft.
- to reduce 'flailing' of the body.

b) Passengers in forward facing seats **WITHOUT** a control wheel/ stick in front of them should, if possible, be briefed to adopt the 'brace' position. The upper body should be bent forward as far as possible with the chest close to the thighs and knees and the head touching the back of the seat in front. The hands should be placed one on top of the other on top of the head with the forearms tucked in against the side of the face. Fingers should NOT be interlocked. The lower legs should be inclined aft of the vertical with the feet flat on the floor. The seat belt should be as tight as possible and low on the torso.

c. Check that front seat occupants have got their belt and upper torso restraint as tight as possible prior to impact.

d. Tell passengers to kick or force out a window if the doors or canopy cannot be opened or if the aircraft has overturned.

e. Remind rear seat passengers how to operate the seat-back release on the front seats (thus allowing rear seat passengers to vacate the aircraft).

f. Agree the order in which the aircraft should be evacuated.

g. Remind passengers that harnesses and belts should be as tight as possible and at the last minute headsets removed, unplugged and stowed.

h. Brief passengers to unlock, but not unfasten, the cabin doors/emergency exits just before landing (or ditching).

i. Make it clear that seat belts/harnesses must be kept fastened until the aircraft has stopped, undo belts, open doors and get out fast.

j. Explain that you must not leave a helicopter until the main rotor has stopped.

k. Explain the position, release method and how to use the fire extinguisher as well as the location of the first aid kit.

6 EXTRA PRECAUTIONS OVER WATER

a) Life jackets

- Before flying over water in a single-engined aircraft, make sure that passengers are **wearing** life jackets, know how to inflate them and how to use any ancillary items, e.g. light, whistle.

- If the aircraft is twin-engined, point out the location of life jackets and how to put them on. If one engine stops, consider asking the passengers to put on their life jackets - it's now a single-engined aircraft!

- Impress on your passengers that life jackets must NOT be inflated until **outside** the aircraft.

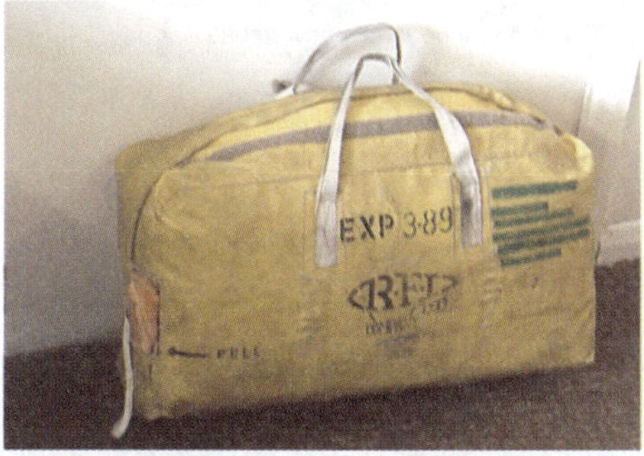

b) Life-rafts

- The life-raft should be secured such

- that it cannot strike people's heads during deceleration. Make sure it is accessible in an emergency. Assign responsibility for getting the life-raft out – it's too late when the aircraft has sunk. It may be heavy, so a strong passenger should be chosen. Do not tie the life-raft to the aircraft after ditching. Passengers should know how to inflate the life-raft and what emergency equipment it contains, e.g. fluorescein dye, flares.

- Brief passengers to swim away from the aircraft before inflating the life-raft so that it cannot be holed on anything sharp. When inflated, make sure it does not blow away, leaving some or all of the passengers still in the water.

c. **Above all**, impress on your passengers not to panic. There will be a lot of water flying around, perhaps through a broken windscreen, but there is usually at least a couple of minutes to get everybody out.

d. Safety Sense Leaflet No. 21 'Ditching' contains comprehensive advice.

7 PASSENGERS NEW TO FLYING IN LIGHT AIRCRAFT

Those who are more used to package holiday jets may find a light aircraft a very different experience. No one wants an early return with a sick or frightened passenger. Chat to them beforehand about:

a. *The higher noise level*: headsets, ear defenders or cotton wool in the ears may help.

b. *Turbulence* – a light aircraft will be more affected. Don't fight it, relax and go with the motion.

c. *Pressure changes and the ears* – most light aircraft are un-pressurised and climb quite slowly so the ears automatically compensate. Plan to descend at about 300 ft per minute. However, during fast descents, holding the nose and attempting to blow with the mouth closed, will equalise the pressure. Alternatively, follow the practice of some airlines and hand out a few chewy sweets.

d. *Stall and other warning horns*. Mention horns and bells, the sudden unexpected noise on landing may startle nervous passengers.

e. *Lookout* – discuss the usefulness of extra pairs of eyes throughout the flight, particularly when joining the circuit. Agree on how passengers should attract your attention. Explain the blind spots. Tell them that high flying traffic can be ignored.

f. *Motion Sickness* – What to do if feeling unwell, but don't mention the word 'sick'. (Make sure there are sick bags handy.)

g. *Toilets* – The lack of a toilet, even in some larger twin-engined aircraft.

h. *Children* – Special care is needed so that they:

   - do not touch the controls, door release etc.
   - keep their legs clear of the controls when sitting on a booster cushion

- keep quiet when the pilot is talking on the radio or is very busy
- tell the pilot if they see another aircraft (keeping their eyes outside helps prevent air sickness).

It helps if you:

- keep talking to them during the flight pointing out landmarks etc.
- avoid turbulent or windy days so that they remember their flight with PLEASURE

8 CHILD RESTRAINTS

a. The ANO and some flight manuals have requirements about safety restraint if children under the age of 2 (or 3 in some cases) are on board. These can be fulfilled as follows.

- For children up to the age of 6 months, approved belt loops as used in commercial airliners must be carried.

- For children between 6 months and 2 years old, either these approved belt loops must be carried, or the child must be strapped into a suitable car-type safety seat as described below.

- For children between 2 and 3 years old, the child must be strapped into either a car-type safety seat as described below, or secured properly by adult seat belts.

- Children 3 years old or more must be restrained using the aircraft seat belts.

b. The safety seats referred to must:-

- have a well- defined shell
- be designed to allow quick securing and removal from the seat
- have a single point of release for the harness which the child cannot easily release
- secure at least the torso, lap and shoulders
- have straps at least 1" wide

c. The safety seat must be installed so that:-

- it is secured to the aircraft seat in the direction of flight with the aircraft seat belt or harness
- it does not interfere with the aircraft controls or exits
- the lower part of it does not extend unreasonably beyond the aircraft seat
- the aircraft seat belt buckle does not lie on any sub-frame member of the safety seat
- only one set of straps secures the child.

9 SUMMARY FOR PASSENGERS

Have you been told how to use:-

- seats/ locking mechanism
- seat belts/ harnesses
- door and emergency exit release
- front seat- back release
- fire extinguisher
- life jackets and life-raft if carried?

where to find the first aid kit? and what to do:

- in a forced landing
- in a ditching?

Remember, its a LEGAL requirement for the pilot to tell you.

SAFETY SENSE 3
GENERAL AVIATION

WINTER FLYING

1 INTRODUCTION

The purpose of this leaflet is to advise pilots/ operators of aeroplanes, helicopters and microlights of some of the problems they may encounter while flying in winter.

2 AIRCRAFT PREPARATION

a. During the pleasant days of summer, items of equipment may have 'disappeared'. Make sure the aircraft has serviceable pitot head covers, static vent plugs, control surface locks and, if parked outside, proper tie- downs. Having made sure you have got them – **use** them.

b. Some engines may need the aircraft manufacturer's approved winter cooling restrictor to allow the oil and cylinders to reach and maintain correct operating temperatures. After fitting, keep an eye on the oil temperature/cylinder head temperature, especially if the weather turns warmer.

c. The grade of engine oil may need to be changed when operating in colder conditions. Consult the Manufacturers Manual or Maintenance Organisation.

d. Check that the cabin heater/demister is working properly before you really need to use it. A faulty cabin heater, either combustion or exhaust, can allow exhaust gases, including carbon monoxide, into the cabin. If in doubt, have the heater pressure-tested (see *Airworthiness Notices Nos. 40 and 41*). Carbon monoxide is colourless, odourless, tasteless, insidious in its effects and lethal. One of the first symptoms may be a severe headache, drowsiness or dizziness.

e. 'Spot' type carbon monoxide detectors only have a limited life when unwrapped. Use a 'fresh' one and read the instructions.

f. The pitot-static system should be checked for water which can freeze and block the system. If static drains are fitted, know where they are and how to use them.

g. The battery is worked harder in winter, so make sure it is in good condition and well charged. If you've had to make prolonged attempts to start the engine, when it does start allow plenty of time for the battery to re-charge before using heavy electrical loads. In a single-engined aircraft it's all you are left with if the electrical charging system fails in flight.

h. Some aircraft require the addition of Iso-propyl alcohol in the fuel for operation in low ambient temperatures. (See Flight Manual and, in the case of the Cessna 300/ 400 series, see *Airworthiness Notice No.8*.)

i. Check that all the airframe, propeller and windscreen systems are operating correctly. De- icing systems suffer from neglect and may prove faulty when required. Leaks may have developed in inflatable boots especially on the tailplane (due to stones thrown up by the landing gear/propellers), so check that they ALL inflate properly.

j. Make sure engine crankcase oil breather pipes are clear and free from deposits which can freeze, causing a pressure build-up that could force engine oil seals out of their housings.

Control cable tensions may need to be adjusted.

3 FLIGHT PREPARATION

a. If you are planning to visit another aerodrome, make sure it is open. Mud, snow, flooding or frozen ruts may have necessitated closure. Remember also that daylight and airport operating hours are much shorter in winter.

b. **Never** fly in icing conditions for which the aircraft is not cleared. Do not be misled into thinking that because an aircraft is fitted with de-icing, or anti-icing, equipment, it is necessarily effective in all conditions. Most general aviation aeroplanes are not cleared for flight in icing conditions, although some protection may be given. Those cleared are generally cleared only for flight in light icing conditions (the equivalent of a build-up of 12 mm (1/2 inch) of ice in 40 nautical miles). General aviation helicopters are *not* cleared. (See Pilots' Operating Handbooks, Flight Manuals, etc.)

c. Continued flight into bad weather is the number one killer in UK general aviation. Get an up to date aviation weather forecast. The current 'GET MET' booklet explains how (copies available from the Met Office).

d. The most likely temperature range for **airframe** icing is from 0 to –10° C; it rarely occurs at –20° C or colder (see para 6(c) for carburettor icing conditions). Pay attention to any icing warnings. Note the freezing level, it can be surprisingly low even in Spring and Autumn; you may need to descend below it to melt an ice build-up; but **beware of high ground**. Remember also that altimeters over-read in very low air temperatures, by as much as several hundred feet. You can be lower than you think.

e. If you are likely to encounter ice en- route, have you room to descend to warmer air? Will the airspace or performance allow you to climb to cold, clear air? (Note that any ice build up may not melt and will degrade cruise performance). Can you land safely at your destination? If the answers to these questions are NO, **don't go**.

f. Prepare an accurate route plan with time markers, including an alternative in case you do encounter ice/snow. The countryside looks very different when covered by a blanket of snow and familiar landmarks may have disappeared.

g. Wet snow, slush or mud can seriously lengthen the take-off run or prevent take-off altogether. Check the Flight Manual and Safety Sense Leaflet 7 '*Aeroplane Performance*', and allow a generous safety margin, especially from grass.

h. Have a cloth handy for de-misting the inside of the windows while taxiing.

i. Dress sensibly, (you should spend some timeoutside whilst pre-flighting the aircraft), and have additional warm clothing available in case of heater failure or a forced landing.

j. Some parts of the UK will be pretty inhospitable in winter (e.g. much of Wales and Scotland) so, if you are in a single-engined aircraft, file a flight plan and carry a few survival items in case of a forced landing, e.g. warm clothing, silvered survival bag, torch/mirror and whistle for signalling.

k. Be prepared to divert and carry a night- stop kit. **Don't** put pressure on yourself to get home if the weather deteriorates.

l. Read AICs 61/1999 (Pink 195) 'Risks and Factors Associated with Operations on Runways Contaminated with Snow, Slush or Water' and 106/2004 (Pink 74) 'Frost, Ice and Snow on Aircraft'. These are orientated to larger aircraft but do have useful information for General Aviation.

m. When snow has fallen, check SNOWTAMS in the NOTAM series, if available, to find out if your proposed destination, and alternate(s), are open and which operational areas have been cleared. If there is an eight digit code at the end of a METAR, it shows that winter conditions affect that aerodrome. It may be easiest to telephone them. The first two digits, of the eight digit code, are the runway and the last two the braking action. AIP, GEN para 3.5.10.13, page 3-5-30 gives further details/decode. Know the effect that braking action described as, for example POOR, will have on the landing/abandoned take-off distance you need to have available. Bear in mind the effects of a crosswind combined with an icy runway.

4 PRE-FLIGHT

a. There may be a greater risk of water condensation in aircraft fuel tanks in winter. Drain fluid from ***all*** water drains (there can be as many as thirteen on some single-engined aircraft). Drain it into a clear container so that you can see any water.

b. When refuelling, ensure the aircraft is properly earthed. The very low humidity on a crisp, cold day can be conducive to a build-up of static electricity.

c. After flying high such that integral wing tank fuel has been 'cold soaked', and the ambient air is humid and cool, frost will form. If it is raining, almost invisible clear ice may form.

d. Tests have shown that frost, ice or snow with the thickness and surface roughness of medium or coarse sandpaper reduces lift by as much as 30% and increases drag by 40%. Even a small area can significantly affect the airflow, particularly on a laminar flow wing.

e. Ensure that the entire aircraft is properly de-iced and check visually that **all** snow, ice and even frost, which can produce a severe loss of lift, is cleared. This includes difficult-to-see 'T' tails. If water has collected in a spinner or control surface and then frozen, this produces serious out-of-balance forces. **There is no such thing as a little ice**.

f. The most effective equipment for testing for the presence of frost and ice are your eyes and your hands.

g. The best way to remove snow is by using a broom or brush. Frozen snow, ice and frost can be removed by using approved de-icing fluid in a pressure sprayer similar to a garden sprayer. An alternative is to melt the ice with hot water and then leather the aircraft dry to prevent re-freezing. Make sure that control surface hinges, vents etc are not contaminated. A scraper might damage aircraft skins and transparencies.

h. Do not rely on snow blowing off during the take off run. The 'clean aircraft concept' is the only way to fly safely – there should be nothing on the outside of the aircraft that does not belong there.

i. Check that the pitot heater really is warming the pitot head – but don't burn your hand (use the back of it) or flatten the battery.

j. Beware of wheel fairings jammed full of mud, snow and slush – particularly mud, as it is dense and doesn't melt (on one occasion 41 kg, nearly 100 lb, of mud was removed from the three wheel fairings of a 4 seat tourer). If the fairings are removed, there may be a loss of performance and removal may invalidate the aircraft's C of A. Check that retractable gear mechanisms are not contaminated. Also, remove mud from the under-side and leading edge of wings and tail plane; it seriously affects airflow.

k. Water-soaked engine air intake filters can freeze and block the airflow.

l. If hand-swinging a propeller, perhaps because of a flat battery, move the aircraft to a part of the airfield which isn't slippery. Don't try it unless you've been trained. Use chocks and a qualified person in the cockpit.

m. During the engine run-up, check that use of carburettor heat gives a satisfactory drop in rpm or manifold pressure.

n. Check any de-icing boots, particularly the tailplane, for condition, holes etc. Wiping the boots with approved anti-icing fluid will enhance their resistance to ice build up.

5 DEPARTURE

a. Remember that taxiways and aerodrome obstructions may be hidden by snow, so ask if you are not certain.

b. Check the cabin heater/demister operation as early as possible. Be prepared to use the DV window.

c. Taxi slowly to avoid throwing up snow and slush into wheel wells or onto the aircraft's surfaces. Taxiing slowly is safer in case the tyres slide on an icy surface. Stop well clear of obstructions if there is any doubt about braking effectiveness.

d. Allow gyro instruments extra time to spin-up when they are cold.

e. You may consider using a 'Soft Field' take off technique – if so be sure that you are fully aware of recommended procedures.

f. Ensure that no carburettor ice is present prior to take-off by carrying out a 15 second carb heat check as in Safety Sense leaflet 14, both during power checks and before take-off. Ensure the engine is developing full power before taking off.

6 EN ROUTE

a. After take-off on a slushy or snowy runway, select the gear UP-DOWN-UP. This may loosen accumulated slush before it freezes the gear in the up position.

b. Monitor VOLMET and turn back or divert early if the weather deteriorates. **Don't** wait until you are in a blinding snowstorm or covered in ice.

c. Carburettor icing is one of the worst enemies. The chart shows when it is most likely to occur. (See also *Leaflet No 14 – 'Piston Engine Icing'*.)

d. Carburettor ice forms stealthily, so monitor engine instruments for loss of rpm (fixed pitch propeller) or manifold pressure (constant speed propeller), which may mean carb ice is forming.

e. Apply full carb heat periodically (every 10-15 minutes) and keep it on long enough to be effective. As a guide, carb heat should be applied for a minimum of 15 seconds, or longer if necessary. The engine may run roughly for a short period while the ice melts.

f. Use carb heat as an intermittent ON/ OFF control – either full hot or full cold. Do not use carb heat continuously or at high power settings unless the Handbook/Flight Manual allows it. At low power settings, eg descent, the application of heat **before** reducing power, and its continuous use while power is low, is recommended.

- During a descent, when using small throttle openings, with full carb heat, increase rpm periodically to warm the engine.
- Remember carb heat increases fuel consumption.
- At low rpm, use full heat but if appropriate cancel it prior to touchdown in accordance with Manual/Handbook instructions.

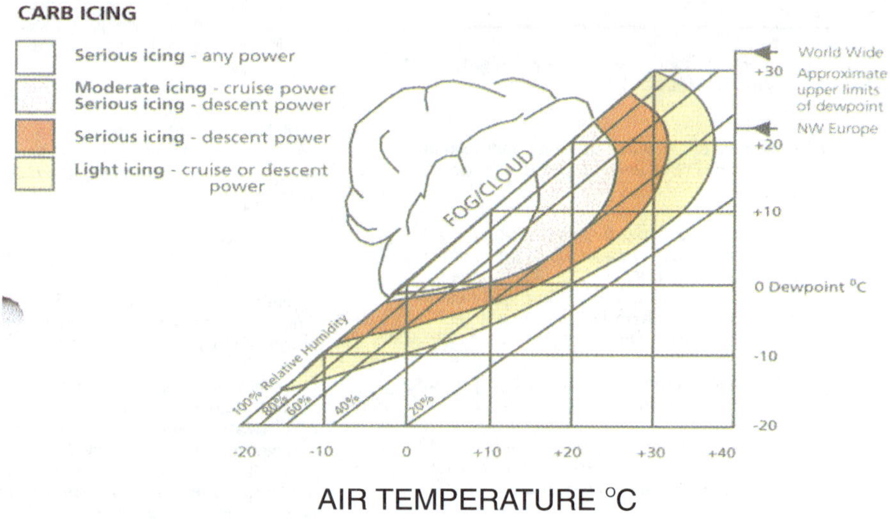

In the absence of dewpoint information assume high humidity when:

- the ground is wet (even dew)
- in precipitation or fog
- just below cloud base

g. If the aircraft has de-icing boots, it's a good idea to cycle the boots from time to time, even when ice is not expected. This prevents the valves in pneumatic systems from sticking.

h. If you are flying just above clouds to stay clear of airframe icing, remember that the cloud tops will quickly rise as you fly:

- across high ground;
- towards a warm, cold or occluded front;
- towards a low pressure area.

If you fly into the top of clouds, the concentration of water droplets is often greatest near the cloud top and ice could build up quickly.

i. Airframe Icing is most frequently encountered within convective clouds, Cumulus or Cumulonimbus (CU/CB) where the build up of ice can be very rapid. In these clouds the icing layer can be several thousand feet thick and a dramatic change of altitude will be required to avoid icing. It is better to avoid flying through these clouds if you can, either by turning back or changing your route.

Icing can also occur in thin layered clouds, especially during the winter. During the autumn, winter and spring an extensive sheet of Stratocumulus (SC) may frequently form just below a temperature inversion, with the temperature in the cloud between 0 to –10° C. Such clouds may only be one to two thousand feet deep but within the cloud layer ice may build up quickly. This icing can be avoided by descending below the cloud, provided there is sufficient height available above the ground, or by climbing above the cloud layer, but remember paragraph h.

j. If you see ice forming anywhere on the aircraft, act promptly to get out of the conditions, don't wait until the aircraft is loaded with ice. Ice forms easiest on thin edges. As the tailplane generally has a smaller leading edge radius than the wing it means that if you can see it on the wing, the tailplane (or propeller blades) will already have a heavier load. Pilots have reported that ice builds up 3 to 6 times faster on the tailplane than the wing and up to double that on a windshield wiper arm. On some aircraft the tailplane cannot be seen from the cockpit. In fact the pencil like OAT probe is often the first place ice forms. If ice does form, keep the speed up; **Don't fly too slowly**. The stall speed will have increased. The Manual/ Handbook may give a minimum speed to cope with increased drag and weight due to ice build - up.

k. The stall warning system may be iced up or otherwise affected. It is in any case designed and calibrated to provide indication of wing stall, not the tailplane!

l. If you've got a big build-up of ice, the drag and weight are increasing while the climb performance is decreasing so you can't climb to get above it. High ground may prevent you from descending.

m. Tell ATC so that others can be warned.

n. Most of the time snow, which is already frozen, will not stick to an aircraft, but occasionally wet snow with a high moisture content will stick. Treat it like ice.

o. Freezing rain can occur during the winter months either at or near the ground, or in a layer above the ground. It occurs when warm moist air is moving into a cold region. The invading warm moist air may cause a layer of air, where the temperature is higher than zero° C, to overrun a much colder layer beneath where the temperatures are below zero° C. Under these conditions precipitation forming in the high cloud layers will melt to form rain as it falls through the warm air which will then fall into the sub-freezing layer beneath. This rain will quickly freeze again in the cold air forming a solid layer of clear ice over everything. This clear ice will build up very quickly and be difficult to 'shake off'.

p. Freezing rain is the most severe form of airframe icing. It can be encountered in flight up to altitudes of 10 000 feet, or it may be encountered on the ground or when flying close to the ground. Aircraft parked outside will be quickly coated with a layer of clear ice, and similarly aircraft in flight. If such conditions are encountered in flight near the ground it is best to land as soon as possible, or if the severe icing is encountered at a higher altitude descend, if possible, into a warmer layer below.

q. If you are in trouble, tell someone clearly and in good time and make sure the transponder is ON and set to code 7700. The Emergency Services can receive a transponder return much better than the primary radar return.

r. Ice forming on an aircraft can cause odd vibrations and noises. An aerial iced up may begin to vibrate (and can fall off). Don't panic, remember **AVIATE, NAVIGATE, COMMUNICATE**.

s. Monitor any autopilot, it may have been surreptitiously altering the trim to compensate, possibly, for the effect of an ice build- up.

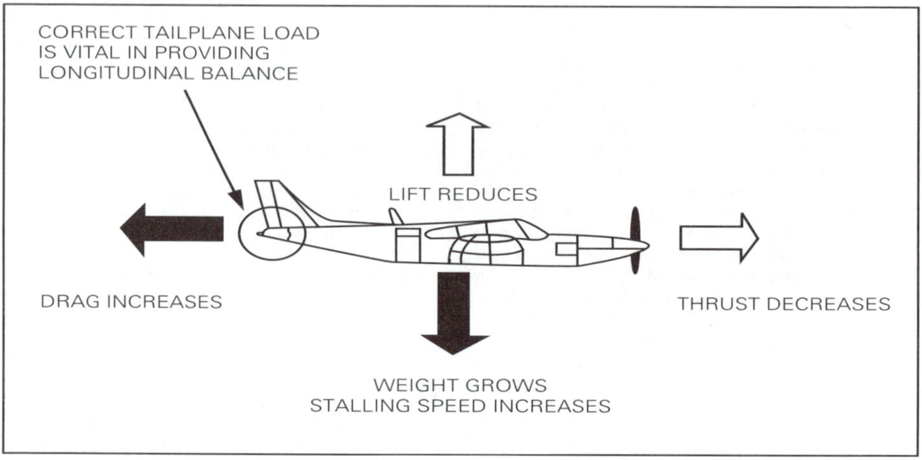

7 LANDING

a. If on arrival you descend with an iced up aeroplane and windshield and cannot see, use the DV window.

b. Most icing accidents occur when the pilot loses control during approach or landing. Even a thin coat of ice on the aircraft justifies a 20% increase in approach speed. It will extend the landing run – perhaps on a slippery runway. The handling may be different, don't make large or abrupt changes in power or flap settings.

c. If you suspect, because of changed stick forces or vibration, that there is ice on the tailplane, a flapless or partial flap landing may be advisable (the handbook/manual gives flapless-approach speeds). This reduces the tailplane load and the likelihood of tailplane stall, which can result in a VERY severe pitch down. Recovery is by REDUCING THE FLAP angle and by pulling hard – over 50 kg (110 lbs) may be necessary.

d. Another unpleasant surprise due to tailplane ice could be when the aircraft is being flown on autopilot, which has been slowly and silently re-trimming nose-up and reaches the limit. When the flaps are lowered, the autopilot could disconnect and it may require 4 strong arms to recover. Again, go for the flap selector.

e. When landing on a very wet or icy runway, particularly in a crosswind, the aircraft may aquaplane or slide and directional control can be lost. In such circumstances an alternate runway or diversion is necessary. Aircraft with castoring nosewheels may be more vulnerable.

f. Remember that ground temperatures fall quickly during the late afternoon on an exposed airfield and by dusk ice may be forming on any wet runways. The ice may form as a clear sheet which is invisible and has a coefficient of friction of zero!

g. Helicopter pilots should beware of 'white-out' due to blowing snow when hovering. (See *Safety Sense Leaflet No. 17 'Helicopter Airmanship'.*)

8 AFTER FLIGHT

a. Take care when getting out of the aircraft. Jumping from the aircraft walkway onto an icy apron could lead to a painful tumble.

b. If parked outside, use control locks and proper tie-downs to guard against winter gales. Face into the prevailing or forecast wind. Put proper pitot and static covers on – make sure the pitot has cooled down!

c. If it is muddy or slushy, inspect wheel fairings, landing gear bays, flaps and tailplane for loose mud or slush. These are easier to remove when soft than when frozen.

d. Notify Air Traffic if the actual weather was different, or worse, than forecasted. It might be important for other pilots to know.

9 SUMMARY

- Stay out of icing conditions for which the aircraft has NOT been cleared.
- Note freezing level in the aviation weather forecast. Don't go unless the aircraft is equipped for the conditions.
- Have warm clothing available for pre- flight and in case of heater failure or forced landing.
- Mud, snow and slush will lengthen take off and landing runs. Work out your distances.
- Remove all frost, ice and snow from the aircraft – there is no such thing as a little ice.
- Check carefully that all essential electrical services, especially pitot heat, are working properly.
- Check that the heater/demister are effective. Watch out for any signs of carbon monoxide poisoning.
- Be extra vigilant for carb ice.
- If ice does start to form, act promptly, get out of the conditions by descending (beware of high ground), climbing or diverting.
- If you encounter ice, tell ATC so that others can be warned.
- During the approach if you suspect tailplane ice, or suffer a severe pitch down, RETRACT THE FLAPS.
- If you have to land with an iced up aeroplane, add at least 20% to the approach speed.
- Snow covered, icy or muddy runways will make the landing run much longer and crosswinds harder to handle.

There is no such thing as a little ice

SAFETY SENSE 4
GENERAL AVIATION

USE OF MOTOR GASOLINE (MOGAS) IN AIRCRAFT

1 INTRODUCTION

a. Before an aircraft is granted a certificate of airworthiness or a permit to fly it must be demonstrated that the aircraft, including its engine(s), complies with the applicable airworthiness requirements. The aircraft or engine designer will normally define, by reference to a recognised specification, the fuel or fuels he is using when showing compliance. The evidence of that compliance will normally be based upon testing using the nominated fuel(s) only. Consequently, when the CAA is satisfied that compliance with the requirements has been shown and issues an approval for the aircraft or engine, that approval will be conditional upon the use of fuels conforming with the particular nominated specifications.

b. For many decades the industry-standard fuel for piston engine aircraft has been 100LL Avgas, conforming with specification DEFSTAN 91-90. This specification is comprehensive, and any changes to be made to it are subject to wide consultation and rigorous analysis before adoption. Production of Avgas is subject to stringent quality control and chemical analysis of the product. The delivery of Avgas to aerodromes is subject to procedures to protect the fuel from contamination and to maintain its quality and traceability. The Air Navigation Order (ANO) places obligations on the managers of aviation fuel installations at aerodromes and personnel carrying out refuelling, to apply procedures to maintain the quality of the Avgas. CAP434 provides guidance on these matters.

c. Compared with the Avgas specification the specifications for motor gasolines, (MOGAS), allow greater variability in the composition of the fuels, and proposed changes to the specifications themselves are not subject to the same level of scrutiny. The major oil companies consider that the systems in place for the production and delivery of Avgas are essential for a fuel which is to be used in aircraft and consequently they do not support the use of MOGAS for aviation purposes. Most major aircraft engine manufacturers, (other than a few whose engines have been developed from car engines), have aligned themselves with the oil industry and have refused to obtain approval for the use of MOGAS in their engines. However, some third-parties, mostly in the US, have provided evidence to the various Airworthiness Authorities to justify continued compliance with the airworthiness requirements for some engine and aircraft types when using certain motor gasolines.

d. Information on the types of aircraft which have been approved by the CAA to use leaded or unleaded MOGAS is given in Airworthiness Notices (ANs) 98, 98A, 98B, and 98C. This leaflet provides guidance on the use of MOGAS and does **not** override the ANs.

e. CAA AN 98 permits leaded motor gasoline, (Leaded MOGAS), to be used with certain engine/aircraft combinations **provided** that the fuel is obtained from an aerodrome aviation fuel installation in full compliance with the applicable requirements of the ANO; (equivalent to the storage and quality control procedures applied to Avgas). Therefore the permissions granted under AN 98 **exclude** the use of fuel obtained from a filling station/ garage forecourt.

f. AN 98A provides a partial exemption from the relevant Article of the Air Navigation Order to allow certain light aircraft to use Leaded MOGAS obtained from garage forecourts **subject to the conditions contained in the Notice**.

g. AN 98B provides a partial exemption from the relevant Article of the Air Navigation Order to allow microlight aeroplanes to use Unleaded MOGAS obtained from garage forecourts **subject to the conditions contained in the Notice**.

h. AN 98C provides a partial exemption from the relevant Article of the ANO to allow certain light aircraft to use Unleaded MOGAS obtained from garage forecourts **subject to the conditions contained in the Notice**.

i. It should be noted that the CAA does not accept any responsibility for any infringement of manufacturers warranties, possible accelerated deterioration of engine or airframe components or any other long term damaging effects resulting from the use of MOGAS.

2 MOGAS SPECIFICATION AND SUPPLY

a. **Leaded MOGAS**
The CAA approvals to use Leaded MOGAS apply **only** to motor gasoline conforming with BSI Specification BS4040:1988. If you use a mixture AVGAS/MOGAS with more than 25% MOGAS, it will be assumed that your aircraft is using MOGAS. Note: "Lead Replacement Petrol", "Unleaded 4-Star", and other products intended to replace leaded petrol are **not** equivalent to BS:4040 and their use is **not** approved

b. **Unleaded MOGAS**
Where approval has been given to use Unleaded MOGAS, this **must** conform with BSI Specification BS:7070 or EN228:1995. Beware of other fuels which are widely available (often advertised as having special properties).

c. Aircraft with certificates of airworthiness carrying out flights for the purposes of commercial air transport or aerial work, and multi-engine aircraft with certificates of airworthiness when flying for any purpose are not approved to use fuels obtained from garage forecourts. Such aircraft must obtain their fuels in full compliance with the specific demands of the Air Navigation Order; (Aviation Fuel at Aerodromes - Article 112 of ANO 2000).

d. Because the sampling, analysis and acceptance controls for MOGAS obtained from garage forecourts are less stringent than those for Avgas obtained at aerodromes, it is essential to ensure that the MOGAS is free from water, alcohol and other contamination. The following conditions must be met:

- The engine/airframe combination must be approved to use MOGAS, either by being listed in Schedule 1 of AN98, or by specific approval as specified in the Airworthiness Notices

- The aircraft must be either:
  - a microlight aeroplane,
  - a powered sailplane,
  - a gyroplane, or
  - a single-engine light aircraft with maximum authorised weight below 2730 kg operating on a private flight.

e. If your engine is a two-stroke don't forget to add the correct quantity of oil, or purchase premixed fuel/oil to the correct ratio.

3 OPERATING LIMITATIONS

Motor gasolines have a higher vapour pressure than Avgas and are also subject to seasonal variation. To reduce the likelihood of interruption of fuel flow to the engine due to vapour lock, the following operating limitations are imposed for all flights using MOGAS:

a. Prior to take-off, the temperature of the fuel in the aircraft tank(s) must be **less than 20 ^{0}C**

b. The aircraft must not be flown at altitudes greater than **6000 ft**, unless the CAA has agreed, in writing, to different limitations for that particular aircraft.

4 HANDLING AND TESTING OF FUEL

a. **Fuel supply**
MOGAS is more volatile than AVGAS, especially in winter; (to help coldstarting). Consequently MOGAS is more susceptible to fuel vaporisation at above average ambient temperatures, so beware of hot weather in the Spring and:

- Use freshly obtained fuel from a major supplier with a high turnover. (Note that local Regulations may only allow transportation of limited quantities in your own vehicle).
- Avoid long storage in the aircraft fuel tanks.
- Record the source of supply. (Note that most credit card receipts show the type of fuel, the quantity, and when and where it was purchased. Retention of such receipts is a means of satisfying this requirement).

b. Testing for alcohol
The use of fuel containing alcohol is prohibited.

Alcohol may be added to motor gasolines by the oil companies in order to improve the octane rating. However, if water accumulates in the fuel tanks, or forms within them due to condensation, the alcohol may migrate from the fuel and combine with the water. This may cause loss of power in two ways:

- Firstly, the aqueous alcohol solution may be drawn into the engine in place of the fuel and cause the engine to stop.
- Secondly, the migration of the alcohol away from the fuel and into the water will lower the octane rating of the fuel. Operation using fuel of insufficient octane rating may damage the engine.
- Also, alcohol is incompatible chemically with certain rubbers and plastics used in "0" rings and seals, and with certain adhesives, sealants, pipelines, gaskets etc.

Because of these potential adverse effects MOGAS must be tested to ensure that no alcohol is present. Testing for alcohol can be carried out as follows:

1. Obtain a clear tube, (like a test tube or fuel drain device), and mark a line on it about 10% from the bottom.
2. Add water to the tube until it comes to the line. Now, fill the tube with your fuel sample until it is near the top.
3. Shake vigorously for 10-15 seconds, let it settle and if the meniscus is on the line, the fuel sample is alcohol free.
4. If it is above the line (because the alcohol has mixed with the water) alcohol is present and the fuel must not be used in an aircraft.

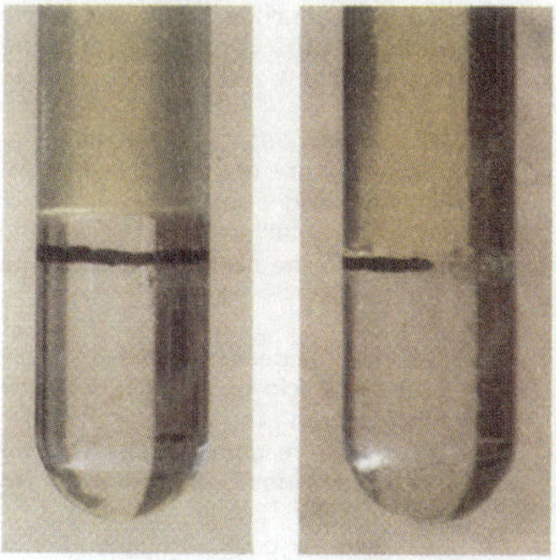
Alcohol present   *No Alcohol*

c. Water and other contaminants
Fuel must be filtered to remove water and any other contaminants. Either use a chamois and funnel or one of the proprietary devices which are available.

d. Fuel containers
These must be properly labelled, clean and free from corrosion etc. There is always a risk of fire when refuelling from cans due to static electrical discharge. There have been several cases of fire, including one in the UK.

Plastic fuel containers SHOULD NOT be used. The process of filling, as well as sloshing in the can during transportation, can cause an electrostatic charge to build up, which then discharges as the can is brought near to the aircraft filler neck. Use a METAL container and funnel, earth them both.

Make up a proper earthing device from copper braid, heavy duty crocodile clips and a 'ground stake' so that the tank, funnel and fuel container are ALL earthed. Static charges build up most easily in dry air. The driest days in the UK can be clear, crisp days in winter.

e. Maintenance indoors
Refuelling and working with fuel, or on fuel systems, in enclosed areas is hazardous because of the accumulation of fuel vapour, which is heavier than air. In an incident overseas, mechanics were killed by an

explosion when pouring fuel into a container attached to a wing fuel tank inside a heated hangar on a very cold (and possibly dry) day. Such work must be done outside and there must be effective electrical bonding between the aircraft, fuel source, piping or funnel and the ground.

REMEMBER - PETROL IS DANGEROUS

THERE IS ALWAYS THE POSSIBILITY OF FIRE OR EXPLOSION

Note: CAP 434 'Aviation Fuel at Aerodromes' contains further information on the storage and handling of fuels.

5 PRE-FLIGHT & MAINTENANCE PRECAUTIONS

a. **Non-metallic parts**
Because of the different constituents of MOGAS and AVGAS, non-metallic fuel pipes and seals must be carefully inspected for signs of leakage or deterioration.

b. **Water Drains**
If the aircraft has been standing overnight or longer, check the drains for water. (This should be normal practice).

c. **Fuel temperature**
Prior to flight you should make sure that the 20 ^{0}C limitation will not be exceeded, ideally by measuring the fuel temperature; (the top of the tank will be several degrees warmer than the bottom), or by considering;

- The length of time the ambient temperature has been above 20 ^{0}C.

- Whether the aircraft has been, or will be, standing in the sunshine. (In metal aircraft with integral wing fuel tanks, white-painted wings significantly reduce the rate at which fuel temperature increases, compared with dark ones. Even in the UK a fuel temperature rise of 15^{0}C, (from 19^{0}C to 34^{0}C), in 3 hours has been measured in an aircraft with light-coloured wings and integral wing fuel tanks).

- How long it has been since the aircraft was refuelled, noting the method of fuel storage; e.g. underground tank or small bowser standing in the sunshine.

6 PRE-TAKE-OFF

a. Carburettor icing is more likely when using MOGAS because it has a higher volatility, (and possibly a higher water content), than AVGAS. Pay particular attention to the serviceability of carburettor heating, (if fitted). If carburettor heating is selectable, ensure that a satisfactory RPM drop is obtained when heating is selected on during pre-take-off checks. Note: If there is an increase above the original engine speed afterwards, it shows that ice was already present when heating was selected on.

b. After any prolonged period of 'heat soak' at low fuel flow, (e.g. during taxying and holding before take-off on a hot day), local hot spots in the engine bay may induce vapour lock in fuel pipes. Before becoming committed to taking off, ensure full power is available and can be maintained. Be particularly alert for the possibility of power loss necessitating abandonment of the take-off.

c. On certain aircraft, the front fuel tank **must** be used for take-off, initial climb and landing. This is because the tank is higher than the engine and provides a positive head of fuel thus reducing the likelihood of vapour-lock. These aircraft are listed in Notices 98, and 98C.

7 IN FLIGHT

a. **Fuel pressure**
Pay particular attention to the fuel pressure gauge, (if fitted), and be on the alert for any signs of power loss when you switch off the electric fuel pump, (if fitted), after takeoff. For aircraft fitted with electric fuel pumps; in the event of:

- fuel pressure fluctuations,
- loss of fuel pressure,
- engine misfiring when temperature or altitude are high, **switch the pump ON immediately**.

b. Carburettor heating
Make regular selections of full carburettor heat lasting at least 15 seconds duration; longer if your engine is particularly prone to carburettor icing.

8 RECORDING THE USE OF MOGAS

The airframe log book must be annotated such that the operating hours using MOGAS can be determined. Block records must be transferred at appropriate intervals into the engine log book(s) where applicable.

9 PROBLEMS

If you experience any problems when using MOGAS, do not hesitate to contact the CAA Safety Investigation & Data Department. Please provide as much detail as possible about the circumstances AND the source of the fuel as soon as practical after the incident.

10 SUMMARY

- Do not fly using MOGAS if the fuel tank temperature is greater than 20^{0}C.
- Do not fly above 6000 ft using MOGAS.
- Only use MOGAS, (leaded or unleaded), if your aircraft/engine combination is approved to do so.
- Use Leaded MOGAS conforming with BS:4040, or Unleaded MOGAS conforming with BS:7070 or EN228 as applicable.
- Always use fresh fuel from a major supplier with a high turnover, (or fuel from a managed aerodrome installation).
- Test for the presence of alcohol.
- Filter the fuel to ensure it is free from contaminants and water.
- When refuelling use metal containers and earth everything properly.
- Certain aircraft must use the front fuel tank during take-off, climb, and landing; (See AN98 and 98C).
- In the event of fuel pressure fluctuations or engine misfiring, switch any fuel pump on.
- Be aware that carburettor icing is more likely.
- Install a placard, visible to the pilot, providing the following information:

1. For *Leaded* MOGAS:

USE OF LEADED MOGAS (See Airworthiness Notice 98A).

Use freshly obtained fuel conforming with the specification BS:4040

Test the fuel to ensure that it is free from water and alcohol.

Inspect fuel system non-metallic pipes and seals daily for deterioration and leaks.

Verify correct functioning of the carburettor heating system.

Verify take-off power prior to committing to take-off.

Fuel tank temperature not to exceed 20 degrees Celsius.

a. Maximum operating altitude 6000 ft.

Carburettor icing and vapour lock are more likely with MOGAS.

2. For *Unleaded* MOGAS:

USE OF UNLEADED MOGAS (See Airworthiness Notice 98C).

Use freshly obtained fuel conforming with the specification EN228 or BS:7070.

Test the fuel to ensure that it is free from water and alcohol.

Inspect fuel system non-metallic pipes and seals daily for deterioration and leaks.

Verify correct functioning of the carburettor heating system.

Verify take-off power prior to committing to take-off.

Fuel tank temperature not to exceed 20 degrees Celsius.

a) Maximum operating altitude 6000 ft.

Carburettor icing and vapour lock are more likely with MOGAS

- Record the use of MOGAS in the log books.
- Report any problems involving MOGAS to the CAA Safety Investigation and Data Department.

SAFETY SENSE 5
GENERAL AVIATION

VFR NAVIGATION

1 INTRODUCTION

a. This leaflet contains useful advice for pilots of all aircraft, including balloons, gliders and microlights. It is particularly relevant to aircraft flying in UK airspace. It should be noted that Visual Flight Rules are defined in Rules 24 to 27 of the Rules of the Air. Some pilots seem to think VMC stands for Very Marginal Conditions!

b. This Leaflet should be read in conjunction with other General Aviation Safety Sense Leaflets.

2 THE CHARTS

a. The law requires, and good airmanship demands, that you **must** carry all the charts you need for your flight and for any diversion which may reasonably be expected.

b. The best 'all round' charts for VFR flight within the United Kingdom airspace are the Aeronautical Charts ICAO 1: 500,000. Their scale and degree of topographical, hydrographical, and terrain detail are suited to map reading at the speeds and altitudes commonly flown by general aviation aircraft. The chart shows aeronautical information up to and including flight level 245, and is amended frequently.

c. If you need greater detail, this is provided by the larger scale 1: 250,000 topographical charts, (e.g. major power lines are shown). Remember that Controlled Airspace with a lower limit above an altitude of 5000 ft is not shown. You should always carry a 1: 500,000 as well.

d. Instrument approach and landing charts and aerodrome charts, are published in the UK AIP (AD) for licensed aerodromes. Although not primarily intended for the VFR pilot, these charts contain a wealth of information which can make it easier to recognise, and make a good final approach to the *right* aerodrome whilst keeping you clear of 'instrument' traffic. Also, commercial Flight Guides carry many other aerodrome charts which help in identifying your destination aerodrome.

3 UP-TO-DATE INFORMATION

a. Confirm that each of your charts are the latest edition by referring to Green Aeronautical Information Circulars (AICs) or your Chart Agent. Note the date of the 'Validity of Aeronautical Information' at the bottom of each chart and then check the Aeronautical Information Publication (AIP), NOTAMs etc. for amendments which affect your area of operation or route (e.g. a changed frequency). Chart and frequency updates are published on the CAA web site at www.caa.co.uk, through “airspace policy” and “aeronautical charts”

b. AIS pre-flight bulletin information is available from the AIS web site on the internet at www.ais.org.uk or by fax. The system is fully described in AIC 66/2003 (White 84)*.

Bulletins available include Aerodrome Information and UK Daily Nav Warnings, which can be accessed individually, in groups, or as complete bulletins. Information for VFR flight in adjacent FIRs is also available, as are the UKAIP, AICs and AIP Supplements.

4 PLANNING THE ROUTE

a. Erase all previous track lines and pencil information from the chart.

b. Draw in your intended route. Does it cross:

- a major hazard;
  Why fly in a straight line over high ground (weather hazards/ few forced landing options) when a slightly longer track could keep you over a friendly valley and well clear of cloud and other weather-related hazards? AIC 6/2003 (Pink 48)* 'Flight Over and in the Vicinity of High Ground' contains useful advice on mountain waves, turbulence etc.
- Controlled Airspace;
- an aerodrome with an active Aerodrome Traffic Zone (ATZ);
- an active aerodrome *without* an ATZ;
- a Prohibited, Restricted, or Danger Area;
- a Military Aerodrome Traffic Zone (MATZ);
- an ATS Advisory Route;
- the extended runway of an aerodrome with an Instrument Approach Procedure (IAP) in the open FIR, indicated by a 'cone' symbol;
- a gliding, parachuting, hang gliding, microlight or paragliding site;
- an area of intense aerial activity (AIAA)
- an air navigation obstruction;
- an high- intensity radio transmission area, a nuclear power station or gaol;
- a bird sanctuary;
- an altimeter setting region (ASR) boundary;
- a NOTAM or mauve AIC restriction, e.g. one which may apply to an air display, a military exercise or Royal low- level corridor and purple airspace (see para 5l).

Do any of these items affect you? If you are not sure, read the chart legend. Many will require a change of route; others will require prior permission, or even a positive ATC clearance to transit at certain altitudes. If your final intended track relies on weather or clearances, make sure you **plan an alternate route**, complete with timings and fuel.

c. Now study the topography, hydrography and terrain of the en-route area.

d. Where is the high ground? Identify the spot heights and contours and remember that the highest point en-route is often the top of an air navigation obstruction. Current charts show Maximum Elevation Figures (MEF), which are the highest known feature including terrain and obstacles in each quadrant in thousands and hundreds of feet amsl. THESE ARE NOT SAFETY ALTITUDES.

Note: Land- based obstacles up to a height of 299 ft AGL are not normally shown.

e. Do not plan to fly below 1000 ft AGL, this airspace can be heavily used by high speed military aircraft (see *Safety Sense Leaflet No. 18 'Military Low Flying'*). It also reduces options in the event of engine failure.

f. Where are the best line features? If a river, valley, railway, road, ridge or tree line is reasonably close and runs roughly parallel to the direct track, then (airspace constraints permitting and not forgetting the right-hand traffic rule, Rule 19) plan to keep it in sight. A modest increase in track distance is a small price to pay for being sure of your position. Line features at right angles to the route can be useful ETA checks.

g. How can you best pin-point your position? Look for distinctive areas of water; line features which cross one another; prominent obstructions etc. Look again and check that they will not be hidden by hills, ridges, or woods. Is there a similar pin-point nearby which could lead to confusion?

h. Large built-up areas do not make good pin-points. If you overfly them, your minimum permissible height may be dictated by engine-out height limitations (Rule 5.1). Think twice about using active aerodromes as pinpoints — the smaller grass ones are often difficult to identify, and some of them will have other aircraft in the area. Do **not** use aerodromes with a parachuting symbol as a turning point, hard to see free-fall parachutists could be using the area. Disused aerodromes with hard runways can be useful as check points, but in some areas there are many of them, so another feature should be used as a cross-check.

i. As a landmark feature, the hard runway pattern at both active and disused aerodromes is shown on the 1: 250 000 Series, although information for disused aerodromes cannot be guaranteed.

j. The best pin-points have line features which lead you to them. Use these, wherever possible, for turning points and for any airspace entry and exit points. Because others will also choose them, it is a good idea to pass to one side (ideally right) of them. The same applies to the Visual Reference Points (VRPs) marked near Controlled Airspace and busy aerodromes; use them as references, not aiming points, although a published 'Entry Point' is just that. Unprotected Instrument Approach Procedures, indicated by 'cones' do not mean that the approaches will always be to the runway with the 'cone'.

k. If you are flying to an unfamiliar aerodrome, it will be easier to spot if the sun is to one side or behind you. Arriving into sun will make it harder to see.

l. Taking all these factors — **and the weather** — into account, decide on your final route, altitudes and diversion aerodromes. Unless everything is 'GO', consider postponing your flight!

5 THE ROUTE PLAN/LOG

a. You should **never** fly a route without a written route plan, containing, at the very least:

- Magnetic headings, time/ distance marks, *minimum safe VFR altitudes*, freezing level and planned altitude for each leg, *including* that to any diversion aerodromes;
- Total distance, time, fuel to destination *and* diversion aerodromes;
- time available on reserve fuel;
- weather for the *Route* and *Destination/ Diversion* aerodromes;
- estimated time of arrival (ETA) at each pin-point and turning point so you can log and compare it with your actual time of arrival.

b. Have you a foolproof system for adjusting ETAs as you pass each check point? Have you marked 'Drift Lines' on the chart? These remove the guess-work if you do get off-track.

c. Have you made best use of 'ETA Check' line features? You should aim to check the ETA at a maximum of 15 minute intervals.

d. Note down your plans for your alternate routings and other en-route contingencies. You may have to remain clear of, or change your route through, Controlled Airspace; in any case you must be ready to pass entry/exit ETAs.

e. Which aerodromes do you plan to use if the weather deteriorates, your radio fails, or some mechanical failure occurs? The nearest aerodrome might not necessarily be the best, but will you have enough fuel, bearing in mind a possible headwind, to get to the one that is?

f. Have you made a note of all the contact frequencies, including parachute drop zone activity information services? Do you know which ones are on the chart? Does the aircraft equipment operate on all the frequencies you may want to use? Do you know how to select 25 kHz channels?

g. Make use of the Lower Airspace Radar Advisory Service (LARS). Brief details, including frequencies, are on the chart. Many units are military aerodromes operating only on weekdays, and a map showing the areas of coverage is in the AIP (ENR 1.6). There is a full explanation in Safety Sense Leaflet 8, *'Air Traffic Services outside Controlled Airspace'*.

h. If your route penetrates a MATZ, you should plan to make contact on the MATZ frequency (it's on the chart) at least 15 nm or 5 minutes' flying time from the zone boundary. Have you planned a pin-point to help you? Details on MATZ penetrations are in Safety Sense leaflet 26, and in AIC 9/2001 (Yellow 39)* *Military Aerodrome Traffic Zones.*

i. If you plan to fly over water more than 20 miles wide or over a sparsely- populated area, file a Flight Plan (see *Safety Sense Leaflet 20 VFR Flight Plans*). A Flight Plan is mandatory if leaving UK airspace. You may need to cancel that Flight Plan on arrival, or if you divert.

j. Does your aircraft have a transponder? Transmit code 7000 with Mode C at all times unless told otherwise. Be prepared to use the emergency codes if needed

k. Are there any activities which could lead to special procedures, e.g. gliding at your destination? Is there a noise sensitive area?

l. Use Freephone **0500 354 802** to check on Red Arrows displays and Emergency Restrictions. The information is updated daily and available from the evening before.

m. Finally, *check for legibility*. Does the route and all other information stand out clearly on the chart and route plan?

n. Don't forget to 'book-out' and it's a sensible idea to start with a clean wind shield.

o. If you are using a GPS to back-up your visual navigation, check and double check that you have programmed it correctly and do not use it unless you are thoroughly conversant with **all** its modes of operation. Read *Safety Sense leaflet 25 "Use of GPS"* .

6 AIRBORNE

a. Air traffic are there to help you, but they are not clairvoyant. If you are permitted to do so, set heading from overhead the aerodrome. Check that you really are heading the right way from landmarks or the sun and haven't, for instance, confused zero-three with three-zero.

b. Frequency changes are best made with a landmark in sight ahead. You can then concentrate on the transmission and report your position with confidence.

c. You should try to stay in R/T contact at all times. If you use the Flight Information Service, do remember it is generally a non - radar service. If you lose contact, continue to transmit your position 'blind' at regular intervals to inform others of your presence.

d. Check your DI for precession against the magnetic compass (remember the errors inherent in the compass), try to ensure level, balanced flight when synchronising and double-check using those line features parallel to track. Don't forget a **FREDA** check every 10 minutes:

- **F**uel
- **R**adio
- **E**ngine instruments, carburettor heat
- **DI**
- **A**ltimeter

e. Call ATC in plenty of time before entering Controlled Airspace, Danger Areas with a crossing service, MATZs and Advisory Routes. If there is any doubt about your clearance, then orbit over a chosen pin-point until clearance is **positively** obtained, or fly the planned alternative route around it. Many unlawful and hazardous infringements of controlled airspace occur because this advice is not heeded.

f. If you use radio nav-aids to confirm your visual observations don't forget to ident the beacon. Radio aids and GPS are to assist visual navigation, NOT substitute for it.

g. Look ahead constantly for potential weather problems. **If the weather deteriorates, don't press on — turn back or divert. Don't be lulled into a false sense of security by still being able to see blue sky. Stay within your licence privileges and your current capabilities. If necessary, carry out a forced-landing with power (see para 7) (not doing this has killed many people).**

7 UNSURE OF POSITION

a. Immediately you become unsure of your position *note the time* and if you are in touch with an ATC unit, especially a radar unit, request assistance. If not, but you think you are near Controlled Airspace, call the Distress and Diversion Cell on 121.5 MHz. Otherwise, check that the DI and compass are still synchronised. Continue to fly straight and level and on route plan heading. Then calculate a rough distance travelled since you last had a positive pin- point.

b. Now compare the outside with your estimated position. Does the general picture make sense? Look at the terrain e.g. ridges, hill lines, valleys, escarpments. Can you see a distinctive line feature e.g. motorway, dual-carriageway, railway, river? Look at the shape of the woodland. Is there a coastline visible? As a general rule work from the ground to the chart.

c. Keep checking that heading and do not relax your lookout for other aircraft.

d. If you are happy with the general picture, then narrow your sights to more specific features, but remember to up-date your estimated position regularly. Look for unique features such as a lake or reservoir, a TV mast, a road with a river or railway running alongside.

8 LOST

a. If you are still uncertain, then TELL SOMEONE. Transmit first on your 'working' frequency and do not mince words. Say you are LOST. If you have lost contact on that frequency, then change to 121.5 MHz and make a PAN call. If you have a transponder, set it to Code 7700. It will flash on a radar screen to alert the controller.

b. If you are lost and any of the items below apply to you, call for assistance – **'HELP ME'**:

- **H** High ground/ obstructions – are you near any?
- **E** Entering controlled airspace – are you close?
- **L** Limited experience, low time or student pilot, let them know
- **P** PAN call in good time – don't leave it too late
- **M** Met conditions – is the weather deteriorating?
- **E** Endurance – fuel remaining; is it getting low?

c. Transmit as much of the following information as you can:

- PAN PAN/ PAN PAN/ PAN PAN
- Call sign and aircraft type
- Nature of emergency
- Your intentions
- Your best estimate of position, flight level/ altitude and heading
- Whether you are a,
    - student pilot
    - pilot with NO instrument qualification
    - pilot with IMC rating or full Instrument Rating
- Fuel endurance
- Transponder equipped
- Persons on board

d. The Emergency Service may be terrain-limited if you are flying below 3000 ft amsl so, if requested, climb above that altitude, but ***do not*** agree to climb into IMC unless you are in current practice to fly on instruments, in which case climb above Safety Altitude. Don't forget to cancel your PAN CALL when you are safe.

e. If conditions (weather, terrain, R/T) preclude safe use of the emergency service:

- maintain VFR;
- note your fuel state;
- calculate the time left to look for an area suitable for a precautionary landing.

f. Transmit your intention to make a precautionary landing and carry out the appropriate actions.

g. Give yourself plenty of time to make at least one low pass to check approaches for obstacles (e.g. aerials, cables), the surface and wind direction.

9 APPROACHING YOUR DESTINATION

a. With your destination area in sight, do not put aside your chart until you have positively identified the **correct** aerodrome (and any Visual Reference Points).

b. Select the appropriate radio frequency in plenty of time to obtain landing information. Don't forget a last **FREDA** check.

c. Check the Minimum Safe Altitude and noise sensitive areas. Note the aerodrome elevation, and remember that an ATZ extends to 2000 ft *above aerodrome level*. Check your altimeter setting and confirm that the change from QNH to QFE equals the aerodrome elevation.

d. Have you positively identified the high ground and significant obstructions within the ATZ?

e. Make sure it's the right aerodrome, plenty of pilots have got it wrong.

f. Do not just rely on the compass or DI to establish the circuit pattern. Use line features to help you to line up with the **correct** runway.

g. Unless you know of different procedures, or safety reasons or Controlled Airspace prevent it, join the circuit pattern in the standard overhead manner, as shown on the poster on the CAA web site and in LASORS. *See Safety Sense leaflet 6 "Aerodrome sense".*

10 POST FLIGHT

a. Were you satisfied with your navigation, or would more pre-flight preparation have helped? Study your route, tracks made good and actual timings to try to learn from the flight.

b. Are there any hints and tips which might be useful to other pilots flying that route? If so, publish them through club Newsletter, or via the CAA General Aviation Safety Information Leaflet (GASIL).

c. If you think that the chart would benefit from any change, contact the:

VFR Chart Editor
Aeronautical Charts and Data Section
CAA House K6
45– 59 Kingsway
London WC2B 6TE.
Tel.: 020 7453 6572
Fax: 020 7453 6565

Helpful advice as well as your Charts can be obtained from Chart Room staff.

* The AICs referred to in this leaflet may have been superseded, please check that you are consulting the latest edition.

11 SUMMARY

- Use up to date charts
- Prepare a thorough written route plan which takes into account other airspace users, high ground etc.
- If the weather deteriorates, know your safety altitude and resist any temptation to fly lower
- Plan to fly above 1000 ft agl to keep clear of military traffic
- Get an aviation weather forecast and if it turns out to be worse than predicted **KNOW WHEN TO TURN BACK OR DIVERT**
- Check NOTAMs, Bi-weekly Bulletin for latest airspace/frequency information and Freephone 0500 354802 for Royal Flights/ Red Arrows Displays
- Let someone responsible know where and when you are going, your ETA, or file a Flight Plan
- Check DI against compass at regular intervals as part of your **FREDA** check
- If you encounter bad weather, turn back, divert or land
- Use the Lower Airspace Radar Service (LARS)
- Obtain permission before entering anyone else's airspace
- Know what to do if you become lost or suffer an emergency – set the transponder to 7700
- Check when near your destination that it really is the correct aerodrome
- Fly within your licence privileges and current capability
- Don't forget to look out.

To fail to prepare is to prepare to fail

SAFETY SENSE 6
GENERAL AVIATION

AERODROME SENSE

1 INTRODUCTION

This leaflet is intended to be a reminder of good sense and consideration for others which is expected of aerodrome users. It will help you to pave the way so that your visit does not cause problems for others and is at the same time pleasant for yourself and your passengers.

2 BEFORE SETTING OFF

a. Look up the aerodrome in the UK AIP (Aerodromes), [which does not include unlicensed or most government aerodromes] or in *Pooley's* or other commercial *Flight Guide*. Check on runway lengths, displaced thresholds, location of general aviation parking areas, runway lighting, local regulations, noise sensitive areas, special activities, warnings, opening hours, fuel availability etc. Also check on ATC procedures and visual reference points to save you a nasty surprise when ATC ask you to 'report when passing X' and you have no idea where X is!

b. Use the UK AIP to find all the frequencies you may need. Check **NOTAMs** and AIS Information Bulletins for any radio frequency changes, work in progress, change in opening hours etc. These are available on the web site www.ais.org.uk

c. If it is a 25 kHz frequency, make sure you know how to select it on the aircraft equipment.

d. Safety Sense Leaflet 12 gives comprehensive advice when using unlicensed aerodromes and private strips. Leaflet 26 gives additional guidance on the use of military aerodromes.

e. Check whether the aerodrome requires prior permission (PPR). At unlicensed aerodromes and strips this generally needs to be obtained by writing or telephoning **before hand**. At Licensed Aerodromes permission can normally be obtained by radio. Check on this as well as **operating hours**. Note that you may not be allowed to land outside promulgated operating hours.

f. Check what air traffic services are available. Air Traffic Controllers will provide instructions within the ATZ, but Flight Information Service Officers may only give instructions on the ground, and Air to Ground Communications Operators can only provide information

g. If you are non-radio or there is no air traffic service at your destination, phone to get the correct procedures, as well as the runway and altimeter setting details. Know the signal square markings.

h. There may be special procedures for helicopters or microlights.

i. Know the procedures in the event of radio failure.

j. Make sure you know about aerodrome lighting and markings. See Rules 42 to 46 of Rules of the Air or CAP 637, available free on the CAA web site www.caa.co.uk .

3 ARRIVAL

a. Make sure that you have carried out field approach (including altimeter) checks, and have identified the correct aerodrome.

b. If an Automatic Terminal Information Service (ATIS) is provided, listen early, copy the details, and use the code letter in your initial call

c. Identify the runway in use. Beware of confusing directions by 180 degrees!

d. Check the circuit direction. Make all turns near the aerodrome (especially inside an ATZ) in that direction.

e. Identify the 'dead side' – if there is one!

f. Descend outside the circuit pattern, using the procedure illustrated here (taken from CAP 413 and also on the "standard overhead join" poster available under "Safety", "General aviation", "information", "posters" on the CAA web site) unless another is published.

g. Avoid noise sensitive areas and keep to published circuit height.

h. Consider using your landing lights, especially in poor visibility.

i. Keep a good lookout, and give way to aircraft already in the pattern.

4 CIRCUIT PATTERN

a. Follow the pattern illustrated, if there is no different procedure published.

b. Remember wake turbulence separations if it's an airport with larger aeroplanes or helicopters (see Safety Sense Leaflet No. 15, *Wake Vortex*),

c. Keep radio calls brief and unambiguous. Know the non-radio procedure, look for light signals.

d. If the controller tells you to "orbit", maintain circuit height while flying turns in the circuit direction or as ordered, through 360 degrees. Allow for wind, aiming to return to the same point over the ground after every orbit.

e. Ensure you have completed your pre-landing checks – it is easy to be distracted at an unfamiliar aerodrome

f. Check you are aiming for the correct runway threshold (displaced?)

g. Be prepared (expect) to go-around, especially on the first approach to an unfamiliar runway. If you have to go-around, remember to side-step to the dead side so that you are flying parallel with the runway while able to see it.

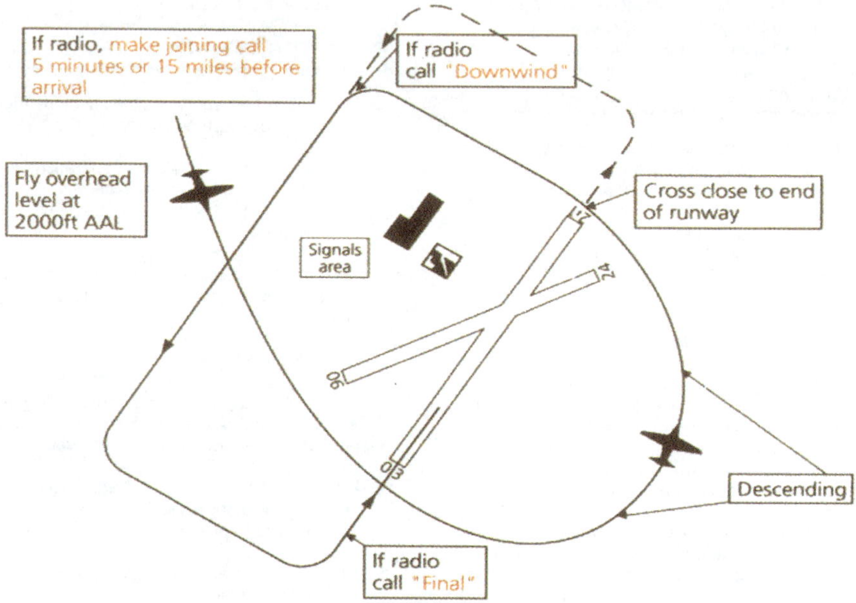
If radio, make joining call 5 minutes or 15 miles before arrival
If radio call "Downwind"
Fly overhead level at 2000ft AAL
Cross close to end of runway
Signals area
24
06
03
Descending
If radio call "Final"

Light Signal	Meaning to Aircraft in flight	Meaning to Aircraft on Aerodrome
STEADY GREEN	Authorised to land if pilot satisfied no collision risk exists	Authorised to take-off if pilot satisfied no collision risk exists
STEADY RED	Do not land. Give way to other aircraft and continue circling	Stop
GREEN FLASHES	Return, wait for permission to land	Authorised to taxi IF pilot satisfied no collision risk exists
RED FLASHES	- Do not land - Aerodrome not available for landing	Taxi clear of landing area in use
WHITE FLASHES	Land at this aerodrome, after receiving continuous green light	Return to starting point on aerodrome

5 AFTER LANDING

a. On an aerodrome without marked runways, turn left after landing (Rule 17)

b. Taxi clear of the runway and stop before doing your after-landing checks. Before raising the flaps, check visually that you are not about to move the undercarriage selector instead!

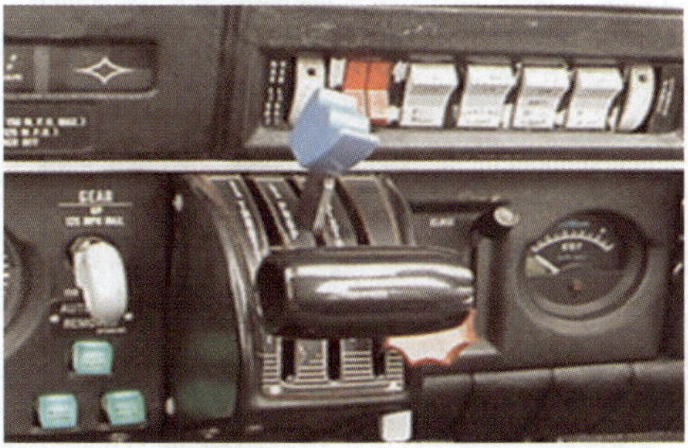

c. If you are unsure of your route to the parking area, wait clear of the runway and call the tower for assistance or a 'Follow Me' service

d. **Never** cross an active runway without permission from the controller or FISO, or informing the Air/Ground Communications Operator: there may be more than one active runway.

e. Keep a lookout for parallel grass runways, glider strips and tow cables or parachuting areas, and have a good look before crossing any runway. If you are non-radio or the aerodrome has no Air Traffic Service, have an **especially good look**.

f. Look for any marshaller's signals, but remember you are still responsible for your aircraft's safety. Most common aeroplane marshalling signals are shown in this leaflet. A full list is at Rule 47 of Rules of the Air.

g. When under marshaller's control, reduce speed to a walking pace.

h. If you are flying a helicopter, do **not** land or hover near parked aeroplanes.

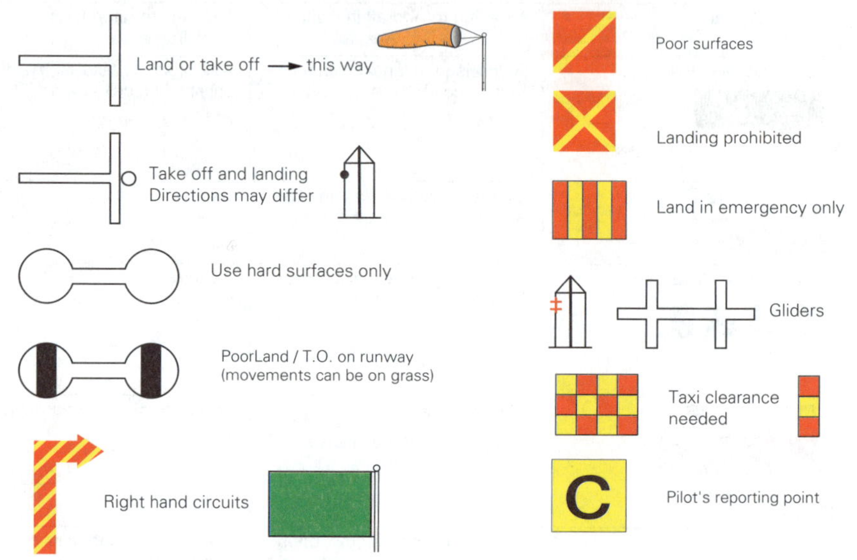

(b) Ground Markings

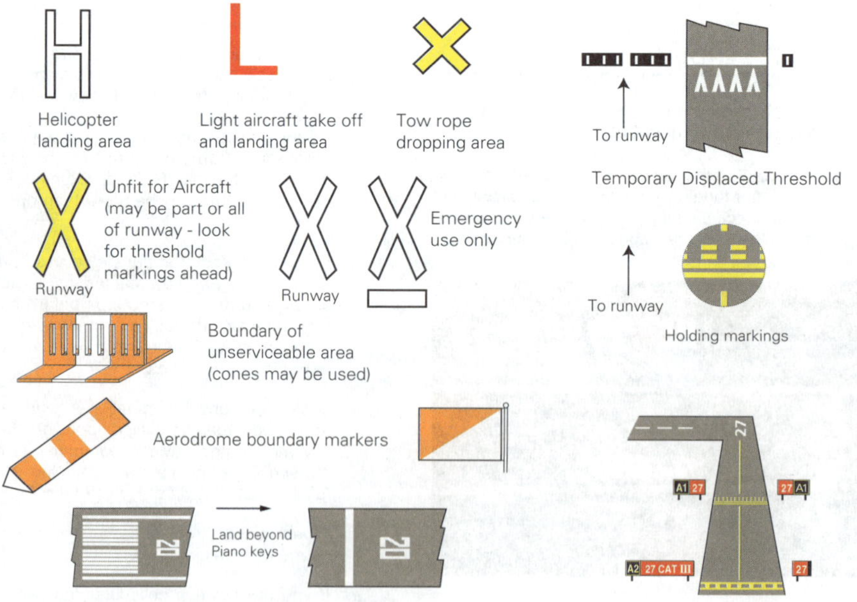

AEROPLANE MARSHALLING SIGNALS

SIGNAL MEANINGS REMAIN THE SAME IF BATS, ILLUMINATED WANDS OR TORCHLIGHTS ARE HELD

6 AFTER SHUT DOWN

Control locks are in place

a. Before leaving the aircraft ensure:

- it is parked into wind (if you can't get hangarage).
- all the electrics are off and the magnetos are safe,
- control locks are in place (another aircraft's propwash can be more severe than a strong wind),
- the parking brake is on and/or the wheels are chocked,
- pitot covers etc. are in place if you are staying for more than a couple of hours,
- it is locked, unless aerodrome personnel ask otherwise (remove or hide items which might be stolen),

b. Don't leave the aircraft in the way of others and then disappear with the key in your pocket.

c. If you are leaving your aircraft overnight or for a long time, check the weather forecast and, if necessary or in doubt, arrange for the aircraft to be tied down.

d. If you have to walk across a busy apron, keep well clear of aircraft with engines running and keep an eye on taxiing aircraft. Take particular care to escort passengers who may be in a completely strange environment. Local rules often require a high-visibility jacket.

e. Report to the building which shows a black **C** on a yellow background.

f. Close any Flight Plan

7 REFUELLING

a. **Always** supervise the refuelling of your aircraft because **you** are responsible for what goes into the tanks and how much. JET A1 and AVGAS mistakes are easily made, and diesel-engined types are becoming ever more popular.

Diesel-engined types

b. Ensure that earthing wires are attached before delivery begins and that the nozzle is earthed. Make sure a fire extinguisher is available.

c. After refuelling, personally check **all** filler caps and access panels for security.

d. Make sure hoses and earthing wires are wound back clear after use.

e. When you sign or pay for the fuel, double-check the invoice for the correct type/grade of fuel and **quantity**. (JET A1 in a piston- engined aircraft has been discovered at this stage.)

8 DEPARTURE

a. Don't forget to pay landing and parking fees.

b. Book out and/or let the 'tower' know your departure intentions (and if going to or from certain UK islands the Terrorism Act applies, see UK AIP GEN 1-2-1). Especially if you are non-radio, get the runway and altimeter setting details. There may be an aerodrome terminal information service (ATIS) available by telephone or on a dedicated frequency.

c. Always get the latest weather information, even if staying in the circuit. Allow time to obtain recorded or faxed weather information.

d. Thoroughly pre-flight the aircraft, making sure that no damage has occurred nor that birds have built a nest overnight. Don't forget the obvious things like pitot covers, tie-down blocks, external control locks, towing bar or baggage doors.

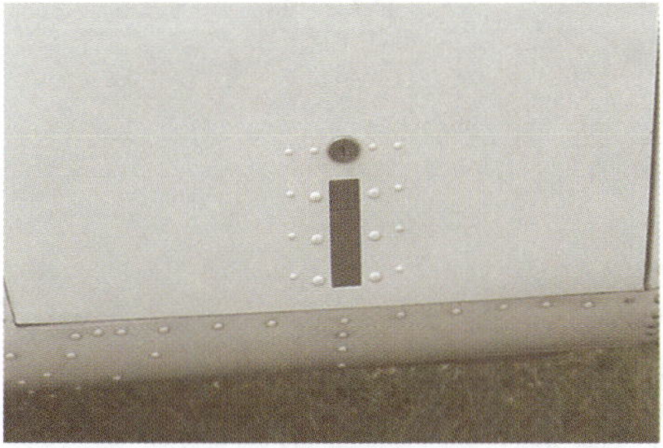

Check baggage doors

e. **Visually** check that your fuel has not 'disappeared' overnight. Always check fuel drains for water etc. especially if parked outside in heavy rain. Water can get into the tank via worn filler cap seals.

f. At some aerodromes you must obtain permission to start engines. Before start-up, ensure that no-one is near the propeller/rotors and that the brakes are on and/or chocks in place, particularly when hand-swinging a propeller.

g. If a marshaller is standing by for start- up, give clear and unmistakable signals.

h. Never start engines in a hangar, nor immediately in front of open doors.

i. Don't use high power settings when another aircraft is parked close behind in your slipstream.

j. Switch on the red anti-collision beacon, prior to starting the engine [Rule 9(2)(b)]. Do not cause dazzle with strobes.

k. Do not taxi on the manoeuvring area without agreement from the 'tower'. If a controller or FISO is on duty, a *taxi clearance* is required. Write it down, and if in doubt about its meaning, ask for clarification.

l. Although aircraft have right of way over vehicles on the manoeuvring area, (except those towing aircraft) if in doubt **STOP** until the way ahead is clear.

m. When taxiing, don't just follow someone else - they might be wrong *or have a different clearance.*

o. If you are given a departure clearance, *write it down, read it back to the controller, and follow it when airborne*.

9 MISCELLANEOUS

a. Don't leave chocks, tie-down ropes or weights where they might be struck by other aircraft.

b. Don't drop litter or allow it to blow out of your aircraft – it could be ingested by the engines of other aircraft.

c. Comply with aerodrome warnings and signs, e.g. CRASH EXIT KEEP CLEAR.

d. Do not smoke or allow others to smoke inside hangars or near aircraft, nor on aprons or manoeuvring areas.

e. Do not taxi onto a Customs area unless you are clearing Customs.

f. If you note any obstructions, debris, pot holes, etc. on the aerodrome – ***tell someone in authority at once!***

10 SUMMARY

- Before setting off, obtain aerodrome details including frequencies, reporting points, runway and taxiway layout, operating hours etc.
- If necessary, obtain permission by telephoning destination
- Call the aerodrome in good time and be ready to follow joining procedures/ reporting points.
- If no procedure is published, use the standard joining and circuit pattern.
- On arrival, make sure it is the correct runway – and aerodrome.
- If you are uncertain of your taxiing route, **STOP** and **ASK**.
- Book in and close any Flight Plan.
- Supervise re-fuelling yourself.
- **YOU** are responsible for the passengers' safety until they are in the clubroom/terminal.
- When departing, allow time to obtain weather information, file Flight Plan, book out etc.

All aerodrome users bring happiness some by arriving, others by departing!

SAFETY SENSE 7
GENERAL AVIATION

AEROPLANE PERFORMANCE

1 INTRODUCTION

a. Accidents such as failure to get airborne, collision with obstacles after take-off and over-run on landing, occur frequently to light aeroplanes – (over 20 cases per year). Many have happened at short strips, often when operating out of wind or where there was a slope. Poor surfaces such as long or wet grass, mud or snow, were often contributory factors. These were performance accidents and many, if not all, of these accidents could have been avoided if the pilots had been fully aware of the performance limitations of their aeroplanes.

b. The pilot in command has a legal obligation under Article 38 of the Air Navigation Order, which requires the pilot to check that the aeroplane will have adequate performance for the proposed flight. The purpose of this leaflet is to remind you of the actions needed to ensure that your aeroplane's take-off, climb and landing performance will be adequate. It may not of course, be necessary before every flight. If you are using a 3000 metre runway a cursory check of performance will do, but where is the dividing line - 700, 1000 or 1500 metres? This will be decided by a large number of variables and only by reference to performance data, including climb performance, can the safety, or otherwise, of the particular flight be properly determined.

2 WHERE TO FIND THE INFORMATION

The data needed to predict the performance in the expected conditions may be in any one of the following:

- The UK Flight Manual, or for a few older aeroplanes, the Performance Schedule.

- The Pilot's Operating Handbook or the Owner's Manual. This is applicable to most light aeroplanes and sometimes contains CAA Change Sheets and/or Supplements giving additional performance data which may either supplement or override data in the main document, e.g. a 'fleet downgrade'.

- For some imported aeroplanes, an English language Flight Manual approved by the airworthiness authority in the country of origin, with a UK supplement containing the performance data approved by the CAA.

3 USE OF PERFORMANCE DATA

a. Many light aeroplanes are in performance group E, and certificated with UNFACTORED data, being the performance achieved by the manufacturer using a *new aeroplane and engine(s) in ideal conditions* flown by a highly experienced pilot. The CAA does not verify the Performance Data on all foreign aeroplanes; in some cases a single spot check is made.

b. To ensure a high level of safety on UK **Public Transport** flights, there is a *legal* requirement to apply specified safety factors to un-factored data (the result is called Net Performance Data). It is strongly recommended that those same factors be used for private flights in order to take account of:

- Your lack of practice
- Incorrect speeds/techniques
- Aeroplane and engine wear and tear
- Less than favourable conditions

c. Performance data in manuals for UK manufactured aeroplanes certificated for the purposes of Public Transport may include the Public Transport factors, (i.e. Net Performance) but manuals and handbooks for the smaller aeroplanes often do not. For foreign manufactured aeroplanes the Net Performance may be included as a Supplement. Manuals usually make it clear if factors are included but if in any doubt you should consult the CAA Safety Regulation Group (see para 9e).

d. Any 'Limitations' given in the Certificate of Airworthiness, the Flight Manual, the Performance Schedule or the Owner's Manual/Pilot's Operating Handbook are **mandatory** on all flights. (Note that there can be a UK Limitation contained in a Supplement which is not referred to in the text of the main document.)

e. If any advice/information given in this leaflet differs from that given in the Flight Manual, (or Pilot's Operating Handbook), then you must always comply with the manual or handbook – these are the authoritative documents.

4 PERFORMANCE PLANNING

A list of variables affecting performance together with Factors for non-Public Transport operations are shown in tabular form at the end of this leaflet. These represent the increase in take-off distance to a height of 50 feet or the increase in landing distance from 50 feet. It is intended that the tabular form will be suitable for attachment to a pilot's clipboard for easy reference. When specific Factors are given in the aeroplane's manual, handbook or supplement, they must be considered the minimum acceptable. The primary source is the Flight Manual or Pilot's Operating Handbook but cross check using this leaflet and use this where other Information is not available.

5 GENERAL POINTS

a. **Aeroplane weight:** use the actual aircraft Basic Empty weight stated on the Weight and Balance Schedule for the *individual* aeroplane you plan to fly. The weight of aeroplanes of a given type can vary considerably dependent upon the level of equipment, by as much as 77 kg (170 lb.) – the "invisible passenger", for a well equipped single-engined aeroplane. Do not use the 'example weight' shown in the weight and balance section, it may be a new aeroplane with minimum equipment. Remember, on many aeroplanes it may not be possible to fill all the fuel tanks, all the seats and the baggage area. Safety Sense Leaflet 9, (Weight and Balance) provides further guidance.

b. **Aerodrome elevation:** performance deteriorates with altitude and you should use the pressure altitude at the aerodrome for calculations. (This equates to the height shown on the altimeter on the ground at the aerodrome with the sub- scale set at 1013 mb.)

c. **Slope:** an uphill slope increases the take- off ground run, and a downhill slope increases the landing distance. Any benefit arising from an upslope on landing or a downslope on take-off should be regarded as a 'bonus'. There are a few 'one way strips' where the slope is so great that in most wind conditions it is best to land up the hill and take off downhill.

d. **Temperature:** performance decreases on a hot day. On really hot days many pilots have been surprised by the loss of power in ambient temperatures of 30° C and above. Remember, temperature may be low on a summer morning but very high in the afternoon.

e. **Wind:** even a slight tailwind increases the take-off and landing distances very significantly. Note that if there is a 90° crosswind there is no beneficial headwind component and aircraft controllability may be the problem. Where data allows adjustment for wind, it is recommended that not more than 50% of the headwind component and not less than 150% of the tailwind component of the reported wind be assumed. In some manuals these factors are already included; check the relevant section.

f. **Cloudbase and visibility:** if you have to make a forced landing or fly a low-level circuit and re-land, you **MUST** be able to see obstacles and the ground. Thus, cloudbase and visibility have to be appropriate.

g. **Turbulence and windshear:** will adversely affect the performance, you must be aware of these when working out the distances needed.

h. **Surrounding terrain:** if there are hills or mountains nearby, check that you will have a rate or angle of climb sufficient to out-climb the terrain. This is particularly important if there is any wind, it may cause significant down drafts.

i. **Rain drops, mud, insects and ice:** these have a significant effect on aeroplanes, particularly those with laminar flow aerofoils. Stall speeds are increased and greater distances are required. Note that any ice, snow or frost affects all aerofoils, including the propeller and also increases the aircraft's weight – you must clear it all before flight. (AIC 104/ 98 (Pink 176) – Frost, Ice and Snow on Aircraft, refers.)

j. **Tyre pressure:** low tyre pressure (perhaps hidden by grass or wheel fairings) will increase the take- off run, as will wheel fairings jammed full of mud, grass, slush, etc.

k. **Engine failure:** since an engine failure or power loss (even on some twin-engined aircraft) may result in a forced landing, this must be borne in mind during all stages of the flight.

l. **Performance during aerobatics:** remember that variations in aeroplane weight will directly affect its performance during aerobatics (even, for example, steep turns) and outside air temperature/ altitude will similarly affect engine power available. Hot day aerobatics in a heavier than normal aeroplane require careful planning and thought.

6 TAKE OFF – POINTS TO NOTE

a. **Cross wind:** a cross wind on take off may require use of brakes to keep straight, and will increase the take off distance.

b. **Decision point:** you should work out the runway point at which you can stop the aeroplane in the event of engine or other malfunctions e.g. low engine rpm, loss of ASI, lack of acceleration or dragging brakes. Do NOT mentally programme yourself in a GO-mode to the exclusion of all else.

If the ground is soft or the grass is long and the aeroplane is still on the ground and not accelerating, stick to your decision-point and abandon take off. If the grass is wet or damp, particularly if it is very short, you will need a lot more space to stop.

c. **Twin engines:** on twin engined aircraft, if there is an engine failure after lift off, you may not reach the scheduled single engine rate of climb until:

- the landing gear and flaps have retracted (there may be a temporary degradation as the gear doors open)
- the best single engine climb speed, 'blue line speed', has been achieved.

Under limiting conditions an engine failure shortly after lift off may preclude continued flight and a forced landing will be necessary. Where the performance is marginal, the following points must be considered when deciding the best course of action:

- while flying with asymmetric power it is **vital** that airspeed is maintained comfortably above the minimum control speed, V_{MC} . A forced landing under control is infinitely preferable to the loss of directional control with the aircraft rolling inverted at low altitude. If there are signs you are losing directional control, lower the nose immediately if height permits to regain speed and if all else fails reduce power on the operating engine. (Care must be taken to maintain normal margins above the stall.)

- performance and stall speed margins will be reduced in turns. All manoeuvres must be kept to gentle turns.

Keep In Asymmetric Practice

d. **Use of available length:** make use of the full length of the runway, there is no point in turning a good length runway into a short one by doing an 'intersection' take off. On short fields use any 'starter strip'.

e. **Rolling take off:** although turning onto the runway, and applying full power without stopping can reduce the take off run, it should only be used with great care (due to landing gear side loads and directional control) and your propwash must not hazard other aircraft. If you are having to do this sort of thing, then the runway is probably TOO SHORT.

f. **Surface and slope:** grass, soft ground or snow increase rolling resistance and therefore the take- off ground run. When the ground is soft, a heavy aircraft may 'dig in' and never reach take off speed. Keeping the weight off the nosewheel or getting the tail up on a tail wheel aircraft, may help. An uphill slope reduces acceleration.

For surface and slope, remember that the increases shown are the take- off and landing distances to or from a height of *50 feet*. The correction to the ground run will usually be proportionally greater.

g. **Flap setting:** use the settings recommended in Pilots Handbook/Flight Manual but check for any Supplement attached to your manual/ handbook. The take-off performance shown in the main part of the manual may give some flap settings which are not approved for Public Transport operations by aeroplanes on the UK Civil Aircraft register. Do not use settings which are 'folk- lore'.

h. **Humidity:** high humidity can have an adverse effect on engine performance and this is usually taken into account during certification; however there may be a correction factor applicable to your aeroplane. Check in the manual/ handbook.

i. **Abandoned take-off:** Many multi-engined aeroplane manuals include data on rejected take- off distances. Some aircraft quote a minimum engine rpm that should be available during the take off run.

j. **Engine power:** check early in the take off run that engine(s) rpm/manifold pressure are correct. If they are low, abandon take off when there is plenty of room to stop. Brief use of carb heat at the hold should ensure carb ice is not forming.

7 LANDING – POINTS TO NOTE

a. When landing at places where the length is not generous, make sure that you touch down on or very close to your aiming point (beware of displaced thresholds). If you've misjudged it, make an early decision to go around if you have any doubts – don't float half way along the runway before deciding.

b. Landing on a wet surface, or snow, can result in increased ground roll, despite increased rolling resistance. This is because of the amount of braking possible is reduced, due to lack of tyre friction. Very short wet grass with a firm subsoil will be slippery and can give a 60% distance increase (1.6 factor).

c. When landing on grass the pilot cannot see or always know whether the grass is wet or covered in dew.

d. The landing distances quoted in the Pilot's Operating Handbook/Flight Manual assume the correct approach speed and technique is flown, use of higher speed will add significantly to the distance required whilst a lower speed will erode stall margins.

8 SAFETY FACTORS

a. **Take-off**: It is strongly recommended that the appropriate Public Transport factor, or one corresponding to that requirement, should be applied for all flights. For take-off this factor is x 1.33 and applies to all single engined aeroplanes and to multi- engined aeroplanes with limited performance scheduling (Group E). Manuals for aeroplanes in other Performance Groups may give factored data.

Pilots of these latter Performance Group aeroplanes and other complex types are expected to refer to the Flight Manual for specific information on all aspects of performance planning. It is therefore important to check which Performance Group your aeroplane is in.

The table at the end of this leaflet gives guidance for pilots of aeroplanes for which there is only UNFACTORED data. It is taken from AIC 67/2002 (Pink 36).

Don't forget, where several factors are relevant, they must be **multiplied**. The resulting Take-Off Distance Required to a height of 50 feet, (TODR), can become surprisingly high.

For example:

In still air, on a level dry hard runway at sea level with an ambient temperature of 10° C, an aeroplane requires a measured take-off distance to a height of 50 feet of 390m. This should be multiplied by the safety factor of 1.33 giving a TODR of 519m.

The same aeroplane in still air from a dry, short- grass strip (factor of 1.2) with a 2% uphill slope (factor of 1.1), 500 feet above sea-level (factor of 1.05) at 20° C (factor of 1.1), including the safety factor (factor of 1.33) will have TODR of:– 390 x 1.2 x 1.1 x 1.05 x 1.1 x 1.33 = 791m

You should always ensure that, after applying all the relevant factors, including the safety factor, the TODR does not exceed the take-off distance available [TODA] (or accelerate/ stop distance available [ASDA]). If it does, you **must** offload passengers, fuel or baggage. Better a disappointed passenger than a grieving widow! Do not rely on the 'It will be alright' syndrome.

b. **Climb (and Go-around):** In order that the aeroplane climb performance does not fall below the prescribed minimum, some manuals/handbooks quote take-off and landing weights that should not be exceeded at specific combinations of altitude and temperature ('WAT' limits). They are calculated using the pressure altitude and temperature at the relevant aerodrome.

Remember rate of climb decreases with altitude – don't allow yourself to get into a situation where the terrain outclimbs your aeroplane!

c. **Landing**: It is recommended that the Public Transport factor should be applied for all flights. For landing, this factor is x 1.43 (so that you
should be able to land in 70% of the distance available).

Again when several factors are relevant, they must be **multiplied**. As with take-off, the total distance required may seem surprisingly high.

You should always ensure that after applying all the relevant factors, including the safety factor, the Landing Distance Required (LDR) from a height of 50 feet does not exceed Landing Distance Available.

9 ADDITIONAL INFORMATION

a. **Engine failure:** bear in mind the glide performance, miles per 1000 ft, of single-engined types and the ability to make a safe forced landing throughout the flight. Where possible, the cruise altitude should be selected accordingly.

b. **Obstacles:** it is essential to be aware of any obstacles likely to impede either the take- off or landing flight path and to ensure there is adequate performance available to clear them by a safe margin. AGA 3 section of the UK AIP includes obstacle data for a number of UK aerodromes. Excessive angles of bank shortly after take off greatly reduce rate of climb.

c. **Aerodrome distances:** for many aerodromes information on available distances is published in the Aerodrome section of the AIP or in one of the Flight Guides. At aerodromes where no published information exists, distances can be paced out. The pace length should be established accurately or assumed to be no more than 0.75 metres (2 ½ft). It is better to measure the length accurately with the aid of a rope of known length.

Slopes can be calculated if surface elevation information is available, if not they should be estimated. For example, an altitude difference of 50 ft on a 750 metre (2,500 ft) strip indicates a 2% slope. Unless the Flight Manual gives specific figures, do not try to calculate any benefit from an advantageous slope.Be sure not to mix metres and feet in your calculation and remember, for instance, that a metre is more than a yard (see Conversion Table below).

Beware of intersection take-offs, displaced runway thresholds or soft ground which may reduce the available runway length to less than the published figures. Check NOTAMs, Local Notices etc.

d. **Runway surface:** operations from strips or aerodromes covered in snow, slush or extensive standing water are inadvisable and should not be attempted without first reading AIC 126/ 96 (Pink 131), 'Risks and Factors Associated with Operations on Runways Contaminated with Snow, Slush or Water'. A short wait could help in the case of standing water, hail, etc.

e. **Advice:** where doubt exists on the source of data to be used or its application in given circumstances, advice should be sought from the Flight Department, Safety Regulation Group, Civil Aviation Authority, Aviation House, Gatwick Airport South, West Sussex RH6 0YR, Telephone (01293)573113 Fax (01293)573977.

Conversion Table

1 kg	= 2-205 lb.	1 lb.	= 0.454 kg
1 inch	= 2.54 cm	1 cm	= 0.394 in
1 foot	= 0.305 m	1 metre	= 3.28 ft
1 Imp gal	= 4.546 litres	1 litre	= 0.22 Imp gal
1 US gal	= 3.785 litres	1 litre	= 0.264 US gal
1 Imp gal	= 1.205 US gal	1 US gal	= 0.83 Imp gal

10 SUMMARY

FACTORS MUST BE MULTIPLIED i.e. 1.20 x 1.35

Condition	TAKE-OFF		LANDING	
	Increase in Take-Off Distance to height 50 feet	Factor	Increase in Landing Distance from 50 feet	Factor
A 10% increase in aeroplane weight, e.g. another passenger	20%	1.20	10%	1.10
An increase of 1,000 ft in aerodrome elevation	10%	1.10	5%	1.05
An increase of 10° C in ambient temperature	10%	1.10	5%	1.05
Dry grass* - Up to 20cm (8in) on firm soil	20%	1.20	15%+	1.15
Wet grass* - Up to 20cm (8in) (on firm soil)	30%	1.3	35%+ Very short grass may be slippery, distances may increase by up to 60%	1.35
Wet paved surface	-	-	15%	1.15
A 2% slope*	Uphill 10%	1.10	Downhill 10%	1.10
A tailwind component of 10% of lift-off speed	20%	1.20	20%	1.20
Soft ground or snow*	25% or more	1.25+	25%+ or more	1.25+
Now use additional Safety Factors (if data is unfactored)		**1.33**		**1.43**

Notes:

1. Effect on Ground Run/ Roll will be greater. Do not attempt to use the factors to reduce the distances required in the case of downslope on take-off or upslope on landing.

2. +For a few types of aeroplane e. g. those without brakes, grass surfaces may decrease the landing roll. However, to be on the safe side, assume the INCREASE shown until you are thoroughly conversant with the aeroplane type.

3. Any deviation from normal operating techniques is likely to result in an increased distance.

If the distance required exceeds the distance available, changes will HAVE to be made.

SAFETY SENSE 8
GENERAL AVIATION

AIR TRAFFIC SERVICES OUTSIDE CONTROLLED AIRSPACE

1 INTRODUCTION

a. In this leaflet, 'controlled airspace' means airspace of Classes A, B, C, D and E (the UK does not use B at present). The leaflet describes only the types of air traffic service available **outside** controlled airspace; i.e. airspace Classes F and G – commonly known as the 'open' FIR. These types of service are as follows:

- Flight Information Service (FIS).
- Radar Information Service (RIS).
- Radar Advisory Service (RAS).
- Procedural Service.
- Alerting (i.e. Emergency) Service.

These services apply to the departure, en-route and arrival stages of your flight.

b. If you require FIS, RIS or RAS you must ask an appropriate air traffic service unit (ATSU) to provide the particular service you wish to receive. However, some ATSUs are only staffed by Flight Information Service Officers (FISO) or Air/ Ground Operators. Such ATSUs will **ONLY** be able to provide an information service for their local area.

c. If the service you requested cannot be provided, for instance due to workload or equipment problems, another service may be offered.

d. Procedural Service and Alerting Service are provided automatically by ATSUs, (see also paras 2b and 2c). It is not necessary for you to request these services.

e. It is important that you understand the benefits and limitations of these air traffic services so that you can ask the controller for the best one to suit your needs.

f. You do not have to hold an instrument rating to fly in accordance with the Instrument Flight Rules (IFR) outside controlled airspace. There is nothing mysterious about IFR within UK airspace, they are there to ensure that you have adequate clearance from ground obstacles and that you are safely separated in the vertical plane, according to your magnetic track, from other aircraft in flight. The **UK** regulations for IFR flights outside controlled airspace are as follows:

- Except when necessary for take off and landing, or when authorised by the appropriate authority, you must be flying at least 1000 ft above the highest obstacle within 5 nm of your aircraft. However, you may disregard this if you are flying IFR below 3000 ft and you are **clear of cloud and in sight of the surface**.*

- If you are in level flight above 3000 ft amsl you MUST fly at a level appropriate to your magnetic track in accordance with the Quadrantal System.

g. There is often confusion about the IFR in relation to VMC and IMC. VMC and IMC refer to the weather conditions encountered during flight and are terms used to denote actual weather conditions, in relation to the VFR minima.

h. The VFR minima (weather conditions for flying in accordance with Visual Flight Rules) for flight outside controlled airspace are contained in the box below:

	Distance from cloud		
	Horizontal	Vertical	Flight Visibility
at and above FL 100	1500 m	1000 ft	8 km
below FL 100	1500 m	1000 ft	5 km
OR **at or below 3000 ft amsl**	clear of cloud and in sight of the surface		5 km
Aircraft, other than helicopters, flying at 140 kts IAS or less	clear of cloud and in sight of the surface		1500 m
Helicopters	clear of cloud and in sight of the surface		compatible with speed
Note that licence privileges may prevent a pilot from flying in conditions of low flight visibility.			

Pilots must be aware of the minimum safe height and must comply with Rule 5 of the Rules of the Air Regulations (the Low Flying Rules).

2 NON- RADAR SERVICES

a. **Flight Information Service (FIS):**

As described in AIC 48/2004 (Pink 65), this non-radar service provides information to assist with the safe and efficient conduct of your flight. The information available may include:

- Weather.
- Serviceability of navigation and approach aids.
- Conditions at aerodromes.
- Other aircraft reported in your area, which are in contact with or known to the FIS.
- Other information pertinent to flight safety.

Remember that use of FIS is not intended to replace pre-flight planning, nor is it intended to be a comprehensive source of information on the presence of other aircraft. The controller may be able to provide information on aircraft in your vicinity that have contacted him, but it is **most unlikely** that he will be aware of **all** aircraft that may affect your flight, i.e.: warnings of conflicting traffic are far less likely to be given under a FIS than under RAS or RIS. Most ATSUs can provide a FIS within their local areas. Those ATSUs which provide RAS and RIS can normally offer a FIS when conditions prevent them from providing a radar service.

b. **Procedural Service:**

This non-radar service provides separation between **participating** traffic and is only based on position reports. For example, it is used for IFR traffic which is carrying out pilot-interpreted approaches when radar is not available, or for aircraft flying along Advisory Routes. It may also be used when radar contact is temporarily lost with an aircraft receiving RAS in the vicinity of other participating traffic. However, during radio transmissions, civil ATSUs do not use the term 'Procedural Service'.

c. **Alerting (Emergency) Service:**

When the controller becomes aware, or suspects, that you need Search and Rescue assistance, he will notify the appropriate organisations; this is known as an Alerting Service. It is not a service which you request – it is provided automatically. Remember, the best way of making sure that the controller realises that you have an emergency situation is to make a clear MAYDAY or PAN call, whichever is appropriate.

3 RADAR SERVICES

a. **Radar Information Service (RIS):**

RIS is a radar service which aims to provide you with information on conflicting traffic, but **no** avoiding action will be offered. Hence you are responsible for maintaining separation from other aircraft. This service is tailor- made for letting you get on with your flying in VMC while the controller provides you with an extra pair of eyes. This is a very useful facility when carrying out general handling, or when flying through busy airspace where repeated avoiding action under RAS may be unnecessary and time-wasting. The controller may provide radar headings for his planning purpose or at the pilot's request. The pilot still remains responsible for separation from other aircraft and may decide not to accept the heading. However, you **must** tell the controller **before** you change level, level-band, or route. RIS may be requested under any flight rules or meteorological conditions, but in IMC it is better to obtain and use RAS (if available).

b. **Radar Advisory Service (RAS):**

This service is only available to flights operating under IFR irrespective of meteorological conditions and aims to provide you with the information **and** the advisory avoiding action necessary to maintain separation from other aircraft. It is the radar service used by many pilots, particularly when flying in IMC. But remember, if you are:

- not qualified to fly in IMC, or
- qualified but out-of-practice,

you **must NOT** accept an advisory turn or level change which will put you into IMC.

However, if you do not take the controller's advice, or if for any other reason you cannot accept heading or level changes, you **must tell the controller**, who may be able to offer alternative avoiding action. You **must** also inform the controller before making any other changes in heading or level, because it may affect your separation from other aircraft. If you request RAS, but the controller is unable to provide that service, you may be offered RIS instead.

4 HOW TO OBTAIN A SERVICE

a. You should contact the appropriate ATSU and ask for the service you require. The controller will tell you whether your request can be met. If you don't specify the type of service, the controller may apply the best available. You can request a change in the type of service at any time. The ATSU should be given the following information:

- call sign and type of aircraft
- estimated position
- heading
- level (or level-band for traffic carrying out general handling)
- intention (next reporting/turning point, destination or general handling area)
- flight rules (IFR/VFR)
- type of service requested (RAS/ RIS/ FIS).

b. Services are available from civil and military ATSUs, subject to their operating hours and controller workload. But remember that, at weekends, many military ATSUs are closed and so you may not be able to obtain a RAS or RIS for some part of your route. In this case you should consider contacting the FIR controller for a FIS, or aerodromes along your route who may be able to provide a more comprehensive FIS for their local area.

NB: Remember, even when only providing a FIS, a controller may wish to identify your aircraft on radar to confirm your position – but that does **not** mean that a radar service will subsequently be provided. Furthermore, just because you have been allocated a transponder code, AND IDENTIFIED, i**t does not mean that you are receiving any service.**

5 LIMITATIONS OF RADAR SERVICE

Gliders, microlights, balloons and very slow moving aircraft do not always show on radar. When they do, they are often indistinguishable from the radar returns of birds, road vehicles etc.; this is an inherent limitation in radar services. It is important that you are aware of this and **maintain the best possible look-out for other aircraft** even though you are receiving RIS or RAS. When a radar service is adversely affected by other factors, e.g. weather returns on the radar, poor radar performance, high traffic density, controller workload etc. it is described as 'limited'. The controller will then give you a specific warning of the situation e.g. 'You are near the base of radar cover'. You should note the warning and conduct your flight accordingly, such as by adjusting your look-out scan.

6 TERRAIN AND OBSTACLE CLEARANCE

Pilots are **always** responsible for providing their own **terrain and obstacle** clearance whilst flying under VFR. However, ATSUs will only provide RAS above levels/ altitudes which they consider safe.

7 CHANGING FREQUENCY

When you are in sight of your destination or wish to change to another frequency, always tell the FIR/Radar Controller that you are leaving their frequency and your subsequent intentions.

8 AVAILABILITY OF SERVICES

Any ATSU may provide the services described in this Leaflet but you should particularly note the following:

a. **Lower Airspace Radar Service:**

Although many ATSUs can provide RAS/RIS, those whose location makes them particularly suitable for providing radar service to transit traffic, at and below FL 95, participate in a system called the Lower Airspace Radar Service (LARS). Details are in AIC 2/2001, (Yellow 33) *Services to Aircraft Outside Controlled Airspace* and in the UK AIP ENR 1–6–4, latest chart of coverage shown in 6–1–6–3. The service is mostly available weekdays 0800 to 1700 local.

b. **ATCC FIR Service:**

The London and Scottish ATCCs try to provide FIS in their FIRs. Details are in the UK AIP ENR 1-1-2-1-2. You should consider a call if you have not obtained any service elsewhere. (Note that all London Flight Information Regions may be operated by one person).

c. **Military Aerodrome Traffic Zone (MATZ) Penetration Service:**

This is available for aerodromes which have MATZs. The Penetration Service will often include provision of RAS. Details are in the Yellow AIC listed in para 1e, in AIC 9/01 (Yellow39) '*Military Aerodrome Traffic Zones*' and in the UK AIP ENR 2– 2– 3.

d. **Danger Area Services:**

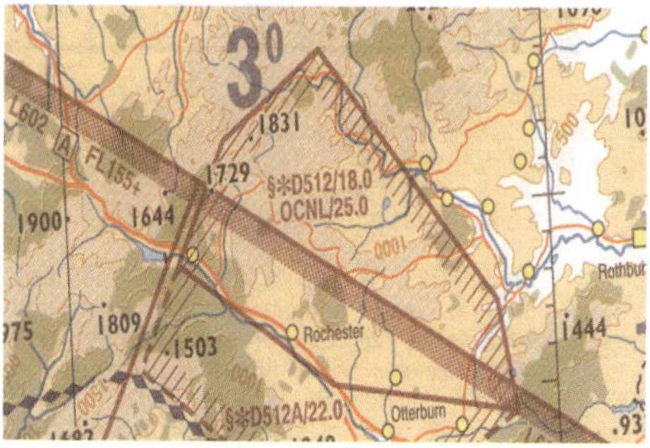

Nominated Service Units (see UK AIP ENR 5–1– 3– 1 to –22 and the legend on the CAA 1:500,000 charts) provide (†) Danger Area Crossing Service (DACS) or (§) Danger Area Activity Information Service (DAAIS). MERELY OBTAINING INFORMATION UNDER DAAIS DOES **NOT** GIVE YOU A CLEARANCE TO CROSS AN ACTIVE DANGER AREA. **YOU MUST HAVE A SPECIFIC CLEARANCE.**

e. **Areas of Intense Aerial Activity and Aerial Tactics Areas:**

Intense civil and/or military activity takes place within these areas which are listed in ENR 5–2. Pilots of non- participating aircraft who are unable to avoid AIAAs/ATAs, must keep a good look out and call the appropriate frequency which is also shown on the 1:500,000 chart.

f. **Free-fall Parachute Drop Zones:**

Intense free-fall is conducted up to FL 150 at permanent drop zones (listed in the UK AIP at ENR 5.5) or at other sites by NOTAM. Activity information may be available from certain ATSUs as listed on VFR charts, but pilots are advised to assume a drop zone (DZ) is active if no information can be obtained. Parachute dropping aircraft and, on occasions, parachutists may be encountered outside the DZ circle shown on VFR charts and pilots are strongly advised to give a wide berth to all active DZs

Air Traffic Services Outside Controlled Airspace (ATSOCAS)

ATC OPTIONS

1

British weather!
Working hard?
ATC will tell you about other aircraft and offer advice on how to avoid (by 5nm or 3000ft, where possible)

Radar Advisory Service (RAS) - IFR only

2

Nice day, working hard?
Need some help?
Let ATC tell you about other aircraft, but remember, it is **YOU** who must avoid

Radar Information Service (RIS)

3

Lovely day?
Enjoying yourself?
You're happy to see and avoid other aircraft.
Other info on request

Flight Information Service (FIS)

Which Option do YOU want?
Let ATC know on the initial call

Full details of available services in UK AIP/MATS Pt I/JSP 318A

ACDA01329 11-01.

Pilots are always responsible for their own terrain and obstacle clearance

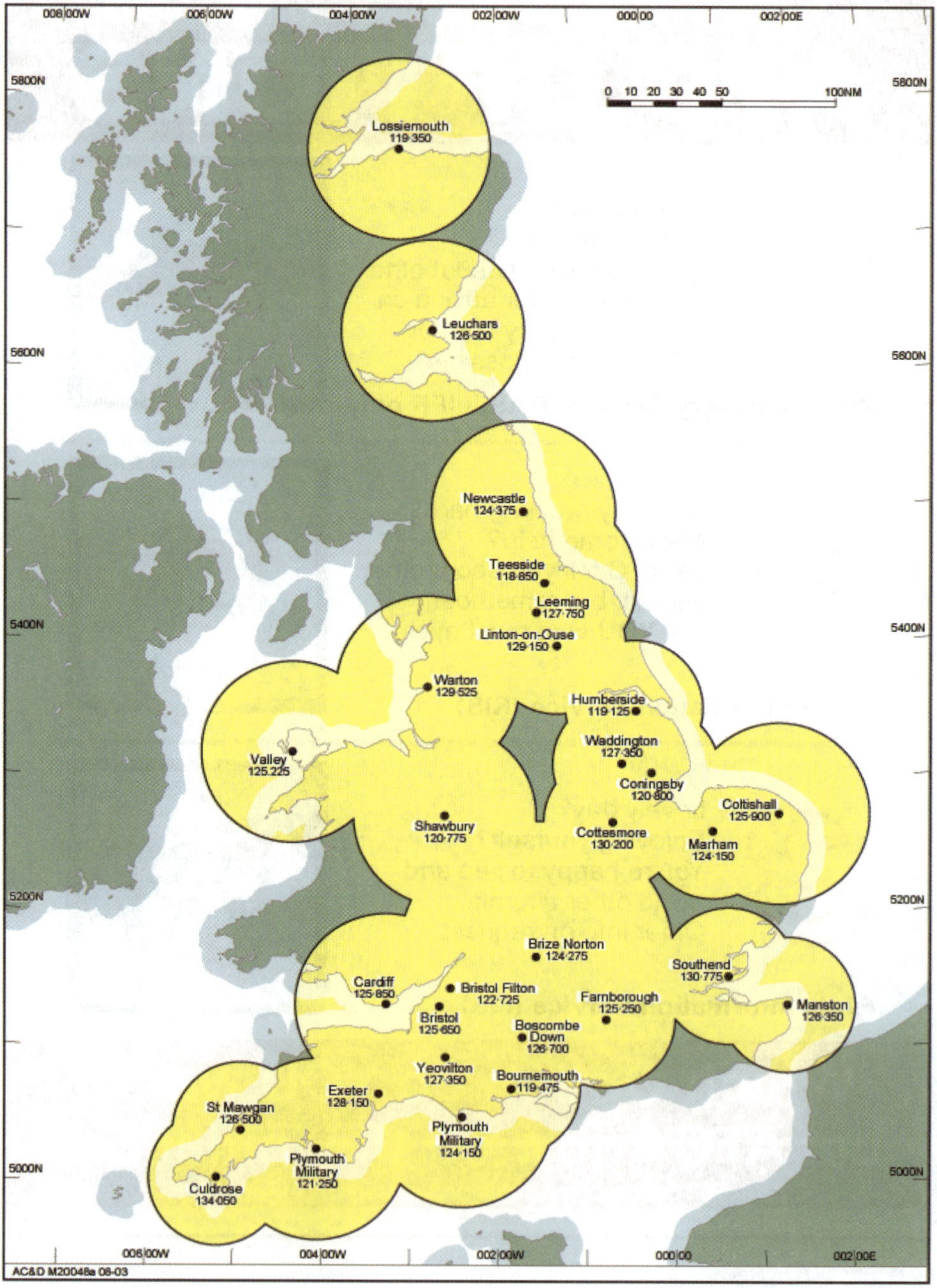
008|00W
006|00W
004|00W
002|00W
000|00
002|00E
5800N
5600N
5400N
5200N
5000N
0 10 20 30 40 50 100NM
Lossiemouth 119·350
Leuchars 126·500
Newcastle 124·375
Teesside 118·850
Leeming 127·750
Linton-on-Ouse 129·150
Warton 129·525
Humberside 119·125
Waddington 127·350
Coningsby 120·800
Valley 125.225
Coltishall 125·900
Shawbury 120·775
Cottesmore 130·200
Marham 124·150
Brize Norton 124·275
Southend 130·775
Cardiff 125·850
Bristol Filton 122·725
Farnborough 125·250
Manston 126·350
Bristol 125·650
Boscombe Down 126·700
Yeovilton 127·350
Bournemouth 119·475
Exeter 128·150
St Mawgan 126·500
Plymouth Military 124·150
Plymouth Military 121·250
Culdrose 134·050
AC&D M20048a 08-03

SAFETY SENSE 9
GENERAL AVIATION

WEIGHT AND BALANCE

photo- John Thorpe

1 INTRODUCTION

a. The principles of weight and balance should have been understood by all pilots during their initial training. It is clear that, afterwards, some forget, don't bother or are caught in 'traps' There have been several fatal accidents to UK registered general aviation aircraft in which overloading, or out-of-limits centre of gravity (cg), were contributory factors.

b. An **overloaded** aircraft may fail to become airborne, while **out-of-limits** centre of gravity seriously affects the stability and controllability. Pilots **must** appreciate the effects of weight and balance on the performance and handling of aircraft, ***particularly*** in combination with performance reducing factors, such as long or wet grass, a 'tired' engine(s), severe or un-coordinated manoeuvres, turbulence, high ambient temperatures and emergency situations (see also Safety Sense Leaflet No 7 – *Aeroplane Performance*).

c. This Leaflet is intended to remind pilots of the main points of weight and balance.

2 THE LAW AND INSURANCE

a. Article 43(d) of Air Navigation (No. 2) Order 2000 states that 'the Commander of an aircraft registered in the United Kingdom shall satisfy himself before the aircraft takes off that the load carried by the aircraft is of such weight, and is so distributed and secured, that it may safely be carried on the intended flight'. The CAA has successfully prosecuted pilots who have failed to comply with this Article.

b. In addition ANO Article 8 requires that all aircraft have a valid Certificate of Airworthiness or Permit to Fly. These documents, either directly, or by reference to a Flight Manual/Pilots Operating Handbook which forms part of a C of A, specify the weight and centre of gravity limits within which the aircraft must be operated. If these limitations are not observed, the pilot is failing to comply with a legal condition for the operation of his aircraft, thus insurers could reject any claim in the event of a mishap.

3 WEIGHT

a. The effects of overloading include:

- reduced acceleration and increased take- off speed, requiring a longer take-off run and distance to clear a 50 ft obstacle;
- decreased angle of climb reducing obstacle clearance capability after take-off;
- higher take-off speeds imposing excessive loads on the landing gear, especially if the runway is rough;
- reduced ceiling and rate of climb;
- reduced range;
- impaired manoeuvrability;
- impaired controllability;
- increased stall speeds;
- increased landing speeds, requiring a longer runway;
- reduced braking effectiveness;
- reduced structural strength margins;
- on twin-engined aircraft, failure to climb or maintain height on one engine.

Photo – John Thorpe

b. It **must** be realised, that with many four and six seat aircraft, it is **not** possible to fill all the seats, use the maximum baggage allowance, fill all the fuel tanks **and** remain within the approved weight and centre of gravity limits. You may have to reduce the number of passengers, baggage, or fuel load or possibly a combination of all three. Better that a passenger travels by bus or by train than in an ambulance!

c. The aircraft weight used in the example calculation in the Flight Manual/Pilot's Operating Handbook is for a **new** aircraft usually with little or no equipment. The weight and/ or other data used in the example **MUST NOT** be used as the basis for operational weight and balance calculations. Whenever significant equipment is added a new empty weight and cg position must be provided for the Weight and Balance Schedule. This is the **only** valid source of data. You **must** use this actual equipped weight and be sure whether this includes such items as engine oil, fire extinguisher, first aid kit, life jackets, etc. The actual weight of a well equipped single engined aircraft can be as much as 170 lb. (77 kg) greater than a basic aircraft – the invisible passenger! Periodic re-weighing of an aircraft is sensible – many owners have been surprised by the increase.

d. Estimating the weight of baggage can result in variations from half to double the correct weight. If there is a remote possibility of being close to the maximum take-off weight, you **must** weigh the baggage. (Pocket-sized spring balances can be obtained from fishing/ hardware shops and are a handy stand-by if 'scales' are not available.) Note that, on some aircraft, if the maximum baggage allowance is used, restrictions are placed on rear seat occupancy. When carrying freight, check for any gross errors in the declared weight. There may also be a weight per unit area limitation on the baggage compartment floor. Make sure the baggage/ freight is properly stowed and secured so that it cannot move and does not obstruct exits or emergency equipment.

e. Beware of items such as flammable substances, acids, mercury, magnetic materials, etc. which are classified as Dangerous Goods with special controls that apply even in general aviation aircraft. Further assistance is available from Dangerous Goods Office, phone (01293) 573800 fax (01293) 573991.

f. Again, if the aircraft is anywhere near maximum weight, the passengers **must** be weighed or asked for their weight (even if it means embarrassing your spouse or friends). The risk of embarrassment is a better option than the effect of the aircraft being overweight. Remember, passengers' weight when flying is NOT their stripped weight. Allow for clothes, shoes, wallets and handbags! Check your own weight as equipped for flying and compare it with the weight you admit to.

g. Fuel gauges are often inaccurate and estimates of the weight of part filled fuel tanks should err on the high side for weight (but **NOT** endurance) purposes. Be careful of mixed units such as litres/lbs/kgs/Imp gallons/ US gallons.

h. If a long range or extra tank(s) have been fitted, the extra fuel could add a lot to the weight. Check that the contents marked at the filler cap(s) are the same as in the Pilot's Handbook/Flight Manual or Supplement and are **the ones you used for your calculations**.

i. See para 4(g) on weight restrictions of Normal and Utility category.

Note:

1 kg = 2.205 lb.	1 lb. = 0.454 kg
1 inch - 2.54 cm	1 cm = 0.394 inches
1 ft = 0.305 metre	1 m = 3.28 ft
1 Imp gall = 4.546 litres	1 litre = 0.22 Imp gall
1 US gall = 3.785 litres	1 litre = 0.264 USG
1 Imp gall = 1.205 US gall	1 USG = 0.83 Imp gall

4 BALANCE (CENTRE OF GRAVITY)

a. Balance refers to the location of the centre of gravity (cg) along the longitudinal axis of the aircraft. The cg is the point about which an aircraft would balance if it were possible to suspend it from that point. There are forward and aft limits established during certification flight testing; they are the extreme cg positions at which the longitudinal stability requirements can be met. Operation outside these limits means you would be flying in an area where the aircraft's handling has not been investigated, or is unsatisfactory. The limits for each aircraft are contained in the Pilot's Operating Handbook/Flight Manual, UK Supplement or Weight and cg Schedule referred to in 3(c). The aircraft **must not** be flown outside these limits.

b. The cg is measured from a datum reference, which varies from one aircraft type to another, check the Handbook/ Flight Manual. The arm is the horizontal distance (defined by the manufacturer) from the reference datum to the item of weight. The moment is the product of the weight of an item multiplied by its arm. Remember the see- saw, where a small weight at a large distance can be balanced by a large weight at a small distance.

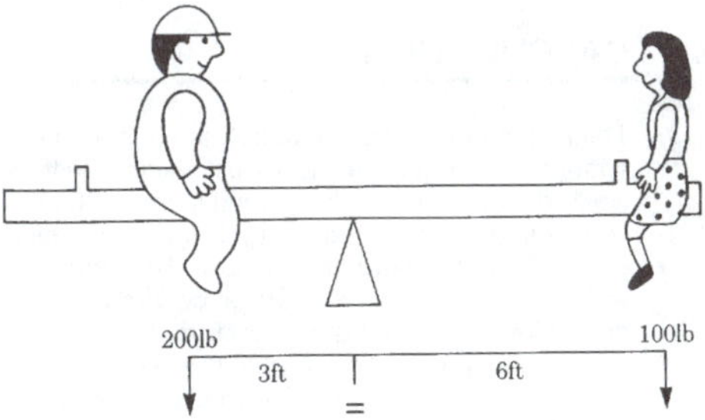

c. Exceeding the forward cg limit usually results in:

- difficulty in rotating to take-off attitude;
- increased stall or minimum flying speed against full up elevator;
- extra tail downforce requires more lift from wing resulting in greater induced drag. This means higher fuel consumption and reduced range;
- inadequate nose up trim in the landing configuration necessitating a pull force throughout the approach making it more difficult to fly a stable approach;
- difficulty in flaring and holding the nose wheel off after touch down. Many modern aircraft have deliberately restricted elevator travel (for stall behaviour reasons). Inability to hold the nose up during a bounce on landing can result in damaged nose landing gear and propeller;

- increased loads on the nose landing gear.

d. Exceeding the aft cg usually results in:

- pitch up at low speed and high power, leading to premature rotation on take-off or to inadvertent stall in the climb or during a go-around;
- on a tail wheel type, difficulty in raising the tail and in maintaining directional control on the ground;
- difficulty in trimming especially at high power;
- longitudinal instability, particularly in turbulence, with the possibility of a reversal of control forces;
- degraded stall qualities to an unknown degree;

- more difficult spin recovery, unexplored spin behaviour, delayed or even inability to recover.

e. Relatively small, but very heavy objects can make a big difference, e.g. a tool box or spare parts. Be careful where you stow them and make sure they cannot move.

f. On many aircraft the cg moves as fuel is used; on some aircraft types it could move the cg forward to beyond the forward limit when flying solo. On other types the cg moves rearward with fuel use, thus, on a loaded aircraft the cg could move to beyond the aft limit. Aft mounted long range tanks have a large effect. Careful cg calculation prior to flight will reveal any likely problems.

g. The following cg terms may be used (mainly on aircraft certificated to US regulations):

Normal category – normal flying, no spinning or aerobatic manoeuvres, bank angle may be restricted to 60°.

Utility category – manoeuvres in which bank angles exceed 60°, spinning (if permitted). No aerobatics.

h. There may be cg or weight restrictions on certain manoeuvres e.g. steep turns, spinning, aerobatics etc., imposed by the Pilot's Operating Handbook, Flight Manual or UK Supplement (e.g.: on the Socata Rallye, the rear seats must be removed to remain within the permitted cg range for spinning or aerobatics).

i. Very light (or heavy) pilots flying solo may need ballast or other measures, particularly in some homebuilt and tandem two seat aircraft.

j. Any ballast (permanent or temporary) **must** be securely fixed.

k. When parachute dropping remember the effect of the movement of parachutists prior to and immediately after dropping.

5 CALCULATION

The Pilot's Operating Handbook or Flight Manual contains a Weight and Balance section, with a worked example. The Limitations Section contains the permitted weight and cg limits. (Check to see if there are any CAA Supplements which further restrict weight or cg range.) The presentation varies from aircraft to aircraft and may be diagrammatic, graphical or tabular. You must be familiar with the method for **your** aircraft. Examples follow:

1	**SAMPLE LOADING CALCULATION**	**Weight (kg)**	**Moment* (kg.m)**
1	Empty weight (includes unusable fuel, full oil and other fluids) as well as extra equipment and navaids	662	663
2	Fuel 139 litres at 0.72 kg/litre (standard tanks)	100	120
3	Pilot and front passenger	150	140
4	Rear passenger	80	150
5	Baggage or child's seat (54 kg max)	40	100
	Total weight and moment	1032	1173

** The moments are obtained by applying the known weights to the loading graph in item 2.*

2

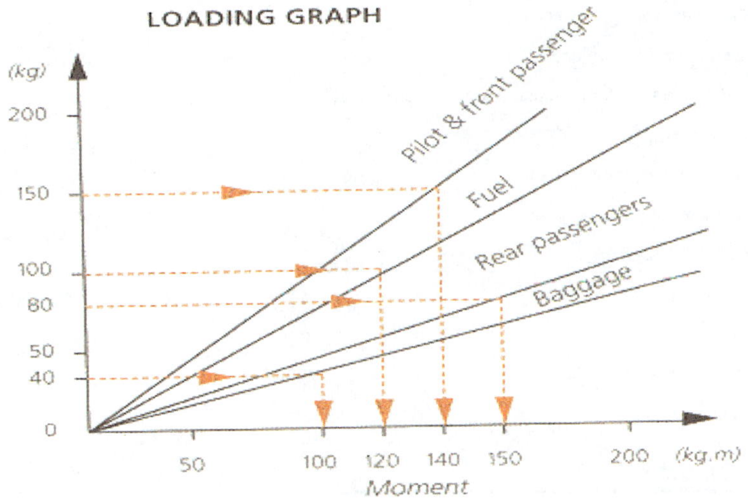

3

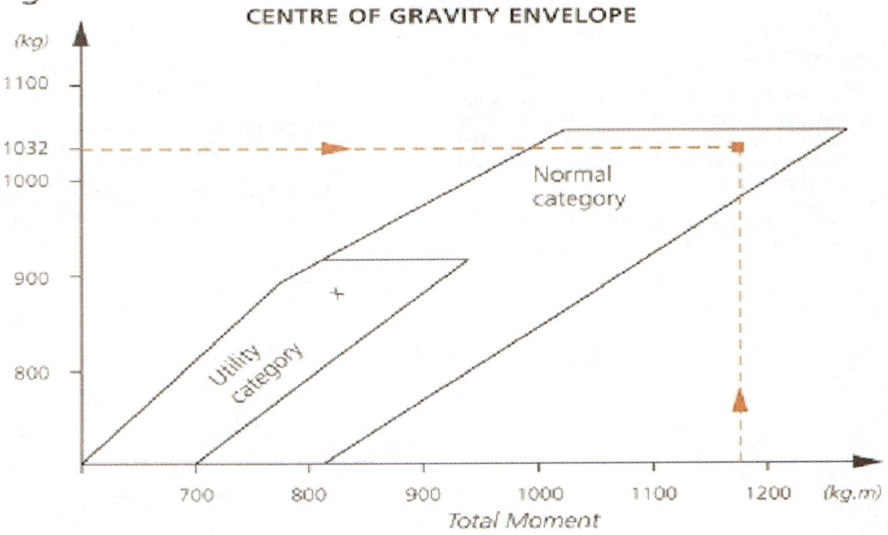

In this example it can be seen that the weight is below the maximum allowed and the cg is within limits

ORS — Safety Sense

4 WEIGHT LIMITATIONS		
Normal category		
Maximum weight for take-off		1043 kg
Maximum weight for landing		1043 kg
Maximum weight for baggage or optional child seat		54 kg
Utility category		
Maximum weight for take-off		907 kg
Maximum weight for landing		907 kg
FUEL CAPACITIES		
2 standard tanks of	81.5 litres	21.5 US gall
Total fuel	163 litres	43 US gall
Total useable fuel	152 litres	40 US gall
Unusable fuel	11 litres	3 US gall

6 SUMMARY

- Obtain **actual** (not 'typical') empty weight and cg of the **individual aircraft** you are operating from the latest Weight and Balance Schedule.
- Check that the aircraft maximum take-off weight is not exceeded. If it is, you **MUST** reduce the weight by off- loading passengers, baggage or fuel.
- Check that the cg is within limits before take-off and will remain within limits throughout the flight. If it does not stay within the approved range, you **MUST** make some changes to one or more of the following:
  - position of baggage or cargo
  - allocation of seats according to
  - passenger weight
  - fuel load and tank position
  - planned type of flight
- Before certain manoeuvres, e.g. spinning or aerobatics, check and if necessary act upon any weight or cg range restrictions.
- **DO NOT** forget the effect of weight changes on runway length requirements and safety factors given in Safety Sense Leaflet No 7 – Aeroplane Performance.
- **NEVER** consider flying an aircraft which is outside the permitted weight and cg range.

Note: Weight is used throughout this leaflet but European Regulations may refer to Mass.

SAFETY SENSE 10
GENERAL AVIATION

BIRD AVOIDANCE

1 INTRODUCTION

Many pilots do not realise that if they collide with a soft feathery bird, the effect of speed turns it into a missile capable of inflicting considerable damage. This has included smashed windshields (killing pilots), blocked engine air intakes, broken pitot heads, damaged brake hoses, holed structures and helicopter tail rotor damage. Out of about 100 incidents *reported* each year by UK general aviation pilots, about 5% result in damage. The advice given in this Leaflet may provide greater awareness of the problem, and perhaps further reduce the number of collisions as well as help pilots to minimise the consequences if a bird strike does occur.

2 PLANNING THE FLIGHT

a. Check aerodrome documentation and NOTAMS (issued by some countries as BIRDTAMS) for information about permanent or seasonal bird problems at both departure and destination aerodromes.

b. Plan to fly as high as possible, only 1% of general aviation bird strikes occur above 2500 ft (although a jet airliner struck a vulture at 37,000 ft off the W. African coast!)

c. Do not fly over bird and wildlife sanctuaries detailed in UK AIP ENR 5-6-1 or marked on aeronautical charts.

d. Avoid flying along rivers or shore lines, especially at low altitude. Birds as well as pilots use these useful navigational features.

e. Note also that inland waters and shallow estuaries, even outside the breeding season, may contain large numbers of gulls, waders and wildfowl which make regular flights around dawn and dusk. In order to minimise the possibility of bird strikes and unnecessary disturbance of birds, DO NOT fly low over such areas. Note: It is an offence to deliberately disturb nesting birds, pilots have been successfully prosecuted for doing so.

f. Avoid off- shore islands, headlands, cliffs, inland waters and shallow estuaries, so as not to disturb nesting colonies.

g. Helicopters cause more disturbance to bird colonies than fixed wing aeroplanes.

h. Bear in mind that birds **do** fly at night.

i. If there are two pilots, discuss emergency procedures before departure, including those if the cockpit communications are lost.

j. Up to 80–90 kts, birds usually have time to get out of your way, but the higher the speed, the greater the chance of a strike.

k. If your flying requires lengthy periods at low level, consider wearing head protection with polycarbonate visor. Pilots' lives have been saved by their helmets, particularly in helicopters. Use goggles and a head protection during air racing.

l. In July and August the risk of a strike is at its greatest because many inexperienced young birds are present. Also, the flying abilities of adults may be impaired as they moult their flight feathers.

m. Birds of Prey have been known to attack aircraft!

3 AT THE AERODROME AND IN FLIGHT

a. In springtime, **pre-flight** the aircraft thoroughly as birds can build a nest almost overnight. Any signs of grass etc. may necessitate further investigation of hard to inspect corners. A nest under the cowling could catch fire, or one in the tail area can restrict the flying controls.

b. As you taxi out, listen for any warnings of bird activity on the ATIS e.g. a mass release of racing pigeons.

c. While you are taxiing, look for birds on the aerodrome. Note that the most frequently struck birds, gulls, have a grey or black back which makes them hard to see on concrete or tarmac runways.

d. In general terms, the slower a bird's wing beat, the bigger the bird and the more hazardous it could be.

e. If birds are observed on the aerodrome, request aerodrome personnel to **disperse** them before you take- off. This is particularly important for turbo- prop and jet powered aircraft operating at aerodromes mainly used by smaller general aviation aircraft (the birds may have got used to slow aircraft).

f. **Never** use an aircraft to scare birds away.

g. Some aircraft have windshield heating, remember that its use, in accordance with the Pilots Operating Handbook or Flight Manual, will make the windshield more pliable and better able to withstand bird impact.

h. Use landing lights during take-off, climb, descent, approach and landing. Although there is no conclusive evidence that birds see and avoid aircraft lights, their use **will** make the aircraft more visible.

i. If you experience a bird strike during the take-off run, provided there is sufficient runway remaining – **stop**. Taxi off the runway and shut down. Inspect the intake, engine etc. for damage/ ingestion, or for bird remains blocking cooling or other airflow ducts. Several airline incidents have occurred where turbine engine damage or high vibration developed during subsequent flights because of undetected engine damage. Don't forget to check landing gear and brake hydraulic lines, downlocks, weight switches etc.

j. Where the take-off must be continued, with an engine problem, properly identify the affected engine and execute emergency procedures and tell the aerodrome why you are returning. It is essential to FLY THE AIRCRAFT.

k. If you see bird(s) ahead of you, **and it is safe to do so**, attempt to pass above them as birds usually break-away downwards when threatened. Be careful when near the ground, and **never** do anything that will lead to a **stall** or **spin**.

l. As you pass through a flock, or feel a strike, FLY THE AIRCRAFT. Maintain the correct speed and use whatever performance remains to reach a safe height.

m. If structural or control system damage is suspected (or the windshield is holed) consider the need for a controllability check before attempting a landing. During such a check at a safe height, do **not** slow down below threshold speed. Be wary of unseen helicopter tail rotor damage.

n. If the windshield is broken (or cracked), slow the aircraft to reduce wind blast, follow approved procedures (depressurise a pressurised aircraft), use sunglasses or smoke goggles to reduce the effect of wind, precipitation, or debris, but remember to **fly the aircraft** . Don't be distracted by the blood, feathers, smell and windblast. Small general aviation aeroplane and helicopter windshields are not required to be tested against bird impact and the propeller gives little protection. Gulls, pigeons, lapwings and even swifts can hole light aircraft windshields.

o. If dense bird concentrations are expected, avoid high-speed descent and approach.

Halving the speed results in a *quarter* of the impact energy.

p. If flocks of birds are visible on the approach, go-around early for a second attempt, the approach may then be clear.

4 AFTER FLIGHT

a. After landing, if you have had a bird strike, check the aircraft for damage.

b. Report **all** bird strikes on the Bird Strike Report Form Freepost CA 1282, available on the CAA web site at www.caa.co.uk/publications/search.asp via "general aviation" (A copy is at the back of this leaflet). Send to the address below. AIC 81/2002 (Pink 37) refers.

c. If you are unsure of the bird species send the remains (even feathers can be sufficient) for identification (marked "bird remains") to the:

Bird Strike Avoidance Team
Central Science Laboratory
Sand Hutton
York YO41 1LZ.

d. Photograph any damage, and send to the same address as the reporting form:

Civil Aviation Authority
Aerodrome Standards Dept
Freepost RCC1456
Crawley RH6 0YR
Fax: 01293 573971

5 SUMMARY

- Check NOTAMS/ATIS for bird activity at departure and destination aerodrome.
- Plan to fly as high as possible, most birds fly below 2500 ft. -
- Avoid bird sanctuaries and coastlines in spring. -
- Pre- flight the aircraft thoroughly, birds nests can be built (or rebuilt) in a few hours. -
- Many hazardous species are coloured such that they merge into the background. -
- If you see hazardous birds on or near run-ways, get aerodrome personnel to move them BEFORE you take off. -
- The higher the speed, the greater the risk and consequential damage.
- Birds usually escape by diving, so try to fly over them, but do NOT risk a stall or spin. -
- Most general aviation aircraft windshields etc. are NOT required to be able to withstand bird strikes. -
- If the windshield is broken, avoid distraction – FLY THE AIRCRAFT. -
- Report ALL bird strikes using the Reporting Form CA 1282. (Photos of damage are helpful.)

  If you are NOT CERTAIN of the bird species send remains to the Central Science Laboratory.

LOOK OUT FOR THESE BIRDS – they can be a hazard to aircraft

Weights of other birds frequently encountered:

Heron	1.5 kg	Swift	40 gm
Buzzard	800 gm	Skylark	40 gm
Kestrel	200 gm	Swallow	20 gm
Partridge	400 gm	Martin	17 gm
Pheasant	1.1 kg	Sparrow	20 gm

CIVIL AVIATION AUTHORITY

BIRDSTRIKE OCCURRENCE FORM - CA 1282 (Amended 02/2003)

Civil Aviation Authority

To be completed on discovering evidence that a birdstrike has, or may have, occurred.
To be completed for all birdstrikes, whether or not damage has been caused.
Copies of this form should be sent as indicated at Note 1 below.

Aircraft Operator...

Aircraft type & series...

Aircraft reg. ....

Date (dd/mm/yy) ..../.........../...........

Time (local) ....: ....Hrs (24 hr)

Dawn ☐ Day ☐ Dusk ☐ Night ☐

Aerodrome ....

Runway in use ....

Height (agl) .... ft

Speed (IAS) ....kts

Position (if en route) ....

Phase of Flight

Taxi	☐	Descent	☐
Take-off run	☐	Approach	☐
Climb	☐	Landing roll	☐
En Route	☐	Ground checks	☐

Part(s) of Aircraft	Struck	damaged* (describe)
Radome	☐	☐
Windshield	☐	☐
Nose (if not one of the above)	☐	☐
Engine nos: 1	☐	☐
2	☐	☐
3	☐	☐
4	☐	☐
Propeller	☐	☐
Wing/rotor (inc high lift devices)	☐	☐
Fuselage	☐	☐
Landing Gear	☐	☐
Tail	☐	☐
Lights	☐	☐
Other (specify*)	☐	☐

Effect on flight

None	☐	Returned	☐
Aborted t/off	☐	Diverted	☐
Other	☐		

Other Reports raised

Mandatory Occurrence Report (MOR) ☐
Air Safety Report (ASR) ☐
Other* (specify) ☐

Send to:
Civil Aviation Authority
Aerodrome Standards Dept
FREEPOST RCC1456
Crawley RH6 0YR

Fax No 01293 573971
Web site: www.caa.co.uk

Precipitation:

None ☐ Fog ☐ Rain ☐ Sleet/Snow ☐

Bird Species/description (e.g. Herring gull, Woodpigeon)

....

If you are not *certain* of the bird species, please send a *copy* of this form and *any* remains (e.g. a wing, but even the smallest of remains are useful) to: -

BIRDSTRIKE AVOIDANCE TEAM, CENTRAL SCIENCE LABORATORY, SAND HUTTON, YORK YO41 1LZ, UK.

Please mark the container **"Bird remains"**
This identification service is provided free to UK aerodromes and aircraft operators.

Bird remains sent for identification Yes ☐ No ☐

Number of birds

	seen	struck* *(enter actual number if known)*
1	☐	☐
2-10	☐	☐
11-100	☐	☐
100+	☐	☐

Pilot warned of birds Yes ☐ No ☐

Note 1: Copies of this form should be submitted as soon as practicable to the recipients shown below. (It is not necessary to wait for confirmation of bird species.)

Aerodrome ☐
Aircraft Operator ☐
Civil Aviation Authority (address overleaf) ☐
Bird Strike Avoidance Team ☐ (if identification required)

Remarks and other relevant information*:

Reporter Details

Name..

Employer ....

Tel no .... Date ....

SAFETY SENSE 11
GENERAL AVIATION

INTERCEPTION OF CIVIL AIRCRAFT

1 INTRODUCTION

a. In order to comply with ICAO standards, the Air Navigation Order includes an item in Schedule 11 – 'Documents to be carried by aircraft registered in the UK'. This requires that on **INTERNATIONAL** flights **ALL** aircraft must carry a copy of 'Signals for Use in the Event of Interception'. These are detailed in the UK AIP ENR 1– 12. This leaflet is intended to expand on the AIP and may be carried by pilots whose international flights require details of the Signals and Procedures.

b. Under Article 9 of the Convention on International Civil Aviation, each contracting state reserves the right, for reasons of military necessity or public safety, to restrict or prohibit the aircraft from other states from flying over certain areas of its territory.

c. The regulations of a state may prescribe the need to investigate the identity of aircraft. Accordingly, it may be necessary to lead an aircraft of another nation, which has been intercepted, away from a particular area (such as a prohibited area) or the aircraft may for security reasons be required to land at a particular aerodrome.

d. In order to reduce the possibility of interception, pilots should adhere to flight plans and ATC procedures, as well as maintaining a listening watch on the appropriate ATC frequency. If details of your flight are in doubt, all possible efforts will be made to identify it through the appropriate Air Traffic Services Units.

e. As interception of civil aircraft can be potentially hazardous, interception procedures will only be used as a last resort. If you are fired upon, there is little advice that can be offered!

f. The word 'interception' does **not** include the intercept and escort service provided on request to an aircraft in distress in accordance with Search and Rescue procedures.

g. Remember, the intercepting aircraft may not be able to fly as slowly as a low speed general aviation aircraft.

2 PROCEDURES

If you are intercepted by another aircraft you must immediately:

a. follow the instruction given by the intercepting aircraft, interpreting and responding to visual signals in accordance with paragraph 3,

b. notify, if possible, the appropriate Air Traffic Services Unit,

c. attempt to establish radio communication with the intercepting aircraft or with the appropriate intercept control unit, by making a general call on the emergency frequency 121.50 MHz, giving your identity and the nature of the flight. If no contact has been established and if UHF is fitted, repeat the call on the emergency frequency 243 MHz,

d. select mode A, code 7700 and Mode C if equipped with a transponder, unless otherwise instructed by the appropriate Air Traffic Services Unit.

3 INTERCEPTING AIRCRAFT SIGNALS AND YOUR RESPONSES

a. **'You have been intercepted, follow me'**
Day - the intercepting aircraft rocks its wings from a position slightly above and ahead of, and normally to the left of your aircraft and, after acknowledgement, makes a slow level turn, normally to the left, onto the desired heading.

Night - same, also flashes navigation lights at irregular intervals

Note 1: Meteorological conditions or terrain may require the intercepting aircraft to take up a position slightly above and ahead of, and to the right of your aircraft and to make the subsequent turn to the right.

Note 2: If your aircraft can't keep pace with the intercepting aircraft, he is expected to fly a series of racetrack patterns and to rock his wings each time he passes your aircraft.

Your response to show you have understood and will comply:

Aeroplanes:

Day - rock your wings and follow him.

Night - same and in addition flash navigation lights at irregular intervals.

Helicopters:

Day or Night - rock your helicopter, flash navigation (or landing lights) at irregular intervals and follow.

Note: You must also try to communicate as in Para 5 overleaf.

b. **'You may proceed'**

Intercepting aircraft signals by day or night with an abrupt break away manoeuvre away from your aircraft consisting of a climbing turn of 90° or more without crossing the line of flight of your aircraft.

Your response to show you have understood and will comply:

Aeroplanes:

Day or Night - rock your wings.

Helicopters:

Day or Night - rock your helicopter.

c. **'Land at this aerodrome'**

Day -the intercepting aircraft signals by circling the aerodrome, lowering his landing gear and over flying runway in direction of landing, or if your aircraft is a helicopter he signals by over flying the helicopter landing area.

Night - same and, in addition, shows steady landing lights.

Your response to show you have understood and will comply:

Aeroplanes:

Day - lower landing gear (if possible), following the intercepting aircraft and, if after over flying the runway you consider landing is safe, proceed to land.

Night - same and, in addition, show steady landing lights (if fitted).

Helicopters:

Day or Night - following the intercepting aircraft and proceeding to land showing a steady landing light (if fitted).

4 SIGNALS INITIATED BY YOUR AIRCRAFT AND RESPONSES

a. **'Aerodrome designated is inadequate for my aeroplane'**

Day - raise landing gear (if possible), while passing over landing runway at a height exceeding 300 m (1000 ft) but not exceeding 600 m (2000 ft) above the aerodrome level, and continue to circle the aerodrome.

Night - in addition, flash landing lights while passing over landing runway as above. If unable to flash landing lights, flash any other available lights.

The intercepting aircraft responds to show he has understood.

- If it is desired that you follow him to an alternate aerodrome, he will raise his landing gear and use the signals prescribed for intercepting aircraft in paragraph 3a. However, if he has understood and decides you may proceed, he will use the manoeuvre prescribed in paragraph 3b.

b. **'I cannot comply'**

Day or Night - switch all available lights on and off at regular intervals but in such a manner as to be distinct from flashing lights.

The intercepting aircraft responds to show he has understood by using the manoeuvre at paragraph 3b.

c. **'I am in distress'**

Day or Night - flash all available lights at irregular intervals.

The intercepting aircraft responds to show he has understood by using the manoeuvre described in paragraph 3b.

5 COMMUNICATION

a. If radio contact with the intercepting aircraft is established, but communication in a common language is not possible, you should attempt to convey essential information and acknowledgement of instructions by using the following phrases and pronunciations (ICAO Annex 2, Appendix 2 and Attachment A refer):

Phrase	Pronunciation	Meaning
CALL SIGN	**KOL** SA- IN	My call sign is (call sign)
WILCO	**VILL**- CO	Understood Will comply
CAN NOT	**KANN** NOTT	Unable to comply
REPEAT	REE- **PEET**	Repeat your instruction
AM LOST	**AM LOSST**	Position unknown
MAYDAY	**MAYDAY**	I am in distress
HIJACK	**HI-JACK**	I have been hi-jacked
LAND	**LAAND**	I request to land at
(place name)	(place name)	(place name)
DESCEND	DEE- **SEND**	I require descent

b. The following phrases should to be used by the intercepting aircraft in the circumstances prescribed above:

Phrase	Pronunciation	Meaning
CALL SIGN	**KOL** SA- IN	What is your call sign?
FOLLOW	**FOL**- LO	Follow me
DESCEND	DEE- **SEND**	Descend for landing
YOU LAND	**YOU LAAND**	Land at this aerodrome
PROCEED	PRO- **SEED**	You may proceed

c. If any instructions received by radio from other sources conflict with those given by the intercepting aircraft's visual signals or radio instructions, you must request immediate clarification while continuing to comply with the visual instructions.

d. Beware of making hand gestures, these could be misinterpreted!

6 AFTER FLIGHT

As interceptions are very rare, others may learn from your experience. Please tell the CAA's Safety Investigation and Data Department.

SAFETY SENSE 12
GENERAL AVIATION

STRIP SENSE

1 INTRODUCTION

a. Unlicensed aerodromes and private strips are often used by pilots and private owners. They may be more convenient or cheaper than licensed aerodromes; however they do require special consideration. Approximately one third of GA Reportable Accidents in the UK occur during take off or landing at unlicensed aerodromes. The proportion of flying activity is not known.

b. This Leaflet is intended to start you thinking about the differences and particular needs of such flying, and also to give some guidelines about operating from, or establishing, your own strip. It should be read in conjunction with the relevant parts of Safety Sense leaflet 6, Aerodrome Sense

2 ASSESSING THE STRIP

a. It is important to realise that the CAA criteria for the licensing of an aerodrome, e. g. clear approaches without power or other cables, no trees or obstructions close to the runway and so on, are unlikely to have been applied to the strip. Since in almost all cases **Prior Permission is Required (PPR) before landing**, your phone call should also include discussion of any difficulties, obstructions, noise sensitive areas to be avoided and the useable length of the strip.

b. Find out the arrangements for grass cutting. It is no use landing only to find the grass is so long that it prevents you taking off again. As a rule of thumb, the grass length should not be more than 30% of the diameter of the wheel.

c. Use an Ordnance Survey map to find out accurately the elevation above mean sea level of the strip –modern maps are in metres.

d. The orientation of the strip may have been laid out to fit in with the needs of agriculture. Establish the direction of the prevailing winds in the area and note the location of any windsock. Will it be affected by nearby trees or buildings? A well located windsock will give you the ground level wind speed and direction. Beware of strips near the coast; sea breezes can change rapidly from onshore to offshore, morning and evening.

e. Tell the operator of the strip what experience you have, which strips you have used recently, and what aeroplane you intend using. He has probably seen pilots with similar aeroplanes flying into and out of the strip and you can benefit from local knowledge. He does not want an accident any more than you do! Exchange telephone numbers in case of a last minute hitch. If possible visit it by road to see for yourself, but best of all carry out the advice of paras 5a, 5b and 5c.

f. The length of the strip ***must*** be accurately established. If you pace it out, remember an average pace is ***not*** one metre, but considerably less (the British army's marching pace is only 30 inches). This may decrease still further after walking several hundred metres. A proper measuring device is better; for example a rope of accurately known length.

g. The strip should be adequately drained or self-draining. Visit it after heavy rain to see whether it remains waterlogged or muddy.

Rain after long dry periods may not soak away and can remain hidden by the grass.

h. The surface should be free from ruts and holes and should be properly and regularly rolled. One way of assessing the surface is to drive a car along the strip. If at about 30 mph the ride is comfortable, there should be no problems.

i. If it is a disused wartime airfield, some of the runway may be unusable, while other parts may have a surface in poor condition – including loose gravel and stones. These can be picked up by the propeller wash and can damage windscreens, tail and, of course, the propeller itself. Stone damage can be very expensive.

j. Carefully examine from the ground, air or maps the approaches to the strip and the go-around area, with particular reference to any runway slope, obstructions or hills within 5 km, windshear or turbulence from nearby woods/ buildings and other considerations.

k. Look closely at neighbouring properties; a climb out above the breeding pens or stud farm next door will soon bring an end to everyone's operation.

3 OPERATIONAL CONSIDERATIONS

a. Aeroplane performance **must** be appropriate for the proposed strip. You must be fully familiar with the contents of Safety Sense Leaflet No. 7 (Aeroplane Performance) or AIC 67/2002 (Pink 36) 'Take off, Climb and Landing Performance of Light Aeroplanes'. Remember, the figures shown in the Pilots Operating Handbook are obtained using a **new** aeroplane, flown by an expert pilot under near ideal conditions, i.e. the best possible results. On the strip, the grass may be different from the 'short, dry, mown grass' of the Handbook. There may be a slight uphill gradient, tall trees or cables at the far end, or a cross wind. Short wet grass should be treated with utmost caution, it can increase landing distances by 60% – it's like an icy surface! Take account of all of these most carefully and then add an additional margin for safety before deciding. (Safety Sense Leaflet No. 7, Aeroplane Performance, recommends a 33% safety factor for take-off but 43% for landing.)

b. Your own abilities as a pilot need critical and honest assessment. The ability to land smoothly on a long hard runway is very different from the skills needed for this type of operation.

c. Most importantly the combination of ***YOU and YOUR*** aeroplane must be satisfactory. A weakness in either of these could show up in the accident statistics

d. The CAA poster 'AIRSTRIPS, think Hedgerow NOT Heathrow' reminds pilots of the operational considerations, and is available for free download from the CAA web site www.caa.co.uk through "safety", "general aviation" and "information".

e. Some strips are located on hills where, up to a certain wind speed, take offs are downhill and landings uphill. Re- read the above paragraphs, for although such strips are not necessarily dangerous, they should not be attempted unless you are totally confident about paragraphs a, b and c.

f. You must check that the insurance covers operation from an unlicensed aerodrome or a strip. It is important that you give Insurers fullest possible written details before the visit.

g. Find out about the local arrangements for booking in and booking out; usually a Movements Log is provided.

h. Ensure that passengers and spectators are properly briefed about where they may go, where they may stand and what they may or may not touch.

i. Leave details of route, ETA and passengers in the Movements Log **AND** with someone who will react appropriately and alert the Emergency Services if you fail to arrive/ return.

j. If you are planning to go abroad direct from the strip, then nominating a 'responsible person' is even more important. Remember customs and immigration requirements, and those of the Terrorism Act if going to or from Northern Ireland, the Isle of Man, or the Channel Islands. Consult the UK AIP GEN 1.2.1 and Safety Sense Leaflet No. 20, 'VFR Flight Plans'.

4 OVERNIGHT CONSIDERATIONS

a. If you intend to leave the aircraft overnight at a strip, it may be necessary for you to arrange your own tie- downs and wheel chocks. Ensure that control locks are in place and the aircraft is properly secured. If the wind is likely to increase, then position your aircraft so as to minimise the possibility of it moving and be prepared to reposition it if the wind direction changes. Covers should be used to keep insects and water out of the pitot tube and static vents.

b. Next morning your pre- flight inspection should be more careful than usual just in case birds or other wildlife have taken up residence; birds can build a nest overnight. Check the pitot head, static and tank vents for insects.

c. If the strip is shared with cows, horses or sheep, then an electric or other suitable fence to separate them from your aeroplane is essential. Cows are very partial to the taste of aeroplane dope and their rough tongues have been known to strip fabric from wings. Metal aeroplanes do not escape their attentions, since they make suitable back-scratchers.

d. Discuss with the strip operator the security of the aeroplane. Vandalism and fuel thefts may be a problem.

5 FLYING CONSIDERATIONS

a. Consider having a familiarisation flight to and from the strip with a pilot who knows the strip and is both current on your aeroplane and operations into grass strips.

b. In any case you must know and fly the correct speeds for your aeroplane and remember the importance of using appropriate techniques, keeping the weight off the nosewheel etc.

c. If the strip is shorter than you are used to or has difficult approaches, you should arrange for a flying instructor to appraise your flying skills and revise and improve short field, soft field, general circuit and airmanship skills. It is not the intention of this leaflet to list the skills – that is the instructor's task. Listen and learn. If an instructor is not available, at least practice your short landings on a long runway before attempting to land at a short strip.

d. Airmanship and look- out must be of the highest order; there is unlikely to be any form of ATC service to advise you of the presence of other aircraft, their position or intentions, so be especially vigilant. Low flying military aircraft may NOT avoid strips.

e. Circuit **practice** at unlicensed aerodromes could be unpopular with the neighbours and may be in breach of part of Rule 5 of the Rules of the Air if you are within 500 ft of persons, vessels, vehicles or structures. However, if you find a problem with turbulence or crosswind, surface or slope, do not hesitate to **go around in accordance with normal aviation practice**.

f. Plan your circuit using the best available QNH, for example from a nearby aerodrome. Failing that you could use the most recent 'regional pressure setting (RPS)' but be aware your altimeter will certainly over-read if you use RPS. You should already know the elevation of the strip, so add this figure to the appropriate height that you would use in a normal circuit. Thus, if the strip is 250 ft amsl, downwind will be e.g. 1250 ft QNH.

g. Get into the habit of flying a compact circuit using engine and propeller handling techniques that will minimise noise disturbance. Avoid long flat and noisy approaches, these are not conducive to good neighbourliness nor necessarily the best short landing technique. If your approach is bad, **make an early decision** to go-around. It is often useful to plan to make a go-around from your first approach (avoiding persons, vessels vehicles and structures by 500 feet).

h. Note carefully the position and height of any obstructions on the approach especially hard-to- see local power and phone cables. Make sure that you can clear them (and any crop) by an adequate margin, and provided that you maintain this clearance, always aim to touch down close to the threshold – **not halfway down the strip.**

i. Always start your take off run as close as possible to the beginning of the strip, unless there are very good reasons not to do so. Work out an acceleration check point from which you can stop if you haven't reached sufficient speed to make a safe take-off

j. Bear in mind when turning off the strip, Rule 17(7) of the Rules of the Air and other arriving aircraft.

k. When performing power checks or engine runs try to minimise any noise nuisance and ensure that the slipstream is not creating a problem. Unexpected noise etc. can terrify livestock; be considerate when choosing the site for engine checks.

l. After take off, reduce power and propeller rpm when it is safe. Climb to at least 500 ft agl before turning.

m. If you are a regular strip user, decide your weather and wind limits and be clear about your Go/ No Go decision process.

6 SETTING UP YOUR OWN STRIP

a. If you are planning to move your aeroplane to a strip, or perhaps start your own, the points below should be considered, in addition to any others in CAP 428 'Safety Standards at Unlicensed Aerodromes'.

b. Remember that Rule 5 of the Rules of the Air includes, amongst other requirements, the prohibition of flights below 1000 feet over 'congested' areas except when aircraft are taking off or landing at a licensed or government aerodrome. It is therefore most important that climb out, approach and circuit paths at an unlicensed aerodrome are clear of 'congested' areas. Such areas are legally defined as 'in relation to a city, town, or settlement, any area which is substantially used for residential, industrial, commercial or recreational purposes'.

c. Talk to nearby aerodrome operators to ensure that you will not conflict with their activities.

d. Look again at the performance of the aeroplane and your abilities. If operating from this strip means that **every** take off and landing, even when the aeroplane is lightly loaded, is 'tight', change to a more suitable aeroplane or strip.

e. Remember that, unless there is 'established use', aircraft operations may be in contravention of local regulations. It may of course be possible to obtain planning permission from the outset for your strip, although this would probably involve you in a great deal of hassle. However, this is much better than having it compulsorily closed by the local council if they decide that your operations are in contravention of Planning Regulations. It is in your interests to establish this from the outset and it is furthermore a good idea to talk to all of the neighbours and the planning authority ***before*** you do anything.

f. Cutting the grass and generally maintaining the surface has been discussed earlier; however, if you are responsible for the upkeep of the strip it is important to establish who will cut the grass, roll it and how often. This needs to be a regular activity – we all know only too well how much our lawns grow in a week.

g. Beware when mowing. Instances have occurred of pilots following the mown lines instead of the strip direction.

h. Grass seed mixtures which will give reduced rolling resistance and slower growth are available. Consult a seed merchant.

i. In deciding the orientation of the strip/landing run, consider carefully the local wind effects. It may be possible to re- orientate the strip by some 10 or 20 degrees which could reduce the cross wind effect. This is particularly important for some tailwheel types where the maximum crosswind component that can be tolerated may be as little as 10 knots.

j. Remember that whilst taking off down a slope or landing up a slope is acceptable, taking off and landing across the slope is dangerous. Ensure that the orientation of the strip eliminates excessive lateral slope.

k. It is essential to mark any obstacles, potholes or bad ground at this stage and runway markers or even runway numbers will help people to line up and operate more accurately. It is also possible to have local power lines and telephone lines moved by paying the costs.

l. You must decide in advance on your fuel arrangements. If you are intending to store fuel, then you must comply with Article 101 of the Air Navigation Order and CAP 434 'Aviation Fuel at Aerodromes'. It may be possible to obtain relatively small quantities of aviation fuel by sharing the delivery with a nearby aerodrome or strip. It is normally necessary to obtain local council permission to store fuel.

m. Decide on your maintenance arrangements, your engineer may require coaxing/ persuasion to visit your strip at short notice to rectify a defect.

n. If you own or fly a wood or fabric covered aeroplane it should be hangared – ideally all aircraft should be. However, storing it in a farm barn brings its own particular problems – rodents. Mice are nimble creatures, able to climb landing gear legs and set up home in your aeroplane. We heard of a squirrel that got into the wing structure and stored its winter supply of acorns near the wing tip. Over 30 lbs of acorns were removed! A tray of rat poison encircling each wheel should be considered.

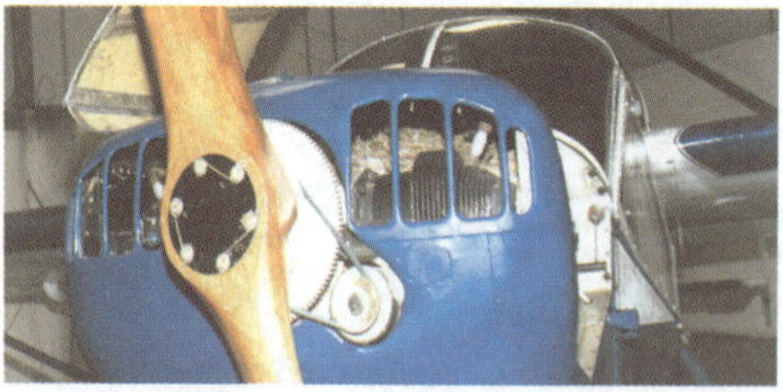

Birds also find aircraft irresistible nesting sites; a nest removed in the morning may be substantially rebuilt by late afternoon. Pre-flight checking the aeroplane becomes very important. Insects may take over your aircraft. Given a few days undisturbed progress, a wasps' nest could appear.

o. It is vital to remove all live- stock from the runway prior to take off and prior to landing. Thus, if animals have access to the strip, assistance by a friend or farmhand is essential. Animals are unpredictable.

p. Cows leave other evidence of their presence – cow pats! Not only does this look unsightly on the aeroplane, but a build up of this, and mud, add to the drag and weight of the aeroplane. Mud and animal contaminants may also be corrosive, so regular washing of the aeroplane, especially the underside, becomes a necessity. Check regularly that spats are clear of mud and grass. Temporary removal of the spats must be agreed with a CAA Regional Office.

q. The farmer and/ or his workers may need gentle reminders about the fragile nature of your aeroplane compared with farm machinery, should they need to move it. They may not know about the dangers of propellers/ helicopter rotors.

r. Consider sitting a small hut or caravan on the strip. This will give secure storage for oil, fire extinguishers, fire axe, polish, foot pump and so on. It is suggested that this should have a large letter C painted on it to make it clear that it is a reporting point for pilots and where the Movements Log is kept. A notice board inside is useful to display information such as local instructions, NOTAMs, the engineer's telephone number, accident procedures and any temporary obstructions, soft ground and grass cutting rotas. Make sure there is enough room to park visiting aircraft well clear of the landing area.

s. Get into the habit of checking the strip each day before starting flying. Any ruts, soft ground or other problems should be dealt with or publicised on the notice board so that they can be avoided on take off and landing.

7 MAIN POINTS

DO obtain permission from the owner/operator prior to visiting the strip. Talk to pilots who have used the strip before and can advise you on procedures/obstructions.

DO check that the combination of you **and** your aeroplane **can** safely cope with this strip.

DO always leave details of ETA route, destination and how many are on board in the Movements Log.

DO always nominate a 'responsible person' as described in Safety Sense Leaflet 20 'VFR Flight Plans', who knows how to raise the alarm if you fail to arrive/return.

DO follow the requirements for customs, immigration and the Terrorism Act if flying to or from overseas.

DO talk to neighbouring aerodromes or to the Flight Information Service on the radio.

DO build up a working relationship with your nearest aerodrome. You may need them for fuel, weather information and maintenance.

DO be ready for unexpected effects from trees, barns, windshear, downdraught, etc.

DO work hard at being a good neighbour and improving the Public's perception of General Aviation by minimising noise nuisance.

DO check that the strip **really** is long enough, with a 30% margin for safety.

DO check on the effect of power and other cables.

DO check whether any slope makes it a 'one way' strip.

DO obtain and display a copy of the CAA's AIRSTRIPS poster.

DO NOT 'beat up' the strip or engage in other forms of reckless, illegal and unsociable flying.

DO NOT attempt to take off or land if the grass is long, the ground is muddy or weather is marginal. There will always be a better day to fly or you can always divert into a neighbouring aerodrome.

DO NOT run- up an engine where the noise affects others or slipstream can be a nuisance.

DO NOT attempt to 'scrape' in from a bad approach.

FINALLY, ensure that safety is the first consideration. A safe flight will almost always be an enjoyable and rewarding one.

SAFETY SENSE 13
GENERAL AVIATION

COLLISION AVOIDANCE

1 INTRODUCTION

a. 'See-and-avoid' is recognised as the main method that a pilot uses to minimise the risk of collision when flying in visual meteorological conditions. 'See- and- avoid' is directly linked with a pilot's skill at looking outside the cockpit or flight deck and becoming aware of what is happening in his/ her surrounding. Its effectiveness can be greatly improved if the pilot can acquire skills to compensate for the limitations of the human eye. These skills include the application of:

- effective visual scanning
- the ability to listen selectively to radio transmissions from ground stations and other aircraft,
- creating a mental picture of the traffic situation, and
- the development of 'good airmanship'.

b. This Leaflet, based on ICAO Circular 213–AN/ 130, aims to help pilots to make 'look-out' more effective and is mainly for pilots who do most of their flying under visual flight rules (VFR). It should be of interest to all pilots, however, regardless of the type of aircraft they fly and the flight rules under which they operate since no pilot is immune to collisions.

c. A study of over two hundred reports of mid-air collisions in the US and Canada showed that they can occur in all phases of flight and at all altitudes. However, nearly all mid-air collisions occur in daylight and in excellent visual meteorological conditions, mostly at lower altitudes where most VFR flying is carried out. Collisions also can and do occur at higher altitudes. Because of the concentration of aircraft close to aerodromes, most collisions occurred near aerodromes when one or both aircraft were descending or climbing. Although some aircraft were operating as instrument flight rules (IFR) flights, most were VFR.

d. The pilots involved in the collisions ranged in experience from first solo to 15,000 hours, and the types of flight were equally varied. In one case a private pilot flying cross-country, legally VFR, in a single-engine aircraft collided with a turboprop aircraft under IFR control flown by two experienced airline pilots. In another case, a 7000 hour commercial pilot on private business in a twin-engine aircraft overtook a single-engine aircraft on its final approach piloted by a young instructor giving dual instruction to a student pilot. Two commercial pilots, each with well over 1000 hours, collided while ferrying a pair of new single-engine aircraft.

e. Experienced or inexperienced pilots can be involved in a mid-air collision. While a novice pilot has much to think about and so may forget to maintain an adequate look- out, the experienced pilot, having flown many hours of routine flight without spotting any hazardous traffic, may grow complacent and forget to scan.

f. There appears to be little difference in mid-air collision risk between high-wing and low-wing aircraft.

g. If you learn to use your eyes and maintain vigilance, you can reduce the risk of mid-air collisions. Studies show that there are certain definite warning patterns.

2 CAUSES OF MID-AIR COLLISIONS

a. What contributes to mid-air collisions? Undoubtedly, traffic congestion and aircraft speeds are part of the problem. In the head-on situation, for instance, a jet and a light twin-engine aircraft may have a closing speed of about 650 kt. It takes a minimum of 10 seconds for a pilot to spot traffic, identify it, realise it is a collision risk, react, and have the aircraft respond. But two aircraft converging at 650 kt could be less than 10 seconds apart when the pilots are first **able** to see each other! Furthermore, the field of view from the flight deck of a large aircraft can be more restricted than that from the cockpit of a small aircraft.

b. In addition, some air traffic control and radar facilities are overloaded or limited by terrain or weather. Thus they may not be able to offer the service you require.

c. These factors are all contributory causes, but the reason most often noted in the mid- air collision statistics reads 'failure of pilot to see other aircraft in time' — i.e., failure of the see-and-avoid system. In most cases at least one of the pilots involved could have seen the other aircraft in time to avoid the collision if that pilot had been watching properly. Therefore, it could be said that it is really the eye which is the leading contributor to mid-air collisions. Take a look at how its limitations affect you.

3 LIMITATIONS OF THE EYE

a. The human eye is a very complex system. Its function is to receive images and transmit them to the brain for recognition and storage. About 80 per cent of our total information intake is through the eyes, thus the eye is our prime means of identifying what is going on around us.

b. In the air we depend on our eyes to provide most of the basic input necessary for flying the aircraft, e.g. attitude, speed, direction and proximity to opposing traffic. As air traffic density and aircraft closing speeds increase, the problem of mid- air collision increases considerably, and so does the importance of effective scanning. A basic understanding of the eyes' limitations in target detection is one of the best insurances a pilot can have against collision.

c. The eye, and consequently vision, is vulnerable to many things including dust, fatigue, emotion, germs, fallen eyelashes, age, optical illusions, and the effect of alcohol and certain medications. In flight, vision is influenced by atmospheric conditions, glare, lighting, windshield deterioration and distortion, aircraft design, cabin temperature, oxygen supply (particularly at night), acceleration forces and so forth. If you need glasses to correct your vision, make sure that you have regular checks that the prescription is still correct and that you carry any required second pair.

d. Most importantly, the eye is vulnerable to the vagaries of the mind. We can 'see' and identify only what the mind permits us to see. A daydreaming pilot staring out into space is probably the prime candidate for a mid-air collision.

e. One inherent problem with the eye is the time required for accommodation or refocusing. Our eyes automatically accommodate for near and far objects, but the change from something up close, like a dark instrument panel two feet away, to a bright landmark or aircraft a mile or so away, takes one to two seconds. That can be a long time when you consider that you need 10 seconds to avoid a mid-air collision.

f. Another focusing problem usually occurs when there is nothing to specifically focus on, which happens at very high altitudes, as well as at lower levels on vague, colourless days above a haze or cloud layer with no distinct horizon. People experience something known as 'empty-field myopia', i.e. staring but seeing nothing, not even opposing traffic entering their visual field.

g. To accept what we see, we need to receive cues from **both eyes** (binocular vision). If an object is visible to only one eye, but hidden from the other by a windshield post or other obstruction, the total image is blurred and not always acceptable to the mind. Therefore, it is essential that pilots move their heads when scanning around obstructions.

h. Another inherent eye problem is the narrow field of vision. Although our eyes accept light rays from an arc of nearly 200°, they are limited to a relatively narrow area (approximately 10–15°) in which they can actually focus on and classify an object. Although movement on the periphery can be perceived, we cannot identify what is happening there, and we tend not to believe what we see out of the corner of our eyes. This, aided by the brain, often leads to 'tunnel vision'.

i. Motion or contrast is needed to attract the eyes' attention, and tunnel vision limitation can be compounded by the fact that at a distance **an aircraft on a collision course will appear to be motionless**. The aircraft will remain in a seemingly stationary position, without appearing to move or to grow in size, for a relatively long time, and then **suddenly** bloom into a huge mass, almost filling up one of the windows. This is known as the 'blossom effect'. It is frightening that a large insect smear or dirty spot on the windshield can hide a converging aircraft until it is too close to be avoided.

j. In addition to its inherent problems, the eye is also severely limited by environment. Optical properties of the atmosphere alter the appearance of aircraft, particularly on hazy days. 'Limited visibility' actually means 'reduced vision'. You may be legally VFR when you have 5 km visibility, but at that distance on a hazy day you may have difficulty in detecting opposing traffic; at that range, even though another aircraft may be visible, a collision may be **unavoidable** because of the high closing speeds involved.

k. Light also affects our visual efficiency. Glare, usually worse on a sunny day over a cloud layer or during flight directly into the sun, makes objects hard to see and scanning uncomfortable. An aircraft that has a high degree of contrast against the background will be easy to see, while one with low contrast at the same distance may be impossible to see. In addition, when the sun is behind you, an opposing aircraft will stand out clearly, but if you are looking into the sun, the glare of the sun will usually prevent you from seeing the other aircraft. A dirty, scratched, opaque or distorted windshield will make matters worse. Keep it clean, and if it has deteriorated, consider fitting a new windshield or using a proprietary re-furbishing kit.

l. Another problem with contrast occurs when trying to sight an aircraft against a cluttered background. If the aircraft is between you and terrain that is varicoloured or heavily dotted with buildings, **it will blend into the background** until the aircraft is quite close.

m. In daylight, the colours and shapes are seen by 'cones' which are light sensitive cells occupying a small central area of the retina of the eye. At night, the cones become inactive, and vision is taken over by 'rods' which make up the rest of the retina, and which provide peripheral vision by day. The problem with rods is that they cannot distinguish colour, they are not as good at distinguishing shapes as cones, and at night there is now an area in the centre of the retina (populated by inactive cones), which cannot see anything.

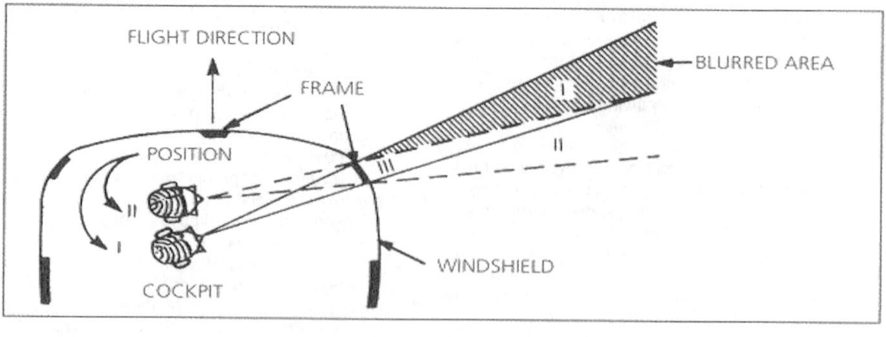

This explains why it is easier to see a faint star by looking away (by about 10 degrees) than straight at it. Rods take 30 minutes in the dark to reach their efficiency. They are insensitive to red light, and that was the reason why WWII night fighter pilots sat around in dim red rooms before jumping into dim red cockpits. Nowadays it is felt more important to interpret a normally lit instrument correctly, than run the risk of misinterpreting a dim red instrument, even though the pilot's outside night vision might be marginally better in the latter case. However, it obviously makes sense for pilots to try and avoid looking at bright lights at night. It is important to maintain a scan at night, but because peripheral rods are being used, it is better to use a continuous scan which will cause an image (aircraft lights) to move on the retina, rather than trying to focus on one area of sky (because the fine focusing cones are not working). Since the rods are sensitive to movement, they are more likely to be alerted by this technique.

n. Finally, there are the tricks that the mind can play, which can distract the pilot to the point of not seeing anything at all, or cause cockpit myopia — staring at one instrument without even 'seeing' it.

o. It can be realised that visual perception is affected by many factors. Pilots, like others, tend to **overestimate their visual abilities** and to misunderstand their eyes' limitations. Since a major cause of mid- air collisions is the failure to adhere to the practice of see-and-avoid, it can be concluded that the best way to avoid collisions is to learn how to use your eyes for an efficient scan.

4 VISUAL SCANNING TECHNIQUE

a. To avoid collisions you must scan effectively from the moment the aircraft moves until it comes to a stop at the end of the flight. Collision threats are present on the ground, at low altitudes in the vicinity of aerodromes, and at cruising levels.

b. Before take-off, check the runway visually to ensure that there are no aircraft or other objects in the take-off area. Check the approach and circuit to be sure of the position of other aircraft. Assess the traffic situation from radio reports. After take-off, continue to scan to ensure that there will be no obstacles to your safe departure.

c. During the climb and descent beware of the blind spot under the nose – manoeuvre the aircraft so that you can check.

d. During climb or descent, listen to radio exchanges between air traffic and other aircraft and form a mental image of the traffic situation and positions of aircraft on opposing and intersecting headings, anticipating further developments. Scan with particular care in the area of airway (route) intersections and when near a radio beacon or VRP. You should remain constantly alert to all traffic withln your normal field of vision, as well as periodically scanning the entire visual field outside the aircraft to ensure detection of conflicting traffic. Remember that the performance capabilities of many aircraft, in both speed and rates of climb/descent, result in high closure rates, limiting the time available for detection, decision, and evasive action.

5 HOW TO SCAN

a. The best way to develop effective scanning is by eliminating bad habits. Naturally, not looking out at all is the poorest scan technique! Glancing out at intervals of five minutes or so is also poor when considering that it takes only seconds for a disaster to happen. Check the next time the aircraft is climbing out or making an approach to see how long you spend without looking outside.

b. Glancing out and 'giving the old once-around' without stopping to focus on anything is practically useless; so is staring out into one spot for long periods of time.

c. There is no one technique that is best for all pilots. The most important thing is for each pilot to develop a scan that is both comfortable and workable.

d. Learn how to scan properly by knowing where and how to concentrate your search on the areas most critical to you at any given time. In the circuit especially, **always** look out before you turn and make sure your path is clear. Look out for traffic making an improper entry into the circuit.

e. During that very critical final approach stage, do not forget to scan all around to avoid tunnel vision. Pilots often fix their eyes on the point of touchdown. You may never arrive at the runway if another pilot is also aiming for the same runway threshold at that time!

f. In normal flight, you can generally avoid the risk of a mid-air collision by scanning an area at least 60° left and right of your flight path. Be aware that constant angle collisions often occur when the other aircraft initially appears motionless at about your 10 o'clock or 2 o'clock positions. This does not mean you should forget the rest of the area you can see. You should also scan at least 10° above and below the projected flight path of your aircraft. This will allow you to spot any aircraft that is at an altitude that might prove hazardous to you, whether it is level with you, climbing from below or descending from above.

g. The more you look outside, the less the risk of a collision. Certain techniques may be used to increase the effectiveness of the scan. To be most effective, the gaze should be shifted and refocused at regular intervals. Most pilots do this in the process of scanning the instrument panel but it is also important to focus outside the cockpit or flight deck to set up the visual system for effective target acquisition. Proper scanning requires the constant sharing of attention with other piloting tasks, thus it is easily degraded by such conditions as distraction, fatigue, boredom, illness, anxiety or preoccupation.

h. Effective scanning is accomplished by a series of short, regularly- spaced eye movements that bring successive areas of the sky into the central visual field. Each movement should not exceed 10°, and each area should be observed for at least one second to enable detection. Although horizontal back-and-forth eye movements seem preferred by most pilots, each pilot should develop the scanning pattern that is most comfortable and then keep to it. Peripheral vision can be useful in spotting collision risks. It is essential to remember, however, that if another aircraft appears to have no relative motion, it is likely to be on a collision course with you. If the other aircraft shows no horizontal or vertical motion on the windshield, but is increasing in size, **take immediate evasive action**.

6 SCAN PATTERNS

a. Two scanning patterns described below have proved to be very effective for pilots and involve the 'block' system of scanning. This system is based on the premise that traffic detection can be made only through a series of eye fixations at different points in space. In application, the viewing area (wind- shield) is divided into segments, and the pilot methodically scans for traffic in each block in sequential order.

i) Side- to- side scanning method

Start at the far left of your visual area and make a methodical sweep to the right, pausing very briefly in each block of the viewing area to focus your eyes. At the end of the scan, return to and scan the instrument panel and then repeat the external scan.

ii) Front- to- side scanning method

Start in the centre block of your visual field (centre of front windshield); move to the left, focusing very briefly in each block, then swing quickly back to the centre block after reaching the last block on the left and repeat the action to the right. Then, after scanning the instrument panel, repeat the external scan.

b. There are other methods of scanning, of course, some of which may be as effective as the two described above. However, unless some series of fixations is made, there is little likelihood that you will be able to detect all targets in your scan area. When the head is in motion, vision is blurred and the mind will not register potential targets.

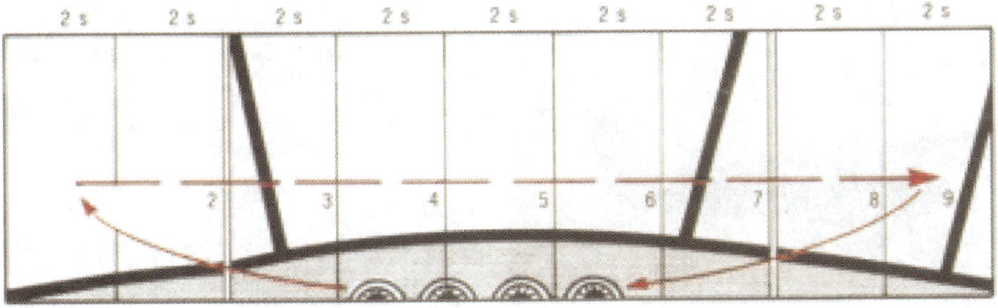

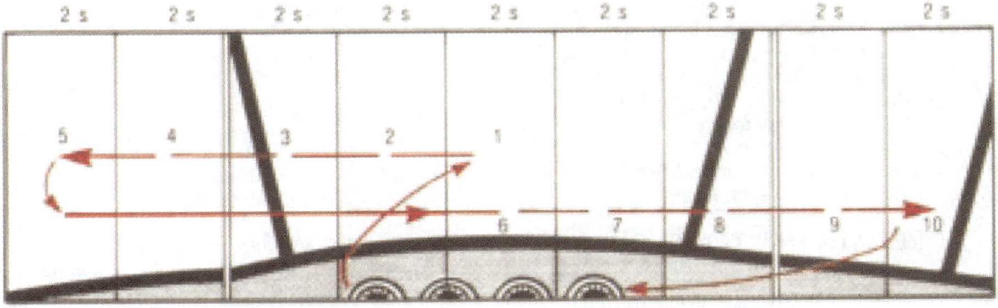

7 THE TIME-SHARING PLAN

a. External scanning is just part of the pilot's total visual work. To achieve maximum efficiency in flight, a pilot also has to establish a good internal scan and learn to give each scan its proper share of time, depending, to some extent, on the work-load inside the cockpit and the density of traffic outside. Generally, the external scan will take considerably longer than the look at the instrument panel.

b. During an experimental scan training course, using military pilots whose experience ranged from 350 hours to over 4000 hours of flight time, it was discovered that the average time they needed to maintain a steady state of flight was three seconds for the instrument panel scan and 18 to 20 seconds for the outside scan.

c. An efficient instrument scan is good practice, even when flying VFR. The ability to scan the panel quickly permits more time to be allotted to exterior scanning, thus improving collision avoidance.

d. Developing an efficient time-sharing plan takes a lot of work and practice, but it is just as important as developing good landing techniques. The best way is to start on the ground, in your own aeroplane or the one you usually fly, and then use your scans in actual practice at every opportunity.

e. During flight, if one crew member is occupied with essential work inside the cockpit, another crew member, if available, must expand his scan to include both his usual sector of observation and that of the other crew member.

8 AIRPROX REPORTING

If you consider that your aircraft has been endangered during flight by the proximity of another aircraft such that a risk of collision existed, report it by radio to the Air Traffic unit with which you are in communication. The call should be prefixed 'AIRPROX'. If this is not possible, immediately after landing (in the UK) telephone or by other means contact any UK ATS unit, but preferably an ATCC. Prompt action is important. Confirm in writing within 7 days using CA 1094 'Airprox Report Form'.

9 OPERATIONAL TECHNIQUES

a. Collision avoidance involves more than proper scanning techniques. You can be the most conscientious scanner in the world and still have an in-flight collision if you neglect other important factors.

- Check yourself

  Start with yourself - your eyesight, and consequently your safety, depend on your mental and physical condition. If you are preoccupied you should not fly – absent-mindedness and distraction are the main enemies of concentrated attention during flight. Age affects your eyes, so if you are a mature pilot have regular eye checks. If you need glasses to correct your vision, then wear them and ensure that you have the required spare pair with you.

- Plan ahead

  To minimise the time spent 'head- down' in the cockpit, plan your flight, have charts folded in proper sequence and within reach. Be familiar with headings, frequencies, distances, etc. so that you spend minimum time with your head down in your charts. Pilots should record these things on a flight log before take-off. Lift anything you need to read up to the coaming, rather than look down. Check your maps, NOTAM, etc. in advance for potential hazards such as military low-level routes and other high-density areas. See Safety Sense Leaflet 18, Military Low Flying.

- Clean windows

  During the pre-flight walk-around, make sure your windshield is clean and in good condition. If possible, keep all windows clear of obstructions such as opaque sun visors and curtains.

- Night Flying

  Be aware of the limitations of vision at night and give your eyes time to adjust. Avoid blinding others with the careless use on the ground of your strobes or landing lights.

- Adhere to procedures

  Follow established operating procedures and regulations, such as correct flight levels (quadrantal or semi- circular) and proper circuit practices. You can get into trouble, for instance, by 'sneaking' out of your proper level as cumulus clouds begin to tower higher and higher below you, or by skimming along the tops of clouds without observing proper cloud clearance. Some typical situations involving in-flight mishaps around airports include: entering a right-hand circuit at an airport with left-hand traffic or entering downwind so far ahead of the circuit that you may interfere with traffic taking off and heading out in your direction. Beware of pilots flying large circuits with long final approaches. **In most in-flight collisions at least one of the pilots involved was not where he was supposed to be.**

- Avoid crowded airspace

  Avoid crowded airspace, e.g. over a VRP or radio beacon. Aircraft can be training over navigation beacons, even in good weather. If you cannot avoid aerodromes en route, fly over them well above ATZ height and if appropriate give them a call stating your intentions.

- Compensate for blind spots

  Compensate for your aircraft's design limitations. If you are short, or the aircraft has a high coaming, a suitable cushion can be helpful. All aircraft have blind spots; know where they are in yours. For example, a high-wing aircraft has a wing down in a turn that blocks the view of the area you are turning into, so lift the wing slightly for a good look **before turning**. One of the most critical potential mid-air collision situations exists when a faster low-wing aircraft is overtaking and descending onto a high-wing aircraft on final approach.

- Equip to be seen

  Your aircraft lights can help avoid collisions. High intensity strobe lights, which can be installed at relatively low cost, increase your contrast and conspicuity considerably by day and even more by night. In areas of high traffic density, strobe lights are often the first indication another pilot receives of your presence. Transponders, especially with altitude encoding (Mode C) allow radar controllers to identify your aircraft in relation to other traffic and provide you with traffic information. They also indicate your aircraft to commercial aircraft which carry ACAS (aircraft collision avoidance system). If you show mode C, ACAS can guide the commercial aircraft away from you! The carriage of transponders is now mandatory in some airspace, even when operating VFR. If ATC do not allocate you a code, use code 7000 (with Mode C), but switch it off if instructed. Aircraft with one high contrast colour can be seen more easily than those with a pattern or one low contrast colour. Recent tests have shown that matt black (or gloss black) gives greatest contrast. Consider the use of landing lights during the circuit and landing especially on hazy days.

- Talk and listen

  Use your ears as well as your eyes by taking advantage of all the information that you receive over the radio (but beware, non-radio aircraft may be in the same airspace). Pilots reporting their position to the tower are also reporting to you. Approaching an aerodrome, call the tower when you are 10 km from the airport, or such other distance or time prescribed by the ATS authority, and report your position, height/ altitude and intentions. When flying in areas where there are no air traffic services, change to the FIR or nearest aerodrome frequency.

- Make use of information

  Since detecting a small aircraft at a distance is not the easiest thing to do, make use of any hints you get over the radio. Your job is much easier when you are told that traffic is 'three miles at one o'clock'. **Once that particular traffic is sighted, do not forget the rest of the sky**. If the traffic seems to be moving on the windshield, you're most probably not on a collision course, so continue your scan but watch the traffic from time to time. **If it has little relative motion you should watch it very carefully – he may not have seen you.**

- Use all available eyes

  If you normally fly with another pilot, establish crew procedures which ensure that an effective scan is maintained at all times. Otherwise, use passengers to help in looking for traffic you have been made aware of, while you monitor the movement of other aircraft. Remember, however, that the responsibility for avoiding collisions is yours and you must maintain your vigilance at all times.

- Scan

  The most important item, of course, is to keep looking out at where you are going and to watch for other traffic. Make use of your scan constantly.

b) Stick to good airmanship; if you keep yourself and your aircraft in good condition, and develop an effective scan time- sharing system, you will have the basic tools for avoiding a mid-air collision.

10 SUMMARY

- If you need glasses, carry any required spare pair.
- Clean the windshield and side windows (if either is badly scratched, have a new one fitted).
- If you are short or the aircraft has a high coaming, use a cushion.
- Beware of blind spots, move your head or manoeuvre the aircraft.
- Spend the minimum time with your head down checking the charts (or GPS) changing radio frequencies etc.
- The aircraft with little or no relative motion is the one which is hard to see – and the most hazardous.
- Aircraft below you may blend into the background of buildings etc.
- High intensity strobes can be useful on dull days.
- Use the radio to form a mental picture of what is going on. Don't rely solely on it – someone could be NON- RADIO e.g. a glider.
- Develop and use an effective scan pattern.
- Don't move the eyes continuously, stop and give them a chance to SEE.
- The external scan should take much longer than your instrument scan.
- When you have spotted another aircraft, do not fix on it and forget the rest of the surroundings.
- Use landing lights in the circuit.
- Scan
- Encourage your passengers to assist in the look- out.
- Report any AIRPROX

SAFETY SENSE 14
GENERAL AVIATION

PISTON ENGINE ICING

1 INTRODUCTION

a. This leaflet is intended to assist pilots of carburetted piston engined aircraft operating below 10,000 feet. Although it may appear to be mainly aimed at aeroplane operations, much of its content applies at least equally to piston-engined helicopters and gyroplanes.

b. Piston engine induction system icing is commonly referred to as carburettor icing, although, as described later, carb icing is only one form. Such icing can occur at any time, **even on warm days, particularly if they are humid**. It can be so severe that unless **correct** action is taken the engine may stop (especially at low power settings during descent, approach or during helicopter autorotation).

c. Every year engine induction system icing is assessed as being a likely contributory factor in several aircraft accidents. Unfortunately the evidence rapidly disappears.

d. Some aircraft/engine combinations are more prone to icing than others and this should be borne in mind when flying different aircraft types.

e. The aircraft Flight Manual is the primary source of information for individual aircraft. The advice in this leaflet should only be followed where it does not contradict that Flight Manual.

2 TYPES OF ICING

There are three main types of induction system icing:

BUILD-UP OF ICING IN INDUCTION SYSTEM

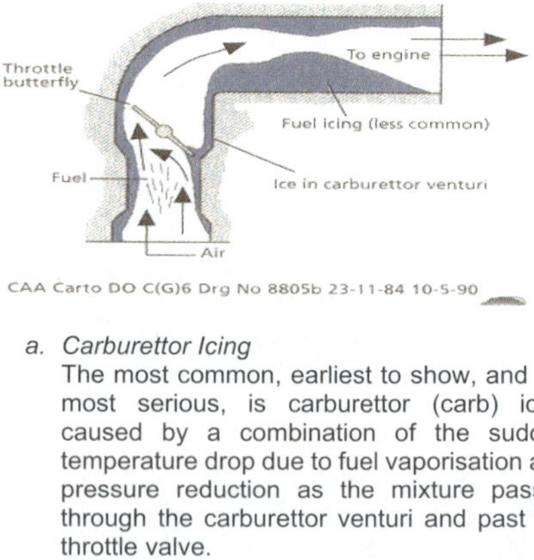

CAA Carto DO C(G)6 Drg No 8805b 23-11-84 10-5-90

a. *Carburettor Icing*
The most common, earliest to show, and the most serious, is carburettor (carb) icing caused by a combination of the sudden temperature drop due to fuel vaporisation and pressure reduction as the mixture passes through the carburettor venturi and past the throttle valve.

If the temperature drop brings the air below its dew point, condensation results, and if the drop brings the mixture temperature below freezing, the condensed water will form ice on the surfaces of the carburettor. This ice gradually blocks the venturi, which upsets the fuel/ air ratio causing a progressive, smooth loss of power and slowly 'strangles' the engine. Conventional float type carburettors are more prone to icing than pressure jet types.

b. *Fuel Icing*
Less common is fuel icing which is the result of water, held in suspension in the fuel, precipitating and freezing in the induction piping, especially in the elbows formed by bends.

c. *Impact Ice*
Ice which builds up on air intakes, filters, alternate air valves etc. is called impact ice. It forms on the aircraft in snow, sleet, sub-zero cloud and rain, (if either the rain or the aircraft is below zero°C).

This type of icing can affect fuel injection systems as well as carburettors. In general, impact ice is the main hazard for turbocharged engines.

d. Testing has shown that because of its greater and seasonally variable volatility and higher water content, carb icing is more likely when MOGAS is used.

e. Engines at reduced power settings are more prone to icing because engine induction temperatures are lower. Also, the partially closed butterfly can more easily be restricted by the ice build- up. This is a particular problem if the engine is de-rated as in many piston-engined helicopters and some aeroplanes.

Note: For the sake of simplicity, in the rest of this leaflet, the term Carb Icing includes Induction Icing and Carb Heat includes Alternate Air.

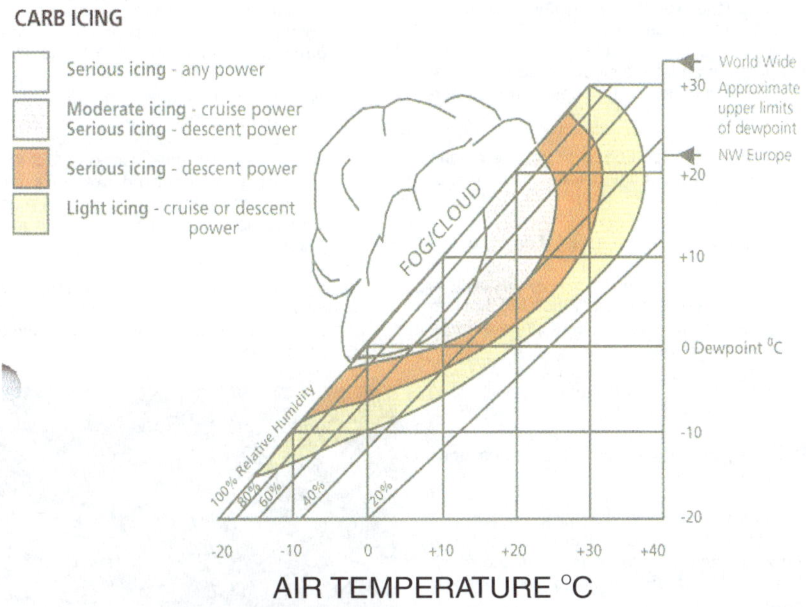

3 ATMOSPHERIC CONDITIONS

a. Carb icing is **not** restricted to cold weather. It will occur on **warm days** if humidity is high, especially at **low power settings**. Flight tests have produced serious icing at descent power with ambient (not surface) temperature above 25° C, even with relative humidity as low as 30%. At cruise power, icing occurred at 20° C when relative humidity was 60% or more. (Cold, clear winter days are less of a hazard than humid summer days because cold air holds less moisture than warm air.) In the United Kingdom and Europe where high humidity is common, pilots must be constantly on the alert for carb icing and take corrective action **before** an irretrievable situation arises. If the engine fails due to carb icing, it may not re-start (even if it does, the delay could be critical).

b. Carb icing can occur in clear air and is therefore made more dangerous by the lack of any visual warning. In cloud, the icing risk may be higher but the pilot is less likely to be caught unawares.

c. Specific warnings of induction system icing are not normally included in aviation weather forecasts. Pilots must therefore use knowledge and experience. The closer the temperature and dewpoint readings, the greater the relative humidity. However, the humidity reported at an aerodrome may bear little relation to the humidity at flying altitudes. When dewpoint information is not available, assume high humidity particularly when:

- in cloud and fog; these are water droplets and the relative humidity should be assumed to be 100%.
- in clear air where cloud or fog may have just dispersed, or just below the top of a haze layer;
- just below cloud base or between cloud layers (highest liquid water content is at cloud tops);
- in precipitation, especially if persistent;
- if the surface and low level visibility is poor, especially in early morning and late evening, and particularly near a large area of water;
- when the ground is wet (even with dew) and the wind is light.

However, the lack of such indications does not mean low humidity.

d) The chart shows the wide range of ambient conditions in which carb icing is most likely. Particular note should be taken of the much greater risk of serious icing with descent power.

4 RECOGNITION & GENERAL PRACTICES

Paragraphs 4 and 5 are intended as a general guide to assist you to avoid icing, but reference must be made to the relevant sections of the Pilot's Operating Handbook or Flight Manual for specific procedures related to the particular airframe/ engine combinations. **These may vary for a different model of the same aircraft type**.

a. With a fixed pitch propeller, a slight drop in rpm and performance (airspeed and/or altitude) are the most likely indications of the onset of carb icing. This **loss of rpm** can be smooth and gradual and the usual reaction is to open the throttle slightly to compensate. However, this, whilst restoring power, hides the loss. As icing builds up, rough running, vibration, further loss of performance and ultimately engine stoppage may follow. The primary detection instrument is the **rpm gauge** in conjunction with ASI and altimeter.

b. With a constant speed propeller, and in a helicopter, the loss of power would have to be large before a reduction in rpm occurs. Onset of icing is even more insidious, but there will be a **drop in manifold pressure** and in a performance reduction. In this case the primary detection instrument is the **manifold pressure gauge.**

c. An exhaust gas temperature gauge, if fitted, may show a decrease in temperature before any significant decrease in engine and aircraft performance.

d. Carb icing is normally cleared by the pilot selecting an alternative air source which supplies air, (heated in an exhaust heat exchanger) which melts the ice obstruction. This source by-passes the normal intake filter.

e. Engines with fuel injection generally have an alternate air intake located within the engine cowling via a valve downstream from the normal air intake. This alternate air is warmed by engine heat, even though it does not normally pass through a heat exchanger.

f. Always use **full** heat whenever carb heat is applied; partial hot air should only be used if an intake temperature gauge is fitted and only then if specifically recommended in the approved Flight Manual or Pilot's Operating Handbook

g. Hot air should be selected:

- as a matter of routine, at regular intervals to prevent ice build up,
- whenever a drop in rpm or manifold pressure, or rough engine running, is experienced,
- when carb icing conditions are suspected, and
- when flying in conditions within the high probability ranges indicated in the chart.

But always be aware that hot air, while selected, reduces engine power. This may be critical in certain flight phases.

h. During the cruise, carburettor heat should be applied at regular intervals, to prevent carburettor ice forming. It should be selected for long enough (at the very least 15 seconds but considerably more in certain aircraft) to pre-empt the loss of engine power or restore power to the original level.

i. If icing has caused a loss of power, and the hot air disperses it, re- selection of cold air should produce an increase in rpm or manifold pressure over the earlier reading. This is a useful check to see whether ice is forming, but does not prove that all the ice has melted!. Carry out further checks until there is **no** resultant increase, monitor the engine instruments, and increase the frequencies of the routine checks, as it may re-occur. Lack of carb icing should produce no increase in rpm or manifold pressure beyond that noted prior to the use of hot air.

j. Remember, selection of hot air when ice is present may at first make the situation appear worse, due to an increase in rough running as the ice melts and passes through the engine. If this happens **the temptation to return to cold air must be resisted** so that the hot air has time to clear the ice. **This time may be in the region of 15 seconds**, which will, in the event, feel like a very long time!

k. Unless necessary, the continuous use of hot air at high power settings should be avoided. However, carburettor heat should be applied early enough **before** descent to warm the intake, and should remain fully applied during that descent, as the engine is more susceptible to carb icing at low power settings.

5 PILOT PROCEDURES

a. *Maintenance*
Periodically check the carb heating system and controls for proper condition and operation. Pay particular attention to seals which may have deteriorated, allowing the hot air to become diluted by cold air.

b. *Start Up*
Start up with the carb heat control in the **COLD** position.

c. *Taxiing*
Generally, use of carb heat is not recommended while taxiing - the air is usually unfiltered when in the HOT position. However, ice may build up at the low taxiing power settings, and if not removed may cause engine failure after take-off. If carburettor heat is needed – USE IT.

d. *Ground Power Checks*
Select carburettor heat fully ON for at least 15 seconds. Check that there is a **significant** power decrease when hot air is selected (typically 75– 100 rpm or 3– 5" of manifold pressure) and that power is regained (but to a level no higher than before) when cold air is re-selected. If the power returns to a higher value, ice was present and further checks should be carried out until the ice has cleared.

e. *Immediately Prior to Take-Off*
Since icing can occur when taxiing with low power settings, or when the engine is idling, select carb heat ON for a minimum of 15 seconds and then OFF, immediately before take off to clear any build- up. If the aircraft is kept waiting at the holding point in conditions of high humidity, it may be necessary to carry out the run- up drill more than once to clear ice which may have formed.

f. *Take-Off*
Take-off should **only** be commenced when you are sure the engine is developing full power. When at full power and as airspeed is building, you must check that the full throttle rpm and/ or manifold pressure is as expected. **Carburettor heat must NOT be used during take-off** unless specifically authorized in the Flight Manual or Pilots Operating Handbook.

g. *Climb*
Be alert for symptoms of carb icing, especially when visible moisture is present or if conditions are in the high probability ranges in the chart. Be aware if your Flight Manual restricts the use of carb heat at full power.

h. *Cruise*

Avoid clouds as much as possible. (Note that few piston engined aircraft are cleared for flight in airframe icing conditions). Monitor appropriate engine instruments for any changes which could indicate icing. Make a carb heat check (see below) at least every 10 minutes, (more frequently if conditions are conducive to icing). **Use full heat** and note the warning of para 4 (j), it may take 15 seconds or more to clear the ice and the engine will continue to run roughly as the ice melts and passes through the engine. If the icing is so severe that the engine has died, keep the hot air selected as residual heat in the rapidly cooling exhaust may be effective (opening the throttle fully and closing the mixture control for a while may also help)

i. *Carburettor heat check*

- Note the RPM/ Manifold Pressure (consider slightly increasing power beforehand to prevent a reduction in performance during the check)
- Apply full Carb heat for at least 15 seconds.
- Return Carb heat to Cold. The RPM/ Manifold Pressure will return to approximately the earlier indication if there was no icing. If it is **higher** - icing was present, and may not yet be completely clear, so repeat the check until no increase results.

j. *Descent and Approach*
Carb icing is much more likely at reduced power, so select hot air **before, rather than after**, power is reduced for the descent, and especially for a practice forced landing or a helicopter autorotation, i.e., before the exhaust starts to cool. (A full carb heat check just before selecting heat for the descent is advisable). Maintain FULL heat during long periods of flight with reduced power settings. At intervals of about 500 ft or more frequently if conditions require, increase power to cruise setting to warm the engine and to provide sufficient heat to melt any ice.

k. *Downwind*
Ensure that the downwind check includes the cruise carburettor heat check at 5(i) above. If you select and leave the heat on, speed or altitude will reduce on the downwind leg unless you have added some power beforehand.

l. *Base Leg and Final Approach*

Unless otherwise stated in the Pilot's Operating Handbook or Flight Manual, the HOT position should be selected before power is reduced and retained to touchdown. On some engine installations, to ensure better engine response and to permit a go-around to be initiated without delay, it may be recommended that the carb heat be returned to COLD at about 200/ 300 ft on finals.

m. *Go-around or Touch and Go*
Ensure the carb heat is COLD, ideally before, or simultaneously as, power is applied for a go- around.

n. *After Landing*
Return to the COLD setting before taxiing, if not already set COLD.

6 SUMMARY

- Icing forms stealthily.
- Some aircraft/ engine combinations are more susceptible than others.
- Icing may occur in warm humid conditions and is a possibility at any time of the year in the UK.
- Mogas makes carb icing more likely.
- Low power settings, such as in a descent or in the circuit, are more prone to give carb icing.
- Use full carb heat frequently when flying in conditions where carb icing is likely. Remember that the RPM gauge is your primary indication for a fixed pitch propeller; manifold pressure for variable pitch.
- Treat the carb heat as an ON/OFF control – either full hot or full cold.
- It takes time for the heat to work and the engine may run roughly while ice is clearing.
- Timely use of appropriate procedures can PREVENT THIS PROBLEM.

FINALLY

In the event of carb heat system failure in flight:

- Avoid likely carb icing conditions.
- Maintain high throttle settings – full throttle if possible.
- Weaken the mixture slightly.
- Land as soon as reasonably possible.

SAFETY SENSE 15
GENERAL AVIATION

WAKE VORTEX

photos: Bob Stoyles, Cathay Pacific via 'Crewsnews'

1 INTRODUCTION

a. There have been serious and fatal accidents in the UK to light aircraft because pilots were unable to maintain control after being caught in the wake vortex or helicopter downwash generated by heavier aircraft. The hazard to light aircraft is most likely at airports where general aviation mixes with airline traffic.

b. All aircraft generate vortices at the wing tips as a consequence of producing lift. **The heavier the aircraft and the slower it is flying, the stronger the vortex**. Among other factors, the size of the vortex is proportional to the span of the aircraft which generates it, for instance a Boeing 747, with a span of 65 metres trails a vortex from both wingtips each with a diameter of around 65 metres.

c. At low altitudes, vortices generally persist for as long as 80 seconds, but **in very light or calm wind conditions, they can last for up to two and a half minutes**. Once formed, vortices continue to descend until they decay (or reach the ground). Decay is usually sudden and occurs more quickly in windy conditions. Cross-winds can carry a vortex away from the flight path of the aircraft. For each nautical mile behind an aircraft, the vortex the aircraft generates will typically have descended between 100 and 200 ft.

d. Generally, the lighter the aircraft you are flying, the greater the degree of upset if you encounter a wake vortex. Thus, a light aircraft will be vulnerable to the vortices of a similar sized aircraft ahead of it, and microlight aircraft will be even more vulnerable.

e. Aeronautical Information Circular (AIC) 17/ 1999 (Pink 188) 'Wake Turbulence' provides detailed information including aircraft weight categories and recommended spacings.

f. The AIC provides advice for avoiding vortices in all phases of flight. The simple advice for light aircraft pilots is, 'Avoid crossing below or close behind the flight path of a heavier aircraft'.

g. Jet blast and prop wash may also cause considerable turbulence, but are not covered in this leaflet.

2 VORTEX ENCOUNTERS

a. A light aircraft penetrating a vortex from a larger aircraft on a similar trajectory and axis can experience a severe roll. In the worst cases it may be beyond the power of the ailerons to counteract the roll. Even executive jets have been rolled upside down.

Same Trajectory Encounter

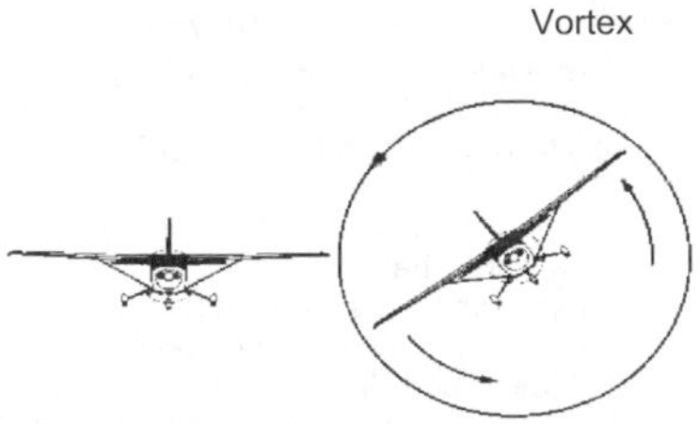

b. If the vortex is entered at right angles to its axis, rapid vertical and pitch displacements with airspeed changes are likely. An oblique entry, the most likely event, will have symptoms of both.

Right Angle Encounter

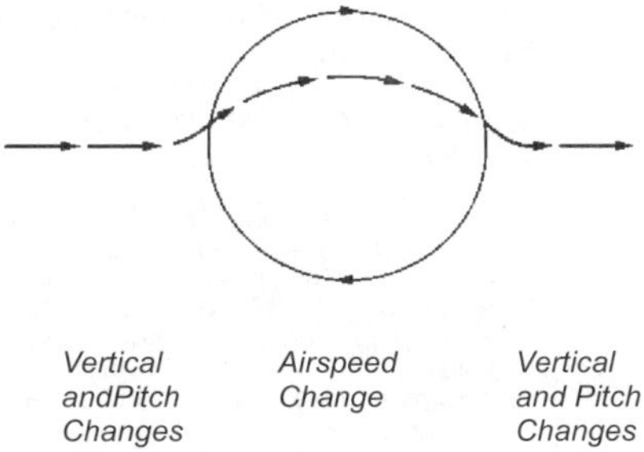

c. Although a vortex encounter at altitude is uncomfortable and alarming, it should be recoverable. However, any loose objects in the cockpit may be scattered about. A Piper PA23 Aztec was flying north– south at 1000 ft, 7 ½nm west of Heathrow, underneath the approach path. The Aztec was almost turned on its back by the vortex from a Boeing 757 on the approach which had crossed its track at 2500 ft. The wind at Heathrow was calm.

d. A significant proportion of the wake vortex incidents reported in the UK occur below 200 feet i.e. just before landing where there may not be room to recover. An accident in the UK badly damaged a Robin aircraft, which it appears got too close behind a landing Short SD360. At 100–150 ft the right wing and nose dropped and the aircraft did not respond to control inputs, descended rapidly and hit a hedge. Estimated separation was about 3 nm. **The wind speed was reported as 2kt**. Incidents including fatal accidents have also occurred shortly after take-off, which is when the affected aircraft is most likely to be directly behind a larger aircraft.

e. Close to the ground, vortices generally persist for about 80 seconds where their effect is most hazardous. They tend to move apart at about 5 knots in still air, so a crosswind component of 5 knots can keep the upwind vortex stationary on or near the runway while the downwind vortex moves away at about 10 knots. In crosswinds of more than 5 knots, the area of hazard is not necessarily aligned with the flight path of the aircraft ahead. Take particular care at airfields where intersecting runways are both in use.

HEADWIND LESS THAN 10 KNOTS

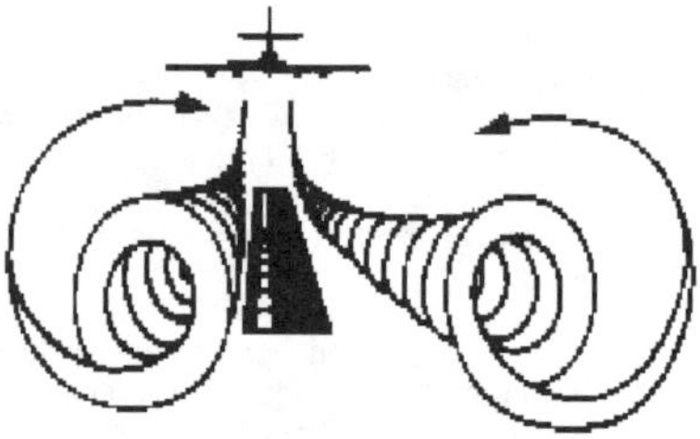

CROSSWIND LESS THAN 5 KNOTS

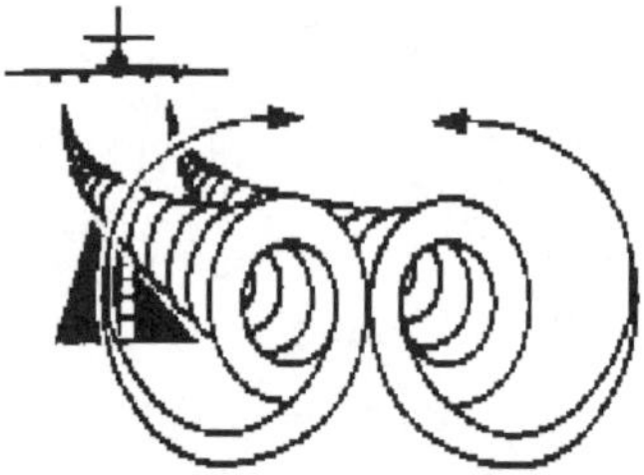

CROSSWIND OVER 5 KNOTS

At very low altitude the area of hazard is not necessarily aligned with the flightpath of the aircraft ahead

3 AIR TRAFFIC CONTROL

a. At UK airports where there are commercial movements, an ATC service will be provided with the possible exception of some Highlands and Islands aerodromes. The controllers will advise pilots of the recommended interval; e.g. '*Golf November Tango, you are number two to a Boeing 737, the recommended wake vortex spacing is 6 miles, report final'*.

b. **For VFR arrivals vortex spacing is the responsibility of the pilot**, however, the recommended distance will be given by ATC **but not by AFISO/ Air Ground Service**. If in doubt, use greater spacing.

c. Read the AIC so that you will be familiar with the weight categories, e.g. 'heavy' includes all wide- bodied airliners. Also become familiar with the spacing minima which ATC will apply.

d. Some large narrow bodied aircraft present a particular hazard to lighter aircraft. Experience has shown that the Boeing 757 creates particularly strong vortices. Caution is recommended for all pilots following such aircraft, particularly on approach. Additional spacing (with the agreement of ATC) is recommended.

4 VORTEX AVOIDANCE APPROACH

a. Since the vortices are invisible, although occasionally the cores can be seen in very humid conditions, they are difficult to avoid unless you have a good 'mental' picture of where they occur.

b. There are two techniques which can be employed:

- Distance can be judged visually by runway length – most major airports have runways between one and 2 nautical miles long (1850 and 3700 metres). Thus, if the recommended spacing is 6 miles, then you need 3 to 6 runway lengths between yourself and the aircraft ahead.

- If the aircraft on the approach ahead of you is much heavier than your own type, try to keep it in sight. In general, vortices drift downwards, **so fly above** and to the upwind side of the lead aircraft's flight path. Obviously as you get closer to the runway lateral displacement has to be reduced, so land beyond the point where the heavier aircraft touched down as generation of vortices ceases when the nosewheel contacts the runway. The heavier the type ahead, the longer the runway is likely to be, so stopping a light aircraft should not be a problem – it may even save you some taxi time! Airliners almost always approach on a 3° glide slope, light aircraft can readily accept steeper angles.

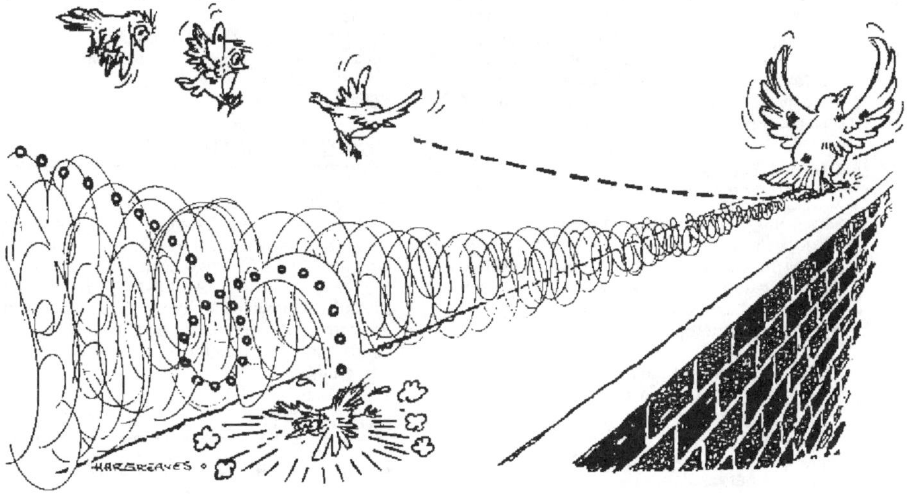

Courtesy- Hargreaves

5 AVOIDANCE – DEPARTURE

a. **Vortices are generated as the aircraft rotates on take off**, so the time interval between departures specified in the AIC starts from rotation. For example, a light aircraft taking off behind a Boeing 737 should allow an interval of at least 2 minutes if commencing take-off from the same point, and at least 3 minutes if taking off from a point part- way up the same runway.

b. Although you may think you can avoid the vortex by lifting off early and climbing above the vortex, most commercial aircraft will climb much more steeply than a light aircraft once they have accelerated. In order to avoid entering the vortex you would need to turn early and fly well clear of the preceding aircraft's flight path.

6 HELICOPTERS

a. The AIC specifies minimum spacing between light aircraft and the Sikorsky S61N or similar large helicopters (there was a fatal accident to a Piper Warrior in 1992 at Oxford). **It is considered that a helicopter in forward flight generates more intense vortices than a fixed-wing aircraft of a similar weight**. When following a helicopter, pilots of light aircraft should consider allowing a greater spacing than would normally be used behind a fixed-wing aircraft of similar size, perhaps treating each helicopter as being one category higher than that listed in the AIC.

SikorskyS76 – Photo FAA Technical Center, Mr J Sackett

b. Helicopters with rotors turning create a blast of air outwards in all directions, the strongest effect being downwind. This effect is not so significant when the helicopter with rotors turning is on the ground. It is most severe during hovering and hover taxiing, when the rotors are generating enough lift to support the full weight of the helicopter, and this creates the greatest downwash. During an approach it may not be possible to determine which of the stages of flight the helicopter is at, nor the helicopter pilot's immediate intentions. In these circumstances, pilots of light aircraft should aim to keep as far away as possible. In particular, if there is a helicopter on or near the runway, and if runway length permits, consider landing further down the runway to avoid being caught by rotorwash. **If in doubt, make an early decision to go-around**.

7 MICROLIGHTS

a. Microlights and very light aircraft are more susceptible than other GA aircraft to the effects from wake vortex. Control problems have been experienced when one has encountered the vortex of a single engined piston training aeroplane.

b. Pilots of microlights should consider treating every aircraft in front of them as being one category higher than listed in the AIC.

c. Hang gliders and paragliders (including powered parachutes) can expect to be affected even more than microlights. Parachute canopies may collapse, as shown below.

photo courtesy 'Skywings'

8 REPORTING

National Air traffic Services (NATS) maintains a wake vortex database to monitor incident rates. All suspected wake vortex incidents should be **reported immediately to ATC by radio** and followed up after landing using form CA 1695 'Wake Vortex Report Form' (Forms are available from Documedia Limited) If an Occurrence Report (Form CA 1673) is used to report wake turbulence, this will automatically be copied to the database office, a separate Wake Vortex Report need not be sent but detailed information is most useful. Reports should be sent to:

Wake Vortex and Radar Analysis
Incidents
Air Traffic Management Development Centre
National Air Traffic Services Ltd, Swanwick,

Tel. 01489 615813

9 FURTHER INFORMATION

A graphic 17 minute video, AF 9468 'Wake Turbulence – The Unseen Menace', is available from The British Defence Film Library, Chalfont Grove, Chalfont St. Peter, Gerrards Cross, Bucks SL9 8TN. Tel. 01494 878237 Fax: 01494 878007. It provides a useful illustration of the problem to those who fly both small and large aircraft, and also for Air Traffic Services personnel.

10 SUMMARY

- Wake vortices are generally invisible.
- Vortices last longer in calm or light wind conditions and are therefore at their most hazardous then.
- They are most dangerous close to the ground.
- The heavier an aircraft, and the slower it is flying, the stronger its vortex and the greater the risk to following aircraft.
- The lighter the aircraft you are flying, the more vulnerable it is.
- When an aeroplane's nosewheel is on the ground, there are no vortices.
- On departure, use the appropriate time interval when following a heavier aircraft –
- 2 minutes if starting the take-off at the same point,
- 3 minutes if taking off part-way along the same runway.
- When taking off behind a departing heavier aircraft, note its rotation point so that you can lift- off before that point and climb above the vortex. If you cannot – WAIT.
- On the approach, avoid vortices by flying above and upwind of the lead aircraft's flightpath.
- When following a heavier aircraft which has already landed, note its touchdown point and land beyond it. If there isn't room – GO AROUND.
- Apply the spacing advised by ATC, using runway length as a guide to judging distance.

- When following a large helicopter consider allowing a bigger gap than for the equivalent sized aeroplane.
- Keep well away from helicopters with rotors turning, they may be hovering or hover taxiing – it can be difficult to judge.
- If in doubt – WAIT.
- All encounters should be reported.

Full details are published in AIC 17/1999 (Pink 188), 'Wake Turbulence'

16

SAFETY SENSE 16
GENERAL AVIATION

BALLOON AIRMANSHIP GUIDE

1 INTRODUCTION

a. This guide is intended for pilots of hot air balloons, however much of the advice will apply to any lighter-than- aircraft.

b. The growth of hot air ballooning into a significant leisure activity, with many commercial operators, makes the use of safe operating practices vitally important. The objectives are to safeguard persons and property on the ground as well as the balloon and its occupants. The invaluable work of the representative organisation, the British Balloon and Airship Club (BBAC), is gratefully acknowledged and all owners, operators and pilots are encouraged to join and participate in its work.

c. The safety record of ballooning is excellent and many of the criteria which apply to the safe conduct of balloon flights apply equally to the safe conduct of any flight. These can be summarised as sound **Knowledge,** careful **Preparation,** and the exercise of good **Practice.** These are detailed below.

2 KNOWLEDGE

a. Reporting

Learn from the mistakes of others; you might not live long enough to make them all yourself. Share your knowledge and experience with others by making a report to the BBAC, and to the Safety Data Department of the Civil Aviation Authority, on any incidents from which you think others might learn.

Your report could prevent someone else's accident. Improve your knowledge by reading as many accounts of other people's ballooning problems as you can. The BBAC Pilot's Circular, CAA Balloon Notices, Bulletins issued by the General Aviation Safety Council and by the Air Accident Investigation Branch of the Department of Transport, are regular sources of safety information.

b. Statistics

Accurate statistics for ballooning are difficult to obtain. A total of almost 1700 hot air balloons are now registered in the UK. There is no record of the total number of balloon flights, however, in 1996 there were nearly 9000 flights by about 200 commercial balloons, during which over 66,000 passengers were carried. During 1995/96 there were 14 Reportable accidents to balloons; fortunately there were no fatalities, but 11 passengers received injuries and a number of balloons were damaged. The most potentially serious situation which a balloon can encounter, other than mid-air collision, is to be in close proximity to, and up-wind of, over-head electricity cables. In 1995/96 nearly 40% of accidents were due to wire strikes.

c. Training

Keep in regular flying practice; you will handle difficult situations more effectively if you are current. Check that you have sufficient recent flying experience to maintain the validity of the licence, and that your medical certificate is current. Occasionally fly with an experienced pilot/instructor/ examiner who can identify any bad flying habits you may have inadvertently acquired.

3 PREPARATION FOR FLIGHT

a. Paperwork

Formal documentation for private flight is relatively simple, but keeping a balloon and Personal Flying Log Book requires a responsible attitude. Commercial operators of balloons for Public Transport must keep a Technical Log and sign for the condition and loading of the balloon before flight.

Documents and data, i.e. Flight Manuals and Log Books, must be kept up to date for all balloons so that the condition and loading of the balloon can be established before the next flight. The Annual or 100 hour inspection must be completed when due and properly certificated before further flight.

b. Balloon Condition

Commercial balloons must be maintained to a high standard and operators are required to provide evidence of this in the Technical Log and Balloon Log Book. Private balloons must be maintained to no less a standard by using similar procedures. You must ensure that all damage or defects, even minor (balloons are not 'self-healing'), are put right in accordance with the Manufacturer's instructions, before further flight. It is the pilot's responsibility to ensure that the balloon is airworthy before flight. **Never use unauthorised or improper parts in a balloon.**

c. **Weather**

Make maximum use of weather forecasts for ballooning. These are available by phone and fax from a number of commercial sources in addition to the existing Met. Office Services. The various methods of obtaining aviation weather, (including codes) are available in a small booklet **'GET MET'**. This is available from the Met office and may be downloaded free from their web site. Avoid personal or commercial pressure to fly and, if in doubt about the conditions, **don't.** Remember the adage about its better to be on the ground wishing you were flying than the other way round! Know and comply with the Visual Flight Rules as well as with the wind speed limits of the balloon, and what the pilot feels comfortable with.

d. **Maps and Charts**

The Air Navigation Order (ANO) requires you to carry an up-to-date chart, for obvious and sensible reasons. Balloon pilots probably need more information than most from their maps and charts because their landing area is uncertain until the final stages of the flight. Ordnance Survey maps, marked with sensitive landing and over-flying areas, are needed as well as aeronautical charts. Keep yours up-to-date and don't fly without them.

e. **Flight Planning and Navigation**

The more time you spend in preparation, the better you will enjoy the flight. Armed with appropriate maps and charts, and in possession of a recent aviation weather forecast, you should be able to make a reasonable estimate of the expected track. Study the available information for the route, including NOTAMs. Check for the proximity of regulated airspace, Danger Areas, sensitive areas and other hazards, including major overhead power lines. Attention to this will avoid last minute unfolding of maps in flight and thumbing through flight guides for the frequency of an airfield you are approaching. Call the AIS **Freephone number, 0500 354802,** for the latest information on Royal Flights, Red Arrows Displays and Airspace Restrictions.

f. **Landing Area**

Plan to land in an area which provides a choice of suitable sites.

Avoid being committed to land in an area which does not offer any alternatives if an initial approach has to be abandoned. **You must not plan to land within the congested area of a city, town or settlement.**

g. **Radio**

Carry a radio if there is a possibility that you will approach controlled airspace or an active Aerodrome Traffic Zone. Ground crews prefer that they, and you, have a well-charged radio and know how to use it. A VHF R/T licence is required if an aeronautical frequency is used. A licence for any R/T equipment must be obtained from the CAA's Directorate of Airspace Policy Surveillance and Spectrum Management. Keep transmissions brief and to the point, and brush-up your radio procedures by reading the Radiotelephony Manual, CAP413 available free from the CAA web site www.caa.co.uk/publications.

h. **Loading**

Make sure that the empty weight of the balloon, including equipment, fuel cylinders and contents, is available and accurate. Use actual weights for passengers and crew and add an allowance for miscellaneous items such as camera bags. (You may need to have 'bathroom scales' available.) Use Flight Manual figures for calculating available **lift** and **do not exceed this figure.** Remember, there is significant loss of lifting capability on a hot day. Excessive heating will shorten the life of the balloon.

i. **Re-fuelling and Fuel Planning**

Use fuel from a reliable source. As Propane is considerably more volatile than petrol and is stored under pressure, treat it with the respect it deserves. Re-fill cylinders in well-ventilated surroundings free of static discharge or other source of combustion. **Make sure no-one is smoking.** Keep equipment in good condition and observe the Propane Code, available from the BBAC. Propane vapour pressure is reduced by low ambient temperature resulting in loss of burner efficiency, and thus balloon performance. Nitrogen pressurisation has largely replaced warming of cylinders as the preferred method of maintaining pressure on cold days.

j. **Safety Equipment**

The following safety equipment **must** be carried:

- alternative method of ignition
- protective gloves
- fire extinguisher
- first-aid kit

The items below are recommended:

- binoculars, to help spot power lines etc., and
- protective helmets for all on board when flying conditions dictate.

Pilots and Ground Crew should have attended a fire and first-aid refresher course within the last 3 years. Also check that the equipment is "in date".

k. Ground Crew

Crews should receive training as recommended by the BBAC which is provided in many parts of the country. The training should include inflation, launching and tethering, emergency procedures, refuelling, use of radio, map reading and landowner relations

l. Flight Over Water

Life jackets should be carried when the flight is likely to be more than 1 nm from the nearest land, supplemented when water temperatures are low, by a life raft capable of accommodating all occupants. Check that loading figures take this equipment into account, and that these items have recently been tested by an Approved Organisation. (See Safety Sense Leaflet No. 21 'Ditching' for a list.)

m. Tethering, Clearances and Permissions

Anywhere in the UK:

- in the unlikely event that the top of a tethered balloon is to be more than 60 metres above ground level, a permission in writing must be obtained in good time from the CAA's Flight Operations Inspectorate (General Aviation) (ANO Article 97(3)(c).
- Permission must be obtained from the person in charge of any vessel, vehicle or structure within 60 metres of a tethered balloon (ANO Article 97(2)).
- You must obtain the landowners permission.
- The local Police Authority should be notified of any intended tethered flight.

Airspace
In addition to the above, if the free or tethered flight is within, or will enter, controlled airspace or an aerodrome traffic zone, a clearance must be obtained from the appropriate Air Traffic Service Unit (ANO Article 97(45) and (56)).

Equipment
Equipment for tethering must be in good condition and provision made for crowd control at public events. Check the Flight Manual for instructions and restrictions which apply to tethered flight, especially wind limits

n. Night Flying

Free balloons, and tethered balloons above a height of 60 metres, must display the lights specified in the Rules of the Air Regulations (Rules 13 and 14) when flying between half an hour after sunset and half an hour before sunrise. Particular regard must be paid to the 'endangering' Articles of the ANO (Articles 73 and 74) when contemplating a night flight in a balloon, and the pilot's licence privileges and insurance must include night flying before such flights are made.

o. Large Events

Go to the briefing, pay attention to what is said, and comply. There are no prizes for being first off the ground, or for appearing braver than anyone else by setting off in unsuitable weather. Lives could be endangered and the future of the event could be jeopardised by unreasonable behaviour. BBAC agreed practices are now contained in CAP403, the Flying Display Manual, which **must** be used by organisers when planning an event.

p. Flight Abroad

Make certain that you are aware of the rules and regulations for ballooning, and of NOTAMs, airspace etc., for the country concerned. Take with you all balloon documents, Log Book, Certificates of Registration and Airworthiness, Flight Manual, procedures to be used in the event of interception, and your personal log book and licence. Check insurance cover. You have to file a Flight Plan before flying across an International Boundary.

q. Pilot Fitness

Don't fly if unfit. It is better to cancel a flight than to scrap a balloon. Check the following I'M SAFE check-list:

I **Illness,** any symptoms?
M **Medication,** does your family doctor know you are a pilot?
S **Stress,** any serious personal upsets?
A **Alcohol**/drugs.
F **Fatigue,** good night's sleep?
E **Eating,** recent meals?

4 PRACTICE

a. Selection of Take-off Site

Check that the selected site is sheltered, unobstructed by overhead lines or other hazards, clear of built-up (congested) areas unless an Exemption to Low Flying Rule 5(2)(c) is in force (see para 4g) in which case carefully check the conditions under which it is issued. Also, you **MUST** have the landowners permission. Check that the expected track from the site is clear of controlled airspace, Danger Areas and other airspace restrictions as well as built-up areas. Check that there is a good choice of landing sites along the expected track within the planned flight time.

b. Inflation

Brief an adequate number of ground crew and check that they, as well as the pilot and passengers, are wearing gloves and suitable long-sleeved non-synthetic clothing. Check that the balloon is serviceable, the cylinders are re-fuelled and that loading will be within limits. Test burners and check for leaks. Attach the quick-release tether to a vehicle which has an effective hand brake and is in gear. Before starting the cold inflation, attach the flying wires prior to laying out the envelope and the rip line. Carry a lighter, and spare matches or striker. Keep passengers well clear, but paying attention, and move spectators to a safe distance. The fire extinguisher should be readily available.

c. Pre Take-off

Take your time, use a check-list, and do not hesitate to **cancel the flight** if all is not well with the condition of the balloon, its instruments and equipment, with the take-off site or the weather. Test the deflation system, and double check all burner systems for leaks, contents and correct functioning. Leave nothing to chance.

d. Passenger Briefing

Article 53 of the ANO requires that all passengers **MUST** be given a briefing on what they should do in the event of an emergency etc. The briefing must include the following:

- do not hold on to hoses, valves or control lines
- hold on to the internal rope handles or fuel cylinder rims
- on landing, normally face backwards hold on tightly and always pay attention to the pilot's instructions, keep arms inside the basket and , **do not leave the basket without the pilot's permission.**

It is recommended that children are not carried on any flight unless they are old enough to understand the briefing, and are tall enough to see over the edge of the basket unaided.

e. Burner Handling and Fuel Management

Test all systems before take-off. Memorise cylinders in use and know the state of the others. Plan cylinder changes in advance, watch the gauges and change cylinders **before** the pressure drops. Check the burner after changing cylinders. Double check all hose connections. Know and practice emergency procedures for pilot-light failure, burner failure and fire in the air.

f. Take-off

Make a final communications check with the ground crew. Agree a contact telephone number and hand over the vehicle keys. Use a take-off technique appropriate to the prevailing wind conditions. Employ both ground crew and a quick-release tether in other than calm conditions to ensure a clean departure. Immediately after take-off, check again that all systems are 'go'.

g. Low Flying Rules

The Rules of the Air Regulations apply to ALL aircraft, which includes balloons. Fly no lower than 1,000 ft above the highest fixed object within 600 metres of the balloon when over a congested area (unless in possession of an Exemption to Rule 5 (2)(c) for take-off and climb-out).

Over open country, remain at least 500 feet clear of any persons vessels, vehicles or structures (Rule 5 (2)(b)) unless taking off or landing in accordance with normal aviation practice (Rule 5 (3)(a)(ii)).

h. Avoidance of Obstacles and Overhead Lines

Although binoculars are helpful, if obstacles or power lines are seen at the last moment, make a decision to climb or to land and then **stick to this decision.** For a fast climb, use all burners together, but be careful not to exceed the maximum permitted rate of climb or envelope temperature. To descend, use the deflation valve but be ready to slow the sink rate with the burner when it is safe to do so. Remember, it is easier to maintain or increase the vertical motion of a balloon, either up or down, than to reverse it. From level flight a balloon responds faster when put into a descent than when asked to climb. Do not deliberately fly near power lines (bear in mind the 500 ft rule) and **avoid touching them at any cost.** If contact is inevitable, descend as fast as possible so that the envelope and **not** the basket assembly contacts the wire. Shut down the fuel system and vent fuel lines before contact. If the balloon is caught in the wires, **do not** touch any metal parts. If possible, remain in the basket until the electrical power is switched off. Do not allow ground crew near the balloon until the power is switched off.

i. Controlled Airspace

See ANO Article 97 'Balloon Regulations'. Before embarking on a flight in a direction which could involve approaching controlled airspace, talk to the authority responsible for the airspace. Preferably telephone well in advance, but if an unexpected change of wind during flight is the cause, make early contact by radio to give the controlling authority as much time as possible to consider the situation. Air Traffic often think you are closer to them than is in fact the case. They sometimes forget how big a balloon is and it may not show on radar, so call early! If you cannot make contact and have not previously made arrangements for this situation, you **must** land before entering the airspace.

j. Sensitive Areas and the BBAC Code of Practice

While not really a safety matter, it is relevant that the pilot should be fully aware of the BBAC Code of Conduct, agreed with the National Farmers Union (NFU) and CAA, and observe sensitive areas along the line of flight. Don't frighten animals or damage crops, these are the farmer's livelihood. Ask for permission before retrieving the balloon.

k. Landing

Tell the ground crew where you are planning to land. Check that the approach to the selected site is clear and that sufficient fuel remains in the cylinder in use in case it is necessary to make an approach to an alternative site. Brief passengers emphasising that they must **NOT** leave the basket until told to do so. Stow all loose articles. Locate the rip-line and prepare to use it. Turn off fuel just before touch-down. Avoid the risk of setting fire to crops or scorching grass by extinguishing the pilot-light and checking there is no residual flame. Make sure that spectators are not at risk. When you have finished the retrieve make certain gates are left as you found them, and remember to thank the landowner.

Useful Addresses:

Civil Aviation Authority
Safety Regulation Group
Aviation House
Gatwick Airport South
West Sussex RH6 0YR

Flight Operations Inspectorate (General Aviation)
Tel. 01293 573517
Fax. 01293 573973

Aircraft Registration
Tel. 020 7453 6299
Fax. 020 7453 6262

Personnel Licensing Dept.
Tel. 01293 573700
Fax. 01293 573996

Medical Dept.
Tel. 01293 573700
Fax. 01293 573995

Radio Licensing Section
Surveillance & Spectrum Management
Directorate of Airspace Policy
CAA House, K6G6
45-59 Kingsway
London WC28 6TE
Tel. 0207 453 6555
Fax. 0207 453 6556
E-mail: radiolicensing@dap.caa.co.uk

Aircraft Accidents Investigation Branch
Dept for Transport
Berkshire Copse Road
Aldershot
Hampshire GU11 2HH
Tel. 01252 510300
01252 512299 (24 hr.)

British Balloon & Airship Club
Information Officer
C/o Cameron Balloons
St. John Street
Bedminster
Bristol BS3
Tel. 0117 963 7216
Fax. 0117 966 1168

General Aviation Safety Council
Holly Tree Cottage
Park Corner
Nettlebed
Oxon RG9 6DP
Tel & Fax. 01491 641735

Meteorological Office
Central Forecasting Division
Fitzroy Road
Exeter
Devon EX1 3PB
Tel. 01392 885680
Fax. 01392 885681

Radiocommunications Agency
Dept. of Trade & Industry
New Kings Beam House
22 Upper Ground
London SE1 9SA
Attn. RA2/AMACB
26 N/26.4
Tel.Tel.Fax. 020 7211 0122
Fax. 020 7211 0228

5 MAIN POINTS

- Learn from the mistakes of others
- Keep in current flying practice
- Stick to your limitations and those of the balloon
- Get a proper weather forecast
- Use the latest maps and charts, and check NOTAMs
- Know the balloon, its systems and equipment
- Observe the Propane Code
- Load the balloon correctly
- Have completed first aid and fire training
- Keep spectators at a safe distance.
- Check everything thoroughly before take-off
- Stay out of controlled airspace unless clearance has been obtained to enter it
- Know and observe the Regulations in the Rules of the Air
- Regularly check fuel contents and cylinder in use
- Observe the BBAC/NFU Code of Practice
- Keep well away from power lines **etc.**

SAFETY SENSE 17
GENERAL AVIATION

HELICOPTER AIRMANSHIP

1 INTRODUCTION

a. Although this guide is mainly intended for helicopter pilots, much of the advice will be equally relevant to gyroplane pilots.

b. A review of 42 fatal accidents during a recent 15 year period to helicopters of less than 5700 kg, reveals that most should not have happened. Broadly, they are the result of the following:

• low flying including wire strikes	8
• controlled flight into terrain	8
• loss of control VMC	6
• technical failures	5
• third party into rotors	4
• loss of control IMC/night	4
• collision with ground objects	4
• mid-air collision	1
• unknown	2

c. Comprehensive **knowledge**, careful **preparation** and frequent flying **practice** are the best insurance against becoming an accident statistic. Avoid a complacent 'it will be all right' attitude.

2 KNOWLEDGE

2.1 Reporting

a) Learn from the mistakes of others; you might not live long enough to make all of them yourself. Improve your knowledge via other peoples' problems by reading the CAA's GASIL, the Air Accident Investigations Branch's monthly Bulletin and the General Aviation Safety Council's quarterly Flight Safety Bulletin.

b. Share your knowledge and experience with others, preferably by reporting to the Civil Aviation Authority Safety Investigation & Data Department, British Helicopter Advisory Board, the Helicopter Club of Great Britain, or for gyroplanes the Popular Flying Association, anything from which you think others could learn. Your report could prevent someone else's accident. Photographs often help to illustrate a problem.

c. Details of all helicopter occurrences are on the CAA's Safety Investigation & Data Department database.

d. If there is a Manufacturer's Safety Course, improve your knowledge by participating – it could result in cheaper insurance!

2.2 Refresher Training

Revise your basic knowledge and flying skills by having a regular check flight, (at least every 6 months), with an instructor which should include:

- practice engine failure so that in a single-engine helicopter it is a reflex response to lower the collective IMMEDIATELY and to enter autorotation
- in multi-engined helicopters, practice simulated engine-out procedures
- sloping ground take-offs and landings

- appropriate emergency procedures for the type of helicopter, including emergency R/T call, either on the intercom or by a practice PAN call
- AWARENESS of (but not necessarily demonstrated) height-velocity curve, dynamic roll-over, vortex ring, ground resonance and engine icing situations
- awareness of the importance of maintaining rotor rpm, and proficiency at recognising and recovering from low rotor rpm conditions, both with power ON and power OFF
- operation from confined areas.
- assessment of flight visibility
- other flying that you or your instructor feel would be beneficial.

2.3 Limitations

a. You must know the helicopter's limitations and your own – HEED THEM BOTH.

b. Experienced fixed wing pilots, but with low rotorcraft hours, may be confident and relaxed in the air but will not yet have developed the reflex responses, control feel, co-ordination and sensitivity necessary in a helicopter. They may well react incorrectly to a low rotor rpm warning. (See paragraph 2.2 and 4.9b.) A more cautious approach is necessary.

3 PREPARATION

3.1 Paperwork

Make sure that your licence/rating, certificate of experience and medical are up-to-date. Also check that the helicopter's documents, including Certificate of Airworthiness/Permit to Fly, Maintenance Releases and Insurance are current.

3.2 The Helicopter

a. If you do not fly very often, prior to flight study the Pilot's Operating Handbook/Flight Manual etc. so that you are thoroughly familiar with:

- limitations
- normal and emergency procedures
- rotor speeds/power settings
- the height-velocity avoid areas
- weight and balance calculations
- operation of radio and navigation instruments.

b. Sit in the helicopter and re- familiarise yourself with the external and ground checks, cockpit layout, fuel system and position of all controls etc.

c. Carry out refresher training as described in paragraph 2.2 if you have not flown the type in the last six months. (Many commercial operators require a check-flight if their pilots have not flown the type in the last 28 days!)

3.3 Weather

a. Get an aviation weather forecast, heed what it says, and make a carefully reasoned GO/NO GO decision. Do not let 'Get-there/home- itis' influence your judgement. Establish clearly in your mind the current en-route conditions, the forecast and the 'escape route' back to good weather. Take account of the freezing level. Plan a more suitable route if you are likely to fly over high ground which may be cloud covered.

b. The various methods of obtaining aviation weather (including codes), are available in a small booklet 'GET MET'. This is available free from the Met Office.

c. Know the conditions that lead to the formation of piston engine icing (Safety Sense Leaflet 14). Know the Flight Manual/ Pilot's Operating Handbook instructions regarding the use of Carb heat or Engine anti-ice and comply with them. Include Carb Air Temp and OAT in your regular scan of engine instruments.

d. Beware of turbulent and windy conditions, especially if your experience is limited.

e. In wet weather beware of misting of windshield and windows, especially when carrying wet passengers.

3.4 Winter Flying

a. In addition to much of the information in Safety Sense Leaflet 3 'Winter Flying', helicopter pilots should also beware of 'white-out', due to blowing snow, when landing on a snow covered surface.

b. It should also be noted that there are NO general aviation helicopters cleared for flight in icing conditions. You must use weather forecasts to avoid snow and icing conditions.

c. Wear warm clothing in case of heater failure or a forced/precautionary landing – you can't put them on in flight!

d. A Canadian gyroplane accident was the result of the pilot's eye balls freezing. He lost control and crashed.

e. If operating from an icy surface, take care to open and close the throttle slowly and lead with the appropriate yaw pedal to avoid the possibility of the helicopter rotating on the spot.

3.5 VFR Navigation

a. Use appropriate current aeronautical charts, ready folded to show the planned track. It may be too late when you are airborne.

b. Check NOTAMs, Temporary Navigation Warnings, AICs etc for changes issued since your chart was printed or which are of a temporary nature, such as an air display, or ATC frequency change. (Internet site www.ais.org.uk)

c. Information on Red Arrows displays and Emergency Restrictions of Flying is available on the AIS website and Freephone 0500 354 802, updated daily. See AIC 103/ 2002 (Pink 44) entitled 'Helicopter Flights in Restricted (Emergency/ Incident/Accident) Airspace'.

d. Prepare your Route Plan thoroughly with particular reference to Safety Altitude, icing hazards and suitable diversions. Familiarise yourself with geographical features, time points, airspace en-route and the procedures in any helicopter special routes.

e. If you fly a single engined helicopter and your proposed route takes you over a congested area, forest, lake etc. where a forced landing due to engine failure could be hazardous to yourself or those on the ground, plan a different route – so that you can make a safe forced landing.

f. Note congested areas, high ground, masts and other obstructions in planning your safe altitude; note Maximum Elevation Figures (MEF) on charts. Remember you must not fly over some High Security Prisons and other sites in a helicopter, these may not be all shown on your chart, but are listed in the UK AIP ENR 5-1-2.

g. Plan to reach your destination at least one hour before sunset, unless qualified, equipped and prepared for night flying. (Public transport night flying is prohibited in single-engined helicopters.) You may not spot fog or low cloud at night.

h. In order to comply with Rule 5 of the Rules of the Air, 'Low Flying', you must NOT fly:

- within 500 ft of persons, vessels, vehicles and structures, unless taking off or landing in accordance with normal aviation practice or,
- over or within 1000 m of any assembly in the open air of more than 1000 persons at an organised event without complying with the procedures in rule 5 of the Rules of the Air,
- over a congested area, i.e. city, town, or settlement, below 1000 ft above the highest fixed object within 600 m of the helicopter, unless flying on a notified route under 'Special VFR',
- at such a height/speed combination that persons or property on the surface are endangered in the event of an engine failure,
- in the London 'Specified Area', except on the approved routes

Note: If your proposed flight appears to be limited by Rule 5, first check the full terms of the Rule and, if necessary, seek further advice from the CAA's General Aviation Dept*.

i. If you intend to fly below 1000 ft agl (where most military low flying takes place), use Freephone 0800 515544 for the Civil Aircraft Notification Procedure (CANP) or Pipeline and Power line Inspection Procedures (PINS) to let them know where and when you will be operating on relevant activities (see appropriate AICs and Safety Sense Leaflet 18 'Military Low Flying').

j. Know the procedure if you get lost, see paragraph 4.7.

k. Above all, prepare a thorough route plan (Safety Sense Leaflet 5 'VFR Navigation').

l. GPS is a back-up to other methods of navigation NOT a substitute for them. Double check way- point calculation and entry.

3.6 Radio

a. Know what to do in the event of radio failure, including when flying Special VFR in controlled airspace etc.

b. Have all necessary radio frequencies to hand, including those for destination and diversion aerodromes, VOLMET, LARS, Danger Area Crossing Service etc.

c. When using RADIO-NAV to back-up your visual navigation, note the frequencies and Morse idents of radio NAVAIDs.

d. Brush-up periodically on radio procedures, phraseology etc (CAP 413 'Radiotelephony Manual').

3.7 Weight and Balance

a. Use the actual (not typical) empty weight and centre of gravity (cg) from the latest Weight and Balance Schedule of the actual helicopter you are operating. Helicopters get heavier due to extra equipment etc. Take account of ground handling equipment, camera installations, etc.

b. Check that the helicopter's maximum/ minimum weights are complied with. If too heavy, you must adjust the weight by off-loading passengers, baggage or fuel.

c. Check that the cg is within limits for take-off and throughout the flight. If it does not stay within the approved range, e.g. after passengers have been unloaded, or with low fuel and two heavy crew in front; then in some helicopters, you may run out of cyclic control for landing. You may have to carry ballast; make sure it is suitable and properly secured.

d. Never attempt to fly a helicopter which is outside the permitted weight/ cg range and performance limitations. It is dangerous as well as illegal, invalidates the C of A and almost certainly your insurance.

3.8 Performance

a. Make sure that the sites you intend using are going to be large enough for take-off and landing. Use the Pilot's Operating Handbook/ Flight Manual to calculate the space and power required. Calculate your density altitude.

b. Use the recommended take-off and landing profiles. Minimise flight in the height-velocity avoid areas.

3.9 Fuel Planning

a. Always plan to land by the time the tank(s) are down to the greater of 1/4 tank or 45 minutes, but don't rely solely on the gauge(s) or low fuel warning. Remember, a headwind may be stronger than forecast, which particularly affects slower flying helicopters. Frequent use of carb heat/ hot air will also increase fuel consumption.

b. Know the hourly fuel consumption of your helicopter. In flight, check that the gauge(s) agree with your calculations.

c. Understand the operation and limitations of the fuel system, gauges, pumps, mixture control (do not lean mixture unless it is permitted), unusable fuel etc.

3.10 Destination

a. Check for any special procedures due to activities at your destination, such as parachuting, gliding, microlighting etc. Use the UK Aeronautical Information Publication (UK AIP) or other Flight Guides including NOTAMs and Temporary Navigation Warnings, etc. to find out where the helicopter operating area is located.

b. If your destination is a private landing site, the surroundings may be very different from the licensed aerodrome at which you learnt to fly, or from which you normally operate. The final approach and take-off area should be at least twice the length of the helicopter including rotor blades. There may be hard-to-see cables or other obstructions in the approach path, or hills, trees and buildings close to the site giving wind shear and/or unusual wind patterns. Read the guidelines published by the British Helicopter Advisory Board (BHAB) on their web site www.bhab.org

c. Try to chose a landing site where you can use the recommended profiles, but if that is impossible consider:

- a check out with an instructor or someone who knows the site well, or
- a check from the ground of the potential problems associated with different wind directions, or the reduced climb on a hot day.

Always minimise the time that the helicopter is at greatest risk from engine failure.

d. In a helicopter, you cannot just land anywhere – you need the landowner's (or his Agent's) permission. This also applies at strips and most aerodromes, where Prior Permission is Required (PPR).

3.11 Flying Abroad

a. Make sure you are conversant with the aeronautical rules, charts (including scale and units, e.g. feet or metres), airspace etc for each country you are flying to/over.

b. Take the helicopter's documents which include for example – in some countries the insurance details written in their language, e.g. Spain, your licence and a copy of 'Interception Procedures' (Safety Sense Leaflet 11).

c. Before crossing an International FIR boundary you must file a Flight Plan, check that it has been accepted. (Safety Sense Leaflet 20 'VFR Flight Plans').

d. Don't forget the Prevention of Terrorism restrictions for flights to Ireland, Channel Isles and Isle of Man. (UK AIP GEN 1-2-1 paragraph 5.)

e. Permit to Fly aircraft may need special permission in many countries.

3.12 Over Water

a. Before flying over water, read Safety Sense Leaflet No 21 'Ditching'. Some helicopter manuals/handbooks contain specific advice on ditching including the need to apply full lateral cyclic control as the helicopter contacts the water to stop the main rotor blades.

b. The weather over the sea can often be very different from the land, e.g. sea fog.

c. When flying over water, everyone in a single-engined helicopter should, as a minimum, wear a life jacket. In the event of an emergency there will be neither time nor space to put one on.

d. The water around the UK coast is cold even in summer and survival time may be only 15 minutes (about the time needed to scramble an SAR helicopter). A good quality insulated immersion suit, with warm clothing underneath and the hood up and well sealed, should provide over 3 hours survival time. In water, the body loses heat 100 times faster than in cold air.

e. In addition, take a life raft. It's heavy, so re-check weight and balance. A life raft is much easier to see and will help the rescuers find you. It should be properly secure, but easily accessible as a helicopter will sink faster than an aeroplane.

f. Make sure that lifejackets, immersion suits and life raft have been tested recently by an approved organisation – they must be serviceable when needed.

g. You are strongly urged to carry a Personal Locator Beacon (PLB) and flares. If flying more than 10 minutes over water, carry an approved ELT.

h. Remain on an appropriate aeronautical radio station.

i. Pilots and passengers who regularly fly over water, are advised to attend an underwater escape training and Sea Survival Course (details in 'Ditching' leaflet).

j. If the helicopter is fitted with flotation equipment, make sure you are familiar with its operation.

k. Minimise over water time in single-engined helicopters. (Public transport helicopters are limited to 10 minutes over water when crossing sea areas around the UK.)

3.13 Night Flying

Night flying is a combination of visual and instrument flight, the ratio depending on the weather and background lighting including moonlight. You must have a Night Rating and you should be in current instrument flying practice (e.g. during the previous 28 days). For night take offs and landings, the site and any relevant obstacles, should be illuminated by external means.

3.14 Pilot Fitness

a. Don't fly when ill or tired – it is better to cancel a flight than to wreck a helicopter or hurt yourself!

Are you fit to fly – 'I'm Safe' checklist

I	**Illness** (any symptom)
M	**Medication** Medication (your family doctor may not know you are a pilot)
S	**Stress** Stress (upset following an argument)
A	**Alcohol** / Drugs
F	**Fatigue** (good night's sleep etc.)
E	**Eating** (food keeps blood-sugar level correct).

b. If you have to wear glasses for flying, make sure that the required spare pair is readily accessible. Sunglasses and a peaked cap may be useful.

c. During hot weather, beware of de-hydration, have water available, the cabin can be like a greenhouse.

d. Wear clothes that cover the limbs and give some protection in the event of fire. Avoid synthetic material which melts into the skin.

4 PRACTICE

4.1 Pre-Flight

a. After removing blade tie-downs, pitot and engine covers, complete a thorough pre-flight inspection, paying particular attention that swashplate, control rods etc. are secure and in good condition – climbing may be necessary. Don't forget any 'telatemps' designed to show overheating. Use the check list.

b. Check the surrounding area for loose objects that could blow about in the rotor wash and that the rotor disc will be well clear of obstacles.

c. Determine visually that you have enough fuel of the right type. Don't let anyone confuse AVGAS and AVTUR. Personally supervise re-fuelling and be aware of the danger of static electricity. If necessary use a dip-stick to check fuel levels. Make sure the filler caps are properly secured and the earthing cable disconnected. With the fuel selector ON, check fuel drains for water and other contamination. Minimise 'Rotors Running' refuelling, which should only be done if approved in the Flight Manual.

d. Check engine and transmission oil levels and, if necessary, top them up. Don't be fooled by a 'tide line' on the sight glass, this has led to failures as there was no oil in the gear box. (See also Airworthiness Notice No 12 Appendix 43 'Helicopter Gearbox Oil Level Sight Glasses'.)

e. Check engine intake(s) for foreign objects, particularly on turbine helicopters.

f. Remove all ice, snow and FROST from the helicopter. Even light frost can disturb the air flow over an aerofoil surface. (Beware of re-freezing.) Only use authorised de-icing fluids on rotor blades, due to the possibility of damaging the bonding of metal fittings and composite rotors.

g. If you find anything which you are not happy about, get further advice.

h. When doing the internal checks, use the check list. Confirm visually that the rotor blades move correctly in response to control inputs.

i. Properly secure any baggage so that nothing can foul the controls. Beware of loose items, e.g. cameras being carried by passengers.

j. Make sure all baggage doors are properly closed and locked.

4.2 Passengers

a. Removal or blanking of dual controls will prevent passenger interference.

b. The law requires that you MUST brief passengers on the location and use of doors, emergency exits and safety harnesses as well as emergency procedures. Personally check that doors and hatches are secure (Safety Sense Leaflet 2 'Care of Passengers').

c. Centralise the controls and switch on the beacon/strobe. Do not start the engine until all ground personnel are well clear of the helicopter and all passengers are seated inside with the doors secure.

d. Do not let passengers step up into the helicopter and then wave to their friend, their hands may be much too close to the rotor disc.

e. If it is necessary for passengers to get in or out with the rotors turning, brief someone to escort passengers to and from the helicopter. Passengers may behave oddly and do silly things in the wind and noise of a running helicopter, childrens' hands should be firmly held. Always approach from the front, wait outside the rotor disc until the pilot has given a 'thumbs up'. NEVER walk uphill away from a helicopter or downhill towards a helicopter, the rotor tip may do more than part your hair!

Note: AIC 'Propeller and Rotor Markings', provides good advice on colours to make rotors much more visible (AIC 83/ 1997, Pink 150).

f. Some passengers may be affected by flicker vertigo, see AIC 73/ 2001 (Pink 23) 'The Effect of Flickering Light on Passengers and Crew'.

4.3 Starting Engine(s)

a. Know where to find and how to use the helicopter's fire extinguisher, as well as the location of any others in the vicinity.

b. Use the check-list and closely monitor the appropriate gauge(s).

c. If parked on snow or ice don't forget the possibility of the helicopter yawing. Open and close the throttle carefully

4.4 Take-off

a. Know the helicopter Marshalling Signals.

b. Make sure you know the maximum demonstrated sideways speed for the helicopter type you are flying and factor this for your experience and recency.

c. Ensure skids are not stuck to the ground by mud or ice. This has caused helicopters to roll over on take-off

d. Take particular care if you have to lift off crosswind or downwind, there may only be marginal control if there is a crosswind of 10–12 kts from the critical side. This can also affect hover taxiing.

e. Beware of hovering close to tall buildings and hangars when there is a possibility that the helicopter downwash will not dissipate uniformly and may re-circulate through the top of the rotor disc. This will require more power to hold hover height and produces a dynamic force towards the obstruction. As a rule of thumb, re-circulation can occur when the helicopter is hovering closer than two thirds of the rotor diameter from an obstruction.

f. Before lifting off, always carry out a clearing turn. Consider your options such that engine failure will not be a hazard to persons or property on the ground (see paragraph 4.11 on rotor wash).

g. Lift-off slowly into a low hover and check engine gauges including manifold pressure/rpm and control effectiveness.

h. If you take off into a strong wind and then turn downwind with constant pitch and attitude, the speed 'perceived' from ground reference will appear to increase by an amount equivalent to the wind speed. If you then attempt to reduce 'perceived' speed by increasing the attitude, it can lead to the use of high power, together with a reduced rate of climb and in severe cases a high sink rate. You are now in the classic vortex ring condition, near the trees with low IAS and full power. Now get out of that! (see paragraph 4.13c).

4.5 Look Out

a. Always keep a good look-out (and listen-out), for other aircraft, particularly over and close to radio beacons, Visual Reference Points and in the vicinity of aerodromes. The most hazardous conflicts are those aircraft with the least relative movement to your own. These are the ones that are difficult to see and the ones you are more likely to hit. Beware of blind spots and move your head, or the helicopter, to uncover these areas. Scan effectively. (Safety Sense Leaflet 13 'Collision Avoidance'.)

b. Helicopters are harder to see than aeroplanes so if the fixed wing pilot hasn't seen you, you had better keep an exemplary look out and make sure you've seen him!

c. Remember the Rules of the Air which include flying on the right-hand side of line features (even if your helicopter is flown from the right) and give way to traffic on your right.

d. If the helicopter has strobe lights, use them. If you are in a crowded circuit environment, use landing lights as well.

e. Spend as little time as possible with your head 'in the office'.

4.6 Airspace

a. Do not enter controlled airspace unless properly authorised. You might have to orbit and wait for permission. Keep out of Danger and other Prohibited Areas. If you need to transit, contact the Danger Area Crossing and Information Services.

b. Use the Lower Airspace Radar Service (LARS), which is available from many RAF and civil aerodromes, particularly on week days. It may prevent you from getting a nasty fright from military or other aircraft.

c. A Radar Advisory Service (RAS) will tell you about conflicting aircraft and offer avoidance advice. If you take alternative action or consider no action necessary, then you must tell the controller. A Radar Information Service (RIS) gives you details of conflicting aircraft, but you have to decide if avoiding action is necessary. Make sure you know which service you are receiving. Pilots are always responsible for their own terrain and obstacle clearance. (Safety Sense Leaflet 8 'ATC Services Outside Controlled Airspace'.)

d. Allocation of a transponder code
does NOT mean that you are receiving a service.

4.7 En-route Diversion

a. You must not lose sight of the surface unless appropriately qualified, in current practice, and flying a suitably equipped helicopter. Don't fly above clouds unless they are widely scattered and you can remain in sight of the surface.

b. If you encounter deteriorating weather turn back or divert before you are caught in cloud. A 180° turn in cloud can easily become a death spiral!

c. Maintain a safe cruising altitude. Many pilots have come to grief because a lowering cloud base has forced them lower and lower into the hills. You MUST avoid 'scud running'.

d. Unless you have an instrument rating, you are strongly advised not to continue if flight visibility is below 3000 metres. In conditions of low visibility or lowering cloud, turn back, divert or make a precautionary landing. Don't PRESS ON – LAND ON!

e. An occasional weather check from VOLMET is always worthwhile.

f. Divert if the periodic cruise check, such as FREDA (fuel, radio, engine, DI, altimeter) indicates you won't have 45 minutes fuel reserve at destination.

4.8 Lost

a. If you are lost (or temporarily unsure of your position) then tell someone. Transmit first on your working frequency. If you have lost contact on that frequency or they cannot help you, then change to 121.5 MHz and make your PAN or MAYDAY call. If you have a transponder, the emergency code is 7700, it will instantly alert a radar controller. Select Mode C, if fitted.

b. If you are lost and any of the items below apply to you, call for assistance – **'HELP ME'**:

H High ground/ obstructions - are you near any?
E Entering controlled airspace – are you close?
L Limited experience, low time or student pilot, let them know –
P PAN call in good time – don't leave it too late
M Met conditions – is the weather deteriorating?
E Endurance – fuel remaining; is it getting low?

c. As a last resort, make an early decision to land while you have the fuel and daylight to do so. Choose a site with care and afterwards use a telephone so that you can advise that you are safe and obtain a weather update or further help.

4.9 Control Considerations

a. Fly at a safe speed in relation to visibility. Stay out of the 'height-velocity avoid curve'. Above all, maintain rotor speed, needles should be at the top of the green band rather than the bottom.

b. In most helicopters, particularly two bladed teetering rotor types and especially gyroplanes, you MUST avoid any push-over manoeuvre resulting in negative 'g'. This can be one of the causes for the main rotor striking the tail boom with catastrophic results.

c. When flying a helicopter (or gyroplane), with an articulated or teetering head beware of retreating blade stall, especially at or near VNE in turbulent conditions. This may cause pitch up and roll. Recover by reducing speed and pitch.

4.10 Environmental

a. The public don't like helicopter noise. Several aerodromes and landing sites are under threat of closure due to this, so it is vital to be a good neighbour. Read the 'Code of conduct' on the BHAB web site www.bhab.org. Know the noise pattern for your helicopter; most comes from the tail rotor. Often a turn of 90° can direct the noise away from a neighbour. Avoid 'blade slap' on descent by slowing down early with no sudden manoeuvres.

b. Adhere to noise abatement procedures and do NOT fly over noise or other sensitive areas. These are detailed in the UK AIP or other Flight Guides or may be established on a local basis.

c. When en-route, fly at a height/ power setting which will minimise noise nuisance, as well as complying with Rule 5, 'Low Flying' (see paragraph 3.5h).

NEVER be tempted to 'beat up' the countryside.

d. Select sites for practice auto rotations very carefully – HASELL includes 'LOCATION'.

SOME HELICOPTER MARSHALLING SIGNALS

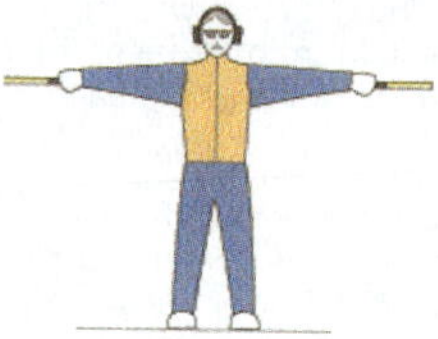

Hover: Arms horizontally sideways, palms downward.

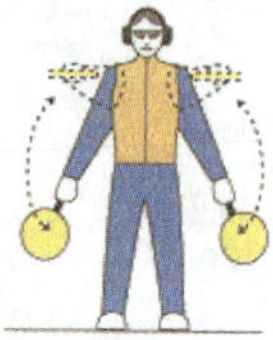

Move Backwards: Arms by sides, palms facing forward, arms swept forward and upward repeatedly to shoulder height.

Stop: Arms repeatedly crossed above the head.

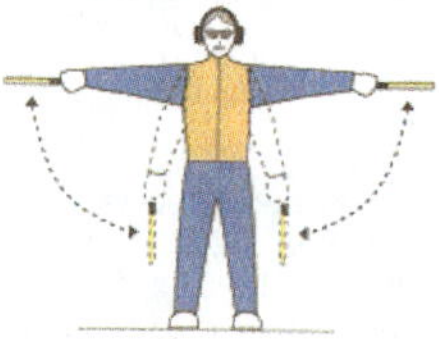

Move Downward: Arms extended horizontally sidways, with palms turned down, beckoning downwards.

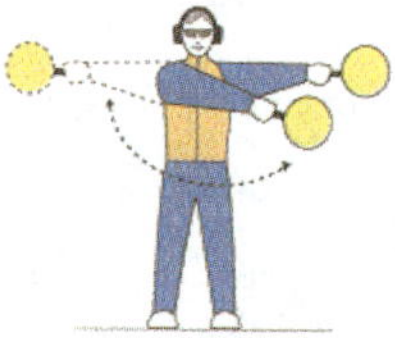

Move Sideways: Either arm placed horizontally sideways, then the other arm moved in front of the body to that side, in the direction of the required movement; repeated several times.

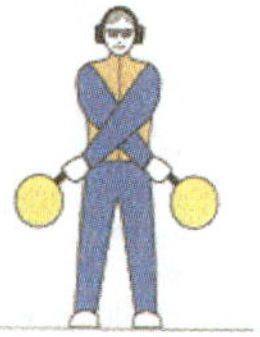

Land: Arms placed down and crossed in front of the body.

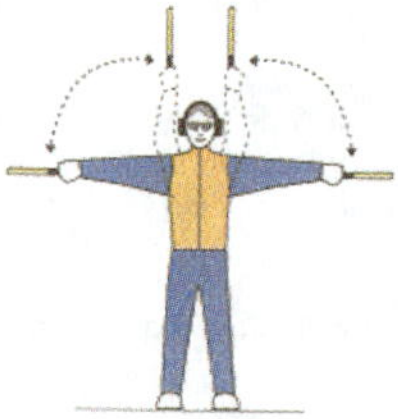

Move Upward: Arms extended horizontally sideways, with palms up, beckoning upward.

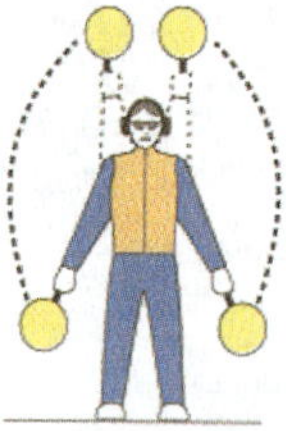

Move Ahead: Arms repeatedly moved upward and backward beckoning onward.

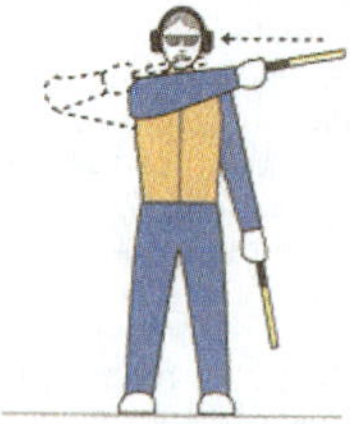

Cut Engine(s): Either arm and hand placed level with the chest, then moved laterally with the palm downwards.

Note: In many cases the speed of arm movement indicates the rate/urgency.

4.11 Wake Turbulence and Rotor Wash

a. Don't operate in conditions worse than those stated in the Pilot's Operating Handbook/ Flight Manual. Remember, these were obtained by a test pilot! If in doubt – replan.

b. Stay well clear of the 'blast' end of powerful aircraft.

c. Always be mindful of the effect your own rotor wash can have on parked aeroplanes and other surface objects.

d. Beware of wake turbulence behind heavier aircraft on take-off, during the approach or on landing. You should remain 8 nm, or 4 minutes or more behind large aircraft. Hover-taxiing helicopters, particularly large ones, generate very powerful vortices. (Safety Sense Leaflet 15 'Wake Vortex' provides further guidance.)

e. Note that wake turbulence lingers **when wind conditions are very light.** These very powerful vortices are invisible. Heed Air Traffic warnings.

4.12 Circuit Procedures

a. When joining or re-joining make your radio call early and keep radio transmissions to the point – 'cut the chat'. If non-radio (or your radio has failed), know the procedures.

b. Check that the change from QNH to QFE reduces the altimeter reading by the landing site elevation. If landing using QNH, don't forget to add the site elevation to your planned circuit height.

c. Use the appropriate joining procedures at your destination aerodrome. Check circuit height and look out for other aviation activity, e.g. gliding, parachuting.

d. Check the windsock or nearby smoke to ensure you land into wind. Be very sure of the wind direction and strength before committing yourself to an approach direction.

e. Make radio calls in the circuit at the proper places and listen and look for other traffic. Remember pre-landing checks – easily forgotten if you make a straight-in approach.

f. If you have to fly a fixed wing circuit, maintain your speed, do not slow down or hover thus creating a collision hazard from following traffic.

g. Be aware of optical illusions at unfamiliar landing sites, e.g. those with sloping terrain.

h. Take care at aerodromes where identification of the runways can be confused, e.g. 02 and 20. Make sure you know whether the circuit is left-hand or right-hand, as this will determine the dead side. If in doubt – ASK.

i. In most piston engined helicopters, apply carb heat well BEFORE reducing power. You may decide to return to cold at 200 ft plus above ground.

j. Reduce rate of descent before reducing airspeed.

4.13 Landing

a. Don't land in tall dry grass, the hot exhaust could start a fire.

b. A good landing is a result of a good approach. If your approach is bad, make an early decision and go around.

c. Avoid conditions likely to result in Vortex Ring:

- Power On
- Low IAS (below 35 kts)
- High rate of descent (over 300 ft per min).

See AIC 2/2005 (Pink 78) 'Vortex Ring'.

d. The unplanned downwind approach is particularly hazardous. It can lead to over-pitching, loss of rotor rpm and lift, resulting in a hard contact with the ground. (Correlators are less effective at high power settings, so maintain rotor rpm by leading with the throttle before applying pitch.)

e. If there is a white H marking, you must use that area.

f. If you are loading passengers, have them escorted to/from the helicopter, or else make them wait until the rotors have stopped. They must be aware of the danger of the main and tail rotor (see paragraph 4.2e).

g. Remember, the flight isn't over until the engine(s) are shutdown and all checks completed and the rotors have stopped.

h. 'Book in' and close any Flight Plan, if necessary by phoning the local Air Traffic Service Unit. See Safety Sense Leaflet No 20A 'VFR Flight Plans'.

A helicopter has the unique ability to land almost anywhere. If, despite our advice, you find yourself in a weather, fuel, navigation or other difficulty - simply LAND and sort out the situation.

Useful Addresses:

Safety Promotion GAD
Aviation House
Gatwick Airport
West Sussex RH6 0YR
Tel: 01293 573225
Fax: 01293 573973

Safety Data Department (address as above)
Tel: 01293 573220/1
Fax: 01293 573972

Air Accident Investigation Branch
Berkshire Copse Road
Aldersot
Hants GU11 2HH
Tel: 01252 512299
Fax: 01252 376999

British Helicopter Advisory Board
Graham Suite
West Entrance
Fairoaks Airport
Chobham,
Woking GU24 8HX
Tel 01276 856100
Fax 01276 856126
www.bhab.org

5 MAIN POINTS

- If the engine fails in a single- engined helicopter, you must have a reflex response to lower the collective IMMEDIATELY.
- Keep current. Regular simulated engine-off landing practice with an instructor is recommended.
- Know the helicopter thoroughly.
- Always get an aviation weather forecast, and update it through the day.
- Prepare a thorough Route Plan using latest charts and check on NOTAMs, Temporary Nav warnings etc.
- Keep time over water to a minimum in a single-engined helicopter and wear a lifejacket (and a survival suit), carry a life-raft.
- Pre-flight thoroughly with special emphasis on fuel, engine and transmission oil contents, and flying controls.
- Brief passengers/ground staff about getting in and out of helicopters. Either have passengers escorted or shut down the engine(s).
- Don't over-load the helicopter.
- In a single-engined helicopter, bear in mind the possibility and consequences of engine failure.
- Minimise time in the 'avoid curve'.
- Maintain a good look-out, scan effectively.
- Make regular cruise checks of OAT or carb air temperature and when necessary use carb heat.
- Keep out of controlled airspace unless you have clearance.
- Request help early (or land) if lost or have other problems, e.g. fuel shortage.
- Return or land if the weather deteriorates. Maintain a safe altitude.
- Maintain rotor rpm.
- Avoid retreating blade stall in turbulent conditions or near VNE – SLOW DOWN.
- Push-over negative 'g' manoeuvres can be catastrophic, particularly in gyroplanes.
- Remain at the controls until the rotors have stopped turning.
- Don't do anything stupid – become an old pilot, NOT a bold pilot.

SAFETY SENSE 18
GENERAL AVIATION

MILITARY LOW FLYING

1 INTRODUCTION

The purpose of this Leaflet, which is based on AIC 41/ 2005 (Yellow 165), is to inform civilian pilots, in the interests of mutual flight safety, about military low flying training operations in the UK. Low flying training is an essential element of an effective air force and regular training in a realistic environment is necessary to maintain operational capabilities. Over the UK, low flying is carried out by the Royal Air Force, the Royal Navy, and the Army Air Corps. A small amount of low flying is also undertaken by other NATO air forces.

2 THE UNITED KINGDOM MILITARY LOW FLYING SYSTEM

a. The United Kingdom Low Flying System (UK LFS) covers the whole of the UK and surrounding over-sea areas, from the surface to 2,000 ft. This permits wide distribution of the activity so as to reduce the impact on the environment. Military pilots must avoid major built- up areas, Controlled Airspace, Aerodrome Traffic Zones (ATZ) and some other sensitive locations. Inevitably, the protection given to these areas creates unavoidable concentrations of military low flying activity where corridors are formed between them. Where necessary, military pilots, except those of helicopters flying below 200 ft Minimum Separation Distance (MSD), (MSD is the authorised minimum separation, in all directions, between an aircraft and the ground, water or any obstacle), follow established uni-directional flows below 2,000 ft to reduce the risk of confliction. These flow arrangements, which apply in daylight hours only, over areas and through 'choke' points, are published on CAA chart UK AIP ENR 6–5–2–1. 'Areas of Intense Aerial Activity, Aerial Tactical Areas and Military Low Flying System'.

b. For administrative purposes, the UK LFS is divided into Low Flying Areas (LFA). Certain LFA, nominated Dedicated User Areas (DUA), are allocated for specific use, e.g. concentrated helicopter training, and are managed under local arrangements. Salisbury Plain and the surrounding area is a DUA. It is used mainly by Army Air Corps helicopters, although other military aircraft may be encountered. Civil pilots should be aware that night exercises are frequently conducted in this area without, or with limited, navigation lights. Details of the Salisbury Plain night training area are in the ENR 1-1-5 section of the UK AIP. Similar night exercises may be conducted in the airspace of Northern Ireland. Details are promulgated by **UK NOTAM** when such exercises are conducted in other areas of the UK LFS.

c. In the North of Scotland, the Highlands Restricted Area (HRA) designated EGR 610A, B, C and D is used for special training, often in Instrument Meteorological Conditions (IMC). To ensure safety, entry by civil and non-participating military aircraft is prohibited during the promulgated operating hours – between 15.00 and 23.00 (local time) Monday to Thursday in winter, and 1600– 2200 in summer. Details of the HRA are contained in AIC 40/2005 (Pink 81) and UK AIP ENR 5-12. During operating hours crossing permission for Areas 610C and D may be available from **Tain Range on 122.750 MHz.** If the HRA has not been booked for specific military flying, access to the whole of the HRA airspace can be obtained from the Low Flying Booking Cell, on the Freephone number given in para 4d. A civil pilot will be given clearance to operate in the HRA airspace for up to 3½ hours from the time of the telephone application. The airspace is available for normal use outside the above and during Scottish Bank holidays.

d. UK Danger Areas are regularly used for weapons training. This can lead to an increased amount of low flying in the surrounding airspace. Details of Danger Areas can be found in the UK AIP ENR 5-1.

3 MILITARY LOW FLYING ACTIVITY

a. Military fixed-wing aircraft (except light aircraft and helicopters) are considered to be low flying when less than 2,000 ft MSD. The lowest height at which fixed wing military aircraft normally fly is 250 ft MSD. However, in three specially designated areas, known as Tactical Training Areas (TTA) located in Mid-Wales, in the Borders/SW Scotland and in the North of Scotland, a small number of flights may be authorised to fly down to 100 ft MSD. Military light propeller aircraft and helicopters are considered to be low flying below 500 ft MSD. In practice, most military low flying takes place between 250 ft and 600 MSD, decreasing in intensity up to 1,000 ft MSD and reducing further in the 1,000 ft to 2,000 ft height band. However, occasionally military aircraft perform high energy manoeuvres between 250 ft and 2,000 ft during which they rapidly change height, speed and direction.

b. Most low flying training is during weekdays and daylight hours, although it is necessary to carry out some low flying at night and occasionally at weekends. Fast jet aircraft are normally limited to a speed of 450 kts (7½ miles per minute), although speeds of up to 550 kts can be authorised for short periods during simulated attacks and practice interceptions.

c. Low flying takes place in the UK Flight Information Regions (FIR), outside Controlled Airspace, where ground radio and radar coverage is not adequate to provide a radar service. It would be impractical for military jet aircraft to avoid each other by contacting ATC units. With the exception of the HRA, military low flying is only conducted in Visual Meteorological Conditions (VMC), where pilots not only fly with visual reference to the surface, but also apply the see and avoid principle regarding other aircraft.

UK MILITARY LOW LEVEL FLYING SYSTEM

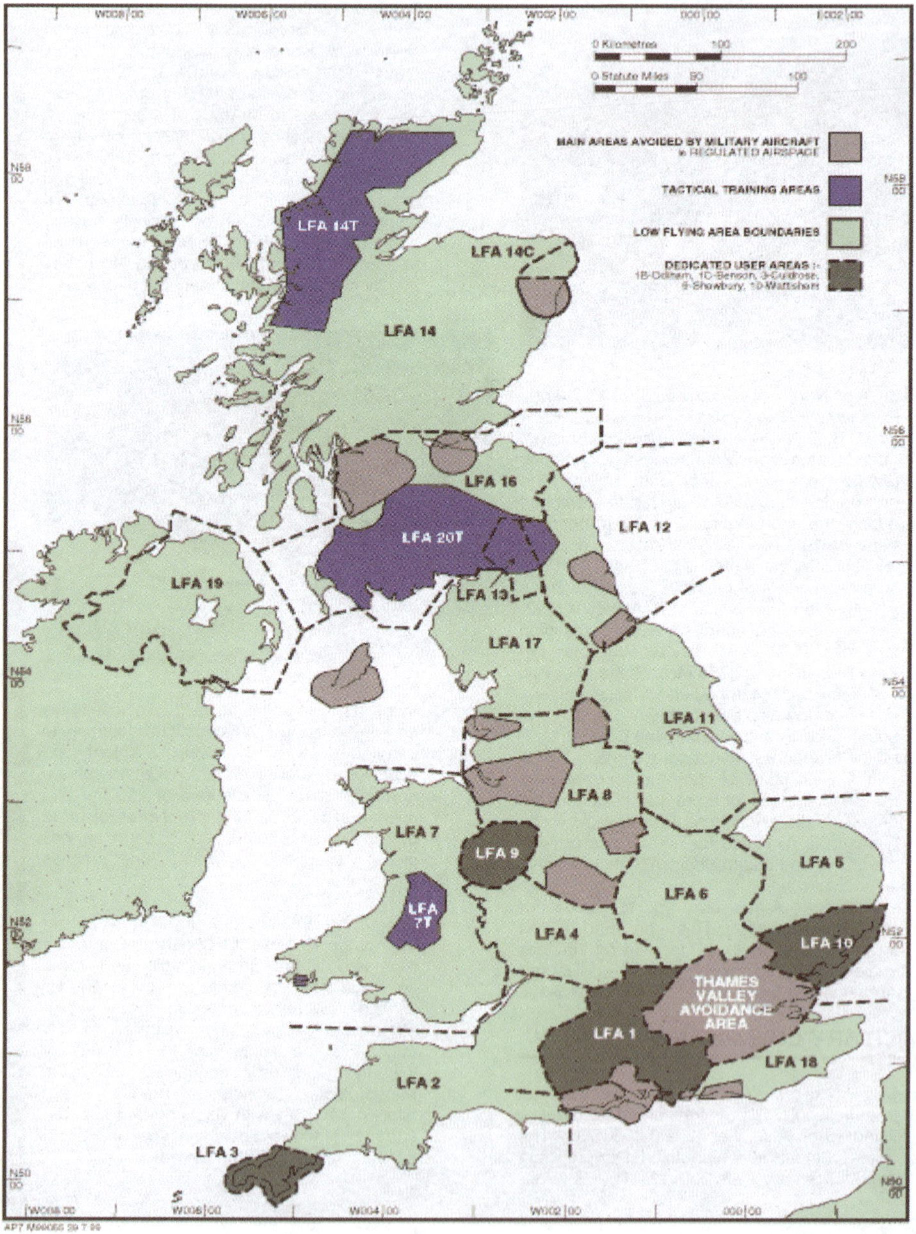

4 CIVIL LOW LEVEL ACTIVITY

a. The Low Flying Booking Cell disseminates the information notified from the Civil Aircraft Notification Procedure (CANP), to all military flying units.

b. Civil pilots engaged in low level aerial work may be subject to aircraft manoeuvring limitations and/or restricted lookout. CANP exists to provide military aircrew with information on aircraft below 1,000 ft agl engaged in crop spraying, photography, surveys or helicopter under slung load work close to a declared site. Military aircraft at speeds in excess of 140 kts will avoid laterally, or by overflying with a separation of **not less than 500 ft** the notified CANP area of operation. However, no provision is made for commercial (public transport) transit flights at low level.

c. **Recreational** activities notified under CANP will not normally be provided with CANP avoidance areas. However, where five or more aircraft (gliders, hang and paragliders, free balloons or microlights) plan to operate at a site which is not normally used, or will be outside the published hours, the Low Flying Booking Cell will issue a warning to military pilots.

d. The Low Flying Booking Cell should be contacted **not less than 4 hours** beforehand, but preferably earlier, to discuss CANP. This minimum period of 4 hours for notification is required so that aircrew can be advised during their flight planning. Notifications with less than 4 hours notice will generally be accepted but as the notice period diminishes, so does the likelihood of the message getting through. A Freephone facility is available on **0800 515544** or Freefax on **0500 300120**. Full information on the use of CANP is published in AIC 91/2006 (Yellow 214) and UK AIP ENR 1-10-13.

e. Pilots should note that information about the Temporary Restricted Airspace associated with Red Arrows displays, **of 6 nm radius**, which may be at country fairs and seaside resorts, is available on **Freephone 0500 354802**. The information, which also includes Temporary Controlled and Restricted Airspace, is updated daily, at about 19.00 hours local. During summer weekends the Red Arrows and other display aircraft may transit at low level between displays and on weekdays may fly contrary to the flow arrows during the run-in to a display. A free sticker is available from the CAA's Flight Operations Inspectorate (GA Safety Promotion) at Aviation House, 1W, Gatwick Airport South, RH6 0YR; please send a SAE.

f. Commercial helicopter operators who conduct pipeline inspection flights should refer to AIC 92/2006 (Yellow 215). 'Helicopter Pipeline and Powerline Inspection Procedures'., and also to AIC 44/2005 (Yellow 168).

g. To reduce the risk of confliction with low flying military aircraft, pilots of civil aircraft on Visual Flight Rules (VFR) flights during the working week are advised to:

- fly above 2,000 ft agl if possible
- avoid particularly, operating in the 250 to 1,000 ft agl height band
- climb above 1,000 ft as soon as possible when departing from aerodromes (or landing sites) in the open FIR, and to remain above 1,000 ft for as long as possible when approaching such aerodromes or sites
- where an ATZ is established, fly circuits and procedures within the ATZ (military pilots are directed to avoid ATZs)

  Note: at aerodromes without an ATZ, military pilots will apply the see and avoid principles
- keep a good lookout at all times, military aircraft smoke trails can be visible before the camouflaged aircraft can be seen. (*Safety Sense Leaflet 13, 'Collision Avoidance' may be helpful.*)

5 OTHER AREAS OF INTENSE ACTIVITY

In addition to the Military Low Level flying system the following areas should also be noted:

- AIAAs, (Areas of Intense Aerial Activity) airspace within which military or civil aircraft, singly or in combination with others, regularly participate in unusual manoeuvres.
- ATAs, (Aerial Tactics Areas) airspace of defined dimensions designated for air combat training within which high energy manoeuvres are regularly practiced by aircraft formations.

  Pilots of non-participating aircraft who are unable to avoid these areas are strongly advised to make use of a radar service and maintain a particularly good lookout.

AREAS OF INTENSE AIR ACTIVITIES AND AERIAL TACTICS AREA

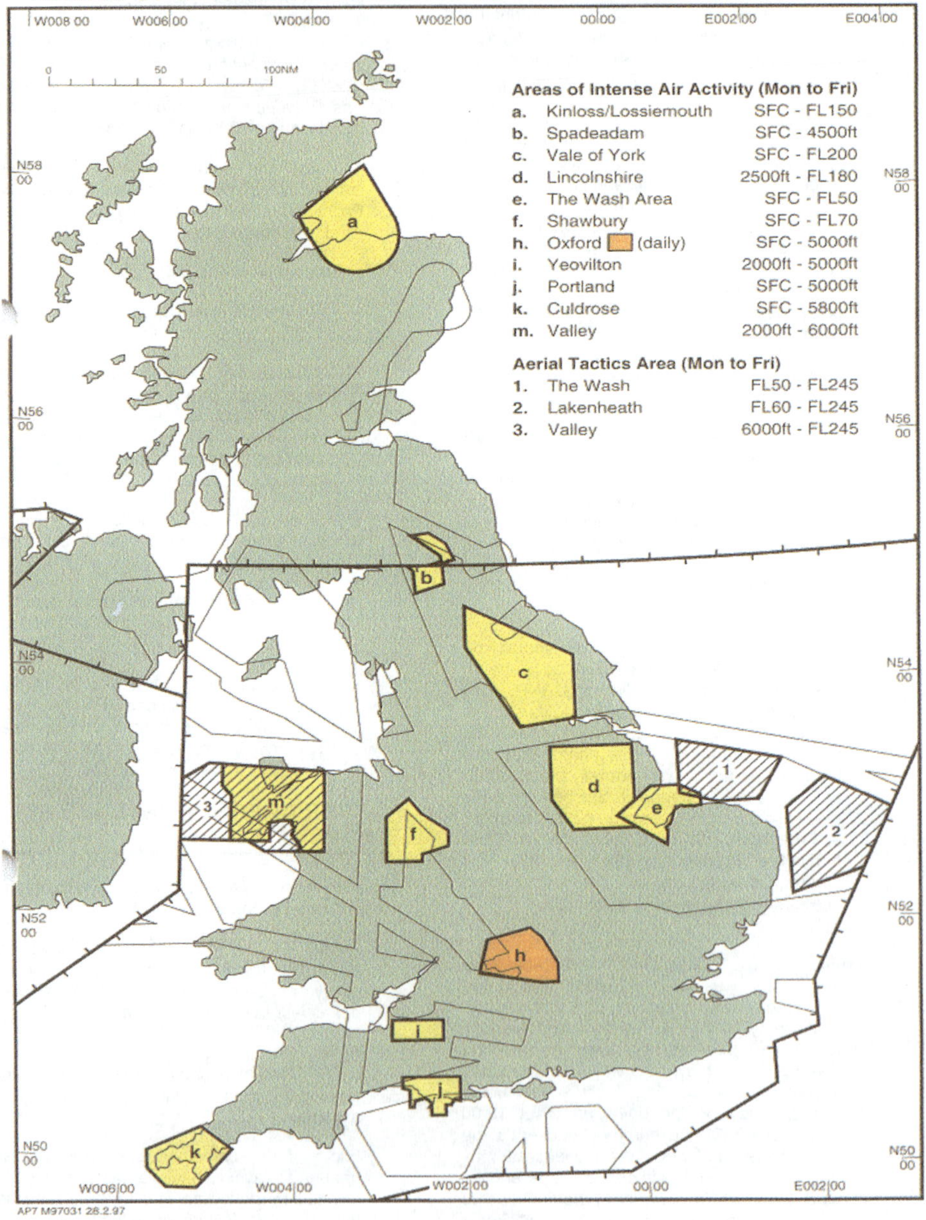

6 REPORTING

Whenever, in the opinion of a pilot (or a controller), the distance between aircraft as well as their relative positions and speed have been such that the safety of the aircraft involved was or may have been compromised the pilot should:

- immediately report by radio to the ATS Unit with which the pilot is in communication, prefixing the message AIRPROX. If this is not possible, immediately after landing in the UK, report by telephone or other means to any UK ATS Unit but preferably to an Area Control Centre

  Note: In the event of a an alleged CANP infringement, in order that radar tracing can be implemented as soon as possible, use Freephone 0800 515544

- It is highly important that every AIRPROX is reported immediately to the UK Airprox Board, when the incident occurred in UK airspace, with confirmation in writing, using Airprox Report Form CA1094 (available from address below) within 7 days to:

  Director
  UK Airprox Board
  Hillingdon House
  Uxbridge
  Middx UB10 0RU

  Tel: 01895 276121 or 276122 (normal hours),
  Fax: 01895 276124,
  Telex: 934725 AFTN: EGGFYTYA.

7 MAIN POINTS

In the airspace used by the military low flying system, as elsewhere in the open FIR, collision avoidance depends on pilots seeing and avoiding other aircraft. Civil pilots can minimise the risk by:

- being aware that military fast jet activity is of a lower intensity on Friday afternoons and, does not normally take place on Saturdays or Sundays. However, there may be a few Hercules flights, some helicopter operations and transits by the Red Arrows and other display aircraft. Public holidays (Vbank holidays in Scotland) are avoided.
- using the Freephone 0500 354802 to find out about Red Arrows Displays etc
- giving at least 4 hours notice to the Low Flying Booking Cell of low level aerial work and other activities notifiable under CANP
- checking NOTAMs etc for details of military exercises, particularly those which include low flying
- flying **above 2000 ft agl** whenever possible
- where possible **avoiding flying below 1000 ft agl**
- climbing above 1000 ft as soon as possible when departing at aerodromes and landing site in the open FIR
- staying above 1000 ft as long as possible when arriving at such aerodromes,
- keeping the circuit inside an ATZ
- **keeping a good look-out at all times**.

SAFETY SENSE 19
GENERAL AVIATION

AEROBATICS

1 INTRODUCTION

a. Aerobatics, whether in a glider or a powered aircraft, provide an opportunity for pilots to learn and participate in a new facet of sporting aviation. It is, however, vital to keep safety in mind, since **a reckless or careless attitude can result in serious injury or death**. Almost every year accidents occur where the height available proves insufficient to recover from an intentional or, more usually, a badly executed aerobatic manoeuvre.

b. The motivation to acquire aerobatic skills is usually a desire to experience the pleasure of being able to control the aircraft while precisely drawing a defined manoeuvre in the sky. A side benefit is that it also adds to the pilot's ability to cope with unusual attitudes and unexpected upsets, such as wake turbulence, in a safe manner.

c. Only a limited range of aircraft attitudes will have been encountered during a pilot's training towards a private licence. Learning aerobatics will extend the pilot's knowledge of the aircraft's performance envelope, while emphasising the need to co-ordinate use of the flying and engine controls to achieve the desired manoeuvre.

2 AIRCRAFT SUITABILITY

a. The particular aircraft which you propose to use **must** be cleared for the aerobatic manoeuvres intended, so a review of the Certificate of Airworthiness/Permit to Fly and the Flight Manual/Pilot's Operating Handbook, including all Supplements, is essential before flight. These will detail the permitted speeds (e.g. Va – manoeuvring speed, the maximum speed at which controls can be fully deflected under normal circumstances), as well as the permitted manoeuvres and load factors, which may vary between two outwardly identical aircraft. The aircraft should, ideally, be fitted with a 'g' meter to confirm that it has been flown within its permitted 'g' envelope. In addition, try to avoid sudden large control movements at any speed, especially when reversing direction.

b. On most aircraft the maximum weight and centre of gravity (cg) position permitted for aerobatics is restricted. Fuel and oil system design may also limit manoeuvres which are possible, duration of inverted flight etc.

c. Aircraft with fixed pitch propellers need particular care to ensure rpm limits are not exceeded at high speed.

d. If the aircraft is fitted with a Turn Co-ordinator, be warned that it can give incorrect indications in an inverted spin, whereas a conventional Turn and Slip indicator will always indicate the correct yaw direction.

e. For aerobatics the aircraft must have a full harness, but a lap strap and diagonal is permitted for spinning. Be sure that you understand the restraint system – some aerobatic aircraft have two separate, independent restraints.

f. A serviceable transponder can be used to warn air traffic radar units that you are carrying out aerobatics. Select 7004 (with Mode 'C' if fitted) a few minutes before starting your practice.

g. If there are any aspects concerning the aircraft or its suitability that you do not fully understand, seek advice from a suitable, knowledgeable person.

3 PHYSIOLOGICAL ASPECTS

a. Aerobatic manoeuvres involving changes of aircraft attitude cause marked effects on the balance apparatus of the inner ear. Without good visual cues, erroneous messages from this to the brain can lead to disorientation, so a good horizon and good visibility are essential. Even in perfect conditions, the mismatch between balance cues (which have an in-built time lag) and visual cues (which are instantaneous) can cause motion sickness, although experience and practice will usually overcome this. Non-pilot occupants, or non-aerobatic pilots will be more prone to this feeling and should be warned that it might happen, and that it is a normal physiological response. Any attempt to continue aerobatic flight after the other occupant has gone pale and quiet will inevitably lead to a messy cockpit unless a sick bag is readily available.

b. During aerobatics, 'g' loading causes shifts of blood within the body. Positive 'g' moves blood toward the feet and away from the brain. At about +3½ to +4 'g' a relaxed human being will suffer vision changes, initially loss of colour and peripheral detail (greyout) and then a complete loss of sight (blackout). If the 'g' load increases, loss of consciousness will occur ("g-loc"). Tensing the stomach and leg muscles and grunting will help prevent this sequence (guidance should be sought from a pilot who is familiar with the technique). Other occupants should be advised to carry out the technique when approaching positive 'g' manoeuvres of this magnitude (the natural muscle tensing of the aerobatic passenger may help). They should also keep their head still during application of 'g' to minimise the risk of neck injuries and reduce the likelihood of disorientation. Negative 'g' manoeuvres cause blood to accumulate in the head, and the increased blood pressure can occasionally cause damage. Little can be done to mitigate the effects of negative 'g', which is poorly tolerated and more uncomfortable than positive 'g'. A person's tolerance to 'g' tends to increase with exposure and reduce with age.

c. Because aerobatic flight places extra stresses on the body you should seek medical advice from your AME, (Authorised Medical Examiner), or airsport medical advisor about the wisdom of performing aerobatics if you are over 60 years of age or suffer from any possibly relevant medical condition.

4 PERSONAL EQUIPMENT AND CLOTHING

Whilst there are no requirements to wear or use specific garments or equipment, the following options are strongly recommended:-

- Gloves help to protect against fire and abrasion in an accident. They also absorb perspiration, improving grip.
- Overalls made from natural fibres, with zippered pockets, and close fitting ankles, collar and wrists also give protection, as do leather flying boots.
- Particularly when flying open cockpit aeroplanes, a lightweight helmet gives protection while minimising discomfort under increased 'G' loadings.
- Parachutes are useful emergency equipment and in the event of failure to recover from a manoeuvre may be the only alternative to a fatal accident. However, for physical or weight and balance reasons their carriage may not be possible or practicable in some aircraft. Even if their carriage is practicable, the effort required and height lost while exiting the aircraft (and while the canopy opens) must be considered. If worn, the parachute should be comfortable and well fitting with surplus webbing tucked away before flight. It should be maintained in accordance with manufacturer's recommendations. Know, and regularly rehearse, how to use it, and remember the height required to abandon your aircraft when deciding the minimum recovery height for your manoeuvres.
- Don't take any potential loose articles e.g. coins, keys.

5 INSTRUCTION

a. As with any other aspect of aviation, the acquisition of skill and knowledge is most effective and enjoyable with high quality instruction. (There is a formal qualification to enable instructors to teach aerobatics.) Effective pre-flight briefing is essential if full benefit is to be gained from any course of training. Initially, keep the flight lessons as short as possible concentrating on simple, positive 'g' manoeuvres, such as loops and barrel rolls, to start with. Make the post flight analysis and discussion session a worthwhile contribution towards the next training flight.

b. The Aircraft Owners and Pilots Association, (AOPA), have published an aerobatic syllabus and training is available at some flying clubs. General handling, to revise those skills acquired during PPL training is necessary before learning basic aerobatic manoeuvres. Since the PPL syllabus now only includes incipient spinning, you **must** now become familiar with entry to and recovery from a fully developed spin since a poorly executed aerobatic manoeuvre can result in an unintentional spin. Training in recovery from incorrectly executed manoeuvres and unusual attitudes is essential. On completion of the AOPA Aerobatic Course a pilot should be capable of flying a simple sequence of manoeuvres in a safe manner.

c. Know the spin characteristics of the aircraft even though you may have no intention of entering a spin. Know also the different symptoms of erect and inverted spins and the appropriate recovery drills for each type of spin.

d. Ensure you learn the safest way of recovering from each manoeuvre if it goes wrong **and be prepared to use it in the future.** Continuing to pull is usually less safe than rolling to the nearest horizon.

e. Novices should not attempt new manoeuvres without proper qualified instruction, the result could be an over- stressed aircraft or an accident.

6 AIRCRAFT CHECKS

a. Maintain a close liaison with the person/ organisation responsible for maintenance so that the maintenance schedule may be interpreted to its best effect when taking into account the particular needs of an aerobatic aircraft. Homebuilt and other 'Permit' aircraft are not subject to a formal Maintenance Schedule, thus the engineer who maintains the aircraft should be familiar with the type and the critical areas to inspect.

b. The pre- flight inspection needs to be carried out with extra care, since the aircraft will be flown nearer to its performance and structural limits than usual. Ask other owners/users of the specific aircraft type about items which need particular scrutiny.

c. Check that items of cockpit equipment, such as the fire extinguisher, are properly secured and check VERY carefully for any loose objects which might be present. Even the most insignificant item could lodge in such a manner as to restrict control movement. Dust and dirt from the floor, under negative 'g' situations can get in the pilot's eyes.

d. Make sure that there is sufficient fuel for the flight whilst still remaining within the **aerobatic** weight and cg envelope.

7 PREPARATION FOR FLIGHT

a. Make sure you all are tightly strapped in, yet still able to move the controls to their full travel without difficulty. It is essential that you feel part of the aircraft and not a loose object within it. Tuck away the surplus harness adjustment.

b. Check that the rudder, which on the ground may be restricted by nosewheel steering or braking, does have FULL travel.

8 PRE-AEROBATIC VITAL ACTIONS

a. Weather conditions must be suitable. There must be good visibility, a clear horizon all round and space to remain clear of cloud under VFR.

b. Allow plenty of height from ground to cloud base. Recognition and recovery from an inadvertent spin and the subsequent dive may require many hundreds of feet, (e.g. a Chipmunk requires 250 feet per turn and 1200 feet for the dive recovery). In an aircraft with a low power to weight ratio, remember to allow sufficient height to complete an aerobatic sequence before reaching the base height.

c. Be considerate to those on the ground. Do not always use a particular area for aerobatic practice to the annoyance of those who desire peace and quiet. Avoid also regular VFR routes and areas well known to have frequent traffic, e.g. PPL training areas.

d. The standard HASELL check needs to be carried out with particular vigilance.

- **H**eight - depends on experience of pilot, but novices should commence at no less than 5000 ft above ground level and all manoeuvres should be completed by 3000 ft agl.

- **A**irframe - flaps up, brakes off, (in some aircraft brake application restricts rudder movement), wheels up, etc. to suit your particular aircraft.

- **S**ecurity - all harnesses fastened, canopy/ doors secure and no loose articles.

- **E**ngine - all engine instruments reading normally, mixture rich, carb heat check, adequate fuel selected and electric fuel pump on if applicable.

- **L**ocation - clear of congested areas and outside or below any controlled airspace (unless appropriate permission from the controlling ATC unit has been given). An area offering good forced landing options in the event of engine problems is wise. Note a good landmark to assist orientation.

- **L**ook-out - clearing turns in both directions and check above and particularly below.

e. Look-out needs to be comprehensive at all times, checking between manoeuvres and sequences, to avoid any risk of confliction with other aircraft.

9 SPORTING AND COMPETITION ASPECTS

a. Once the basic skills have been mastered, many pilots are quite content with the occasional aerobatic flight in a club aircraft to enhance their pleasures of aviation.

b. However, some pilots enter competitions to measure their ability against others at a similar level of attainment.

c. Competition aerobatics is an international sport under the Federation Aeronautique Internationale. The relevant sporting regulations have been prepared by the International Aerobatics Committee who sanction both World and Continental championships. The Royal Aero Club of the United Kingdom have recognised the British Aerobatic Association* as the sport's representative body to foster its development and to organise national competitions.

d. Contests are held at a number of venues each year at the various levels of pilot skill. These are Beginners, Standard, Intermediate, Advanced and Unlimited. Aircraft performance is a major factor in progression up through the system, however a well flown sequence in a basic aircraft can be just as competitive.

*Address:

BAeA
White Waltham Airfield
Nr Maidenhead
Berks SL6 3NJ

Phone: (01455) 617211

10 AIR DISPLAYS AND PUBLIC EVENTS

Before a pilot can perform at an Air Display or public events, he/she MUST have a Display Authorisation permitting aerobatics issued by the CAA (see CAP 403 – Flying Displays and Special Events: a guide to safety and administrative arrangements), for details.

11 SUMMARY

- **Get dual instruction before attempting aerobatics.**
- Check that the aircraft is cleared for aerobatics and know both the aircraft and your own limitations.
- Be proficient with recoveries from spinning and unusual attitudes.
- Start with sufficient height to give plenty of margin if things go wrong.
- Maintain a good look- out and monitor your height constantly.
- Do not exceed the 'g' limits, or use large control movements near or above maximum manoeuvring speed Va. Do not exceed Vne, the never exceed speed.
- Do not exceed maximum engine RPM or manifold pressure limitations.
- Ensure you know the escape route for each manoeuvre if it goes wrong – and use it when necessary.
- Never be tempted to show off with low aerobatics or beat-ups

SAFETY SENSE 20
GENERAL AVIATION

VFR FLIGHT PLANS

1 INTRODUCTION

With the removal of barriers in the European Community, it is now convenient for General Aviation pilots to fly both from their local airfield/ airport, as well as their farm strip, direct to the Continent. However, although British Customs & Excise and Immigration have simplified their systems, the French Authorities have not and it is still necessary to land at a French airport with Customs and Immigration facilities in order to enter France. It is not this leaflet's intention to describe the relaxed procedures operating for Customs here in the UK – readers are advised to contact their local Customs and Excise Office to discuss their own individual arrangements.

2 LEGISLATION

a. VFR flight plans (FPLs) **must** be filed for the following flights:

- A flight to or from the United Kingdom which will cross the United Kingdom FIR boundary.
- A flight within Class D control zones/ control areas. However, this requirement may be satisfied by passing flight details by Radio Telephony (RT).
- A flight within the Scottish and London Upper Flight Information Regions, (but since this will be above Flight Level 245, it seems unlikely that many GA pilots will be concerned with this situation).

b. Other requirements exist for flights where an aircraft's maximum take- off weight exceeds 5700 kg (12500 lbs).

c. In addition, it is **advisable** to file a VFR FPL if the flight involves flying over the sea, more than 10 nm from the UK coastline or flying over sparsely populated areas where Search and Rescue operations might be difficult. In addition, a VFR FPL may be filed for any flight at the pilot's discretion.

d. The Terrorism Act 2000 applies to flights between the mainland UK and the Republic of Ireland, Northern Ireland, the Isle of Man and the Channel Islands.

e. Some European Countries do not accept aircraft which only have a Permit to Fly, (homebuilt aircraft/microlights etc.). It is the responsibility of the pilot/ operator to obtain permission beforehand from the State concerned.

f. In addition, some if not all of the following documents may be required to be carried in the aircraft: Tech. Log; Certificates of Registration, Airworthiness & Maintenance Release; Radio Licence; Interception Procedures (*leaflet 11*); Load Sheet; Pilot's Licence; Insurance Certificates and your passport.

3 DEPARTURES FROM AIRPORTS

a. Assuming that the departure and destination aerodromes are both major airports, the operation of the FPL is as follows. You complete the FPL at the Air Traffic Service Unit (ATSU) of your departure aerodrome and they will file it into the system on your behalf. The effect of this filing will be to inform your destination airfield, together with any of your alternates, that the flight is going to take place.

b. Once you get airborne, the ATSU will file a 'departure (DEP)' message and this will 'activate' the FPL. Thus the destination airfield, knowing your estimated time en-route from the filed FPL, and now knowing your departure time, will have an estimated time of arrival (ETA) at their airport.

c. Once you arrive, they will 'close' the FPL on your behalf, and that marks the end of the operation. If, however, you do not arrive **within 30 minutes** of your ETA, they will institute overdue action and subsequently, Search and Rescue operations may commence. It is therefore essential that if you land at any airfield other than your destination, you **MUST** inform your original destination of this fact, otherwise they will institute overdue and Search and Rescue action, the cost of which may be passed onto you.

d. This has covered the ideal situation where others handle it for you.

4 DEPARTURES FROM STRIPS ETC

a. If the aerodrome that you operate from is:

- an airfield or airport with an ATSU, but your operations are outside their normal hours, or
- an airfield without an ATSU, or
- a private strip.

The responsibility for filing, activating and closing a FPL now rests with the pilot.

b. At this stage, it is important to understand the concept of the 'parent ATSU'. The UK is divided into a total of three areas, each of which has a parent ATSU and the map overleaf shows their areas of responsibility and the table beneath shows the telephone and fax numbers of the Flight Briefing Unit that you should telephone or fax when flight planning.

c. To file a FPL, telephone or fax the Flight Briefing Unit at least 60 minutes before the intended flight. A fax is cheaper than a telephone call. Prior to departure, arrange for a **responsible person** on the ground to telephone the Flight Briefing Unit as soon as you are airborne in order to pass a departure time. This has now activated the FPL. A suitable **responsible person** could be your spouse, relative, friend, fellow pilot or secretary. Alternatively, once airborne, you could ask any ATSU by radio to activate the flight plan, but this could lead to delay if the controller is busy. If it is not possible to file a FPL on the ground, it can be filed while airborne with any ATSU, but normally with the FIR controller responsible for the area in which the aircraft is flying. In such cases the message should begin with the words 'I wish to file an airborne flight plan'. Once again, when this method of filing is used, delays can occur due to controller workload.

5 RETURNING TO THE UK

a. Prior to departure for the return flight to an airfield without an ATSU (when closed for instance) or to a private strip, pilots are responsible for informing a **responsible person** at the destination of the estimated time of arrival. The responsible person is required to notify the parent ATSU if the aircraft fails to arrive within 30 minutes of the ETA. This action will then trigger the parent ATSU into alerting, overdue and Search and Rescue action. Obviously this person **MUST** have the telephone numbers of the appropriate parent ATSU. If the parent ATSU fails to hear anything, it will assume that the flight landed safely i.e. NO NEWS IS GOOD NEWS and no further action is required. If the responsible person does inform the parent ATSU of your non-arrival, then the parent ATSU will go back to the filed FPL to check departure times, routings and so on as part of the Search and Rescue procedures.

b. It can be seen that the **responsible person** is crucial to this operation. If no one is expecting you, no one will be looking for you if you do not arrive. If, in an extreme case, the pilot fails to find a **responsible person** at his destination, then he may contact his parent ATSU prior to departure and request then to act in the capacity of the **responsible person**. Should the pilot follow this course of action, he will be required to contact the parent ATSU within 30 minutes of landing at his destination or diversion airfield, to confirm his arrival. Failure to do this, will automatically result in the parent ATSU initiating alerting action.

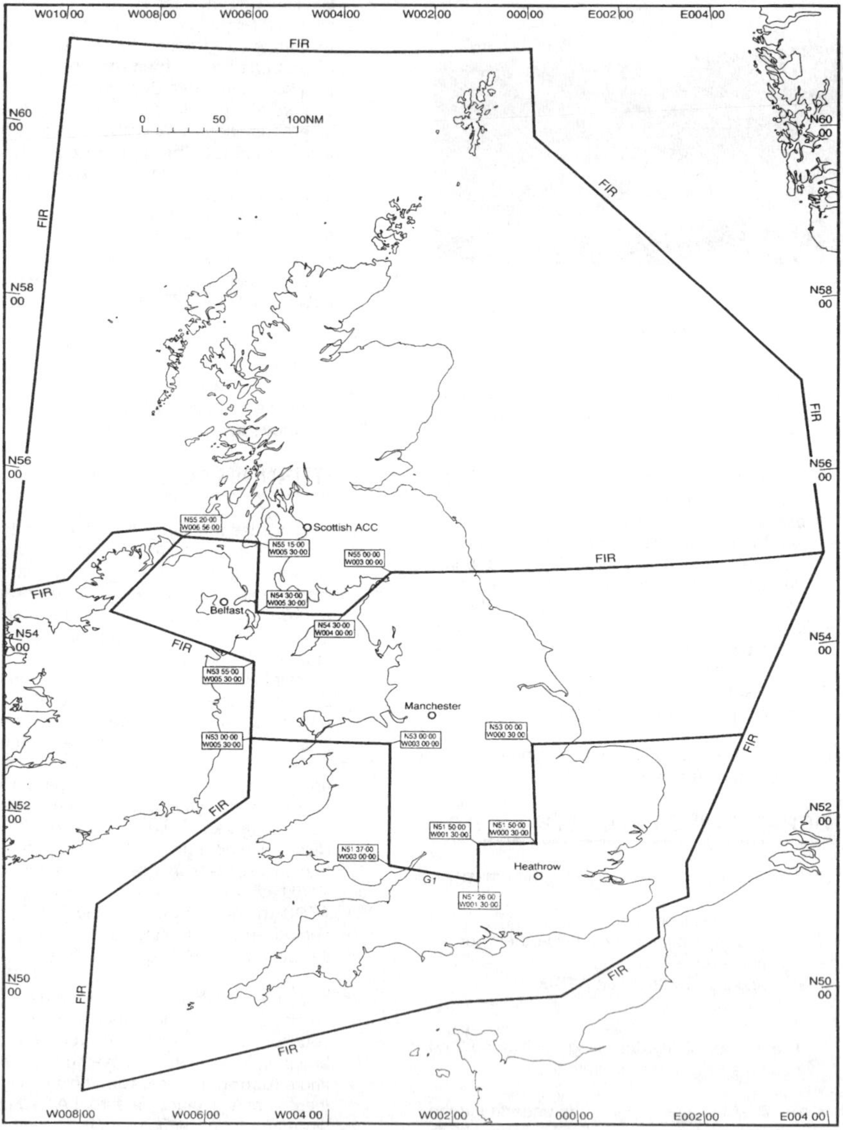

FLIGHT BRIEFING UNIT	TELEPHONE NUMBER	FAX NUMBER
Scottish ATCC - EGPXYFYX Manchester - EGCCZQZX London/Heathrow - EGLLZPZX	01292 692679 0161 499 5502 / 5500 020 8745 3111 / 3163	01292 671048 0161 5504 / 5501 020 8745 3491 / 2

6 COMPLETION OF THE FLIGHT PLAN

Note: that this is an abbreviated explanation intending to cover simple VFR flights. Full details are obtainable from CAP 694 (The UK Flight Plan Guide). An ICAO poster on completing Flight Plans is available from Documedia Solutions at Cheltenham.

Enter all details in block capitals.

Leave the top part of the form blank, i.e. start at item 7.

ITEM 7 AIRCRAFT IDENTIFICATION

INSERT AIRCRAFT REGISTRATION when the radiotelephony call sign will be the aircraft registration (OMIT THE HYPHEN)

ITEM 8 FLIGHT RULES

TYPE OF FLIGHT

INSERT **V** – VFR to denote the category of flight rules (other letters apply if you plan to fly under IFR)

INSERT **G** – General Aviation to denote the type of flight

ITEM 9 NUMBER

TYPE OF AIRCRAFT

WAKE TURBULENCE CAT

INSERT Number of aircraft only if more than 1

INSERT AIRCRAFT TYPE DESIGNATOR or ZZZZ if no designator or formation flight comprising more than one type (see item 18 TYP) **Note:** Aircraft Type Designators for most types are shown in Annex A to this leaflet.

INSERT **L** – Light (17 000 kg or less)

ITEM 10 EQUIPMENT

INSERT Preceding the oblique stroke one letter as follows:

N – if no COM NAV Approach aid equipment for the route to be flown is carried, or the equipment is unserviceable. OR

S – if standard COM NAV Approach aid equipment for the route to be flown is carried and serviceable. (Standard equipment is considered to be VHF RTF, ADF, VOR and ILS unless another combination is prescribed by the appropriate ATS Authority.) Individual letters apply to each item of navigation equipment.

THEN following the oblique stroke

INSERT one of the following to describe the serviceable SSR equipment carried

N – nil

A –Transponder Mode A 4096 Codes

C – Transponder Mode A 4096 Codes and Mode C

ITEM 13 DEPARTURE AERODROME

TIME

INSERT LOCATION INDICATOR of the departure aerodrome or ZZZZ if no ICAO location indicator assigned (see item 18 – DEP).

INSERT ESTIMATED OFF- BLOCK TIME in Universal Co-ordinated Time (UTC).
Note: Location Indicators are given in UK AIP and most flight guides.

ITEM 15 CRUISING SPEED

LEVEL

ROUTE

INSERT CRUISING TRUE AIR SPEED for initial or whole cruise as follows:

N (knots) followed by 4 digits (e. g. N0125)

(K = kilometres per hour). **Note:** there is no provision for statute mph

INSERT CRUISING LEVEL for initial or whole cruise as follows:

A – Altitude in hundreds of feet (use 3 digits e.g. A025)

F – Flight Level (use 3 digits e.g. F055). OR

VFR – for uncontrolled VFR flights.

INSERT the ROUTE to be flown as follows:

for flights OFF designated routes, list points normally not more than 30 minutes flying time apart and enter DCT (DIRECT) between successive points. Points may be navigation aids, or bearing/distances from these (as "DVR05010", or co-ordinates.

ITEM 16 DESTINATION AERODROME

TOTAL EET

ALTN AERODROME

AERODROME

INSERT LOCATION INDICATOR of the designation aerodrome or ZZZZ if no assigned indicator (see item 18 – DEST)

INSERT TOTAL ESTIMATED ELAPSED TIME (EET) en route as a four figure group expressed in hours and minutes.

INSERT LOCATION INDICATOR(S) of no more than two alternate aerodromes or ZZZZ if no assigned indicator(s) (see item 18 ALTN).

ITEM 18 OTHER INFORMATION

INSERT 0 (zero) if no other information OR any other necessary information in the preferred sequence shown hereunder, in the form of the appropriate indicator followed by an oblique stroke and the information to be recorded

EET/ – Significant points or FIR boundary designators and accumulated Estimated Elapsed Times to such points or FIR boundaries, when so prescribed on the basis of regional air navigation agreements or by ATS authority (e.g. EET/EGTT0020 LFF0105 OR EET/ EINN0204)

TYP/ – TYPe(s) of aircraft, preceded by the number(s) of aircraft in a formation flight, if ZZZZ is used in item 9.

DEP/ – Name of DEParture aerodrome if ZZZZ is inserted in item 13.

DEST/ – Name of DESTination aerodrome, if ZZZZ is inserted in item 16.

ALTN/ – Name of ALTerNate aerodrome(s) if ZZZZ is inserted in item 16.

DOF/ - Date of flight if not the date of filing

RMK/ – any additional information.

ITEM 19 SUPPLEMENTARY INFORMATION (NOT ALL TRANSMITTED IN FPL MESSAGES)

ENDURANCE – used a four- figure group to express fuel endurance.

PERSONS ON BOARD –includes passengers and crew, use TBN if number not known at time of filing.

EMERGENCY RADIO –cross out equipment not available.

SURVIVAL EQUIPMENT –cross out equipment not available including S if none carried.

JACKETS – same as above and cross out J if no jackets carried.

DINGHIES – cross out both D and C if no dinghies carried.

REMARKS – enter other remarks regarding survival equipment or cross out N if no remarks.

FILED BY – insert name of the unit, agency or person filing the flight plan.

FLIGHT PLAN

ATS COPY

PRIORITY
<<≡ FF

ADDRESSEE(S)
<<≡

FILING TIME → ORIGINATOR <<≡

SPECIFIC IDENTIFICATION OF ADDRESSEE(S) AND/OR ORIGINATOR

3 MESSAGE TYPE
<<≡ (FPL

7 AIRCRAFT IDENTIFICATION
– G B O M Z

8 FLIGHT RULES
– V

TYPE OF FLIGHT
G <<≡

9 NUMBER
–

TYPE OF AIRCRAFT
P A 3 8

WAKE TURBULENCE CAT.
/ L

10 EQUIPMENT
– S/C

13 DEPARTURE AERODROME
– E G K A

TIME
1 1 0 0 <<≡

15 CRUISING SPEED
– N 0 1 2 0

LEVEL
V F R

ROUTE
→ DCT SAM DCT YVL DCT

<<≡

16 DESTINATION AERODROME
– Z Z Z Z

TOTAL EET
HR MIN
0 0 4 5

ALTN AERODROME
→ E G T E

2ND. ALTN AERODROME
→ E G H H <<≡

18 OTHER INFORMATION
– DEST/DUNKESWELL

)<<≡

SUPPLEMENTARY INFORMATION (NOT TO BE TRANSMITTED IN FPL MESSAGES)

19 ENDURANCE
HR MIN
–E/ 0 3 0 0

PERSONS ON BOARD
→ P/ 0 0 2

EMERGENCY RADIO
→ R/ UHF [X] VHF [X] ELBA E

SURVIVAL EQUIPMENT
→ S / POLAR [X] DESERT [X] MARITIME M JUNGLE [X]

JACKETS
→ J / LIGHT L FLUORES F UHF [X] VHF V

DINGHIES
NUMBER CAPACITY COVER COLOUR
→ D / 0 1 → 0 0 8 → C → YELLOW <<≡

AIRCRAFT COLOUR AND MARKINGS
A/ BLUE/WHITE

REMARKS
→ [X] / <<≡

PILOT-IN-COMMAND
C/ EDWARDS)<<≡

FILED BY

SPACE RESERVED FOR ADDITIONAL REQUIREMENTS

CA48/RAF F2919(REVISED NOVEMBER 1985)

Carto D.O. Drg No 8810

ORS — Safety Sense

7 SOME GENERAL TIPS FOR VFR FLIGHT PLANNING

a. The procedures as outlined above will work when filing FPLs over inhospitable areas or mountainous terrain in the UK. In this case, it can be seen that you will need a **responsible person** at both your departure and destination airfield and both of those will need to have the telephone number of the parent ATSUs in both your departure area and your destination area if they are different.

b. To make the process of filing a FPL over the telephone as speedy as possible, have a copy of your FPL ready filled in, so that you can pass the information quickly in the correct order.

c. Many pilots now file their FPLs by fax. It is suggested that you include a contact telephone number in the remarks section, or better still, **phone the office direct to confirm that the plan has been received.**

d. A test showed that it took well over a minute to fax the top copy of the FPL due to the shaded area, while the non- shaded COM copy took under 15 seconds. Either copy is acceptable for this purpose.

e. If your FPL is for a future date, make sure that the date (maximum 144 hours ahead) is entered clearly in item 18 using the ICAO convention (e.g. DOF/060127 for 27th January 2006).

f. It is essential that ATC is advised of cancellations, delays over 30 minutes and changes to FPL details. To prevent a double entry into the computer which would lead to confusion, always cancel the first FPL and resubmit.

g. When departing from smaller airfields, do not assume that the Air Ground Operator or FISO will automatically telephone a departure time to the parent ATSU on your behalf, check with them or, once again, find a **responsible person** to do this for you.

h. All in all, the procedure is intended to simplify VFR FPLs and to move the onus for safe operation on to pilots.

ANNEX A

ICAO TYPE DESIGNATORS

This list only covers some common light aircraft/ helicopters on the UK Civil Register. The complete list is in ICAO Document 8643, available at most large aerodromes or through the ICAO web site

http://www.icao.int/anb/ais/8643/index.cfm

AGUSTA	A109
AGUSTA/ BELL	
206 Jet Ranger, Long Ranger	B06
BEAGLE Pup	PUP
Terrier	AUS6
BEECH (RAYTHEON)	
most as types e.g. 19	BE19
CESSNA (INC REIMS)	
most as numbers e.g.	C152
except some complex e.g.	C82R
DE HAVILLAND as types e.g.	
Tiger Moth	DH82
and Chipmunk	DHC1
DIAMOND DA-20/22 Katana	DV20
EUROPA	EUPA
FOURNIER as types e.g.	RF4
FUJI FA-200	SUBA
GROB most as types	
except complex e.g.	G109
GRUMMAN AMERICAN	
most as type e.g.	AA5
JODEL most as types	
e.g. D-9 and series	D9
LUSCOMBE Silvaire	L8
MOONEY M-20, 201	M20P
231 etc (turbo charged)	M20T
MORANE SAULNIER Rallye	RALL
MUDRY most as number	
e.g. CAP- 10	CP10
PIPER most as type nos e.g.	J3
but most PA28 piston, fixed gear	P28A
PA28 Arrows	P28R
PA28 RT	P28T
PA23 Aztec	PA27
ROBIN DR- 400 series	DR40
ROBINSON as type nos e.g. R- 22	R22
ROCKWELL Commander	
112, 114 etc	AC11
RUTAN Varieze	VEZE
SLINGSBY T67 Firefly	RF6

SAFETY SENSE 21
GENERAL AVIATION

DITCHING

Piel Emeraude – Irish Sea 1991

1 INTRODUCTION

a. Ditching is a deliberate emergency landing on water. It is **NOT** an uncontrolled impact.

b. Available data from both UK and USA indicates that 88% of controlled ditchings are carried out with few injuries to pilots or passengers. There is no statistical survival difference between high wing and low wing aeroplanes. However, despite most ditchings being survivable, approximately 50% of survivors die before help arrives.

c. This leaflet is mainly aimed at private operators of aeroplanes but much of the advice will be equally relevant for helicopters. It includes details of how to improve the chances of survival after a ditching.

d. Details of the UK Search and Rescue System together with appropriate advice, are available in the AIP GEN 3-6.

2 KNOWLEDGE

a. Do you know how far YOUR aircraft can glide per 1000 ft of altitude in still air? It's in the Pilots Operating Handbook or Flight Manual.

b. The main cause of death after ditching is drowning, usually hastened by hypothermia and/or exhaustion. It is essential to consider the reasons for this and how the risks may be minimised.

c. In many cases, the deceased persons did not have life jackets, either worn or available to them. It is vital TO WEAR a suitable life jacket whilst flying in a single engined aircraft over water beyond gliding range from land.

d. Selection of the correct life jacket is most important, since there are many different types available. Some so-called 'life jackets' are in fact little more than buoyancy aids which are used for leisure boating and have a permanent buoyancy of about 7 kg (15 lbs). This kind of 'life jacket' will not keep an unconscious person afloat. Worse still, the inherent buoyancy may prevent a person from escaping from an inverted aircraft.

e. A proper life jacket provides 16 kg (35 lb.) of buoyancy which can be enough to keep an unconscious person afloat with the head above water. It is essential to use a life jacket designed for constant wear since this has the ruggedness and durability to prevent tearing and other damage during normal use.

f. Many automatically inflated life jackets, used by the sailing community, are activated when a soluble tablet becomes wet. This type is totally unsuitable for general aviation use as they will inflate inside a water- filled cabin, thus seriously hindering escape.

g. Airline life jackets provided for passengers are unsuitable for GA use, because they are not durable enough for significant constant wear.

h. When being worn, the life jacket should not become entangled in harness/ belt. It should include the following (see supplement B):

- a light activated by pulling a toggle or by immersion in sea water;
- a whistle for attracting attention;
- a crotch strap to stop the life jacket from riding up over the face;
- a spray hood or plastic face mask which can be pulled over the face and lobes of the jacket. It will reduce heat loss through the head as well as the amount of water flowing across the face;
- high visibility colour with reflective tape.

i. Wearing a suitable life jacket, is not the end of the story. When not in use, the life jacket must be properly stored in a dry environment and regularly serviced.

j. A life jacket should be serviced at least every year (more frequently if required by the manufacturer) by an approved servicing organisation or appropriately licensed engineer. The weight, and thus contents, of the gas cylinder will be checked, and the life-jacket itself examined for damage and leaks; and ancillary equipment inspected for serviceability.

k. Whilst properly fitted life jackets can prevent people from drowning, none provide any protection against hypothermia

l. Hypothermia is defined as lowering of the 'core' body temperature. In cold water, the skin and peripheral tissues cool very rapidly, but it can be 10 to 15 minutes before the temperature of the heart and brain begin to decrease. Intense shivering occurs in a body's attempt to increase its heat production and counteract the large heat loss. Decreasing consciousness, mental confusion and the loss of the will to live occur when core body temperature falls from the normal 37° C to about 32° C. Heart failure is the usual cause of death when core body temperature falls below 30° C.

m. The temperature of the sea around British coasts is at its coldest in March, and **below 10°C between October and April.** Survival times for individuals in cold water will vary greatly depending on water temperature, individual build, metabolism, fitness and the amount of clothing worn. The graph shows average survival times. Note that without a life-raft or survival suit **there is little difference between survival times in summer and winter**.

ORS — Safety Sense

LIKELY SURVIVAL TIME FOR RELATIVELY THIN PERSON IN CALM WATERS WITH NO LIFERAFT

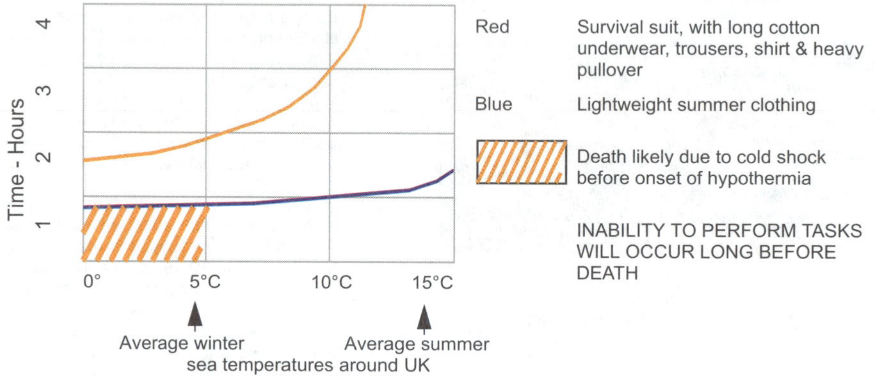

n. In addition, several other responses to the shock of sudden immersion in cold water can cause death:

- heart failure is possible for those with weak circulatory systems, particularly the elderly;
- hyperventilation can increase the risk of swallowing water;
- cold makes coordinated movement difficult;
- ability to hold ones breath is severely curtailed, perhaps to just a few seconds, thus reducing the chances of successful escape from a submerged aircraft.

The effect of shock and panic can amplify the above effects, so it is important to consider ways of reducing the risk of both cold shock and hypothermia.

o. Clearly, the ideal solution is to insulate the body from the water by using a life-raft and/or survival suit.

p. As with life jackets, an aviation life-raft, with a recognised approval, is the safest option and this must also be regularly serviced and properly stored when not in use. The use of a life-raft, together with other survival tips, are detailed later in this leaflet. However, it is important to know how to use all your survival equipment.

q. A marine life-raft is **NOT** suitable for aviation use because of a significant difference in the inflation system. Any malfunction of a marine CO 2 cylinder will cause it to vent INTO the life-raft, inflating it, and filling the cockpit possibly causing catastrophic results. Aviation life-raft cylinders are designed to vent to atmosphere in the event of a malfunction. (Just in case, carry a pocket knife or screwdriver.)

r. If, for any reason, a life-raft is not available, the survival time in cold water can be significantly increased by wearing suitable protective clothing.

s. A survival suit specially tailored for general aviation use is most effective, and can prolong life by keeping hypothermia at bay for the longest time. Whilst some pilots may feel that this level of protection is 'over the top' for a cross Channel flight, there have been cases where lives have been saved by the wearing of such clothing. A leak-proof suit, properly worn, can increase survival time from 3 to 10 times depending on the insulating qualities of the clothes worn underneath. Wear several layers of suitable clothing to create layers of air.

t. As with all safety and survival equipment, it should be the correct type, with a recognised approval, be a comfortable fit, properly maintained and serviced, and carefully stored when not in use.

u. If a survival suit is not used, then generally, the more layers of clothes that are worn, the longer will be the survival time. This will vary considerably depending on the type of clothing and the amount being worn. If time permits, put on as much clothing as possible, including headwear, since a very large proportion of body heat escapes through the head. Wet wool retains 50% of its insulating properties, whereas wet cotton retains only 10%. Watersport suits could also be considered.

v. An emergency locator transmitter (ELT) is a portable radio transmitter which will greatly assist in locating you after ditching. Several types of ELT are permanently attached to the aircraft, and some can be removed in the event of a ditching. A survival ELT (sometimes referred to as a personal locator beacon) is removable from the aircraft and manually activated. It should be able to float, have a satisfactory power output and provide a continuous signal for 24 hours. It should operate on 406 MHz for initial satellite alerting, and on 121.5 MHz for rescue service homing.

w. Signals from an activated ELT can be received by orbiting INMARSAT or dedicated COSPAS/SARSAT satellites. These relay alerts to the Rescue Co-ordination Centres. The time between activation and alerting the RCC should not exceed 90 minutes in the worst case.

x. Pilots should attempt to transmit an initial distress call on a conventional communications radio BEFORE ditching to alert the RCC. The 121.5 MHz transmissions can then guide the rescue services to you.

y. ELTs are designed to float in the water with the transmitting aerial pointing upwards – the aerial's optimum transmitting position. Most ELTs have a battery test facility. Users **MUST NOT** test the transmit facility – this must only be done by an avionics engineer.

3 PREPARATION

a. Many ditchings and subsequent drownings could have been prevented by careful planning and preparation.

b. Those who frequently fly over-water should consider attending a survival course. Here, in a non-threatening environment, you will be taught the correct operation of life jackets, methods of getting into life-rafts and the problems which might be encountered after a ditching.

c. Some specialist companies arrange sessions in swimming pools with wave machines whilst others have light aircraft structures which can be used as 'dunkers' to practice underwater escapes.

d. On the day of the flight, obtaining and correctly interpreting the weather forecast is vital. Whilst the weather might be pleasant on one side of the Channel, it may be very different on the other side. It would be no fun to leave English shores in CAVOK, only to struggle against unexpected headwinds, find sea fog or lowering cloudbases resulting from warm air over the cold sea any of which could force you to return.

e. Use forecast wind to ensure that enough fuel is onboard for the flight, **plus any diversions**, which may include a return from overhead the destination or else to a suitable alternative airfield. In many accidents and some ditchings, the reason for engine stoppage has proved to be fuel exhaustion.

f. Thorough pre-flight inspection of the aircraft is essential, including double- checking that fuel and oil levels are satisfactory.

g. A 4-person life-raft can weigh as much as 15 kg (35 lb.) and is a significant extra load. Take care to determine the total weight and centre of gravity position and take these into account (*see Safety Sense leaflet 9 – Aircraft weight and balance*).

h. Pilots must review any recommended procedures contained in the Aircraft Flight Manual or Pilot's Operating Handbooks for both a power-on and power-off ditching.

i. The law requires that, as commander of the aircraft, you **MUST** brief the passengers on the emergency escape features of the aircraft, operation of the seats, seatbelts etc. On a flight across water in a single engined aircraft, this briefing should be extended to ensure that each passenger knows how to operate the life jacket they should be wearing. Brief the passengers on the contents and the features found on the life jacket, including how to inflate it if the bottle fails.

j. Before boarding the aircraft, brief the passengers carefully:

- on the location of the life-raft;
- on the order in which people should vacate the aircraft in the event of a ditching and who will be responsible for taking the life-raft with them;
- that life jackets must **not** be inflated until clear of the aircraft and that the instructions normally state – 'pull the toggle' to inflate;
- to remove headsets and glasses and to stow glasses on their person prior to touchdown
- tighten seat straps/harnesses prior to touchdown on the water. Rear seat passengers should assume a braced position;
- indicate reference points on the aircraft's internal structure that they should reach for when exiting the aircraft as well as any features which might impede exit.

k. The life-raft must be **SECURED** in an accessible position. If flying alone, place the life-raft on the front passenger seat and secure it with the harness. Check it will not interfere with the controls, lookout or exit.

l. Some pilots have a hand-held VHF radio or mobile phone; put them in a sealed plastic bag along with any hand held GPS in order to keep them dry. A waterproof torch or better still a portable waterproof strobe light could also be useful.

m. Once airborne, particularly over the sea, it is prudent to fly as high as can be safely and legally flown. This will give better radio reception and more time between the onset of a problem and ditching. Consider a high level longer crossing compared with a short one at low level.

n. Before crossing the coast, carry out a particularly careful cruise check (FREDA check) to ensure that everything is normal.

4 PRACTICE

4.1 Ditching

a. The worst has happened – you are unable to maintain height and a ditching appears likely. If you are flying a twin-engined aircraft and one engine stops, everyone should put on a life jacket. Make a PAN call.

b. Immediately adjust the airspeed for the best glide speed and taking into account the wind direction either aim towards the nearest coast or towards shipping. Remember, that a medium size vessel is the best choice to ditch near, since a large ship may take many miles to slow down. In any event, avoid landing immediately in front; landing alongside and slightly ahead is better.

c. At this stage, transmit a MAYDAY call, using the frequency you are working or the emergency frequency of 121.5 MHz. If fitted, immediately select transponder code to 7700, unless you are already using an allocated code. Transmit the best position fix that you can, this may be by means of VOR, DME or GPS or even your estimate in relation to the coastline. **Make this as accurate as you can**.

d. Check immediately for any problem which can be dealt with by vital actions such as: selecting carburettor heat, change of fuel tank, use of the electric fuel pump, etc.

ABOVE ALL, THROUGHOUT, FLY THE AIRCRAFT.

e. Conventional wisdom is that the swell direction is more important than wind direction when planning a ditching. By the time you are down to 2000 ft, the swell should be apparent and your aim should be to touchdown parallel to the line of the swell, attempting, if possible, to land along the crest. The table below describes sea states.

Wind Speed	Appearance of Sea	Effect on Ditching
0 - 6 knots (Beaufort 0 - 2)	Glassy calm to small ripples	Height very difficult to judge above glassy surface. Ditch parallel to swell
7 - 10 knots (Beaufort 3)	Small waives; few if any white caps	Ditch parallel to swell
11 - 21 knots (Beaufort 4 - 5)	Larger waives with many white caps	Use headwind component but still ditch along general line of swell
22 - 33 knots (Beaufort 6 - 7)	Medium to large waves, some foam crests, numerous white caps	Ditch into wind on crest or downslope of swell
34 knots and above (Beaufort 8+)	Large waves, streaks of foam, wave crests forming spindrift	Ditch into wind on crest or downslope of swell. **Avoid at all costs ditching into face of rising swell**

f. If you can see spray and spume on the surface, then the surface wind is strong. In this case it is probably better to plan to land into wind, rather than along the swell. Winds of 35 to 40 kts are generally associated with spray blowing like steam across waves and in these cases the waves could be 10 ft or more in height. Aim for the crest again or, failing that, into the downslope.

g. The force of impact can be high so ditch as slowly as possible whilst maintaining control.

h. Retractable gear aircraft should be ditched with the gear retracted (beware of automatic lowering systems). The Flight Manual/ Pilot's Operating Handbook may provide suitable advice. Consider unlatching the door(s).

i. Hold the aircraft off the water so as to land taildown at the lowest possible forward speed, but do not stall into the water from a height of several feet.

j. There will often be one or two minor touches, 'skips', before the main impact with the water. This main impact will usually result in considerable deceleration with the nose bobbing downwards and water rushing over the cowling and windshield. It may even smash the windshield – leading you to think that the aircraft has submerged.

k. With a high wing aircraft, it may be necessary to wait until the cabin has filled with water before it is possible to open the doors. A determined push or kick on the windows may remove them.

l. The shock of cold water may adversely affect everyone's actions and this is where the importance of the proper pre- flight passenger briefing which emphasised reference points and the agreed order in which to vacate the aircraft becomes apparent. Do **NOT** inflate life jackets inside the aircraft, inflate them as soon as you are outside. The natural buoyancy of the un- inflated life-raft may make it hard to pull it below the surface to get it out of a sinking aircraft.

m. Consider leaving the master switch and the anti- collision beacon or strobes on. If the aircraft floats for a while or sinks in shallow water, the lights may continue operating and provide a further sign of your position. Exit the aircraft as calmly, but as swiftly as possible. If it is afloat after the passengers are clear, provided you don't put yourself in danger, deploy loose items that could float on the surface and help rescuers spot you, e.g. blankets, overnight bags, seat cushions. The first aid kit and plastic bag with PLB, hand-held radio, phone etc. should be taken with you.

4.2 The Life-raft

a. Before inflating the life-raft, it should be tied to someone holding firmly onto the aircraft, so that it doesn't blow away. (It will float even before it is inflated.) Do **NOT** attach it to the sinking aircraft. The life jacket harness or belt would be a good attachment point. If possible, inflate the life-raft on the downwind side so that it is not blown against the aircraft and damaged. (A pocket knife to cut the cord would be easier than trying to undo a wet knot.) If necessary and you are able to stand on the wing, it may, be easier to turn the life-raft upright.

b. Should the life-raft need to be turned upright while you are in the water, get downwind of it and rotate it so that the inflation cylinder is towards you. The weight of the cylinder and the wind will help turn it over. Avoid getting tangled in the attaching cord.

c. If possible, get into the life-raft from the wing, or lower yourself gently into the water to keep your head dry. Remove high heeled shoes and **do not** leap or jump into the life-raft as this may damage it. If you have to enter the water first, hold the bottom of your life jacket with one hand and place the other hand over your mouth and nose.

d. Climb into the life-raft. If anyone is in the water and injured or cannot climb aboard, position their back towards the entrance. Two people should then hold the person under the armpits, (not by the arms), while any others balance the life-raft by sitting at the far end. Push the person initially down into the water, then give a good pull as the buoyancy from the life jacket pushes the person back up again. Warn them first!

e. Once everyone is aboard the life-raft, inflate the floor, trail the sea anchor as soon as possible, and erect the canopy to prevent wind chill hypothermia affecting wet bodies. **PROTECTION is the key to survival**. Get all the water out using the bailer and mop up with a sponge or spare item of clothing. If necessary, fully inflate the buoyancy chambers. All should be firm, but not rock hard.

f. Ensure that at least one person is tied to the life-raft just in case a large wave should overturn it; then it should be possible to get back into it and help the others aboard.

g. To avoid vomiting, ensure that everyone takes a sea sickness pill straight away – do not wait for the onset of sickness. The smell inside the life-raft and the loss of visual references will increase the risk of sickness. (Vomiting causes serious fluid loss). The sea sickness pills will normally be found in the equipment pouch inside the life-raft. You can survive around the UK without water for over 4 days. **NEVER** drink sea water.

h. Once the canopy is erected, you will have PROTECTION. Wring out your clothes as much as possible and if you have anything suitable, insulate the floor.

i. Even on a warm day, keep the cover up to provide protection from the sun.

j. Treat any injuries and administer appropriate first aid. It will have been a traumatic experience, some survivors may be suffering from shock, which can affect mental processes.

k. The second element of survival is **LOCATION**, so switch on your ELT. Rig it as high as possible with the aerial vertical. DO NOT leave the ELT lying on the floor. If the hand- held radio is available in the waterproof bag, now is the time to make sure it is ON and working. Selecting 121.5 MHz will confirm that your ELT is working. A mobile phone or GPS could also be useful.

l. Prepare any other signalling equipment which might be available. However, with pyrotechnics do read the instructions first and check, then check again since some are double- ended. (It would be disastrous if you thought you were about to set off a smoke signal only to discover a white hot magnesium flare burning inside the life-raft!).

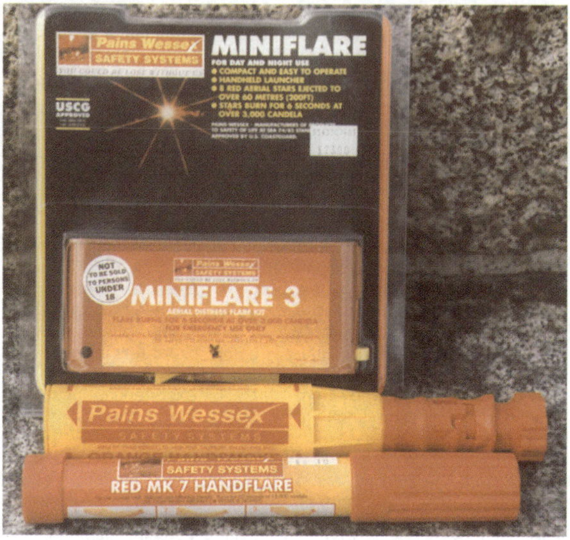

m. Take turns to keep watch and only use flares or smoke signals when you are sure somebody will see them, not, for instance, as a search aircraft is flying away from you. Flares should be held at arms length, outside and pointing away from the life-raft as they often drop hot deposits. If you have any gloves or other protection, wear them when using pyrotechnics. Sweep the horizon with a heliograph, (mirror), at any time when the sun is shining. Any marker dye will normally last around 3 hours in the vicinity of the life-raft, so make an intelligent guess as to when to use it – normally once a search aircraft is seen.

4.3 No Life-raft

a. If you do not have a life-raft, but have to survive in the water with only a life jacket, then this is a life-threatening situation. However, **do NOT give up hope, the will to survive is the most powerful force to prolong life**.

b. The sea is cold, UK waters only reach 15° C even in summer and are below 10° C from October to April. If you are not wearing an immersion suit; then it is **ESSENTIAL** that you and any other survivors immediately adopt the following measures in order to conserve body heat:

- The cold will cause you to lose the use of your hands very quickly, so perform any manual tasks straightaway while you are still able and if possible tie yourselves together.
- Ideally tie the ELT onto the life jacket. Try to keep the aerial vertical.
- Do NOT swim in an attempt to keep warm. The heat generated due to more blood circulation in the arms, legs and skin will just be transferred to the cold water.
- Generally, don't attempt to swim to the shore unless the distance is say less than 1 km and you are a strong swimmer.
- The main aim is to conserve heat. The most critical areas of the body for heat loss are the head, sides of the chest and the groin region. If the life jacket has one, cover your head with the spray hood.

c. If there is a group of survivors, tie yourselves together and huddle with the sides of your chests and lower bodies pressed together. If there are children, sandwich them within the middle of the group for extra protection.

d. A lone survivor should adopt the 'HELP' position (this is the Heat Escaping Lessening Posture). The use of this position significantly increases survival times.

- Hold the inner sides of your arms in contact with the side of the chest. Hold your thighs together and raise them slightly to protect the groin region.

e. A single floating person is very difficult to see from the air. When a search aircraft is close enough to be able to see you, signal using your heliograph (mirror). If this is not available, sparkling light reflected by splashing water with your arms, may attract attention.

f. To attract the attention of surface vessels, use the whistle attached to the jacket; shouting is much less effective and more exhausting to the survivor.

4.4 No Life jacket or Life-raft

a. This is a very life threatening situation, but again **DO NOT give up hope**.

b. Use anything from the aircraft such as seat cushions, plastic boxes or pieces of polystyrene that will help you stay afloat.

c. If all else fails an inflated plastic bag or wet shirt are better than nothing.

d. Follow the advice of earlier paragraphs.

4.5 The Rescue

a. If survival equipment is dropped to you, it may consist of two attached packs, get into the raft and investigate the equipment in the other pack.

b. When help arrives, whether it is a boat or helicopter, stop signalling and wait for instructions from the rescuer. DO NOT:

- attempt to stand up
- try doing things on your own initiative.

c. If a helicopter is making the rescue, wait for the winch man to tell you what to do, do not reach out and grab the cable.

d. The winch man will most likely use a strop and carry out a double lift, i.e. go up with the survivor. When the strop is secure, the survivor should put both hands by his side, or better still hold hands behind his back. Many people try to hold on to the cable on the way up. This could be dangerous as it increases the risk of falling out of the strop. Equally, on approaching the door sill, don't grab at the helicopter or try to help yourself in, the crew are much better at this than you!

e. Once in the helicopter, your inflated life jacket is a hazard. You will either be asked to deflate it, or you will be given a new jacket by the crew.

f. In most cases, the rescue services will deflate the life-raft after rescuing you and take it away. It is neither practical nor safe to try to recover it intact and leaving it afloat may result in a false alarm.

g. There is further information on SAR in the UK AIP GEN 3- 6 'Search and Rescue'.

5 MAIN POINTS

- Don't panic – Ditchings are SURVIVABLE. The key elements are a good ditching then PROTECTION and LOCATION. Water and particularly food are by comparison minor considerations.
- Correct actions increase your chances of survival and early rescue.
- Always wear a properly maintained constant wear life jacket when beyond gliding range from land in a single engined aircraft.
- Carry a serviceable aviation life-raft, stowed so that it is accessible, or else wear a survival suit, particularly when the sea temperature is below 10° C.
- Carry an Emergency Locator Transmitter (and flares).
- In single engined aircraft, route to minimise the time over water or fly high to increase your glide range. Know the range per 1000 ft of altitude.
- Carefully pre-flight the aircraft and make sure there is enough fuel for all contingencies.
- Before take off, brief passengers on ditching procedures and survival equipment.
- Transmit a Mayday preferably on 121.5 MHz; and select 7700 on the transponder.
- Ditch along the crest of the swell, unless there is a very strong wind.
- Touch-down as slowly as possible – but don't stall.
- Inflate life jackets once clear of the aircraft cabin.
- Get everyone into the life-raft as quickly as possible and get the cover up.
- Switch on the ELT (or hand held radio, mobile phone).
- If in the water with no life-raft, conserve energy and heat by huddling together to reduce the risk of hypothermia. The will to live is the single most important factor in surviving until you are rescued.
- Have the other signalling devices e.g. pyrotechnics, heliograph etc. ready for use.
- Let the rescuer take control of the actual rescue.

6 SUPPLEMENT A

CAA APPROVED COMPANIES WHICH SERVICE LIFEJACKETS AND LIFERAFTS

*Aviation Engineering & Maintenance Ltd
Stansted Division
Stansted Airport
Essex CM24 1RB
Tel: 01279 680030 Ext 200
Fax: 01279 680395

Bristow Helicopters Ltd
Safety Equipment Section
Aberdeen Airport
Dyce
Aberdeen AB2 0ES
Tel: 01224 723151
Fax: 01224 770120

Seaweather Aviation Services Ltd
625 Princes Road
Dartford
Kent DA2 6FF
Tel: 01322 275513
Fax: 01322 292639

** SEMS Aerosafe
13 & 25 Olympic Business Centre
Paycocke Road
Basildon
Essex SS14 3EX
Tel: 01268 534427
Fax: 01268 281009

* FAA Approved
** They also undertake practice evenings in a pool with wave machine and have a rental service.

CAA APPROVED LIFEJACKET AND LIFERAFT MANUFACTURERS

Beaufort Air-Sea Equipment Ltd
Tel: 0151 652 9151 Ext 211

International Safety Products
Tel: 0151 922 2202

ML Lifeguard Equipment
Tel: 01824 704314

RFD Ltd
Tel: 01232 301531 Ext 105

COMPANIES KNOWN TO PROVIDE SURVIVAL TRAINING USING A 'DUNKER'

Fleetwood Offshore Survival Centre
Broadwater, Fleetwood
Lancashire FY7 8JZ
Tel: 01253 779123
Fax: 01253 773014

Humberside Offshore Training Association
Malmo Road
Sutton Fields Industrial Estate
Hull
East Yorks HU7 0YF
Tel: 01482 820567
Fax: 01482 823202

Robert Gordon Institute of Technology
338 King Street
Aberdeen AB24 5BQ
Tel: 01224 619500
Fax: 01224 619519

Warsash Maritime Centre
Newtown Road
Warsash
Southampton SO31 9ZL
(using ANDARK facility)
Tel: 01489 576161
Fax: 01489 579388

7 SUPPLEMENT B

SUITABLE LIFEJACKETS

- CAA Approved equipment is required for Public Transport aircraft use but with the exception of those used in North Sea helicopter operations, is NOT intended for constant wear. (Note: when serviced approx. 50% of airline style life jackets used for GA purposes are found to be defective, versus less than 25% of the constant wear jackets.) Thus, on non- Public Transport flights it is up to you what to wear since not all life jackets designed for constant wear are CAA Approved. (See Supplement A.)

- There are life jackets available that are 'Approved' to US or to European Community Standards, some are designed to meet marine criteria (do not use any which inflate automatically).

- It is thus impossible to provide specific details on which are likely to be satisfactory. The subject should be discussed with manufacturers, stockists and maintainers.

- When choosing a life jacket it will need to be a compromise of:

    - comfort when worn
    - convenience yet avoiding it becoming
    - entangled in seat belt/ harness
    - price
    - durability

SAFETY SENSE 22
GENERAL AVIATION

RADIOTELEPHONY FOR GENERAL AVIATION

1 INTRODUCTION

a. Radiotelephony (RTF) is essential for the safe operation of aircraft in a busy environment. RTF enables a pilot to obtain aerodrome information, weather information, and instructions relating to the safe movement of air traffic. Many student pilots find the process of learning to use the radio more daunting than learning to fly.

b. Radio waves are not confined by national boundaries and for this reason radiocommunications are regulated at International, European and national levels. The International Telecommunications Union (ITU) Radio regulations, which are reviewed regularly at World Radio Conferences, form the foundation of international agreements on the use of the radio frequency spectrum. The European Conference of Postal and Telecommunications Administrations (CEPT) committees supported by the European Radiocommunications Office (ERO) provide a forum for the discussion of regulatory issues for posts and telecommunications for the member states, with the UK Office of Communications (Ofcom) representing the interests of the UK with participation from the UK Civil Aviation Authority.

2 WIRELESS TELEGRAPHY (WT) ACT

a. Under the Wireless Telegraphy (WT) Act 1949 it is an offence to install or use radio transmission equipment without a licence. The Office of Communications (Ofcom) is responsible for managing that part of the radio spectrum used for civil purposes in the UK as set out in the Communications Act 2003 and has contracted the Civil Aviation Authority (CAA), Directorate of Airspace Policy (DAP) to administer WT Act radio licences for aircraft, aeronautical ground stations and navigation aids on their behalf.

b. An Aircraft Licence is required for radio equipment installed in an aircraft. A Transportable Licence is required for any hand-held VHF radio equipment (even if only for 'back-up' use), with an integral antenna and power supply, for use on multiple aircraft as well as gliders, microlight aircraft, balloons, hand gliders and for other aviation related activities such as parachuting and paragliding.

c. The aircraft radio equipment, whether installed or hand-held, is required to have been approved either by the UK CAA under the British Civil Airworthiness Requirements (BCARs) or by the European Aviation Safety Agency (EASA), who are now responsible for all aircraft radio equipment approvals, under the European Technical Standard Order (ETSO) Authorisations process.

d. An Aeronautical (Ground) Station Licence is required for the operation of any radio equipment on the ground; even for hand-held VHF radio equipment already covered by a Transportable Licence for use in aircraft.

3 FLIGHT RADIOTELEPHONY OPERATORS LICENCE

a. Under Article 27 of the Air Navigation Order the CAA issues 'appropriate licences' for aircraft station flight radiotelephony operators, generally being a Flight Radiotelephony

Operators Licence (FRTOL) issued either as a stand-alone licence or in conjunction with a flight crew licence. Operators of Aeronautical Radio Stations providing Air Traffic Services are also required to be similarly qualified, either holding an Air Traffic Controllers Licence, Flight Information Service Officer's Licence or Radio Station Operator's Certificate of Competence. Glider pilots and student pilots under training are, subject to certain conditions, exempt under ANO Article 26 from the requirement to hold a FRTOL. However, glider pilots without a FRTOL are not permitted to use the radio to communicate with an Air Traffic Control (ATC) unit.

b. The Flight Radiotelephony Operators Licence (FRTOL) entitles the holder to operate the radio equipment in any aircraft. FRTOLs issued prior to April 1998 contain the word 'Restricted', this is often mistaken for a 'VHF Only' limitation which, if applicable, will be endorsed on the reverse of the licence (the frequencies that will be used by a General Aviation aircraft are almost exclusively VHF, the 'VHF Only' limitation will not therefore be likely to cause any difficulties). In the UK the term 'Restricted' referred only to the type of equipment that may be operated (see ANO Schedule 8). Older radio equipment designed for use by specialist radio operators who were 'Unrestricted' is no longer in use, therefore the word 'Restricted' has been eliminated from the FRTOL. The privileges however remain unchanged.

c. When the FRTOL is limited to 'VHF Only', the holder may not use transmitting equipment operating in the HF aeronautical bands below 30 MHz. This limitation may be removed by obtaining a pass in the HF written examination with an RTF Examiner authorised to conduct the HF examination, or by obtaining a pass in the JAA Navigation group examinations at CPL/ ATPL level.

d. It is essential that the holder of a FRTOL is familiar with the phraseology and procedures used for aeronautical communication. ATC frequencies are often busy, necessitating the use of concise phrases without ambiguity. **Long winded radio calls waste time and may endanger others.**

e. On 27th March 1977 two heavily laden Boeing 747s collided on the runway at Los Rodeos airport Tenerife in poor visibility, resulting in 575 fatalities. A KLM 747 commenced take-off whilst a Pan Am 747 was still taxiing towards it on the same runway. There was clearly a breakdown in communication; perhaps a misunderstood radio call! The Pan Am aircraft had been asked by the controller, who was unable to see either aircraft due to low cloud, **'Are you CLEAR of the runway'?** The KLM aircraft had already commenced the take-off roll without clearance; could the KLM pilot have mistaken the call to the other aircraft thinking that he was **'CLEAR to Take-Off'?** The answer remains a mystery; the cure is straightforward, use the correct RTF phraseology, which is designed to be unambiguous, acknowledge and read back all clearances and above all, if in doubt **ASK!!**

f. As a direct result of aircraft accidents RTF phraseology has been progressively modified to avoid any possibility of ambiguity or confusion. Specific phrases have well defined meanings and should not be modified by the operator. Some recreational pilots consider that they don't need to know the full vocabulary used for RTF communication, yet when communicating with an Air Traffic Service Unit (ATSU) they may encounter any aspect of it. Every radio user must be fully conversant with the nature of the air traffic service provided, and be able to understand the radio calls they may hear.

4 AIRCRAFT VHF RADIO EQUIPMENT

a. Aircraft VHF radio equipment used for communications operates in the aeronautical mobile band 117.975 MHz to 137.000 MHz with a channel spacing of either 25 kHz or 25 kHz/8.33 kHz. Channel spacing of 25 kHz and 8.33 kHz provide 760 and 2280 frequencies respectively within the band. At present, the mandatory carriage of 8.33 kHz capable VHF radio equipment is only required in certain airspace within Europe which is unlikely to be used by a GA pilot. However, due to the congestion in the VHF aeronautical mobile band, the introduction of 8.33 kHz channel spacing to other airspace or users may be necessary at some time in the future.

b. GA aircraft VHF radio equipment typically has 760 channels spaced at 25 kHz; some older radios may have only 720 channels with an upper limit of 135.975 MHz, these are not allowed for IFR flight, or for VFR flight in certain countries including Germany.

c. Some installed and hand-held VHF radio equipment also includes coverage of the aeronautical radio navigation band 108.000 MHz – 117.975 MHz which is used by radio navigation facilities such as VOR and ILS. Air Traffic Information Services (ATIS) broadcasts of aerodrome information to aircraft may be carried on some VORs in addition to ATIS frequency assignments in the aeronautical mobile band.

d. Aircraft VHF radio equipment is fitted with a minimum of controls. Rotary knobs or switches select the operating frequency, allowing it to be adjusted in steps of 1 MHz, 100 kHz, and either 50, 25 or 8.33 kHz. On some equipment an additional switch selection is necessary in order to select 25 kHz resolution. This may take the form of a toggle switch or require a rotary selector knob to be pulled out. Many radios do not display the third decimal of the frequency. This creates the impression that the frequency ends in a (. x2) or a (. x7) rather than (. x25 or .x75). E.g.

121.025 shown as 121.02
121.050 shown as 121.05
121.075 shown as 121.07

This may mislead the user into thinking that a particular frequency cannot be selected.

Frequencies spaced at 8.33kHz are at present only used above FL245 in the UK but at lower levels over parts of Europe. 8.33 kHz frequencies such as 118.033, 118.058, or 118.055 require equipment with a narrow enough bandwidth to use them without causing interference to the neighbouring frequencies.

e. All too often the receiver VOLUME and SQUELCH controls may be incorrectly set. SQUELCH is an electronic switch that mutes the receiver audio output when no signal is received. This facility is designed to reduce operator fatigue, which can result from continuous exposure to background noise. When a continuous radio signal (carrier) is received, it activates or 'lifts' the SQUELCH causing the speaker or headphones to be activated. Where a variable SQUELCH control is fitted, this allows the operator to determine the strength of the received signal required to lift the SQUELCH, which may also be activated by bursts of noise. The correct setting procedure for the SQUELCH control is:

- set the volume control to approximately halfway;
- turn the SQUELCH control up until a hiss appears, this is background 'static' noise;
- turn back the SQUELCH control until the hiss just stops, this occurs quite abruptly;
- leave the SQUELCH control in this position.

Some radios are not fitted with an external SQUELCH control, but incorporate a switch marked TEST. Operating this switch 'lifts' the SQUELCH and allows the volume control to be set at a level where the background hiss is audible, or alternatively where the receiver volume is acceptable.

Note:

- The SQUELCH cannot be set correctly whilst you are receiving a station.
- If the VOLUME control is set excessively high, distortion may occur within the radio making it more difficult to hear stations. Ideally the VOLUME control should not exceed 70% of its rotation.

f. VHF aeronautical radios use amplitude modulation (AM), the same system used by broadcast radio stations in the long and medium wave bands. When two AM stations transmit simultaneously on the same frequency the signals can mix together and may render one or both stations unreadable. If the two transmitters are not exactly on the same frequency, an annoying whistle or 'heterodyne' equal to the difference between the two frequencies may be heard. **Do not transmit at the same time as another station or you may render both signals unreadable. Always listen before speaking and keep transmissions short.**

g. If you experience difficulty contacting another station the following checks should be made:

- The correct frequency is selected *
- Frequencies ending (. 025 MHz) and (. 250 MHz) are easily transposed.
- The correct radio has been selected on the comms panel e.g. COM 1, or COM 2. (Transmit and receive switching are often independent)
- The ground station is open for watch
- The station is within range (This varies with altitude)
- Volume and Squelch are correctly set

h. Many light aircraft are fitted with a an intercom system which may be integrated into one of the radios or a be a separate unit. Before flight these should be checked and adjusted independently of the radio equipment. It is important to obtain a good balance between intercom volume and radio volume to prevent radio calls being swamped by the intercom. Always seek instruction if you are unfamiliar with a particular radio installation. KNOW THE EQUIPMENT.

i. Most light aircraft are equipped with a **Transponder**. This important aid to flight safety permits an air traffic controller to positively identify an aircraft. The transponder transmits a 4 digit code (SQUAWK), set by the pilot, to the ground station where it is displayed on the radar screen. The code is either issued to the specific aircraft by an air traffic controller or, if no specific code has been issued, one of the special use codes may be selected by the pilot to indicate the type of flight being undertaken by the aircraft. Most transponders incorporate Mode C (Charlie), which transmits and displays the aircraft's level (relative to 1013.2 mb) on the ATC radar screen when the transponder mode switch is selected to 'Altitude' (ALT). **Adjustment of the altimeter pressure setting has no effect on the Mode C altitude information.** A switch marked 'IDENT' is provided on the transponder, this enables the symbol shown on the radar display to be modified so that the controller can positively identify the aircraft. The IDENT switch should not be operated unless requested by ATC.

j. In recent years an Airborne Collision Avoidance System (ACAS) has been employed in airliners and helicopters in order to provide automatic collision avoidance information. Mode C information from the transponder is important for ACAS to be effective. **Pilots should always fly with their transponder switched on, with ALT selected, unless advised otherwise by ATC.** One of the most commonly known ACAS systems is the Traffic Alert and Collision Avoidance System (TCAS) pronounced 'TEEKAS'.

k. In the absence of a code allocated by ATC, the pilot should set the "conspicuity code" 7000 on the transponder, or in the case of specialist activities the appropriate code.

5 USE OF PHRASEOLOGY

a. The correct radio phraseology to be used in the UK is detailed in CAP413 Radiotelephony Manual. In some cases it may seem very pedantic, however, it must be remembered that it has evolved for a purpose, primarily to avoid ambiguity. Many incorrect phrases are regularly heard.

b. **FINAL** is a position in the circuit pattern between 4 nautical miles and the landing threshold, in circuit parlance it is singular not plural! An Air Traffic Controller Officer hearing a call such as **'ON FINALS'** might easily believe the traffic to be **'LONG FINAL'** (a position between 4 and 8 miles from the landing threshold); in poor visibility, such a mistake could result in the controller giving another aircraft clearance to Take-Off as he believes the landing traffic to be in excess of 4 miles away, when in reality, it may be as little as only half a mile away! There is no official report 'SHORT FINAL' however; the distance from the landing threshold may serve as a more accurate indication of position i.e. 'Half Mile Final'.

c. At Aerodromes with an Aerodrome Flight Information Service (AFIS), the phrase ***'at your discretion'*** is used to indicate that the Flight Information Service Officer (FISO) is not issuing a clearance. Pilots should NOT respond using the phrase '**at my discretion**' but rather reply with their intentions, for example '***landing***'.

d. ***'Land at your discretion'*** is not a clearance to land. Pilots must exercise their own judgement and comply with the rules of the air. e.g. An aircraft may not land on a runway whilst another aircraft is on that runway unless authorised to do so by an air traffic controller. (Rules of the Air Rule 17).

e. **Requests for '*landing instructions*' should not be made**.

f. **Requests for '*instructions*' should not be made to stations providing a AGCS or FIS.** AGCS operators and Flight Information Officers (FISO) are not permitted to give instructions.

g. Public correspondence messages (including air to air conversations) are not permitted on the VHF aeronautical band.

6 MICROPHONE TECHNIQUE

a. Use a headset, it cuts out aircraft noise and avoids the distraction of a hand-held microphone.

b. Keep the microphone close to your mouth.

c. Speak directly into the microphone.

d. Don't 'clip' your transmissions - ensure that the transmit button is held firmly pressed BEFORE you speak until AFTER you have finished speaking.

7 AERODROME AERONAUTICAL RADIO STATIONS

a. The nature of the ground radio facilities at an aerodrome is usually dependent upon the number of air traffic movements. Some minor aerodromes have no provision for radio at all, whilst others may have an allocated frequency but the AGCS is seldom maned. The majority of aerodromes have a ground radio station and provide one of three types of air traffic service:

- Air/Ground communication service (AGCS) Callsign **'RADIO'**
- Flight Information Service Callsign **'INFORMATION'**
- Air Traffic Control (ATC) service Callsigns: **'GROUND; TOWER; APPROACH; RADAR; DIRECTOR; DELIVERY'**

Each service employs different procedures and it is important for pilots to be familiar with the differences and the implications for the pilot's actions in response. Small aerodromes may provide an AGCS or aerodrome FIS utilising a single frequency, whereas a busy airport will have an ATC service with separate frequencies for Radar, Approach, Tower, Ground and possibly an Automatic Terminal Information Service (ATIS).

b. **SAFETYCOM (135.475 MHz)** is a common frequency allocated for use by aircraft flying in the vicinity of aerodromes not assigned a discrete frequency. Because there is no frequency assigned for the aerodrome there is no ground radio station. SAFETYCOM is designed to allow pilots to broadcast their intentions to other aircraft that may be operating on or in the vicinity of the aerodrome. Transmissions shall only be made when the aircraft is below 2000 ft aal or below 1000 ft above circuit height within 10 miles of the aerodrome. Calls should be kept concise. Aircraft taxiing, taking-off, landing and flying in the circuit pattern should self announce their position and intentions on the SAFETYCOM frequency to alert other pilots of their presence. Initial calls should be addressed to '*Airfield Name*' with the suffix **'TRAFFIC'**,
e.g. ***'WILTON TRAFFIC G-ABCD downwind 24 left to land'.***

The intention of the airborne aircraft is then obvious to a pilot taxiing or waiting to back-track the runway. The pilot of the taxiing aircraft may choose to broadcast his intentions,
e.g. ***'WILTON TRAFFIC G-ZZXY holding point 06 awaiting landing traffic'*** in order to make his intentions known to the traffic in the circuit.

Avoid using the word 'CLEAR', it may be mistaken as a clearance!

Announce your intentions in order to assist other traffic whilst making your presence noticed. Altimeter settings will need to be determined in relation to the aerodrome elevation. The QNH of a neighbouring aerodrome will be approximately correct whereas the regional pressure setting, which has a built in safety margin will result in the aircraft being higher than shown on the altimeter.

c. An **Air/Ground communication service (AGCS) Station** is the simplest form of aeronautical radio communication. The call sign uses the aerodrome name followed by the suffix '**RADIO**'. The ground radio operator is not an air traffic controller and **must not**

give any air traffic instructions or clearances however he may relay instructions and clearances given by a controller e.g. an airways clearance to departing traffic.

This service provides aerodrome and traffic information only. In some instances the AGCS station may be located in a flying club or building that does not have an unrestricted view of the aerodrome.

In order to operate an AGCS station the operator must be in possession of a Radio Operators Certificate of Competence (CAA Form CA1308), which must be countersigned by the aeronautical radio station licensee.

AGCS operators will **NOT** use the expression: **'At your discretion'**.

The AGCS operator may pass information to a pilot such as the runway, pressure settings, wind velocity and details of any known reported traffic. **Pilots should not request clearances or instructions, as they cannot be given.**

Before entering the Aerodrome Traffic Zone (ATZ) during the published hours of operation of an aerodrome with a notified AGCS service, a pilot must obtain **'information'** from the AGCS radio station operator to ensure that the flight can be conducted safely. The AGCS radio station operator may pass messages on behalf of the aerodrome operator but any such message must be passed as information and must include details of the originator of the message,
e.g. ***'G- AYZZ Message from the airport manager. You are requested to report to the Control Tower after landing'***

On arrival at an aerodrome with an AGCS service, taxiing and parking are also the responsibility of the pilot. The AGCS operator may not give taxi instructions but, may suggest a suitable parking location if requested by the pilot.

'is there a convenient parking space? G-ZZ' 'G-ZZ there is parking space available next to the blue Cessna'

AN AGCS STATION CANNOT GIVE CLEARANCES OR INSTRUCTIONS TO AN AIRCRAFT.

d. A Flight Information Service Officer is qualified to provide an aerodrome Flight Information Service (FIS) in order to pass:

- 'Instructions' to vehicles and persons on the aerodrome, to aircraft on the ground up to the holding point and, in the case of aircraft landing, after the landing roll is completed;
- 'Information' for the safe conduct of aerodrome traffic on the runway and within an ATZ.

In practice, there is little difference between AFIS and AGCS service, however the FISO is required to undergo training and is tested by the CAA. The FIS call sign uses the suffix **'INFORMATION'** to identify the type of service. **Air traffic clearances must not be given, but may be relayed by a FISO.**

The service may revert to AGCS if a qualified FISO is not available, it is promulgated by NOTAM, and the AGCS operator is appropriately certificated. The call sign suffix then reverts to **'RADIO'**.

The phrase 'At your discretion' may be used by a FISO and will follow any advisory information. Pilots requesting departure may be advised:
'Take off at your discretion'

The pilot **should not respond** by repeating the phrase: **'at my discretion'.** No clearance has been given, there is no requirement to read one back. The pilot should simply respond:
'G –XX Roger' or 'G- XX taking off'

e. Examples of AGCS and FISO RTF phraseology are contained in CAP413 Radiotelephony Manual.

An aerodrome Flight Information Service Officer (FISO) may control aircraft on the ground up to the holding point and after the landing roll is complete. Pilots are reminded that they are responsible at all times for the safety of their aircraft and collision avoidance, LOOKOUT is always paramount.

8 AIR TRAFFIC CONTROL SERVICE

a. Pilots familiar with small aerodromes providing either an AGCS or FIS may find larger aerodromes somewhat daunting. Busy aerodromes will employ separate controllers for Ground, Tower, Approach and possibly Radar. If the purpose of each is fully understood, it will help to eliminate any confusion regarding who to talk to and when.

b. The **GROUND** controller is responsible for all movements on the manoeuvring area; this will include all taxiing aircraft and vehicular traffic equipped with radio. Initial calls will be made to GROUND, including taxi clearance, (start clearance at some aerodromes), departure clearance* if applicable, and, normally, all calls up to the holding point. Landing traffic will normally be instructed to change to GROUND after vacating the runway.

** The departure clearance tells a pilot what he is required to do on departure and will include any frequency changes required, together with routeing instructions and altitude restrictions.*

Note: this is **NOT** a clearance to take- off or to enter an active runway.

c. The **TOWER** controller is responsible for all traffic using the runway and in close proximity to the aerodrome, including the circuit. Normally an aircraft will be instructed to change to TOWER when at the holding point, at which time the pilot should have completed all of his checks and be ready for departure. The first call will usually be:
WRAYTON TOWER G-ABCD holding point RW 30 Ready for departure'.

Aircraft remaining in the circuit will remain with **TOWER**, whereas departing aircraft will change to either **APPROACH** or **RADAR**. Pilots arriving at an aerodrome will usually be instructed by APPROACH to contact TOWER at a suitable point in order to obtain circuit joining instructions. After landing, aircraft should vacate the runway, unless otherwise instructed, at the first available taxiway that the aircraft reaches having slowed to taxiing speed and advise the controller:
'Runway Vacated G-XX'

The pilot will normally then be instructed to change to the GROUND frequency. **Do not use the phrases:**
'Clear the Active' or 'Clear of the Runway'

d. **GROUND** and **TOWER** controllers are located in the glass uppermost part of the ATC Tower; they are invariably located side by side and should have a good view of the aerodrome and circuit.

e. **APPROACH** controllers are usually located in the lower part of the ATC tower and have no visual contact with the aerodrome. Control may be either radar or non-radar. At busy aerodromes RADAR controllers may be used in addition to the APPROACH controller to provide services for traffic transiting the area.

f. It is not uncommon for controllers to conduct more than one function when traffic is light; The **RADAR** and **APPROACH** controllers work in close proximity such that the jobs may be combined. The **GROUND** and **TOWER** controllers are also ideally situated to combine functions. At the very small provincial airports, **TOWER** and **APPROACH** control may also be provided by one controller. Occasionally at smaller airports the service may revert to a **FIS** outside the busy period at weekends, in which case, the service will be apparent from the Callsign Suffix **'INFORMATION'** and no clearances or instructions will be given.

g. **ATIS** uses a dedicated frequency on which a recording of aerodrome information is broadcast continuously. This information is updated at least hourly. Such a facility allows pilots to obtain weather and aerodrome information without having to establish radio contact with the aerodrome, thus considerably reducing the workload of the controller and enabling the pilot to plan ahead. ATIS information is coded using a letter of the alphabet to enable both pilot and controller to ascertain which broadcast the pilot has received,
e.g. ***'This is Langford information Delta time zero nine five zero'***

the message concludes:
'on initial contact with Langford advise information Delta received'.

The pilot advises ATC on his initial call that he has received ATIS Delta. Pilots who call ATC without passing the ATIS code may be asked if they have received the latest 'ATIS information'. **To the unwary this may cause confusion!**

If a pilot does not report the latest broadcast identification letter the controller will advise the pilot of any updated information.

9 OTHER SERVICES

Lower Airspace Radar Service (LARS) is available to pilots when flying outside controlled airspace below FL95. The General Aviation Safety Sense Leaflet 8 provides details of Air Traffic Services Outside Controlled Airspace.

10 MILITARY ATC

a. Military ATC units often provide a LARS. The terminology used by military controllers differs in some details from that used by civil controllers. Military controllers are not obliged to adhere to civil Rules of the Air when issuing instructions, and it is possible that you may be asked to fly in a manner that might not conform to civil practices or law. It is the pilot's responsibility to advise the controller if he/she is unable to comply with the instruction and why, e.g. being asked to over fly a built up area below 1000 ft or at a height where it is not possible to glide clear, or if altitude changes might place an unqualified pilot in IMC.

b. Military ATC use frequencies in the UHF band (225- 380 MHz) for their primary function of providing services to military aircraft whilst operating VHF frequencies that facilitate communication with civil aircraft is normally a secondary function. When calling a military ATC unit on VHF always allow time for the controller to reply as he may be in communication with a military aircraft on UHF. Often you will hear only one side of the conversation when transmissions are made on both VHF and UHF simultaneously; you hear the VHF transmission from ATC, but not the reply from the aircraft on UHF. Information on operating at and in the vicinity of military aerodromes is contained in Safety Sense leaflet 26 "Operations at Military Aerodromes".

11 RADIO OPERATION

a. It is not intended to reproduce CAP 413 Radiotelephony Manual, but rather to highlight certain aspects of radio operation.

b. **Radio Check.** Before embarking upon a flight it is essential to know that the radio equipment is working. Listening to other stations will check the radio receiver but in order to check the transmitter, it is necessary to talk to another station and let them confirm that they have received your transmission in an intelligible form. It is also important to be sure that the equipment switches channels and that the channel indicated is the correct one. Where two frequencies are in use at an airfield, radios may be checked by selecting the frequencies alternately. The transmitter may be checked on the initial call for the aerodrome information. When more than one radio is installed, the second radio should be checked on a subsequent call.

c. The golden rule of RTF operation is: **know what you are going to say before you say it**. Whilst this may seem obvious, once the transmit switch is pressed the human brain often forgets the obvious. Secondly, **anticipate what the reply is likely to be**. That way, it will not be a surprise. For example when calling for aerodrome information, the reply will include the QFE, QNH, surface wind and runway (R/W) in use. The pilot may get an idea of the pressure settings in advance by using the altimeter, whilst a good indication of the R/W in use and wind direction can be obtained by observing the windsock and any other traffic. **Always read-back the reply in the same order that it was given – avoid reversing the order.**

d. A **Departure clearance** can often pose problems for the inexperienced; it may be a lengthy clearance, which must be read back to the controller. Prior to departure it is normal to 'Book- Out' with the ATSU, specifying your departure details; flying instructors should allow students to observe and practice this procedure as part of the learning process. If the pilot has any questions about the departure route or the clearance that he is likely to receive, it is a good idea to ask when Booking Out rather than to wait until having to ask on the radio. The departure clearance will normally be a confirmation of the routeing already requested, although occasionally it may involve changes. It should therefore be no surprise when the controller passes a clearance that closely resembles the information passed by the pilot when 'Booking Out'. If a frequency change is required on departure it will be to a published frequency. Know where to look it up and whenever possible, select it on a second radio as a reminder. Invariably, when departing VFR, the first two digits of the transponder code will remain the same for a particular ATSU.

Remember: The departure clearance is NOT a clearance to enter a runway or to take- off!

After take- off you are required to follow the departure clearance, remember the basic rule:

- Aviate
- **Navigate** and then
- **Communicate**

When safely airborne and established in the climb you can expect TOWER to instruct you to change frequency,
e.g. ***G-ABCD to APPROACH 126.1***

To omit this call could result in uncertainty over your whereabouts!

e. **En-Route** calls usually take the form of position reports. The initial call to an ATSU should begin:

- **Station** being called
- Aircraft **Callsign** in full
- **Request** ,

e.g. *'WILTON RADAR G- AAXX request Radar Information Service'*

Do not say any more until the ATSU invites you to 'pass your message'. If you are advised to "Stand-by", do so but **do not acknowledge**. When requested to ***"pass your message"*** it should consist of:

- **Full call sign** – so that the controller can write it down.

- **Type** – PA28, C172, Robin 400 etc.

- **Departure/Destination** –the point of departure and destination; – the controller will write these on a handling slip. **do not include a list of turning points.** If you are returning to the point of departure it is satisfactory to say ***Navex from Wilton to Wilton.***

- **Present Position** – should be given relative to a point on a 1:500,000 chart, the controller may not be familiar with small features in the area.

- **Altitude/ Level** – together with the pressure setting this will enable the controller to assess if there is any confliction with other traffic in the vicinity at the same level!

- **Additional details** – What service or information do you require? e.g. Flight Information Service (FIS), regional pressure settings next turning point etc.

Common mistakes are a failure to make any request of the controller, and inadequate or misleading position reporting, leaving the controller unaware of your present position and/ or the next turning point. In order to provide you with a Service, the controller needs to know:

- Who you are
- **Where you are** and
- What you want

Then **WAIT...**
If you cannot remember what to say, **stop transmitting.** The controller will ask you for anything you miss out!

f. Many pilots will avoid flight through a Control Zone (CTR) by flying a longer route around it. The majority of CTRs in the UK are designated Class D airspace, which permits VFR flight subject to an ATC clearance. In the case of a CTR designated Class A airspace, a Special VFR (SVFR) clearance is required if the aircraft is being flown visually. Requesting a VFR or SVFR clearance is straightforward. The controller will form a mental picture of a pilot from the radio calls made. He is unaware of a pilot's qualifications, experience or status from the aircraft call sign alone. A radio call delivered in a professional manner will be treated accordingly, whereas a poorly structured and hesitant call may lead the controller to be cautious about issuing a clearance that is complex or requires the pilot to fly very accurately. A badly delivered request for a clearance may result in a routing that avoids controlled airspace rather than the route requested.

For example,
'SOLENT APPROACH G- ABCD request zone transit'

followed by:
'G- ABCD; Cessna 172; Popham to Sandown VFR; 10 miles North of Winchester; Altitude Two Thousand Feet on One Zero Zero Six. Estimate Sierra Alpha Mike, Two Five; request zone transit'.

will probably result in a reply:
'G- CD is cleared to enter the Southampton zone abeam Winchester VFR not below altitude two thousand feet Solent QNH One Zero Zero Nine. Report Sierra Alpha Mike'

Whereas a call:
'SOUTHAMPTON this is G- ABCD Err! a 172 at two thousand feet Err! Point of departure Popham. 4 Persons on board. Err! Can we transit over Southampton to the Isle of Wight Sir? or if not we will go round. Err! we are North of Winchester. Over'

may result in the reply:
'G- ABCD remain outside controlled airspace. Route via Romsey, Totton and Calshot for the IOW., Solent QNH One Zero Zero Nine. Report Romsey'.

g. **Aerodrome Arrival.** Unless you have filed a Flight Plan (CA48) or have telephoned in advance, (essential at PPR aerodromes) VFR flights usually arrive at an aerodrome without prior knowledge of ATC, the FISO or AGCS radio station operator. You may arrive at the same time as other VFR or IFR traffic. If the aerodrome provides a RADAR service it is a good idea to talk to them as soon as you are within range, they may look after you until you are in visual contact with the aerodrome at which point you will be asked to contact **TOWER**. If there is no radar service the initial call will be to **APPROACH** not greater than 25 nm from the aerodrome. Joining procedure will depend upon the type of traffic when you arrive, if there is IFR traffic arriving and departing it is unlikely that you will be able to join overhead. You may be asked to report your position relative to one of the established Visual Reference Points (VRPs). Occasionally, you may be asked to route via a position not obvious to you, **if in doubt ASK.** The change to **TOWER** can occur quite late. On landing you may be asked to vacate the runway at a specific point and change to **GROUND**. Be prepared for references to published ground positions, stand numbers and holding points. In other words, use a plan of the aerodrome! For arrival at a small aerodrome with either **AGCS** or **AFIS**, initial contact should be made within 10 miles of the aerodrome. If unfamiliar with the aerodrome an overhead join is preferred (but not always permitted – see the UK AIP) as it enables orientation with the aerodrome and circuit traffic. Remember you must establish radio contact with the aerodrome **BEFORE** you enter the ATZ. See General Aviation Safety Sense Leaflet 6B, Aerodrome Sense.

h. Any pilot arriving at an unfamiliar aerodrome will experience a high workload and may not recognise geographical features. The aircraft has to descend; there are checks to be completed and frequencies to be selected. It is essential to **LOOKOUT**, **listen out** and keep your wits about you. Be prepared, have a plan and select the required frequencies as far in advance as possible. **Check the Aeronautical Information Publications (AIP) and NOTAMs prior to departure and do not use out of date documents.**

12 EMERGENCY PROCEDURES

a. Fortunately emergencies are rare. However, there have been a number of occasions when a pilot has recognised the need to land as soon as possible, (e.g. no oil pressure but the engine is still running OK) but has not wanted to 'make a fuss about it'. Clearly if a situation arises where there is a possibility of danger or a worsening situation it is in your best interest to make an URGENCY call, that way immediate help, or a priority landing, is available to prevent the situation getting out of hand.

b. **The states of EMERGENCY are**:

- **Distress**. (MAYDAY) A condition of being threatened by serious or imminent danger and of requiring immediate assistance.
- **Urgency**. (PAN PAN) A condition concerning the safety of an aircraft or other vehicle, or some person on board or within sight, ***but does not require immediate assistance.***

c. The EMERGENCY MESSAGE advises others:

- **Who you are!**
- **What the problem is,**
- What you intend to do about it and
- **Where you are!**

The format is as follows:

- **MAYDAY** (repeated 3 times) or **PAN PAN** (repeated 3 times)
- **STATION** addressed when appropriate
- **CALLSIGN** (once)
- **TYPE** of Aircraft
- **NATURE** of emergency
- **INTENTION** of person in command
- **POSITION – HEIGHT and HDG**
- **Pilot qualification**: e.g. Student pilot, no instrument qualification, IMC rating or full Instrument Rating (IR) (Not required by ICAO).
- **Any other information** – POB, endurance etc.

It is probable that in a real emergency you will not wish to be bothered with talking further on the radio. By ending the call: ***MAYDAY OUT*** you will convey the message that you do not expect a reply.

d. Further attention can be attracted in an emergency by selecting the appropriate code on the transponder:

Emergency	**7700**
Radio Failure	**7600**

13 THE PRACTICAL COMMUNICATIONS TEST FOR THE FRTOL

a. Candidates wishing to obtain a FRTOL are required to sit a written examination and a practical communications test with an authorised RTF examiner. The practical test involves the use of an approved RTF simulator; this may provide basic radio facilities, or be a PC based system with a moving map and associated communications equipment. The candidate is briefed to follow a typical light aircraft route from one aerodrome to another passing through a Military Air Traffic Zone (MATZ) and possibly at some stage into or through a CTR. The candidate is required to make all the appropriate radio calls and frequency selections as if he were actually flying the route. The examiner performs the function of an AGCS radio station operator, FISO or controller. Other aircraft may be heard so the candidate is required to listen out. At some stage there will be an emergency involving either the candidate or another aircraft. At all stages of the test the candidate is required to make the appropriate radio calls. There are a number of options available to the candidate and in most cases it is the candidates responsibility to select an appropriate agency with whom to communicate with. The candidate is provided with a route map, a completed navigation flight plan and a list of all communications facilities available to him. The candidate must be familiar with the procedure for obtaining VHF Direction Finding (VDF) bearings from stations equipped with this facility.

b. A typical examination route would be for a C172 aircraft routeing from Shipdham in East Anglia to East Midlands Airport via Huntingdon and Melton Mowbray. The aircraft is equipped with a single channel radio and a transponder with no mode C. The pilot is assumed to be a PPL holder. On this particular route a LARS service is available for most of the route, it would be a shame not to use it. The route passes South of RAF Marham and then through the Combined MATZ (CMATZ) at RAF Wittering and RAF Cottesmore, finally arriving at East Midlands, which is in Class D airspace. Special entry and exit lanes are provided to assist VFR and SVFR traffic.

MAP OF ROUTE (1:500,000 CAA VFR Chart)

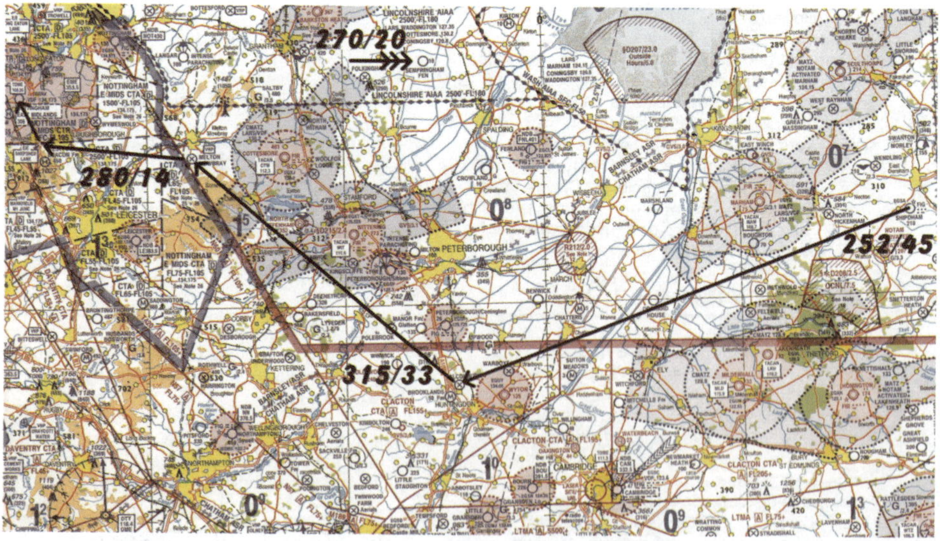

c. A typical narrative for the flight could be as follows:

Note: for the sake of clarity numerals are used in this example in preference to spelling out numbers.

Shipdham Radio G-ZAON request radio check 119.550

G-ZAON Shipdham Radio Readability 5

G- ZAON; request airfield information; Taxi VFR to East Midlands

G-ON RW 20; Surface Wind 250/ 07; QNH 1009;

R/ W 20; QNH 1009 G-ON
G-ON Ready for departure.

G-ON traffic is a Cessna 152 on a half-mile FINAL.

ROGER G-ON

G-ON reported traffic, surface wind 260/ 05.

Roger taking off G-ON.

G-ON ROGER

G-ON overhead altitude 2500 ft QNH 1009, changing to Marham 124.150

G-ON ROGER

Marham Approach G- ZAON request FIS

G-ZAON Marham Approach pass your message

G-ZAON
Cessna 172
Shipdham to East Midlands
2 miles North of Watton
Altitude 2500 ft 1009
Estimating Alconbury at 35
Request Radar Information Service and Chatham Pressure

G-ON Chatham 1005, Squawk 2632

Chatham 1005, Squawk 2632, negative Charlie, G-ON

G-ON identified 8 miles SE of Marham; Flight Information Service; report passing Chatteris

FIS;; WILCO G-ON
G-ON 5 miles North of Ely request change to Cambridge 123.6 for VDF

G-ON Squawk 7000 contact Cambridge 123.6

Squawk 7000; Cambridge 123.6 G-ON
Cambridge Homer
G-ZAON request true bearing G-ZAON

G- ZAON Cambridge Homer transmit for bearing.

True Bearing/ True Bearing G- ZAON request true bearing G- ZAON

G-ZAON Cambridge Homer true bearing 355 degrees class Bravo; I say again 355 degrees class Bravo

True bearing 355 degrees class Bravo; changing to Wyton 134.050 G- ZAON

G-ON ROGER

Wyton Approach G- ZAON request FIS.

G-ZAON Wyton approach pass your message.

G-ZAON
Cessna 172
Shipdham to East Midlands
2 miles South of Chatteris
Altitude 2500 ft 1005
Estimating Alconbury at 35
Request RIS

G-ON ROGER; Report turning at Alconbury The Wyton Circuit is active with three Vigilants.

WILCO G-ON
G-ON Overhead Alconbury 35
Altitude 2500ft 1005
Estimating Melton Mowbray at 03

G-ON ROGER Freecall Cottesmore on 130.2

Cottesmore 130.2 G-ON
Cottesmore Approach G- ZAON request MATZ penetration
G-ZAON Cottesmore Approach pass your message
G- ZAON
Cessna 172
Shipdham to East Midlands
3 miles South of Conington
Altitude 2500 ft Chatham 1005 Estimating Melton Mowbray at 03;
request MATZ penetration;
Radar Information Service and Barnsley pressure

G-ON Barnsley 1002 Squawk 6554

Barnsley 1002 Squawk 6554 G-ON

G-ON identified; Radar Information Service; maintain 2500 ft
Cottesmore QFE 993 millibars

Maintain height 2500 ft
QFE 993 millibars;
Radar Information Service, G-ON

G-ON ROGER, report abeam Oundle

WILCO G-ON
G-ON abeam Oundle

G-ON is cleared to cross the CMATZ at 2500 ft QFE 993 millibars; maintain VFR; report abeam Oakham

Cleared to cross the CMATZ at height 2500ft 993 millibars; Wilco G-ON
G-ON abeam Oakham

G-ON Squawk 7362

Squawk 7362 G-ON

G-ON contact East Midlands Radar 119.650

East Midlands Radar 119.650 G-ON

(If possible listen to East Midlands ATIS 128.225 MHz to obtain airfield information)

East Midlands Radar G- ZAON inbound from Shipdham with Information 'Golf' (The ATIS code)

G-ZAON Stand-by

G-ON expect zone entry via the Shepshed Lane VFR; RW 27 surface wind 270/ 08 QFE 998 millibars, report approaching Shepshed

Route via the Shepshed Lane RW 27 QFE 998 millibars, G-ON
Approaching the Shepshed Lane, G-ON

G- ON Cleared to enter the zone VFR report field in sight

Clear to enter the Zone VFR, WILCO G-ON
G-ON Field in Sight

G-ON contact East Midlands Tower 124.0

East Midlands Tower 124.0 G-ON
East Midlands Tower G-ZAON

G-ZAON join left base RW 27; QFE 998 millibars; No 2 to a Boeing 737 on a 1 mile FINAL.

Join left base RW 27; QFE 998 millibars; No 2. G-ZAON

G-ON report FINAL caution vortex wake the recommended spacing is 6 miles.

WILCO G-ON
G-ON FINAL

G-ON continue approach surface wind 265/ 07

Continue approach G-ON

G-ON Cleared to land RW 27 surface wind 270/ 07

Cleared to land RW 27 G-ON

G-ON landing time 1417 vacate next left

Vacate next Left, G-ON

G-ON contact East Midlands Ground 121.9

Ground 121.9 G-ON
East Midlands Ground G-ZAON Runway vacated

G-ZAON turn right onto taxi-way
Alpha turn left at Alpha 2 for the flying club

Taxi-way Alpha via Alpha 2 for the Flying Club G-ZAON

G-ON report closing down

WILCO G-ON
G-ON Closing Down

Notes:

At some stage in the practical test the candidate will be required to make both Urgency and Emergency calls. They must be made in accordance with CAP413. Failure to make these calls correctly will result in a mandatory failure of the test.

RTF practical tests are conducted using an approved RTF simulator where the candidate must be isolated from the examiner. Only Authorised RTF Examiners may conduct this test. Tests may not be conducted in an aircraft, with the candidate in the same room as the examiner, or without the RTF simulator equipment.

A radiotelephony training record form SRG 1171 is available on the SRG/PLD web site to enable candidates to cover all test items with their flight instructor.

Useful References:

CAP 413 Radiotelephony Manual

AIC 19/2004 (White 95) Flight Radiotelephony Operators Licence (VHF and HF) Examinations

Listing of all authorised RTF Examiners can be found on the SRG/PLD web site

CAA Flight Safety Poster FSP 4 'Cut the Chat'

The Private Pilot's Licence Course – Air Law and Radiotelephony by Jeremy M Pratt – AFE

The Air Pilots Manual – Volume 7 – by Trevor Thom – Airlife Publishing Ltd

CAA publications can be viewed or downloaded from the CAA web site www.caa.co.uk. Many are available in printed form for purchase from TSO.

14 SUMMARY

- A Wireless Telegraphy (WT) Act Licence is required for aeronautical radio equipment installed or used in aircraft and aeronautical radio stations.
- Aircraft radio equipment must be approved either by the UK CAA or EASA.
- Know how to use the aircraft radio equipment
- Be familiar with CAP413, it is revised from time to time with new phraseology
- Use correct phraseology, it is designed to prevent ambiguity
- Use a headset, speak directly into the microphone positioned close to the mouth
- Listen out before transmitting
- Keep transmissions short
- If uncertain of what to say, STOP TRANSMITTING!
- Know the types of Air Traffic Service provided and the limitations
- **Know the Emergency Procedures**

SAFETY SENSE 23
GENERAL AVIATION

PILOTS:
IT'S YOUR DECISION

1 INTRODUCTION

a. A CAA study examined 166 fatal accidents to UK light aircraft. That review was published as CAP 667 'Review of General Aviation Fatal Accidents 1985 – 1994', and this highlights some of the points made. Most accidents are the result of the pilot's actions. This includes their skill level and, most important of all, **the decisions that they make**. This leaflet details some of the factors that can affect how the pilot's decisions do – or don't – keep the aircraft in one piece and the occupants safe.

2 TO GO OR NOT TO GO

a. Weather

Probably the single most important factor in General Aviation flight safety is the decision of a pilot to begin, or continue, a flight in unsuitable weather conditions. As you might expect, weather was a major factor in fatal accidents: over 80% of Controlled Flight Into Terrain (CFIT) accidents happened when the pilot either continued flying into adverse weather, or did not appreciate the actual effects of the weather conditions. Of those pilots who lost control in Instrument Meteorological Conditions (IMC), only one had an Instrument Rating.

Crosswind landings seldom result in fatalities, but they still feature in many accidents resulting in broken aircraft and painful injuries.

Weather does not stay constant, it doesn't always do what the forecast predicts, and it can deteriorate very fast. Respect the weather, and the implications for flight safety. That doesn't just mean ***other*** less experienced people who can't fly so well are the ones who should respect the weather; it means **you**.

b. I Can't Turn Back Now!

Any competent pilot knows that weather can, and will, change en- route. If it does, it is essential that the pilot is prepared and willing to divert or turn back if conditions deteriorate. It does not reflect badly on your ability as a pilot if you turn back in poor weather. In fact, it reflects **good judgement and realistic assessment of the situation**. It is also important that diverting is feasible in practical terms. Have you got enough fuel, money to get home, or pay for a hotel? Have you promised to be somewhere important? ***Never*** put yourself in a position where you would not feel able and willing to turn back if necessary. No Monday job is worth dying for on a Sunday, so carry your driving licence and credit card.

The decision to turn back will be made easier if you have practised, in advance, to fly the relevant manoeuvres **on instruments,** for example: a 180% turn and if necessary climb to a higher Minimum Safe Altitude (MSA).

c. Chain of Events

In aviation accidents, it is common to find a chain of events where one shortcut or poor judgement leads to another. For example, the apparent 'cause' of an accident may be that the pilot has attempted a landing in marginal weather conditions, has not diverted or turned back despite reducing visibility, or has descended below the Minimum Safety Altitude (MSA) to try to establish their position. Consider why they chose to do this – was it really an isolated bad judgement, or could they have been short of fuel due to poor planning and lack of contingency time?

MSA is at least 1000 feet above the Maximum Elevation Figure (MEF) in the relevant chart lat/ long square. Remember that good planning, proper use of forecasts, awareness of terrain features en route and relevant safety altitudes, are not just good practice – they save lives.

d. But I've Done it Before!

Why do some highly experienced pilots believe that they can safely fly in marginal conditions, ignore their MSA, or attempt extreme aircraft manoeuvres? One of the reasons could be that either they, or others that they know, have done it before and 'got away with it'. This may well be true, but it certainly does not prove that it is safe. Imagine if your son or daughter tried to convince you that it was quite safe for them to cross a busy road blindfold, because they did it yesterday, and survived? What would you say to them?

e. But I know someone else who does it!

People vary in all kinds of ways, experience, concentration, skill, how they are feeling on a certain day, how much sleep they had, how much sleep they need, the after effects of recent illness, and their personal or domestic circumstances. The fact that someone else, on a particular day, can land in a marginal crosswind does not mean that you can necessarily do the same. The fact that **you** can do this does not mean that you should encourage **someone else** to do the same.

Being a competent pilot means correctly assessing your own limitations on a particular occasion. It does not mean pretending that if someone can do it, then everyone can do it every time; or that if someone else is doing it, that necessarily makes it safe or wise.

f. Exercising Sound Judgement

Pilots enjoy a great deal of freedom, despite the unforgiving nature of flying. The reason for this is that the regulatory authorities place a great deal of trust in the pilot to exercise competent judgement concerning flight safety. Qualified pilots are thought to be capable of making responsible decisions about whether it is safe to fly, taking into account their experience level, aircraft type, location, personal physical and emotional state, and prevailing or expected weather conditions. There are two serious threats to the use of this judgement: The pilot may have an excessively optimistic view of the situation or of his own ability; or he may be persuaded by other people to proceed with a flight **against his better judgement**. How can this happen?

g. But You Promised!

Never promise to fly on a certain day or to be somewhere important, if you can only get there by flying. If it really is important to be there, leave yourself time for alternative surface transport. Tell friends or relations that you **may** be able to take them flying **weather permitting**. Better still, keep it as a 'surprise', decide on the day if you feel prepared and fit, the weather is fine, and the aircraft is serviceable, and offer to take them flying. They won't know you had to book the aircraft a month in advance. It is always disappointing to cancel a flight if non-aviator people, especially children, are looking forward to the trip. This is particularly true if the reasons are not easy for them to understand.

h. Peer Pressure

There will always be people who will pressure you in subtle ways to take risks that you don't feel comfortable with. They can be prevalent in clubrooms, asking you if you flew on a certain windy day, and smiling smugly if you say that you cancelled whilst they braved the crosswind, low cloud or lack of horizon. 'You diverted? What an idiot! I'd have carried on and got there... '. Perhaps they would; alternatively they might have carried on and ***not*** got there. Perhaps they are just full of bravado and wouldn't have carried on at all. Perhaps they have more experience, a better equipped aircraft, or suicidal tendencies. It doesn't really matter. The fact is that the world of aviation relies on competent and independent pilot judgement, and the pilot is **you**. If you are swayed by clubhouse buffoons, then you are more afraid of their dubious opinions than of your own death. If this applies to you, you may not have the character that is expected of a pilot licence holder.

i. Audiences: are you impressing anyone?

In the review of fatal accidents, more than half of the low flying and aerobatic accidents involved an 'audience' – seldom at a formal air show, but more often to impress friends on the ground, at the clubhouse, or even passengers taken for a flight. The temptation to 'show off', to impress those watching, proved fatal in too many cases. (In fact, the 'audience' are not necessarily filled with admiration while watching these antics. They may simply be wondering when the accident will happen, and what this person is doing with a licence.) Before you decide to take such a risk, ask yourself*: would the people who are watching be prepared to risk their lives to impress you? What would you think of them if they were?*

j. Joint Decisions

It is a well known phenomenon that a joint decision made by a group of like minded people is usually more extreme than the decision that any one of them, alone, would have made. Pilots tend to be, by their nature, fairly adventurous individuals who are willing to face a certain amount of risk in order to pursue their activities. Committee decision: 'we'll give it a go!'

3 DIFFERENT PEOPLE - DIFFERENT RISKS

a. Age Groups

The review of fatal accidents suggested that the risks for young pilots were a little different from those of more mature years. Young pilots – especially young male pilots – sometimes took quite unnecessary risks in terms of low flying and aerobatic manoeuvres, often in front of friends or others watching (see 'Audiences' above). Older pilots seem less tempted to perform spectacular or risky manoeuvres, but they may take a different kind of risk. Pilots who fly into terrain, under full control of their aircraft and without any significant technical failures are, on average, older than pilots involved in other kinds of fatal accident. Typically, these pilots continued flying into adverse weather conditions, and / or ignored their MSA (if indeed one had been calculated).

b. Total Experience Level

Pilots involved in the fatal low flying and aerobatics accidents are usually highly experienced. Perhaps they believe that because of their very high hours, they can fly safely in these very unforgiving regimes. Pilots in fatal CFIT accidents are also typically very experienced. Again, they may believe that their long experience might allow them to fly safely in conditions that others are advised to avoid. If this thought ever enters your mind, remember that all of those highly experienced pilots in the fatal accident reports also thought that '**it would be all right'.**

Pilots with low flying hours may be vulnerable to a different kind of accident. Those with very low hours feature less in the accident reports than those with 200 – 500 hours. The latter group seem to be more likely to lose control of the aircraft during visual conditions. This is probably not very surprising, given that these pilots are still quite inexperienced, and may be moving for the first time toward some slightly more ambitious flying.

c. Use It or Lose It

Recency may also be a safety issue; the fact that you could do something perfectly six weeks ago does not mean you can immediately do it now. A skill is like a message written in chalk on an outdoor wall – it gets eroded a little every day. If the writing is retraced repeatedly it will become more enduring. Even then, it will be eroded eventually if it is not periodically refreshed. Skills are refreshed via practice, annual or recency checks or post qualification training.

4 ONLY HUMAN

a. Trust Me, I'm a Pilot

Despite what some people may think, pilots are only human, and have normal human limitations. The fact that pilots are trained, experienced and competent, does not mean that they will always perform perfectly, that they will never experience an 'off day', overload, illusions or distorted perceptions, or that they will never make a mistake. Everyone recognises that physical parts of the aircraft have a certain expected failure rate, and this is (correctly) seen as a realistic, normal performance level. Human pilots also have a 'realistic' performance failure rate, and it is **not** zero.

b. To Err is Human

One characteristic of human beings is that **we all make mistakes**, no matter how well trained, competent, careful, or skilled we may be. **Nobody** is immune from errors, and the person who imagines that they are infallible is the most dangerous of all. There are two general classes of error:

- 'slips and lapses' include 'finger trouble', errors in data entry or recording (such as writing down the wrong digits), or not noticing that an instrument reading has changed;
- 'mistakes' refer to actions that the pilot makes intentionally, and executes correctly, but they turn out to be a bad plan.

In general, mistakes are more easily reduced by training, but they still can and do happen. The important thing is to recognise and rectify mistakes – and to learn from them. Slips and lapses can happen to anyone and are, if anything, more likely in highly skilled, experienced people.

c. Believing is Seeing

There are well known optical illusions that can affect pilots judgement, e.g. height perception when approaching sloping runways. In other circumstances, there can be a mental distortion that is nothing to do with visual illusions as such, but can be just as dangerous. Human beings are selective about what they 'see'. If a person believes something to be true, then they will tend to 'see' only those cues in the environment that are consistent with that belief, treating these as positive confirmation that the belief is correct, and 'not see', 'blot out' or ignore any evidence to the contrary.

Unfortunately, pilots are no exception to this rule. If a pilot has formed the belief that he is at a certain geographic location, then his mind may try to organise whatever cues are present in a manner that will confirm this belief. This means that conscious cross checking to look for differences to expectation are critically important, and frequently a feature of aviation procedures. This principle can even apply to the expectation that instruments should be showing a certain reading, or hearing an ATC clearance that is expected or usual. It is vital that instruments are actually read and messages are really listened to, with at least some anticipation that they may **not** say what you expected. It is difficult for anyone to accept this about themselves, especially if they are highly technically qualified and experienced. Believe it: if you are human, this **does** apply to you.

d. Stress

Stress is a familiar feeling to most people. When people are stressed, their judgement can be affected, and their thinking may be unclear. They may suffer from 'tunnel' thinking, concentrating on (or over-reacting to) one particular problem to the exclusion of all else. This is dangerous. If there is a problem in flight, *the pilot's first priority must be safe flight.* Attention to a faulty radio, airsick passenger, or navigation problem **must** be a secondary task. If you are feeling stressed before a flight, consider whether you should cancel. If you can foresee a period of high workload during the flight, rehearse it mentally, prepare as much as possible ahead of time and, above all, remember that your first priority at all times is to **fly the aircraft**.

5 ONLY A MACHINE

a. Trust Me, I'm Electronic

Just as human beings can make errors, mechanical and electronic devices can also be faulty. THINK about what your instruments should say – do a mental 'reality check'. Always cross check with a second source (e.g. landmarks in the outside view) if possible. Change – especially movement – attracts attention from our senses, but a static condition, or a very slow rate of change, is more likely to go unnoticed. It is important to check all instruments regularly, never think that your attention will automatically be drawn to a deteriorating situation. If your fuel gauge is stuck on full, the needle will remain steady, although actual fuel levels will be dropping. There will be no rapid movement or change to attract your attention.

b. GPS

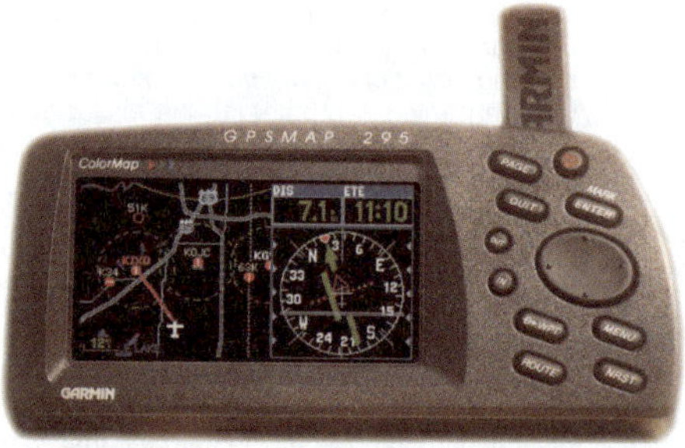

GPS is becoming a common accessory for GA pilots. It can be tremendously helpful at times and is probably an overall safety 'plus'. However, a few words of caution *(see Safety Sense leaflet 25 – use of GPS)*:

- **Never** use GPS as your primary means of navigation
- **Never** use it to land in poor visibility (and that means you too, helicopter pilots!)
- **Never** spend time head down, fiddling with GPS, and ignoring the outside world.
- **Never** believe GPS data without question. It is NOT infallible and it CAN go wrong.
- **Never** fly in conditions that you would normally avoid, because you believe GPS will reduce the risk and get you there safely.

6 HOW DO ACCIDENTS HAPPEN? COMMON SCENARIOS IN A CAA REVIEW

a. Controlled Flight Into Terrain (CFIT)

In a CFIT accident the pilot does not lose control, and the aircraft has not failed. They simply fly into the ground, often hills or mountains. The pilots who had fatal CFIT accidents were typically over fifty years old, and very experienced. More than a third were flying in their home base local area, and accidents were not restricted to mountainous regions. Of all CFIT accidents, 82% included unwise reaction to weather conditions (such as continuing to fly into worsening weather) and 64% had not adhered to their MSA (if they had calculated one at all), trying to get 'below the weather', or hoping to confirm their position. More than a third found out too late that they had made an error in navigation.

b. Loss of Control in VMC

Loss of control in visual meteorological conditions (VMC) is almost as common as CFIT. In the accident review, it was noticed that many of these loss of control accidents involved an unfamiliar situation, a distraction or a minor technical failure. The inexperienced pilot was probably coping quite well, until they were overloaded by some unforeseen event. This is probably difficult to avoid, but it is worth rehearsing – even mentally – exactly what you would do if you had a technical failure, or encountered a distraction. Also, remember that if the flight you have planned is going to require 100% of your current skill capacity to cope with it, then you won't have anything left in reserve for unplanned or unusual events that crop up.

c. Low Flying / Aerobatic

Highly experienced young male pilots (often with an informal audience) who fly low and perform aerobatics without adequate height are putting themselves and others at risk. Accidents are not unusual in these circumstances.

d. Loss of Control in IMC

All but one of the pilots killed when they lost control in IMC were flying in instrument conditions without an Instrument Rating. This is extremely unwise to say the least. Possibly they believed that their IMC rating was sufficient for prolonged, intentional flight in instrument conditions. Unfortunately, the IMC rating is not sufficient for such conditions. It should only be regarded as a **minimum skill** to 'get out of trouble' if an unintentional excursion into IMC occurs. Disorientation can affect anyone, particularly those who have not been adequately trained to fly on instruments, **and kept in practice**.

And finally, the bottom line is:

Don't gamble, safe flying is ENJOYABLE flying

7 SUMMARY

Most pilots want to enjoy the freedom to fly when, where and how they want to, whilst maintaining safety for themselves and others. The way to achieve and sustain this situation is to:

- be realistic about the weather
- work out a Minimum Safe Altitude (MSA) and keep to it
- use your judgement responsibly, don't be pressurised to fly
- know your own limitations
- prepare thoroughly
  - * allow for contingency
  - * have enough fuel
  - * be prepared to divert
- rehearse possible 'situations'
- use good practice in your planning and flying
- don't take unnecessary risks.

This will avoid the need for additional regulations and restrictions, and give you safe, enjoyable flying.

LASORS

2007

SAFETY SENSE 24 GENERAL AVIATION

PILOT HEALTH

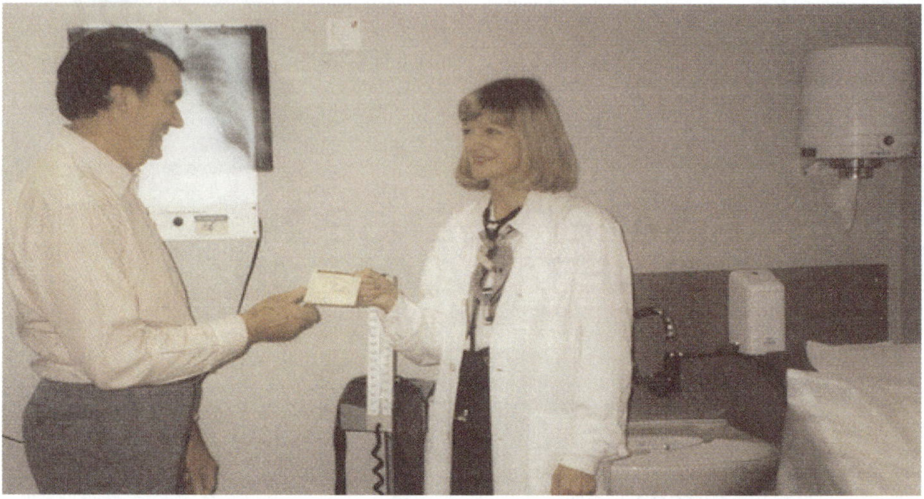

1 INTRODUCTION

The CAA requires pilots to hold a medical certificate (for Joint Aviation Authority, JAA, licences) or a declaration of health (for the National Private Pilot Licence, NPPL). The medical assessment is intended to reduce the risk of in-flight incapacitation.

A network of Authorised Medical Examiners (AMEs) across the country are approved by the CAA's Medical Division to undertake the appropriate medical examination for the JAA medical certificate. The AME has received training in aviation medicine and may also be a pilot.

However, pilots who wish to fly only light (up to 2,000 kg) single-engine aircraft (also microlights, gliders or gyroplanes) within the UK and in good weather can obtain the relevant medical documentation for a national PPL without visiting an AME, although they will need to attend their general practitioner. Slightly different requirements apply, depending on which type of flying activity is intended, so it is best to seek advice from your local flying club, or from the NPPL web site: www.nppl.uk.com

Advice on health related matters can also be obtained from an airsport medical adviser, an AME, or the CAA Medical Division – see the Medical Division's web site for further details: www.srg.caa.co.uk.

Medical requirements for flying are under regular review and frequently change. Any recent changes will be posted on the Medical Division's web site.

2 THE MEDICAL ASSESSMENT

It is particularly important that pilots are aware of their state of health. as what may seem a trivial symptom e.g. mild earache, can assume importance when flying. Whilst a medical assessment by a doctor can be reassuring, such assessments (which, for the NPPL, do not necessarily include a medical examination) are much less useful than the individual's self-determination of fitness, or unfitness. It is primarily the pilot's responsibility to decide if he is fit to fly, and it is also his responsibility to stay on the ground if he suspects he may not be completely well.

3 ENVIRONMENT

The earth's atmosphere consists of a mixture of gases, primarily oxygen and nitrogen, with the former being essential for human life. As an unpressurised aircraft climbs through the atmosphere the cockpit pressure reduces and at 18,000 ft the pilot experiences half the pressure of that at sea level.

4 THE BIOLOGICAL ENGINE

a. The human body converts the substances it absorbs such as food and oxygen into energy by a chemical process, similar to very slow combustion, called 'oxidation'. The body varies its consumption of stored energy sources according to its degree of activity, just like an engine. The intake of food (energy source) is adjusted on a medium to long term basis, whereas oxygen intake can be increased very quickly, in response to a short-term requirement to oxidise more stored nutrients and provide extra energy. When resting we require very little oxygen; under a high physical work load this increases and at maximum effort, oxygen use and energy production can be more than 15 times the resting value.

b. Air is inhaled into the lungs where its oxygen combines with haemoglobin in the red cells of the blood and is then circulated to those tissues where energy is needed. At the cellular level, oxygen combines with food stores to provide energy (with heat as a by-product). All cells need some oxygen to survive and the brain is particularly susceptible to a reduced supply of oxygen. Apart from heat, a main by-product of the oxidation process is carbon dioxide, which is returned to the lungs by the blood and exhaled.

c. Oxygen comprises only one fifth of the air breathed in and its availability for absorption and transport through the body is pressure dependant. Up to about 10,000 ft altitude, the healthy body has compensatory mechanisms to cope with the associated reduction in oxygen availability with increasing altitude without any noticeable detrimental effect. However, if there is an abnormality of the respiratory or cardiovascular system, the individual is likely to be more affected by a reduction in oxygen pressure, and may have symptoms even below 10,000 ft.

d. Reducing the capacity of your oxygen transport system by donating blood may increase your sensitivity to altitude, although this is quickly remedied by the body's reserves. However, a pilot should not fly for at least 24 hours after giving blood.

e. When an individual ascends above 10,000 ft in an aircraft the reduction in oxygen pressure reduces the efficiency of cellular processes, with the brain being the most sensitive of the body's systems. No-one is immune to these effects, which are insidious and often unnoticed by the affected individual. They may lead to hazardous actions, such as forgetting to change fuel tanks or flying off course. The effects become increasingly more serious with increasing altitude and above 18,000 ft, breathing atmospheric air, pilots are likely to eventually lose consciousness. At 25,000 feet this is likely to occur in 2-4 minutes. The mountaineer is able to adapt, to a certain extent, to such altitudes but such adaptation occurs at a rate which is too slow to be of benefit to the aviator used to living near sea level.

5 HYPOXIA

a. When the human body is starved of oxygen at altitude, or is in poor health with regard to its ability to absorb and transport oxygen, its efficiency reduces. When inadequate oxygen is available for normal functioning a condition called 'hypoxia' results. The brain is affected early but symptoms are often unnoticed due to the associated dulling of judgement. The effects are similar to alcohol intoxication. As hypoxia proceeds the individual becomes clumsy, drowsy, develops an inappropriate sense of well being and becomes increasingly error prone. The extent of the symptoms is dependant upon the actual altitude but even short periods above 10,000 ft are likely to produce effects.

b. To prevent hypoxia, flights must be at an altitude less than 10,000 feet, or the aircraft must have a pressurised cabin (as do almost all commercial airliners) or the pilot must utilise an individual oxygen source supplied by a personal mask.

6 HYPERVENTILATION

a. The respiratory system adapts quickly to changes in oxygen demand caused by exercise. However, breathing rapidly does not reduce the effects of hypoxia and can have some disadvantages.

b. The body cells produce carbon dioxide as a by-product of the oxidation process, which is dissolved in the blood and returned to the lungs for exhalation. Increasing the rate and depth of breathing speeds up the removal of carbon dioxide, disturbing the chemical balance in the blood and symptoms similar to hypoxia may result.

c. The most common causes of hyperventilation are stress and anxiety but this can usually be controlled by consciously returning to a normal rate of respiration, and relaxing. Your instructor will give you advice if he notices you are breathing rapidly when under training. If you or a fellow crew member or passenger do experience symptoms which might be attributable to hyperventilation, it is important to first ensure that hypoxia is not the problem.

7 VISION

a. Our sight is something we tend to take for granted. There are, however, two points pilots should be aware of.

b. Firstly, if you use contact lenses or spectacles you should have a spare pair of spectacles immediately available, which can be put on if you become intolerant of your lenses (or lose one, or both, of them) in flight, or you lose or break your spectacles.

c. Secondly, almost all of us will require reading glasses at some point – the lens in each eye stiffens with increasing age and can't adjust for near distances as it can when younger. Generally this process becomes noticeable at about 40 years with the first sign being an inability to read in poor light (because in low lighting conditions the pupil widens and, in photographic parlance, the 'depth of field' reduces and the near point for focussing moves further away from the eye). Unfortunately it will not improve with eye exercises! After your first set of reading glasses you will probably need slightly stronger ones every few years until about age sixty. Do make sure that your reading glasses are suitable for flying. You still need to see clearly into the distance and so you should use bi- focal lenses or the half frame, look-over type so that you can be comfortable looking at a map, your instruments, or at the horizon without having to change or remove your glasses. Full frame near vision spectacles are not acceptable for pilots, because distant vision is adversely affected. 'Varifocal' lenses (those which gradually, rather than abruptly, adjust their refractive power) can be used but make sure you find them suitable for flying before using them in the air, as not everyone can tolerate them (it can make some individuals feel dizzy).

d. There are a number of surgical procedures available which reduce, or even eliminate, the need for spectacles. All involve a reshaping of the clear part at the front of the eye, called the cornea. Although the methods vary, some using lasers, others diamond knives (the older techniques) none offer guaranteed success and all will require a period of grounding with a specialist assessment before being considered fit for flying. The long term effects are not fully known and vision can occasionally be worse after such surgery. Any pilot considering such surgery should look at the CAA Medical Division web site (www.srg.caa.co.uk) before submitting to an irreversible procedure.

8 STRESS AND FATIGUE

a. All of us at some time will find our lives affected by stress, fatigue, illness or injury – the important thing is to recognise how these can affect our flying skills and to proceed in a sensible fashion.

b. Stress is considered a modern day ailment, but it is a part of everyday life. It is the reaction to it that may cause a problem. Sleep disturbance, poor appetite and indigestion can all be signs of excess stress, whether at home or at work. Although most consider flying to be a relief from such pressures, it is not sensible to fly when you are experiencing physical symptoms or ruminating over your problems. Any preoccupation can detract from the continuing mental activity needed for safe flying. If you are not feeling 100%, take responsibility for your own flight safety and seek medical advice if you are uncertain of the implications for flying.

c. Short term fatigue is what we experience after strenuous physical or mental exercise. It may be associated with sleepiness and may also be the cause of mistakes and lapses of concentration. Medium to long term fatigue is more often associated with shift work, time zone crossings (which causes 'jet lag') or just regularly cutting back on sleep. It can cause drivers to fall asleep at the wheel or pilots to fall asleep at the controls. The only means of dealing with fatigue is to recognise when it is likely to occur and what can happen as a result. The only means of preventing it is to make sure you get adequate rest before flying.

9 ILLNESS AND INJURY

a. Any illness can be debilitating and recovery can take longer than you think. Most pilots would think that returning to work means they are fit to fly but this is not always the case. As a rule of thumb, any condition requiring medical certification that you are unfit for work should normally require at least an equivalent time back at full employment, without treatment, before flying. Your GP or AME may be able to give you specific guidance if you want to start flying earlier. This particularly applies to some of the modern outpatient surgery or investigations which have been addressed in Aeronautical Information Circular 63/2002 (Pink 35) 'Modern Medical Practice and Flight Safety'. Seek medical advice before flying and ensure you advise your doctor that you are a pilot.

b. If you have an injury ensure you have fully recovered before flying. You do not want to find yourself in severe pain, or with a weak arm or leg when operating an aircraft. Unlike car drivers, pilots do not have the option to stop in a few seconds. Also make sure that you have the full range of movement necessary for flying before returning to the cockpit. A circuit or two with an instructor before going solo can be beneficial if there is any doubt about your fitness after recovery from injury.

10 ALCOHOL

a. The consumption of alcohol produces effects similar to hypoxia. However, breathing oxygen will not reverse the effects. Increasing altitude increases the effects because of the reduced oxygen pressure. It is therefore essential for pilots to separate their flying from alcohol consumption. Since it takes an extended period of time to remove even low levels of alcohol from the blood, pilots should not fly for at least eight hours after consuming modest amounts of alcohol and up to 24 hours (or longer) following a major celebration!

b. Since one of the more subtle effects of alcohol is on the inner ear and can result in an increased susceptibility to disorientation up to three days after taking a large amount of alcohol, pilots should always be careful in the amount of alcohol they consume if they are flying during the next 1-3 days.

11 EXPANSION OF BODY GASES

a) If you take a balloon from sea level to 18,000 ft, its volume will double due to the decrease in pressure (Boyle's Law). Gas in the cavities of your body will do exactly the same thing. Problems can be experienced with air in the sinuses or behind the eardrum (middle ear) as both of these cavities have entrances which can be easily affected by the inflammation from a common cold. The most important point is to avoid flying with a respiratory tract infection (cold). You should know how to 'clear your ears' using the Valsalva technique and if you cannot clear your ears before flight, stay on the ground because you may tear an eardrum, or suffer severe pain in your ears or sinuses on descent (climbing is not usually a problem).

b. It is also possible for the nitrogen gas which is dissolved in our body fluids to come out of solution and form bubbles if exposed to reduced pressure for a prolonged period. This is known as decompression sickness or 'the bends' and is rarely experienced at an altitude below 18,000 ft. However, SCUBA diving exposes the body to increased pressure and dissolves more nitrogen in the body. This may cause decompression sickness during subsequent flying at a very much lower altitude. Most divers are aware of this problem and will not fly, even in a pressurised aircraft, immediately after diving. If you intend to SCUBA dive within 24 hours before flying, seek expert advice about the time interval between the two activities.

12 MEDICATION AND FLYING

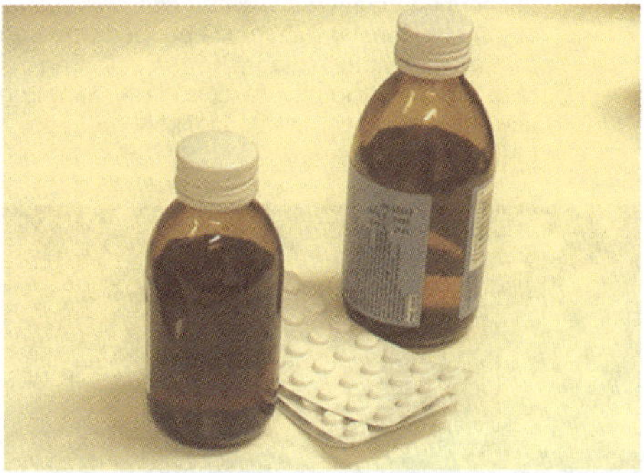

a. Doctors can choose from a wide range of medications when treating an illness. There is also a wide range of 'over the counter' treatments which do not require a prescription. Doctors may be unaware of the effects of their prescriptions upon a pilot's flying capability. Some may cause drowsiness, nausea or fatigue and others may reduce resistance to even minor increases in acceleration forces.

b. Some quite simple 'over the counter' products carry warnings to avoid operating machinery and they may react with other medication. If the medication you are taking says that driving, or operating machinery may be adversely affected, it is probably unsuitable for use if you are flying. Remember that the underlying condition for which you are taking the medication may preclude flying. Seek specialist advice if you are unsure of whether or not you should be flying, before you take to the air as a pilot.

13 CARBON MONOXIDE

a. An aircraft engine is rather less efficient than your body in that some of its fuel oxidation is incomplete and carbon monoxide rather than dioxide is produced. This would be of academic importance if it were not that many aircraft use their engine exhaust gas heat, through an exchanger, to warm the cabin. Add to that the fact that carbon monoxide bonds very strongly to the blood cells and blocks its oxygen carrying capacity then it becomes necessary to consider the symptoms of carbon monoxide (CO) poisoning.

b. As a gas, CO is colourless, tasteless and lethal! Exposure of pilots to it has been the cause of many fatal accidents. It can usually only be recognised in an aircraft by associated engine exhaust smells. Symptoms are subtle, similar to hypoxia but perhaps with a more obvious headache and it doesn't respond so promptly to oxygen – although using an oxygen mask is likely to restrict further exposure.

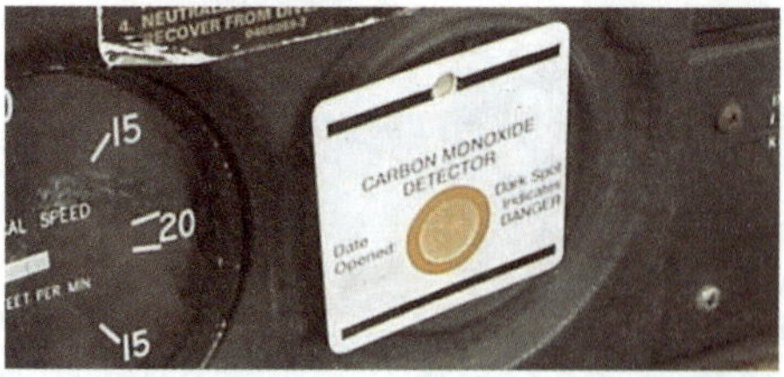

c. The best way to deal with CO poisoning is to prevent exposure in the first place but if you do suspect its presence when in flight, increase ventilation, land and try to get an engineer to trace any sources. There are CO monitors on the market and we recommend that one of them be carried. Paper sensors are easily contaminated by other fumes and need to be changed more frequently than their markings would suggest. Electronic detectors often have several functions in addition to a basic warning, but if fitted permanently would constitute a modification, and may place the device outside its operating limits. However, one could be carried as personal equipment.

14 I'M SAFE

a. This acronym gives all pilots a basic checklist for their fitness to fly. The items on that checklist are covered in this leaflet. The bottom line is that a pilot's fitness can change quickly and it is primarily the responsibility of the pilot himself to decide whether or not he is fit to fly .

I llness
M edication
S tress
A lcohol
F atigue
E ating
I'M SAFE

Safety Promotion, GAD, Gatwick

Use this personal checklist before setting off for the airfield, just as you would look at the weather or do a pre-flight check. It is available as a free sticker from Safety Promotion, General Aviation Department, Aviation House, Gatwick Airport South RH6 0YR (please send SAE).

b. If in doubt about any of the items, then take medical advice.

SAFETY SENSE 25
USE OF GPS

INFORMATION AND GUIDANCE TO PILOTS FOR THE USE OF GPS IN LIGHT AIRCRAFT

Most illustrations courtesy of Garmin UK and Honeywell

1 INTRODUCTION

a. The most familiar Satellite Navigation (or GNSS) system to most of us in the UK is the US Department of Defence "Navstar" Global Positioning System or GPS. Other systems are available, or in development, but this leaflet is based on the use of the Navstar GPS system.

b. Here you will find background information and guidance for General Aviation pilots in the use of stand-alone GPS equipment (i.e. systems not forming part of an integrated Flight Management System).

c. Unless specifically approved for particular purposes, such equipment is only to be used as an aid to other forms of navigation.

2 SYSTEM AND SIGNAL ANOMALIES

a. The GPS system has generally shown exceptional reliability, but it has been known to suffer technical and human failure. Consequently, **GPS must not be relied upon as a sole navigation reference in flight critical applications**. Common sense dictates that pilots should not only familiarise themselves with the techniques required to use the system properly, but understand how it could go wrong and prepare for the unexpected.

b. **Availability**
The receiver relies on maintaining line of sight between itself and the satellite. It needs to be able to 'see' several satellites (the number depends on the accuracy and integrity required) to provide a fix and, even with 24 satellites in orbit, there are times when insufficient satellites are 'visible' to provide that service.

c. **Geometry**
Whilst enough satellites may be 'visible' to give a fix, at certain times their angular separation may be small, giving rise to poor accuracy. This reduction in accuracy is called "Dilution of Precision" or "DOP" and may be displayed as a number. A high DOP (more than 6) indicates that GPS position accuracy is significantly degraded and the information should not be used.

d. **RAIM**
More sophisticated receivers contain a processing algorithm known as Receiver Autonomous Integrity Monitor (RAIM). RAIM compares the information received from a number of satellites and alerts the user to an error. If enough satellites are visible, the function may be able to identify the faulty signal and discard it.

The presence of a working RAIM function only monitors one type of failure and does not guarantee the absence of a position error. RAIM availability at any time and place in the world can be predicted from satellite orbital information by receivers with appropriate software. However, RAIM prediction cannot foresee the failure of a satellite, nor the removal of satellites from service. Neither does it take account of terrain.

e. **NOTAMs/NANUs**
Notice Advisories to Navstar Users (NANUs) are the means of informing GPS users of planned satellite "outages". NANUs are available in the UK through the NOTAM

system, and must be consulted to determine the availability of GPS and RAIM information. Some receivers can be adjusted to manually deselect a particular satellite if it is expected to be out of service.

f. **Failure / Error**
The satellite clock (the heart of the system) may drift off time, the satellite may stray from its orbit or its transmitter may simply fail. **It can take up to two hours for such failures and errors to be resolved**. At such times, unknown position errors have been reported (up to 2 km), despite the presence of RAIM.

g. **Terrain Shielding**
At low level, in regions of high terrain or obstacles, satellites can become hidden to the aircraft receiver. This may give rise to unexpected loss of position and/or RAIM .

h. **Dynamic Masking**
Parts of the aircraft itself may get in the way, for example the outside wing in a turn. If this blanks the signal momentarily, the navigation capability may be degraded or lost, requiring several seconds of straight and level flight to re-establish navigation information.

i. **Multi-path Reflections**
The signal may bounce off hills and structures before arriving at the receiver, giving rise to range errors from the satellite. Such errors are generally very small but may appear as a sudden change in position which the receiver interprets as a change in drift and groundspeed. This may lead to distracting messages declaring phenomenal wind shifts, and may be sufficient to destroy the integrity of the navigation information altogether.

j. **Interference and Jamming**
The GPS signal received from the satellite is at very low power and is **vulnerable to interference**, either intentionally or otherwise. Sources of unintentional interference include, among others, UHF and microwave television signals, some DME channels, and harmonics from some VHF RT transmissions. It is known that jamming devices are available which can easily disrupt signal coverage across a wide area. Military exercises and trials which include deliberate GPS jamming take place frequently, and are notified. Check NOTAMs for any areas likely to be affected.

k. **Sunspots**
Because the satellites orbit at very high altitudes, radiation from the sun can affect their transmissions, or even their own navigation system. Particular flares or sunspots cannot be forecast, nor can their effect, but NOTAMs include warnings of possible GPS signal interference when major disturbances are detected.

l. **Selective Availability**
Finally, the satellites are the property of the US Department of Defence (DoD), which may move satellites around to improve cover over a particular area, thereby reducing the availability over others. Although the signal is promised to remain available for civilian use, the facility exists to insert random errors into the signals to reduce accuracy, or even to switch the whole system off completely.

3 EQUIPMENT

a. **Carriage of Equipment**
The installation or carriage of GPS equipment does not affect the requirement for a primary means of navigation appropriate for the intended route, as detailed in Schedule 5 of the Air Navigation Order.

b. **VFR use only**
When operating under Visual Flight Rules (VFR) outside controlled airspace, there is no requirement to carry any radio navigation equipment and there is no installation standard for GPS used only as an aid to visual navigation. However, equipment permanently installed (in any way) in an aircraft must be fitted in a manner approved by the CAA. If a hand held unit is carried, care should be taken to ensure that it, the antenna and any leads and fittings for them are secured in such a way that they **cannot interfere** with the normal operation of the aircraft's controls and equipment and do not inhibit the pilots movements or vision in any way. Consideration should also be given to their possible effect on the aircraft occupants if the aircraft comes to a sudden stop or has to be abandoned.

Equipment permanently installed…

c. **IFR certification**
If a GPS system has been certified as meeting the "Basic Area Navigation" (BRNAV) requirements this will be stated in a 'Supplement' to the aircraft Flight Manual. Such approval means only that the equipment is regarded as accurate for en-route purposes (within ±5 nautical miles for 95% of the time).

There may be additional approval requirements to operate it in Terminal Areas (Including SIDs and STARs) or on an instrument approach. Even systems which are certified for Precision Area Navigation (PRNAV) may not meet the required navigation performance for use on an instrument approach. The use of such equipment for precision navigation will probably also require specific pilot qualification.

4 SYSTEM FAMILIARISATION

a. The individual manufacturers of GPS equipment each provide different functions in the receiver. There may also be major differences between individual receivers from the same manufacturer.

b. Before attempting to use the equipment in the air, pilots should learn about the system in detail, including:

- Principles of GPS
- System Installation & Limitations
- Pre-Flight Preparation & Planning
- Cross-Checking Data Entry
- Use of the System In Flight
- Confirmation of Accuracy
- Database integrity
- Human Error
- System Errors & Malfunctions

More detailed guidance on training is available in other CAA documents.

c. Essential learning, even for VFR use only and preferably with guidance from the manufacturer's representative or an instructor experienced on the individual equipment, should include at least the following:

- Switching on and setting up
- Checking the status of receiver, satellites, battery, and any database used
- Loading waypoints
- Loading a route
- Loading alternate routes
- "Direct" or "GO-TO" functions
- Selecting alternate routes
- What your database contains (and what it doesn't)
- Use of RAIM function if fitted
- Amending RAIM input if fitted
- Regaining the last screen when you have pressed the wrong button!

d. Whether or not you find a suitable instructor, practise using the equipment on the ground before trying it in the air. Then take someone else to fly and navigate for you, while you are becoming totally familiar with the GPS. If you fly a single-seater, ask someone else to fly you in their aircraft while you practise.

e. If the check list supplied with your GPS equipment is complicated, inadequate or non-existent, use part of the learning process to write your own check-list for setting up and use in the air.

f. Although there is no requirement to demonstrate use of the GPS on any UK flight test, it is sensible to use it at least for some of the time when an examiner or instructor is flying with you. You may pick up some useful tips.

5 FLIGHT PLANNING

a. The attention a GPS receiver requires in flight can be minimised with careful planning and preparation before departure, releasing the pilot to other tasks whilst in the air.

b. Most modern units allow the user to enter a series of waypoints as a route or flight plan. Be familiar with how to do this, how to store it, and retrieve it for later use. Doing this significantly reduces the chances of making an error in flight, and allows more time for other things such as lookout or instrument flying.

c. **Plan the flight and prepare a map and log in the normal way**. Then enter the route information from the log, directly into the receiver as a “Flight Plan”. This achieves three things;

i. The route information is created visually on a chart, helping to eliminate any gross error.

ii. You have a back up should the GPS information become unreliable or unavailable in flight.

iii. You are aware of the terrain over which you intend to fly, and can calculate safe altitudes (many databases do not consider terrain).

d. **User Waypoints**

i. If the aircraft and GPS receiver are your own, you may want to set it up to your own preferences. For example, you might have a favourite visual navigation route which you follow every time you depart or arrive. Most GPS receivers allow you to set up User Waypoints to guide you along such a route, even if there is an airspace database installed. Keep a record of all loaded User Waypoints for future reference.

ii. It has been known for one pilot in a group or club to edit the data comprising a stored User Waypoint and leave it with the same name, but in a different position. Deleting or moving existing User Waypoints, or changing their names, should be **expressly prohibited** where the GPS is operated by more than one pilot. Any changes must be agreed by the group.

iii. This underlines the need to check the position of waypoints in the flight planned route, and any possible alternative or diversion route, before departure. If this is not done, pilots cannot rely on any ‘Go Direct’ or ‘Nearest’ function in the air when working with User Waypoints.

iv. When inserting a User Waypoint, ensure that the latitude and longitude co-ordinates you use are from the correct geodetic datum. The positions of an individual point may be up to a kilometre apart if referred to different datums. Although some receivers have the facility to convert position information between the WGS 84 datum used in GPS equipment and others, these conversions are not always absolutely accurate and can contain errors. Positions may also be in different formats. Many receivers refer to positions as degrees, minutes and decimals of a minute, rather than the degrees minutes and seconds used in documents.

6 PROGRAMMING CROSS-CHECKS

a. Once the route has been entered, ‘run’ it to make sure you have not missed (or mis-entered) any waypoints. This may be called the ‘Simulator’ or ‘Demo’ mode.

b. If you have a map display, it is usually possible to display the route on the screen once it has been entered. Any gross error in the position of a waypoint or turning point should be obvious on the map. If there is no map, or it is too small to be of practical use, **compare the tracks and distances displayed on the GPS with the previously prepared flight log**.

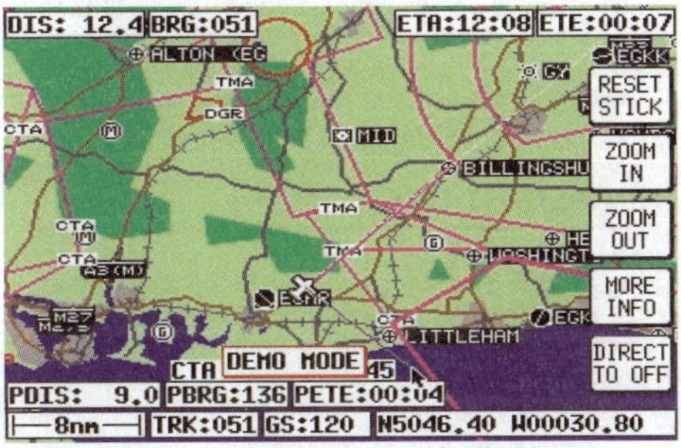

any gross error should be obvious

compare tracks and distances

7 THE DATABASE

a. If you have an aviation database installed, ensure that it is current, and is valid for the area over which you intend to fly. Aerodromes seldom move far, but their serviceability, airspace, frequencies, reporting points and other information change often. An out-of-date database can lead (at best) to embarrassing and expensive error. At worst, it could be catastrophic. **Do not use an out of date database.**

b. Even a current database cannot be automatically assumed to be error free. Instances of database errors have been recorded, and only careful checking against current charts and the AIP may identify these. In addition, NOTAMs must still be consulted before flight.

8 INITIAL STATUS

On start up, check the status of the receiver and its battery. Compare the indicated GPS position with the aircraft's known position. If your aircraft is normally parked in the same place, it helps to enter the coordinates of that position as a User Waypoint. Each time you start up in that position, select 'go direct' to that waypoint. You will then see the current error of the GPS position. You can also compare the relative indicated position of a known database point (such as the Aerodrome Reference Point) with its actual position.

9 IN-FLIGHT USE

a. **The GPS system should NEVER be used in isolation**. The risk of loss or degradation of the signal, with the attendant possibility of a position error, is genuine. More importantly, the risk of human error in data input and display reading is extremely high and these errors can go unnoticed until it is too late.

b. It is easy to transpose numbers in one's head, and these errors are surprisingly persistent. Do not allow any such errors to lead you into trouble.

c. It may help to go through a three-stage exercise in setting up **any** navigation aid, including GPS:

1. Set it up and satisfy yourself that you have done it correctly.

2. Do something else – even if only for a few seconds.

3. Go back and check again that the set up is still correct.

d. When flying in IMC or above cloud, only use GPS in combination with other radio aids to correlate with dead reckoning of the flight planned route and general situational awareness.

e. If the GPS display agrees with everything else you know, including dead reckoning, the navigation log, map reading and general situational awareness as well as radio navigation, then the GPS display is likely to be providing the most accurate information.

f. The accuracy of GPS will often expose the operational error of other navigation aids. Errors of up to 5° are normal in a VOR display (more on an ADF), and DME is only accurate to about half a mile. DME indicates slant range but GPS displays horizontal range, giving rise to a further small disparity, which increases as you approach the DME station overhead. Some apparent errors may of course be due to magnetic variation.

g. If flying visually, it is easiest (but not usually particularly accurate) to cross-check your GPS position with a recognisable feature on the ground. You could also compare indications from a radio aid station with the GPS range and bearing to that station. Any difference greater than the normal error associated with the radio aid indicates a problem with one or other aid. If you cannot cross-check with a third system, especially if short of fuel or near controlled airspace, consider asking an ATS radar unit or Distress and Diversion Cell for a position fix.

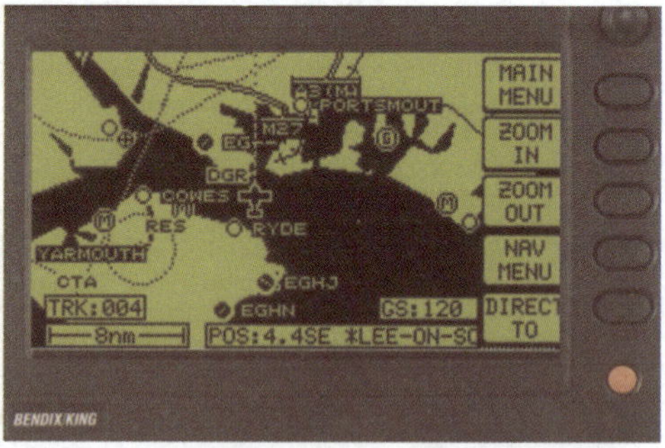

cross-check your position

h. When using GPS to track to an aerodrome, radio navigation aid or visual reference point, it may not be necessary to keep the course deviation indicator in the centre. Consider trying to maintain one dot to the right of centre in order to minimise the risk of collision with other aircraft approaching the same point. However, remember you will now fly 1 mile right of the direct route, so ensure that is a safe track.

To avoid becoming totally dependent on the GPS, ask yourself 2 questions regularly throughout the flight;

1. Does the GPS agree with at least one other independent source of navigation information?

2. If the GPS quits completely, ***right now***, can I continue safely without it?

If the answer is yes to both questions, you may continue to use the equipment for guidance. However, if the honest answer to either one of the questions is "No", then ***you must establish navigation by some other means***.

10 DIVERTING FROM INTENDED ROUTE

a. Re-programming the system in the air is time-consuming, and interferes with other procedures such as lookout. Like any cockpit operation, re-programming should not be undertaken whilst the aircraft is manoeuvring. Unless someone else can fly the aircraft for you, switch operation must be interrupted so that individual selections are interspersed with a thorough lookout (or instrument scan) every few seconds.

b. Anything you can do to reduce this re-programming will help. **Pre-plan likely route changes**, for example around controlled airspace in case you cannot obtain clearance, or around high ground in the event of bad weather. Have a note of the ICAO designators of all suitable diversion aerodromes.

c. Re-programming in the air is also much more likely to produce human errors. If you need to change your planned route, make at least a rough set of mental calculations (and note them down) BEFORE you turn onto the GPS track. Then if your new heading does not agree with your mental calculations, you will know you have made an error somewhere. **Check the new route on a map for terrain and any NOTAMed activity.** If your database is not current, you must check for controlled and restricted airspace also.

11 INSTRUMENT APPROACHES

a. Existing instrument approach procedures at some aerodromes are already provided in many receiver databases. These "Overlay" or "Monitored" approaches can present the pilot with a direct comparison with the terrestrial approach aid being used. **If your GPS receiver can do this, you must exercise extreme caution**. VOR and NDB approaches to beacons actually <u>on</u> the destination aerodrome usually provide a final approach path or track which is not aligned with the main runway centre-line. Even on a direct approach to a particular runway, pilots should not necessarily expect to be on the extended centreline of the runway.

b. The terrestrial approach procedure may include DME ranges from the threshold, missed approach point (MAP) or some other reference, such as the beacon. The GPS may give distance guidance to a different point, such as the Aerodrome Reference Point. Pilots should be aware of any differences in the distance information given to step-down fixes and/or the MAP, as this has the potential for catastrophic error.

c. **Overlays and Monitored approaches must only be used as supplemental information and the normal equipment for that approach procedure must be used as the primary reference**. Otherwise, disparity between the two displays and the potential for mistakes are just as likely to diminish the safety margins on an instrument approach as enhance them.

d. The safety values in the design criteria of any published approach are applied to known, surveyed obstacles and restrictions to the required flight path. **Disregarding the established approach procedures and published minima, in favour of reliance on the GPS, is not authorised and is highly dangerous.**

11 USER DEFINED APPROACHES

a. Pilots have been known to produce and follow their own approach procedures using GPS information. **This is potentially dangerous**. There is no ground based confirmation of position and the risk of mis-entering waypoints is high.

b. Furthermore, when flying towards a waypoint in normal, en-route mode, the course deviation indicator (CDI) normally indicates a track error of 5nm at full-scale deflection (or 1 mile per 'dot'). This is not accurate enough for any final approach, and only changes when either the sensitivity is changed manually or the aircraft is following a published *and correctly activated* GPS approach contained in the database. Changing sensitivity whilst on approach is a hazardous distraction.

c. Unless a *published* approach is activated, the receiver's RAIM function remains in en-route mode (even if the CDI scaling is changed manually) and there may be a position error of up to *2 nautical miles* before any RAIM alarm is given.

d. **User-defined approaches can be dangerous and are not authorised.**

12 THE FUTURE

Satellite navigation will one day almost undoubtedly form the basis of our radio navigation but in the mean time, the GPS system is fallible and should be used **with knowledge and caution**, not blind faith.

13 SUMMARY

1. Accuracy is not guaranteed
2. Apparent accuracy does not mean reliability
3. Understand your own equipment.
4. Train before using it.
5. Use standard settings and check lists.
6. Flight plan normally before loading a route.
7. Check the route before flight.
8. Load possible alternative routes.
9. Ensure database is the latest version.
10. Check the status on start-up.
11. Fly and navigate manually, only use the GPS once you have verified its accuracy against something else.
12. Do not rely on GPS for instrument approaches.

SAFETY SENSE 26
GENERAL AVIATION

26

VISITING MILITARY AERODROMES

1 INTRODUCTION

It is Ministry of Defence (MOD) policy to encourage civil use of military aerodromes where this does not conflict with military flying operations. While the same general rules and procedures apply to aircraft at all aerodromes, the specific requirements of military operations mean that the way they are applied often makes them appear quite different to those to which civilian pilots have become accustomed. Military pilots have their own regulations, but pilots of civil aircraft are always subject to the current Air Navigation Order and Rules of the Air Regulations. This leaflet is intended for use by private pilots, although commercial operators may find it useful background. It should be read in conjunction with Safety Sense leaflet 6 "Aerodrome Sense".

2 EMERGENCIES

a. Many military aerodromes have long hard surfaced runways. Most have resident fire and rescue services and air traffic controllers who are trained to help pilots of aircraft in distress or in urgent need of assistance, and who have the ability to listen and talk on the emergency frequency 121.5 MHz. These facilities suggest that such aerodromes make excellent diversion destinations for any aircraft with problems. Even if the aerodrome is closed, a long hard runway (or any part of a large flat airfield) is a much more attractive place to land in an emergency than a farmer's field, and it is even possible that some rescue facilities may still be available.

b. There is a natural reluctance on the part of civilian pilots to make use of military facilities. However, if the pilot is experiencing problems which can be reduced by the use of a military aerodrome, the MOD encourages them to do so by waiving landing fees for any aircraft landing as a result of a diversion for genuine safety reasons. Nevertheless, it should be remembered that military operations normally have total priority. Unless pilots of civilian aircraft make distress ("MAYDAY") or urgency ("PAN, PAN") calls (which again many civilians seem reluctant to do), they are unlikely to be offered the use of these aerodromes.

c. **If you are experiencing problems in the air, do not hesitate to make a PAN call**, especially if there is anything that ATC can do to help. Because of the nature of military operations and the complexity of the aircraft, military air traffic controllers tend to be well practised in emergency procedures. As the saying goes, "an ounce of prevention is worth more than a pound of cure!"

d. Inexperienced pilots may be worried about information being passed to them too quickly for them to absorb. In that case, consider adding the word "TYRO" to your callsign (for example "TYRO Golf Alfa Bravo Charlie Delta") to warn the controller that he needs to give information clearly and more slowly than

PART 1 - VISITING DURING NORMAL OPERATING HOURS

3 PRE-FLIGHT

a. As for any flight, the most important part is the planning. Except in an emergency situation, every military aerodrome is **strictly PPR** (prior permission required) well in advance. Some require a minimum of 24 hours notice or longer and permission cannot usually be given instantly over the telephone, so an early request is vital. The published telephone number will normally be to Station Operations (Ops), which may or may not be co-located with Air Traffic Control. In order to consider the request, certain information is usually needed, so be ready to give the following:

- Pilot's name (and those of all passengers) (frequent visitors may require security clearance)
- Aircraft type and registration
- Aerodrome of departure
- Estimated time of arrival at the MATZ (if applicable) or ATZ boundary
- Intended time of departure from the military aerodrome
- Reason for the visit (appointment in nearby town, visit friends etc.)
- What the aircraft's insurance covers (temporary £7.5 million Crown Indemnity can be added to the landing fee)
- Fuel type and likely quantity for refuelling if required (AVGAS may not be available)
- Pilot's flying experience and currency, including familiarity with that and other military aerodromes

- Customs, Immigration, and Special Branch clearance requirements (which may not be available)

b. Once permission is granted, Ops will have useful airfield information available. An aerodrome "visiting aircraft brief" may be provided to you either by phone, e-mail, fax or letter if there is enough time. It is expected that you telephone early on the day of arrival, so use that call to obtain more up to date information. Every military aerodrome records regular weather reports and has a dedicated terminal aerodrome forecast (TAF). Although these may not be published by the Met office, the aerodrome Ops will have them available. Ask for and be ready to copy down the latest TAF and METAR. Ops personnel will be aware of local navigation warnings, which they can also pass to you. In addition, they may be able to direct you to an aerodrome Automatic Terminal Information Service (ATIS) giving weather and other essential aerodrome information on a radio frequency and/or a telephone number.

c. Aerodrome and approach charts for military aerodromes are normally not included in the UK AIP, but many are included in commercial guides, and they can be provided by ATC on request or obtained through the internet at www.aidu.mod.uk The "visiting aircraft brief" should be studied in conjunction with the appropriate charts.

d. Even if permission has been granted, always pre-plan a diversion to a suitable alternative aerodrome and carry enough fuel to reach it after allowing for holding time at your intended destination. Emergencies or military operations may require such holding, and prevent you landing even when on final approach. While most military aerodromes have runways long enough to accommodate the majority of light aeroplanes, they may have only one of them. Know your own crosswind limit in the aircraft you will be flying, and do not make an approach if the wind is outside that limit.

4 APPROACHING OR PASSING THE AERODROME

a. Make yourself as obvious as possible to other traffic; consider using the landing light. While it is not mandatory for civilian pilots to recognise a military aerodrome traffic zone (MATZ), if your track passes through or near one (and obviously if you intend landing!) it is **strongly** recommended that you call on the published VHF LARS or zone frequency at least 15 miles or 5 minutes flying time before you expect to enter the MATZ, and comply with requests from ATC. A serviceable transponder, ideally with altitude transmission (mode C), will assist ATC in identifying you but is not essential. Note that, except in a very few cases, the aerodrome traffic zone (ATZ) of a military aerodrome (whether within a MATZ or not) is permanently active, even if the aerodrome is closed, and you must avoid it unless you have permission to enter.

b. Many military aircraft are only equipped with UHF radio equipment, and Air Traffic Control is provided on UHF frequencies which civilian aircraft cannot use. If the controller is talking to an aircraft on UHF, he will not be able to answer a VHF transmission, and indeed may not even hear it if the UHF transmission happens at the same time. When you make the initial call, it is advisable to say on what frequency you are transmitting (e.g. "on 122.1"). Give the controller time to answer, and be prepared to call again if you hear nothing. Once the controller starts talking to you, he may simultaneously transmit on both UHF and VHF frequencies, so listen carefully for your own callsign at all times. You will hear everything he says, whether on the VHF or UHF frequency, but you will not hear UHF transmissions from other aircraft, which may take place while you are transmitting and cause the controller to ask you to repeat your transmission. If you have not received it already, you may be given the "visiting aircraft brief" over the radio, together with pertinent information about the aerodrome facilities.

c. Military procedures use two altimeter settings below transition altitude. Normally, military aircraft will set the Regional Pressure Setting (RPS) on their altimeter when outside the immediate area of the aerodrome and its instrument approach pattern, and controllers may ask you to do the same when receiving a service from them. Otherwise, QFE is the datum, and all heights indicated are above the runway. However, separation from other traffic may dictate that a controller asks you to use a pressure setting which you do not expect.

PAR controller

5 INSTRUMENT APPROACHES

a. Expect to set QFE as above. Most aerodromes equipped with radar will provide you with radar assistance until you are visual with the aerodrome, or will direct (vector) you on to a precision or non-precision final approach using that radar. If a surveillance radar approach (SRA) is provided it will usually be more detailed than at a civilian aerodrome, but is still only an aerodrome (non-precision) approach aid.

b. Precision approach radar (PAR) may be provided, which can be likened to a ground controlled ILS. The controller will direct you onto the final approach, and then give heading directions to maintain your flight path on the runway centreline, telling you not to acknowledge such instructions unless requested. Once you reach the glidepath he will tell you regularly whether you are above or below it, but will not give specific rate of descent directions. You must make your own adjustments to follow the glideslope down to your decision height. For any approach, expect the controller to ask you what decision height (minimum descent height for a non-precision approach) you are using; he will pass the procedure minimum with which you must compare your system minimum and add any extra allowance (for example for the IMC rating).

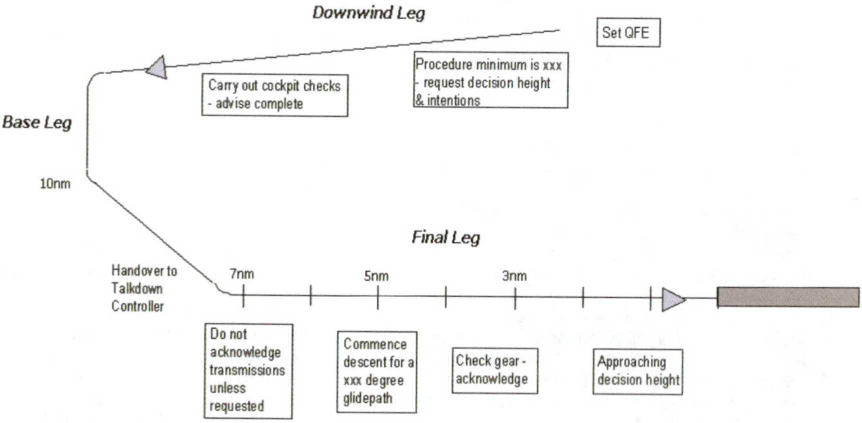

PAR procedure

c. On any instrument approach, expect the controller to ask you to "carry out cockpit checks, advise complete" before you turn onto the base leg, and "check gear, acknowledge" during the final approach. Transmit your confirmation when you have completed these checks. On that approach, you may hear the controller talking to the tower controller while he is talking to you. If making an approach towards the runway in use, expect to receive landing clearance or go-around instructions before reaching decision or minimum descent height. Ensure you know the Missed Approach Procedure. If you cannot remember it, ask for "missed approach instructions" well before you reach the final approach.

d. Expect military traffic to be given priority (They usually use a lot of fuel, and often do not carry much spare for diversion – you must!). Consider the aircraft types which normally use the aerodrome. Any major speed difference between these and your own aircraft may result in your being directed perhaps away from the approach to provide separation. The same might apply if there is a major difference in rates of descent; military aircraft often descend quite rapidly, especially above 2000 feet. Be aware that traffic in the visual circuit may pass quite close behind or above you.

e. Once you are able to see the runway, the controller will expect you to land on it if you can, close to the threshold unless there is a cable on the runway (see paragraph 7 below). As always, if you are unable to do so, fly a go-around to join the circuit, manoeuvring onto the dead side as soon as it is safe, or carry out the full Missed Approach Procedure. Beware of jet efflux, and **wake turbulence** from large aeroplanes, or rotor downwash from helicopters which may be using a different but nearby landing area – although the controller will normally be aware of the problem and pass a warning if conditions make such turbulence likely, a lack of warning does not mean a lack of risk. If you are not used to landing on wide runways, beware of the visual illusion which may cause you to round out higher than intended.

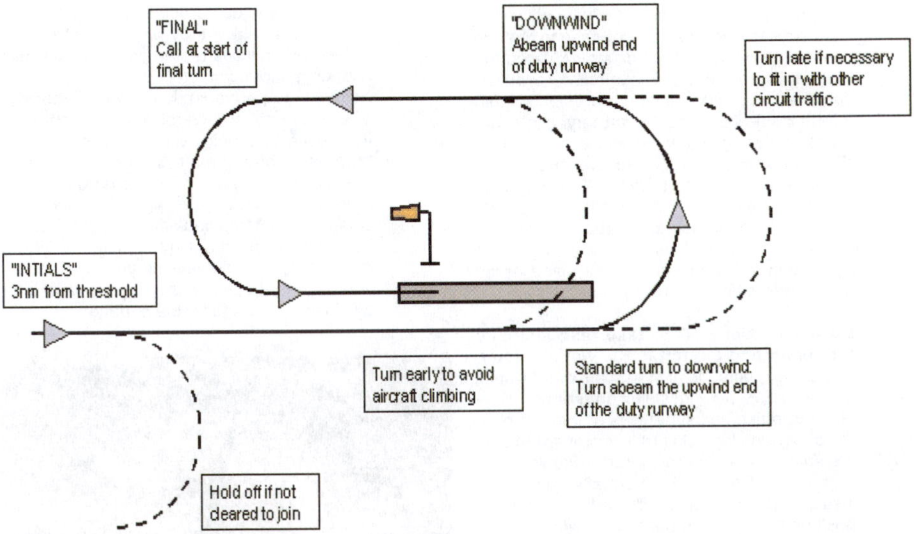

Oval circuit with military join procedures

6 CIRCUIT PROCEDURES

a. Many military aerodromes expect visitors to carry out a standard overhead join, as published in the GA safety poster included in LASORS and on the CAA web site. However, depending on the direction of your approach, ATC may direct you to join downwind, or on base leg. Circuit patterns are usually flown at heights which depend on aircraft type. For example, a turboprop trainer may fly the pattern at 1000 feet on QFE, light piston aeroplanes at 800 feet, and, if traffic is mixed, fast jet traffic at 1200 or 1500 feet. The "military standard join" shown above involves approaching parallel with the runway in use from an "initial point" outside the ATZ on the dead side of the runway centreline, at circuit height or lower. A call of "initial" will be made at that "initial point". Some aircraft may approach at high speed for a "run and break", also shown above. Approximately 1-1½ minutes after calling "initials" the aircraft will turn steeply, level or climbing to the circuit height, from the deadside to downwind, calling "on the break" instead of the normal "downwind" call. You may not hear these calls because they will be on a UHF frequency, but ATC may inform you that they have been made. If the aerodrome has "no dead side" (often when helicopters operate together with aeroplanes) the run in may take place over the runway itself. Any non-standard procedures would normally form part of the visiting aircraft brief.

b. Most military circuit patterns are oval. The downwind leg is flown closer than at most civilian aerodromes, because the turn after take-off, and the final turn, both involve continuous 180 degree turns. The "downwind" call is standard, but the call of "final" is given as the aircraft starts its final turn at the end of the downwind leg. It is not easy to fly an accurate military oval circuit, but if you can practise it beforehand, it is very satisfying to be able to fit in. You do not need to change your own normal pattern or radio procedure, but be aware that the controller might be surprised at how late you call "final". Intentions transmitted by military pilots are slightly different from those found in CAP 413. "Roll" effectively equates to "touch and go". "Land" equates to "full stop". You may also hear "overshoot" which means a pilot will make a low approach to the runway followed by a go-around, while confusingly an instruction to "go-around" is the same as an "orbit" (see next paragraph).

c. **Do not expect ATC to take responsibility for separating aircraft in the visual circuit**. You are expected to fit in with the other traffic, and if that is not possible, go-around. The place to make adjustments is at the turn onto the downwind leg. Do not turn crosswind until it is safe to do so, military aircraft usually climb steeply. Priority is normally given to instrument traffic, and ATC will transmit the position of that instrument traffic with its type. If you have called "downwind" before "instrument traffic at 8 (sometimes 6) miles", unless ATC give you other instructions they will expect you to be able to land and move off the runway before that instrument traffic. If you cannot, or you are told to go-around, or the "8(6) mile" call comes before your "downwind" call, go-around at circuit height. This may be referred to, again confusingly, as an "orbit", which involves crossing to the dead side over or just downwind of the threshold at circuit height, rejoining crosswind (ideally over the other threshold), again at circuit height. A call of "instrument traffic at 4(3) miles" is the equivalent of a "final" call; if you have not started the downwind leg you should end up behind the instrument traffic (but beware wake turbulence).

d. Once clearance to land is given, the controller will expect you to touch down close to the threshold unless there is a cable on the runway (see paragraph 7 below). Otherwise fly a go-around, manoeuvring onto the dead side as soon as it is safe. Beware of jet efflux, and **wake turbulence** from large aeroplanes, or rotor downwash from helicopters which may be using a different but close landing area – although the controller should be aware of the problem, he may not always have time to remind you.

7 BARRIERS AND CABLES

a. Several military aerodromes have "arrester cables" which can be laid across the runway to assist fast jet aeroplanes to stop. The mechanism (which may be called RHAG for "rotary hydraulic arrester gear" or a similar sounding acronym) for these cables will normally be permanently fitted on either side of the runway at several hundred metres in from each threshold, one at the threshold or "approach" end, the other (more common) at the "overrun" end (some aerodromes may have more than two). When required, the cables are stretched across the runway between the mechanisms. The position of the cables is marked by yellow discs on vertical boards beside the runway, and often by similar markings on the surface.

Cable 'UP'

b. The vertical position of the cables themselves may be one of three possible. "UP", or possibly "supported", means the inch thick metal cable is raised 3 inches above the runway surface on vertical rubber discs, as shown above. Although certain civil aircraft types may be able to do so, no propeller driven aircraft should attempt to cross a supported cable. "DOWN" or possibly "unsupported" means that the cable is lying on the runway surface, and the supporting discs have been pushed to one side. Crossing even an unsupported cable should be avoided whenever possible, and only attempted in propeller driven aeroplanes at very slow taxying speed. A "DE-RIGGED" cable has been removed from the runway surface completely.

c. Air Traffic Control will pass the state of the cables. Land beyond a rigged approach cable, and aim to turn off before an overrun cable. Similarly, aim to start the take-off run beyond an approach cable and lift off before an overrun cable. This will reduce the available runway length, so adjust your performance calculations to suit. In an emergency, the aerodrome may be able to de-rig a cable for you to make a safe landing, but that may take up to 20 minutes.

RHAG from threshold

d. There may be an "arrester (or jet) barrier" positioned at or beyond the end of the runway. Unlike a cable, this is for emergency use only and does not affect the runway itself. However, an "up" overrun barrier is a 20 foot obstacle affecting the climb after take-off or go-around. If for some reason the approach end barrier is up, it forms a significant obstruction. Propeller driven aeroplanes should not attempt to use an arrester barrier as an aid to stopping in an emergency.

Jet barrier

8 GROUND MOVEMENT

a. Once you have landed, the runway may be required by other aircraft for landing or take-off. You may be asked to vacate the runway quickly ("expedite"). "Expedite" does not mean "rush"! Do not dawdle, but make sure you are totally under control before you make any turns. Pre-flight study will indicate where you may turn off the runway, otherwise check with ATC. Military pilots stop and carry out their after-landing checks when well away from the runway, you should consider doing the same.

b. When taxying, beware of jet efflux or propeller slipstream from larger aircraft, including rotor downwash from helicopters. Several markings around the aerodrome may be different from the ICAO standard ones to which you are used. You should know the taxi route from your briefing, but if in doubt, stop and ask! If the aerodrome uses the military common frequency of 122.1 MHz for ground control, always use the aerodrome callsign when transmitting. Markings may be unfamiliar, if in doubt stop and ask.

c. You will usually be marshalled into your parking position by qualified personnel, rather than choose your own space. Leaflet 6, "Aerodrome Sense", shows the most common signals. You may be offered chocks, but these may be too large for your aircraft, so check them before allowing them to be fitted. Adding weight in the form of fuel may lower wheel spats onto the chocks! If you have asked for fuel, remember that the refuelling personnel will not be familiar with your aircraft. You should supervise the refuelling, paying particular attention to the type of fuel being dispensed. AVGAS and AVTUR (JET A-1) must not be confused! Check that additives are compatible with your aircraft.

d. You should report to Ops to discuss your requirements and future movements. You will probably be required to show your certificate of insurance detailing the level of third party and crown indemnity cover. Ensure you have an appropriate means to pay landing and other fees. Cheques are acceptable, but few military aerodromes have the facilities to accept credit cards. Make sure that if your aircraft has to be moved for operational reasons, the aerodrome authorities are able to either move it or contact you quickly.

9 DEPARTURE

a. You should receive a departure briefing from Ops. At that time give them the information you would normally pass on a taxi call, including how you wish to leave the aerodrome area; they will pass this to ATC to reduce radio transmissions. Confirm the frequency to use on start-up. Even if you are departing soon after arrival, a visit to Ops or ATC may provide much useful information and assistance. The staff may be able to help you to file a flight plan, or inform your destination of your intentions. They should certainly be able to update you with TAFs and METARs; NOTAMs should also be available, often already plotted on a map. Check the taxi pattern – find a suitable place for engine and/ or navigation equipment checks which will not obstruct the taxiway. If a suitable place for such checks does not exist, consider carrying out whatever checks you can before starting to taxi.

b. When starting engines, you may have the assistance of ground personnel, who will have access to a fire extinguisher and perhaps be able to remove chocks, although 12v ground power is unlikely to be available. Brief them about your intentions, for example if you are delaying taxying to carry out equipment checks, or allowing the engine to warm up. ATC may have asked you to inform them that you are starting engines, but you must always inform your marshaller! A signal to remove chocks is a good way to indicate to him that you are ready to taxi, whether chocks are in place or not.

c. In many cases, aerodrome information is provided in a similar format to an Automatic Terminal Information Service (ATIS). That information will have been displayed in Ops, but may also be available by telephone, or on an ATIS frequency before engine start. When calling for taxi instructions (stating the frequency on which you are calling), add the code letter applicable to the information you have already copied down, and ATC will assume you know it so will not give long instructions. You will be passed the runway in use and QFE when given taxi instructions; the regional pressure setting will be given later if you do not already know it from the aerodrome information.

d. When taxying, again beware of jet efflux, rotor downwash or propeller slipstream. Do not dawdle, but do not rush. Even if you appear to be holding up other traffic, remember safety comes first. You should know the taxi route from your briefing, but if in doubt, stop and ask the controller. You may be given departure instructions (including the regional pressure setting) while taxying, or at the same time as you are given take-off clearance.

e. When ready for departure, look carefully for traffic approaching to land, or taxying onto the runway from the opposite direction. You will probably need greater separation from fast moving traffic than normal. Do not call until you are ready to enter the runway immediately, and do not stay on the runway for longer than necessary. However, essential checks on the runway should not be omitted. Consider the position of any arrester cables and barriers.

f. Once airborne, and at a safe height (500 feet or higher as directed), turn onto your cleared track or heading as advised. When outside the circuit pattern, tell ATC. Your controller may change, either by your changing frequency or by a different voice talking on the same frequency. Once outside the MATZ, you may wish to leave the frequency, although if they can provide a radar service it might be advisable to continue to accept that service for as long as it is offered. If you wish to continue your flight with the aerodrome QNH set, you may need to ask for it before you change frequency.

PART 2 – VISITING OUTSIDE NORMAL OPERATING HOURS

10 PRE-FLIGHT

a. A government aerodrome is always PPR (prior permission only). If you wish to use it outside normal operating hours (unless you are making an emergency landing), you must obtain permission during these normal operating hours, as in paragraph 3. Obtain as much of the "visiting aircraft brief" as is relevant. If intending to land later the same day, ask for the TAF and the latest METAR. Check what facilities, if any, will be available (the aerodrome fire and rescue service for example) and how to contact them for assistance if required. Check where you should park, and how anyone who is to meet you can gain access to the apron. Ask how you should pay your fees, and be aware that an aircraft using a military aerodrome outside its normal operating hours may be subject to a surcharge on its landing fees.

b. Find out if any airfield maintenance (grass cutting, runway sweeping etc.) is expected. Check what other activities may take place on the aerodrome (shooting, driving, model flying etc.). Some military aerodromes have gliding clubs operating outside normal hours. Ensure you know how to keep out of their way, and what frequency they operate on.

11 APPROACHING THE CLOSED AERODROME

a. If possible, make use of a Lower Airspace Radar Service (LARS) from a nearby military aerodrome, informing them of your intentions. Except in a very few cases, the ATZ of a military aerodrome is permanently active, even if the aerodrome is closed. If you have permission to land outside operating hours, you will expect to receive no reply when you call on the published VHF zone or approach frequency. However, continue to make 'blind' calls on that frequency. Other civilian aircraft, even flying clubs, may be based at the aerodrome, and will use the frequency when they require it (they may even provide an air/ground communication service). It is also possible that the aerodrome has been re-activated at short notice and the lack of reply is the result of a radio problem!

b. Radio aids to navigation may still be switched on. They can help you find the aerodrome, but do not fly an instrument approach. Any instrument approach to a military aerodrome in IMC must be flown only under Air Traffic Control. In addition, most maintenance is done outside normal operating hours, even if it was not planned when you telephoned, and your instrument indications may not be correct!

12 CIRCUIT PROCEDURES AT A CLOSED AERODROME

a. Aim to make a standard overhead join unless the "visiting aircraft brief" tells you otherwise. Check the windsock and select the most suitable published runway. Check for obstructions on and close to the runways and taxiways – vehicle drivers and pedestrians will almost certainly not be expecting you. If gliding or powered flying is already taking place, fit in with their established procedures unless it is unsafe to do so, in which case take extreme care.

b. Military aircraft will not be using the aerodrome, so fly your normal circuit pattern with normal calls (on the approach frequency unless advised otherwise) in the correct place. A go-around from the first approach, especially if there is no other flying activity taking place, may act as a warning of your presence to those on the ground. For the same reason, consider using the landing light even in good visibility.

c. The barriers should normally be down and the cables de-rigged. However, that cannot be relied upon; maintenance is a possible reason for them to be up. Look at the position of the barriers during the circuit and initial go-around, and aim to land beyond the approach end cables unless performance limitations apply and you are sure it is safe to do so. Keep a sharp lookout for possible runway intruders, and be ready to go-around. Local people may have become used to having the free run of the aerodrome in the evenings and at weekends.

13 SUMMARY

- Ask for permission well in advance
- Obtain a "visiting airfield brief"
- Check for weather close to arrival time
- Make the radio call early before entering the MATZ
- Be prepared (and pre-planned) to divert at any time
- Listen out carefully
- Priority may be given to military aircraft
- Beware wake turbulence
- Avoid cables and barriers
- Monitor refuelling
- Beware incursions onto the manoeuvring area outside hours

14 APPENDIX – MILITARY AERODROME COLOUR CODES

In addition to a normal TAF or METAR, military aerodromes may use a colour code, which is a form of shorthand for their crews to reinforce the information in the main message. The meaning of each colour is listed below. PPL holders without instrument qualifications are advised that any code except "blue" or "white" may indicate serious problems, and even "white" is no guarantee that the weather is good, even at the time of the report.

Colour Code	Minimum base of lowest cloud (SCT or more) above aerodrome level	Minimum reported visibility
Blue	2500 feet	8 km
White	1500 feet	5 km
Green	700 feet	3700 m
Yellow	300 feet	1600 m
Amber	200 feet	800 m
Red	below 200 feet (or sky obscured)	Below 800 m
Black	Aerodrome unavailable for reasons other than cloud or visibility	

ORS — Safety Sense

SAFETY SENSE 27 GENERAL AVIATION

FLIGHT IN CONTROLLED AIRSPACE

1 INTRODUCTION

a. Although much of the United Kingdom is covered by Class G (uncontrolled) airspace, around many aerodromes controlled airspace has been established to provide an adequate level of safety for commercial air transport. Fortunately, general aviation pilots may fly in much of that controlled airspace, even in poor weather, provided they and their aircraft are properly qualified and equipped.

b. This leaflet is intended to give pilots without an instrument rating guidance on the use of controlled airspace (CAS) in the UK. It should be read in conjunction with the Aeronautical Information Publication (AIP), which contains specific procedures for each piece of controlled airspace in the UK. Pilots should also consider obtaining the assistance of an instructor when entering controlled airspace for the first time.

c. Further guidance for individual control zones and areas may be found on the 'on track maps', under 'aeronautical charts' of the Directorate of Airspace Policy's web site www.caa.co.uk/dap.

2 CLASSES OF CONTROLLED AIRSPACE

a. Class A airspace is prohibited to pilots without a valid instrument rating, unless they have been given special VFR clearance in a control zone (see paragraph 10).

b. Flight under VFR (visual flight rules) is permitted in Class B airspace (there is none currently in the UK) provided the pilot is under air traffic control. Flight under IFR (instrument flight rules) requires a valid instrument rating.

c. VFR flight is also allowed in Class C airspace, but in the UK this is all above Flight Level (FL) 195, where VFR flight is not normally permitted unless specifically authorised. Again, IFR flight requires a valid instrument rating.

d. In class D airspace, VFR flight is permitted with the specific permission of the air traffic controller. In UK airspace, IFR flight is permitted, under control, to holders of a PPL with valid UK IMC ratings (IMC ratings may not be added to an NPPL).

e. In class E airspace, IFR flight is again permitted, under control, to PPL holders with valid UK IMC ratings. Provided the pilot maintains the VMC applicable to controlled airspace, pilots may fly under VFR in Class E airspace without informing air traffic control. However, it is usually appreciated, and often advisable, to inform the controlling agency of your presence.

f. Class F airspace is not controlled airspace. It is advisory airspace in which an air traffic service is provided to participating IFR traffic. In the UK there is no need for pilots who are following VFR to obtain permission to enter Class F airspace, nor indeed to inform anyone that they are doing so. However, since commercial operators may be using the airspace, we recommend that pilots inform the appropriate air traffic service unit of their presence whenever practicable. Flight under IFR in class F airspace should take advantage of a Radar Information or Radar Advisory Service as described in Safety Sense leaflet

8, "Air traffic services outside controlled airspace".

3 PRE-FLIGHT PREPARATION - GENERAL

a. Before flight in CAS, you need to know the specific rules applying to flight in that particular airspace. Consult the en-route (ENR) section of the AIP, available on-line through www.ais.org.uk.

i. ENR 1-4 lists the airspace notified in each particular airspace classification, and notifies those with specific rules.

ii. If intending to land at an aerodrome inside CAS, check the procedures published for the individual aerodrome, and for the controlling aerodrome if different, in the aerodromes (AD) section also.

iii. Note down all the frequencies you may need, checking they are up-to-date on the "aeronautical charts and data" section of the CAA web site. Check NOTAMs for frequency changes and other information.

b. You may wish to file a flight plan (*see AIP ENR 1-10 and Safety Sense leaflet 20- VFR flight plans*), and you must if flying under IFR.

i. File it at least 60 minutes before taxiing, or 3 hours if your flight might be subject to "flow control" through European controlled airspace.

ii. For VFR flight in class D airspace there is no requirement for a written flight plan, the initial radio call will suffice. However, if the controller has plenty of warning of your intentions, it should reduce the amount of time spent in radio communication.

c. Whether or not you have filed a flight plan, it may be worth writing down as much as possible of the initial calls you expect to make.

d. Even if you do not have a serviceable radio, you may be able to fly under VFR in certain Class D airspace which has been specifically notified at ENR 1-4 for the purposes of Rule 27(4)(c) of the Rules of the Air regulations. If that is possible, you must comply fully with that rule. You must obtain positive clearance from the controlling authority for the airspace, listed at ENR 2-2. While in controlled airspace, you must maintain separation of at least 1500 metres horizontally and 1000 feet vertically from cloud in a flight visibility of 5km at all times (8km if above FL100).

e. If you plan to fly under IFR in CAS:

i. ensure your aircraft's communications and navigation equipment is serviceable

ii. you must carry sufficient approved equipment to comply with the requirements in Schedule 5 of the Air Navigation Order (ANO).

iii. VOR and ILS equipment must be FM immune.

iv. Remember to check the IFR NOTAMs as well as the VFR ones.

f. Even when not specifically required, carriage of a serviceable transponder with altitude reporting facility is strongly advised. Some air traffic control units rely exclusively on secondary radar, and most jet and turboprop aircraft carry airborne collision avoidance systems which can receive secondary radar transmissions and in some cases provide their crews with advisory avoiding action.

4 PRE-FLIGHT - CROSSING CAS

a. If planning to fly through controlled airspace, you will need to obtain clearance to enter it, and will need to follow ATC instructions.

b. When planning your route, find prominent features on the 1:500,000 chart close to the points where your route enters and leaves CAS and work out what times you expect to cross the boundaries and what your range and bearing will be from the features. Visual reference points (VRPs) are ideal, but aim to pass near them, not over them. The same applies to navigation beacons. You will need to inform the controller of your estimated times for entering and leaving CAS; if you have planned it all before take-off it makes life much easier in the air.

c. Also select a feature at least ten minutes (but know exactly how long) before you enter CAS, so that you can make the initial call to the controller with confident ETAs. Study all the VRPs and prominent features around your route, because the controller may give you a clearance which requires you to fly to one of them. Be prepared to give ETAs to them also.

d. The initial prominent feature may also be a useful place from which to plan an alternative route in case circumstances mean the controller cannot give you clearance and tells you so immediately. You must also plan a route avoiding CAS from the point at which you intend to enter it, in case a hoped for clearance does not materialise, but an early alteration of course invariably uses less time and fuel.

e. You must expect to have to fly one of these alternative routes, so carry sufficient fuel for the longer one, and plan them both carefully with calculated times and headings.

f. Back up your visual route planning with reference to radio aids. Especially note radials and ranges at your intended entry and exit points. Even if you expect to remain in sight of the surface, they are useful backups, especially if visibility is reduced.

g. If using GPS as a back up to your primary means of navigation, insert your entry and exit points as waypoints, double check their position, and run the route before take-off (*see Safety Sense leaflet 25 – use of GPS*).

5 PRE-FLIGHT- LANDING INSIDE CAS

a. Again you will need to plan an entry point, and be ready to be directed to features on the chart.

b. Make sure you have read all the applicable procedures in the AIP Including those for communication failure, and carry the aerodrome landing or taxi chart. If you might need to carry out an instrument approach, make sure you carry **all** the published procedures. The charts for UK licensed aerodromes can be all downloaded from the AD section of the AIP from the AIS web site www.ais.org.uk.

c. Study the charts you expect to use.

i. Calculate decision or minimum descent heights and altitudes, and compare with the forecast (and actual weather reports).

ii. Select appropriate alternate aerodromes and carry charts and fuel for those also.

iii. If the weather means you might need a Special VFR clearance, study the appropriate procedures.

d. If you intend landing at a major aerodrome, there may be "flow control" considerations. If in doubt, call London Flow Management Centre (FMC) on 01489-612427 and ask, because if flow control is in force you may be delayed even if a flight plan has been accepted.

6 PRE-FLIGHT - TAKING OFF WITHIN CAS

a. Check the weather carefully and decide what departure you need; VFR, IFR or Special VFR.

i. Study the appropriate departure procedures given in the AIP, and ensure you are carrying all the charts you might need.

ii. Either file a flight plan or telephone ATC in plenty of time to advise them of your intentions.

b. You may need to request 'start clearance' by radio. Obtain the latest aerodrome information from the aerodrome terminal information service (ATIS) either by telephone beforehand or by listening on its discrete frequency, and include the information code in your taxi call. Be ready to copy down and read back your ATC clearance at any time after switching on your radio. You cannot take off without it.

7 THE FLIGHT PLAN

a. ENR 1-10 describes the requirements and guidance for filing a flight plan. Much of the information contained in Safety Sense leaflet 20, "VFR flight plans", is relevant even to IFR flight plans within controlled airspace. However, the flight rules (Item 8) may be "***I***" if IFR for the whole flight, or "***Y***" or "***Z***" as appropriate.

b. In Item 10, which lists the navigation and communication equipment carried, the letter "***S***" before the "/" means you carry a radio with all the required frequencies, and also ADF, VOR and ILS as navigation equipment, all of which must be serviceable (and approved if flying under IFR). Other wise, list the individual serviceable equipment you do carry, such as "***D***" for DME, "***F***" for ADF, "***L***" for ILS, "***O***" for VOR, and "***V***" for VHF RTF. "***N***" means you carry none. After the slash "/", insert "***A***" for SSR mode A, "***C***" if you have mode C also, and "***N***" if no SSR is carried. If you carry Mode S then "***S***" will usually apply.

c. In Item 13, insert the designator of your departure aerodrome in the first box, then in the second box your estimated "off-blocks" time (EOBT). This is the time you expect to taxi; at major aerodromes, if you are ready at this time, any delay for air traffic reasons will have the flight plan delayed by ATC automatically.

d. In Item 15, fill in the route you intend to follow within CAS and any other turning points you intend to use under IFR outside CAS.

i. After your cruising TAS and intended cruising altitude or Flight Level, insert either the ATS route designator (e.g."***P18***") if you intend and are able to fly along an airway, or the first and subsequent points at which a change of track, speed or cruising level is intended.

ii. Insert points at least every 30 minutes flying time, and use either latitude and longitude or, better, bearing and distance from ground navigation aids.

iii. Insert "***DCT***" between points unless the designated ATS route runs between them.

iv. Although you will have to follow the published IFR departure or arrival procedures, do not include them here.

e. If you are unable to make your EOBT, and expect to be more than 30 minutes late, you must inform ATC. If your flight is likely to be subject to flow control *(see AIC 70/2005, Yellow 174)* make sure you are familiar with the AIC and the AIP ENR 1-10.

f. If you are filing a flight plan for flight partly under IFR and partly under VFR, you must ensure your flight plan is addressed to your departure and arrival aerodromes and every FIR through which you will fly. Refer to AIC 100/2002, Yellow 94, and/or the AIP ENR 1-10-4.5.5.

g. Further information about flight plans can be found in CAP694 'UK Flight Planning Guide', available for free download from the CAA web site www.caa.co.uk/publications.

8 IN FLIGHT - BEFORE ENTERING CAS

a. At least ten minutes before entering CAS, prepare yourself to write down your clearance, then make an initial call to the controlling authority, for example:

"***East Midlands Approach, Golf Alfa Bravo Charlie Delta, for Zone transit***".

You may be told to "*Stand by*", which means "wait, I will call you". In that case, say nothing and stay outside controlled airspace. However, the controller may reply immediately with "pass your message". Having been asked to "pass your message", make your full call, for example:

"***East Midlands Approach, Golf Alfa Bravo Charlie Delta is a PA twenty eight***

From Wickenby to Gloucester,

One five miles East of Nottingham Tollerton,

Three thousand feet on one zero one one, VMC,

Estimate Tollerton at two zero,

Request transit your airspace VFR from Tollerton to Swadlincote".

b. Listen to the reply, which may again be "*Stand by*" with the same meaning as before, or may just be an acknowledgement of your call, in which case you must wait for your clearance before entering controlled airspace.

c. If the reply is your clearance, write it down as you receive it, maintaining a good lookout all the while. If you miss something, ask "***say again***" before attempting to read it back.

d. If the clearance is different to your intended route or altitude, make sure you can follow it safely. Remember that a controller does not know for example how many engines you have, so may offer you a route which takes you over a congested area at a height from which you cannot glide clear. In that case, use the phrase "unable comply" and explain why.

e. If you have not been given the words "*cleared to enter controlled airspace*", do not enter. Either revert to your alternative route outside CAS, or if you have fuel to hold, do so, but remember the wind will drift you so allow for it if you fly one or more orbit.

f. Advise ATC if you no longer wish to enter CAS.

g. If you think the controller has forgotten you, it is acceptable to call in a suitable gap "Golf Charlie Delta standing by" as a reminder. However, do not badger the controller, there may be a lot of activity on another frequency or on telephone lines.

h. You must not only stay outside controlled airspace until you have received and read back a formal ATC clearance, but you must also understand that clearance, and follow it. The clearance will include an altitude or flight level at, below, or above which you must fly.

j. Ensure you and the controller have the same datum, so if you are flying below the local transition altitude and have not been given the QNH ask for it and set it.

k. If circumstances dictate that you cannot follow your clearance, you must inform ATC immediately, and if you forget what you were cleared for, do not hesitate – ask for confirmation!

9 VFR FLIGHT IN CAS

a. Pilots without instrument qualifications may and do fly under the Visual Flight Rules (VFR) in Class E airspace without informing air traffic control. They may also fly under VFR in class D airspace, provided they obtain clearance from the responsible air traffic services unit (ATSU) and continually listen for instructions and information on the allocated frequency.

b. VFR flight is also possible in airspace classes B (under control) and C, although in the UK such airspace is at high altitudes and VFR cruising in class C airspace above FL195 is not permitted.

c. The VFR pilot has the privilege to travel through Class D airspace, but also the responsibility to obey ATC instructions. That means that no matter what the pilot initially asked to do, he or she must follow the route allocated by ATC, following any altitude or flight level instructions given by the controller.

d. Again, be sure you have the same altimeter setting as everyone else in the airspace, and concentrate on maintaining your allocated altitude (if you are not confident you can keep within 200 feet of a given altitude under normal circumstances, consider some remedial instruction – it is a skill which must be practised).

e. If you are required to change altitude or level, do not allow yourself to continue climbing or descending beyond your cleared level – such "level busts" create a serious hazard to others.

f. The VFR pilot may have the privilege of some collision protection, although that may well not be available even if your transponder is transmitting a designated code. Beware the terminology. You may hear the controller use the words "radar control" – although technically that terminology may be accurate he is not actively controlling you. Apart from remaining on whatever track at whatever altitude for which you have been cleared, and listening attentively at all times for any changes to these instructions, you have the further responsibility to avoid other traffic.

g. Although the controller will pass information to you on the general position of other traffic, in Class D airspace ATC are not responsible for keeping you away from that other traffic. Even in Class C airspace, the controller is only responsible for keeping VFR traffic away from IFR traffic; a VFR pilot is responsible for maintaining separation from other VFR traffic.

h. The last implies a further responsibility. You cannot avoid what you cannot see! Visual Flight Rules for aeroplane pilots in Class C, D and E airspace include:

i. Remain in a flight visibility of 5 km (8km above FL100) at all times.

ii. You must also remain 1000 feet vertically and 1500 metres horizontally away from cloud unless you are in radio communication with the controlling authority, and are flying at 140 kts or less below 3000 feet altitude, clear of cloud and in sight of the surface.

If your cleared track and altitude would lead you outside these Visual Meteorological Conditions (VMC), you must inform ATC and seek a revised clearance.

i. You may fly under VFR in Class E airspace without advising ATC. However, consider asking the ATSU nominated on the chart, or the controlling ATC unit, for a Flight Information Service.

j. Flight in controlled airspace requires accurate flying, understanding, anticipation and clear thinking. It also requires confidence in using the radio and talking to controllers, which only comes with practice.

10 IFR FLIGHT IN CAS

a. The IMC rating allows a PPL holder to fly under IFR in controlled airspace of Classes D and E when circumstances require him or her to do so.

b. IFR clearances will be given in relation to radio navigation aids, which is one reason why aircraft equipment must be adequate for the purpose.

c. CAA VFR charts show all the radio aids in the UK and are usually adequate for IFR flight at low altitudes (and you may need to refer to them), although a dedicated IFR chart produced by a commercial publisher may be easier to use if you are flying out of sight of the ground. Ensure it (and any database in your navigation system) is current.

d. A typical clearance may be to follow a VOR radial to a point designated by a DME range, although it is possible for the controller to ask you to fly direct to a point designated by radial and range from a co-located VOR/DME station. Ensure you have practised (or obtain instruction in) that procedure before attempting to fly under IFR in CAS. Again, accurate altitude keeping is important. Fortunately, not all IFR flight is by sole reference to instruments.

e. Although the controller is responsible for separating IFR traffic from each other, in Class D and E airspace VFR traffic is expected to remain clear of IFR traffic. That means if you choose to fly IFR when others consider they are flying in VMC, you are relying on their lookout. You may receive traffic information about other aircraft known to the controller, but it is best to keep a good look out yourself, or at least have one or more well-briefed passengers do so.

11 SPECIAL VFR FLIGHT

a. If a pilot wishes to fly in a Control Zone but is not able to comply with the IFR, and at the same time cannot comply with the VFR, it may be possible for him to obtain a clearance to fly under "Special VFR (SVFR)", even in class A airspace. Since there is no VFR at night in the UK, this is the only way private pilots with only a night qualification can fly at night in CAS.

b. It is important to realise this is **not** a VFR clearance; consider it an IFR clearance in conditions which allow a pilot to navigate visually.

c. Controllers will treat SVFR aircraft in a similar way to IFR aircraft, but having lower priority. They will provide separation from other aircraft, which may mean that clearance is delayed or perhaps even impossible.

d. In the AD section of the AIP, most aerodromes specify their requirements for SVFR flight, including the specific weather minima (usually as reported by the aerodrome met observer).

e. In addition to the weather minima for SVFR flight laid down by individual aerodromes, a pilot's licence privileges and restrictions also apply.

   i. A pilot with an IMC rating may not fly under SVFR unless flight visibility is greater than 3000 metres.

   ii. An aeroplane pilot without an IMC rating must maintain a flight visibility of 10 kilometres under SVFR unless on a route or in an aerodrome traffic zone (ATZ) which has been specifically notified in the AIP (ENR 1.4) as allowing flight in a lower (specified) minimum flight visibility, with an absolute minimum of 3000 metres.

   iii. Pilots with instrument ratings have no licence restriction.

f. A flight plan should be filed for SVFR flight, although in individual zones a telephone call to ATC is likely to be sufficient.

g. The flight plan form requires the pilot to decide at item 8 whether he is flying under VFR (V) or IFR (I) or combinations of the two. There is no letter for "Special VFR".

h. Use "*I*" in field 8 for all flights at night (including those which may have been delayed from a previously planned day flight).

j. If you do not have the requisite ratings or equipment for such IFR flight in controlled airspace, write in field 18: "RMK/SVFR in controlled airspace".

12 LEAVING CAS AND POST-FLIGHT

a. If you are flying under VFR, the controller may appear to pay no further attention to your flight after you have received clearance to enter. You must, however, not leave the frequency without informing the controller, nor must you leave the frequency while still inside CAS unless the controller has specifically given permission (for example to inform an aerodrome of your approach).

b. Before finally leaving the frequency, ensure you are actually outside CAS both horizontally and vertically, and remember to change the transponder code from the one you were allocated for flight in the CAS, to 7000 unless another code is allocated

c. If a flight plan was filed, cancel it once it is no longer required. If landing at an aerodrome with an Air Traffic Service Unit (ATSU) inside CAS, the ATSU will cancel the flight plan for you; otherwise you can ask another ATSU (perhaps even the controller of the CAS you have crossed) to do it for you, or telephone the parent ATSU as listed in Safety Sense leaflet 20, GETMET, and AIP ENR 1.10.3 after landing.

d. If you wish to cancel an IFR flight plan but continue VFR through airspace in which a flight plan is not required, you may call an ATSU and do so using the words "Cancel IFR flight plan".

e. VFR flight plans for flight within UK airspace should not be formally cancelled: they are assumed to end safely unless a "responsible person" informs the parent ATSU otherwise – see Safety Sense leaflet 20.

13 FLIGHT ADJACENT TO CAS

a. We have emphasised the importance of remaining outside controlled airspace if you have not received a positive clearance. If intending to fly near CAS, pilots must plan their trip especially carefully and pay close attention to their navigation to ensure they do not inadvertently infringe it *(see Safety Sense leaflet 5 "Navigation")*.

b. Ensure you plan and fly the trip with reference to the latest charts, and have consulted NOTAMs for any changes to CAS since the chart publication date.

c. When in the vicinity of CAS, inform the controlling ATC unit of your presence if you can. If not, use the Lower Airspace Radar Service if it is available. Keep your transponder ON (code 7000 if no other code has been allocated) with Mode C (ALT) selected if you have it – an infringement by an aircraft visible to the radar controller is much less dangerous than an infringement by an aircraft he cannot see!

d. If at any time you become unsure of your position and think you might be close to CAS, ask for help. If you are talking to an ATC unit with radar, ask for navigation assistance. If not, and you are in UK airspace, select 121.5 MHz and make an urgency call ("PAN PAN") to the Distress and Diversion Cell of the appropriate Air Traffic Control Centre.

14 SUMMARY

- Ensure you can fly and navigate accurately by keeping in practice.
- Study and prepare procedures, frequencies, and approach minima before flight. Carry appropriate charts.
- Check the aircraft and its communication and navigation equipment is adequate and serviceable.
- Select ground features to relate your position to, and plan an alternative route avoiding controlled airspace.
- Consider filing a flight plan.
- Prepare radio calls, and make them in plenty of time. Be ready to copy and read back clearances.
- Stay outside CAS unless you have positive clearance.
- If in doubt about a clearance – confirm with ATC.
- In CAS, listen out at all times, and follow instructions. If VFR, keep a good lookout and maintain VMC.
- Cancel any flight plan when it is no longer required.
- If uncertain of your position close to CAS, call for help.

LASORS

2007

HANDLING SENSE 1

1

TWIN PISTON AEROPLANES

1 INTRODUCTION

a. The major difference between operating multi-engine piston (MEP) and single-engine piston (SEP) aeroplanes is in knowing how to manage the flight after the failure of an engine. Although having more than one engine gives the pilot more options, in practice the number of ***safe*** options is limited, either by control or performance.

b. The aim of this leaflet is to remind pilots of MEP aeroplanes of some of the basic handling considerations, and to offer safety guidance on the options available in the event of an engine failure. Only an overview can be offered here; there are a number of books available offering more detailed information (see LASORS list of recommended reading).

2 PERFORMANCE

a. Climb performance depends on the excess of power available over that required for level flight. Failure of one engine obviously results in the loss of half the total power available. However, most of the remaining power is used to overcome drag so that typically the "excess" power left for climbing will be reduced by 80% to 90% depending on ambient temperature, altitude and aeroplane mass.

b. Most MEP aeroplanes used for training, air taxi operations and general aviation were designed and built by Piper, Cessna, Beechcraft and Grumman to Federal Aviation Regulations part 23. For certification under these regulations, MEP aeroplanes that weigh 6000 pounds or less and have a stall speed of 61 knots or less do not need to demonstrate any single-engine climb performance at all! The single-engine climb performance required for certification of MEP aeroplanes that are heavier or have higher stalling speeds must be positive but is still very low (a Cessna 310 for example must demonstrate only 110 feet/minute).

c. On most MEP aeroplanes there is usually no provision for single engine climb performance until the aeroplane is configured correctly (e.g. landing gear and flap retracted, full power on the live engine, propeller feathered on the failed engine, single engine best rate of climb speed Vyse). The act of raising the gear or retracting the flap may, in some aeroplanes, cause a temporary increase in drag, loss of lift or even reduction in control margin. Thus, from the time of engine failure on take off to achieving the single-engine climb criteria, a forced landing must be considered as a likely outcome.

3 ENGINE FAILURE DURING TAKE-OFF

The options available to a pilot when faced with an engine failure during take-off depend on the stage of flight:

a. **Rejected Take-off**. During the take-off run, loss of an engine will result in loss of directional control. At low speeds the rudder is less effective and the best method of regaining directional control is to close both throttles and use rudder and asymmetric braking to keep straight. The accelerate/stop performance figures, if available, will indicate whether a high speed rejected take-off is possible on the runway in use.

b. **Land back on the remaining runway**. In the event of an engine failure just after take-off (say 50'), the safest option is normally to close both throttles and land back on the remaining runway. On a long runway, consideration should be given to delaying gear retraction whilst landing-on remains an option. It is unlikely that performance figures are available for this manoeuvre, but as a guide the sum of take-off distance and landing distance, plus an allowance for reaction time (say 500 feet?) will give a fair approximation.

c. **Forced Landing**. As discussed in paragraph 2 above, an engine failure after take-off but before achieving the single engine climb criteria, may be controllable but offer no climb performance. It is very difficult to lay down hard-and-fast rules on the best course of action, as this will depend very much on individual circumstances. However, there will be occasions when it is safer to use the available power to make a controlled landing in a suitable area, rather than attempt to climb away. Local knowledge of suitable landing areas is beneficial. As a guide, Vyse will give best performance, which in this case might be minimum rate of descent.

d. **Continued Climb**. If, having completed the EFATO immediate action drills, a climb can be achieved at Vyse then it should be possible to continue flight to land back at the aerodrome. Remember that 5° of bank towards the live engine will minimise drag and increase climb performance. Turns should not be attempted before reaching a safe height, bearing in mind that turns will reduce climb performance. Complete any subsequent actions when the aeroplane is under control and trimmed.

4 EFATO – IDENTIFYING FAILED ENGINE

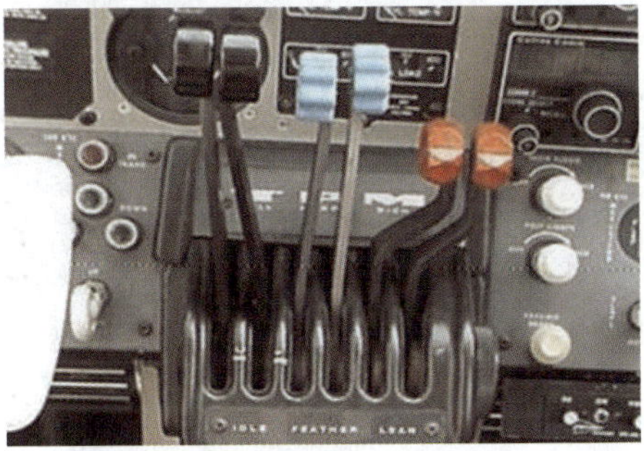

a. **Control.** The first priority is always to fly the aeroplane. Establish control by levelling wings, prevent yaw with rudder and adjust the attitude to achieve and maintain Vyse. (Note that for most light twins Vyse is quoted for maximum all up mass only; at lower mass Vyse is also lower). Confirm that full power has been selected on all engines and reduce drag by retracting gear and flap.

b. **Identify**. 'Dead leg = dead engine' is the usual method of identifying which engine has failed. However, do not rush into feathering drills just yet – make sure you confirm the diagnosis.

c. **Confirm**. The first action is to close the throttle of the affected engine. If the engine noise changes significantly or the aeroplane yaws towards this engine, then you have got the wrong one! A further clue will be the sudden loss of performance. Put the throttle lever forward and start again.

d. **Feather**. When the failed engine has been confirmed, continue with the feathering drills. Most feathering propellers fitted to MEP aeroplanes are designed in such a way that it is not possible to feather the blades below a certain low rpm (typically 700 to 1000 rpm). It is recommended that pilots refer to AIC 100/105 (Pink 90) for further details. Having successfully reached this stage the aeroplane should be at its best performance with full power and minimum drag. Trim the aeroplane and complete the rest of the engine failure drills when convenient.

e. **Inform ATC**. Make an appropriate emergency call, requesting assistance if required.

f. **Other confusing factors**. Correct identification of the failed engine is vital; you may be confused by other factors such as noise or progressive engine failure.

- Noise. A mechanical failure of an engine is very likely to produce noise and vibration. Do not attempt to identify which engine has failed by your perception of the direction of the noise/vibration.

- Instruments. Instrument indications can be misleading, particularly in normally aspirated engines. For example the manifold air pressure (MAP) on the failed engine could be showing ambient pressure, which may well be similar to the live engine MAP indications. If the propeller is windmilling the RPM could be high.

- Progressive engine failure. This is probably the most difficult situation to assess since yaw may be small initially, loss of performance will be progressive and noise and vibration could be high. On the positive side the engine may be producing useful power at first – use it to accelerate and/or climb. Engine failure drills must not be rushed; do not feather the propeller until you have positively identified the failing engine.

5 OTHER EFATO CONSIDERATIONS

a. **Take-off Minima**. In the time between take-off and establishing a safe single-engine climb, the pilot must be satisfied that he can avoid any obstacles visually. This will limit the cloud base and visibility that can be accepted for take-off. For public transport operations cloud base and visibility minima for take-off are specified and mandatory; private pilots would be unwise to use lower minima. Most operators of this class of aeroplane assume that an engine failure at or above 300 feet can be managed into a single engine climb (gear and flap should already be up by this stage) but below this height an engine failure may result in a forced landing or a very shallow climb. To be able to see ahead therefore, a minimum visibility of 1000 metres would seem reasonable. These figures of 300 feet and 1000 metres are a guide and must be adjusted (probably upwards) for individual circumstances.

b. **Visual Circuit**. If performance and weather permit, a visual circuit would be the quickest way back onto the ground.

c. **Instrument circuit**. In IMC a visual circuit may be out of the question. The type of approach aid available at the aerodrome of departure, the weather conditions, pilot's qualifications and approach minima will determine whether this is a viable option.

d. **Diversion**. If a return to the aerodrome is not viable, the pilot should plan to divert to a suitable destination. In IMC this may well be to an aerodrome that could offer radar and an ILS approach.

6 PRE-TAKE-OFF BRIEF

Now that most of the factors have been considered, a plan of action can be formulated. Before every take-off the pilot should consider the prevailing circumstances and brief himself on his actions in the event of an engine failure during or just after take-off. Where 2 crew are involved (e.g. an instructional flight) a formal pre-take-off brief should be given by the flying pilot. The brief should include:

- Under what circumstances take-off will be rejected
- Whether landing back on is an option
- Preferred area/direction if forced landing required
- Visual /instrument circuit or diversion
- Pilot/crew actions as required

7 ASYMMETRIC CIRCUIT/ APPROACH

a. Once safely established in a visual or instrument circuit, aeroplane performance must be considered before reconfiguring for landing. Is sufficient excess performance available to cope with the extra drag of gear and flap? At high mass and/or ambient temperature some MEP aeroplanes may not be able to maintain level flight with the gear down. Sound system knowledge is also required; can the gear/flap be extended/ retracted using the normal system?

b. Power changes can be kept to a minimum by using gear and flap selection to assist in the control of speed and flight path. For example, partial flap may be selected on the down wind leg to reduce speed towards approach speed. Gear selection should coincide with commencing descent onto final and further stages of flap may be considered to adjust speed. Keep power changes to a minimum to avoid large trim changes. A shallow approach will require more power, so maintain at least a nominal (3°) approach path.

c. Keep the speed close to Vyse as you approach committal height.

8 ASYMMETRIC COMMITTAL HEIGHT

a. Many people misunderstand the concept of asymmetric committal height (ACH). Ideally a pilot making an asymmetric approach will land from the first approach. However, there are circumstances when this is not possible and a go-around becomes necessary. Due to the low performance and relatively high drag, the transition from approach configuration to single-engine best rate of climb will entail certain height loss. In essence ACH allows for this height loss; it is the minimum height from which an asymmetric approach may be abandoned to achieve a safe climb at Vyse.

b. On an asymmetric approach, once below ACH, a pilot is effectively committed to land. Note however, that in certain circumstances a pilot may be committed to land from above ACH. For example if the gear cannot be raised or if the airframe has accumulated ice, the aeroplane may not have the performance to go-around. Similarly, a pilot may elect to commit himself to land from above ACH. For example from a stable approach, with a clear runway and with landing clearance, full flap may be selected above ACH. The point is that he should not put himself into a position from which he has no choice but to land until he has a high degree of confidence that a landing will be successful. A useful guide in making this decision is to satisfy the following criteria.

- Correct speed & stable approach
- Configured for landing (gear down at least)
- Clear runway
- Clearance to land

9 CONCLUSION

a. In some ways training for MEP aeroplanes does not give the full picture. All of the various responses to engine failure cannot be practised safely during training in the air; some must be left for discussion on the ground (or training in a synthetic trainer such as a FNPT). Asymmetric training is often carried out on relatively lightly loaded aeroplanes and pilots are anticipating simulated engine failures, therefore they may have a high expectation of the aeroplane's performance and their own ability. In reality single-engine performance on MEP aeroplanes may be very limited; a forced landing is a possibility that should be considered. Pilots must be prepared to react quickly and accurately to engine failure; in particular the accurate identification of the failed engine is crucial. Additionally, pilots must understand the systems on their aeroplane and be totally familiar with the handling notes in the Owner's Manual or Pilot's Operating Handbook.

b. Finally, the options a pilot chooses should be pre-planned and reinforced by (self) briefing of the stages of take-off, identified at paragraphs 3a, b, c and d, prior to every take-off.

HANDLING SENSE 2

STALL/SPIN AWARENESS

1 INTRODUCTION

Although some pilots consider stalling and spinning belong to the days of training and skills tests, the reality is that loss of control at or near the stall is too common and can have fatal consequences. Instructors will introduce exercises in both PPL(A) and CPL(A) courses (Exercises 10 & 11) which give the student pilot sound skills in recognition of and recovery from these manoeuvres. Sadly the reality of flying is that departure from controlled flight does not always happen at safe altitudes, level flight and in clear weather.

2 SIGNS AND SYMPTOMS

a. At least one of the symptoms of the fully developed stall MUST happen before the aeroplane can spin. To revise, these are: wing drop (undemanded roll), nose drop, inability to maintain level flight and buffet. It is clearly inappropriate to wait for this confirmation before recovery. What signs are going to be evident to help us avoid a full stall and possible spin?

b. To help us, we can draw on the classic list of signs of the *approaching* stall: increasingly high nose attitude (in level flight), reducing control effectiveness, low and decreasing airspeed and the onset of buffet – these may be augmented by a stall warning device. Note that all these signs relate most clearly to controlled level flight. What if you are climbing, descending, turning, manoeuvring hard or merely holding large out-of-trim forces?

c. Stalling recognition requires an understanding of angle of attack (AoA). **The stalling angle can be achieved in any attitude, at any speed and in conditions of high control force.** Remember that the stall speed will increase with wing loading (*g*) by √ load factor – e.g. multiply your basic stall speed by 1.4 in a level turn at 60° angle of bank (load factor of 2).

d. One of the most critical phases of flight is just after take off or when going around from an approach to land. At low level, at relatively low speed and with a high nose attitude, an engine failure will lead to a rapid deceleration and increasing angle of attack. To avoid any possibility of stalling and spinning, the pilot must promptly and positively select a lower nose attitude, to achieve and maintain a safe gliding speed. If the aircraft has already decelerated below the recommended gliding speed, this may initially require an attitude lower than normal.

3 STALL AVOIDANCE

How then to safely avoid the stall and spin?

- Be alert and be prepared.
- Practise regularly at safe altitudes to keep your handling skills current.
- Read and understand the contents of the Flight Manual/POH for your aeroplane.
- Seek advice from a Flight Instructor if you are unsure of any techniques.
- Be ready to apply **immediate** recovery action whenever you feel that the aeroplane is not responding correctly:
- Move the control yoke (column) centrally forward to unstall the wings
- Simultaneously apply full power (if available), keeping the aircraft in balance
- Level the wings
- Retract Flaps /Gear as per POH – remember on some aircraft Full Flap must be removed as soon as possible to achieve any climb performance.
- Now you have time to regain a safe flight path and analyse what happened.

If prompt action is taken during the approaching stall, the attitude change required is small and height loss (if any) should be minimal.

HANDLING SENSE 3

SAFETY IN SPIN TRAINING

1 INTRODUCTION

a. While many pilots may have no intention of spinning their aeroplanes, or getting into an extreme attitude, there are several who need, or wish, to, and for them this should be required reading. For the rest of us, the most important part is the first sentence in the paragraph on "spin recovery action".

b. Each year there are a number of occurrences which involve spinning in some form; there are probably still more incidents where pilots give themselves a good fright and put it down to experience, being too embarrassed to tell anyone about it. This is an attempt to give guidance to those involved in spin training or those who wish to explore the envelope of their aeroplane.

c. What is spinning? The spin is a stalled condition of flight with the aeroplane rolling pitching and yawing all at the same time. There are aerodynamic forces and gyroscopic forces (caused by the rotating mass of the aeroplane) which may be either pro-spin or anti-spin. In a stable spin the aerodynamic and gyroscopic forces balance out leaving the aeroplane rolling pitching and yawing at a constant rate.

d. So what? A control input may have aerodynamic and/or gyroscopic effects and consequently it can be difficult to predict the effect that any pilot input may have on a spin. If you are going to spin (or fly aerobatics) it is important to minimise the unpredictable elements. Firstly have you read the manufacturers recommendations in the AFM? Is the aeroplane fully serviceable; would you spin or aero an aeroplane that exhibits odd stalling characteristics? Some have and regretted it! Is the type cleared for spinning and are there any mass and balance considerations?

e. Have you got the right tool for the job? The Cessna 150/152 Aerobat is widely available but its spin characteristics are unusual. For example it is reluctant to spin, usually needs a small amount of power to sustain it, and will recover often before full spin recovery action is taken. This may be satisfactory as an introduction, but does it really prepare a pilot to spin other light aeroplanes?

2 AGGRAVATED SPINS

a. Using anything other than FULL pro-spin controls during the spin may well aggravate the spin:

- In many aeroplanes relaxing the rudder or elevator a little (or not continuing forward movement of the control column sufficiently during recovery) will induce a high-rotational spin.
- Using power can have several effects; firstly the propeller is a gyroscope and at high rpm it produces precessional forces, which may upset the gyroscopic balance of the spin, often flattening the spin attitude; the propeller slipstream will change the effect of the rudder and elevator. (For these reasons the first recovery action is usually to close the throttle).
- Using aileron may promote recovery or it may increase the rate of yaw.

Any of these unusual inputs may cause flat, high rotational, or oscillatory spins (or some combination of these). It is important to realise that recovery from such spins may be considerably prolonged and lead to greater height loss.

3 SPIN SAFETY

Spin training requires a good horizon and visibility

a. **Weather.**
Spin training requires better weather than for other general handling work. You should have a good horizon and visibility and good clearance from cloud both horizontally and vertically. You should not be over complete cloud cover or a smooth featureless surface to minimise the possibility of disorientation.

b. **Handover/takeover of control.**
When 2 pilots are in the cockpit the captain must brief how control will be taken over if the flying pilot has a problem or intercom is lost. For flying instructors on early aerobatic or spinning exercises the chance of a student freezing on the controls is quite high. One way for an instructor to get access to the controls in a side by side set-up, is to move his left arm smartly across the chest of the student; this is usually enough to attract the attention of the student and encourage him to release the controls.

c. **Calculating minimum spin entry altitude.**
Starting the spin from a safe height is imperative. Calculate the absolute minimum safe entry altitude from the ground up in the following steps, then add an extra safety margin if at all possible:

d. **Minimum altitude to complete the manoeuvre.** Logically if you use 3000ft above ground level (agl) for stall recovery you should use not less than this for completing your spin e.g. Ground + 3000ft

1. **Minimum altitude to commence recovery**. Add the height required to take recovery action and pull out of the dive. For an erect spin this could be of the order of 1000ft to 1500 ft (but depends on type and could be more) i.e. ground + 3000 +1500
2. **Minimum entry altitude**. Add on height for each intended turn (typically about 200ft per turn for a light piston aeroplane) i.e. ground + 3000 + 1500 + 800 (for 4 turns)
3. If you intend to do aggravated spins of any kind make extra allowance. For example a high-rotational spin could take an extra 4-6 turns in the recovery. (On early spin exercises wise instructors assume that the student *will* aggravate the spin!)

   If you carry a parachute as a safety back-up, decide on a minimum abandonment height which allows time to get out and height for the parachute to deploy fully. Below this height you cannot abandon so the aeroplane must have recovered by this height. You must be familiar with the abandonment drill for your aeroplane and how to use the parachute. It is a good idea to simulate these drills in a practice session on the ground. If you have to use the parachute, quick and efficient abandonment with sufficient height is essential.

Military schools have gradually increased their minima over the years such that they use figures considerably higher than those suggested here for their light piston aeroplanes. Even these may seem very high, but there have been training accidents where pilots have chosen spin entry heights that guaranteed that they would hit the ground before completing the recovery!

4 SPIN RECOVERY ACTION

a. By far the best action is to initiate recovery *before* a spin develops; that is **centralise the controls as soon as control is lost**. However, if we are deliberately spinning or carrying out extreme manoeuvres we must be prepared for the case where we are too late for this to be effective i.e. a fully developed spin.

b. The spin recovery action may vary according to type; it is important to read the Flight Manual and follow the recommended technique. Typically for an erect spin:-

- **Throttle**: Closed.
- **Aileron**: Neutral.
- **Rudder**: Check the direction of *yaw* and use FULL anti-yaw rudder. A pause is often recommended between moving the rudder and elevator, and this is important to ensure rudder effectiveness.
- **Elevator**: Move the control column centrally forward. As the aeroplane starts to recover the attitude will steepen and the rate of rotation will increase; keep moving the column towards full deflection until the spin stops.
- **Centralise**: Centralise all controls as soon as the spin stops or the aeroplane will flick in the opposite direction!
- **Climb**: Roll towards the nearest horizon and pitch into a climb attitude applying power carefully.

c. Be confident that the correct recovery action will stop the spin. Do not go back to pro-spin control and start again because you will certainly delay recovery. (In the very unlikely event that normal recovery action fails, in-spin aileron may well help but this is a last resort action).

d. In determining the direction of yaw for an inadvertent spin the *turn needle* is always the best indication (not the slip ball). Beware if you only have a turn co-ordinator; it measures yaw *and* roll. In an inverted spin yaw and roll are in opposite directions so a turn co-ordinator is of no help to you here!

e. Before you fly aerobatics and especially if you teach, it is essential to have a thorough understanding of how to recover from mishandled manoeuvres, and especially spinning. Competence in spinning will lend confidence and enjoyment to your flying, but do it safely.

1

PRACTICAL GUIDANCE

UK VFR AND REQUIREMENTS

- Introduction
- Maximum Speed Limit
- Licence Restrictions
- The IMC Rating
- Helicopters
- Special VFR
- General Limitations
- Licence Privileges and Restrictions
- Is the Airspace "Notified"?
- Get a Clearance
- Watch your Height
- Stay Clear of Cloud and in sight of the Surface
- Card A - UK Minimum VFR Requirements - 140 knots (IAS) or less, below FL100
- Card B - UK Minimum VFR Requirements - Any flight at or above FL100 at more than 140 knots (IAS)

1 UK VFR AND REQUIREMENTS

Introduction

The rules vary according to the classification of airspace you are flying in, the speed of your aircraft, the level at which you fly and the type of licence and ratings you hold.

The two pictorial cards (Card A and Card B) are designed for quick reference and essentially, differ according to the cruise speed of the aircraft you are flying. For any particular flight therefore, you should fall onto either one card or the other. For example if you fly a simple, single piston engine aeroplane, then all you need to remember is probably on card A. The assumption is made here, that your aeroplane will not cruise faster than 140 knots IAS and that you will not fly as high as Flight Level 100. For faster aircraft and / or flying at higher levels, you will need to refer to Card B.

If conditions are such that you cannot meet the requirements of Card B, you must either fly IFR (if your licence permits) or slow down to 140 knots or less, and operate within the requirements of Card A, instead.

The full requirements for the conditions in which you can fly VFR are contained in The Rules of The Air (Rules 25 and 26). The privileges and restrictions of your licence and ratings are detailed in the Air Navigation Order – Schedule 8. There is further guidance in the AIP at ENR 1-2-1 for VFR operations and for Special VFR at ENR 1-2-2 and 1-4.

These notes are intended only as a useful 'aide-memoire' and pilots should familiarise themselves with the relevant parts of the Rules of the Air, ANO and the AIP.

Maximum Speed Limit

Generally speaking, all flying below flight level 100 is restricted to a maximum 250 knots IAS, (see Rules of the Air, Rule 23). There are some exceptions in controlled airspace or if you are taking part in an air display, which carries the appropriate permissions – See ANO 2005, Article 80. Remember also, this is not just a VFR restriction.

Licence Restrictions

Despite what it says above; If you hold a PPL, BCPL or a JAR-CPL without either an IMC Rating or an IR then you are restricted by the Air Navigation Order (Schedule 8). This states that you must always remain in site of the surface, so you must not fly above fog or cloud, which obscures your view of the surface at any time, nor are you allowed to fly in any conditions where the visibility is less than 3000 metres. These are blanket restrictions, which you must adhere to, even if other regulations suggest something less limiting.

The IMC Rating

The privileges of an IMC Rating (or Instrument Rating) allow flight under IFR, in IMC both outside Controlled Airspace and within Classes D or E Airspace. It will also allow you to fly VFR outside Controlled Airspace, at or below 3000' and 140 knots, in as little as 1500 metres visibility. This is a little bit misleading because an IMC Rating holder must always have at least 1800 metres visibility to take off or land and so the 1500 metres is only a temporary, en-route provision.

Helicopters

At or below 3000 feet QNH, helicopters may operate VFR in classes C, D, E, F or G airspace, without any specified minimum visibility, provided they remain clear of cloud and in sight of the surface and fly at a 'Reasonable Speed' for the actual visibility.

Special VFR

For a number of reasons, VFR operations within a control zone are not always possible. If the weather conditions are below the VFR minima for that type of airspace or it's night time, or it's Class A airspace for example, then it may be possible to obtain a Special VFR Clearance (SVFR). This is essentially an ATC dispensation to operate in the zone without having to comply with IFR when otherwise, you would have to. Entry and exit lanes are sometimes set up within a control zone inside which, the rules for Special VFR operation may be different again.

The flow Chart entitled "Can I Go SPECIAL VFR ?" should help determine when and in what conditions, a pilot can accept a Special VFR Clearance.

General Limitations

The basic or standard requirements for operation under SVFR are contained in the UK AIP En-route Section (ENR 1-2-2). Any more restrictive requirements for operation under SVFR for any particular Control Zone, should be published in the UK AIP Aerodromes (AD-2)

Section under the respective aerodrome's Flight Procedures - paragraph 2.22.

In any event, you will not get a Special VFR clearance to land or take off within a Control Zone, if the visibility is 1800 metres or less (i.e. 1900m or more) or the cloud ceiling is less than 600 feet.

Licence Privileges and Restrictions

If you hold a PPL, BCPL or a JAR-CPL then you may not fly Special VFR unless the flight visibility is 10 km. or more. If you hold an IMC rating then this restriction is reduced to 3000 metres visibility. Full details of these restrictions are contained in the Air Navigation Order, Schedule 8.

Whatever qualifications you hold, the minima published in the AIP Aerodromes section for Special VFR flight, in that particular airspace may be higher than the minima that your licence or ratings permit. For example, you may hold an IMC rating but the quoted minima for Special VFR in the airspace you want to fly into, may be more than 3000m.

The higher limit is always the limiting factor and you should know your licence limitation (see ANO Schedule 8) and look up the limitations applicable to the airspace you are flying into, (AIP Aerodromes Section – "AD 2 (aerodrome name) paragraph 2.22" (Flight Procedures)).

Is the Airspace "Notified"?

Some Routes (such as Entry and Exit Lanes) and some Aerodrome Traffic Zones (Note that's not necessarily the entire Control Zone) are "Notified for the purposes of schedule 8 to the Air Navigation Order". This means, for example, that if you are limited to 10km by your licence you may still fly Special VFR on these "Notified" routes and in these zones even though the visibility is less than 10 km. Instead, you are limited to the minima quoted in the notification. (See AIP ENR 1-4-1 to 1-4-7) - (For Class D airspace; see ENR 1-4-5).

WARNING ! There are at least 2 other notifications in the AIP, which are not the same.

1. All airspace is "Notified" as some class or other and the words "The following Airspace is notified as Class (D) Airspace..." does NOT mean that it is necessarily notified for the purposes of schedule 8. The words you are looking for are "The (Anytown Aerodrome Traffic Zone) is hereby notified for the purposes of Schedule 8...."
2. Notified for the purposes of Rule 27(4)(c) means that you may be able to get a normal VFR Clearance 'non radio', without filing a flight plan provided you maintain 5, 1½ & 1. This has nothing to do with Schedule 8 or Special VFR!

   Having established that conditions are suitable to fly Special VFR, you must;

Get a Clearance

You must get a clearance from the ATC unit controlling the zone. From outside the zone, you must request your clearance 5 to 10 minutes before you reach the entry point. Having done so you must maintain radio contact with the ATCU so that you are able to comply with their instructions whilst operating under the clearance.

The granting of a SVFR clearance is subject to other traffic conditions and various ATC regulations, which are the responsibility of the controller. This means that whilst conditions for your flight may appear to be acceptable to you, you may not get the clearance you want and you should be prepared to avoid the need for it. This may mean, for example, diverting your route to avoid the relevant control zone.

Watch Your Height

If ATC direct you to fly below 1000' above the congested area of a city, town or settlement, under a SVFR Clearance, you are then absolved from this particular element of Rule 5. You are nevertheless NOT absolved from the other elements of the low flying rules (including the 500 foot rule) which also means if you are flying a 'single' you must still make sure you could glide clear of any congested area should the engine fail.

Stay Clear of Cloud and in Sight of the Surface

Special VFR also means that you must be able to see any obstacles and determine your flight path by visual reference to the surface. Therefore you must keep clear of cloud and in sight of the surface, all the time you are under the SVFR clearance, whatever your qualifications may be.

CARD A - UK MINIMUM VFR REQUIREMENTS

UK Minimum VFR Requirements
140 Knots (IAS) or Less, Below FL 100
CARD A

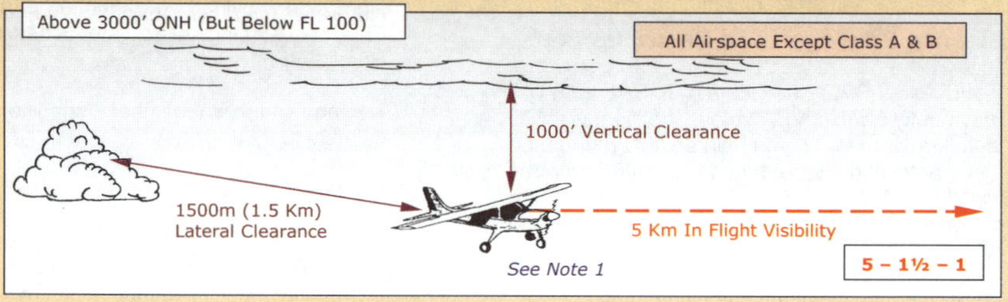

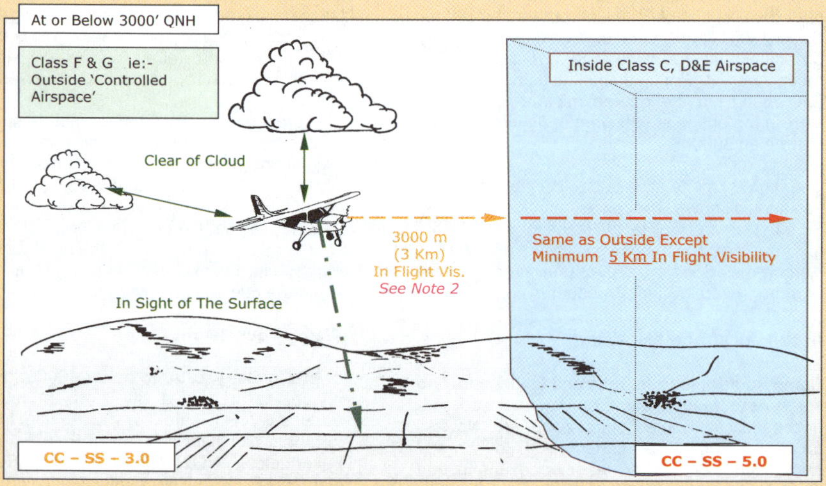

PPL, BCPL and JAR CPL Holders

Note 1 You must remain in sight of the surface at all times unless you hold a valid IMC or Instrument Rating.

IMC & Instrument Rated Pilots

Note 2 You may fly VFR in less than 3000 metres visibility provided you are;
Outside controlled airspace, not above 3000 feet altitude, and not above 140 Knots IAS.
The absolute minimum in flight visibility is 1500 metres but;
IMC Rated Pilots must always have at least 1800 metres visibility to take off or land.

This Card is intended for easy reference and does not cover every eventuality in VFR Operations.
For full reference to VFR Operations see UK AIP ENR-1-2-1
(For Special VFR Operations see UK AIP ENR 1-2-2)
For full details of licence privileges and restrictions – See ANO 2000 – Schedule 8

AW 2001

CARD B - UK MINIMUM VFR REQUIREMENTS

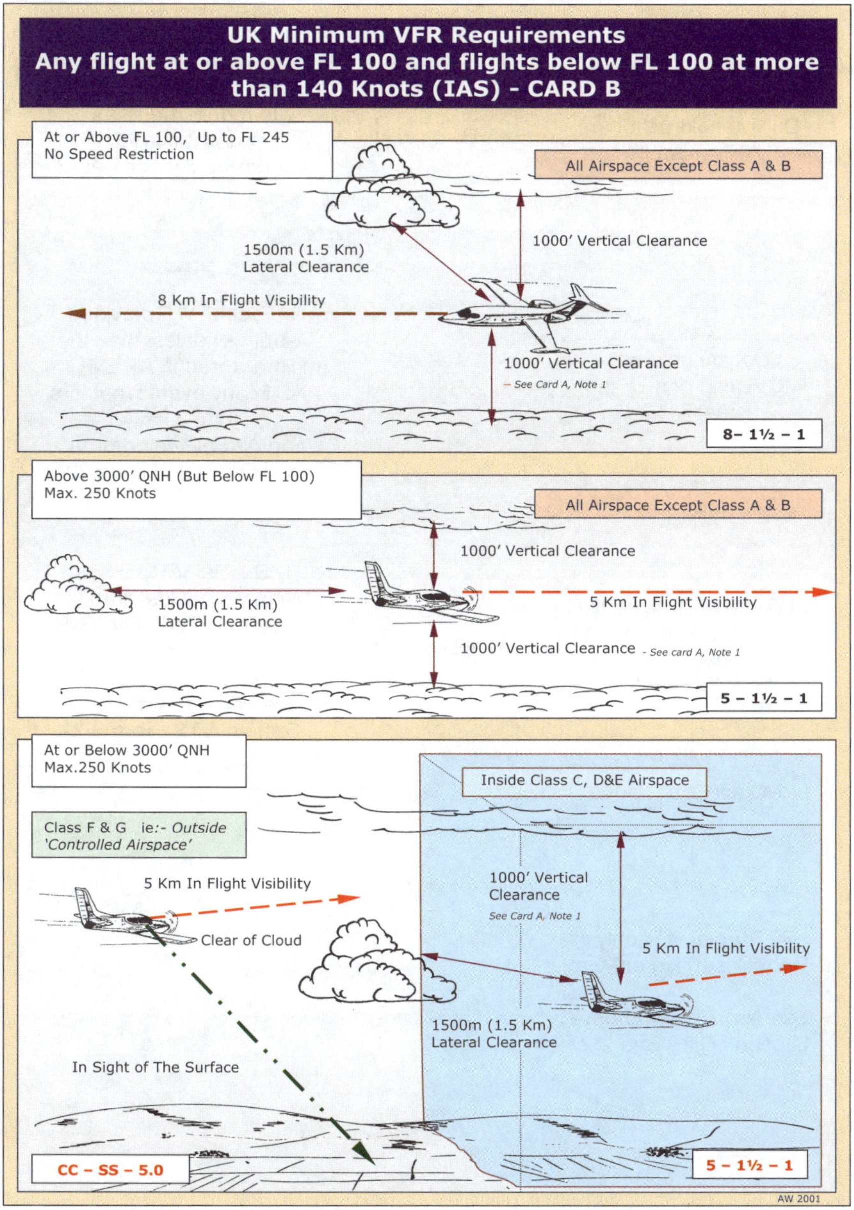

SPECIAL VFR

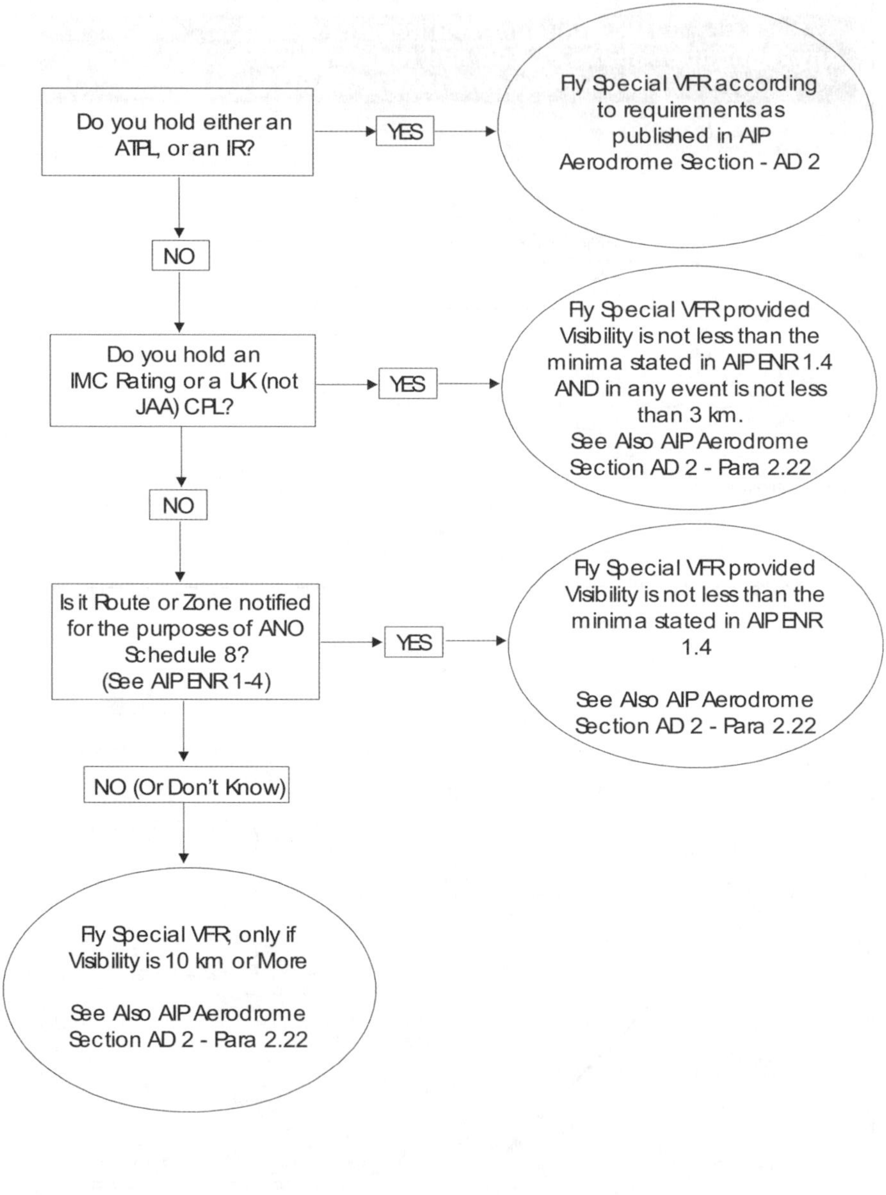
Do you hold either an ATPL, or an IR?
YES
Fly Special VFR according to requirements as published in AIP Aerodrome Section - AD 2
NO
Do you hold an IMC Rating or a UK (not JAA) CPL?
YES
Fly Special VFR provided Visibility is not less than the minima stated in AIP ENR 1.4 AND in any event is not less than 3 km.
See Also AIP Aerodrome Section AD 2 - Para 2.22
NO
Is it Route or Zone notified for the purposes of ANO Schedule 8? (See AIP ENR 1-4)
YES
Fly Special VFR provided Visibility is not less than the minima stated in AIP ENR 1.4
See Also AIP Aerodrome Section AD 2 - Para 2.22
NO (Or Don't Know)
Fly Special VFR, only if Visibility is 10 km or More
See Also AIP Aerodrome Section AD 2 - Para 2.22

1

OCCURRENCE REPORTING

REPORTING OF INCIDENTS TO AIRCRAFT

1 REPORTING OF INCIDENTS TO AIRCRAFT

Was the airframe damaged or any person injured? *Or do you think the incident was so serious that there nearly was an accident*? You **must** report it to Air Accidents Investigation Branch on 01252 512299 as soon as possible. Full details are in AIC 97/2002 (Pink 43) but if in doubt, report it. You must also report it to the local police if it happened in or over the UK.

Was it an Airprox? (there was no collision, but you consider that your aircraft was endangered by the proximity of another aircraft)? Report it as soon as possible by radio to ATC, and to the UK Airprox Board on 01895 815121 /2 /5 /8. Full details are in AIC 87/2002 (Pink 39).

Was it a birdstrike? Report to the CAA's Aerodrome Standards Department on 01293 573273, as detailed in AIC 8/2003 (Pink 50). The appropriate form is CA 1282, available on the CAA website.

Otherwise, could it have endangered an aircraft, its occupants or any other person? Implementing Directive 2003/42/EC of the European Parliament and of the Council on occurrence reporting in civil aviation, Article 142 of the Air Navigation Order 2005 details the requirements of the UK's mandatory occurrence reporting (MOR) scheme, and must be referred to and complied with. Certain specified people are required to submit reports on all 'reportable incidents' to the CAA's Safety Investigation and Data Department, on a "MOR" form (CA 1673) as detailed in CAP 382 and AIC 110/2000 (Pink 15). As a very incomplete extract from the ANO article, those required to provide information include:

Operators and commanders of aircraft involved in public transport operations

Operators and commanders of UK registered turbine engined aircraft

Those involved in design, repair or maintenance of such aircraft, their equipment, or any navigational equipment.

Holders of an Air Traffic Controller's licence

Licensees and managers of licensed aerodromes

Although again the full definition is contained in Article 142 and must be referred to, a 'reportable occurrence' is basically any incident, malfunction or defect affecting such an aircraft or ground equipment which endangers, or if not corrected would endanger, the aircraft, its occupants or any other person, unless it is already the subject of an accident report to AAIB.

If you are not one of these specified people, or the aircraft concerned is not one of those specified, you are also encouraged to report incidents on the same form which is available on the CAA web site through "publications" and "CAA forms". If a form is not available, SIDD on 01293 573220 may be able to send you one.

If you do not wish the CAA to be involved in the reporting or investigating chain, you may send a report to the confidential human factors reporting programme (CHIRP) at Farnborough. Full details are in AIC 47/2001 (Pink 20), and their telephone number is 0800 214645. However, the submission of a CHIRP report does not fulfil the statutory obligations under the Air Navigation Order for mandatory reporting as required by Article 142.

2 OCCURRENCE REPORT FORM CA1673

Occurrence Report Form – CA1673 is for official use only - in accordance with CAP 382
Copies of the form are available on the CAA website – www.caa.co.uk/srg/publications

Occurrence Report Form – CA1673

UK Civil Aviation Authority

OCCURRENCE REPORT

When completed, please send to : Safety Investigation and Data Department (SIDD),
Civil Aviation Authority,
Safety Regulation Group,
Aviation House,
Gatwick Airport South,
West Sussex,
RH6 0YR.

CAA Occurrence Number

If report is CONFIDENTIAL - mark clearly at the top and provide contact address/Tel no. Your wish will be respected.

Civil Aviation Authority

AIRCRAFT TYPE & SERIES	REGISTRATION	OPERATOR	DATE	LOCATION/POSITION/RW	TIME (UTC)	DAY / NIGHT / TWILIGHT

FLIGHT NR	ROUTE FROM	ROUTE TO	FL/ALT/HT (FT)	IAS (KTS)	ETOPS: YES / NO

NATURE OF FLIGHT	PAX	FREIGHT	POSITIONING	FERRY	TEST	TRAINING	BUSINESS	AGRICULTURAL	SURVEY	PLEASURE	CLUB/GROUP	PRIVATE	PARACHUTING	TOWING

FLIGHT PHASE	PARKED	TAXYING	TAKE OFF	INITIAL CLIMB	CLIMB	CRUISE	DESCENT	HOLDING	APPROACH	LANDING	CIRCUIT	AEROBATICS	HOVER

ENVIRONMENTAL DETAILS

WIND		CLOUD			PRECIPITATION				OTHER METEOROLOGICAL CONDITIONS				RUNWAY STATE				
DIRN	SPEED (kts)	TYPE	HT (ft)	8th	RAIN	SNOW	SLEET	HAIL	VISIBILITY	ICING	TURBULENCE	OAT (C)	DRY	WET	ICE	SNOW	SLUSH
					LIGHT	MOD	HEAVY		KM/M	LIGHT / MOD / SEVERE	LIGHT / MOD / SEVERE		CATEGORY	I	II	III	

BRIEF TITLE

DESCRIPTION OF OCCURRENCE

Continue on back as necessary

Any procedures, manuals, pubs (eg AIS, AD, SB etc) directly relevant to occurrence and (when appropriate) compliance state of aircraft, equipment or documentation.

GROUND STAFF REPORT

A/C CONSTRUCTORS NR	ENGINE TYPE/SERIES	ETOPS APPROVED: YES / NO	GROUND PHASE: MAINTENANCE / GROUND HANDLING / UNATTENDED	AIRCRAFT BELOW 5700KG ONLY - MAINTENANCE ORGANISATION (TEL NO.)

COMPONENT/PART	MANUFACTURER	PART NR	SERIAL NR	MANUAL REF	COMPONENT OH/REPAIR ORGANISATION

CA 1673 (Nov 2002)

SPECIMEN

ORS — Safety Sense

DESCRIPTION OF OCCURRENCE CONTINUED

ORGANISATION	NAME	POSITION	SIGNATURE	DATE

If report is voluntary (ie, not subject to mandatory requirements) can the information be published in the interests of safety?	YES NO	Address and tel no. (if reporter wishes to be contacted privately)	NOTE 1: If additional information, as below, is available please provide. NOTE 2: If the occurrence is related to a design or manufacturing deficiency, the manufacturer should also be advised promptly. NOTE 3: Where applicable, a report of this incident should be forwarded directly to other agencies involved, e.g. Aerodrome Authority, ATC agency.

REPORTING ORGANISATION - REPORT

ORGANISATION COMMENTS - ASSESSMENT/ACTION TAKEN/SUGGESTIONS TO PREVENT

UTILISATION - AIRCRAFT				UTILISATION - ENGINE/COMPONENT				MANUFACTURER ADVISED	
	TOTAL	SINCE OH/REPAIR	SINCE INSPECTION		TOTAL	SINCE OH/REPAIR	SINCE INSPECTION		
HOURS CYCLES LANDINGS				HOURS CYCLES LANDINGS				YES	NO

ORGANISATION	TEL/FAX	REPORTERS REF	REPORT		REPORTERS INVESTIGATION			FOR DATA RETAINED	
			NEW	SUPPL	NIL	CLOSED	OPEN	YES	NO

NAME	POSITION	SIGNATURE	DATE

CA 1673 (Nov 2002)

LASORS

2007

SAFETY

INFORMATION POSTERS

1 AIRSTRIPS

AIRSTRIPS –
THINK Hedgerow,
NOT Heathrow......
Check:
— length
— obstructions
— slope
— surface
— animals
Consult
Safety Sense
Leaflet 12
available on
www.caa.co.uk
AOPA
FSP 7
910291
Produced, Sponsored and Distributed by General Aviation Safety Committee,
Aircraft Owners and Pilots Association and Civil Aviation Authority.

2 CUT THE CHAT

CUT THE CHAT!

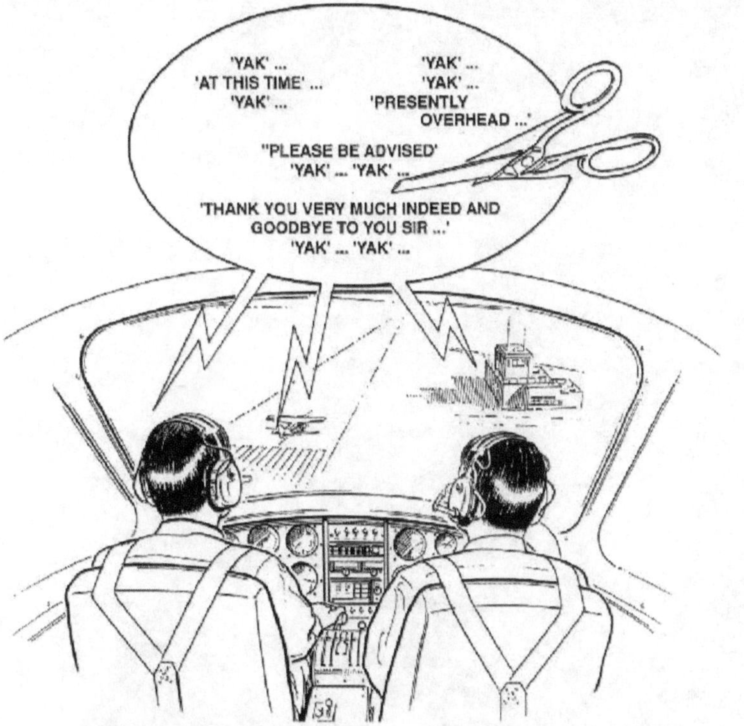

KEEP IT BRIEF

REFER TO CAP 413 (Radiotelephony Manual)
- available on the CAA's website www.caa.co.uk -
TO KEEP YOUR PROCEDURES CORRECT

FSP 4 040497 *Prepared by the CAA's GA Safety Promotion, SRG Gatwick*

ORS — Safety Sense

THE STANDARD OVERHEAD JOIN

4 CROSSING LARGE BUILT-UP AREAS

CROSSING LARGE BUILT-UP AREAS

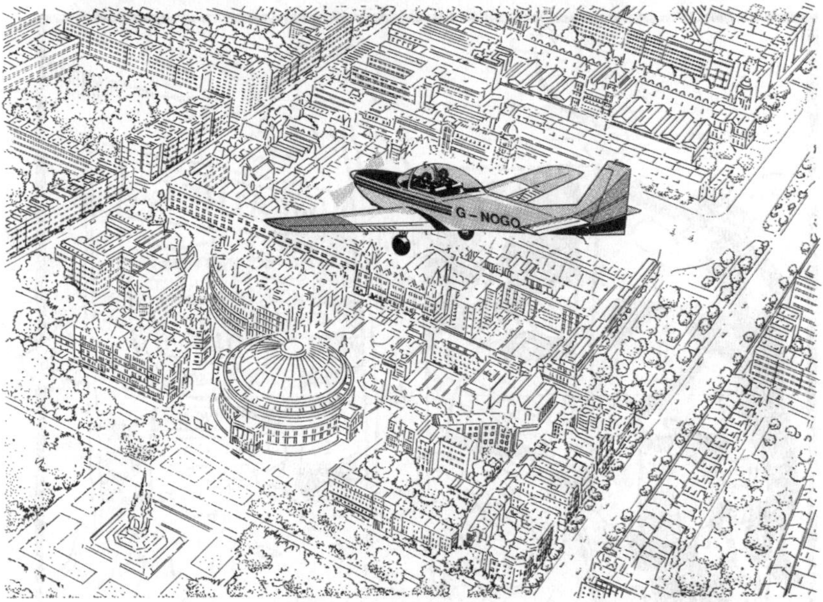

NO-GO FOR SINGLE-ENGINED AEROPLANES ***UNLESS*** YOU CAN GLIDE CLEAR OF THE AREA IF THE ENGINE STOPS

Parks and playing fields are *not* acceptable landing sites

DO YOU KNOW HOW FAR YOU CAN GLIDE? — IT MAY NOT BE FAR!

Produced, sponsored and distributed by General Aviation Safety Committee, BH Pickard and MA Grayburn and Civil Aviation Authority

5 DON'T BE CAVALIER ABOUT MET

DON'T BE CAVALIER ABOUT MET ....

GET AN AVIATION FORECAST

See 'GET MET' Booklet

Civil Aviation Authority

FSP 14 010398

Produced by CAA Safety Promotion, GAD, Gatwick

NOTES:

NOTES:

INDEX BY SUBJECT

A

B

C

H

I

J

K

L

Page No

M

Page No

N

Page No

O

Page No

P

Page No

Q

Page No

R

S

T

Page No

U

Page No

V

W

X

Y

Z